BROADCASTING IN AMERICA

Second Edition

A Survey of Television
and Radio

SYDNEY W. HEAD
Professor of Communications
Temple University

HOUGHTON MIFFLIN COMPANY
BOSTON · New York · Atlanta
Geneva, Illinois · Dallas · Palo Alto

Printed in the U.S.A.

Library of Congress Catalog Card Number: 73–155294

ISBN: 0–395–04586–X

CONTENTS

LIST OF FIGURES

LIST OF TABLES

PREFACE

A meaningful assessment of any broadcasting system seems to require an understanding of the operative forces which produced it. To that end, the First Edition of this book originally tried to answer the basic question: "What makes broadcasting in America the way it is?" The answer fell rather naturally into four parts, representing four sets of controlling influences: the physical nature of the medium, the accidents of history, economic constraints, and the compulsions of social control. The first four parts of the book treated these subjects and a concluding part went on to consider the effects of broadcasting.

This basic organizational pattern has been retained in the Second Edition. Nevertheless, the book has been substantially rewritten; for not only the medium itself but the social setting, too, has changed greatly in the fifteen years since the First Edition appeared. An upwelling of concern about the quality of the environment, about conservation of natural resources, about the rights of minorities, and about consumer protectionism has altered the balance of forces. Neither industry practice nor government supervision, it seems to me, has kept in step with these people-oriented developments, though they involve the media profoundly. This edition, therefore, not only updates such topics as cable television, satellites, cassette recording, the Fairness Doctrine, and public television; it also introduces new viewpoints and new materials on such issues as service to minorities, broadcast consumerism, and what I have called the "mythology" of regulation.

As before, I have wherever possible segregated rapidly changing data from the text proper by presenting them in tabular form. The casual reader need not be distracted by outdated facts in the text; yet the reader who needs the latest available information can easily bring most of the tables up to date by referring to the cited annual sources. I have also retained the practice of letting specialists in each field speak for themselves in their own language, with full citations at the points of occurrence in the text. Additional conveniences in the new edition are the Bibliographical Index and a system of decimal numbering for sections, tables, and figures that facilitates cross-referencing.

A number of readers offered helpful suggestions on how to improve on the original edition and I have tried to profit by their advice. Many individuals and organizations cooperated generously in providing new information, for which I am most grateful. Special thanks are due my former University of Miami colleague, David Nellis, now at State University of New York, College at Oswego. Professor Nellis gave invaluable advice on revision plans and kept me abreast of Stateside broadcasting developments during a period of several years when I was working in Africa. A timely grant from the Kaltenborn Foundation enabled me to continue giving undivided attention to the revision during final crucial months of manuscript preparation.

S. W. H.

Philadelphia, Pennsylvania

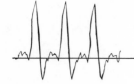

PROLOGUE

BROADCASTING
IN AMERICA—
AND THE WORLD

The title *Broadcasting in America* gives rise to the question: does American broadcasting in fact have unique characteristics which set it apart from world broadcasting?[1] Radio communication had a highly cosmopolitan parentage. The French date its invention from 1891, when Edouard Branly first demonstrated his "coherer," a radio-wave detection device. The Russians celebrate "Radio Day" on May 7, commemorating a demonstration made by Alexander Popoff in 1895. Even the Italian Marconi's English patent of 1896, often regarded as the practical beginning of radio communication, depended on essential prior discoveries by British, French, German, Italian, and Russian scientists. Subsequent contributions to the technical development of the art have continued to come from many countries. In the 1930's, electronic television demonstrations were taking place in Britain, France, Germany, Italy, Japan, Russia, and the United States. America led in the development of electronic television as a practical mass medium, but that leadership hinged on two key personalities who were Russian immigrants—Zworykin in the technical sphere and Sarnoff in the business sphere.

P.1 / The Global Context

Without detracting from the pioneering contributions of other countries, it can be fairly said that America has led the world in developing many aspects of the social phenomenon we know as broadcasting. Not everyone, either in America or elsewhere, may agree that the present system is altogether ideal, but whatever one's value judgments, American broadcasting does have unique features compared with other national systems and has influenced world broadcasting substantially.

Certainly in terms of sheer size, American broadcasting warrants special attention. Although the United States has only about 6 per cent of the world's

---

[1] The term "broadcasting" means both sound radio and vision radio, or television. See Chapter 1 for a full definition of radio and Section 7.1 for a discussion of this definition of broadcasting.

Table P.1
U. S. share of world broadcasting facilities

FACILITY	WORLD TOTAL	U. S. SHARE	
	Number	*Number*	*Per Cent*
Radio transmitters	18,500	6,337	34
Radio receivers	634,000,000[1]	285,000,000	45
Television transmitters			
Primary	3,250	745	23
Secondary[2]	8,050	1,958	28
Television receivers	214,000,000	78,000,000	36

[1]Not counting 47 million wired speakers and excluding both receivers and wired speakers in Mainland China; hence U. S. percentage is overstated.
[2]Boosters and translators.

Source: 1967 (or earlier) data from the *Unesco Statistical Yearbook 1968* (Paris: Unesco, 1969), pp. 512–513, 516, 522, 529–530, 532, 534. Reproduced with the permission of Unesco.

population, Table P.1 shows that it has about a third of the world's broadcast transmitters and about 40 per cent of its radio and television receivers. Because of size (though also because of the political, economic, and social context in which the system has evolved), broadcasting in America presents a more varied face than it does in other countries. Its combined total of about eight thousand primary broadcasting stations (Table 1.3) gives scope for every conceivable variety of program service. Such lavish choice has made the American listener/viewer rather parochial. He feels no need to reach out beyond the confines of his own country to vary his broadcast diet. He hardly appreciates the fact that other countries often organize broadcasting along lines quite different from those he knows at home.

In contrast to the United States, most nations have relatively few domestic stations, and those few are likely to be run either directly by the government or under tight government control (Table P.2). They usually offer a limited

Table P.2
Ownership of world broadcasting systems

TYPE OF OWNERSHIP	RADIO SYSTEMS[1]		TELEVISION SYSTEMS[1]	
	No.	*Per Cent*	*No.*	*Per Cent*
Government control	128	68	74	64
Private enterprise	16	9	24	21
Mixed government and private	43	23	17	15
Total	187	100	115	100

[1]"Systems" refer to separately enumerated areas, not all of which are independent countries.

Source: 1967 (or earlier) data from the *Unesco Statistical Yearbook 1968* (Paris: Unesco, 1969), pp. 514–519, 531–534. Reproduced with the permission of Unesco.

range of program choices, so that consumers interested in alternative points of view or nongovernment-approved entertainment must turn to foreign stations for satisfaction. This they can do more easily than American audiences. Most nations have a smaller geographical spread than the United States so that ordinary signals from neighboring states easily penetrate to the interior. Some countries built up substantial television-set ownership even before they had so much as a single television station within their own borders.

Other external sources of programs are not wanting: powerful, internationally oriented commercial radio stations located in ministates like Andorra and Luxembourg; elaborate propaganda services, not only from major powers but even from scores of quite small countries like Albania or Ghana (Table P.3); quasi-governmental services like Radio Free Europe (aimed at Communist satellite states from transmitters in West Germany and elsewhere); the American Forces Radio and Television Service, with transmitters throughout the world; the United Nations, with facilities in New York and Geneva; and sometimes even "pirate" stations broadcasting from offshore locations (Section P.6). In much of the world, shortwave receivers are commonplace rather than limited to amateur station operators and a few enthusiasts, so that distant radio stations a thousand or more miles away can be regularly received (Table P.3).[2]

International exchange of television programs is common outside America. The European Broadcasting Union, for example, has operated an elaborate program-exchange system, Eurovision, among nations of West Europe since 1954. The East European bloc has a similar service, Intervision, operated by the International Radio and Television Organization (OIRT) from Prague. Exchanges between these two European regional systems have even become commonplace. Asia and Africa also have broadcasting unions, though not yet on the European scale. As for the smaller and the less developed countries of the world, they perforce depend heavily on syndicated television materials from the few major production centers in the larger nations. Both the viewer and the listener in other countries thus receive far more programming from external sources than most Americans.

This internationalism will accelerate as the economics of satellite relays are worked out. The first transatlantic television relay, using Telstar I, took place in 1962. In 1964, a hundred such relays occurred, with four different satellites available for the purpose. The coverage of the 1964 Tokyo Olympic Games, fed live via Telstar II and by means of airlifted tape recordings to both Eurovision and Intervision, represented a landmark in the development of intercontinental television-program exchange. Global television became possible by 1967, when live broadcasts were exchanged among the Americas,

---

[2] Limited research data indicate that in America even occasional shortwave listening to foreign stations is limited to under 10 per cent of the adult population. See Don D. Smith, "America's Short-Wave Audience: Twenty-Five Years Later," *Public Opinion Quarterly*, XXXIII (Winter, 1969–1970), 537–545.

Table P.3
Major international broadcasters

Country	Estimated Hours Per Week
USSR	1,929
Mainland China	1,468
United States (VOA)[1]	877
West Germany	724
Great Britain (BBC)	719
Egypt	586
Albania	480
Australia	359
Holland	339
East Germany	335
Portugal	322
Cuba	319
Poland	305
India	270
Japan	256
Spain	247

[1]Adding the unofficial American-sponsored Radio Free Europe and Radio Liberty to the VOA brings the U. S. total to 1,908 hours.

Source: 1970 data in *BBC Handbook, 1971* (London: British Broadcasting Corporation, 1971), p. 109.

Europe, Japan, and Australia. An estimated 800 million people, at peak viewing times, saw the 1968 Olympics from Mexico City.

Practical satellite relay systems require sophisticated equipment for both sending signals to the satellites and receiving relayed signals. Further complications arise from five prevailing sets of national technical standards for black-and-white television with fourteen different variations, plus three incompatible color systems (Table 3.1). Signals must be converted from one system to another as they go from one country to another.[3]

Communications satellites need not function only as relay stations. They could serve as repeater broadcast stations *per se*. Then the home receiver could pick up signals from satellites directly: signals would no longer have to go first to a specialized ground receiving station and thence through conventional ground-based distribution facilities to broadcasting transmitters. But such a development, on a worldwide scale, will be impeded by the fact that ordinary home television receivers are normally built to interpret signals of only one technical standard. Either broadcast satellites will have to carry duplicate equipment to match the several different national standards, or home

---

[3] In 1970, a television-systems converter cost a third of a million dollars.

receivers will have to be fitted with adapters for multistandard reception. Sound-broadcasting equipment, on the other hand, does have a common world standard. A set designed to receive shortwave transmissions can pick up stations from all over the world. The first international direct home-reception satellite rebroadcast services may therefore be in sound rather than vision broadcasting.

It would be naive, however, to imagine that the technical possibility of such free-flowing global information exchange automatically makes it acceptable politically. International satellites delivering messages directly to home receivers could be regarded as a most unwelcome intrusion. The last thing many countries want for their citizens is uncontrolled exposure to communications from outside their own borders. They are sometimes willing to spend as much or more on jamming unwanted foreign broadcasts as they are on transmitting material designed to rectify foreign propaganda or to counteract unfavorable information.[4] Vested private economic interests can also be expected to influence the adoption of satellite technology. Companies operating the great earthbound communications systems must protect their huge investments in conventional equipment until their role in space communication is assured.[5]

P.2 / National Systems

To a marked degree, then, each country has adapted broadcasting to suit its own basic national philosophy, to meet its own peculiar geographic, social, economic, and cultural problems. Comparative study of broadcasting systems discloses a wide range of solutions, with no two countries having arrived at precisely the same answer. Broadcasting necessarily becomes deeply involved in questions of national policy for two main reasons. First, without national (and, indeed, international) regulation of the physical aspects of radio transmissions—their wavelength, power, characteristics, points of origin, etc.—conflicting signals would soon make the whole system useless. This actually happened in America in the 1920's, forcing revision of government regulations. Second, broadcasting itself is an instrument of social control, making laws to govern it a political necessity. No country can afford to leave so

---

[4] Jamming, first used during the events leading up to World War II in Europe, consists of broadcasting a meaningless interference signal on the frequency of the station the jammer wishes to blot out. As an example of how much weight can be put on this purely negative use of broadcasting, the Polish government at one time spent as much merely to jam the Voice of America as the United States spent on its entire worldwide VOA service. [Thomas Sorensen, *The Word War: The Story of American Propaganda* (New York: Harper & Row, 1968), p. 90.]

[5] See Lawrence Lessing, "Cinderella in the Sky," *Fortune,* October, 1967, pp. 131–133, 196–208, regarding controversy over use of satellites for domestic United States communication.

powerful and so persuasive an avenue of public communication completely open without regard for public policy and national interest.[6]

The common principle underlying the diverse national systems is the universally recognized proposition that the "airwaves"—the electromagnetic frequencies used by broadcasting and other forms of radio communication—are public property, to be administered by each government according to its concept of what is best for its own people. Thus, broadcasting is set apart from other media of communication. Unlike any other, it requires as a prerequisite to its very existence the use of a resource which cannot be manufactured or privately owned, but which on the contrary is by definition a possession of mankind as a whole.

This principle places a duty on any government to administer the use of radio frequencies so as to serve national interests best. The interpretation of this duty naturally differs widely from one nation to another, and that is why we find such a diversity of national broadcasting systems in the world.

The differences revolve around three key questions which every national broadcasting system has to answer for itself:

1. *How shall broadcasting be managed?* Directly by the state? Indirectly by the state through a semiautonomous chartered organization? By private operators subject to some degree of state regulation? Or by some combination of these?

2. *How shall broadcasting be financed?* By state subsidy? By license fees on receiving sets? By revenue from broadcast advertising? By some combination of these?

3. *By what criteria shall programming be controlled?* By the desires of the generality of set owners, as determined by audience research? By judgments about what will be in the best interests of the state and of its people made by political leaders? By broadcasting officials? By committees representing major social institutions such as education, religion, the fine arts? By regional interests as reflected in political subdivisions, parties? By national subgroups having special ethnic, linguistic, or cultural identities? Or by some combination of these?

Every one of these alternatives has been adopted in practice in one country or another. Often particular local circumstances dictate the choice. For example, the economies of many countries are insufficiently developed to enable financing a full-scale broadcasting service from advertising revenue alone,

---

[6] Private vested interests also exert an influence on the shaping of national broadcasting systems. Because their intervention is often clandestine, however, it is difficult to measure. It seems evident that powerful newspaper and motion-picture interests have had something to do with retarding the development of commercialism in broadcasting in many parts of the world. See Harold A. Innis, *Empire and Communications* (Oxford: Clarendon Press, 1950), p. 207. As an example, the British press actively opposed introduction of commercial televison. [H. H. Wilson, *Pressure Group: The Campaign for Commercial Television in England* (New Brunswick, N. J.: Rutgers University Press, 1961), p. 162.]

were that form of support desired. Most developing countries have so many different linguistic and ethnic subgroups that it would be impossible to give each one its own local vernacular broadcasting service. On the other hand, the coexistence of English and French in Canada and of French and Dutch in Belgium requires full-scale services in each language in those countries. In the Netherlands, religiopolitical distinctions are so sharply drawn that each of five such groups has its own broadcasting service.

Aside from such specific variations, each national broadcasting system tends generally to reflect that country's underlying political philosophy. This philosophy, in turn, can be broadly viewed in terms of the attitude assumed by the country's leadership toward *people*. What are considered to be the rights, the duties, the capacities, the potentialities of each individual citizen? And what are considered to be the duties of the country's leadership toward these ordinary individuals who make up the ultimate "mass" audience of broadcasting? In this generalized perspective, we can discern three basic orientations, three kinds of attitudes toward people, which determine how broadcasting is managed, financed, and programmed. We can call these three orientations toward people the *authoritarian,* the *paternalistic,* and the *permissive* attitudes.

The authoritarian attitude takes little or no account of the ordinary citizen's desires as weighed against the demands of the state. The paternalistic attitude does take account of the ordinary citizen's desires but finds some of them unworthy of satisfaction, imposing its own presumably educated standards of taste. The permissive attitude gives first priority to the common man's desires and strives to satisfy them as fully as possible.

P.3 / Authoritarianism

The authoritarian attitude characterizes the systems adopted in the USSR and other communist countries. The state operates broadcasting and harnesses it directly to implementation of government policies. In the USSR, broadcasting is a function of the Ministry of Culture, under guidance of a special committee set up for the purpose by the Council of Ministers. In other communist countries, the Ministry of Education, the Ministry of Information, or a special administration directly responsible to the top political level oversees broadcasting. The guiding philosophy of these systems is, of course, that if people happen to have frivolous tastes and a desire to waste their time on ideologically barren entertainments, it is too bad; far from encouraging such retrograde tendencies by pandering to them, the state should stamp them out. Hence the programming under such systems could never be called "popular," and audiences are under constant temptation to seek satisfaction elsewhere by illegally tuning in to foreign broadcasts. For this reason, in recent years even Russia's rigidly doctrinaire approach has been softened somewhat by the realization that, in terms of effective communication, appeal to popular tastes can serve as a wedge for propaganda.[7]

A somewhat different type of authoritarian attitude prevails in developing countries. A great cultural gap separates the educated elite, who provide the political leadership, from the mass of the people, who remain relatively untouched by modern education and outlook. Leaders in such countries regard the ordinary people as too unsophisticated to know what they "want" from an alien instrument like broadcasting, and too naive to be entrusted freely with alien ideas and unevaluated information. Governments in most developing countries vest program control in departments or ministries which have charge of such fields as education, culture, or information generally; program decisions must often be referred to top political leadership. The leaders, who do not trust the native common sense of illiterate and unsophisticated masses to deal on their own terms with possibly confusing and unfamiliar ideas, prescribe a spoon-fed broadcast diet. This attitude prevails even in developing countries which make no claim to socialistic philosophies modeled on the authoritarian example of communism.

P.4 / Paternalism

By contrast, the paternalistic attitude shows more faith in the basic intelligence of the masses and in their capacity to deal with ideas. Its concern is not to suppress information and to dictate conclusions, but to maintain a healthily balanced program diet, with neither too much spinach nor too much ice cream for social and psychological well-being. The paternalistic attitude assumes that (1) popular taste is, by definition, a rather low taste for frivolous, time-destroying light entertainment; (2) highly educated and cultivated leaders have the duty to limit the extent to which such tastes are gratified and to balance them out with programming at a more serious or cultivated level; (3) this experience will gradually ameliorate the low level of popular taste.

Most noncommunist industrialized countries practice varying degrees of paternalism in their broadcasting systems. For purposes of comparison, the system of pretelevision Britain is apposite, for it was originally designed explicitly with a view to avoiding the "mistakes" which the British felt had been made in America.[8] The British Broadcasting Corporation, founded in 1927 to

---

[7] See S. Vronitsyn, "The Modernization of Soviet Propaganda," *Institute for the Study of the USSR Bulletin* (Munich), XII (October, 1965), 32–39. It should be added, however, that even the dullest, most didactic programming seems to succeed *in the absence of any alternative.* This peculiarity of broadcasting, its power to appeal regardless of content, is discussed further in Section 24.9.

[8] See Asa Briggs, *The History of Broadcasting in the United Kingdom,* Vol. I (London: Oxford University Press, 1961), Chapter 4, "The American Boom." Briggs states that "American experience served as a warning during the 1922–1926 period" and quotes (p. 67) a British writer in 1926: "The American experience provided a valuable lesson. It showed the dangers which might result in a diversely populated country of a small area like our own if the go-as-you-please methods of the United States were copied."

displace a short-lived private commercial company, is a public chartered corporation with a monopoly over sound broadcasting in Britain. It derives its funds from license fees on receiving sets. Although the state appoints its board of governors and it has many other links with officialdom, the Corporation operates with a recognizably independent scope of discretion in program matters within the terms of its charter.

The viewpoint of the BBC has always been that its duty to society as a whole imposes a responsibility for basing program judgments on its own conscientious evaluation of society's best interests. This evaluation has naturally been colored by the paternalistic outlook of the social class from which the BBC leadership has been drawn. It is revealing, for example, to follow the reluctant acceptance by the BBC of the idea of finding out how its audiences really responded and what they actually wanted. In the earlier years, BBC officials simply refused to acknowledge that their own judgments needed to be qualified at all by objective facts about listening behavior or listener preferences. Even in 1949, for example, a British government committee could report that if research indicated that the public disliked a BBC series, "such findings would be considered with the utmost care and weighed with other considerations which were relevant. But the decision, when taken, would be a responsible decision, come to in the light of what was considered ultimately to be in the best interests of the public and the service."[9]

The discovery in the late 1930's that a large proportion of the BBC's supposedly loyal audience was actually tuning by preference to a foreign commercial station, Radio Luxembourg, plus the insistent demand for audience facts by producers of educational programs, finally broke down the BBC's paternalistic isolationism from the reality of the mass listener's tastes and habits. But not until the 1940's did the BBC seriously embark on systematic scientific audience research, and as recently as 1960 a BBC official could write:

The real degradation of the BBC started with the invention of the hellish department which is called "Listener Research." That Abominable Statistic is supposed to show "what the listeners *like*"—and, of course, what they like is the red-nosed comedian and the Wurlitzer organ.[10]

To be sure, this half-joking indictment represents a diehard personal view inconsistent with modern official BBC policy. The BBC philosophy of today holds that neither the paternalistic nor the permissive philosophy of broadcasting makes any sense at the extremes. The question remains, however: can a balance between the extremes be ideally attained by a single organization? Or does it need the interplay of two or more organizations representing alterna-

---

[9] Quoted in William G. Madow, *et al., Evaluation of Statistical Methods Used in Obtaining Broadcast Ratings,* House Report 193, 87th Cong., 1st Sess. (Washington: Government Printing Office, 1961), p. 10.

[10] Quoted in Briggs, *op. cit.,* II (1965), 261.

tive points of view? A BBC official told a government investigating committee that it recognized a "risk of paternalism" in its policy of "giving the lead" to public taste, but that it felt it was a risk that had to be taken.[11] The risk could be eliminated or at least the danger decreased by the presence of another organization representing another philosophy of programming. (See Section P.6.)

P.5 / The Permissive Attitude

All countries, even those with authoritarian outlooks, have by now accepted audience research as a useful and necessary guide in programming. But the ways research results are used differ according to the three points of view toward the audience. The authoritarians use research to make their propaganda more effective, while the paternalists use it to temper, but not replace, their personal judgment of what the people *ought* to have. Only the permissive systems regard the results of audience research as a controlling mandate over programming policies.

Broadcasting in America provides the major example of permissiveness. In the United States, government operation of broadcasting was briefly considered in the beginning but ruled out in favor of operation by private individuals or organizations, subject to federal licensing and the general requirement that stations operate "in the public interest, convenience, and necessity." Interpretation of this phrase in practice is left largely to the broadcasters themselves, so that government control over programming is minimal, in keeping with the Constitutional guarantee of freedom of speech and press.

After a little more hesitancy, alternative ideas for financing the new medium were ruled out in favor of allowing stations to support themselves through the sale of broadcast advertising. These two decisions automatically made the primary criterion of commercial programming whatever seems most popular with most people. The profit incentive, freed from *a priori* standards of program content, resulted in catering to the common denominators of popular taste.

American broadcasters have surpassed all others in skillfully producing mass entertainment and exploiting it as a vehicle of advertising. The result is a broadcasting service characterized by an extraordinarily high degree of technical competence, devoted to programming of which an extraordinarily high proportion consists of light entertainment. The American commercial approach to programming has focused attention on finding out what the mass of the people want—or what they think they want, or what they are most likely to accept (since some critics argue that the people do not really know what they "want" or merely learn to "want" what they are given). This approach has required, of course, intensive development of audience research.

---

[11] Great Britain, Committee on Broadcasting ("Pilkington Committee"), *Report, 1960,* Cmnd. 1753 (London: Her Majesty's Stationery Office, 1962), p. 38.

This permissive system has been extraordinarily successful in quantitative terms—partly because of its permissiveness, but also because broadcasting developed at the critical moment in time to participate in America's mid-century economic boom. Broadcast advertising played a major role in the consumer revolution. It both helped to create and received benefit from the enormously expanding mass market for consumer goods and services.

American broadcasting thus developed relatively unhampered within the permissive framework of the competitive free-enterprise system. The style of American broadcasting has been characterized by all the pragmaticism, aggressiveness, materialism, improvisation, expansionism, and free-swinging competitiveness of American marketing. Whatever its critics may say, the result on the whole has been a more lively, inventive, and varied broadcasting system than can be found elsewhere in the world. Not only can America afford to support far more broadcasting stations than other countries (Table P.1), but the dynamics of its system have also produced a far greater variety of stations. Broadcasting in America has responded to the infinitely varied demands of the marketplace, so that despite an average sameness, when one looks in detail one can find at least some stations devoted to almost every kind of special interest—not only stations of great size and reach in metropolitan areas, but also tiny, localized stations within metropolitan areas and in small communities; not only stations motivated by profit, but also nonprofit stations licensed to educational institutions, foundations, and municipalities; stations not only combined into massive networks but also operated independently; not only stations devoted to trashy entertainment, but also stations devoted to education, culture and a wide range of minority tastes; stations using not only English, but over forty other languages, including Eskimo, Serbo-Croatian, and Turkish.[12]

Even so, most other governments disagree with the extreme permissiveness of the American commercial system, with its emphasis on what people "want" rather than what they "need." They feel that programming cannot be left entirely to the uncontrolled interaction of popular supply and demand, but should be balanced in accordance with *a priori* judgments about the need to preserve national cultural traditions and the relative importance of information, education, and entertainment. In America, too, critics of the commercialism of the present system have not been wanting. Burton Paulu, an American student of European broadcasting systems, comments:

Europe can look to American broadcasting for enthusiasm and drive as well as for production ingenuity. But the United States can acquire from Europe the concepts that broadcasting is a public service rather than an industry, and that program policies should be determined by social values rather than investment returns.[13]

---

[12] Lists of foreign-language broadcasts by American stations can be found in *Broadcasting Yearbook*.

[13] Burton Paulu, *Radio and Television Broadcasting on the European Continent* (Minneapolis: University of Minnesota Press, 1967), p. 245.

P.6 / The Pluralistic Trend

Of course, the three prototypes we have described exist nowhere in pure form. American commercial broadcasting's permissiveness is tinged with a sense of responsibility; the BBC's paternalism is qualified by a "duty to keep sensitively aware of the public's tastes and attitudes as they now are";[14] the USSR's authoritarianism, even if only calculatingly, finds paternalistic head patting and even occasional permissive eye winking sometimes to its advantage. The point is that even with the best of intentions, a single institution (or group of institutions ruled by a single philosophy) tends toward rigidity.

In the light of half a century of broadcasting experience, a *pluralistic* system seems best able to assure that the medium will develop its full potentialities within a given national framework. A single monolithic system seems inevitably to cramp the potentialities of the medium in one respect or another. A pluralistic system, by providing divergent methods of program control and alternative programming philosophies, introduces an element of competition. This corrective prevents a system from drifting too far away from the realities of audience interests and tends to stimulate creativity and innovation.

The power of competition was illustrated by the phenomenal popularity of European "pirate" stations in the 1960's. These stations operated on ships or abandoned offshore forts in the coastal waters of western Europe. The first such station started in 1958 on a ship anchored between Sweden and Denmark. Frankly imitative of American popular-music formats and capitalizing on American advertising techniques, the pirates almost immediately captured huge audiences and created national demands which could not be ignored. In 1965, the popularity of a television station off the coast of Holland escalated the issue of commercial television to the point where it caused the resignation of the Dutch cabinet. Eventually the Dutch Navy closed the station. Laws were passed to deal with the rest of the pirates, but not before they had made their point. In their short and stormy life, the pirates made the monolithic systems of Europe acutely aware of neglected audience tastes. Britain and other western European countries significantly liberalized their broadcasting policies to serve audiences whose wants had hitherto been unsuspected or ignored.[15]

One of the emergent features of modern world broadcasting is increased tolerance toward commercial advertising. Though the majority of the earlier radio-broadcasting systems were noncommercial, today over 60 per cent of the world's national television systems operate commercially, wholly or in part. Alternatively, in countries like the United States, which started with

---

[14] Great Britain, Committee on Broadcasting, *op. cit.,* p. 18.

[15] In Britain, "The Marine, etc., Broadcasting (Offences) Act, 1967" came into effect in August, 1967. The next month the BBC started a new popular-music program of the type featured by the pirates. The law overcame the legal problem of dealing with ships in international waters by cutting off the pirates' supplies of food, equipment, and advertising revenue.

commercialism, the emergent element is a viable noncommercial service. In either case, the trend is pluralistic.

Advertising support as one element in a pluralistic system has arguments in its favor quite aside from the fact that it is the most painless and least discriminatory way of taxing the set owner. Advertising can perform a useful function in a national economy, and broadcast advertising has unique advantages as a sales tool over all other media. A BBC film producer, travelling around the world collecting material on television developments, described the marketing role of television in the Japan of the early 1960's:

I visited one family whose house was completely Japanese. There was no Western furniture of any kind, yet in the kitchen there was an electric fish-fryer, an electric rice boiler, an electric mixer. I asked the housewife whether television had helped her choose which brand to buy. She told me that until she saw TV advertising she didn't even know such gadgets existed . . .[16]

Dependence on advertising income focusses management's attention on objective analysis of audiences and their desires, providing a counterbalance to noncommercial services, which respond less sensitively to popular taste. Advertising by its very nature stresses competition and so provides a spur to innovation and creativity.

Britain again provides an apt example. The BBC still enjoys its monopoly over sound radio in Britain and still rules out commercials. Since 1954, however, it has had to compete for television viewers with private companies. Moreover, these companies operate commercially, somewhat along American lines, even using quantities of American programs.

Such "Americanization" confirmed Britain's worst fears, but it is kept in bounds by an ingenious system for maintaining separation of powers. Still another public chartered corporation, the Independent Television Authority (ITA), owns and operates the transmission facilities of commercial television in Britain. A group of private, commercial program companies supplies the programming and sells the advertising.

The ITA, operating like the BBC under charter, has responsibility not only for contracting to supply transmission facilities to the commercial program companies, but also for controlling both their advertising practices and their programming policies in keeping with standards established in its charter. This division of responsibilities holds commercial interests at arm's length, so to speak, for the ITA has no reason to defer to advertisers. It can fine a contracting program company for infringement of rules or even cancel its contract altogether. The program companies are all regional rather than national in scope, so that no single company achieves a dominant position, nor are regional interests neglected.

---

[16] From "Television—A World Picture" by Richard Cawston, from Robert L. Shayon, *et al., The Eighth Art,* copyright © 1962, Holt, Rinehart and Winston, Inc., p. 8.

Meanwhile, the BBC's own noncommercial television service must compete with the ITA service. Commercial television attracts over half the audience. The BBC can afford to take second place in ratings, since it derives both its radio and its television income from license fees on receivers. The fees are collected by the Post Office, which has from the outset had jurisdiction over the technical aspects of station licensing. The Post Office retains a portion of the fees to defray its own expenses in connection with licensing and collection.[17]

But the BBC recognized early on that holding a national monopoly in the field of sound radio carried with it potential dangers. Lack of competition can mean falling into a rut, becoming stuffily bureaucratic and unresponsive to new developments and creative improvements in the broadcasting art. The position of being a national institution can also mean neglect of regional and popular interests. To ensure variety of programming, the Corporation operates four contrasting services: "Radio 1" picked up the popular-music audience where the pirates left off; "Radio 2" emphasizes varied light entertainment; "Radio 3" provides mostly serious music and talks; and "Radio 4" provides a family service of news, talks, documentaries, plays, and education. Six regional studios have, since the beginning, ensured representation of the major areas of the country. Starting in 1968, additional purely local services have been added experimentally.

Lack of competition has been offset by the high level of dedicated professionalism of the BBC staff. BBC news, for example, has earned unique worldwide respect. The genuine professional sets his own high standards. He comes equipped with a built-in incentive which provides constant stimulus to alert, conscientious, prideful workmanship. The BBC's kind of professional excellence could not, however, originate solely within the BBC. It springs ultimately from the roots of British tradition and character. Any other country, given the BBC charter to work with, would never have come up with exactly the same result.

The singularity of the BBC in this respect has been shown in practice by newly independent countries which were once part of the British colonial empire. British rulers had introduced BBC-type broadcasting systems into these countries, but in every instance the original conception has been completely lost since independence. This does not mean the BBC system is not good for Britain. But it is not necessarily good for any other country. Each national system must be considered in some respects unique.

In the excolonial countries, lack of competition impedes full development of broadcasting services. The treadmill of broadcast production by tenured civil servants can have a deadly effect on morale and creativeness. It is all too

---

[17] A committee which studied the state of British broadcasting in 1960 concluded that competition, after about six years of BBC-ITA rivalry, had brought both good and ill in its wake (Great Britain, Committee on Broadcasting, *op. cit.*, pp. 44–46). The point of view advanced here does not ignore the need to keep competition within bounds.

easy to slip into dull, repetitive routines and to fail to make that extra effort which alert and timely programming and production always demand. In the absence of an ingrained, long-established professional tradition, the most effective antidote to this retrograde tendency is competition. A competing station lying in wait to take advantage of every mistake and to expose slipshod workmanship automatically keys personnel up to the required pitch.

The benefit of constructive competition in broadcasting, which pluralism promotes, has been widely recognized, and most highly developed systems now try to provide for it in some way. In the Federal Republic of Germany, for example, each of the nine federal political units has its own broadcasting system. When the state decided to broaden program choice by developing an alternative service, it did not allow the existing broadcasting units to provide this second service but established an entirely separate organization to compete with the existing stations. Even for American noncommercial television, the Carnegie Commission recommended establishing two separate national program-production centers, in part because "competition between two or more centers will act as a spur and will provide a basis for comparison."[18]

Canada and Japan are other major foreign examples of the pluralistic approach. The Canadian Broadcasting Corporation, a noncommercial public chartered corporation, modelled originally along BBC lines, operates a national network of stations. Privately owned, commercial local stations also exist, but they must carry CBC noncommercial national programs as well as their own. Japan has a government-sponsored national network, operating side by side with relatively unrestricted private commercial stations.

American broadcasting has always been at least incipiently pluralistic. Educational and religious institutions were among the first to obtain radio-station licenses (Table 7.1), and from the outset the desirability of reserving some broadcast channels exclusively for noncommercial use was discussed. However, the landslide success of commercial broadcasting smothered most of the pioneer noncommercial licensees as well as the proposal to reserve noncommercial channels. It took some thirty years for effective alternatives to commercialism to begin to reassert themselves effectively. Though the reasons for this lag are complex, they come down fundamentally to lack of unified power-structure support for the noncommercial service and consequent lack of political influence. Commercial broadcasters, for all their intense intramural competititiveness, found no trouble in closing ranks and uniting their forces to support a powerful Congressional lobby and to bring the regulatory agency to heel. Commercial interests harassed those of the pioneer educational radio stations who survived the first flush of enthusiasm during the late 1920's and early 1930's, until all but about thirty gave up the costly legal battle to hold on to their channels. The regulatory Commission did its part in 1935 by turning down a second proposal to reserve AM channels for educational use.

---

[18] Carnegie Commission on Educational Television, *Public Television: A Program for Action* (New York: Harper & Row, 1967), p. 43.

Noncommercial interests had no such simple, compelling, and unifying rallying point as profits. Their goals were diffuse, and some of the most powerful and prestigious educational interests stayed on the sidelines, comparatively uninvolved. It remained for television to broaden the base of educational involvement. Only with the advent of television did the drive for a viable noncommercial broadcast service get the unified support from the educational establishment and the political leverage needed to overcome opposition and apathy. During the 1960's, the stage was set for the growth of a genuine alternative to the hitherto overwhelmingly dominant commercial service.

P.7 / American Influences Abroad

Foreign examples provided encouragement and inspiration to the American supporters of the noncommercial alternative service, but the flow of influence has been generally stronger in the other direction. We have pointed out that some countries, at least, have regarded American broadcasting more as a dire warning of what to avoid than as an admirable example of what to follow. Nevertheless, the worldwide trend toward commercialization of television created an automatic market for American expertise in commercial management, programming, sales, and promotion. Networks, advertising agencies, and program syndicators entered into a variety of business relationships with foreign broadcasting organizations, both private and government owned. Each of the television networks has international divisions. ABC, for example, acts as sales representative for some fifty stations in Canada, Mexico, Latin America, the Caribbean, Europe, Australia, the Middle East, and the Far East.

Program producers distribute syndicated television materials to over a hundred foreign markets. Indeed, American programs command such popularity with audiences abroad that some countries, including Britain, Canada, and Australia, have imposed quota limitations on American program imports. Despite language and cultural barriers, action-packed syndicated programs fascinate audiences everywhere in the world. Illiterate viewers without a word of English, whose culture and daily life differ completely from the milieu depicted on the screen, become as involved in American cowboy, detective, and adventure stories as their original audiences.[19]

In addition to these pervasive influences exported through commercial channels, American broadcast materials and concepts also reach foreign countries through political channels. The United States foreign-aid program and the Information Agency of the State Department have provided equipment and advisors to assist media in many developing countries. The Peace Corps has supplied technicians and operational personnel to help establish

---

[19] A curious though limited reciprocity of American influence has been noted: programs are produced abroad especially tailored for American tastes. The very first BBC series made with the American market in mind succeeded, but a BBC official observed, "I do not think it is a series of which we could, at the same time, feel very proud." [Great Britain, Committee on Broadcasting, *op. cit.*, p. 44.]

educational radio and television systems, notably in Colombia. United States Information Service[20] posts supply local media generously with program materials. Both USIA and the Agency for International Development arrange scholarships and tours in the United States for foreign media personnel. World audiences can learn of American program methods by example from the Voice of America, the radio-television arm of USIA, which in 1970 broadcast over eight hundred hours per week in thirty-six languages. In addition to its own facilities, comprising over a hundred powerful transmitters, VOA has access to many foreign broadcast facilities; it reported that in 1969, four thousand foreign stations broadcast VOA material.[21]

Less often noted at home perhaps, but nevertheless influential abroad, is the American Forces Radio and Television Service, which provides worldwide radio and television programming for American servicemen. AFRTS operates more than thirty overseas television stations. Powerful stateside shortwave radio transmitters relay a wide selection of American commercial programming, including the news services of the commercial radio networks—all with the commercials edited out, of course. AFRTS thus brings American-style domestic programming within reach of many foreign viewers and listeners.[22]

Clearly, America influences world broadcasting on a massive scale—though whether for good or ill is subject to debate. Many deplore the materialistic values implied by American-inspired commercialism and by the content of American syndicated programming. Foreigners often regard broadcasting as an aspect of "Coca Colonization," a process of cultural-economic exploitation alleged to be the modern equivalent of old-fashioned political-military colonialism. An unusually perceptive economist, Peter Drucker, has considered at some length the economic role of mass media in the new "global community" they have created. He sees the allegedly neocolonialistic effects of the media as more an accident of timing than a sinister plot:

America had simply reached the mass-consumption economy a little ahead of the others. Our economy only demonstrated a little earlier the values, the demands, the appetites, and economic preferences of peoples everywhere today.[23]

We have already ascribed the remarkable success of commercial broadcasting in America in part to an accident of timing: radio emerged at the critical

---

[20] The head office of the State Department's propaganda arm in Washington is known as the United States Information Agency (USIA), while its field posts in foreign countries are known as United States Information Service (USIS) posts.

[21] "The Voice of America in Brief," USIA release, March, 1970.

[22] According to a British commentator: "There is little doubt that British soldiers and civilians alike [during World War II] thoroughly enjoyed the more relaxed, informal atmosphere of American-style broadcasting and found the entertainment more sprightly than that of the pre-war BBC. To some extent, at least, the dreaded 'Americanization' of British tastes by Hollywood and 'pop' records was given additional impetus by the American Forces Network." [Wilson, *op. cit.*, p. 23.]

[23] Peter Drucker, *The Age of Discontinuity* (New York: Harper & Row, 1969), p. 78.

moment when the national economy was about to be revolutionized by unprecedented growth of mass consumption. The case of the Japanese housewife for whom television bridged the gap between the medieval past and the electrified present has been cited. Global communication merely accelerates a tendency which broadcasting neither created nor can halt.

A universal appetite for small luxuries has emerged. They signify a little economic independence, a little control over economic destiny. They are a badge of freedom. . . . That one can do without it makes the small luxury into a psychological necessity.[24]

Of course, nothing speeds the development of such appetites more than television, which puts those small luxuries on tempting display, like so many brightly polished apples in a vendor's stall.

The whole world . . . has become one economy in its expectations, in its responses, and in its behavior. . . . The world economy is the new perception created by the new media—the movies first, followed by radio and TV. . . . These electronic media communicate things rather than what people are or think. They communicate, in other words, economics. They create a global shopping center.[25]

Some critics worry not so much about the impact of American broadcasting on the domestic expectations of audiences overseas as about its reciprocal effect on America. The motion-picture industry (which profits more from showing its products abroad than at home) has for years been scolded because its films create a false impression of America overseas. Television now shares the blame. The Westerns, domestic comedies, and crime and adventure stories that form the bulk of syndicated program exports project neither an accurate nor a flattering image of American character and society. The dilemma is how to reconcile fiction with social documentation, trade with diplomacy, entertainment with propaganda. A free society can hardly set up censors to control the export of media materials, nor can private producers for the domestic market be expected to follow propaganda guide lines. Even elimination of fiction in favor of fact could be equally misleading. One wonders what kind of impression a diet of "real" information would make if due prominence were given to news about poverty, environmental pollution, racial discrimination, street violence, strikes, and automobile accidents!

Edward R. Murrow provided the classic illustration of the dilemma. Murrow became head of the USIA in 1960, after a long and distinguished news career in commercial broadcasting. One of his last major television documentaries as head of CBS News, *Harvest of Shame,* dealt controversially with the exploitation of American migrant farm workers. Soon after Murrow took over at USIA, the BBC scheduled the American documentary for telecast in Britain.

---

[24] *Ibid.,* p. 79.

[25] *Ibid.,* p. 80.

The man who a few months before was disparaging his own network for not protesting attempted Government intervention in the field of news now attempted Government intervention of his own. He . . . asked that *Harvest* of *Shame* be cancelled, as a "personal favor." . . . The request was refused as it surely would have been by Murrow if he were in [the BBC's] place, and the USIA director realized it never should have been made.[26]

Returning finally to our initial question: yes, American broadcasting does have unique characteristics—but so does every other national broadcasting system. The American system deserves special attention, however because of its influence over other systems. Candor requires admission that this influence is not always emulative; the American example has sometimes provided other countries with a model of what they want to avoid. And in America itself the system undergoes constant modification. As American broadcasting celebrated its fiftieth anniversary in 1970, the most conspicuous modification in process seemed to be the growth of the noncommercial system as a viable alternative to commercial broadcasting—in short, a trend toward the pluralism which world experience in general recommends.

---

[26] Alexander Kendrick, *Prime Time* (Boston: Little, Brown, 1969), p. 458.

PART ONE

THE PHYSICAL
BASES OF
BROADCASTING

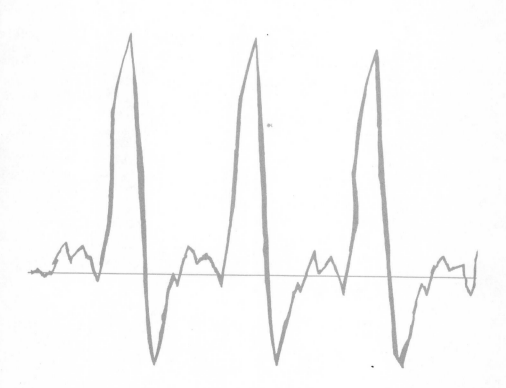

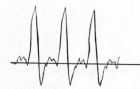

1

THE NATURE OF
RADIO ENERGY

Why does the United States have a Federal Communications Commission and the world an International Telecommunication Union? Why must broadcast stations be licensed, with stringent limits on power, times of operation, and technical characteristics? Why can a station be sold for many times the value of all its physical assets and commercial goodwill? Why can you receive radio stations from all over the world and yet not be able to pick up a television station only a hundred miles away? Why do we have both VHF and UHF television, both AM and FM radio?

Such questions as these, unique to the field of broadcasting, go back to the nature of radio energy itself. A meaningful answer to almost any significant question that can be asked about broadcasting requires consideration of radio's physical nature. We can change national or international radio regulations in keeping with changing economic, political or social conditions; but we cannot change the laws of nature.

Hence, the student of broadcasting, if he is at all serious, must understand the physical bases of radio. Most of the important broadcasting problems he will encounter reach back ultimately to stubborn physical facts. These facts, interacting with economic, political, and social forces, place limits on where and how far broadcast signals can travel and how much information they can carry. They govern the way transmitting stations can be distributed geographically and the number that can be accommodated in any one place or area. They commit us to standardization of systems and of equipment. They demand a degree of international cooperation unknown in other areas of human activity. They necessitate special types of regulation, not common to other mass-communications media. They affect program policies and public attitudes. In short, its physical nature gives broadcasting its unique character.

1.1 / Information Concepts

In other contexts we think of "information" as contrasting with "entertainment," but in the present context information means words, pictures, gestures

—symbols of any kind, regardless of their form or purpose. Information theory looks at communication from an engineering point of view, as measurable energy. The machine is indifferent to meaning; it regards as information anything that can be communicated.

From some original source, information must be *encoded* into the "language" of a given communication system. The encoded information is fed into a communication *channel* which has a certain maximum information capacity. At the other end *decoding* takes place, reproducing the original communication with a certain degree of fidelity. In the course of these operations some degradation of the original information takes place. Errors in the encoding-decoding processes, spurious or unwanted information (*noise*) contaminating the channel, and limitations of channel capacity can all affect the outcome at the receiving end.

This conceptual framework enables us to recognize the elements that all communication systems have in common, whether they are communicating speech, music, pictures, or arbitrary symbols. Wire and wireless communications, for example, are affected by electrical noise, such as interference from electrical power sources and atmospheric static. In radio we hear the crackle of thunderstorms or the drone of electric motors. In television we see the noise of a passing automobile's ignition system. The very transmitting and receiving components themselves generate a certain amount of noise, a built-in hum which becomes obvious when one opens wide the volume control on any piece of sound equipment, such as a radio receiver, phonograph, or studio console. High-quality electronic equipment is rated in terms of "signal-to-noise ratio," a measure of the prominence of inherent noise in relation to the wanted signal in the output.

Encoding-decoding processes are never absolutely perfect. Hence, a *distortion* rating is also commonly applied to communication equipment, giving a measure of the extent to which the components inherently alter the original information in the course of communicating it.

The communication channel in the case of sound or vision broadcasting is a group of radio frequencies. Radio, like visible light, is a form of radiant energy which can travel through space. To use radio energy for communication involves four fundamental operations: we must *generate* the radio energy in the first place; then we must encode information by *modulating* this energy, imposing on it an information pattern, such as a pattern of sound energy; next we must *detect* this modulated signal at the receiving end; and finally we must *demodulate* the signal to recover something approximating the original pattern of information in its original form. FM radio can give us higher-fidelity sound than AM because it is less subject to noise than AM and because the FM channel has greater information capacity than the AM channel. For similar reasons, a photograph in a magazine or a motion picture in a theatre gives us higher fidelity pictures than broadcast television pictures; they reproduce more picture elements simultaneously.

1.2 / Radio "Waves"

We spoke of a channel as consisting of radio frequencies. To understand the concept of "frequency" we must examine the nature of radio "waves." Whenever electrical energy in a wired electrical system is caused to reverse itself repeatedly, so that energy surges back and forth, first in one direction and then the other, some of the electrical energy escapes the wires and radiates into the space surrounding the system. This is true even of ordinary 60-cycle alternating current in the electrical wiring system of our houses.[1] The "60" refers to the frequency with which the current in the house wiring reverses direction each second.

We may think of these radiations as being like waves in water, though actually this is merely an analogy. Modern atomic physics regards such radiations as consisting of discrete energy particles called "quanta," rather than as being some kind of continuous form like a liquid. Although either model may be used, most common and familiar concepts in radio technology are based on the wave model.[2] For this reason we will discuss radio energy in terms of waves rather than quanta.

Wave motion has the characteristic of alternation or periodicity—that is, regular repetition of the same sequence of motion. In radio this repetition is called *oscillation*. It is convenient to explain the properties of oscillation in terms of sound. In doing so, however, we must keep in mind that this comparison is only an analogy; sound energy and radio energy, although they have similarities, are very different phenomena.

If we strike a tuning fork, it produces a sound which has three obvious characteristics—pitch, loudness, and duration. Loudness varies with the amount of force or energy put into the stroke; but whether the sound is loud or soft its pitch remains the same, depending on the size of the tuning fork. The duration of the sound is limited: unless new energy is supplied by another stroke, the sound gradually dies away.

A tuning fork, like other sources of sound, produces its effect by means of physical vibrations, *i.e.,* oscillations. This fact can be readily demonstrated

---

[1] The universal standard in the United States for household electricity is alternating current (AC) at 60 cycles per second (cps). In many other countries the alternating frequency is 50 cps. Direct current (DC) was widely used at one time but has been almost entirely replaced by AC. The frequency standard of 60 or 50 cps, as we shall see, has a bearing on the standards of television systems.

[2] See Donald G. Fink and David M. Lutyens, *The Physics of Television,* copyright © 1969 by Doubleday & Company, Inc., for a nonmathematical treatment of the atomic concept of electromagnetic energy. On the wave *versus* particle issue, the authors say (pp. 27–28): "To describe radiant energy as wave or particle is rather like conveying information about a person either by means of a photograph or a verbal character sketch. Each is better than the other for different purposes. . . . The actual individual is more complex than either."

simply by touching the sounding prong with the finger or dipping it in water. However, the vibrations are too minute and rapid for us to tell much about them by this simple test.

The classic device for demonstrating the detailed nature of such vibrations in slow motion is the pendulum. At rest, the pendulum hangs straight down at what we will call the zero point. Given a push, it swings back and forth, both left and right of the zero point. How far it swings depends on the amount of energy used to start it. If no further energy is supplied, it gradually runs down until it stops altogether at the zero point. The peculiarity of any given pendulum's motion is that the *rate* at which it swings (the number of times it makes a complete left-and-right movement from the zero point and back again in a given period of time) is constant. Whether it swings in a wide arc or barely moves, it takes the same amount of time to complete each cycle of movement. In this it resembles the tuning fork, whose pitch remains constant no matter how hard it is struck and no matter how long it vibrates.

It would be helpful to be able to depict graphically the element of *time* (duration) involved in the pendulum's motion. Imagine a pendulum with a pen attached to the end so that it can trace its movement on a piece of paper. If the paper moves vertically past the pen point at a constant speed, the pen will trace out a line something like that shown in Figure 1.1. Here we depict the time factor by stretching out the action of the pendulum, showing each swing at a different place on the paper—*i.e.*, at a different point in time. The resulting graphic representation of the pendulum's movement has several interesting things to tell.

One complete cycle of movement consists of two loops, one on each side of the zero point. Thus a complete *cycle* includes two opposite *phases*—an important fact to which we will return later. Each complete cycle takes up an equal amount of space along the time dimension, indicating that each cycle takes the same amount of time. Even though the pendulum is gradually running down, as shown by the shortening distance that successive loops extend from the zero line, each cycle covers the same distance.

The graph of the pendulum's motion gives us the basic concepts associated with radio energy. We conceive of radio energy as oscillating, like the pendulum. Each complete *cycle* of movement is conceived as a wave. Waves have a certain *length,* symbolized in Figure 1.1 by the distance covered during one cycle of movement. The waves are generated at a certain *frequency,* shown in Figure 1.1 by the number of cycles of motion completed in the time period depicted. Each wave has a certain *amplitude,* equivalent to the width of swing of the pendulum, which depends on the amount of energy supplied to the wave. As time passes, energy is used up and waves decrease in amplitude. This using up of energy is called *attenuation.* And finally, waves travel at a certain *velocity,* symbolized by the speed at which the drawing paper moved past the pen point.

Figure 1.1
Wave-motion concepts

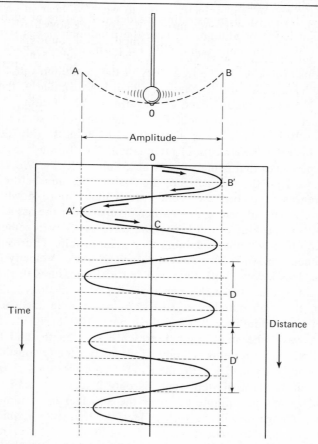

Assuming the pendulum moves from O, its position of rest, first in the direction B, a complete *cycle* of motion includes movement back past O to A and back again to O.

If, as it moved, the pendulum drew a line on a moving surface, its relative position from moment to moment would be depicted graphically as shown. The arrows indicate the direction of movement.

Turn the figure sideways to get the conventional graphic representation of a wave train. The vertical line represents relative amplitude and the horizontal line both time and distance. Note that the time for the complete cycle, D, is the same as that for the next cycle, D′. This is true for all four of the cycles depicted, showing that both the *frequency* and *wavelength* of the pendulum are constant. The amplitude is shown to be decreasing, however, as the pendulum runs down.

1.3 / Sound "Waves"

Let us now see how the seven concepts of cycle, wave, wavelength, frequency, amplitude, attenuation, and velocity apply to what we hear in sound energy. The amplitude of the pendulum's motion depends on how hard it is pushed, *i.e.,* how much energy is applied to it; the amplitude of sound likewise depends on the amount of energy applied to the vibrating sound source and is perceived in terms of *loudness.* The frequency of the pendulum's motion (as also its wavelength) depends on its physical dimensions. Similarly, the frequency and wavelength of a sound depend on the size of the vibrating sound source and are perceived in terms of *pitch.* The farther away the source of a sound, the more faintly it is heard; this diminution in loudness with distance from the source illustrates the concept of attenuation. Finally, we know from many everyday experiences that sound travels at a finite velocity. We see the lightning before we hear the thunderclap, the flash of the gun before the report. These differences occur because sound travels much more slowly than light, so that we see the event perceptibly earlier than we hear the associated sound.

We have been speaking of frequency and wavelength as in some way equivalent to each other without explaining their relationship. Thus, in Figure 1.1 the same dimension symbolizes *both* time and distance. Velocity is, in fact, a concept that does involve both time and space. It measures distance covered in a given unit of time, like miles per hour. A simple analogy will clarify the relationship. If a man marches at 100 steps per minute and each step is 3 feet long, in one minute he will travel three times 100, or 300 feet. Each step represents a wave, the step length represents wavelength, and the distance traveled per minute represents velocity. If we keep velocity constant (300 feet per minute) and vary step length, then step frequency must change to meet the new condition. Thus if step length is only 2 feet, the man will have to march at 150 steps per minute to cover the 300 feet in a minute. Or conversely, if we change step length to four feet, the frequency required to cover 300 feet in one minute is cut down to 75. As long as velocity remains constant, any given frequency has a corresponding wavelength. Under the same condition, of course, any given wavelength has a corresponding frequency. This condition is true of radio energy; its velocity *in space* is a constant, 300,000,000 meters (186,000 miles) per second. Hence, if a radio frequency is given, the corresponding wavelength can always be found by dividing the frequency into velocity; if a wavelength is given, the corresponding frequency can be found by dividing the wavelength into velocity. For practical purposes, wavelength and frequency are therefore different ways of measuring the same thing. Any radio wave can be described in terms of either its frequency or its length. The relationship is inverse: the longer the wavelength the lower the frequency; the shorter the wavelength, the higher the frequency.

So far we have been talking in analogies in order to show the simplicity and familiarity of the concepts involved. We must now emphasize again that radio differs in important respects from sound energy. One such difference is the great speed with which radio energy travels through space. At the rate of

300,000,000 meters per second, a radio wave can travel around the earth seven times in one second. Shakespeare's imagination stopped far short of this: Puck boasted that he could "put a girdle around the earth in forty minutes." Sound, on the other hand, travels in air at only about one-fifth of a mile per second, which means that radio waves travel over nine hundred thousand times as fast as sound waves.

Sound, as usually heard, travels in air, although of course it can also be conducted by other gases, by liquids, and by solids. In any event it has to have some physical conductor: sound cannot travel in a vacuum. Radio waves can; not only do they require no ascertainable conducting medium at all, they actually travel best through a vacuum. Air merely impedes them. Radio waves can, under some circumstances, pass through liquids and solids as well as gasses. On the other hand, some radio waves can be affected by such factors as atmospheric temperature, density, and water saturation.

1.4 / Modulation

So far we have established that radio is a form of energy having wave-like characteristics, capable of traveling through space at a velocity of 300,000,000 meters per second. But of course we are not interested merely in transmitting radio energy; we want to use this energy to transmit information. The process of encoding information into the language of radio energy, as we have said, is called *modulation*. A radio-broadcast transmitter radiates energy continuously as long as the station is turned on, whether or not any information is being transmitted. If one tunes a radio receiver to a station at a moment of "dead air," a slight hiss indicates that unmodulated energy is being transmitted even though no information is being sent. This basic and continuous transmission of the station is known as its *carrier wave*.

Modulation is the systematic alteration of the carrier wave with the energy pattern of the information transmitted. Consider the operation of an ordinary phonograph record. The disc has a continuous groove in which a pickup stylus rides. Suppose a recording is made of "silence," *i.e.,* no signal is recorded. On playback, the reproducing needle will ride in the smooth groove as the disc turns without producing any intentional sound. Nevertheless, a certain amount of noise—needle scratch, amplifier hum, etc.—will show that the phonograph is turned on and a record is being played. The "silent" recording compares to an unmodulated carrier wave, which sends no signal but nevertheless does transmit a certain amount of noise. When sound has been recorded on the disc, the sides of the groove are no longer smooth. A pattern of energy, originally in the form of sound, has now been translated into a corresponding pattern of variations in the shape of the groove. The pickup stylus, responding to this pattern as the record spins, starts the process of retranslation back to sound.

Each radio transmitter runs in its own "groove," the channel, or group of frequencies, to which it has been assigned. The carrier wave has a single specified frequency, but one single frequency can carry only a small amount of information. Information-carrying capacity depends on the number of adjacent frequencies available in addition to the carrier frequency. When a carrier frequency is modulated, the adjacent frequencies above and below the carrier come into play. These are called *side bands*. It is possible to suppress one of the side bands, inasmuch as each is a mirror image of the other, representing the opposite halves of a complete cycle (see Figure 1.1). In television, one of the video side bands is suppressed in order to conserve frequencies (see Figure 3.7). Radiotelephonic communication usually uses single-side-band (SSB) equipment.

Radio waves can be modulated in many ways, but broadcasting uses primarily two methods: amplitude modulation (AM) and frequency modulation (FM). Amplitude and frequency are the two most obvious choices among the variables which could be modulated. If the original signal consists of sound, we are concerned with a form of energy that itself has the two variables of amplitude (loudness) and frequency (pitch). Any sound can be fully described at a given moment in terms of loudness and pitch.

Let us consider amplitude modulation. Suppose a sound to be transmitted from the studio has the pitch of middle C. Suppose further, to avoid complications, that this hypothetical sound is a pure tone, *i.e.,* one without overtones. That means that the sound energy generated in the studio consists of a train of 264-cps waves. The particles of air in the studio, agitated at this frequency, cause a similar agitation in a delicately responsive component in the microphone. The microphone translates the pattern of vibration of the moving element into an identical pattern of *electrical* energy oscillating at 264 cps. Now we can no longer hear the signal. It travels, silent and invisible, along the microphone cable, through the wires and instruments of the control-room equipment, through more wires to the transmitter, where the unmodulated carrier wave is being generated and radiated into space. At the transmitter, the pattern of electrical energy—still vibrating at 264 cps but by now amplified millions of times over what it was when the microphone started it on its way —is imposed on the carrier wave. Since this is an amplitude-modulated transmitter, the signal alters the amplitude (amount of energy) of the carrier wave 264 times per second.

So far, we have left out of this account the element of loudness in the original sound. This component of the sound-energy pattern is accounted for by the *amount* (rather than the frequency) of change in the amplitude of the carrier wave. Thus, if the loudness doubled, the average amplitude of the carrier wave would be doubled, but the 264-cycle alternation in amplitude would be unchanged. In short, a single variable factor in the carrier wave can be used to do two things, since it can be varied independently as to both *rate* of change and *amount* of change.

One common source of confusion to avoid at this point is the assumption that there is any necessary connection between the frequency of the original sound to be transmitted and the frequency of the carrier wave on which it is transmitted. These two factors are independent. The 264-cycle sound can just as easily be transmitted by a carrier wave of 6,000,000 cycles as by one of 600,000 cycles. The 264-cycle energy pattern can be imposed on any broadcast-frequency carrier wave, regardless of the carrier's own frequency.

As the modulated signal travels through the atmosphere, it may encounter random charges of electromagnetic energy generated by natural electricity in the atmosphere, which we sometimes see as lightning. These random bits of energy interact with the amplitude-modulated radio signal, distorting the original pattern. We hear the distortions as the crackling, snapping sounds of "static." Similarly, man-made devices such as electric motors radiate electromagnetic energy which can cause static interference. Figure 1.2 shows modulation of a carrier wave's amplitude and how static distorts the signal.

Static does not affect frequency modulation, which is described in Section 2.4. Other more sophisticated ways of modulating carrier waves are increasingly used in radio communications. For example, PCM (pulse-code modulation) encodes speech in a binary code—a code consisting exclusively of the information "on" or "off." Since the information is reduced to such simple terms for transmission, PCM signals have high resistance to distortion. Other types of modulation use short bursts of energy (pulses) as the carrier; changes in the amplitude, frequency, or duration of these pulses convey the information. One function in color television uses still another type—phase modulation (see Section 3.7).

Modulation, then, means the transfer of a pattern of energy from one medium to another. Once we conceive of the message, whether sound or any other kind of signal, as consisting essentially of an energy pattern, the possibility of translating patterns from one medium to another becomes apparent. The air in the studio, the electrical current in the wires and finally the electromagnetic energy radiated by the transmitter are radically different media, yet each can duplicate an identical pattern of amplitude and frequency.

1.5 / Electromagnetic Spectrum

We have mentioned that the velocity of radio energy in space is approximately 300,000,000 meters (186,000 miles) per second. This quantity has great significance in modern physics, for it is the one absolute in the Einsteinian concept of the physical universe.[3] The fact that 300,000,000 meters per second is also the speed of light is no mere coincidence, for light energy and radio energy are basically one and the same thing. A tremendously varied group of physical phenomena fall under the single concept *electromagnetic energy*. This form of energy may manifest itself as light, radio waves, X rays, or cosmic rays. All these types of energy have that same significant velocity

---

[3] The expression c in the most famous equation of modern times, $E=Mc^2$, stands for the speed of light. This, Einstein's equation which predicts the tremendous energy released by atomic fission, is so well known that CBS used it as the title of its program in memory of Einstein after his death in 1955.

Figure 1.2
Amplitude modulation

Hypothetical sound, consisting of a single complete cycle of a pure tone. The reference line at the left represents relative amplitude.

Electrical wave having the same amplitude and frequency as the original sound.

Sample of unmodulated carrier of a transmitter, consisting of many cycles in the time occupied by only one cycle of the signal.

Amplitude of carrier modulated by the signal. Frequency of carrier remains constant. Note that both the plus and the minus phases of the carrier are modulated in patterns which are images of each other. Either pattern is sufficient to convey the signal.

Erratic wave caused by static electricity in the atmosphere.

Energy from the static wave interacts with the amplitude of the carrier, distorting its modulation pattern.

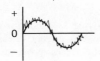

Resulting signal delivered by the loudspeaker. The receiver has stripped off the carrier wave but cannot remove distortion caused by static.

of 300,000,000 meters per second, all have the characteristics of periodic waves previously described, all have the ability to radiate through space. The universe appears to be saturated with electromagnetic energy which reaches the earth even from the depths of outer space in the form of cosmic rays.

The characteristic properties of the various types of electromagnetic energy are determined by wavelength (or frequency, which is the same thing, since velocity is constant). Wavelengths or frequencies laid out in numerical order form a *spectrum* (Figure 1.3). A spectrum is like the keyboard of a piano, which represents a spectrum of sound frequencies in ascending order, from

Figure 1.3
Electromagnetic spectrum

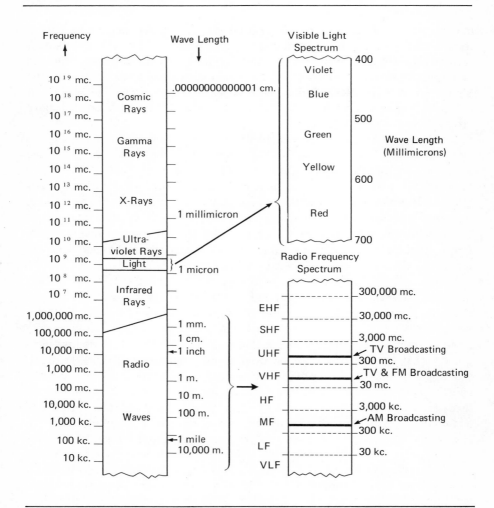

Table 1.1

Subdivisions of radio-frequency spectrum

NAME OF SUBDIVISION	FREQUENCY RANGE EXPRESSED IN		
	Kilocycles Per Second (Kilohertz)	*Megacycles Per Second (Megahertz)*	*Gigacycles Per Second (Gigahertz)*
Very Low Frequency (VLF)	Below 30	—	—
Low Frequency (LF)	30–300	—	—
Medium Frequency (MF)	300–3,000	—	—
High Frequency (HF)	3,000–30,000	3–30	—
Very High Frequency (VHF)	30,000–300,000	30–300	—
Ultra High Frequency (UHF)	300,000–3,000,000	300–3,000	—
Super High Frequency (SHF)	3,000,000–30,000,000	3,000–30,000	3–30
Extremely High Frequency (EHF)	30,000,000–300,000,000	30,000–300,000	30–300

low frequencies at the left end to high at the right. A visible example of a spectrum occurs when a prism or a rainbow breaks up sunlight into its component colors. This color sequence is also laid out in terms of frequency, the red end of the spectrum representing the lower frequencies, the blue end the higher frequencies. Beyond the limits of visible light occur frequencies of invisible "light"—infrared (below visible frequency) and ultraviolet (above visible frequency).

The radio part of the spectrum starts at a frequency of about 10,000 cps or 10,000 Hz.[4] Each wave is 30,000 meters (over 18 miles) long. At the upper end of the radio part, waves have a frequency of 3,000,000,000,000 cycles and a length which is microscopic. Beyond this point the radio frequencies begin to merge with those of infrared electromagnetic energy. Visible light begins at frequencies of about 375,000,000,000,000 cps. Just as the electromagnetic spectrum as a whole exhibits radically different behavior at different frequencies, so does the radio part of the spectrum have widely different characteristics in its various frequency ranges.

Waves of frequencies that are useful for radio communication lie, as has been pointed out, between 10,000 and 3,000,000,000,000 cps in the electromagnetic spectrum. This vast range of frequencies has been classified into frequency bands by international agreement (Table 1.1). In the early days of radio communication it was thought that frequencies above the Medium-Frequency (MF) range could not be used. By the outbreak of World War II, the upper limits of the useful radio-frequency spectrum had reached the neighborhood of 300 megacycles (mc.). During that war, development of such high-frequency devices as radar led to tremendously accelerated evolution of technology in this area, so that by the end of the war the ceiling had been raised to 30,000 mc. The higher in frequency the more subject the waves

---

[4] Hz (an abbreviation for "Hertz," the pioneer of electromagnetic-wave research) means "one cycle per second," for which it may be used interchangeably. The word "cycles" is often used alone to mean "cycles per second." See Table 1.1 for further explanation.

become to atmospheric absorption. At the Extremely High Frequencies (30,000 to 300,000 mc.), the atmosphere extinguishes radio waves almost as soon as they leave the antenna. For this reason practical use has been found for less than 2 per cent of the theoretically useable radio-frequency spectrum.[5]

1.6 / Wave Propagation

The radiation of waves through space is referred to as *propagation*.[6] Theoretically, radio energy radiates from a transmitter into space equally in all directions, forming a circular pattern, and the energy attenuates uniformly with distance from the transmitter. Attenuation occurs because, as the signal travels straight out in all directions from the point of origination, it is progressively distributed over a larger and larger area; hence its energy becomes more and more thinly dispersed. However, refraction (bending), reflection, absorption (loss of radio energy by conversion into other forms of energy), and interference (distortion of signal by energy from other sources), caused by conditions encountered in the propagation path, affect the geographical pattern of coverage, so that in practice a transmitter's coverage area has an irregular shape. This shape can be controlled artificially by directional antennas. Concentrating the radiated energy into a limited sector increases its strength in that direction, just as the reflector in a flashlight creates a beam with far greater reach than the light of the bare bulb.

How much a given wave will be affected by given propagation conditions depends on the frequency of the wave. Take, for example, refraction, a change in a wave's direction caused by its passage from one medium to another of differing density. This bending of the rays is due to the fact that a change of velocity occurs when they pass from one medium to the next.[7] The higher the frequency of a wave, the more markedly a new medium changes its velocity, and hence the more sharply it changes direction. Since the frequency of light is so high, it is particularly subject to refraction. The optical effects of lenses depend on refraction occurring when light passes from air to glass and glass to air. Radio-wave direction may be affected even by changes in the density of the air along a propagation path. In the higher ranges of the radio frequencies and over long propagation paths, even very minute changes in velocity can have considerable bending effect.

---

[5] Office of Telecommunications Management, "The Radio Frequency Spectrum: United States Use and Management" (Washington: Executive Office of the President, 1969), p. A-4.

[6] See Joint Technical Advisory Committee, Institute of Radio Engineers-Radio-Television Manufacturers Association, *Radio Spectrum Conservation* (New York: McGraw-Hill, 1952), p. 21. Most of the material on propagation in this section is adapted from this summary of the problems of allocation in relation to propagation theory.

[7] The previously cited velocity constant of 300,000,000 meters per second applies to electromagnetic energy *in a vacuum*.

Such susceptibilities have to be taken into consideration in choosing the frequency range for a given communication service. The characteristics peculiar to a frequency range must be matched to the special needs of the service using that range. As examples, some services require communication at distances of hundreds, even thousands, of miles; others require distances of only two or three miles; some require continuous, around-the-clock communication, others only occasional contacts; some can justify large, expensive transmitter installations and others must have lightweight, inexpensive transmitters; some require radiotelephony, others radiotelegraphy.

In the strategy of efficient frequency allocation, one of the basic considerations is the type of propagation path over which waves travel. Waves of some frequencies travel in a straight line from transmitter to receiver; those of some frequencies tend to follow the curvature of the earth; waves of other frequencies travel away from the earth and are reflected back. Thus, three basic types of waves can be distinguished in terms of transmission path: direct waves, ground waves, and sky waves (see Figures 1.4 and 1.5). Of particular importance to radio broadcasting are sky waves, for long-distance reception depends on them.

1.7 / Ionosphere Reflection

Situated in several strata, 30 to 300 miles above the surface of the earth, is a layer of atmosphere called the *ionosphere,* or the Kennelly-Heaviside layer.[8] The ionosphere consists of ionized atmosphere, *i.e.,* air whose atoms have a characteristic electrical property induced by the action of the sun's radiations. At certain times the ionosphere reflects Medium- and High-Frequency waves back to earth. Waves of other frequencies pass through the ionosphere and dissipate their energy in space.

The service obtained from sky waves is affected by many variables. The ionosphere is not a fixed and constant reflector, nor do all its layers reflect a given radio frequency equally well; moreover, disturbances related to sunspots and possibly to other extraterrestrial events affect its efficiency. For the frequencies used in standard broadcasting, the most important variable is time of day. During daylight hours the ionosphere does not reflect standard broadcast frequencies well, but after the sun goes down the ionosphere gradually cools, until by two hours after sundown it reaches maximum efficiency as a reflector. Reflected waves may bounce back off the earth, be reflected a second time by the ionosphere, bounce back off the earth again, and so on. By this means sky waves can travel thousands of miles, since they suffer little attenuation from absorption as they bounce back and forth. The ionosphere thus makes possible long-distance nighttime reception of standard broadcast signals—albeit reception subject to fading and interference. At the same time,

---

[8] Existence of the ionosphere was demonstrated in 1902 by two scientists working independently, Sir Oliver Heaviside in England and Arthur Kennelly in the United States.

Figure 1.4

Types of propagation paths

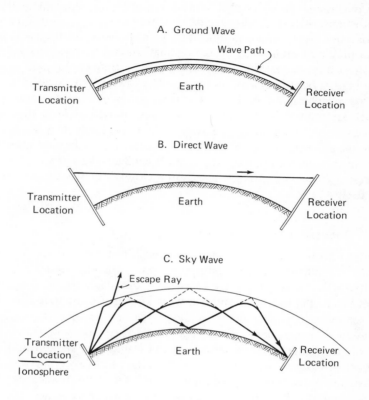

A. Ground Wave

Wave Path

Transmitter Location

Earth

Receiver Location

B. Direct Wave

Transmitter Location

Earth

Receiver Location

C. Sky Wave

Escape Ray

Transmitter Location

Ionosphere

Earth

Receiver Location

A.   The ground wave hugs the earth, following its curvature.

B.   The direct wave behaves more like light. The height of sending and receiving antennas is important in compensating for the curvature of the earth.

C.   Note that some energy may pass through the ionosphere and be lost. Actually, waves may be reflected from several different ionospheric layers. The rays are not thrown back sharply, as light rays are reflected by a mirror, but are bent back gradually.

Source: Data in President's Communications Policy Board, *Telecommunications: A Program for Progress* (Washington: Government Printing Office, 1951), p. 22.

sky waves complicate the problem of station allocation, since the service area of a station using frequencies capable of being reflected by the ionosphere expands so greatly at night. The methods used to solve this problem will be discussed in the next chapter.

Figure 1.5 shows the relation of range and mode of propagation in the radio-frequency spectrum. AM (standard) radio falls in the MF frequency band, enabling it to benefit from both ground-wave and sky-wave propagation. Television and FM sound radio fall in the VHF and UHF bands, which limit these services to short-range direct waves.

This brief survey of the propagation characteristics of the radio-frequency ranges may be summarized by saying that ground waves are most useful at the lowest frequencies, sky waves in the middle frequencies, and direct waves at the highest frequencies (Figure 1.5). The lowest frequencies are most subject to atmospheric noise, the highest frequencies to electron noise. The lower frequencies require high power to overcome noise, whereas the higher frequencies need less power, especially if directional antennas are used to increase the efficiency of propagation. In general, it may be said that the higher the frequency of radio energy the more it behaves like light—for, indeed, the higher the frequency of radio energy the closer it comes to the frequency of light itself.

1.8 / Spectrum Management

The chief problem of allocation is using each frequency range to best advantage by capitalizing on its strong points and avoiding degradation of service because of its weak points. Unfortunately, the allocation of frequencies was begun before the facts just outlined were known. By the time this knowledge had been developed, hundreds of thousands of transmitters were already in operation. It would have been prohibitively expensive and difficult administratively to change them all around to suit a master plan. Furthermore, there are never enough frequencies to satisfy all the needs. New services constantly emerge and old services expand; the demand for radio frequencies always exceeds the supply, and this condition grows steadily more acute. The allocation problem is a serious one on the international as well as the national level.[9]

To get some idea of the pressure on the frequency spectrum, let us look at the kinds of nonmilitary services and numbers of transmitters licensed by the United States (Table 1.2). The over-1.8 million radio stations licensed in the United States comprise eleven major classes of services and over sixty subclasses, ranging from space communication to citizen-band walkie-talkies. Each of these services must be allocated one or more blocks of frequencies, and in many cases each individual station (of which there may be thousands) within a single service has to be assigned its own individual channel. Broadcasting is just one of these services, representing less than 2 per cent of all transmitters authorized. The figure of over twenty-four thousand authorizations in

---

[9] President's Communications Policy Board, *Telecommunications: A Program for Progress* (Washington: Government Printing Office, 1951), p. 7; Joint Technical Advisory Committee, IRE-RTMA, *op. cit.,* p. 17; Office of Telecommunications Management, *op. cit., passim.*

Figure 1.5
Some characteristics of radio-frequency spectrum

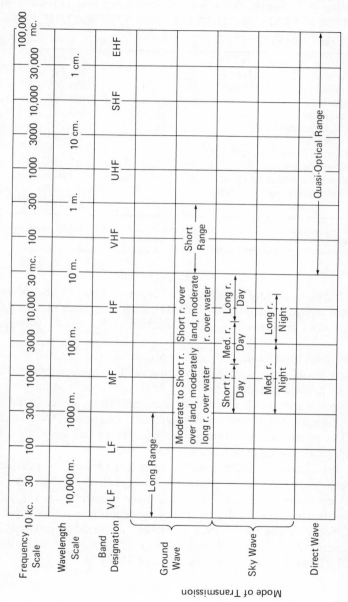

Rough approximation of service ranges: Short = 1–20 miles; Medium = 21–60 miles; Long = 61–unlimited miles.

Source: Data in President's Communications Policy Board, *Telecommunications: A Program for Progress* (Washington: Government Printing Office, 1951), p. 22.

Table 1.2

Radio-station authorizations by class of service[1]

CLASS OF SERVICE	STATIONS AUTHORIZED AS OF JUNE 30, 1969
Citizens service	860,624
Amateur and disaster	285,175
Industrial	204,266
Marine	186,295
Aviation	143,997
Public safety	67,730
Broadcast	24,499
Land transportation	21,291
Common carrier	13,376
Research and development	1,019
Community Antenna relay	43
Total	1,808,315

[1]"Authorizations" include construction permits and therefore slightly exceed the number actually on the air. See Table 1.3 for breakdown of broadcast service.

Source: FCC, *The FCC in Fiscal 1969: A Summary of Activities* (Washington: Government Printing Office, 1969), pp. 20–21.

Table 1.3 for broadcasting includes, in addition to some eight thousand regular broadcast transmitters, auxiliary services such as remote pickup units, television translators and boosters, studio-transmitter links, and wireless cueing systems.

To understand broadcasting allocation problems, it is essential to realize that broadcasting is only one service among many. The other services may come less often to general attention, but they have inestimable value to everyone. They facilitate transportation and wire communication, increase the safety of lives and property, aid industrial development, and make space exploration possible. The nonbroadcast services have become an indispensable adjunct to the technological development of our times.

Ideally, broadcasting should have the technical capacity to provide a large enough variety of unlimited, nationwide, competitive services to satisfy all substantial consumer interests. This ideal may become increasingly difficult to realize as the pressure on the frequency spectrum from other types of service grows. Some of the alternatives to present methods of program distribution are discussed in Chapter 4 (from the point of view of technology) and Chapter 11 (from the socioeconomic point of view).

Table 1.3

Broadcast-station authorizations

Type of Service	Stations Authorized as of June 30, 1969	
Standard (AM)	4,321	
Frequency modulation (FM)	2,181	
Educational (FM)	422	
Total primary sound stations		6,924
Commercial TV		
VHF	522	
UHF	334	
Educational TV		
VHF	82	
UHF	113	
Total primary television stations		1,051
TV translators (UHF–VHF)	2,606	
Signal boosters (UHF)	9	
TV experimental	15	
TV auxiliary	2,257	
International (radio)	3	
Developmental	3	
Remote pickup	10,957	
Studio-transmitter-link and intercity relay	341	
Low-power (cueing)	186	
Instructional fixed TV	147	
Total secondary stations		16,524
Grand total		24,499

[1]"Authorizations" include construction permits and therefore slightly exceed the number actually on the air.

Source: FCC, *The FCC in Fiscal 1969: A Summary of Activities* (Washington: Government Printing Office, 1969), p. 21.

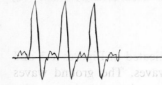

2

SOUND-BROADCASTING SERVICES

In the previous chapter we saw how radio communication uses electromagnetic radiant energy, which has characteristics of frequency, wavelength, and velocity. We saw how the behavior of electromagnetic waves restricts radio communication to certain parts of the electromagnetic spectrum. And we saw how the ever-growing communication requirements of the space age limit the amount of spectrum space that can be allotted to any one service. We turn now to a consideration of how the sound-broadcasting services have dealt with spectrum limitations.

2.1 / Standard Broadcasting

The first of the broadcast services to develop was amplitude modulation (AM), officially designated in the United States as "standard" broadcasting, but in Europe called "medium-wave" broadcasting. In America, amplitude-modulated broadcasting is allocated to the frequency band 540–1,600 kilocycles (kc.). With each channel occupying 10 kc., this band provides for 107 channels.[1] Receiver dials are generally calibrated in kilocycles, but for brevity the final 0 is usually dropped; thus most home-receiver dials read from 54 or 55 to 160. Each standard broadcast station is assigned to a particular channel. The license stipulates the assigned channel, and the licensee must so equip his transmitter that it will not drift off frequency.

The designation of frequency bands for the use of specific radio services is called *allocation*. Permitting a station to provide service on a particular channel at a specific geographic location is called *assignment*. The number of individual stations which can be assigned to the 107 channels allocated to standard broadcasting depends on the propagation characteristics of the frequency band within which these channels fall. The standard broadcast band of 540–1,600 kc. lies in the Medium-Frequency range (Table 1.1). The

---

[1] It should be recalled (Section 1.4) that the channels are identified by their midfrequency and each channel comprises 10 kc.; accordingly, the band actually extends down to 535 kc. and up to 1,605 kc.

propagation characteristics of these frequencies (indicated in Figures 1.3 and 1.4) permit use of both ground waves and sky waves. The ground waves define a station's *primary* service area, the sky waves its *secondary* service area. Ground waves provide a relatively short-range (roughly 10 to 75 miles) service, reliable at all times. Sky waves provide a long-range service, available only at night, when the ionosphere reflects the waves. Since vagaries of weather, sun-spot conditions, and the like affect the atmosphere, nighttime sky-wave reception is not always reliable. Yet sky waves themselves can cause interference; so they must be taken into consideration even in places where sky-wave service is not needed, or beyond the zone within which sky-wave service is expected.

2.2 / Interference and Coverage

Interference, the major assignment problem, comes from three sources: natural and man-made static; stations on adjacent channels; and stations on the same channel. Static, as indicated in Figure 1.2, adds random noise to the transmitted signal and comes both from natural electromagnetic energy released by atmospheric events such as lightning, and from a variety of man-made sources—essentially from any electrically operated machine. Only ground waves have the strength to override severe static, and then only relatively close to the transmitter, before much attenuation has taken place. For this reason sky-wave service is chiefly useful in rural areas; man-made static generally interferes with satisfactory sky-wave reception in large towns.

Adjacent-channel and co-channel interference come from intentionally transmitted signals rather than from random sources. When two or more stations' signals are received at the same frequency, receivers cannot discriminate between them to reject the unwanted signal.[2] Even if one of the conflicting signals is relatively weak, it may still distort the stronger signal to the point of making it unintelligible. A wanted AM signal needs to be about twenty times as strong as an unwanted competing signal to overcome the weaker signal's interference. Each AM station thus has a *nuisance* zone as well as a service zone. Furthermore, if two or more signals on *adjacent* frequencies are very strong, receivers near the transmitters will be unable to keep them apart. Mutual interference, then, may come from either adjacent-channel or co-channel stations. Stations assigned to adjacent channels, if too close to each other, will interfere only in the area near the transmitters; with distance, the signals become sufficiently attenuated for receivers to keep them apart. Adjacent-channel interference is thus a local problem. Co-channel interference creates a more complex problem. Stations assigned to the same channel, if not far enough apart, may interfere in parts of the area covered by both signals. And unfortunately, the extent and shape of the area covered by an

---

[2] Technically, interference is signal distortion resulting from phase differences in two or more received signals.

AM-broadcast transmitter's signal cannot be precisely controlled. Coverage area (especially of sky waves) varies as propagation conditions vary.

AM-station wave propagation depends primarily on frequency, conductivity of the soil and power—although many other factors, as previously indicated, affect propagation, especially of sky waves. Ground-wave efficiency depends on conductivity of the soil.[3] For this reason standard broadcast antennas are often located on swampy ground or even over water. Salt water is estimated to be five thousand times as conductive as the least conductive type of soil.[4] Some AM antennas are actually built on artificial islands or pilings so that their ground systems can be submerged in the water. A dry, sandy soil is the least desirable because of its low conductivity. Signal-strength measurements showed that the signal from a 250-watt (w.) station's antenna located in highly conductive soil actually covered as large an area as that from a 50,000-w. station less favorably located.[5]

Frequency also influences AM-station efficiency. A given amount of power becomes progressively less effective as frequency increases. For instance, a 5,000-w. station at 550 kc. was found to cover a greater area than a 50,000-w. station located in the same city but operating on the 1,200-kc. channel.[6]

A third major factor influencing coverage is power, expressed in watts or kilowatts (one kilowatt equals 1,000 watts). With given frequency and terrain conditions, power is the one variable which can be manipulated. However, signal strength increases as the square root of power. If a 1,000-w. station desired to double its signal strength it would have to quadruple its power; to get four times the signal strength its power would have to be increased from 1,000 w. to 16,000 w. After a certain point, increase in power does not affect ground-wave distance so much as sky-wave distance. Station operators generally want to use as much power as the law and their pocketbooks allow. Not only does high power enable the ground-wave signal to blank out static and possible nearby mutual interference, but it also has prestige value. Most people are impressed by 50,000 w., the maximum AM power permitted in United States domestic broadcasting, even if the number is relatively meaningless in terms of useful physical coverage.

Because of the variety of factors affecting coverage, each station's service area is defined by its signal *contour,* an irregular shape surrounding the transmitter determined by signal-strength measurements in the field. Relatively wide margins must be allowed between stations operating on the same chan-

---

[3] AM-broadcast antenna towers consist of two parts, only one of which is visible. The tower structure itself is the radiating element. For efficient radiation, an antenna needs to be mathematically related to the length of waves radiated. The longer the wavelength, the taller the tower, as a rule. The invisible part of the antenna is its ground system, a series of radially placed heavy copper wires buried in the earth surrounding the antenna.

[4] FCC map, "Estimated Effective Ground Conductivity in the United States" (Washington: Government Printing Office, 1954).

[5] "New Way to Measure Coverage Told," *Broadcasting,* September 8, 1947, p. 16.

[6] *Loc. cit.*

nel. In a station's fringe area, its strength may be too low or inconsistent for satisfactory service, but it may nevertheless cause damaging interference to other stations (Figure 2.1).

The simplest solution to co-channel interference would be to assign only one station to each channel—or at least to keep stations which are assigned to

Figure 2.1
Co-channel interference (*idealized*)

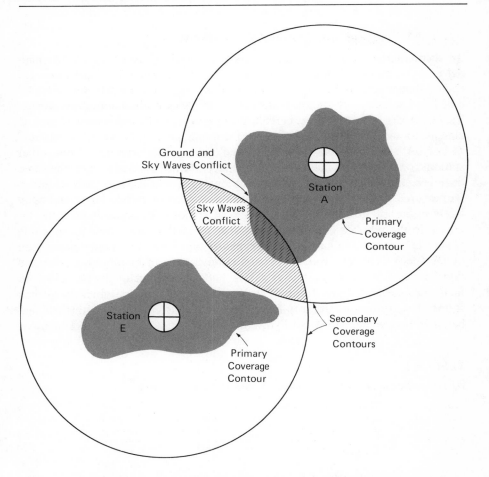

Station A and Station B are assigned to the same frequency. Their primary coverage (ground-wave) areas do not conflict, but their secondary coverage (sky-wave) areas overlap, so that during times of sky-wave propagation receivers located between the two stations experience interference.

the same channel two or three thousand miles apart. But with only 107 channels to work with, this solution would drastically limit the number of AM stations. One of the primary duties of the Federal Communications Commission is to provide as much local broadcast service as possible to all parts of the country. However, the Commission cannot arbitrarily spread stations across the map in accordance with ideal engineering criteria. Population density controls station demand, creating overcrowding in some areas and an undersupply in others. Economic factors as well as engineering factors control the station-distribution pattern.

2.3 / AM Station and Channel Classification

To accommodate a larger number of stations, the FCC uses a system of channel and station classifications. It divides the 107 channels into three classes: Clear, Regional, and Local. It divides stations, in turn, into Classes I, II, III and IV. Each class of station is defined in terms of both channel and power. Table 2.1 shows that channel classifications are generally equivalent to station classifications. The significant exception is the distinction between "dominant" (Class I) stations—*i.e.,* those protected from all interference from other stations, on Clear Channels—and "secondary" (Class II) stations on the same channels. Originally, Clear-Channel stations were intended to provide interference-free sky-wave service to remote rural areas of the country, areas not likely to be able to support their own local stations. In point of fact, the increase in the number of AM stations—far more than was dreamed possible when the concept originated—has somewhat outmoded the intended function of the Clear Channels. But the economic advantage of maximum power and interference-free coverage makes Class I stations exceedingly lucrative. In fact, their owners have formed an association to defend their privileged status. Twenty-four of the fifty-nine Clear Channels continue on this original basis. For example, WSM-Nashville, the dominant station on 650 kc., oper-

Table 2.1

AM-broadcast channel and station classification system

CHANNEL CLASS	NO. CHANNELS IN CLASS	STATION CLASSES
Clear (A)[1]	24	I-A, II
(B)[1]	36	I-B, II
Regional	41	III
Local	6	IV

[1]A = U. S. clear channels on which only one dominant (I-A) station is assigned; B = foreign clear channels and U. S. clear channels on which one or more dominant (I-B) stations may be assigned. A few exceptions to the classification system have been made by the FCC.

Source: Data in *Broadcasting 1970 Yearbook* listing of stations by frequency, pp. B255–B274. Adapted with permission.

ates on unlimited time at 50,000 w., with only two secondary stations on the same channel—one in Texas and another in Hawaii. WSM is "unduplicated" in the sense that it does not have to share dominance with any other station. These exclusive channels have the popular designation "I-A Clear Channels."

The remaining Clear Channels, known as "I-B," have been "duplicated" by assignment to them of one or more dominant (Class I) stations as well as a number of secondary (Class II) stations. For example, WGY-Schenectady (Class I) shares dominance on the 810-kc. Clear Channel with KGO-San Francisco (Class I); but a score of Class II secondary stations with power ranging from 250 w. to 50,000 w. also occupies this channel. This multiple occupancy shows why it is important to understand that the term "Clear Channel" is *not* a station classification.[7] Station WTPR in Paris, Tennessee, uses the same 710-kc. Clear Channel as New York's WOR, but WTPR is a 250-w. daytime-only Class II station, while WOR is a 50,000-w. unlimited-time Class I station. By international agreement, neighboring countries have been assigned about twenty Clear Channels on which their stations have dominance (see Table 2.2.). United States stations using these channels must avoid interfering with the dominant foreign stations.

Stations on Regional Channels, as the name implies, are intended to serve more limited areas than Clear-Channel Class I stations. For this reason, many more Class III stations can be assigned per channel than Class I or II stations (Table 2.2). The Class IV stations, on Local Channels, have an even more restricted service area—a single small community or a part of a metropolitan area. Their restricted coverage enables a small minority of only 6 channels out of the 107 to accommodate nearly a quarter of all the AM stations on the air.

The FCC uses several expedients to maximize the number of stations operating without defeating the purpose of the clear channels or degrading the service of existing stations. To compensate for the difference between daytime and nighttime coverage, some stations are required to switch to lower power at night; others must go off the air entirely after dark; still others must use directional antennas (sometimes with different patterns for night and day) to blank out the signal in a direction which might cause interference.[8]

2.4 / Frequency Modulation

Although experimenters developed the techniques of modulating amplitude first, they realized that a similar result could be obtained by modulating fre-

---

[7] Television has tended to compound the confusion of meaning between "channel" and "station." People have come to speak of "Channel 2," "Channel 3," and so on as stations. A channel is nothing more than an arbitrarily defined group of radio frequencies, whether or not a station actually uses it.

[8] Directional patterns for standard broadcast stations are created by antenna "arrays," two or more separate antenna structures which set up interference and reinforcement patterns with each other. See Section 1.6 on directional antennas.

quency. At first, technical limitations prevented its practical realization, but in the 1930's, inventor Major Edwin Armstrong led a revival of interest in the possibilities of frequency modulation. One hundred 200-kc. FM channels were finally allocated in the VHF region, running from 88 to 108 mc., and num-

Table 2.2

AM channels by frequency, class, and number of stations

CHANNEL (KC.)	CHANNEL CLASS[1]	NO. OF STATIONS	CHANNEL (KC.)	CHANNEL CLASS[1]	NO. OF STATIONS	CHANNEL (KC.)	CHANNEL CLASS[1]	NO. OF STATIONS
540	C(c)	14	900	C(d)	45	1260	R	66
550	R	23	910	R	49	1270	R	60
560	R	22	920	R	47	1280	R	60
570	R	20	930	R	45	1290	R	62
580	R	24	940	C(c, d)	30			
590	R	27	950	R	44	1300	R	64
			960	R	42	1310	R	62
600	R	25	970	R	49	1320	R	58
610	R	23	980	R	48	1330	R	61
620	R	22	990	C(c)	42	1340	L	171
630	R	28				1350	R	57
640	C(a)	4	1000	C(b, d)	21	1360	R	67
650	C(a)	3	1010	C(c, f)	36	1370	R	64
660	C(a)	5	1020	C(a)	5	1380	R	66
670	C(a)	2	1030	C(b)	4	1390	R	56
680	C(b)	16	1040	C(a)	3			
690	C(c)	23	1050	C(d)	55	1400	L	172
			1060	C(b, d)	22	1410	R	68
700	C(a)	1	1070	C(b, c)	18	1420	R	63
710	C(b)	15	1080	C(b)	25	1430	R	61
720	C(a)	2	1090	C(b,d)	27	1440	R	58
730	C(d)	30				1450	L	178
740	C(c)	27	1100	C(a)	6	1460	R	63
750	C(a)	8	1110	C(b)	26	1470	R	65
760	C(a)	5	1120	C(a)	5	1480	R	73
770	C(a)	6	1130	C(b, c)	15	1490	L	165
780	C(a)	7	1140	C(b, d)	17			
790	R	39	1150	R	60	1500	C(b)	37
			1160	C(a)	2	1510	C(b)	40
800	C(d)	29	1170	C(b)	13	1520	C(b)	42
810	C(b)	21	1180	C(a)	3	1530	C(b)	39
820	C(a)	5	1190	C(b, d)	18	1540	C(e)	47
830	C(a)	4				1550	C(d)	62
840	C(a)	4	1200	C(a)	1	1560	C(f)	42
850	C(b)	19	1210	C(a)	8	1570	C(d)	65
860	C(c)	36	1220	C(d)	51	1580	C(c)	66
870	C(a)	8	1230	L	167	1590	R	70
880	C(a)	4	1240	L	154			
890	C(a)	3	1250	R	58	1600	R	74

[1]Channel classification key: C = Clear, L = Local, R = Regional. Clear-Channel subclasses: (a) = U. S., unduplicated (one dominant Class I station plus Class II's); (b) = U. S., duplicated; (c) = Canadian; (d) = Mexican; (e) = Bahamian; (f) = Cuban.

Source: Data in *Broadcasting 1970 Yearbook*, pp. B255–B274. Adapted with permission.

bered 201 to 300. The FCC has set up a national FM-assignment table providing 1,098 specific channel assignments by state and city. Small, medium, and large communities are authorized Class A, B, and C stations respectively. Station classifications are defined in terms of both power and antenna height, ranging from a minimum power of 100 w. and antenna height of 300 feet for Class A stations to a maximum power of 100,000 w. and antenna height of 2,000 feet for Class C stations. Provision has also been made for a special class of low-power (10 w.) educational FM stations. The first twenty FM channels are reserved exclusively for noncommercial educational use; the rest are open.

In the VHF region, as indicated in Figure 1.5, the effective propagation path is direct. Thus, FM does not have the AM problems of allocation created by the differential behavior of ground waves and sky waves. The direct radiation of FM signals from transmitter to receiver produces a stable coverage pattern, its size and shape depending on transmitter power, the height of the transmitting antenna, and terrain formation.[9] The FM antenna is a physically small element, in keeping with the shortness of VHF waves. The tower functions merely as a supporting device, not as a radiator as in AM. Since FM does not depend on ground-wave propagation, it does not require the elaborate ground system of the AM antenna. Height rather than ground conductivity is the primary consideration in choosing an FM antenna site. Even a high-powered FM transmitter cannot push its signal much beyond the horizon. Therefore "super power" has not the same meaning for FM as it has for AM broadcasting, though high FM power is still desirable to eliminate the need for external receiving antennas and to stabilize reception near the horizon limits.

The direct-wave limitation on FM coverage simplifies station assignments. Since FM does not generate ground or sky waves, there is no need for a wide "no-man's land" between stations on the same channel; hence FM allows more uniform geographical coverage than AM. The clear-channel concept, being based on the existence of sky waves for long-distance propagation, does not apply to FM.

Another factor simplifying FM-station assignment is the fact that the FM signal blanks out interference from other stations better than AM. The AM signal-to-interference ratio is 20 to 1, while the FM ratio is only 2 to 1. An FM signal has to be only twice as strong as an interfering signal to blank it out, allowing FM stations to be closer to other stations than AM.

FM's most important advantage over AM, however, is its freedom from static interference. With FM the wanted information depends not on signal amplitude but on signal frequency (Figure 2.2). Thus static does not contaminate the information in the FM signal. By eliminating static interference,

---

[9] At certain seasons of the year, waves of the FM-broadcast frequencies are affected by both the ionosphere and the troposphere (lower layers of atmosphere). Long-distance FM-broadcast propagation then occurs, but only sporadically.

Figure 2.2
Frequency modulation

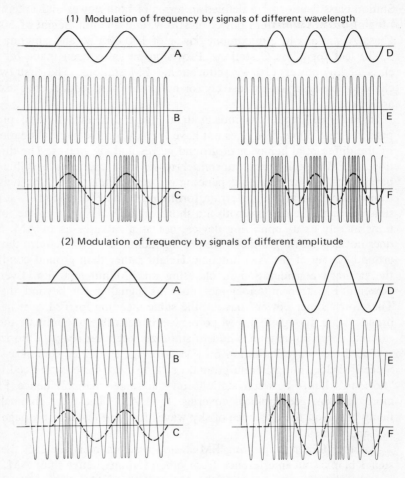

(1) Modulation of frequency by signals of different wavelength

A

D

B

E

C

F

(2) Modulation of frequency by signals of different amplitude

A

D

B

E

C

F

(1) Two cycles of a signal are shown at A. At B is the unmodulated carrier. At C the carrier has been frequency modulated by signal A (the original waveform is superimposed on the carrier to show the relation more explicitly). Note that one phase of the signal wave causes increase in carrier frequency and the other phase causes decrease. The amplitude of the carrier remains constant. D is a signal of the same amplitude as A but has a higher frequency.

(2) In this example the frequency of the two signals A and D is constant, but D has twice the amplitude of A. Modulating the same carrier (B and E) results in a more radical change in the frequency of the carrier at F than at C.

FM provides undistorted reception in areas where—and at times when—satisfactory AM reception is impossible.[10]

2.5 / Sound Quality

Still another major advantage of FM over AM sound broadcasting is its ability to reproduce sound with higher fidelity to the original. This ability is not, however, inherent in FM. To explain this paradox requires further consideration of modulation and sound. It will be recalled (Section 1.4) that modulation of a carrier wave creates "side bands"—the involvement of groups of frequencies both above and below the central carrier-wave frequency. A single frequency can convey only a single bit of information at any given instant; therefore any complex signal, such as sound, necessarily requires more than a single frequency. The carrier frequency merely defines the midpoint of a channel, with the side-band frequencies extending above and below that point. Since the two side bands merely duplicate each other, only one is usefully employed, which means that the actual capacity of a channel amounts to only half its total width. Thus the 10-kc. AM-radio channel provides not 10,000 cps of information capacity, but only 5,000. This limitation in turn restricts AM radio to reproduction of sounds up to frequencies of 5,000 cps.

In planning any communication system the designer must decide how much information capacity is really necessary for the purposes of the system. The maximum amount of information desired must be balanced against the cost of communicating it—not only the expense of providing the necessary physical apparatus but also the expense in frequencies. Since there is always a shortage of spectrum space, conservation of frequencies is of great importance; no service should use more than the number of frequencies required to perform its essential functions. Rarely does a communication system attempt to reproduce information with absolute fidelity to the original, for rarely is such high fidelity necessary. The telegraph, for instance, strips the language of the wealth of information which the speaking, rather than the printing, of messages conveys; the telephone restores a great deal of this information, but still sacrifices much. One does not attempt to communicate the aesthetic nuances of fine music or speech by telephone.

Radio broadcasting, unlike such utilitarian communication services as the telegraph and telephone, *is* concerned with the aesthetic aspects of information. An adequate broadcast service should be capable of communicating the beauty of instrumental music, song, and speech; it should be capable of realistically

---

[10] It should be noted again that although we use "AM" and "FM" to mean "AM sound radio" and "FM sound radio," AM and FM refer simply to types of modulation, regardless of particular applications. Nonbroadcast services use AM and FM for a variety of purposes. Broadcasting itself uses AM for transmitting picture information (Section 3.6).

re-creating the sounds of actual events. These requirements call for a relatively high degree of fidelity to the original. Yet absolute fidelity, even if it could be achieved, would be prohibitively costly in both apparatus and frequencies. Therefore a compromise must still be made.

In the case of AM broadcasting, the choice of the specific 10-kc. channel width, then, is dictated neither by physical necessity nor by mere chance. It is the result of a decision: how high can we make fidelity without unduly reducing the number of available channels? How many channels can we make available without reducing fidelity below the point of toleration? The result, in AM broadcasting, has been a service which, though far short of ideal sound reproduction, satisfies most people for most purposes. Sound reproduced on an AM radio contains less information than the original sound, but most of us are seldom conscious of the loss. However, if AM broadcasting were designed solely to serve a group of people to whom fidelity is very important— let us say orchestra conductors—the standard would be entirely inadequate.

To understand how broadcasting as a communication system can afford to discard part of the original information, we must consider again the nature of sound. A pure sound, consisting of a single frequency, such as the example used in Section 1.4 to illustrate the process of modulation, does not occur in nature. The sounds of voices and musical instruments, the rustling of leaves, the burbling of brooks, the barking of dogs—all the sounds we normally hear —are very complex. They consist of many different frequencies, each with its own amplitude, all combined in a way that gives a particular sound its particular character.

In Section 1.3 we spoke of sound as having at least three variables: frequency (pitch), amplitude (loudness), and duration (length). But take the case of two sounds of exactly *identical* pitch, loudness, and duration—say a note played on a violin and the same note played on a clarinet. Despite basic similarity of the two sounds, the ear detects a difference implied by such terms as "timbre," "quality," "color." The difference exists because pitch (*i.e.,* frequency) is not a simple but a complex factor. We recognize the pitch of the two instruments as apparently identical because for each sound the psychologically dominant frequency is identical; we recognize the difference in quality between the two instruments because the *other* frequencies in the two sounds are not identical.

These secondary frequency components of sounds—their overtones—are usually multiples of (*i.e.,* octaves above) the fundamental pitch. Thus the 264-cps sound of middle C may have overtones at 528 cycles, 792 cycles, 1056 cycles, and so on. Differences in the distribution and amplitudes of the overtones account for the qualitative difference between sounds of the same fundamental pitch (Figure 2.3).

In the graphic representation of the sound wave, the several frequencies combine to form a composite wave. To explain this phenomenon we must revert to the concept of phase, mentioned in Section 1.2 in connection with the pendulum. A complete cycle of motion of the pendulum requires a move-

Figure 2.3
Overtones in sounds

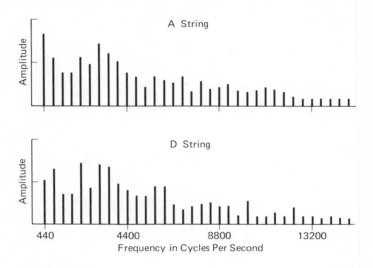

Two different strings on a violin playing a note at the same pitch (440 cps) have recognizably different quality. The graphs show how the relative amplitudes of the fundamental pitch and the overtones account for this difference. Note, for example, that the first overtone is stronger than the fundamental in the D-string tone but weaker in the A-string tone. Note that "amplitude," measured in terms of physical energy, differs from "loudness," measured in psychological terms; this difference explains why, in the D-string example, some overtones have greater amplitude than the fundamental.

Source: Data in Harry F. Olson, *Musical Engineering* (New York: McGraw Hill, 1952), p. 255.

ment to one side and then to the other. These opposite phases of the cycle may be regarded as positive (plus) and negative (minus) aspects of the wave. If the positive aspects of two waves coincide, their energies will combine to make a larger total amplitude at that point. If, however, a negative and a positive aspect of two waves coincide, the smaller will subtract from the larger, making a smaller total amplitude at that point. When two waves of the same frequency exactly coincide they are "in phase" (Figure 2.4).

The phase principle can be illustrated with two tuning forks of slightly different frequency. When both are struck the resulting composite sound will have a "beat" because at regular intervals the two sounds will get in phase and reinforce each other to a maximum amount and then get out of phase and cancel each other to a maximum amount. This throbbing sound is

Figure 2.4
Phase concepts

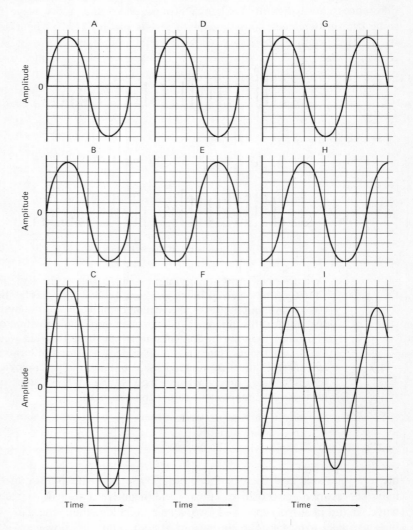

A and B represent waves of equal amplitude and length which are *in phase*. The result of combining these two waves is shown at C.

D and E are two waves of equal amplitude and length which are exactly halfway *out of phase*. The result at F is complete cancellation.

G and H are the same waves one-quarter out of phase. The resultant, I, has neither the same amplitude nor the same form as the resultant of the two waves when *in* phase, shown at C.

familiar in musical chords. Phase considerations play important roles in many practical applications throughout electrical and electronic systems. Two or more microphones fed to the same amplifier must be phased correctly; phase differences cause distortion when a ground wave and a sky wave from the same transmitter meet, sometimes with results much like the "beat" produced by the two tuning forks; color television makes important use of phase differences (Section 3.7); directional antennas use phase reinforcement and cancellation to weaken radiation in one direction and strengthen it in another.

The relevance of overtones to the question of fidelity of sound reproduction is this: overtones being higher in frequency than their fundamental tones, they extend into the higher ranges of the audible frequency spectrum. A system that fails to reproduce these higher frequencies therefore affects *quality* without necessarily affecting intelligibility. Standard broadcasting, with its 5-kc. side bands, permits the reproduction of an audible frequency range of about 50–5,000 cps. The range of frequencies actually audible to the human ear extends to about 20,000 cps.[11] AM broadcasting eliminates a large segment of the audible frequency range. However, the frequencies above 5,000 cps come into play as overtones rather than as fundamental pitches; hence the loss is in terms of quality. For purposes of speech reproduction, this loss is not important. The baritone singing voice, for instance, covers fundamental pitches only to about 400 cps; the soprano singing voice goes only to about 1,200 cps. But the fundamental frequencies of the highest musical instruments reach into the 4,000-cps region, and the fundamental frequencies of certain high-pitched sounds reach even higher. It follows that the AM standard is adequate for the human voice, less adequate for instrumental music, and even less adequate for sound effects.

In amplitude modulation, then, it was decided to provide sufficient radio frequencies per channel to allow *reasonably* faithful sound reproduction. But this standard is not high enough for realistic reproduction of many sounds, including many that are present in instrumental music. The 30-kc. channel width adopted for FM broadcasting enables reproduction of sound frequencies up to 15,000 cps. Since most people cannot hear sounds of higher frequency, this range permits almost "perfect" reproduction of sound. From the physical point of view, FM still leaves out some frequency information, but from the psychological point of view, it includes all the information which could be *useful* to most listeners.

Besides improved frequency range, FM also has the advantage over AM of improved *dynamic* range, *i.e.,* the range in degrees of loudness between the faintest reproducible sound and the loudest. The human ear has an amazing capacity to adjust itself to extremes in this respect, whereas sound-re-

---

[11] Sensitivity to higher sound frequencies varies widely among individuals; a characteristic hearing loss occurs in the upper frequencies with age. Ultrasonic (above audible frequency) "sounds" are used as cueing signals to start and stop tape recordings, to activate slide projectors, and in many other applications.

producing systems are much more limited. Very faint sounds are lost in the noise of the system itself, and very loud sounds overload the system and become distorted. AM broadcasting even compresses dynamic range artificially in order to get maximum average power from transmitters.

2.6 / Multiplexing

FM's capacity to handle sounds ranging up to 15,000 cps implies, as we have said, a channel width of 30,000 cps (allowing for the two side bands). In fact, however, each FM channel has far greater capacity than this—200,000 cps. The additional frequencies allow for multiplexing auxiliary signals in the channel.

Multiplexing means transmitting two or more independent signals simultaneously on the same carrier. At first blush this may seem like a contradiction in terms, but stereophony provides a familiar example. Stereophonic sound requires two independent sound tracks, yet both can be recorded in the same groove (*i.e.,* "channel") on a disc and picked up by a single stylus. Later they are separated and fed to independent amplifiers and speakers. The 200-kc. FM channel provides space not only for a subchannel to carry the second stereophonic track, but also another subchannel which can be used either for sending independent information simultaneously, or for sending additional information related to the main transmission in the channel. "Guard bands" separating the subchannels account for the other frequencies.

Some FM stations use a subsidiary channel to carry independent information, for example, facsimile (Section 3.8), and a subscription background-music service known as "musicasting," used in stores, doctors' offices, and the like (Section 9.9). Potentially, many other kinds of specialized services could be multiplexed in the FM broadcast channel. The FCC issues "Subsidiary Communications Authorizations" for such services.[12]

Multiplexing, one of the most widely used and important techniques of telecommunications, both increases the efficiency of wire and radio circuits and helps to conserve the frequency spectrum. The foregoing example, the subcarriers in the FM channel, is a case of assigning different signals to *different* groups of frequencies within a channel—somewhat like assigning different kinds of traffic to separate lanes within an expressway. More sophisticated types of multiplexing get double use out of the *same* frequencies. This is possible because the normal traffic in most communication systems fails to utilize channel capacity fully. For example, telephonic speech uses a channel only about 40 per cent of the time. The rest of the time consists of pauses and spaces between sounds, during which the channel lies idle. A multiplexing method called "Time Assignment Speech Interpolation" puts transatlantic telephone circuits to work during these times in telephone conversations when

---

[12] For examples of novel uses of FM multiplexed signals, see Lorne A. Parker, *SCA: A New Medium* (Madison: University of Wisconsin, 1969).

they would otherwise be unused. Other broadcast uses of multiplexing include transmitting meter readings on the broadcast carrier from unattended transmitters; incorporating cueing signals into magnetic recordings; and color television (Section 3.7).

2.7 / Shortwave Services

Broadcast services which need to cover long distances use amplitude modulation in the High-Frequency part of the spectrum, where sky waves can be counted on to reach distant target areas. Some underdeveloped countries use shortwave for domestic broadcasting, in the absence of economic justification for numerous local medium-wave or FM installations. Most shortwave broadcasting, however, is intended for external consumption.

Table 2.3

Shortwave (High-Frequency) broadcast bands

Band Limits in Kilocycles	Megacycle Band	Meter Band
3500– 4000	3.9	75
5950– 6200	6	49
7100– 7300	7	41
9500– 9775	9	31
11700–11975	11	25
15100–15450	15	19
17700–17900	17	16
21450–21750	21	13
25600–26100	25	11

By international agreement, specific groups of frequencies, spread throughout the High-Frequency portion of the spectrum, have been allocated to international broadcasting (Table 2.3). Sky-wave propagation conditions change constantly. In order to take advantage of the best conditions, most international shortwave stations make hourly, daily, and seasonal alterations in transmitter frequencies. They also generally broadcast on several transmitters simultaneously, each transmitter being directionally oriented to a specific target area. The Voice of America uses some sixty different frequencies and has over a hundred transmitters at five major United States installations and at relay points overseas. The transmitters range in power up to 1,000,000 w.— twenty times the maximum power permitted American domestic AM broadcast stations.[13]

---

[13] Shortwave transmitter locations, frequencies, and power as well as program schedules can be found in *World Radio-TV Handbook* (New York: Billboard Publications, annual).

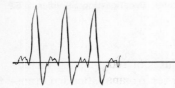

3

THE TELEVISION SERVICE

Before discussing the physical bases of the television service, it will be helpful to consider briefly some characteristics of human vision. To begin with, let us recollect that what we call visible light is a certain range of frequencies in the electromagnetic-energy spectrum (Figure 1.3). The eye is a kind of transducer, transmuting electromagnetic energy into perceptions which we know as light, color, brightness, etc. Sights, like sounds, can be regarded as patterns of energy having characteristics of frequency and amplitude.

3.1 / Picture Definition

The camera—whether still, motion picture, or television—may be regarded as man's relatively crude attempt to build a mechanical eye, much as the microphone can be said to be a mechanical ear. Like the eye, the camera has an adjustable iris to control the amount of light admitted and a lens which concentrates the image on a light-sensitive screen or plate. The screen of the eye, the retina, consists of about 132 million receptors, specialized nerve endings (rods and cones) which respond to light.[1]

When an image falls on the retina, each of millions of active receptors responds independently in accordance with the amount of light which reaches it. The brain assembles the millions of resulting simultaneous impulses into a subjective "reproduction" of the object being seen. It is not, of course, a "perfect" reproduction. Visual acuity varies among individuals just as aural acuity varies. Even at best there are limits to the eye's ability to see detail, for which reason we use microscopes and telescopes to extend the normal limits of vision, as well as eyeglasses to correct abnormalities. The eye sees not "everything," but only as much as the nerve endings in the retina permit. Anything as small as or smaller than an individual nerve end cannot be *resolved, i.e.,* distinguished as a separate detail. Resolution (definition) means the ability to recognize two adjacent objects as separate objects (Figures 3.1 and 3.2).

---

[1] Ida Mann and Antoinette Pirie, *The Science of Seeing* (Harmondsworth-Middlesex: Penguin Books, 1950), p. 28.

Figure 3.1
Effect of scanning-line frequency on definition

60 Scanning Lines

120 Scanning Lines

180 Scanning Lines

240 Scanning Lines

Enlargement

The number of lines scanned per frame determines the amount of detail a television system can reproduce. Notice how smaller details emerge as the number of lines increases.

Source: National Broadcasting Company.

Figure 3.2
Picture structure

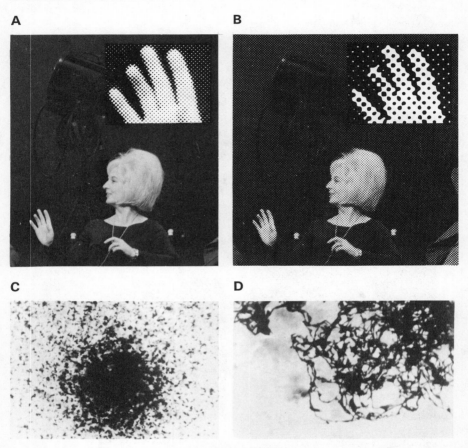

A

B

C

D

Top: Degrees of definition in picture reproduction.

A. Fine engraving, 133 lines per inch. Detail in rectangle enlarged four times.

B. Same subject as reproduced in a newspaper, 55 lines per inch. Detail in rectangle enlarged four times.

Bottom: Grain structure in motion-picture film.

C. High magnification (×250) discloses silver grains of varying size and shape, distributed at random.

D. Extreme magnification (×25,000) shows the fibers making up the complex structure of a single grain.

Sources: Top, Wide World Photos, Inc.
Bottom, reproduced with the permission of Eastman Kodak Company.

On the same principle, most picture-reproducing devices depend on some method of breaking the total scene down into separate picture elements. The minuteness and the distribution of these picture elements, of course, govern the degree of definition, or resolution. Even the unaided eye can discern this piece-by-piece structure, in newspaper pictures, for instance.

In conventional film, the picture elements consist of tiny particles of light-sensitive material. Each particle responds proportionately to the amount of light to which it is exposed. When developed, the particles clump into grains of silver. The ability of film to reproduce fine detail depends on the minuteness of these grains. "Graininess" in film means poor detail; "fine-grain" film is used where fine detail is important (Figure 3.2).

3.2 / Picture Standards

Motion pictures add a time dimension to the process of reproduction: we see not a snapshot of frozen action but continuous action. The action is not in reality continuous in the film itself, but the eye experiences an *illusion* of continuity. This illusion depends on the fact that an image received by the eye persists briefly as a subjective (neural) image even after the original scene is no longer there. The eye cannot turn itself off, so to speak, instantaneously. A motion picture consists of a series of still pictures (frames) taken in rapid succession; each frame freezes the action at a slightly later moment than the preceding frame (Figure 3.3). *Persistence of vision* fills in the moments between pictures, smoothly blending one frame into another, thus achieving an illusion of continuity of action. Silent motion pictures were standardized at 16 frames per second. Vision persists long enough between each successive frame to blend them all into an adequately convincing illusion of continuous action. Film passing over the pickup head at this rate, however, would not provide adequate sound quality (see Section 4.5 on the effect of the speed at which a recording medium travels on its information capacity). Therefore the somewhat faster rate of 24 frames per second was adopted as the standard for sound films.

Although these frame frequencies suffice to give the illusion of continuous action, the eye still detects that light falls on the screen only intermittently. Since, as we have pointed out, motion pictures are really sequences of *still pictures,* the pictures must be immobile at the moment of projection. After each frame flashes its still picture on the screen, a moment of blackout must follow while the projector pulls the next frame into position. The eye reacts more sensitively to these gross changes from complete blackout to complete illumination than it does to the much smaller changes in the position of objects within pictures that occur between successive frames. We perceive this gross alternation between light and darkness as *flicker*—that annoying sensation of unsteadiness we experience in watching old silent films. In fact early movies were called "flicks" for this reason. The sensation of flicker can be eliminated only by increasing the frequency of alternations between screen

Figure 3.3
Motion-picture film and sound-track types (actual size)

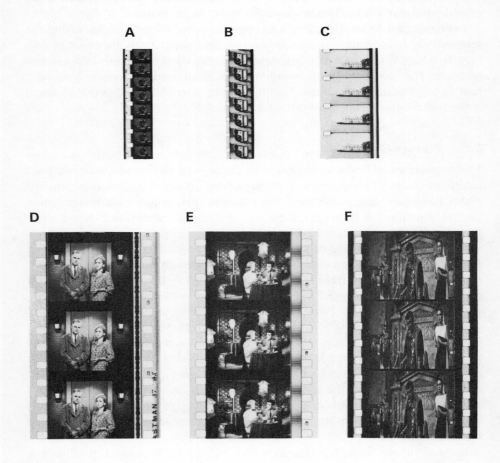

A. 8 mm. with magnetic sound track.

B. Super 8 with magnetic track.

C. 16 mm. with optical variable-area track.

D. 35 mm. with optical variable-area track.

E. 35 mm. with optical variable-density track.

F. CinemaScope with four magnetic tracks. Note smaller sprocket holes to make room for tracks.

Sources: A-E, reproduced with the permission of Eastman Kodak Company. F, 20th Century-Fox Film Corporation.

illumination and blackout to such a rate that the eye no longer detects them, but instead averages the extremes into an illusion of continuous illumination.

From the point of view of film economy it is essential to use as few frames as possible per second. Since the 24-frames-per-second rate provides all the visual and aural information required, it would be wasteful to use a higher frame rate just to avoid flicker. The problem is solved without increasing the amount of film by the simple expedient of projecting each frame *twice*.[2] In other words, when a given frame is pulled into place it is flashed on the screen once, remains in place while the screen is blacked out momentarily, and then is flashed on the screen a second time; during the next momentary blackout the next frame is pulled into place and the process repeated. Although only 24 new frames are projected per second, the screen is illuminated by a picture (field) 48 times a second, which is frequent enough to deceive the eye into accepting the illusion of continuous illumination of the screen. Thus motion pictures require *two* projection-frequency standards: one to achieve continuity of action (frame frequency), one to achieve continuity of illumination (field frequency). A similar double standard obtains in television.

Agreement must be reached on such questions as standard frame frequency so that film can be changed from one camera to another and one projector to another. Two other film standards[3] require comment before we move on to television: size and shape. The size of motion-picture film, like the size of a radio channel, must be based on a compromise between the need for economy and the need for communicating an adequate amount of information. It has been emphasized (Section 2.5) that a communication system is designed to carry not all the information available but only enough to answer its own purpose. The demands made of a moving picture (whether on film or television) differ from the demands made of other kinds of pictures. A great deal of information which might be needed in a still photograph would be superfluous in a moving picture.

In the first place, it is impossible to study any one frame with the same attention to detail with which one might study a still photograph; the eye is constantly hurried on to new perceptions and has no time to dwell on all the available information in every frame. Again because of the factor of motion, the optimum viewing distance is different for motion pictures than for still pictures. One looks at moving pictures for a longer period of time than one normally looks at still pictures. To view a motion picture comfortably, we sit at a distance from the screen. Thus, by the standards applied to some other types of photographic reproduction, motion pictures can be quite crude.[4] One

[2] Most modern projectors repeat each frame more frequently, but for purposes of comparison with television the example of two projections per frame is used throughout.

[3] All film standards are published by American Standards Association, Inc., 10 East 40th Street, New York, New York 10016.

[4] Senate Committee on Interstate and Foreign Commerce, Advisory Committee on Color Television, *The Present Status of Color Television*, Report, Sen. Doc. 197, 81st Cong. (Washington: Government Printing Office, 1950), p. 7.

has only to sit too near a motion-picture screen to become uncomfortably aware of the grainy structure of the picture and the resulting lack of fine detail. Eyestrain in television viewing (especially among children) can come from sitting too close to the screen; the viewer unconsciously strains to see detail which simply does not exist and would not be visible at a proper viewing distance even if it did exist.

Many variables affect the "channel capacity" of a given motion-picture film product. Film size (in the sense of the area available for each frame) is fundamental, though each element—the quality of film stocks, equipment, lenses, and the skill with which they are used—affects the outcome. In many applications the highest possible quality would provide more information than required at far too much cost; therefore several film standards have evolved. The highest standard (short of extremely costly scientific applications) is associated with theatre exhibition, represented by 35-mm. practice. The measurement refers to the width of film stock (Figure 3.3) and also connotes high-quality equipment and operating procedures, along with professional standards of production.

In the 1920's, 16-mm. film-making equipment was introduced for the amateur "home-movie" market. This less costly film medium later encouraged an important new nontheatrical market for business, industrial, and educational films. Professionalization of 16-mm., started by this trend, was completed by television, which became the major customer for 16-mm. film and film equipment. The economy of 16-mm. over 35-mm. is even greater than its 50 per cent reduction in film width suggests. For example, 16-mm. film runs at 36 feet per minute at sound speed (24 frames per second), whereas 35-mm. film runs at 90 feet per minute at the same frame speed. Along with the saving in film stock go economies in equipment, processing, and production costs.

The third film standard, 8 mm., has gone through much the same evolution as 16 mm. It began in 1932 as an amateur medium, and in fact was based on 16-mm. technology: the standard 8-mm. camera used 16-mm. film stock, the reel being reversed and run through the camera a second time so that the film ended as two side-by-side strips of pictures. After processing in conventional 16-mm. equipment, the film was finally slit down the middle to produce the 8-mm. print. Though economical of equipment, this method meant inefficient use of the already small film area available for pictures. In 1965, "Super 8," an improved 8-mm. standard, was introduced, with film stock designed specifically for the small format. By reducing the size of sprocket holes and other changes, Super 8 doubled the frame area. Other improvements, such as continuous loops for single-concept teaching films, cartridge-loading cameras and projectors, magnetic sound striping, and foolproof automation of cameras, have moved small-format film up to a semiprofessional level, where it serves the needs of the new "learning technology."

The fact that motion pictures consist of many frames in sequence makes it also necessary to adopt a standard picture *shape*. Still photographs are standardized to a relatively few basic shapes and sizes for cameras, film stock, and related equipment, but the finished print itself can be enlarged and trimmed to any size and shape required. A still picture of a skyscraper can conform to the vertical design of the subject; conversely, a panoramic view of a skyline can be cut to suit the horizontal orientation of the subject. This adapting of picture shape to the communication content is not possible when the film must consist of many thousands of separate frames and when the picture must be projected on ready-made screens of fixed shape and size. Hence, early in the development of motion-picture photography, it was necessary to standardize not only film size but also the shape of the frame.

Logically, a rectangular shape is the most practical, but what should be the aspect ratio, *i.e.,* the proportion between the width and the height of the picture? The proportion selected was 3 units high by 4 units wide.[5] For example, a screen 9 feet high must be 12 feet wide. This 3-to-4 ratio was chosen as being psychologically appropriate, conforming to the normally horizontal field of view of the human eye, and adaptable to most subject matter. Actually, of course, no single shape is ideal for all subjects—otherwise all paintings would have the same aspect ratio. The fixed aspect ratio of the camera's field of view is a severe limitation; hence a major artistic problem of cinema (and of television) is to compensate for this rigidity. Early cinematographers used masks to alter the shape of the scene. In order to focus attention on a particular object within a scene, for instance, a mask with a circular hole might be introduced to black out everything but the object of attention, which was then seen as through a peephole. Nowadays directors handle these problems by means of camera angles and movement, lens changes, and lighting.

When the time came to set up standards for television, previous experience with motion pictures naturally served as a guide. In the television system, the cost factor is computed not in film footage but in frequencies. By using a sufficiently wide channel, television could equal or surpass the quality of 35-mm. film. The question is, does television *need* to be as good as 35-mm. film? And as a corollary question, how good can television *afford* to be in terms of the frequencies available?

It was decided to approximate in television the quality expected in 16-mm. film. It was reasoned that television is a home medium and should logically be adjusted to the standards of good home movies rather than those of theatrical exhibition.[6] The standards adopted for television deliberately sacrifice a certain amount of visual information (just as the standards for AM broadcasting deliberately sacrifice a certain amount of aural information) in the interests of economical use of the available frequency space. The fewer frequencies needed for each television channel, the greater the number of channels that can be allocated and stations that can operate.

---

[5] In response to television competition, theatrical film producers developed optional wide-format aspect ratios such as CinemaScope.

[6] Senate Committee on Interstate and Foreign Commerce, *op. cit.,* p. 8.

3.3 / Pickup Tubes

Applying the principles of motion pictures on film to motion pictures by radio, we perceive that provision must be made for minimal frame and field frequencies to obtain satisfactory viewing results. However, basic differences in method arise from the nature of the media: in one case the medium is a tangible object, film; in the other case the medium is a transient energy concept, radio frequencies. When light from a photographed scene falls on the negative film in a motion-picture camera, all the light-sensitive particles in the film frame respond at the same time. After exposure and development, the frame becomes a permanent record. A radio channel, however, does only one thing at a time; it cannot simultaneously respond to all the information content of a picture. Nor can it retain information, since radio is a transmitting rather than a recording medium.

In television, therefore, we need a camera not only able to convert light values of the individual picture elements into equivalent electrical values with which to modulate a carrier wave. We need also the ability to *disassemble* each frame so that each picture element can be transmitted separately, one by one, in sequence. The television receiver must play the roles of both film print and film projector simultaneously, for it must reassemble each frame, building it up element by element. At the same time it must convert electrical energy into light energy for display on the receiver screen.

Light can be readily converted into equivalent electrical energy, and vice versa, by the use of any of a variety of chemical compounds that have photoelectric and fluorescent properties. To disassemble and reassemble all the thousands of picture elements in a frame with enough speed is much more difficult, and the solution to this problem took many years of research and experimentation.

A television-camera pickup tube is enclosed in an evacuated glass cylinder, with pins for electrical contacts at the rear end (Figure 3.4). When the tube is mounted in the camera, a conventional photographic-lens system focusses the scene to be televised through the glass face of the tube on a small rectangular plate covered with thousands of specks of light-sensitive material. Exposed to the light pattern reflected from the scene, the specks react by building up a corresponding pattern of electrical charges, each charge equivalent in amplitude to the intensity of the light reflected from that particular point in the scene. The pickup plate thus holds a latent picture in the form of a pattern of electrical *potentials*.

At this point we have the analogue of an exposed film negative, with two significant differences: (1) the picture information is stored as electrical potentials, rather than as a latent visual image; (2) it is stored only temporarily, because the same pickup plate must be used in a moment for the next picture frame, instead of being moved on to expose a new frame as in film. Therefore the television camera has no shutter to provide intermittent exposure as does the film camera.

Figure 3.4
The image-orthicon tube

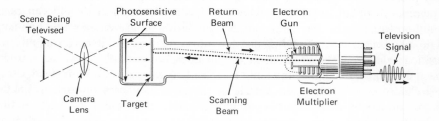

The image is focused on a sensitive plate which has the property of converting light energy into electrical energy. Electrons are emitted from the rear surface of this plate and reproduce an electronic equivalent of the image on the target plate. Each element in the image on the target plate holds a specific electrical charge. When the scanning beam strikes an element it reflects the beam back toward the gun in an amount proportionate to the charge on that element. The return beam is diverted around the electron gun and is amplified by the electron-multiplier section of the tube before being fed out of the tube as the television signal. (The external electromagnets which deflect the beam to produce the scanning pattern fit around the neck of the tube and are not shown.)

Source: Radio Corporation of America, *RCA Color Television* (New York: The Corporation, 1953), p. 24.

Next, the thousands of electrical potentials must be discharged, individually and systematically, so that they can be reassembled in the correct order at the receiver. This operation is accomplished electronically. An electron gun, fixed in the rear end of the pickup tube, points toward the back side of the pickup plate. Electrons are submicroscopic, negatively charged particles of electrical energy. An electron gun "shoots" these particles out in a stream, like so many bullets from a machine gun. The electrons thus directed toward the back of the pickup plate trigger the stored electrical charges, releasing them to be fed out of the tube. These pulses of electrical energy constitute the video (picture) signal.

As the stream of electrons flies back and forth across the rear surface of the pickup plate, it strikes each picture element in passing. Thereupon that element discharges its electrical energy. Thus the electron gun "reads off" the information, element by element and line by line. This process, called *scanning,* follows the pattern of the eye in reading: it starts at the upper left of the pickup plate, reads a line from left to right, drops down and reads another line, and so on until the whole plate has been scanned. Then the electron beam returns to the starting point to repeat the process.

All of this happens with terrific speed, because enough frames must be scanned each second to give the illusion of continuity. Preelectronic television systems attempted to scan mechanically, but no mechanical system can possibly perform such a complex and precise series of movements fast enough. The modern television pickup tube has no moving parts. It performs all operations electronically. The electron gun does not actually move its muzzle back and forth, like a machine gun; it is fixed rigidly in the tube. Instead, after the electrons leave the fixed muzzle of the gun, they pass through magnetic fields formed by deflection coils mounted externally around the neck of the tube. Electrons can be attracted or repelled magnetically. Therefore, appropriate variations in the magnetic fields can precisely control the back-and-forth and up-and-down movements of the electron stream.

The receiver simply reverses the process: it demodulates the radio signal, recovering the electrical information and using it to modulate an electron gun in a *kinescope* (receiver) tube. The modulated electron stream sweeps back and forth across the inner face of the tube, activating a phosphor coating which glows when struck by electrons.

The foregoing is a generalized description. In practice, several types of pickup tubes are in common use, differing in detail but similar in basic principles. The *iconoscope* (Figure 3.5), the original electronic pickup tube of the 1930's, was relatively insensitive and so required uncomfortably intense scene lighting. It was displaced by more sensitive tubes, the *image orthicon,* the *vidicon,* and an improved vidicon, the *plumbicon.* The image orthicon, shown in Figure 3.4, was the workhorse for broadcast television for some twenty years, despite its relatively large size and high cost. The vidicon, though much smaller and cheaper, is less sensitive to light and less capable of good resolution under varying conditions than the image orthicon. It is widely used in closed-circuit television installations, where optimum picture quality is not essential. Its small size[7] also made it valuable in color television, since each color camera requires at least three pickup tubes.

The vidicon's widest use in broadcast television, however, has been for picking up slides and motion pictures. A camera for studio or outdoor use must be adaptable to a wide range of light conditions. Televised slide and motion-picture images are projected directly on the face of the pickup tube, and the projector light can be made as intense as necessary for good reproduction. The sensitivity of the tube can be minimal.

An improved version introduced in 1964, the plumbicon, gets its name from the fact that it uses a compound of lead as the light-sensitive coating on the pickup plate. It combines the sensitivity and other desirable picture characteristics of the image orthicon with the small size, relative economy,

---

[7] Standard image orthicons come in 3-inch and 4-inch diameters, whereas standard vidicons come in ½-inch, 1-inch, and 1½-inch sizes.

Figure 3.5

Zworykin and his iconoscope tube

Vladimir Zworykin displays the key invention which opened the door to the age of electronic television.

Source: Radio Corporation of America.

and simplicity of the vidicon. In 1968, a hand-held portable television camera was developed weighing only 6.5 pounds and using a ⅝-inch-diameter plumbicon.

A pickup device working on an entirely different principle is often used to televise transparent materials such as slides. The *flying-spot scanner* illuminates the subject with a tiny spot of light which flies back and forth, scanning the frame one line at a time. Varying densities modulate the spot of light as it passes through the film. On the other side of the film a photo-electric cell picks up the modulated light beam, converting light energy into correspondingly modulated electrical energy. The scanner is also used for facsimile, described in Section 3.8.

3.4 / The Scanning Pattern

The rate of scansion used in the United States is 30 frames per second. Frame frequency must be accurately standardized throughout the country so that transmitters and receivers will remain in step with each other. Since electrical house current throughout the United States has a frequency of 60 cps, it was convenient to tie television in with this universal standard. In the motion-picture projector, it will be recalled, frame frequency is 24 per second, but, in order to avoid flicker, field frequency is 48 per second. Repeating each whole film frame does not add to the information contained in the film; since film is a *permanent* record, the information in a frame is "remembered" and can be reused any number of times. However, the television information is momentary; it exists only very briefly, one dot at a time; therefore to repeat each entire frame would mean doubling the amount of information the system has to carry. Television avoids this burden by scanning each frame in two successive installments, thus achieving 60 fields with only 30 frames. The method is to scan *every other line* for each field. The first field includes the first, third, fifth, seventh, etc., line; when the electron beam reaches the bottom of the picture it returns and picks up the second, fourth, sixth, eighth, etc., line. This is called interlace, or offset, scanning. It ensures that the screen will be illuminated often enough to prevent flicker, but it minimizes the total amount of information per frame which the system has to transmit.

The television picture, then, is constructed of dots (elements), lines, fields, and frames. The last three are standardized in the United States at 525 lines per frame, 60 fields per second, and 30 frames per second. Each frame consists ideally of about two hundred thousand elements. Since 30 frames are transmitted per second, the number of elements transmitted per second is about six million (Figure 3.1).

Theoretically, only one element out of the two hundred thousand in a frame is visible on the receiver (kinescope) screen at any given moment; in actuality, the phosphor glows briefly even after the electron beam has passed a given position. Nevertheless, only a fragment of the total picture is ever on the screen at one time. Yet elements, fields, and frames succeed each other so rapidly that persistence of vision gives the illusion of a continuous image. However, the number of lines in a frame is small enough to make the line structure of the picture evident on close examination.

The television system is somewhat more complex than the foregoing description indicates. For one thing, what happens to the electron beam while it returns from the end of one line or field to the start of another? If the beam continued to read off the picture information along the fly-back path, the orderly picking up of picture elements would be destroyed. This dilemma is solved by a *blanking signal,* transmitted during fly-back periods. This signal is not apparent on the screen because it cuts off the electron beam. The video signal is negatively modulated; that is to say, a large amplitude of energy in a picture element (indicating whiteness at the corresponding point in the original scene) results in a low amplitude of energy in the transmitted signal. Conversely, a low amplitude in a picture element (indicating darkness at the corresponding point in the original scene) results in high amplitude in the transmitted signal. Therefore, the amplitude of the transmitted signal can be artificially increased beyond the amplitude which produces visible black in the receiver. The boundary line is called the "cut-off" level. All accessory signals in the composite video signal are sent in this "blacker-than-black" region so that they do not interfere with picture information (Figure 3.6).

It can readily be imagined that if receiver and transmitter should get out of step the received picture would be ruined. In order to guarantee exact synchronization of scanning in the receiver with scanning in the camera, special synchronizing signals are included in the composite video signal. These signals, also sent in the blacker-than-black region (along with the blanking signals between frames), establish precise points of "registration," so that the electron gun in the receiver tube scans in exact synchronism with the one in the camera tube.

3.5 / Channel Width and Information Capacity

Each United States broadcast-television channel consists of 6 mc. Some of these frequencies are used for the audio component, some for guard bands (Figure 3.7). The latter are "spare" frequencies left as a protective cushion to prevent adjacent signals spilling over and contaminating each other—in this case video and audio signals. Guard bands must be distinguished from side bands, those frequencies adjacent to the central carrier frequency which become involved when modulation takes place, as explained in Section 1.4. Each cycle in a channel can communicate two pieces of information per second.[8] Thus the 6-mc. television channel would have a theoretical capacity of 2 × 6 million bits of information. However, after subtracting some frequencies assigned to the audio component and guard bands, and others lost in suppressing the lower side band (Figure 3.7), only 4 million cycles remain for the video component of the channel. These are ideally capable of conveying 8 million bits of picture information per second.

---

[8] Note that the capacity of a channel is defined by the *difference* in frequency between the upper and lower limits of the channel, regardless of where these points occur in the frequency spectrum. For example, television Channel 2 falls at 54–60 mc., whereas Channel 83 falls at 884–890 mc. The carrier frequency of one is tremendously higher than that of the other, yet each channel contains the same number of cycles — 6 million.

Figure 3.6
Composite television signal (simplified)

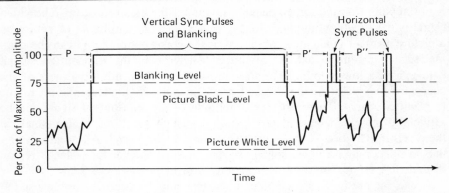

The waveform depicted is a simplified analysis of the picture, synchronizing, and blanking components of the composite video signal. This is the studio output which modulates the transmitter's carrier. During the interval P, the last line of a field is being scanned. The uneven line at P represents the varying amplitudes generated by the scanning beam as it moves across one line of the picture. The higher amplitudes represent dark elements in the image and the lower amplitudes light elements. This reversal is due to negative modulation. At the end of the line, the signal is synthetically increased to an amplitude "blacker than black" (*i.e.,* above the value which shows as "black" at the receiver), which cuts off the electron beam at the receiver. During the ensuing interval the electron beam is returning to the top of the frame to start another field; at the same time, a complex series of pulses (not shown in detail) supplies blanking and synchronizing information to the receiver. At the end of the vertical retrace interval, the first line of the next field is scanned at P'. Then a very short time intervenes while horizontal retrace is taking place, during which a horizontal sync pulse is transmitted. At P'' the second line of the field is scanned, and another retrace interval follows. Note that the "blanking level" is at a slightly higher amplitude than the blackest parts of the actual picture information. (Not drawn to scale.)

Source: FCC signal specifications in *Rules and Regulations,* 47 CFR § 73.699.

Let us see what has to take place during each second. There are 525 lines in each frame, and each frame is scanned at the rate of 30 times per second; therefore the total number of lines per second is 15,750. Dividing that number into the 8 million signal elements available per second discloses that, ideally, 508 signal elements are available for each line. But because some time is used up by the accessory signals, in practice only 416 signal elements per line and 483 lines are available for useful picture information. This real-

Figure 3.7
How the television channel is used

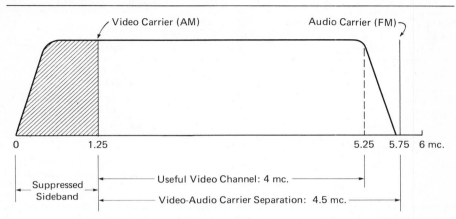

Although 6 mc. are assigned to each television channel, only 4 mc. are available for video information. The lower 1.25 mc. are occupied by the vestiges of the suppressed side band.

Source: FCC specifications in *Rules and Regulations,* 47 CFR § 73.699.

izes ideally 416 × 483, or 200,928 picture elements per frame. Multiplying the number of elements per frame by the number of frames per second, we arrive at 6,027,840 useful picture elements per second. Thus, of the 6 million cycles allocated to each television channel, only 3,013,920 cycles are used for the picture proper; the rest are used for accessory signals, sound, and marginal spacing (Figure 3.7). Definition in the television picture is thus limited by the system itself to the amount of detail ideally resolvable by 200,928 picture elements. In practice, equipment never operates at its theoretical optimum capacity, however, and the television picture most of us see probably has only on the order of 150 thousand elements per frame—considerably less than the 250 thousand of the best-quality 16-mm. film.

The television standard provides a picture only a fraction as detailed as a fine engraving, but, as we pointed out in Section 3.2, the circumstances of viewing pictures in motion make the rendering of finest details superfluous, since they could not be seen by the normal viewer in any event.[9] Magnifying the received picture adds no detail; a 12-by-16-foot theatre-television screen provides no more information than a 12-by-16-inch home-receiver screen. Larger screens simply make it possible to sit farther away from the screen and thus accommodate more viewers.

---

[9] A good 8-by-10-inch photoengraving has about 2 million dots; 35-mm. film, when projected, has the equivalent of about 1 million halftone dots. [Senate Committee on Interstate and Foreign Commerce, *op. cit.,* p. 7. See also Figure 3.2.]

Table 3.1

Major world television standards

System Designation	Lines Per Frame	Channel Width (Mc.)	Sound Modulation	Frames Per Second	Examples of Users
A	405	5	AM	25	Great Britain (BBC-1), Ireland
B (CCIR)[1]	625	7	FM	25	Germany, Australia, Italy
D (OIRT)	625	8	FM	25	USSR, East Europe, Mainland China
E	819	14	AM	25	France
M	525	6	FM	30	United States, Canada, Japan, Latin America

[1] The CCIR (International Radio Consultative Committee of the International Telecommunication Union) standard is the one most widely used outside the American sphere of influence. Omitted letters of the alphabet from A to N designate minor variations, bringing the total for black and-white systems to fourteen.

Source of system designation: International Telecommunication Union, International Radio Consultative Committee, *Report 308, Tenth Plenary Assembly* (Geneva: The Union, 1963).

The television standards just described represent compromises and arbitrary choices, as we have said; therefore it is not surprising that other compromises and choices have been made elsewhere. Britain started with a 405-line system, but this is being replaced by a 625-line system. Since Britain's frame frequency is only 25 per second, their line system will convey about the same net amount of information as our 525-line, 30-frames-per-second system. The French at first erred in the opposite direction—an unnecessarily high definition system of 819 lines. The smaller countries tend to follow the lead of larger countries with which they have cultural and economic ties. Table 3.1 summarizes the chief characteristics of world broadcast-television systems. Still other standards obtain for specialized nonbroadcast applications of television.

3.6 / Picture Transmission

In the studio, a synchronizing generator originates the driving pulses for the scanning action of the cameras, as well as blanking and synchronizing information (Figure 3.8). Video sources may be studio cameras, remote cameras, film, slides, video tape, or network feeds. An operator at a control console combines signals from the various sources to provide the pictorial flow of program material. Meanwhile, the sound components have been handled by an entirely separate set of equipment which likewise terminates at a control console where the audio operator selects the appropriate audio material to match the video material.

The resulting electrical information fed to the transmitter consists therefore of four categories: picture, blanking, synchronizing, and audio (Figures 3.6

Figure 3.8

Block diagram of television-system components and signals

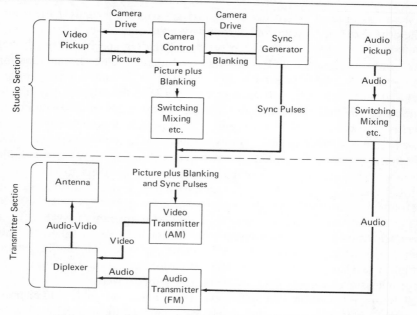

This is a highly simplified diagram showing the basic components and their functions in originating and manipulating the signals. Each block represents a functional component (in practice this may consist of many different related components). The connecting lines indicate the signals delivered from one component to another. The picture information originates in a pickup device (*e.g.*, a studio camera). The pickup device receives drive pulses from the sync generator; these pulses cause the scanning sequence to be performed. Picture information is then delivered to a control point where it is monitored, corrected, and amplified, and the blanking information is added. This signal then goes to the control point where a number of such incoming signals (*e.g.*, from several studio cameras, a film and slide pickup camera, an incoming network relay line) are selected in sequence or mixed to make up the program. Then the synchronizing information is added and the composite video signal is fed to the video AM transmitter. Meanwhile, the audio information has been handled simultaneously but separately. Pickup devices (microphones, records, film tracks) are fed to a control point for switching, mixing, and amplification. This signal is then fed to its own FM transmitter. The two transmitters feed the diplexer, which combines audio and video signals for delivery to the antenna.

Source: Drawing in Harold E. Ennes, *Principles and Practices of Telecasting Operations* (Indianapolis: Howard W. Sams, 1953).

and 3.8). At the video and audio transmitters, these combined signals modulate the carrier waves (AM for video, FM for audio) and are fed to a common antenna. The radiating elements of the antenna are small, in keeping with the shortness of the waves. Channel 2 carrier waves are roughly 18 feet long; at the other extreme, Channel 83 carrier waves are only about a foot in length.

A table of assignments has been set up, allocating specific channel availabilities to specific communities. It is easier to assign television stations than radio stations because their range is more predictable and not very long. A would-be television-station licensee can simply scan the table of assignments to discover whether an unoccupied channel is available in any community, whereas a would-be AM radio licensee has to make a complex engineering study to find out which channel, if any, is available in a given area. Originally provision was made for 2,053 channel availabilities in 1,291 communities, but subsequent revisions of the table reduced these numbers to about 1,850 and 850 respectively. Maximum permissible power varies according to channel frequency, with 100 kw. for the lowest channel number and 5,000 kw. for the highest (see Section 2.2 on the relation of frequency to power). Useful direct television service can generally be expected to reach 20 to 70 miles from the transmitter, depending on frequency, power, antenna height, and terrain. Freakish conditions, however, occasionally cause temporary long-range television reception even as far as 1,000 miles away.[10]

Eighty-two television channels have been made available, numbered 2 through 13 in two segments of the VHF band, and 14 through 83 in the UHF band (Table 3.2).[11] The UHF channels were added in 1952 after it had become evident that twelve VHF channels could not provide for near enough stations. All receivers up to that point had been built to receive VHF channels only, and the coverage area of UHF transmitters of that time was considerably less than that of VHF. Therefore UHF channels were not at first in great demand, though UHF does in fact have certain advantages. UHF is less subject to static and to "ghosts"—multiple images caused by reflected signals which arrive at the antenna a little later than the direct signal because of having travelled over a longer propagation path—because its antennas are more highly directive than VHF, tending to reject signals other than those they are adjusted to receive. The quality of the picture received from UHF stations equals that from VHF stations.

On the other hand, the high directivity of the UHF signal means that its coverage may be spotty—the signal can be cut off by buildings and terrain obstructions in the line-of-sight path between receiver and transmitter. UHF signals are more readily attenuated by absorption and so require higher trans-

---

[10] See Ernest K. Smith, "The Effect of Sporadic E on Television Reception," Department of Commerce, National Bureau of Standards, Report No. 1907 (September 8, 1952, mimeo.).

[11] The original Channel 1 was reallocated to other services in 1947, by which time it was inexpedient to renumber the rest of the channels.

Table 3.2

Summary of U. S. broadcast-channel specifications

Frequency Band	Broadcast Service	Channel Width	No. of Channels	Channel Identification Nos.
535–1,605 kc. (MF)	AM	10 kc.	107	(By frequency)
54– 72 mc. (VHF)	TV	6 mc.⎫		
76– 88 mc. (VHF)	TV	6 mc.⎭	5	2– 6
88– 108 mc. (VHF)	FM	200 kc.	100	201–300
174– 216 mc. (VHF)	TV	6 mc.	7	7– 13
470– 890 mc. (UHF)	TV	6 mc.	70	14– 83

Note: The frequencies intervening between these allocations are used by nonbroadcast services, listed in Table 1.2.

mitting power and more sensitive receiving-antenna adjustment. When commercial UHF television started, transmitters capable of utilizing full permissible power had not been developed. This problem has since been overcome, and under a 1962 amendment to the Communications Act, receiver manufacturers had to equip all sets to receive both UHF and VHF channels, effective in 1964.[12]

3.7 / Color-Television Systems

How the eye perceives color has never been fully explained, but a good deal is known about the physical nature of the stimuli which result in the subjective color sensations. Some of the more recent findings are fundamentally important to color television. It has been found that color sensation is not a single, unified perception. It involves sensations not only of coloredness (hue), but also of brightness (luminance) and of color purity (saturation or chroma). Each of the three factors can vary independently.

The sensitivity of the eye differs for different colors, or light frequencies. For instance, the eye is about twice as sensitive to green as to red. Moreover, its sensitivity to color varies with the size of the object being observed. The eye perceives relatively large objects in terms of hue, brightness, and purity, but as objects get smaller the eye loses its sensitivity to hue. Finally, it sees the smallest details in an image only in terms of brightness. This loss of the ability to sense hues does not occur all at once; the colors to which the eye is least sensitive, such as blues, disappear first; then, as objects get smaller, the colors to which the eye is more sensitive, such as greens, are finally lost. Eventually, in the smallest visible details of the scene, the eye can detect only

---

[12] Communications Act, §303(s). Cf. House Committee on Interstate and Foreign Commerce, *All-Channel Receivers,* Report to accompany H. R. 8031, 87th Cong. (Washington: Government Printing Office, 1962). See Section 10.4 for discussion of economic and legal factors of the UHF-VHF problem.

the brightness factor. The normal eye is actually color blind to small details.

Although these factors are relatively new discoveries, it has long been known that all color sensations can be reproduced by appropriate mixtures of light of only three primary colors. Any set of colors can be used as primaries as long as the three colors are such that no two can be mixed to match the third and a combination of all three in appropriate proportions results in the sensation of white.

Nearly all color-producing systems depend on the trichromatic nature of vision. The fortunate circumstance that all the thousands of hues can be derived from only three primaries enormously reduces the quantity of information contained in a color picture from what it would have to be if each hue were unique. The fact that the eye cannot detect hue and saturation information in small detail again relieves the reproducing system of the need for handling a vast amount of color information.

Two arbitrary prior limitations were placed on the American color-television system: it had to get along with the 6-mc. channel width already set up for black-and-white television; and it had to be compatible with existing black-and-white television receivers. Compatibility means the ability of a noncolor receiver to pick up a color signal as a monochrome signal; it was necessary to avoid the possibility of outmoding millions of existing monochrome receivers. These were severe limitations. Even with the savings previously indicated, more information must be handled in color-television broadcasting than monochrome; and the requirement of compatibility with monochrome made any major changes in the monochrome scanning and other timing operations out of the question.

These problems were solved by the American industry through its National Television System Committee (NTSC), whose recommendations were accepted by the Federal Communications Commission.[13] In setting up standards, the Commission specified the basic composition of the signal but left to the manufacturers the choice of the means of achieving the prescribed signal. Several methods of both pickup and reproduction have been developed; they differ in details but are enough alike to permit any color receiver to respond to any color transmitter.

NTSC color standards retain the 525-line, 60-field standard of monochrome television. All the additional information needed must be packed into the same 4-mc. video channel used by monochrome television. To accomplish this, advantage is taken of the fact that in actual practice the energy of the monochrome signal is not distributed equally throughout the 4 million cycles of the video channel. Instead, the energy clusters about certain frequencies, leaving others relatively unused. These unused frequencies, or blank spaces in the channel, are therefore available to carry extra information (see Section 2.6 on channel utilization).

---

[13] FCC, "Amendment of the Commission's Rules Governing Color Television Transmissions," 18 *Fed. Reg.* 8649 (1953).

The image is picked up simultaneously by three separate camera tubes, each with a filter for one of the specified primary colors (red, blue, green). From each of these color signals is derived a brightness signal proportional in strength to the brightness value of that color. The brightness components of the three primaries when added together yield white, which (in terms of the specific primaries selected) consists of 59 per cent green, 30 per cent red, and 11 per cent blue. This mixed signal provides the brightness information for the color picture. Since brightness is *all* that can be perceived in the fine detail, the mixed signal provides all the fine detail in the color picture. This same signal provides the compatible monochrome picture for black-and-white receivers. Meanwhile, the three color signals (minus their respective brightness components) are transmitted on a separate carrier wave (the subcarrier) generated by the same transmitter. The resulting color picture suffers some loss in actual detail compared to monochrome standards, but this is compensated for by the greater apparent detail color provides.[14]

According to the foregoing description, the composite color signal consists of four different elements: the brightness component and the three primary colors. So far, however, provision has been made for only two signals within the video portion of the channel: the brightness signal on the main carrier, the color signal on a subcarrier. Since the color signal consists of three separate elements—the red, green, and blue values—it is necessary for the carrier to do three things at once. The solution of this problem is the most ingenious part of the NTSC color system. First, the green signal is mixed with the other three signals (red, blue, and brightness) in such a way that the green information can be recovered at the receiver. Then the red and blue signals are *multiplexed* on the subcarrier—*i.e.,* both are sent in the same channel (without mixture), out of phase with each other. This operation requires extremely delicate timing, which necessitates an added synchronizing signal (the "color burst"), transmitted during the blanking period just after the regular synchronizing pulses. The color burst provides the receiver with the reference-timing signal needed to separate the multiplexed red and blue signals.

At the receiving end, each of three different types of phosphor on the face of the kinescope tube glows in one of the prescribed primary colors when struck by electrons. The color elements are separate but closely associated and very minute; hence the eye perceives all three together, although in fact each primary is displayed separately. In other words, the color mixing is done by the eye rather than by the receiver tube. One type of tricolor kinescope uses three separate electron guns, one for each primary color. Another type uses only one electron gun; the electron beam "wobbles" as it scans a line, alternately touching on three narrow stripes of phosphor in the three primary colors. The appropriate electromagnetic information modulates the beam as it touches each of the color stripes in rapid succession.

---

[14] *Ibid.,* paragraph 17.

Color-television components must be fabricated with a precision never before attempted in mass production. For example, one type of tricolor kinescope tube uses a plate in which 400 thousand holes must be accurately positioned. The timing operations involved in developing the color signal are so exact that compensation has to be provided for the tiny delay caused by signal travel time in some of the circuits.

Japan and Canada followed the American lead and adopted NTSC color, but for political as much as for engineering reasons, two slightly different color systems have been adopted in other major countries. The French developed SECAM (*séquential couleur à mémoire*) in 1958, and the Germans PAL ("phase alternate line") in 1963. After extensive comparisons of the three systems, Britain, West Germany, and the Netherlands began colorcasting in 1967 using PAL, while France and the USSR inaugurated color with SECAM. As color has extended to other countries, the division has continued along ideological lines. Little difference in overall quality can be detected among the three systems, although each has certain minor technical advantages in such areas as compatibility with black and white and effects of distortions or signal errors.[15]

3.8 / Related Video Systems

Broadcast-television standards, as indicated in Section 3.5, represent a compromise between the conflicting demands for conserving the frequency spectrum on the one hand and for providing a high-quality picture on the other. That the American standards struck the correct balance seems indicated by the fact that both higher and lower standards adopted in Europe are being phased out in favor of a compromise approximating the American one. The remaining difference in line frequency of 525 per frame versus 625 (Table 3.1) can be explained by the difference in house current, 60 cps in the United States and 50 cps in Europe.

The principle of television has been applied to many other communication situations, however, for which entirely different standards may be appropriate. A few systems have higher standards of definition. For example, an 828-line standard is used in military applications of television, and 1,029-line frames have been used experimentally for medical and scientific television.[16] Most applications call for lower rather than higher standards, however. For example, just as in motion pictures first 16-mm. then 8-mm. formats developed as subprofessional standards, so complete systems of television equipment have been developed for subbroadcast-quality applications. For limited purposes, the end result, just as in the case of film, may well be as satisfactory

[15] Howard Coleman, ed., *Color Television: The Business of Colorcasting* (New York: Hastings House, 1968), p. 251.

[16] National Association of Educational Broadcasters, *Standards of Television Transmission* (Washington: The Association, 1964), p. 1.

as broadcast quality; tolerable sacrifices in versatility, definition, and stability can realize substantial savings in both equipment and operational costs. Thus, many closed-circuit television applications can use extremely simple, fixed-position television cameras, without going to the expense of electronic view-finders, lens-changing capability, mobile tripods, pan heads, and complicated electronic synchronizing equipment.

Facsimile, a system for transmitting still pictures, represents an early practical application of the television principle. Facsimile uses the flying-spot scanner (Section 3.3) to pick up newsphotos, maps, printed pages, engineering drawings, and any other two-dimensional visual material for transmission by wire or radio. A typical facsimile system takes about eight minutes to scan a single page. The receiver "read-out" is in permanent, or "hard-copy," form rather than by kinescopic display. FM broadcast stations can be authorized to broadcast facsimile materials. Experiments have been conducted also with transmitting slow-scan still pictures in conjunction with FM sound radio, a combination which might be ideal for teaching by radio. Unlike facsimile, this method displays pictures electronically. It requires a kinescope tube with special storage capabilities, since it takes almost a minute for the picture to build up. This technique has been called "the most promising unexplored telecommunications medium."[17]

The foregoing illustrate a few of many slow-scan television applications. An extreme example was the Mariner satellite which sent back pictures of Mars in 1965. The satellite carried a tiny vidicon camera having a line frequency of only 200. The camera took 48 seconds to build up one complete picture, which was converted into a numerical code and stored on tape. It then took nearly nine hours to transmit to earth the string of numbers representing the 40 thousand elements in a single picture!

---

[17] Rudy Bretz, *Communications Media: Properties and Uses* (Santa Monica, Cal.: RAND Corporation, 1969), p. 70.

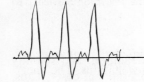

4

RELAY, DISTRIBUTION, AND STORAGE SYSTEMS

From the outset, broadcasters realized that full development of the medium's potentialities required something more than studios, transmitters, and receivers. A broadcast station needs not only facilities to originate and transmit programs, but also means for transporting and storing them. Without ways of relaying, recording, and reproducing program materials, each station would be limited to a narrow range of low-budget, locally produced programs. With these technical resources, however, even the smallest station can command quality program materials drawn from all over the world.

Relays and recording/reproduction may be regarded as the technical aspect of the economic mechanism of *syndication,* an essential element in all mass-media enterprises. Syndication spreads the burden of very costly communications production and distribution among many users. Individual outlets—stations, newspapers, theatres, and so on—cannot individually produce enough high-quality communications material to meet the demand. But the combined financial resources of many outlets can sustain the cost of world-wide news services, highly paid performers, and expensive productions. Relay and recording/reproduction make such syndication physically possible.

A relay, in the present context, is the connecting link for instantaneously transferring program material from one point to another *without* broadcasting it. Broadcasters use local relays routinely in studio-transmitter links—radio connections linking studios to transmitters when the two are in widely separated buildings, the usual case in large cities. "Remote pickup" relays are another example. They connect locations such as stadiums or convention halls to the studio itself, so that a station can pick up remote events for incorporation into its programming. Either wire circuits or radio links can be used for these types of relay. If the latter, they constitute especially licensed types of auxiliary broadcast services (Table 1.3).

4.1 / Networks

The most important use of relays in broadcasting is to connect two or more stations in a network, so that they can transmit the same program simultaneously. Technically speaking, network broadcasting involves *simultaneous* transmission of identical programs by a group of *connected* stations. The "net" of network broadcasting refers to the point-to-point relay circuits which distribute programs from their points of origin to member stations. Points of origin are usually network production headquarters but can also be the studios of member stations and remote locations such as stadiums and convention halls. This formal definition of network broadcasting has become somewhat extended by availability of high-quality recording processes. Originally, networks used only live programs. This was considered superior to program distribution by recordings, which were both inferior in quality and delayed in time. But networks found it convenient to use both methods of distribution, "live" and "delayed," when recordings became indistinguishable in quality from live programs. To compensate for differences in time zones in the United States, national networks feed delayed broadcasts to western stations so that stations in each time zone can release the same network programs at the same local clock time. Affiliates also sometimes record network feeds for later broadcast, to suit their own schedules. Indeed, except for such timely material as newscasts, network interconnection increasingly functions simply as a rapid and convenient method of program distribution, rather than as a means of simultaneous broadcast in "real time." The noncommercial stations in particular find the traditional lock-step scheduling of conventional simultaneous networking irksome.[1]

Some so-called networks have no interconnection facilities, but rely instead on shipping recorded program materials to member stations. These must be regarded as pseudo-networks, for the capability of simultaneous release remains an essential feature of the true broadcast network, as legally defined.

Network relay systems use wire or radio connecting links, or the two in combination. From the start, broadcasters recognized the desirability of using radio relay instead of wire, but at first no suitable radio technique existed. This may seem surprising. If it is possible to broadcast at all, why cannot a second station pick up the signal from an originating station and *rebroadcast* it? In fact such rebroadcasting is possible, but it is not considered a case of relaying. A relay, by definition, transmits a private (*i.e.,* nonbroadcast) communication from one point to another.

Rebroadcasting is not used extensively, partly because broadcasting stations are usually not ideally spaced geographically for network purposes, partly because static and other kinds of interference tend to degrade broadcast signals. FM eliminated the static problem, but the problem of the spacing of stations remained.

At the time broadcasting began, shortwave radio had already long been used for worldwide communication. Shortwave relays could have solved the spacing problem, were it not for the instability of shortwave signals. Fading

---

[1] See Carnegie Commission on Educational Television, *Public Television: A Program for Action* (New York: Harper & Row, 1967), pp. 54–55.

and interference can be tolerated in radiotelegraphy, radiotelephony, and even in international broadcasting in the absence of any better method. But domestic broadcast relays should be capable of delivering the full frequency range normally expected in broadcast-quality programs, with complete reliability and fidelity at all times of the day and year. Sky-wave propagation does not provide such stability.

Fortunately, when broadcasting began, a nationwide telephone-wire network already existed, on the basis of which radio networks could develop

Figure 4.1
Cross-section of coaxial cable

The cross-section discloses twenty individual coaxial tubes and ninety-four conventional wire conductors. Some of the latter service the repeater amplifiers, located at about two-mile intervals. The outer sheath is made up of polyvinyl, aluminum, and steel layers.

Source: American Telephone and Telegraph Company.

rapidly. National networks rent interconnection facilities from the American Telephone and Telegraph Company, which provides the domestic long-distance relay as well as the long-distance telephone circuits of the country.

Equalizing and booster amplifiers have to be used every few miles to maintain signals transmitted long distances by wire. Even so, an ordinary wire circuit cannot carry the 4-mc. band required by the video signal. The need for wide-band relays led to development of a specialized type of conductor, called *coaxial* because it consists of two conductors, one inside the other, having a common axis (Figure 4.1). Each coaxial conductor can accommodate a wide range of frequencies, and each cable may incorporate several such conductors. Coaxial cable, which is buried underground and requires amplifiers every few miles, is troublesome and expensive to install. However, the regular telephone service as well as broadcasting uses the coaxial-cable network and thereby helps defray the cost. A single coaxial channel can accommodate hundreds of multiplexed long-distance calls simultaneously, but only a single television signal.

4.2 / Radio Interconnection

The possibility of using radio relays to eliminate the expensive cable naturally remained attractive. An answer came in 1945 with *microwave* relays, the first satisfactory method for using radio instead of wire or cable for high-quality interconnection. Microwaves are extremely short waves, on the order of 1,000 mc. in frequency. It will be recalled that radio energy at these high frequencies attenuates rapidly, so that it does not normally travel far enough to be useful. Moreover, the energy travels in a direct, line-of-sight path. The first of these disadvantages can be overcome by directional antennas. Because of their short wavelength (under 10 feet), microwaves can easily be focused by a moderate-sized reflecting "dish" (Figure 4.2) into a narrow, intense beam, just as a spotlight focuses light energy. The "directive gain" (ratio of effectiveness of power in a directional as compared with a nondirectional antenna) is on the order of only 2 or 3 at standard broadcast frequencies. By the time one gets up to 30,000 mc., however, the gain can be as high as 100,000. At this high-energy level, microwaves can be reliably transmitted many miles.

The line-of-sight limitation, however, requires spacing microwave relay-repeater stations about 30 miles apart. Mounted on a tower or high building, each station receives, amplifies, and retransmits the signal to the next link in the chain (Figure 4.2). Microwave towers, erected on strategic high spots, provide a smooth radio highway through the roughest terrain—places where installation of underground coaxial cable would be impossible. The first transcontinental television-network relay circuit, opened by AT&T in 1951, used a combination of coaxial-cable and microwave relay links. Wire has now been replaced by cable and microwave in long-distance circuits.

When long distances must be covered in thinly populated areas, the necessity of using so many repeater stations makes microwave relays unduly expen-

Figure 4.2
Microwave relay-repeater station

New "horn" type of reflectors on top of the tower; "dish" reflector at the lower level.

Source: American Telephone and Telegraph Company.

sive, and of course they are quite useless for spanning large bodies of water. So the need remained for a longer-distance direct radio-relay technique.

The next answer, *scatter* propagation, was first used operationally in Canada in 1955 and in the United States in 1957, between Florida and Cuba. A small fraction of microwave energy gets scattered beyond the horizon by the atmosphere (tropospheric scatter) and the ionosphere (ionospheric scatter). Formerly, this scattered energy was merely wasted, but eventually it was found that high power and extremely large antennas made it possible to gather in weak, scattered remnants of the signal, even well beyond the horizon. Tropospheric propagation extended the useful range of radio relays to 600 miles—sufficient to bridge considerable water barriers, but still not enough to span whole oceans.

The ultimate solution came with the launching of space relay stations. In 1962, the Telstar satellite demonstrated experimentally the practicability of using repeater stations orbiting in space for intercontinental relay of a variety of communications—computer data, radiotelephone calls, news dispatches, news photos, radio programs, television programs. Development moved rapidly, with the first commercial relay satellite being launched only three years later. This was Earlybird, the first of a series launched by Comsat, the Communications Satellite Corporation.

Satellite relays overcome the problems of long-distance communication because they can use efficient line-of-sight radio transmission without resorting to sky waves or scatter phenomena. Once free of the earth's atmosphere, radio energy travels in space with little attenuation, enabling very small transmitters (Telstar's power was only 2.25 w.) in a high-orbit satellite to send reliable signals back to earth. The height of the orbit, 22,300 miles, permits line-of-sight transmission from a single satellite to blanket a third of the earth's surface. The earliest satellites could be used for only a short time between any given pair of sending-receiving stations because as they orbited they moved out of station range. Telstar, for example, spent only twenty minutes per orbit in a position enabling Maine-to-Europe communication. Syncom II, launched in 1963, solved this problem by "parking" in synchronous orbit, keeping in step with the earth's rotation.

Comsat's Intelsat series of satellites depended on intricate, expensive ground sending and receiving stations. By putting the largest share of the operational burden on ground stations, the planners kept the satellites themselves relatively light in weight and uncomplicated in design. The appropriate ground station, after picking up the faint signal relayed from space by a satellite, amplified the signal and forwarded it via conventional terrestrial relay networks.

4.3 / Receiver-to-Home Distribution Systems

A broadcasting network has as its underlying purpose making a single program service simultaneously available over a larger service area than any one station could cover. Conventional broadcasting networks go a long way toward this goal, especially in areas of high population density. But they still usually fail to blanket the more remote regions of a country, as well as missing pockets where terrain interferes with propagation.

Several specialized types of relay-distribution systems have been used to help equalize spotty coverage. Television stations may use small, low-power translators to pick up their signals for retransmission into areas not reached by primary signals. American television stations use over twenty-five hundred translators (Table 1.3), most of them in the West where the mountains cast "shadows" blocking off television signals from people in valleys. In order to avoid self-interference between the originating station and its translator station, the latter station "translates" the signal to a different channel. In some cases translators are located even beyond the signal area of the "mother" station and are fed by special microwave relays.

Relays may be used not only to link up networks of stations, but also to link networks of homes to a common receiver. This relay-distribution method, introduced in the early days of radio and sometimes called "rediffusion" and "relay exchange," feeds home loudspeakers by wire from central community receivers. This system is still used for radio reception, notably in Italy, Mainland China, and the USSR.

More recently, the principle of rediffusion has been adapted to American television, though with entirely different motivation. Even with translators to fill in coverage gaps, many communities in America still had limited television choice. Only about 40 per cent of American families live in markets with four or more television stations; about a quarter of the families live in market areas served by only one or two stations. Yet ideally each American home should have access to a minimum of *five* stations—affiliates of the three national commercial television networks, at least one educational station, and one independent commercial station. The normal coverage pattern of conventional broadcasting networks, stations, and translators simply cannot provide this choice of services in all areas.

This need brought about the receiver-to-home type of relay-distribution system known as "community antenna television." CATV, as it is called, involves setting up sensitive receivers and a master-antenna complex near a community which does not receive a full range of reliable television services. Such an installation can pick up television stations at greater distances and with better quality than the ordinary home antenna-receiver combination. The CATV master antenna can even be located miles away from the community it serves, at an ideal reception point. Signals may then be fed to the community distribution point by microwave relay.

The CATV operator distributes programs by coaxial cable to subscriber homes in the community, for which he charges periodic service fees plus (usually) a substantial installation fee. Communities which formerly could receive either no television at all or only a partial or marginal service, obtain through CATV reliable access to a full range of programs. Some CATV operators make their services even more attractive by providing not only regular broadcast-televison programs but also program services of their own, such as local news and weather reports. The subscriber simply tunes his set to one of several (usually at least five) broadcast channels fed by the CATV system cables, or to one or more nonbroadcast (closed-circuit) services originated by the CATV system itself.

CATV finds a market even in some localities where homes can already pick up a full range of services directly from nearby stations. In large cities, man-made electrical noise plus reflections and blanketing caused by tall buildings make ideal television reception virtually impossible. A viewer in the suburbs of New York gets better over-the-air reception from New York stations than a viewer in Manhattan. CATV, by locating a master-antenna system at a point ideal for unimpeded reception, overcomes these difficulties. By 1969, over two thousand systems had been installed and CATV served more than 4.5 million subscribers (Figure 11.4).

Direct satellite-to-home rebroadcasting could perform some of the functions of CATV. As previously pointed out, however, the first satellite relays depended on heavy investments in ground-station equipment. Satellites able to produce signals of sufficient strength and on enough channels to serve homes directly would have to be much heavier and more complex than the Intelsat type used in 1970. In addition to such technical problems, satellite-to-home rebroadcasting would raise complex economic problems because of its potential effect on the existing investment in terrestrial longlines.[2] Homeowners would also have to invest in special antenna and converter equipment, though on a mass-market basis this cost would not be prohibitive. However, satellites cannot satisfy the need for purely local television services, which still have to come from local stations or via some other localized system such as CATV.

4.4 / Closed-Circuit and Hybrid Systems

When a CATV company originates its own program material and sends it via cable to subscriber homes, it becomes an example of a closed-circuit distribution system. In closed-circuit systems, wire or cable connects the originating and receiving points, leaving no radio ("open") links in the communications circuit. Hundreds of specialized business, industrial, scientific, military, and educational communications situations use closed-circuit television. It can be especially useful for surveillance and for observation in hazardous locations. As a medium for reaching large audiences, its most fruitful use has been in education. In 1970, about 150 closed-circuit school-system installations were either operating or about to start; they distributed three times as many hours of instruction as open-circuit (broadcast) educational television.[3]

---

[2] See Lawrence Lessing, "Cinderella in the Sky," *Fortune*, October 1967, pp. 131–133, 196–208.

[3] Don H. Coombs, *One Week of Educational Television, No. 5, May 6–12, 1968* (Bloomington, Ind.: National Instructional Television Center, 1969), pp. 4–5.

Several other hybrid systems, incorporating elements of both closed-circuit and broadcast distribution, have also evolved. Closed-circuit school instructional-television systems may be interconnected by a special quasi-relay service known as ITFS (Instructional Television Fixed Service). Thirty-one channels in the 2,500-mc. region have been set aside for this service, which may be used to distribute television lessons by radio relay from a production studio to any of a number of participating school buildings or school systems; and to interconnect broadcast and closed-circuit systems, or either of these to each other or other ITFS systems. It has been called an "on-the-air closed-circuit system" because it combines features of both. One licensee may have as many as four channels. As of June 30, 1969, 147 ITFS systems had been authorized (Table 1.3).

Another hybrid system, proposed even before CATV, is Subscription Television (also called Pay TV and a dozen other names). The subscriber to CATV pays to get access to a wider range of *existing* on-the-air program services (plus only secondarily, perhaps, the CATV company's own closed-circuit service). In contrast, STV offers programs not otherwise available, for which the subscriber pays by the individual program. Some proposed STV systems distribute the programs on a closed-circuit basis, but the experimental system which has operated the longest (begun in Hartford, Connecticut, in 1962) used a conventional broadcast station whose STV programs are "scrambled" so that only subscribers can get clear reception (Figure 4.3.)

4.5 / Sound Recording

Turning from relay systems to the second of the major adjuncts to broadcasting, ways of storing program material, let us consider first sound recording and reproducing systems. A lively record industry existed before radio broadcasting even began. But the quality of even the earliest live broadcasts exceeded the scratchy, tinny recording quality of that day. For years the radio networks refused to use recordings, producing even the most difficult and complex programs in real time, *i.e.,* "live." The poor quality of records in the 1920's resulted from their dependence on crude sound energy, without benefit of electronic amplification.[4] The cutting stylus vibrated in direct response to sound vibrations in the air impinging on a diaphragm; the reproducing stylus was connected to a diaphragm which vibrated air in a pipe leading to a "morning glory" horn.

Radio brought with it the promise of improved quality through electronic amplification, but not soon enough to save the recording industry from absorption by radio. Mementos survived in the names RCA Victor (harking back to the Victor Talking Machine Company, founded in 1898), and Co-

---

[4] The popularity of Caruso as a recording star in the early 1900's is ascribed to his ability to sing loudly without yelling. See "Phonograph Records," *Fortune,* September, 1939, pp. 72–75, 92–104.

lumbia Broadcasting System (a name derived from Columbia Phonograph Company, founded in 1888).

The effect on music of long-playing recordings, introduced in 1948, has been likened to the effect of the printing press on literature. Previously discs had been made of shellac, a thick, heavy, and brittle material. They ran at 78 revolutions per minute and had coarse grooves which limited playing time to only one popular number per side. Special oversized discs ("transcriptions") for broadcast use, introduced in 1929, ran at 33⅓ rpm and could carry a 15-minute program on one side of a 16-inch disc. However, transcriptions

Figure 4.3
Zenith's Subscription Television system

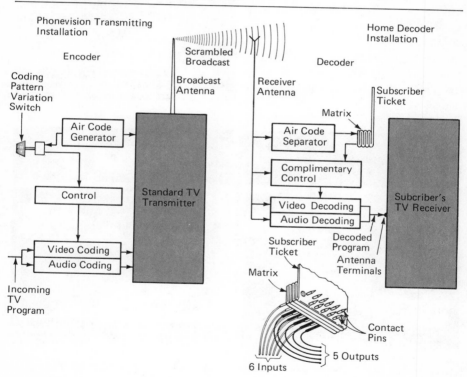

A. Block diagram of coder-decoder system. The coder scrambles the picture by cutting it into thirty-five constantly shifting horizontal strips and reversing polarity. To foil unauthorized decoding, the transmitting station varies the specific scrambling code from program to program.

Source: Zenith Radio Corporation.

Figure 4.3 (*continued*)
Zenith's Subscription Television system

B.   Subscriber ticket, received through the mail, activates the decoder.

C.   Inserting ticket in decoder, mounted atop home television receiver.

D.   Side-by-side comparison: scrambled picture on left; same picture after decoding on right.

Source: Zenith Radio Corporation.

required special heavy-duty playback equipment and were not available to the general public.

In 1948, the recording industry was rejuvenated with the introduction of microgroove recordings—33⅓ rpm long play (LP), and 45 rpm extended play (EP). Light, flexible, durable vinyl plastic replaced the shellac record base. Two to three times as many grooves per inch, along with slower speed, greatly expanded the playing time of each side. Rim-driven instead of axle-driven turntables made it easier to use speeds under 78 rpm without resorting to expensive, cumbersome equipment of the type used in studios to play transcriptions. Electronic amplification made possible exceedingly light stylus pressure, with consequent reduced noise and wear.[5]

Magnetic tape recording completed the LP revolution. Prior to the general introduction of tape in the late 1940's, recordings had to be cut on discs with studio machinery that was not only heavy and expensive, but also temperamental. Tape liberated the recording process from manifold restrictions while opening up a whole new world of technical resources—echo effects, track superimposition, and so on. LP recordings gave the consumer better quality and convenience; transistors made possible compact portable playbacks; and radio itself created a new audience for recorded sound of all kinds. Where before a few major companies had dominated the whole record industry, now hundreds of "labels" could compete; new technology had so simplified the mechanical aspects of record making that records in quantity became inexpensive to produce and buy.

A Dane, Valdemar Poulsen, discovered the principle of magnetic recording in 1898. It relies on two elementary electrical phenomena: the strength of a magnetic field can be modulated by varying the electrical current applied to an electromagnet; patterns of magnetic force can be transferred to and permanently stored in a strip of metal as it passes across the poles of an electromagnet. In modern sound-recording practice, the electromagnet is ring shaped, with a minute air gap at the poles across which a plastic tape with metallic coating passes. Signals from a microphone or other source modulate the current in the electromagnet, which induces a corresponding magnetic pattern in the tape. On playback, the tape passes over the gap of a similar electromagnet, generating in it a modulated electrical current which, after suitable amplification, goes to the loudspeaker. Exposure of the recorded tape to an unmodulated magnetic field rearranges the molecules, neutralizing the stored magnetic pattern, so that the same tape can be used over and over.

Poulsen did not succeed in solving the practical problems of his system, chief among which was very low energy output, which was overcome only after the development of electronic amplifiers. The recording medium originally used—steel piano wire or steel tape—also had practical drawbacks. During World War II, the Germans solved the remaining technical problems,

---

[5] See John M. Conly, "Five Years of LP," *The Atlantic Monthly*, CXCII (September, 1953), 87–94.

producing tape recorders with a frequency range up to 10,000 cps. Among their contributions was an improved paper tape, ¼-inch wide and coated with finely powdered iron. Subsequently, plastic replaced paper as the base. Other tape widths—⅛, ½, 1, and 2 inch—are now used for specialized purposes.

The chief variable governing the frequency response of magnetic tape is the speed at which it passes over the recording and playback magnets. Present standards date back to the standard of 76 mm. per second used by the Germans during the early 1940's. This rate approximates 30 inches per second. Slower rates (each speed one-half the next higher speed) became practicable with improvements in other aspects of the system. Now 15 ips represents the highest standard, used in recording master music tapes, for example. Broadcasting has standardized on 7½ ips, while speeds of 3¾ and 1⅞ ips allow adequate quality for most amateur uses. For dictation and logging, a tape speed as slow as 15/16 ips suffices.

One inconvenience remained after magnetic sound recording achieved high-quality standards—the open reels of tape, which had to be threaded on the machine, creating mechanical hazards for the careless or inept operator. Tape cartridges and cassettes,[6] which simply click into place, removed this last inconvenience and widened the market for tape players, which could now be easily used in automobiles, for example, and school learning centers. They encouraged the market for prerecorded tapes to compete with discs. During the 1960's, stereo tapes captured a quarter of the recording market. Cartridges also lend themselves well to automation in radio stations. Inaudible cues recorded on the tape start and stop cartridges automatically and precisely.

Early experiments with motion-picture sound included attempts to use piano-wire magnetic recorders, but the first "talkies" in America used 33⅓-rpm discs of the transcription type used in early radio. However, motion-picture sound presents the special problem of synchronization—sound must keep precisely in step with picture. This requirement led to development of optical sound, photographed directly on the film alongside the picture and thus locked into permanent synchronism.

Film moves intermittently through the projection aperture, but it must move at constant speed over the sound-pickup head. A projector maintains free loops of film just before and after the film enters the projection gate where the sharp, intermittent movement takes place. These loops enable the rapid jerking of the film into place without tearing and without disturbing the steady winding of the film from feed reel over the sound head to takeup reel. Therefore, the part of the sound track associated with any given picture frame has to be at a different position on the film. The sound offset is 20 frames ahead in 35-mm. film and 26 frames in 16-mm. film. In "single-system" sound-film

---

[6] *Cartridges* are plastic boxes containing endless tape loops, while *cassettes* incorporate feed and takeup reels in a single housing and have to be either rewound after play or reversed to play a second "side." The two words have come to be used interchangeably, however, especially in connection with home video-recording systems.

production, picture and sound are recorded simultaneously on the *same* film strip. The sound offset makes it impossible to edit such film freely, for any cut will be wrong either for picture or for sound. All but the simplest types of motion-picture production therefore use "double-system" sound, in which the sound element and the picture element are handled entirely separately and are not physically united on a single film strip until the release-print stage. Prior to this stage, picture and sound can be separately edited and processed.

Optical sound appears on release prints on a narrow band alongside the picture component (illustrated in Figure 3.3). In optical-sound recording, sound energy, converted into electrical current, modulates a tiny pencil of light as it shines on the track area of the film. Modulation can consist either of varying the width of the beam (variable area) or of varying its intensity (variable density), as shown in Figure 3.3. For playback, the projector shines a similar narrow beam of light through the sound track onto a photoelectric cell. As the film moves, the varying area or density of the sound track modulates the light falling on the cell, inducing a modulated electric current.

Double-system production requires a method of keeping the two physically separate elements, picture and sound, locked into "sync" during the recording and editing stages. Optical sound is recorded on its own film strip. Two or more separate film strips can be run through a sprocketed synchronizer to keep them in step with each other. When magnetic recording was finally perfected, a special sound tape with sprocket holes was first used for double-system motion-picture sound. Later, regular ¼-inch sound tape also came into general use in film-sound recording, with the synchronizing function performed electronically rather than mechanically.

Film producers now generally use magnetic tape for the original sound recording and for editing operations. Magnetic sound is converted to optical sound in release prints. Magnetic sound can also be used in release prints by adding a magnetic stripe to the finished print. Figure 3.3 shows an example of a theatre release print with four separate magnetic tracks, designed to feed different sets of speakers to create a "surround" effect.

4.6 / Picture Recording

Television uses four main classes of conventional motion-picture materials: (1) feature films made for theatrical exhibition; (2) business, industrial, and educational films, made both for direct projection in meetings, schoolrooms, auditoriums, and the like, and for television release; (3) "syndicated films," entertainment material made especially for television, mostly in half- or full-hour formats, but also in feature length; (4) news and documentary material, often shot silent or in single-system sound.[7]

---

[7] The very simplest form of television film is negative shooting stock, which can be shown as positive by reversing polarity in the television-film pickup camera.

A form of film unique to television, a true case of picture recording or storage, is the kinescope film. The film camera takes pictures of an image as it appears on a special television picture tube whose phosphor is especially suited to photography. The 30-frames-per-second television recording camera has to be especially designed to compensate for 24-frames-per-second motion-picture film. A kinescope recording causes a double loss of information because of the double transfer from live to television to film. The resulting picture quality leaves a good deal to be desired.

Magnetic-tape picture recording (video-tape recording, or VTR) eventually displaced kinescoping for most domestic broadcast uses. In principle, picture recording on tape is just like sound recording. It merely increases the quantity of information stored. However, the increase over sound requirements of 200 to 1 poses a difficult design problem. The Ampex company introduced the first solution in 1956, when it began marketing production models of video-tape recorders. It will be recalled from Section 4.5 that the chief variable affecting the information capacity of a magnetic-tape recording system is the speed at which the tape passes over the recording and playback heads. A simple increase over the tape speed used in sound recording would have meant impracticable speeds. Ampex's ingenious solution was mounting four magnetic recording heads on a disc which rotates at high speed transversely across 2-inch tape at the same time as the tape moves laterally at 15 ips (Figure 4.5). The horizontal and lateral scanning movements combined produce an effective tape speed of 1,500 ips. The sound component of the composite television signal is recorded along the edge of the tape. Subsequent development of techniques for electronic editing, copying, slow motion, stop motion, and "instant replay" have made magnetic recording a remarkably versatile adjunct to television—not merely as a storage medium, but also as a creative production resource.

The original "quadruplex" Ampex VTR's cost about $75 thousand each. Since then, production has proliferated among some forty manufacturers, bringing even home video recorders to the market at under a thousand dollars. The less expensive models use 1-inch and ½-inch tape and simpler head-to-tape systems (Figure 4.5).

Magnetic tape has not entirely displaced either discs or film in broadcasting. Ease of operation, immediate playback without processing, editability, reusability, near-perfect quality—all these make magnetic tape the ideal storage medium for many purposes. On the other hand, discs still have the advantage of accessibility—any part of a disc recording can be retrieved without delay, whereas tape requires winding backwards or forwards to locate the start of a wanted item. For this reason, some magnetic systems use the recording medium in a disc format instead of a tape format, for example for "instant replay" of significant moments in live sports-events coverage.

Several novel picture-recording techniques have been developed, among which the most advanced is "Electronic Video Recording" (EVR), planned for 1970 production by CBS in collaboration with British firms. EVR has

Figure 4.4
Magnetic video-recorder scanning systems

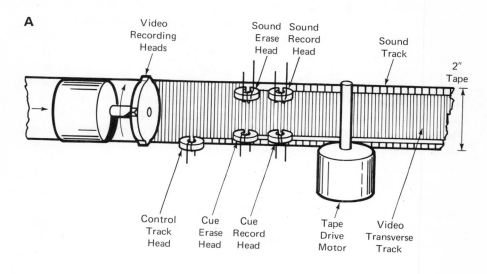

A

Video
Recording
Heads

Sound Sound
Erase Record
Head   Head

Sound
Track

2"
Tape

Control
Track
Head

Cue
Erase
Head

Cue
Record
Head

Tape
Drive
Motor

Video
Transverse
Track

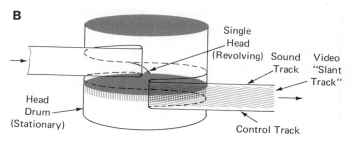

B

Single
Head
(Revolving) Sound
Track

Video
"Slant
Track"

Head
Drum
(Stationary)

Control Track

A. *Transverse quadruplex type.* Four video-recording heads
mounted on the rapidly spinning wheel at the left lay down a track
transversely (across) the 2-inch tape. Sound is recorded longitudinally
on one edge of the tape, auxiliary control signals on the other. This
design is used for broadcast-quality recordings.

B. *Helical type.* The tape (of varying widths) spirals around a large,
stationary drum. Within the drum, the video-recording head spins on
a revolving disc, making contact with the tape as it slips over the
drum surface. As the tape moves laterally and also slightly downward (because of the spiral wrap around the drum), the combined
movements of tape and recording head produce a slanting track, as
shown. Some helical recorders use two heads mounted opposite each
other on the disc; some use different wraparound configurations.

Source: Drawings supplied by Ampex Corporation.

features that make it in some ways a video counterpart of the LP recording in sound, making it available directly to the consumer for playback at will on his own television receiver. A flying-spot scanner, operating in a vacuum, records from any video source (film, magnetic tape, live cameras) on a special superfine-grain master-negative film. Individual frames are very tiny, even compared with 8-mm. film. A 750-foot cartridge of unperforated 7.5-mm. release-print film runs for a half hour. Though manufacture of negative and release prints is expensive, large print orders bring the price of individual prints down within reach of the consumer market. A relatively inexpensive playback adapter, which also uses the flying-spot scanner principle, connects to an ordinary television receiver for displaying the picture (Figure 4.6).

Magnetic tape has many other applications for storing both pictures and nonpicture data. It can be used to record documents—as many as two-hundred thousand pages on a single reel of tape. It plays a vital role in storing digital data for computer systems. Instrumentation tape recording helps importantly in industrial and space design and operations by keeping track of changes in temperature, velocity, stress, pressure, and other variables. Although these are nonbroadcast uses, they have a relevance to broadcasting, as we shall see in the next section.

4.7 / Broadcasting and Emergent Technology

We introduced the discussion of program storage and distribution technology in terms of the needs of broadcasting stations to expand their program resources and their coverage areas. The development of this technology, however, did more: it brought about linkages between broadcasting and other communications systems. During the middle of the twentieth century, communications technology outstripped utilization. New devices and techniques poured forth from research and development laboratories at such a rate that there was not enough time to assimilate them into functionally useful communications systems.

As this assimilation of technology began to take place in the last decades of the century, two facts emerged: (1) steps had to be taken to use the frequency spectrum more rationally, for not only were numerous vitally important nonbroadcast radio services already suffering from inadequate frequency space, the new technology was causing additional demands for allocations; (2) the trend would be toward integration of hitherto separate items of communications hardware and separate communications enterprises into composite systems—in the phrase of a Federal Communications Commissioner, into some kind of "cable-video-tape-library-computer-retrieval-closed-circuit-television combination."[8]

---

[8] Nicholas Johnson, "The Why of Public Broadcasting," *Educational Broadcasting Review,* I (December, 1967), 8.

Figure 4.5

CBS's Electronic Video-Recording system

A

B

A. Inserting EVR reel in playback unit, which feeds picture to conventional television receiver. Controls (on right) provide for stop-frame viewing as well as for fast winding to locate a desired segment of film.

B. The EVR film (here slightly enlarged) has no sprocket perforations; marks down the center between the two picture channels provide synchronizing information.

Source: Columbia Broadcasting System.

Let us see how some of the new technology affects broadcasting. A relatively huge segment of the radio-frequency spectrum is allocated to television. The purpose of such lavish allotment was to assure localized and varied program services throughout the country. But, if this purpose can be served in some other way, cutback in television's spectrum allocation is inevitable. One alternative is further development of CATV to originate local programs. Domestic satellites could serve home receivers directly with national-network programs, while local programming in well-populated areas could be supplied by cable, thereby eliminating the need for local over-the-air television stations.

Other spectrum-conserving strategies look toward raising the ceiling on usability at the upper end of the spectrum. Here, it will be recalled (Section 1.6), atmospheric absorption quickly attentuates radio energy. The *waveguide* solves this problem by creating an artificial, absolutely stable atmosphere in which EHF waves travel efficiently. A waveguide is simply a straight metal pipe filled with nitrogen. A range of frequencies capable of carrying over 200 thousand simultaneous telephone conversations can travel in a 2-inch pipe. It is expected that waveguides, buried underground, will displace existing co-axial-cable and microwave-relay circuits in areas of dense traffic.

Even more astonishing are the potentialities of the laser (an acronym for "amplification by stimulated emission of radiation"), a device for producing an exceedingly powerful but small concentrated beam of light at nearly a single frequency. Laser light can be focussed into a beam only one or two wavelengths in diameter (and light wavelengths are expressed in billionths of a meter). This creates the kind of power that punches holes in diamonds.[9] Unfortunately, laser radiations, like ordinary light, have trouble passing through clouds and fog. In space or in an artificial environment, however, a single laser beam could transmit all the telephone calls of the whole world simultaneously.[10] Lasers have a great potentiality in photography. By a process known as "holography," laser light, without benefit of lenses, can create on film three-dimensional pictures so realistic that the observer can even see *around* objects by moving his head.[11]

Short-range relay systems using the upper reaches of the spectrum have been developed to serve the needs of wired, CATV-like distribution systems. The "quasi-laser link" (not actually a laser) uses a form of pulse modulation at 10,000 mc. and above and is capable of handling twenty to forty television

---

[9] By way of comparison, it has been calculated that if the output of an ordinary 75-w. electric light bulb could be concentrated down to the point where all its energy had to pass through an aperture equal in diameter to one wavelength of ultraviolet light, the power flow at that point would be equivalent to about 300,000,000,000 w.—or more than the combined output of all the power stations in the United States. [Winston E. Kock, *Lasers and Holography: An Introduction to Coherent Optics* (Garden City, N. Y.: Doubleday, 1969), p. 34.]

[10] International Telecommunication Union, *From Semaphore to Satellite* (Geneva: The Union, 1965), p. 330.

[11] See Kock, *op. cit.*

channels over ranges of a few miles. Another system with somewhat wider range, the "amplitude-modulated link," operates at 18,000 mc. A third short-wave relay system, operating at 60,000 mc., covers only a few hundred feet but could be useful in relaying signals from block to block in a cable distribution network.

Such techniques for short-range, wide-band relay systems excite interest because of their relevance to the "wired city"[12] concept and similar ideas for integrating existing technological resources into radically new combinations. The telephone system already gives us a working model of a two-way wired network of homes and switching facilities, permitting any desired interconnections, for either input or output. Since telephone wires carry only a narrow band of frequencies, they could not be used for the more complex kinds of information, such as pictures. But CATV gives us at least a limited working model of a *wide-band* network. Outside the home, meanwhile, we find many examples of specialized applications of communications technology: industry uses remotely located shared-time computers, to which it gains access by wire; students use dial-access stations in learning centers to get at banks of learning material; offices communicate with each other by typewriter over telex circuits; libraries store printed material on microfilm; regular picturephone service (telephone with video pictures of the speakers) has been in use on a few routes for some time; television stations routinely use facsimile pictures of meteorological conditions transmitted from weather satellites. Why not combine such scattered, uncoordinated bits and pieces of communications technology into an overall rational system for getting maximum benefits from all resources for all citizens? This is the challenge of the wired-city concept.

Such a coordinated, rationalized communications system might, for example, give the connected household access to libraries, shopping centers, and banks; the libraries could transmit not only print materials but also still and motion pictures and recorded sound. A dozen sources of television entertainment and information could be available at the push of a button, both on a "free" basis and on a "subscription" basis. Outgoing circuits from the home could carry utilities metering information, shopping orders, monthly bill-payment orders.

These and many more such communications functions could be implemented now, within the limits of existing technology. It remains only to develop the parallel innovations in the economic and social spheres before such an advanced communications system can be realized in practice. We will take up the theme again in Chapter 11, but first we must gain perspective by tracing the evolution of broadcasting before the wired-city concept emerged.

---

[12] This term seems to have originated with an essay by H. J. Barnett and E. A. Greenberg, "A Proposal for Wired City Television" (Santa Monica, Cal.: RAND Corporation, 1967).

PART TWO

THE ORIGIN AND GROWTH OF BROADCASTING

5

PRECONDITIONS FOR MASS COMMUNICATION

5.1 / The Meaning of "Mass"

Though used rather loosely, the term "mass communication" usually implies at least five things: (1) relatively large audiences, (2) relatively undifferentiated audience composition, (3) some form of message reproduction, (4) rapid distribution, and (5) low unit cost per consumer. As a working definition, we might say that mass communication means approximately simultaneous delivery of identical messages by high-speed reproduction and distribution to relatively large and undifferentiated numbers of people.

In former ages, some publications—for example, the Bible or the works of Aristotle—certainly reached very large numbers of people in the course of time, but the elements of approximate simultaneity, low unit cost, and mass audience were lacking. A mass audience is not merely a large audience. It is an extremely heterogeneous audience whose members need have nothing in common beyond receiving identical messages at about the same time. The fact that members of the audience do not have to assemble in one place or otherwise engage in some common social act in order to participate as members makes for heterogeneity.

Before the development of cheap paper, high-speed printing, rapid distribution methods, and mass marketing, a book had great intrinsic value. Books cost too much either to be wasted on inconsequential matters or to come within the economic reach of most people. The same could once be said of newspapers: they dealt with serious matters for serious people. Of course, a potential market has always existed for popular, ephemeral writings. Such cheaply produced ephemera as "broadsides" appeared almost as soon as printing. Critics in all ages have deplored the frivolity of popular taste, but before the era of mass communication, economic and social constraints always kept production of such material at an insignificantly low level.[1]

Because mass-media output must be great and the unit cost of their products low, public communications no longer need to be concerned primarily

---

[1] Leo Lowenthal traces the development of attitudes toward popular art in "An Historical Preface to the Popular Culture Debate," in Norman Jacobs, ed., *Culture for the Millions? Mass Media in Modern Society* (Boston: Beacon Press, 1964), pp. 28–42. Until modern times, he points out, class segregation set popular art apart.

with serious matters. The mass media produce vast quantities of frivolous, trivial, highly ephemeral material. Indeed, the mass media in a sense *demand* a self-liquidating product, like disposable tissue. If people studied and pondered each message, the system would soon become hopelessly clogged. The motion-picture exhibitor tries to get his customer to leave the theatre after seeing the show once, so that he can usher another paying customer into the still-warm seat; the newspaper publisher hopes that yesterday's paper will line today's garbage pail, so that the reader will be ready to buy tomorrow's paper. Nothing could be more fatal to the operation of the mass media than for audiences to pause and savor every message like so many sonnets or old masters.[2]

Conditions which make mass communication possible include not only a highly developed technology for the inexpensive reproduction and distribution of messages, but also an urbanized, relatively literate population with buying power, leisure, and some degree of "consumership" orientation. Developing countries have discovered that merely installing the machinery of mass communication—the presses, film-production units, radio and television transmitters—does not automatically result in effective communication to the masses. Mass communication involves consumption as well as production; consumption, in turn, depends not only on purchasing power, but also on motivation. Where tradition is conservative and outlook parochial, the introduction of mass communication can appear more a threat than a benefit. It disturbs the internal balance of a closed society, introducing alien ideas, stimulating questions about unquestioned assumptions, creating hitherto unfelt wants. For this reason, among others, the potentialities of mass communication for facilitating social and economic development in backward countries have not been realized to the extent once expected.

Elsewhere, the Industrial Revolution brought about changes in commerce, transportation, and living conditions essential to the flourishing of mass communication. The groundwork was laid in the nineteenth century, but the mass media are essentially a twentieth-century phenomenon. The telegraph and telephone, forerunners of radio, developed in the last half of the nineteenth century; so did the mass-circulation daily newspaper, the first of the mass media; the modern motion-picture industry is based on inventions first put to commercial use in the 1890's. Broadcasting did not arrive on the social scene until the third decade of the twentieth century, and its success was almost instantaneous.

By that time, communication had already become big business. The mass-distributed newspaper had established guidelines: techniques for effective advertising, full utilization of telecommunications, syndication of editorial content, large-scale business organization, legal and philosophical precedents. The motion-picture industry had just gone through developmental stages simi-

---

[2] Even radios themselves have become disposable: in 1966 an estimated sixteen million transistor radios were simply thrown away. [*Fortune* Magazine, *Markets of the Seventies* (New York: Viking, 1968), p. 74.]

lar to those on which broadcasting was about to embark. Existing business empires based on wire and wireless communication had direct economic and technological effects on broadcasting. In short, the earlier experience of other media made possible phenomenally rapid evolution of broadcasting—from laboratory experiments to a major social force in a single generation.

5.2 / The Mass-Appeal Newspaper

As the archetypical mass medium, the newspaper furnished the pattern: a high degree of syndicated basic content material; mechanized production and distribution; high production costs offset by increased market penetration through consolidated competing enterprises; a regional or national outlook instead of a localized, parochial outlook. Magazine publishing followed parallel lines of development. The trend has been away from the colorful, highly individualistic entrepreneur like William Randolph Hearst toward corporate ownership, with economic interests in diverse fields and managers rather than owners making the operational decisions.

Newspaper publishing in the United States goes back to the early eighteenth century, but before the Industrial Revolution, papers remained small, low-investment enterprises. Though numerous, each depended on a small subscription list (street and newsstand sales were unknown), and each addressed a limited readership representing a political or other special interest. The shift from an agrarian to an industrial economy created a new, urbanized readership potentiality. In response, a novel concept began to emerge in the 1830's —the "penny press," aimed at the low-income, urbanized masses.

In the course of the next fifty years, this concept evolved into a whole new approach to newspaper publishing. Instead of confining themselves to serious news of interest to the mercantile and political elite, papers sought to interest —and to serve—ordinary people, the "masses." Papers increased local news coverage, developed the human-interest story, exploited sensationalism. Journalistic style changed from stodgy, would-be literary longwindedness to a more colloquial and readable standard. Content became more informative and entertaining, less argumentative and didactic. Newspapers aimed at serving not only the common man, but also his common wife and common children.

Along with these changing concepts of content and form came the means for faster, more economical quantity production—cheap paper, typesetting machines, photographic engraving processes, high-speed presses. The third strand in this process, the development of new telecommunications media, eventually made possible instantaneous coverage of news on a worldwide scale. The first of these new media was the telegraph.

5.3 / Wire Communication

Telegraphy, the first communication device to utilize electrical energy, is a point-to-point system, adapted to the needs of private communication. The theoretical and experimental background of the use of electrical energy for communication can be traced back to the Greeks, but the first practical applications came in the 1830's. The persistence of Samuel F. B. Morse led to the first successful telegraph line in the United States, installed at government expense between Washington and Baltimore in 1844.

Morse's idea was so simple it may seem surprising that it took him more than a dozen years to develop and install that first short link. We must bear in mind, however, that every aspect of the installation required innovation. Since electrical theory itself was in a primitive state at the time, most decisions had to be made on the basis of trial and error; many wrong guesses were made before each workable expedient evolved. The awe with which his contemporaries regarded his achievement is reflected in the first official message Morse sent: "What hath God wrought!"[3]

The first regular messages sent over Morse's Washington-Balimore telegraph link were news reports of political events. It is more than a coincidence that about eighty years later the first broadcast by the first regularly licensed commercial radio broadcasting station also consisted of news reports of a political event. Yet Morse and his contemporaries had no inkling in 1844 that the first breach in the wall of international isolation was being made. In less than a century the wall was to crumble completely.

The telegraph is based on the simple concept that wires conduct electrical energy. How to generate electricity in small amounts was already known. Morse's basic problem was to make the energy convey information—to modulate it. The method of modulation he used was merely turning the current on and off. In other words, the telegraph is fundamentally capable of sending two signals: "current on" and "current off." Varying the time factor (how *long* the current remains either on or off) gives the simple on-off form of modulation unlimited potentialities for encoding information. The problem of telegraphic modulation resolves itself into inventing a code based on signals of varying length in the "current on" and "current off" modes, together with devising a means of receiving these signals.

An early solution to reception, used by nineteenth-century British railways, relied on visible deflections of a sensitive pointer or needle in response to the electric impulses. Morse substituted a pen for the pointer. The pen inscribed its deflections on a moving roll of paper, thus making a permanent record of the telegraphic signals, a vital improvement over the British system. To this day, telegraphy is known as *record* communication.

Morse devised a sending code, ever since known as the Morse code, using combinations of long and short pulses of electrical energy, known as "dots" and "dashes." Using the typesetter's box to discover which letters occur most frequently in English, he found the letter "e" needed the biggest compartment; he thus assigned to it the simplest code symbol—a single dot. Less

---

[3] President John F. Kennedy echoed this phrase in 1962, when he spoke to Lagos, Nigeria, on the first transatlantic telephone call relayed by satellite.

frequently used letters use more complex groups of dots and dashes. For example, "q" is "dash-dash-dot-dash." Codes have the disadvantage of requiring intermediaries between the sender and the receiver of a message—clerks trained in the special skill of encoding and decoding. Moreover, manual operators attain a maximum speed of only about sixty words per minute.

If it was difficult to devise methods of installing wire connections overland, even after the feasibility of the system had been demonstrated, a much more difficult problem was to insulate the conductors and incorporate them into a cable tough and flexible enough to lay on the bottom of the sea. The name of Cyrus W. Field is linked with the Atlantic cable. After almost unbelievable difficulties, disappointments, and expense, transatlantic cable communication was finally established on a regular basis in 1868.[4] From then on it was only a matter of time before all the major commercial centers of the world were linked by a network of land and undersea wires.

Once the practical problems of communicating by simple electrical impulses over wire circuits were solved, the next step was to eliminate the awkward necessity of encoding and decoding messages. Telegraphic signals require no more than the simple "on-off" switching device, but sound signals require a much more complex "switch," the microphone. Sound also requires wire with about forty times the minimum information capacity of telegraph conductors. Elisha Gray and Alexander Graham Bell solved the problem in the United States simultaneously. Bell applied for preliminary patents on the telephone in 1876, only a few hours before Gray, and opened a public telephone service in Boston in 1877. Again prophetically, the first public telephone call was a news story relayed to the *Boston Globe.*

5.4 / News Syndication

Even before the days of the telegraph, newspapers had begun to adopt the practice of *syndication,* an essential feature of all mass-media enterprises. In the 1840's, for example, a group of New York newspapers formed the Harbor News Association to share the cost of operating fast boats to meet incoming ships off shore, pick up the latest news from abroad, and rush it to the editors of papers in the Association. This precedent made it logical for papers to cooperate in sharing the cost of telegraph services when they became available. In the early days of telegraphy, news interests even organized and operated their own telegraph companies. The word "telegraph" in the names of newspapers still survives as a witness of the role the new telecommunications medium played.

Out of these early cooperative newspaper efforts grew the idea of independent specialized news gathering and distributing organizations designed

---

[4] A cable laid in 1858 failed after a few months of intermittent operation. One of the factors in the final triumph over odds was a fantastic iron vessel, the *Great Eastern,* an enormous white elephant whose only practical use turned out to be in laying cable. See James Dugan, *The Great Iron Ship* (New York: Harper & Bros., 1953).

to capitalize on the unique capabilities of the telegraph. By the third quarter of the nineteenth century, an international cartel of such news agencies, or syndicates, had been formed. Agence Havas (France), Reuters News Agency (Britain), and Wolff's Telegraphic Bureau (Germany) divided the world into exclusive territories. This arrangement lasted until 1934. Only then were the American press agencies able to expand into worldwide services. Of these there are now two—the Associated Press, an agency cooperatively owned by the media, and United Press International.

News agencies are still referred to as "wire services," though they have long used radio as well as wire in their communications networks. With bureaus in all major capitals and news centers of the world and with local "stringers" filling in as part-time reporters in secondary locations, the modern news agency has remarkably long reach and flexibility. Its services now include not only straight news, but news written especially for broadcasting, many kinds of specialized features, as well as news photos, television slides and newsfilm, and voiced material for radio.

5.5 / The Role of Patents

Another precondition for the emergence of modern mass communication was the development of manufacturing and service industries to capitalize on the promise of the new communications devices. When Morse introduced telegraphy in the United States, its commercial possibilities were hardly perceived. His own idea was that it would be useful mainly for government communications, but the legislators themselves regarded it more as a scientific curiosity than as a revolutionary means of speeding up the world's business. However, by the time the telephone was invented, the commercial importance of the telegraph had been established. Wire communication had become big business, with international ramifications. In this arena, patents and their exploitation played a crucial position.

Article I, Section 8, of the United States Constitution provides that "Congress shall have the power . . . to promote the progress of science and useful arts, by securing for limited times to authors and inventors the exclusive right to their respective writings and discoveries." This provision lays the Constitutional foundation for laws of copyrights and patents. Copyrights are the source of a major economic burden to the broadcasting industry, and patents have been the pivotal points in the strategy of industrial control.

A patent gives an inventor an exclusive property right in his invention for a period of seventeen years. During that time he has a legal monopoly. He can manufacture and sell the product himself, or he can sell or lease the patent rights to others. The early Americans thought in terms of economic incentives to native genius at a time when the country depended wholly on Europe for scientific knowledge. In creating patent rights, they could hardly have foreseen that after the Industrial Revolution patents would become the cornerstones of great industrial monopolies from which the individual inventor often profitted little if at all.

One man rarely combines the two sets of qualities which, respectively, make for inventive genius and for business genius. An invention is almost never a marketable product at its birth. Time, money, and business ingenuity must be liberally expended to develop the product, set up manufacturing facilities, create a market, arrange for distribution, and defend the patent in the courts. The conversion of the raw invention into a marketable product has been called the work of the *innovator,* as distinguished from the work of the inventor:

... the making of the invention and the carrying out of the corresponding innovation are, economically and sociologically, two entirely different things. They may, and often have been, performed by the same person; but this is merely a chance coincidence which does not affect the validity of the distinction. Personal aptitudes —primarily intellectual in the case of the inventor, primarily volitional in the case of the businessman who turns the invention into an innovation—and the methods by which the one and the other work, belong to different spheres.[5]

Business history is strewn with the wrecks of companies launched by optimistic inventors. In most cases, they have ended either by losing control of their own companies and their own patents or by selling their rights for a flat fee. Lee de Forest, probably the most important American inventor in the radio field, is the classic example (Section 6.3).

Radio grew out of a scientific background inaccessible to the ordinary artisan. Edison was primarily an inventor, for instance, but he kept in close touch with scientific developments. All of radio's inventors similarly depended on science. Inventions in the radio field tend to be not only complicated but also difficult to establish as unique, for any invention which depends on another patented device for operation is automatically blocked by the prior patent. As a result, the whole history of radio has been marked by constant patent litigation, one of the most complicated of legal proceedings. It costs over $100 thousand to take a patent suit through the Supreme Court. Edison himself is said to have spent more on litigation than he made in royalties.[6] In the highly developed technological fields it often takes millions of dollars and years of research to bring a product to the point at which it is marketable. The diesel engine took over thirty years to develop; nylon took thirteen years and an investment by one company of $27 million. Before television was ready for

---

[5] Joseph A. Schumpeter, *Business Cycles* (New York: McGraw-Hill, 1939), I, 85–86. This concept has been applied to radio by W. Rupert Maclaurin in his *Invention and Innovation in the Radio Industry* (New York: Macmillan, 1949), who writes (p. 250): "No case has come to my attention in the history of the [radio] industry in which high inventive talent and the capacity for successful innovation were combined in one man."

[6] Frank C. Waldrop and Joseph Borkin, *Television: A Struggle for Power* (New York: William Morrow, 1938), p. 206. See their chapter, "Patents and Power," for a somewhat alarmist view of patent monopolies.

commercial exploitation, $30 million had been spent in developmental work.[7] Television was not "invented." Scores of individuals can be singled out as having made important contributions. Television as a commercial medium is essentially the result of teamwork, much of it in highly organized corporate research facilities.

5.6 / The Rise of AT&T

Patenting became inextricably involved with big-business strategy in the latter half of the nineteenth century. Alexander Graham Bell's two basic patents on the telephone, taken out in 1876 and 1877, became the seeds of the world's greatest business enterprise, the American Telephone and Telegraph Company.[8] An account of the maneuvers leading to this development may be of interest, since similar techniques of exploitation and control later profoundly affected the development of broadcasting.

The Civil War had given great impetus to the commercial development of the telegraph, in contrast to the apathy which greeted its birth. By the time the telephone appeared on the scene, Western Union already dominated the telegraph field. Organized in 1851, Western Union was at this time controlled by members of the Vanderbilt family. So secure did they feel that in 1877 they turned down an offer from Bell by which they could have acquired his patents for a mere $100 thousand. Ironically, a quarter of a century later the Bell company was almost equally blind to the implications of radio, but in this instance events moved slowly enough for the company to get a foothold in the new medium before being permanently frozen out.

Western Union was not so fortunate. Events moved rapidly, because the supremacy of the Vanderbilts was being energetically challenged by another nineteenth-century financial giant, Jay Gould. The gravity of the Vanderbilts' blunder in turning down Bell's patents immediately became obvious, and the very next year they bought up the telephone patents of Elisha Gray and Edison. This could have had serious consequences for the Bell company, since the rival patents were superior. But the battle between the financial titans saved the struggling Bell company from early extinction. In 1879, as part of the grand strategy, the Vanderbilts sold Western Union's telephone patents and properties to the Bell company. Western Union and Bell agreed not to compete in each other's fields, thus establishing a precedent for many subsequent empire-dividing agreements in the communications industry. Jay Gould proved too much for the Vanderbilts, however. By 1882 he had acquired control of Western Union and was master of the field. In the end the

---

[7] Frank Joseph Kottke, *Electrical Technology and the Public Interest* (Washington: American Council on Public Affairs, 1944), p. 158.

[8] The first Bell patent, No. 174,465, issued March 7, 1876, may well be the most profitable single patent ever recorded. Litigation concerning it led to *The Telephone Cases,* 126 U. S. (1888), the only subject ever to occupy an entire volume of the Supreme Court reports.

Bell company, once a mere pawn in the struggle for telegraphic supremacy, actually bought the controlling interest in the once-invincible Western Union.[9]

Bell organized his original firm, the American Bell Telephone Company, in Massachusetts in 1877, the year in which he secured the second of his two basic patents. The inventor and his friends could not raise enough capital to develop the company, and the control over the patents soon passed to others. Bell's name has been associated with the company ever since, but it ceased to be his company almost as soon as it was founded. The company went through a number of changes in organization and name as it expanded and brought in new investors, but it has had a continuous corporate history down to the present day. It now consists of a parent holding company and over a score of subsidiary companies which constitute the "Bell System" and provide most of the local and all of the long-distance telephone service in the United States. The parent company is the American Telephone and Telegraph Company (AT&T), often referred to simply as the Telephone Company or the American Company. The subsidiaries include Western Electric (a manufacturing company) and regional Bell System companies stretching from coast to coast.

During its first seventeen years, while its patent monopoly lasted, the Telephone Company's strategy centered on keeping its patent position impregnable and vigorously suppressing infringements. During this period, the Bell Company brought six hundred suits against competing firms for patent infringements. Rather than spread to ungainly proportions by seeking to supply service throughout the country, it adopted a policy of franchising independent regional operators to supply telephone service. The franchised companies received the exclusive and permanent right to use the Bell patents and in turn gave the Bell company substantial stock holdings. By the time the patent monopoly period came to an end, the Bell Company had seen to it that it held controlling interests in these franchised companies. Expiration of the patents in 1893–1894 brought an upsurge of competition, but in the long run the Bell company held a trump card: the long lines for connecting one area with another. Supremacy in this field was assured by acquiring patent rights to the audion (Section 6.4), which made coast-to-coast long-distance service possible.

Even after the original Bell patents expired, the company retained a policy of not selling telephone equipment outright. In 1881, it had purchased Western Electric as its manufacturing subsidiary, thus making it possible to keep the whole process of manufacture, installation, and service within the Bell family. Nevertheless, the company felt the effect of competition after the expiration of the patents and had to expand its service and cut rates to meet the threat. At the turn of the century, independent companies operated nearly as many telephones as the Bell System. Once again new capital was needed,

---

[9] For details of the struggle for control, see N. R. Danielian, *A.T.&T.: The Story of Industrial Conquest* (New York: Vanguard, 1939).

and once again new money brought new control. The Morgan banking interests now came to dominate the Telephone Company. During this period (1909), the company acquired Western Union in a maneuver to combat Postal Telegraph, then a vigorous competitor in the telegraph field. Under pressure from the Department of Justice, the Telephone Company sold its Western Union stock in 1913. But in the meantime Postal Telegraph had been seriously weakened, and it finally was absorbed by Western Union in 1934. In its century-long history, Western Union had absorbed over five hundred competitors. This last merger left it with a government-regulated monopoly on domestic telegraphic services (with some reservations in favor of AT&T). The government encouraged this consolidation in an effort to bolster the telegraphic service, which has been declining ever since World War I.[10]

Patents continued to play a major role in the strategy of the AT&T business empire. As we shall see, patents enabled the Telephone Company to dominate the infant broadcasting industry, and although the Company ultimately withdrew from operating broadcast stations, it still participates in the broadcast industry through its monopoly of the long-distance facilities for network interconnection, pending development of domestic satellite relay systems.

Later, still another innovation, communication satellites, challenged AT&T, since they offer alternatives to the conventional terrestrial systems. When Congress authorized formation of the Communications Satellite Corporation (Comsat) as a chartered private company to provide commercial relay services via satellite, AT&T became the largest stockholder, with 29 per cent of the shares. RCA and over 150 other companies in the common-carrier field shared the rest of the 50 per cent of the stock allotted to the industry. The general public purchased the other 50 per cent on the open market.

5.7 / GE and Westinghouse

Two other large companies which had built industrial empires on nineteenth-century patents also played key roles in the development of radio: General Electric and Westinghouse. The foundation of the General Electric Company goes back to Edison's patent on the incandescent electric light. The present company was born of a merger between the Edison Electric Light Company and another manufacturing concern in 1892. The Westinghouse Manufacturing Company was founded by George Westinghouse, best known for the Westinghouse Air Brake and other improvements in railroad equipment. GE and Westinghouse became embroiled in the usual patent litigation and in rivalry over the exploitation of competing electric power systems. Westinghouse installed the first alternating-current (AC) power system in 1886 and for ten years fought to establish it as the standard, instead of the earlier direct-current

---

[10] For a discussion of the problem of the decline in "record" communications, see President's Communications Policy Board, *Telecommunications: A Program for Progress* (Washington: Government Printing Office, 1951).

(DC) system advocated by GE. The contest ended in 1896, when the two companies pooled their patents for their mutual benefit and agreed to standardize on the alternating-current system we know today.

By the turn of the century, with electric power increasing in importance and with the demand for equipment high, both GE and Westinghouse had grown into very powerful concerns. With AT&T (including Western Electric), they were an invincible triumvirate in the field of communications and electrical manufacturing when radio came upon the scene. The existence of these powerful companies when the new medium arrived contrasts significantly with the situation at the time the first of the electrical communication systems, the telegraph, began. Then there were no antecedent and powerful vested interests.

These, then, can be considered some of the "preconditions" for the emergence of mass communication—the social, economic, industrial, and technological environment which made this new social phenomenon possible. The telegraph, first of the electrical telecommunications devices, came into a world unprepared to understand its implications and its potentialities. A half century later, wireless came into a very different world, one ready to put it to immediate work.

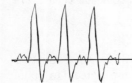

6

WIRELESS

The most eminent men of the time were conscious of the problem, were interested in it, had sought for years the exactly right arrangement, always approaching more nearly but never quite reaching the stage of practical success. The invention was, so to speak, hovering in the general climate of science, momentarily awaiting birth. But just the right releasing touch had not been found. Marconi added it. JUSTICE WILEY RUTLEDGE

Marconi's application in 1896 for a British patent started the wireless era.[1] Though other inventors may have antedated Marconi, their isolated experiments and demonstrations gained only passing notoriety as curiosities.[2] Marconi's invention was the basis for immediate application of wireless to solving practical communications problems, moving directly from the stage of invention to the stage of innovation:

There can be no doubt that . . . Marconi invented a system of highly successful wireless telegraphy, and that he personally inspired and supervised its application until it spanned the world. This must be considered as ample justification for his award, in the year 1909, of the Nobel Prize for Physics.[3]

If Marconi fathered wireless in the practical and industrial sense, James Clerk-Maxwell fathered it in the theoretical and scientific sense. Clerk-Maxwell, the greatest theoretical physicist of the nineteenth century, published *A*

---

[1] The terms *wireless* and *radio* are used interchangeably. *Radio* is said to have come into use in the United States Navy about 1912, since at that time the concept "wireless" embraced certain nonradio methods of transmission. Sound broadcasting is an application of radio (or wireless) telephony. For a discussion of the origin of the term "radio," see Gleason L. Archer, *History of Radio to 1926* (New York: The American Historical Company, 1938), p. 88.

[2] For example, one Dr. Mahlon Loomis of Virginia has been put forward as a successful wireless inventor as early as 1866. Other claimants are mentioned in Erik Barnouw, *A Tower in Babel: A History of Broadcasting in the United States to 1933* (New York: Oxford University Press, 1966), p. 18.

[3] International Telecommunication Union, *From Semaphore to Satellite* (Geneva: The Union, 1965), p. 125. Marconi shared the Nobel award with Carl F. Braun, who developed the cathode-ray tube.

Treatise on Electricity and Magnetism in 1873, in which he put forward the theory of electromagnetic energy, supported by mathematical proofs and based on observation of visible light. Experimental proofs that radio waves existed and had the same properties as light waves came in the 1880's, as a result of research by Heinrich Hertz. He published a paper in 1888, "Electro-magnetic Waves and their Reflection," in which he reported laboratory demonstrations which fully confirmed Clerk-Maxwell's concepts.

Clerk-Maxwell used theory to generate predictions about the way hypothetical radio waves should behave, basing his predictions on the known behavior of light. Hertz devised experiments which bore out Clerk-Maxwell's predictions. To do this, he had, in effect, to invent radio. He had to generate radio energy, transmit it, detect it, and measure it. In recognition of the importance of his contribution, other scientists called radio waves "Hertzian waves," and "Hertz" (abbreviated "hz" or "Hz") has been adopted internationally as a short way of expressing the frequency unit "cycle per second."

Hertz wanted to verify a scientific theory, not invent a method of communication. He never followed up the practical implications of his research. Indeed, when asked if his Hertzian waves might not be used for communication, he produced theoretical reasons to show they could not.[4]

6.1 / Marconi as Innovator

It remained for Guglielmo Marconi—more an inventor than a scientist—to defy theory with practical application. Stimulated by Hertz's paper, Marconi as a young man of twenty-one experimented with similar apparatus, first indoors and then on the grounds of his father's estate in Italy. Fortunately, Marconi had the leisure for experimentation and the money for equipment. Equally important, he had social entrée to high official and business circles.

As soon as Marconi convinced himself that wireless was more than a laboratory toy, he hurried to England, applied for a patent in 1896, and in the next year formed a company there to exploit his invention. His objective was nothing less than to create a world monopoly in wireless communication. Toward this end, he founded a second company, Marconi International Marine Communications, in 1900.

Once Marconi had made the giant step from the laboratory to practical application, he progressed rapidly. By 1899, he had sent messages across the English channel; in 1901, he succeeded in sending a signal across the Atlantic; the next year, actual transatlantic intelligence was exchanged (Figure 6.1).

Meanwhile, his example stimulated many others already working in the field to develop rival systems, and the rush to the patent offices began. The key to ultimate success was the ability to secure a set of patents covering a complete wireless communication system, so that a company could be set up

---

[4] W. Rupert Maclaurin, *Invention and Innovation in the Radio Industry* (New York: Macmillan, 1949), pp. 15–16.

Figure 6.1
Guglielmo Marconi (1874–1937)

Marconi sits in the Newfoundland station where he received the first transatlantic radio signal in 1901.

Source: Radio Corporation of America.

without having to pay license fees to a rival. With each passing year, as the technology of wireless improved and grew more complicated, this objective became more difficult to attain. Before long, literally thousands of patents were involved, making the patent structure so complex that no one was safe from infringement suits. The growing complications of the patent situation made it inevitable that control of the new industry should gravitate toward the great corporations which had the resources to build up patent strength, withstand the costly, long drawn-out court battles, and undertake the developmental work patents always need. Eventually, as we shall see, a stalemate resulted: the largest companies bought up patent rights as fast as they could, but none could carve out a self-contained system which would not at some points conflict with rival systems.

Of all the pioneer inventors engaged in the struggle for self-sufficiency, Marconi alone succeeded. The others succumbed to patent suits, business setbacks, and bankruptcies. The promise of eventual returns was great, but immediate returns were small. American Marconi, the United States branch founded by British Marconi in 1889, lost money consistently for six years, and a whole decade passed before it realized substantial profits. The turning point came with the acquisition in 1913 of the assets of the rival de Forest company, United Wireless, which had gone bankrupt after the Marconi company won a patent-infringement suit against de Forest. This gave American Marconi four hundred ship stations, seventeen land stations, and a virtual monopoly on commercial wireless in America.

The Marconi company aggressively pursued its objective of a world monopoly, using every stratagem it could devise to freeze out competition. Not infrequently, this policy created bad public relations. Prince Henry of Prussia, on his way home from a visit to the United States in 1902, tried to send a wireless thank-you note to President Theodore Roosevelt, but British Marconi refused to accept a message from a German ship. The international convention on wireless held in Berlin in 1903 failed because of the uncooperative attitude of the Marconi company.[5] The United States Navy at first adopted German equipment because of the restrictive terms the British company insisted on. The Navy continued its opposition to the Marconi company through World War I, as we shall see, and finally helped close the American market to Marconi.

6.2 / Early Wireless Services

During the first two decades of wireless, its commercial value consisted primarily in supplying communication *services*. Some money could be made selling equipment to navies and to amateurs, but these were limited markets. Nothing existed like the tremendous mass market for receivers later created by broadcasting. The promise of riches at first lay mainly in the potentialities of worldwide communication networks in competition with the telegraph cables and the telephone wires.

The first service to develop, the maritime mobile service, involved shipborne stations and coastal land stations. Here wireless was unique. The relative efficiency of over-water propagation made this service feasible even with the crude equipment available in the early days of the art.

Long-distance transoceanic communication, however, had more commercial promise, in spite of its great enemy, static. For two decades the major goal of inventors was to devise a high-power generator capable of overriding the heavy static interference characteristic of the low frequencies. Marconi's demonstration in 1901 of transatlantic reception proved that radio waves could travel great distances, but he was a long way from a reliable transatlantic service able to compete effectively with the cable. In 1908, the Marconi company offered a transatlantic service from Nova Scotia to Ireland, but the

---

[5] Joint Technical Advisory Committee, Institute of Radio Engineers-Radio Television Manufacturers Association, *Radio Spectrum Conservation* (New York: McGraw-Hill, 1952), p. 6.

outbreak of World War I in 1914 postponed further commercial development of long-distance radiotelegraphy.

A third service, overland wireless, competed with the telegraph and the telephone, but was not extensively developed before 1920. In fact, the United States Navy still considered it of no consequence in planning post-World War I development of radio communication.[6]

A fourth service, the amateur service, developed during the first two decades of wireless. Amateurs ("hams") had special importance during these pioneer days. They developed techniques for exploiting the high frequencies to which they were relegated so that they would not interfere with maritime traffic. Their ranks included leading engineers and inventors who could be called amateur only because they did not operate their stations for profit:

. . . the amateur, in many cases, had more money than some of the commercial companies. Moreover, both classes of wireless workers used apparatus almost equally crude. It is rather an unflattering commentary on the state of the art as it existed around 1903–1910, that the commercial concerns had to give jobs to the amateurs with the biggest sets around New York, in order to get a chance to receive their own messages.[7]

No explicit provision had been made for the amateurs as a recognized service in the Radio Act of 1912, although at that time there were 405 ship stations, 123 land stations, and 1,224 amateur stations. All subsequent legislation took cognizance of their rights, however, and the amateur class has continued as one of the largest classes of stations to this day (Table 1.2). Spokesmen for the amateurs appeared at all the important Congressional hearings on proposed new radio legislation in the post-World War I years,[8] and also at the four Radio Conferences held in Washington in 1922–1925.

Of all the early radio services, the maritime service had the most dramatic impact because of its unique value in times of emergency. As early as 1898, wireless had been used in a maritime disaster. In 1909, the *S. S. Republic* foundered off New York, and all passengers were saved by wireless-alerted rescue ships. A number of other maritime emergencies in these early years dramatized the capabilities of wireless communication.[9] The culminating event

---

[6] House Committee on Merchant Marine and Fisheries, *Government Control of Radio Communication,* Hearings on H. R. 13159, 64th Cong. (Washington: Government Printing Office, 1919).

[7] Harold P. Westman, ed., *Radio Pioneers, 1945* (New York: Institute of Radio Engineers, 1945), p. 30.

[8] See the eloquent testimony of Hiram Percy Maxim, representing the amateurs' American Radio Relay League, in Senate Committee on Interstate Commerce, *Commission on Communications,* Hearings on S. 6, 71st Cong., 2d Sess. (Washington: Government Printing Office, 1930), pp. 2061–2074.

[9] A list appears in House Committee on Merchant Marine and Fisheries, *Radio Communication,* Hearings on H. R. 19350, 64th Cong. (Washington: Government Printing Office, 1917), pp. 417–430. Until 1909, instances were sporadic. In 1909, however, twenty-one cases are listed, and in each succeeding year the list grew longer.

came in 1912, when the "unsinkable" luxury liner *Titanic* struck an iceberg on her maiden voyage to the United States. The ship sank, with loss of some fifteen hundred lives. Her passenger list, studded with famous names in the arts, the sciences, the financial world, and diplomacy, made the *Titanic* disaster the most dramatic tragedy of its kind in history. And the fact that for days radio telegraphy maintained the world's only thread of contact with the survivors brought the new medium to public attention as nothing else had done. Subsequently, when inquiries revealed that a more rational use of wireless resources could have prevented the accident or at least materially decreased the loss of life, the *Titanic* disaster had an important influence on the adoption of laws governing the use of wireless in maritime commerce.[10]

Naturally, the naval powers of the world took an early interest in military applications of wireless. Pigeons had hitherto provided the only means of communication with ships beyond the range of sight. Both the British and American navies began experimenting with ship installations as early as 1899, and Germany followed the next year. The first naval use of radio in actual war occurred in the Russo-Japanese War in 1904–1905. The United States Navy became an important customer for the wireless equipment of American inventors.

Experimentally, both Hertz and Marconi had used relatively high frequencies; but practical applications proved successful initially only at low frequencies. During the pre-World War I period, the available equipment permitted efficient use of only a small range of these frequencies. Moreover, the fact that the first commercial service involved shipborne stations placed a practical limit on the frequencies that could be used. It will be recalled that the optimum length of the transmitting antenna depends on the length of the waves it is designed to radiate. The length of ocean-going vessels controlled the maximum length of antennas and hence determined the wavelengths suitable for the maritime mobile service. Since 500-kc. waves represent a convenient average length for ships' antennas, that frequency was selected as the international distress frequency, and it is still so designated. Thus, the earliest allocation of spectrum space came about more by chance than by design. Subsequently, when broadcasting began, the only frequencies available were those above the range already used by the maritime service. Ideally, broadcasting could have used the 300–550-kc. band,[11] but the 500-kc. distress frequency had to be protected from interference.

It may be necessary at this point to remind ourselves that the four services we have been discussing in this chapter—maritime mobile, transoceanic, overland, and amateur—were radiotelegraphic services. Nowadays, most people

---

[10] See Geoffrey Marcus, *The Maiden Voyage* (New York: Viking, 1969). At the time, the Marconi company rather than the shipping lines employed shipboard radio operators. The *Titanic* chief operator died at his post, but we know his story because the assistant operator survived.

[11] Joint Technical Advisory Committee, *op. cit.*, p. 10.

think of "radio" as intelligible sound, but we must remember that radio began, like the telegraph, as language encoded as dots and dashes of energy. However, experiments in applying the principle of the telephone to wireless began as early as 1900. But before World War I, the methods available for generating carrier waves did not lend themselves to the complex modulation required for reproducing sound. Very crude apparatus can generate readable dot-dash code signals; the raw pulses of energy needed for code can survive a great deal of distortion and interference. But wireless telephony, as a commercially usable medium, had to await the development of the audion.

6.3 / Invention of the Audion

Marconi's gift to the world was a very imperfect instrument. To communicate across space with electromagnetic energy was in itself an achievement of great magnitude, of course, but severe practical limitations remained. The audion and its numerous analogues, shown in Figure 6.2, eventually broke all the major barriers to fuller exploitation of Marconi's invention. The audion unlocked the realm of electronics. With it, man can command "electricity itself, not just its manifestations."[12] Hence, its importance extends far beyond its role in radio communication. It made possible all the thousands of devices which depend on electron manipulation—from guided missiles to automatic garage doors, from computers to machines which automatically reject faulty units coming off a production line. As for radio, the vacuum tube performed each of the basic operations: generating, modulating, amplifying, and detecting radio energy. The television pickup and kinescope tubes are, of course, examples of specialized applications. By opening the field of electronics, vacuum tubes made possible a new industrial revolution. They freed technology from dependence on mechanical moving parts, making possible operations of a complexity, delicacy, and precision undreamed of before.

The transistor, announced by Bell Laboratories in 1948, represented another decisive step forward in the electronic age. Whereas the audion deals with electrons in a vacuum, the transistor deals with electrons in a solid. It does most of the things vacuum tubes do but is much smaller, takes much less power, creates less heat, has longer life, and is more rugged. The transistor made possible the miniaturization of electronic equipment so essential in computer and space technology. It had a profound effect on radio broadcasting because it made the receiver truly portable. A decade later, still another development, integrated circuits, allowed designers to capitalize fully on the transistor's unique advantages. An integrated circuit packs dozens, even scores, of subminiature electronic components into a crystalline chip no larger than the head of a pin.

---

[12] Lee de Forest, *Father of Radio* (Chicago: Wilcox & Follett, 1950), p. 2. *Audion* is a word invented by one of de Forest's associates. In modern parlance, it is the electronic (or vacuum, or thermionic) tube.

The paternity of the audion, like that of radio itself, is complex, but history recognizes the claim of Lee de Forest, much as it recognizes the radio patent claim of Guglielmo Marconi. In 1883, while studying the problem of the tendency of the early electric lamps to blacken with use, Edison had discovered that current could be transferred through the space between the glowing hot filament and a metal plate sealed inside the lamp. He patented a device for measuring this current, and that for the moment ended the matter.[13] Two decades later, Ambrose Fleming, a member of Marconi's research staff, studied the "Edison effect" and patented a radio detector based on it in 1904. The Fleming detector took advantage of the discovery that a two-element tube (diode) can convert energy at radio frequencies into electrical currents. But the device was not a practical success, and when the more reliable crystal detector became available in 1906, the Fleming valve went out of use.

De Forest approached the work on thermionic tubes by another route. He had received a Ph.D. from Yale in 1899, and he worked first as an engineer with Western Electric. However, he found routine engineering research dull, and he soon began devoting full time to his own inventive bent. In 1903, he began experimenting with a radio detector, using an open gas flame. Since a flame has inherent practical disadvantages, he turned to the analogous idea of gas heated within an enclosed space by a glowing filament. He had such a device fabricated by a commercial electric-lamp maker in 1905.

The next and crucially important step was the addition of a third element in the tube, making it a triode, the first tube to be called an "audion." The new element was a grid interposed between the filament and the plate. The heated filament throws off clouds of electrons which, being negatively charged, are attracted to the positively charged plate. But in order to get to the plate, the electrons have to pass through the grid. A small current applied to the grid can control with great precision the flow of electrons from filament to plate. Very weak currents can thus be used to modulate very powerful currents. De Forest used the triode first in 1906 and filed a patent in January, 1907.

6.4 / Dawn of the Electronic Age

De Forest had started with the notion that the heated gas within the tube was the important feature of the device. Had he realized, as subsequently became clear, that the gas trapped in the tube is a hindrance rather than a help, the ensuing confusion about patents might have been less involved.[14] Electron tubes did not become really efficient until they contained a near-perfect vacuum. This involved more than merely exhausting the air trapped in the tube,

---

[13] Curiously, this minor patent of Edison's is considered to be the only original scientific discovery of that prolific inventor. See Lawrence Lessing, *Man of High Fidelity: Edwin Howard Armstrong* (New York: J. B. Lippincott, 1956), p. 64.

[14] The theory of thermionic emission is a branch of science distinct from the theory of electromagnetic radiation.

Figure 6.2
Family tree of the audion

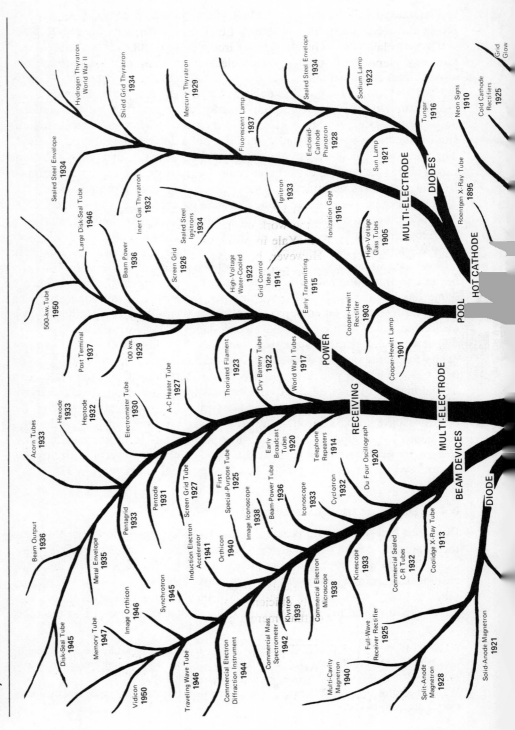

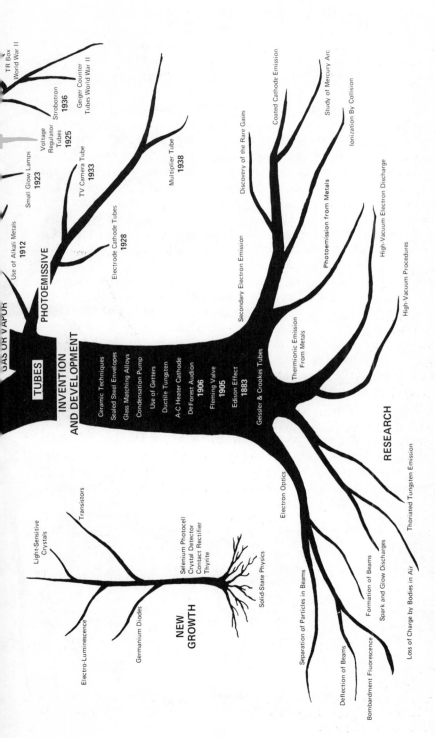

More than a dozen fields of research combine to support the great technological growth which started with the audion in 1906. Note the new sapling which has produced the transistor; it now rivals in size and complexity the "parent" tree, some of whose branches are likely to wither in the shade of the new growth.

Source: W. C. White, "Evolution in Electronics," *Electronics,* XXV (September, 1952), 98.

for the glass envelope and the metal parts within the tube give off minute quantities of gas under the influence of heat even after the tube has been evacuated and sealed. Irving Langmuir, a General Electric scientist, recognized the theoretical basis of the electron tube's operation and secured the high degree of vacuum needed. General Electric, as the major manufacturer of electric lamps, had a natural interest in this new development.

Harold D. Arnold of AT&T made other improvements. The Telephone Company needed an efficient amplifier for long-distance telephone circuits. Before the development of the audion, coast-to-coast telephone service had been impossible because of the attenuation which occurs in long-distance wire circuits. In 1913, AT&T bought the telephone rights to seven basic audion patents from de Forest for $50 thousand.[15] By 1915, AT&T had opened the first coast-to-coast telephone circuits, using vacuum-tube reamplifiers (repeaters). In 1914, the Company also began to take a belated interest in the possibilities of radiotelephony and paid de Forest $90 thousand for the radio rights to his audion patents, the inventor retaining only manufacturing rights for sale to amateurs and experimenters.[16]

The patent problems surrounding the development of the audion involved not only the tube itself but the electrical circuits using the tube. One of the latter, the regenerative or feedback circuit, has been the subject of "the most controversial litigation in radio history."[17] This circuit feeds part of the received signal back on itself to build up the signal strength, thus increasing tremendously the sensitivity of radio receivers. In fact, it has been called "as historic as the first Bell telephone patent and as clearly decisive in the development of the modern world."[18] Four companies claimed to hold the controlling patent on this improvement: AT&T, with the de Forest patent; General Electric, with the Langmuir patent; American Marconi with a patent of Edwin Armstrong, and the Telefunken Company with the German Meissner patent. This four-way battle moved in and out of the courts for twenty years. After millions of dollars had been spent in legal fees, the Supreme Court finally decided in favor of de Forest in 1934.[19] Even the final court decision

---

[15] De Forest made this sale at a low point in the violent fluctuations of his financial career. Obviously, rights of such crucial importance to the Telephone Company were worth more than a mere $50 thousand. De Forest claims that AT&T was willing to pay as much as $500 thousand but that he was hoodwinked by their agent into thinking he was selling the rights to a much less significant customer. See de Forest, *op. cit.,* pp. 309–310.

[16] These radio rights were effectively paralyzed by a 1916 court decision (*Marconi Wireless Telegraph Co. of America* v. *de Forest Radio Telephone & Telegraph Co., 236 F. 942*) which left both litigants stalemated. The situation was not resolved until after World War I, when the assets of American Marconi passed to Radio Corporation of America.

[17] Maclaurin, *op. cit.,* p. 78.

[18] Lessing, *op. cit.,* p. 78.

[19] *Radio Corporation of America, et al.* v. *Radio Engineering Laboratories, Inc., 293 U.S. 1* (1934). The decision is interesting for its review of the issues and some of the complex history of the litigation.

did not clear the atmosphere completely. Armstrong seems to have understood the *principle* underlying the feedback circuit better than de Forest, who arrived at the invention by largely empirical methods.[20]

6.5 / Radiotelephony

By 1934, however, de Forest had long since sold his radio patents and moved on to other fields. His feedback circuit and other radio patents had gone to the Telephone Company in 1917 for $250 thousand. By this time, the great manufacturing and communications companies were actively engaged in radio research, after years of what de Forest considered "amazing indifference," and de Forest's pioneering interest had flagged.[21] He turned instead to a newer field, sound motion pictures (Figure 6.3). His adventure in this field is discussed in Section 11.3.

De Forest greatly enjoyed music; his attention naturally turned to the possibilities of using radio for transmitting sound. The early commercial radiotelegraphic transmitters generated radio energy first with a spark gap, later on with an arc. The arc transmitter had two drawbacks for radiotelephony: the frequency of the current used to activate the arc was so low that it fell in the audible range, so that the tone of the arc itself tended to mask the intended signal; and it was difficult to modulate the powerful current fed to the arc with the very weak current produced by a microphone. Early experimental microphones, closely coupled to arcs, had to be water-cooled. Speakers had to be careful not to singe their lips on the microphone.[22] Despite these difficulties, de Forest and others persisted. De Forest broadcast phonograph music from the Eiffel Tower in 1908. In 1910, he staged the first opera broadcast, from the Metropolitan with Caruso in the cast, but the voices were reported to be "hardly recognizable."[23] In 1916, he began work on the problem of adapting the audion as an oscillator, a substitute for the arc. He set up an experimental radiotelephone station, and in 1916 began to broadcast phonograph records and announcements. De Forest describes his personal announcements, crediting the Columbia Gramophone Company for the recordings and mentioning the products of his own firm, as the first radio commercials.[24] He even broadcast election returns in that year, four years before the similar broadcast over KDKA usually credited as the historical beginning of broadcasting (Section 7.2). In 1919, after the World War I shutdown, he resumed his informal experimental broadcasts, but a government radio inspector told him, "There is no room in the ether for entertainment," and forced him off the air.[25]

---

[20] Maclaurin, *op. cit.,* pp. 78–79.

[21] De Forest, *op. cit.,* p. 359.

[22] Archer, *op. cit.,* p. 87.

[23] See de Forest, *op. cit.,* pp. 267–271, for details of this historic experiment.

[24] *Ibid.,* pp. 337–338.

[25] *Ibid.,* p. 351.

Figure 6.3
Lee de Forest (1873–1961)

The inventor stands beside a motion-picture camera he converted
for optical sound.

Source: Brown Brothers.

De Forest deserves credit for imaginative and creative use of his inventions
as well as for the inventions themselves. He was part inventor, part showman,
and part businessman. As an inventor he was prolific; he filed over thirty
patents in the pioneer days of 1902–1906 and over the years was granted
more than two hundred. He had connections with a score of firms created to
exploit his inventions. Much of the time he carried on research and experimentation under the most adverse financial conditions, often victimized by the
unscrupulousness and bad judgment of business associates. His United Wireless Company went bankrupt in 1912, giving American Marconi a monopoly
on wireless communications in the United States.[26]

---

[26] American Marconi was later bought out by Radio Corporation of America; another
bankruptcy in 1926 resulted eventually in other de Forest assets finding their way to
RCA. This corporation thus owes a great deal to the genius of Lee de Forest.

6.6 / Other Wireless Pioneers

Reginald Fessenden, another entrepreneur-inventor who pioneered in radio-telephony, became Professor of Electrical Engineering at the University of Pittsburgh in 1893. He has been called "the first important American inventor to experiment with wireless," having developed an invention second in importance only to the audion: the heterodyne circuit.[27] In his search for a means of practical radiotelephonic transmission, Fessenden also worked on the transmitting method. It will be recalled that alternating current produces electromagnetic radiation. He aimed at developing a high-frequency generator, or alternator, as it was called. In 1906, Fessenden made the first long-distance transmission of radiotelephony, using a 50,000-cycle alternator built for him by Ernst Alexanderson of General Electric.[28] From the technical viewpoint, this event could be said to represent the birth of broadcasting. But it was, of course, merely experimental, with an "audience" mainly of ships' operators. Fessenden, too, suffered disastrous financial setbacks in his attempts to exploit his own inventions.

Alexanderson, on the other hand, was not an inventor-entrepreneur like de Forest and Fessenden. He represented a later development, the approaching era of the great industrial research laboratory. In the General Electric laboratories, he went on independently of Fessenden to develop alternators of higher and higher capacities. During World War I, General Electric supplied the United States Government with 200-kw. Alexanderson alternators, by far the most powerful ever built up to that time. Alexanderson also developed the means of coupling the microphone to these powerful transmitters electronically, using electron tubes. These and other patents gave General Electric a very strong patent position in the field of radiotelephony by the end of World War I. The Alexanderson alternator was a huge, costly machine, described as "perhaps the most elegant machine ever known in the realm of Radio."[29] The fact that a United States firm owned it contributed, as we shall see, to breaking the monopoly of American Marconi.

The superheterodyne circuit was the final major link in the chain of inventions which made broadcasting commercially feasible. This circuit, invented by Edwin Armstrong, increased the sensitivity of receivers so much that outdoor receiving antennas for ordinary home reception could be eliminated. Nearly all modern radio receivers use the superheterodyne principle. It was patented in 1920 and by 1924 had come into general commercial use.

6.7 / World War I Developments

The 1914–1918 war caused great acceleration in the development of wireless communication technology. This was the first major war in which wireless had

---

[27] Maclaurin, *op. cit.,* pp. 59 and 61.

[28] Archer, *op. cit.,* pp. 86–87.

[29] George H. Clark in Westman, *op. cit.,* p. 42.

been used in naval operations, and by its close, the new means of communication had become a vital military service. Long-distance transoceanic wireless also was much improved during the war. Alarmed by the possibility that the Germans might cut off the United States from communication with its allies by simply slashing the transatlantic cables, the United States government placed a high priority on the development of reliable alternative channels. The Alexanderson alternator came into use, and the wireless circuits to Europe played an important role in military operations and in diplomatic communications during the Paris peace conference.

The war contributed to radio development in other ways. The United States Navy took over the operation of all private stations that it found useful and had all other transmitters shut down and disassembled. In order to capitalize fully on all United States patents, the Navy effected a moratorium on patent suits. Such a pooling of the country's total technical resources had previously been quite impossible because of commercial rivalries.

In short, wireless advanced tremendously during the war and came back to civilian life with materially altered status. The prewar era had been dominated by the inventor/entrepreneurs. Now began the era of big business. AT&T had acquired the de Forest patents and built up an important interest in wireless telephony. General Electric, with the Alexanderson alternator and the family of related patents that went with it, held a commanding manufacturing position. American Marconi, though weakened by Navy inroads on its maritime business, still dominated the wireless communication service. Westinghouse, not at the moment deeply involved, was about to inject a new and dynamic element into the situation—a novel use of wireless telephony ultimately to be called "broadcasting."

At the close of World War I, however, the commercial utility of wireless telephony was by no means clear. In 1917, Lee de Forest had suggested that it might be used instead of wireless telegraphy on small ships to save the cost of skilled operators.[30] In 1919, David Sarnoff sweepingly predicted that radio could replace the telephone. The Navy, on the other hand, still regarded radio as essentially a maritime instrument which had no business competing with the telephone and telegraph wires.[31] The time was ripe for a business innovation: a practical, money-making use of radiotelephony that would not duplicate any existing service.

---

[30] House Committee on Merchant Marine and Fisheries, *Radio Communication,* p. 295.

[31] House Committee on Merchant Marine and Fisheries, *Government Control of Radio Communication,* pp. 204 *et passim.*

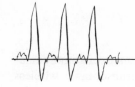

7

EMERGENCE OF BROADCASTING

"Broadcasting" means the dissemination of radio communications intended to be received by the public. COMMUNICATIONS ACT OF 1934

7.1 / The Concept

"Intended" is the key word in the legal definition of broadcasting. The nature of radio makes it impossible to prevent the general public, should it wish to invest in the necessary equipment, from receiving radio signals of any kind whatever.[1] But most signals, though available to all, are *intended* only for specific recipients. Broadcasting alone sends out information intended for any and all recipients.

This apparently simple concept represented a radical innovation in the communications business. The whole history and tradition first of wire and then of wireless communication had based commercial profit on the exchange of *private* intelligence. The sender of the message rather than the receiver was the key man. The sender paid a fee for the use of the service, just as today one pays by the word to send a telegram or by the call to use a telephone. How else could a profit be made? What possible motive could a sender have for paying money to reach an unknown audience indiscriminately?

This is not to say that no one had visualized the desirability of bringing remote events to the ears of audiences. As early as 1890, the Telephone Company had experimented with wire "broadcasts" of public events to audiences at remote locations.[2] Visionaries imagined wireless performing similar services. While radiotelephony was still in a primitive stage of development, de Forest set up a series of experimental and demonstrational transmissions to dramatize

---

[1] A striking illustration of this point was the feat of the British tracking station at Jodrell Bank in picking up the camera signals from the Russian unmanned satellite which made the first "soft" moon landing in 1966. Britain released photographs of the moon's surface ahead of the Russians.

[2] William P. Banning, *Commercial Broadcasting Pioneer: The WEAF Experiment, 1922–1926* (Cambridge, Mass.: Harvard University Press, 1946), pp. 4–5.

such possibilities.[3] One of the visionaries not only saw his broadcasting predictions come true but took a prominent part in the whole subsequent development of commercial broadcasting. In 1916, when he was assistant traffic manager of American Marconi, he wrote a memorandum to his chief, saying in part:

I have in mind a plan of development which would make radio a "household utility" in the same sense as the piano or phonograph. The idea is to bring music into the house by wireless. . . . The receiver can be designed in the form of a simple "Radio Music Box" and arranged for several different wave lengths. . . . The main revenue to be derived will be from the sale of the "Radio Music Boxes" which if manufactured in lots of one hundred thousand or so could yield a handsome profit. . . . The Company would have to undertake the arrangements, I am sure, for music recitals, lectures, etc. . . . Aside from the profit to be derived from this proposition, the possibilities for advertising for the Company are tremendous; for its name would ultimately be brought into the household and wireless would receive national and universal attention.[4]

The writer was David Sarnoff. In the light of subsequent events this may not seem to have been a remarkable flight of imagination, but we must bear in mind that at the time of this memorandum, Sarnoff worked for the largest United States firm dealing in radiotelegraphic communication. Radiotelephony was still in the experimental stage. The best evidence of the radical nature of his proposal is, of course, that nothing was done about it. Four years later, A. N. Goldsmith developed the first "unicontrolled" radio receiver—a set with a single knob for tuning, another for volume, and a built-in speaker. Previously, large sets had come with a formidable array of knobs which had to be twiddled with some finesse before the set was properly tuned. When Sarnoff saw the simple unicontrolled receiver he exclaimed, "This is the radio music box of which I've dreamed!"[5] By that time, 1920, American Marconi had been taken over by the Radio Corporation of America, and Sarnoff had come with it. He was now in a better position to renew his suggestion with some hope of being heard.

The question was not so much whether broadcasting was ultimately possible or desirable, but how broadcasting could be financed. Not unnaturally, the companies which profitted from precisely the opposite use of radio—private rather than public communication—failed to embrace the idea of broadcasting with enthusiasm.

---

[3] About transmissions made in the spring of 1907, de Forest writes: "I cannot, of course, claim that I originated the term 'broadcast,' but I think that I was the first one to apply so descriptive a term to this new art which I was then beginning to create. . . ." [Lee de Forest, *Father of Radio* (Chicago: Wilcox & Follett, 1950), p. 226.]

[4] Quoted in Gleason L. Archer, *History of Radio to 1926* (New York: The American Historical Company, 1938), pp. 112–113.

[5] Robert C. Bitting, Jr., "Creating an Industry," *Journal of the Society of Motion Picture and Television Engineers*, LXXIV (November, 1965), 1016.

Figure 7.1

Conrad's amateur station

This informal hookup led to the establishment of KDKA and ultimately to the broadcast era.

Source: Brown Brothers.

7.2 / Westinghouse Starts KDKA

In 1920, Dr. Frank Conrad, an engineer with the Westinghouse Corporation in Pittsburgh, was operating an amateur radiotelephone station, 8XK, in connection with the work at the factory (Figure 7.1).[6] Conrad fell into the habit of transmitting recorded music, sports results, and the like on a more or less regular schedule in response to requests from other amateurs. His informal programs built up such an interest that they occasioned newspaper stories. He even began to receive requests for particular records from his ama-

---

[6] Conrad's station had originally been licensed in 1916 but had, of course, suspended operations during World War I.

teur following. These circumstances were not in themselves unique; similar amateur broadcasts had occurred in other parts of the country and the world. What did distinguish the Conrad broadcasts was the chain of events they set in motion.

Horne's Department Store in Pittsburgh, becoming aware of the growing public interest in wireless, sensed a hitherto untried commercial possibility in the 8XK broadcasts. Would their customers perhaps be willing to pay for ready-built receiving sets? To test this hunch, Horne's installed a demonstration receiver in the store and ran a box in their regular newspaper advertisements of September 22, 1920, advising: "Amateur Wireless Sets made by the maker of the Set which is in operation in our store, are on sale here $10.00 up."[7]

Westinghouse had been casting about for a profitable entry into the communications field—in fact had already explored several possible new types of radio service. For this reason, no doubt, Westinghouse officials were particularly alert to the somewhat obscure hint contained in Horne's modest advertisement. They saw the possibility of a novel merchandising tie-up: Westinghouse could manufacture inexpensive radiotelephone receivers and create a new market for them by transmitting programs for the general public.

Conrad's superiors at Westinghouse realized that a new class of purchasers might be induced to buy radio sets in unprecedented numbers.[8] A radiotelegraphy transmitter was converted for radiotelephony at the Westinghouse factory in East Pittsburgh and went on the air as KDKA from a site on the roof of the factory on November 2, 1920. The opening was scheduled to coincide with the presidential election, so that the maiden broadcast could take advantage of public interest in the voting. This first program consisted of the Harding-Cox election returns, read on the air as they came in by telephone from a newspaper office, phonograph records, and banjo music.

Broadcasting might have developed much more slowly had it not been for its ready-made audience—the amateur set builders. In order to understand the significance of KDKA's 1920 broadcasts in their terms, we must reconstruct the circumstances of the time. A push-button generation of radio listeners and television viewers can scarcely appreciate the quality of interest such transmissions could arouse in 1920. The crystal detector, an extremely simple and inexpensive rectifier of radio-frequency energy, had brought radio within reach of almost everybody who wanted to build a receiver. The crystal set, the simplest form of radio receiver, consists basically of a tuning coil, a crystal detector, and a pair of earphones (see Figure 7.2). The earphones are the only essential item which need cost more than a few cents. No battery or other

---

[7] The advertisement is reproduced in E. P. J. Shurick, *The First Quarter-Century of American Broadcasting* (Kansas City: Midland, 1946), p. 18.

[8] The man who made the specific decision was Westinghouse Vice-President H. P. Davis. See his "The Early History of Broadcasting in the United States," in Harvard University Graduate School of Business Administration, *The Radio Industry* (New York: A. W. Shaw, 1928), pp. 189–225.

Figure 7.2

Crystal receiving set

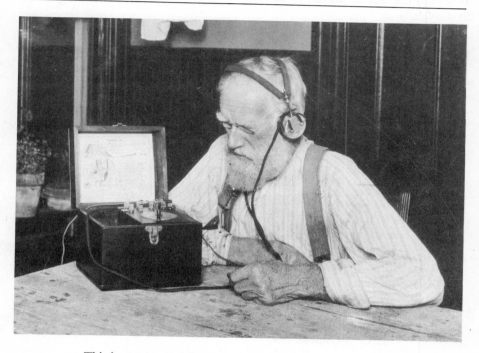

This is a commercial model, neater than the more common home-built set, whose tuning coil was often wound on a round Quaker Oats box.

Source: Brown Brothers.

electric power source is required: the crystal rectifier makes the signal audible by changing the high-frequency radio waves into weak electric currents.[9]

The only signals regularly on the air in 1920 were in radiotelegraphic code. To hear music and the human voice instead of the monotonous drone of Morse code in the earphones was a startling experience for any listener, amateur or professional. He felt, too, a unique satisfaction in the idea of a program directed to himself; previously he had had to eavesdrop on messages intended for other people.[10] KDKA was an immediate success. Because there was as

[9] The crystal set went out of general use after 1922, when the regenerative vacuum-tube circuit, an immensely more sensitive detecting device, became available.

[10] Some inkling of the impact of broadcasting in the early days can be gained from reading the grateful letters of listeners in Banning, *op. cit.*, pp. 19–29.

Figure 7.3
KDKA's studio in 1922

At this time, studio designers used heavy draperies on ceilings as well as walls to control reverberation. Acoustic tile came later.

Source: Westinghouse Photo.

yet no crowding of the broadcast channels and hence no station interference, KDKA's sky wave could be picked up at great distances. Newspapers all over the country and even in Canada printed the station's program logs. To assist "DX" (long-distance) listeners, local stations later observed a "silent night" each week, a time-period when they went off the air so as not to interfere with incoming signals from distant stations.[11]

In its first year of operation, KDKA pioneered in broadcasting many types of program which later became standard radio fare: orchestra music, church services, public-service announcements, political addresses, sports events, dramas, market reports. But one type of material was conspicuously absent: commercials. Westinghouse bore the expense of operation and had no plan to dilute the favorable publicity the station brought the firm by sharing it with others.

Although the Harding-Cox election program on KDKA in 1920 is usually

[11] Erik Barnouw, *A Tower in Babel: A History of Broadcasting in the United States to 1933* (New York: Oxford University Press, 1966), p. 93. "Silent nights" were discontinued in 1927.

Table 7.1

Ownership of broadcast stations as of February 1, 1923

Type of Owner	% of All Stations Licensed
Communications manufacturers and dealers	39
Educational institutions	12
Publishers	12
Department stores	5
Religious institutions	2
Other	30

Source: Data in William P. Banning, *Commercial Broadcasting Pioneer: The WEAF Experiment, 1922–1926* (Cambridge, Mass.: Harvard University Press, 1946), pp. 4–5.

cited as the historic beginning of broadcasting in America, a number of other stations claim the honor. KQW in San Jose, California, first broadcast in 1909 and ran a regular schedule in 1912; Station 2ZK, New Rochelle, New York, broadcast music regularly in 1916; a Detroit amateur station, 8MK (later WWJ), began regular broadcasting over two months before KDKA's maiden broadcast. Then, of course, there were the many experimental transmissions by de Forest and Fessenden previously mentioned. At least a dozen stations still in operation date their beginnings from 1920 or earlier. But the fact remains that KDKA was the first commercially licensed standard broadcast station listed in the United States Department of Commerce records (Figure 7.3).[12]

Westinghouse did not long have the field to itself, however. The other leading communication concerns—General Electric, AT&T, RCA—were watching with interest. Broadcasting had a strong appeal for department stores, newspapers, educational institutions, churches, and electric-supply dealers (Table 7.1). The number of stations increased slowly in 1920, with only 30 licenses issued by the end of that year. In the spring of 1922, however, the new industry began to gather momentum. By May, over 200 licenses had been issued, and the upward trend continued during the next twelve-month period, reaching a peak of 576 early in 1923. Mortality, however, was high among these early stations. Would-be broadcasters hastened to get in on the ground floor of—they knew not quite what. Problems of financing and programming were left to improvisation as they arose. Stations not backed by adequate financing and planning soon fell by the wayside. Educational stations were particularly heavy losers in this respect. On the other hand, companies like

---

[12] The detailed evidence is discussed in Archer, *op. cit.*, pp. 207–208. See also R. Franklin Smith, "Oldest Station in the Nation?" *Journal of Broadcasting*, IV (Winter, 1959–1960), 40–55.

Westinghouse, with a long-term interest and a high financial stake in the future of the medium, could afford to keep abreast of rapid improvements in technique, programming, and production.

7.3 / The Telephone Company Steps In

AT&T watched the sudden surge of activity in this new application of radio-telephony with keen interest. Telephony was its undisputed province, and its patent rights in radiotelephony were so extensive that, willy-nilly, broadcasting seemed to be its province, too. AT&T built WEAF in New York to experiment with the new medium. As the showcase for the Telephone Company, WEAF had every financial, technical, and managerial advantage. The station went on the air on August 16, 1922, replacing another AT&T station, WBAY, whose nearby location had proved unfavorable for good propagation. In this connection the technique of field-strength measurement was first developed. Other technical innovations of WEAF included the volume indicator and the multiple-input control panel, or mixer, with independent control of microphone channels. Inexperienced performers could not be depended on to stay "on mike," so a multiple-microphone setup was devised.[13] Network broadcasting and commercial sponsorship were also developed at WEAF.

In order to understand the full historical significance of WEAF, however, we must look further into the background to explore the motivations of the Telephone Company in terms of the larger interests at stake. WEAF, after all, was but one manifestation of an epic struggle for the control of business empires, brought on by the emergence of a totally new field of enterprise.

It may be useful at this point to review the conditions under which broadcasting began. First, it should be noted that the major communications companies all became active in broadcasting within its first two years. Second, broadcasting was a genuine innovation. No precedents indicated how it should be financed and organized; the concepts of the sale of time to sponsors and the syndication of programs by networks did not at once emerge. Third, at that time the federal law of 1912 governed radio, a law intended to govern maritime communications. It could not possibly have anticipated the problems such a radically different service as broadcasting might raise.

Each of these factors suddenly became critically important because broadcasting sprang into being almost overnight. Herbert Hoover, who as Secretary of Commerce had the responsibility of administering the Radio Act of 1912, said early in 1922:

We have witnessed in the last four or five months one of the most astounding things that has come under my observation of American life. [The Department of Commerce] estimates that today over 600,000 (one estimate being 1,000,000) per-

---

[13] Banning, *op. cit.*, p. 79. This history of WEAF is full of interesting details on early broadcasting.

sons possess wireless telephone receiving sets, whereas there were less than 50,000 such sets a year ago.[14]

This unprecedented growth of the new medium caught all concerned off guard and precipitated several years of turmoil in the new industry. In the critical years 1920–1927, the basic shape of American broadcasting was hammered out.

7.4 / Government Monopoly Averted

The most fundamental issue was whether radio was to remain a government monopoly or to be thrown open again to private commercial enterprise. In April, 1917, the United States Navy had been given control of all private wireless facilities as a wartime measure. The war ended in November, 1918, yet the government did not relinquish control of these properties until February, 1920. Critical decisions made during this delay of over a year affected the whole future of radio in the United States, including the yet-unborn service of broadcasting. The war had demonstrated the vital importance of wireless communication facilities as a national asset.[15] Were they too vital to entrust again to private hands? The United States Navy thought so. In fact, the Navy had always asserted jurisdiction over radio as a natural right on the mistaken assumption that radio was destined to remain primarily a marine service.

The Alexander Bill, introduced in Congress late in 1918, represented the Navy's point of view.[16] It proposed, in effect, to reduce radio to a government monopoly. The bill was badly drawn and ineptly defended by the Navy witnesses at the hearings; yet eventually such a law might well have been passed. After all, at that moment the Navy already had complete control, by virtue of its wartime powers. Other countries had made radio a government monopoly; yet the United States radio law then on the books, the Radio Act of 1912, required little more than a registration procedure of private stations. The Alexander Bill and other similar attempts to remove radio from the realm of private enterprise failed in large measure because of the dissolution of American Marconi and the formation of the Radio Corporation of America in 1919.

It will be recalled (Section 6.6) that General Electric had developed the 200,000-w. Alexanderson alternator, which made reliable long-distance radio communication possible. This machine had been successfully put into service

---

[14] Department of Commerce, "Minutes of Open Meeting of Department of Commerce Conference on Radio Telephony" (1922, mimeo.), p. 2.

[15] Before the United States's entry into the war, the German high-power station in Sayville, New York, violated United States neutrality by sending vital intelligence to German ships at sea. Later on, a single message interception netted the United States alien-property custodian $10 million. [House Committee on Merchant Marine and Fisheries, *Government Control of Radio Communication,* Hearing on H. R. 13159, 65th Cong. (Washington: Government Printing Office, 1919), p. 10.]

[16] H. R. 13159 and S. 5036, 65th Cong., 2d Sess. This bill was in fact a stronger version of a similar bill introduced in the 64th Congress, H. R. 19350.

by the Navy in 1918. Three years earlier, the potentialities of Alexanderson's experiments had been recognized by Guglielmo Marconi himself. He had opened negotiations with GE for exclusive rights to the alternator, but these talks had been interrupted by the war. Now, in March of 1919, the negotiations were reopened. In this immediate postwar period, with the flow of government orders ceasing, no major United States market for wireless equipment existed. American Marconi was the only company in the United States with enough capital and commercial potential to qualify as a customer for the alternators. GE had spent a great deal on their development and justifiably expected substantial returns.

7.5 / The Founding of RCA

The prospect that American Marconi would consolidate its United States monopoly by capturing exclusive rights to the Alexanderson alternator deeply disturbed the Navy. The extent of its concern is measured by the fact that as early as 1918 the Navy had spent $1 million to block American Marconi by securing patent rights to the Poulsen arc, the next-best radio-energy generator to the Alexanderson alternator.[17]

President Wilson himself is said to have taken an interest in the situation, even in the midst of the Peace Conference. He is said to have considered that international communication, together with oil and shipping, represented the key to the balance of power in international affairs.[18] In 1919, Britain led the world in maritime strength, the United States in petroleum production. Britain already had a long lead in the field of worldwide cable facilities and was now on the verge of obtaining the world monopoly on international wireless communication, so long the objective of British Marconi. Thus, what ordinarily would have been purely a matter of business and financial strategy was projected into the realm of international politics.

British Marconi found itself subjected to an international squeeze play. The American government made no overt move actually to expropriate British Marconi's American holdings; the international negotiations were carried out on a private level by Owen D. Young of General Electric. But British Marconi's position in the United States was plainly untenable. The president of American Marconi told his stockholders in 1919:

We have found that there exists on the part of the officials of the Government a very strong and irremovable objection to [American Marconi] because of the stock interest held therein by the British Company.[19]

---

[17] Senate Committee on Interstate Commerce, *Commission on Communications,* Hearings on S. 6, 71st Cong., 2d Sess. (Washington: Government Printing Office, 1930), pp. 1013 ff. According to David Sarnoff, the Navy also pressured American Marconi into selling it 330 ship sets and 45 coastal stations for $1.45 million in 1918. [House Committee on Merchant Marine and Fisheries, *op. cit.,* pp. 195–201.]

[18] Archer, *op. cit.,* p. 164.

[19] Quoted in Archer, *op. cit.,* p. 178.

We may never know the full story of the behind-the-scenes maneuvers which led to the sale of American Marconi to American interests. GE's motivation combined elements of patriotism and profit. Which incentive predominated became a matter of debate a few years later—a debate with strong political overtones. The Radio Corporation of America (RCA), which GE set up to take over the American Marconi assets and operations, was accused of trying to justify its monopoly by claiming that it had come into being at the request of President Woodrow Wilson and therefore had a quasi-official status.[20]

RCA took over the operation of American Marconi's assets on November 20, 1919. Significantly, this antedates the opening of KDKA by a full year. Owen D. Young testified later, "We had no broadcasting in our minds in 1919 and 1920."[21] Westinghouse and AT&T, as well as General Electric, invested in the new corporation. In 1922, the stock distribution was approximately as follows: General Electric, 25 per cent; Westinghouse, 20 per cent; AT&T, 4 per cent; former American Marconi stockholders and others, 51 per cent.[22]

RCA was a unique corporate enterprise "put together from the top" by Owen D. Young, the GE vice-president whose business statesmanship had successfully effected the complicated and delicate international negotiations. It remained for David Sarnoff in the years that followed to convert the abstract legal documents and high-level corporate policies into operational effectiveness. It took less than a year for Young to create RCA, but it took Sarnoff twenty years to make it into a completely integrated operating concern.[23] Sarnoff was the young Marconi Company radiotelegraph operator who had maintained shore contact with the survivors of the *Titanic* disaster in 1912; in 1916, as Marconi traffic manager, he had argued for the "radio music box." He typifies the American saga, the rise of the poor immigrant boy to leadership in the top ranks of industry. Sarnoff taught himself the Morse code while still in his teens (Figure 7.4). He entered the industry as an office boy with American Marconi, but his unusual skill with the key eventually won him the job of operator in the Marconi station located atop the old Wanamaker building near Washington Square in New York, where he was working at the time of the *Titanic* disaster. Sarnoff foresaw the need for industrial leadership which combined first-hand technical knowledge with business ability; he was, in

---

[20] See Senate Committee on Interstate Commerce, *op. cit.*, particularly the testimony of Owen D. Young, pp. 1081–1173 and 1176–1220. The origin of RCA was the subject of a number of inquiries; one of the earliest is to be found in FTC, *Report on the Radio Industry* (Washington: Government Printing Office, 1924). The known story is reconstructed in Archer, *op. cit.*, pp. 157–180.

[21] Senate Committee on Interstate Commerce, *op. cit.*, p. 1115.

[22] FTC, *op. cit.*, p. 20. American Marconi had had eighteen hundred American small stockholders. AT&T sold its interest in 1923. RCA remained under the control of General Electric and Westinghouse until it achieved independence in 1930.

[23] W. Rupert Maclaurin, *Invention and Innovation in the Radio Industry* (New York: Macmillan, 1949), pp. 110, 248.

Figure 7.4
David Sarnoff as a boy

In 1908, Sarnoff was employed as a wireless operator on Nantucket Island, Massachusetts. Compare the later Sarnoff, launching the television age at the New York World's Fair in 1939 (Figure 10.5).

Source: Radio Corporation of America.

short, the true innovator. He became president of RCA in 1930, chairman of its board in 1947, and retired in 1969. His active business career spanned the whole evolution of broadcasting.

7.6 / Cross-Licensing Agreements

RCA's real mission was not merely to take over and operate the half-dozen American Marconi subsidiaries engaged in wireless communication. A serious problem faced the parent companies. Young testified that "it was utterly impossible for anybody to do anything in radio, any one person or group or company at that time [1919]. . . . Nobody had patents enough to make a system. And so there was a complete stalemate."[24] RCA broke that stalemate. Young proposed that the major patent rivals could find a meeting ground in their commonly owned subsidiary. Accordingly, in 1919, 1920, and 1921, a

[24] Senate Committee on Interstate Commerce, *op. cit.,* p. 1116.

series of cross-licensing agreements was made among General Electric, AT&T, Westinghouse, and RCA.[25] Cross-licensing simply means the pooling of patent rights among participants in the agreements. RCA participated as a cross-licensee because it had inherited important patent rights from American Marconi. In the period 1919–1923, RCA entered into more than a score of licensing, traffic, and sales agreements, both with its parent companies and with others.

But the purpose of the cross-licensing agreements was not solely to resolve patent conflicts. They also defined and held free from intramural competition the special area of interest of each company in the group. Since RCA was not an independent entity, its role was to be a subordinate. General Electric and Westinghouse would use RCA's patents in the manufacture of equipment, and RCA would act as a mere sales agent for the other firms' products. AT&T was to maintain control over telephonic communication, by wire and wireless. AT&T's exclusive right, under the cross-licensing agreements, to the manufacture and sale or lease of transmitters would ensure this control. General Electric and Westinghouse could use the pooled patents to make transmitters for themselves but not for sale to others. All these rights were exclusive among the parties to the agreements.

Although the cross-licensing agreements in principle anticipated even such future technical developments as television, they did not take into account the multibillion-dollar economic potential of broadcasting. The unexpected development of this new service almost immediately threw the carefully calculated plan for division of the communications empire out of balance. It must again be emphasized that the market for receivers and components was not of major economic importance before the advent of broadcasting. In 1921 the retail value of all the receiving equipment sold in the United States was about $5 million; by 1928 it had risen to $650 million.[26] The discovery of this rich mass market introduced a totally unexpected element into the business arrangements of the cross-licensees. Aside from the disturbing effect of this dazzling manufacturing bonanza, the advent of broadcasting also caused the cross-licensees difficulty in agreeing on the interpretation of certain provisions of their agreements. What was the status of the Telephone Company's rights to the telephone lines used by broadcast stations, for instance? From the outset, broadcasting had found wire facilities a necessary adjunct for remote pickups.[27] Soon wire facilities were also needed for network interconnection. Again, what were the Telephone Company's rights with respect to the use of transmitters for commercial broadcasts?

---

[25] These agreements are printed in FTC, *op. cit.,* pp. 122ff.

[26] Testimony of David Sarnoff in Senate Committee on Interstate Commerce, *op. cit.,* p. 1235.

[27] Note that even KDKA's inaugural broadcast used the telephone to relay election results from a newspaper office to an announcer at the transmitter.

7.7 / Divergent Theories of Broadcasting

As a result of such divisive forces within the ranks of the cross-licensees, a sharp cleavage developed. On one side was the Telephone Group, consisting of AT&T and its subsidiary, Western Electric; on the other side was the Radio Group, consisting of General Electric, Westinghouse, and their subsidiary, RCA. In the race for dominance in the new realm of broadcasting, AT&T's entry was Station WEAF and the Radio Group's was WJZ. Each built up rival networks. In this competition, WEAF had a distinct advantage: immediate access to AT&T's telephone lines and AT&T's telephonic know-how. Moreover, the Radio Group's stations, under AT&T's interpretation of cross-licensing agreements, were barred from operating stations for profit.

The split between the two groups carried over into the rationale of their early broadcast operations. The Radio Group started with the idea of operating broadcast stations as a means of stimulating the market for their manufactured products. Therefore the broadcast station assumed responsibility for supplying both the physical facilities and the messages sent over these facilities, just as Sarnoff had suggested eight years before (Section 7.1). The Radio Group emphasized the public's interest in receiving a program service —at the price of investment in receiving equipment. According to this approach, each separate firm wishing to use broadcasting to create public good will for its products would operate its own separate station for that purpose.

AT&T started with quite an opposite conception of the role of the broadcaster. It saw broadcasting as an extension of the telephone service, the main difference being that broadcasting was one-way instead of two-way telephony. This meant that (1) a relatively small number of stations would serve all users and (2) the broadcast station assumed no responsibility for the messages, *i.e.*, programs, sent over its facilities. Early in 1922, when the Telephone Company was preparing to open WEAF, an official explained: "[the Company] . . . will furnish no programs whatsoever over that station. It will provide facilities over which the general public, one and all alike, may use those services."[28] This plan was based on a direct analogy with the Company's customary telephone services:

Just as the company leases its long distance wire facilities for the use of newspapers, banks, and other concerns, so it will lease its radio telephone facilities and will not provide the matter which is sent out from this station.[29]

AT&T's broadcasting activities were accordingly placed under the long-lines department, and sponsored programs were called "toll" broadcasts, analogously with long-distance telephony. AT&T took the view that its exclusive jurisdiction over transmitters permitted it to restrain others from using them

---

[28] Department of Commerce, *op. cit.*, p. 7.

[29] AT&T press announcement, 1922, quoted in Banning, *op. cit.*, p. 68.

"for toll or hire, or for the rendition of any advertising or personal message service."[30]

As broadcasting finally evolved, it combined elements from both the Telephone Group's concept of the medium and the Radio Group's concept in a new synthesis. The Telephone Company had correctly assumed that the financial support of a limited number of broadcast stations would need to be distributed among many users, who would lease the facilities temporarily, as was done with the telephone. It miscalculated in placing the emphasis on the sender rather than on the receiver of the messages. Here the Radio Group's concept of service to the public, with emphasis on the public's program needs and wishes, prevailed.

7.8 / "Toll" Broadcasting

WEAF was far from being one of the first stations on the air. More than two hundred stations were already licensed by the time WEAF started, fifteen of them operating in the New York area alone. But WEAF has particular significance because of its role as AT&T's guinea pig in the new medium. The company spared no expense, investing a quarter of a million dollars during the first year's operation.[31] Two major practices which were to distinguish the American system of broadcasting—network syndication and commercial sponsorship—first developed at WEAF. Even before the station went on the air, prospective advertisers themselves expressed an interest in hiring its facilities. Hitherto, as we have said, it had been assumed that each would-be advertiser would have to operate his own station to publicize his own wares, just as Westinghouse had done with KDKA. This concept led, of course, to the rapid multiplication of stations. The Telephone Company received no less than sixty requests for transmitters in the New York area alone. AT&T realized that such excessive numbers of stations could achieve nothing but interference and a general depreciation of the service. WEAF was built with the idea that a single station, operated as a common carrier by the Telephone Company, could serve many advertisers without leading to self-defeating congestion of the broadcast channels. The refusal to sell transmitters to all comers, based on this conception, led to charges that AT&T was attempting to monopolize broadcasting. Indeed, its intention seems to have been just that—and on perfectly logical grounds. Said the AT&T official in charge of radio:

We have been very careful, up to the present time [1923], not to state to the public in any way, through the press or in any of our talks, the idea that the Bell System desires to monopolize broadcasting; but the fact remains that it is a telephone job, that we are the telephone people, that we can do it better than anybody

---

[30] House Committee on Merchant Marine and Fisheries, *To Regulate Radio Communication,* Hearings on H. R. 7357, 68th Cong. (Washington: Government Printing Office, 1924), p. 41.

[31] Testimony of W. E. Harkness, *ibid.,* p. 88.

else, and it seems to me that the clear, logical conclusion that must be reached is that, sooner or later, in one form or another, we have got to do the job.[32]

WEAF's facilities were first leased for a "toll" broadcast on August 28, 1922. A Long Island real-estate corporation supplied a "commercial" consisting of a ten-minute talk extolling in somewhat indirect terms the advantages of living in "Hawthorne Courts." The first commercial advertiser known to have provided entertainment along with the commercial on WEAF was Gimbel Brothers, which became a major advertiser on the station in its early days. However, WEAF handled toll broadcasting with circumspection, permitting no direct advertising such as the mention of prices. Officials even debated whether such an intimate subject as toothpaste should be mentionned on the air.[33]

Despite AT&T's restrictions on the sale of transmitters and its insistence that it alone had the right, under the cross-licensing agreements, to use transmitters for toll broadcasting, stations continued to multiply. Hundreds of stations operated in violation of the Telephone Company's rights. By February, 1923, 93 per cent of the 576 stations in operation were infringing on AT&T patent rights.[34] Although many of these stations were individually too short-lived or inconsequential to warrant serious concern, the Company nevertheless was unwilling to abandon its rights by default. Yet its refusal to sell transmitters to all comers had already evoked accusations of monopoly, so it was reluctant to adopt aggressive measures. It decided, therefore, to license toll stations that used transmitters involving its patent rights. A test case initiated by AT&T against WHN in New York in 1924 was settled out of court, with the license fee being paid by WHN.

7.9 / Networks

In the meantime, another problem had arisen. As we have pointed out, stations had from the outset used wire connections for picking up programs remote from the broadcast-transmitter locations—especially since the early transmitters were usually located in factories and other relatively inaccessible places. AT&T interpreted the cross-licensing agreements as prohibiting the connection of broadcast equipment to telephone circuits. Naturally, AT&T made its own lines available to its own station, WEAF. In fact, one of WEAF's primary purposes was to experiment with ways of integrating the Company's telephone facilities with its broadcast facilities. As early as 1921, the Telephone Company advanced the idea of a series of broadcast stations located at strategic points along its long-distance trunk lines which could occasionally broadcast identical programs, *i.e.*, network programs. The Company conceived that these stations might be programmed by corporations set up in the various towns

---

[32]A. G. Griswold, quoted in N. R. Danielian, *A. T. & T.: The Story of Industrial Conquest* (New York: Vanguard, 1939), pp. 123–124.

[33] Banning, *op. cit.*, p. 150.

[34] *Ibid.*, p. 134.

where the stations were located, representing the business and cultural interests of the communities involved. The Telephone Company would lease out the broadcast facilities and would have no hand in the programming—again an attempt to apply the telephone concept to broadcasting.

An early test of the network principle occurred on January 4, 1923, when WEAF fed a program by wire for simultaneous broadcast in Boston by WNAC, owned by Shepard Stores.[35] This was a five-minute broadcast of a saxophone solo, carried over lines especially adapted for the purpose. Telephone long lines normally were adjusted to carry a frequency band of 250–2,500 cps. They had to be specially equalized for 100–5,000 cps to provide broadcast quality. Later in 1923, the first permanent network circuit (as distinguished from a one-time arrangement) was established between WEAF and WMAF in South Dartmouth, Massachusetts. WMAF was the property of Col. E. H. Green, who operated it for his own amusement and had no means of programming it. He persuaded WEAF to feed him both toll broadcasts and nontoll broadcasts. He paid a fee for the sustaining programs and broadcast the commercial programs without cost to the sponsor.[36]

AT&T continued experimenting with network broadcasts, gradually adding to the number of stations interconnected. In October, 1924, a special twenty-two-station hookup carried a speech by President Coolidge from coast to coast. The regular WEAF network at that time consisted of six stations broadcasting three hours of network programs per day. The network still used regular telephone circuits temporarily equalized for broadcast purposes. In 1926, however, the Company began setting aside circuits exclusively for broadcasting.

What of the Radio Group in the meantime? The location of RCA's first station, WDY, in a GE plant in Roselle Park, New Jersey, proved unsuitable for competition with WEAF. In February, 1922, RCA took a half-interest in a Westinghouse station, WJZ, which, although located in Newark, had studios in the Waldorf-Astoria Hotel in New York. In the following year, RCA bought out the Westinghouse interest, and thereafter WJZ became the chief rival of WEAF. RCA operated, however, at a considerable disadvantage. According to the cross-licensing agreements of which RCA was itself a signatory, it could neither use AT&T telephone lines for broadcast purposes nor sell time. WJZ cost RCA a hundred thousand dollars a year to operate and brought in no income whatever, whereas WEAF was grossing three quarters of a million dollars annually by 1926.

WJZ tried using Western Union telegraph lines for network interconnection, but the requirements of telegraphic signals are so much lower than those of telephonic signals that the Western Union lines could not deliver broadcast quality. The Radio Group at this time seriously considered the possibility of

---

[35] The Shepard family also was important in another, much later radio development when it gave the support of its Yankee Network in New England to Edwin Armstrong in his attempts to promote FM broadcasting.

[36] WMAF was thus the first network "bonus station."

radio-relay circuits for network interconnection, but suitable equipment was not yet developed for utilizing the microwaves which have since proved so useful for this purpose. Despite these difficulties, by the end of 1925, WJZ had succeeded in organizing a network of fourteen stations.

During these years of broadcast pioneering (1922–1926), continual behind-the-scenes negotiations had been in progress, with the purpose of resolving the conflict produced by the cross-licensing agreements. By 1926 the Telephone Company had come to the conclusion that its original concept of broadcasting as just another branch of the telephone business was inadequate. Its excursion into broadcast operations, its repression of the use of telephone lines for relaying competitive broadcast programs, its insistence on exclusive control of broadcast transmitters—all had resulted in taking the Telephone Company far afield from its primary business and in creating bad public relations. In sum, "as an experiment, broadcasting had been necessary; as a business, it was almost certain to be a liability."[37] Accordingly the signatories of the cross-licensing agreements finally arrived at a revised set of three agreements in July, 1926. The preamble to one of the new agreements frankly confessed:

[Since] the art in certain of the fields dealt with in said [1920] agreement had not progressed to a point at which it was possible fully to comprehend the problems involved, disputes have arisen between the parties as to the meaning of various provisions of said agreement.[38]

Some of the significant provisions of the new agreements follow: (1) The *license agreement* redefined the patent rights of each company in the light of the new developments. AT&T was granted exclusive control over wire telephony and two-way wireless telephony, both domestic and foreign. Wire-telegraphy rights also went to AT&T, but RCA retained rights in wireless telegraphy. Telephony was defined in such a way as to leave AT&T in control of network relays, whether wire or wireless, for radio or television. Broadcasting itself went to RCA. Western Electric was barred from competing with the Radio Group in the manufacture of home receivers and other devices for home use. AT&T surrendered its exclusive claims on transmitter manufacture, and thereafter RCA and Western Electric became competitors in this market. They also subsequently competed in the field of sound motion-picture equipment. (2) The *service agreement* required RCA to lease radio-relay facilities from AT&T and to cease using Western Union wires for networking. (3) The *purchase agreement* provided for the sale of WEAF and its broadcast assets to the Radio Group for $1 million, with AT&T to be barred from reentering the field except under penalty.[39]

---

[37] Banning, *op. cit.*, p. 272.

[38] Quoted in Danielian, *op. cit.*, p. 127.

[39] See Danielian, *op. cit.*, pp. 126–132, for a more detailed description of the agreements. It should be borne in mind that the power and scope of these agreements derived from the patent rights of the parties concerned.

As far as broadcasting was concerned, the agreements of 1926 amounted to this: The Telephone Company would continue to profit from broadcasting as the source of all interconnection facilities for networks, and RCA would have a free hand in developing commercial network broadcasting. RCA thus emerged as the overwhelmingly strongest force in the new business of broadcasting. David Sarnoff had long since recognized what had not been apparent to the officials of AT&T: that broadcasting was a genuine innovation in business which would require its own special organization, business methods, and personnel. He had no illusion that broadcasting could continue to be carried on as incidental to some other kind of business. Sarnoff had renewed the "Music Box" memo of 1916 immediately after the transfer of American Marconi to RCA. As early as 1922, he predicted the course for broadcasting:

When the novelty of radio will have worn off and the public [is] no longer interested in the means by which it is able to receive but rather, in the substance and quality of the material received, I think that the task of reasonably meeting the public's expectations and desires will be greater than any so far tackled by any newspaper, theater, opera, or other public information or entertainment agency. . . . Let us organize a separate and distinct company, to be known as Public Service Broadcasting Company, or National Radio Broadcasting Company, or American Radio Broadcasting Company, or some similar name . . .[40]

Herein Sarnoff had anticipated by four years what came to pass in 1926, when AT&T withdrew from broadcasting. A few months after the settlement, the Radio Group formed a new subsidiary, the National Broadcasting Company, owned 50 per cent by RCA, 20 per cent by GE, and 20 per cent by Westinghouse. It was the first company organized solely and specifically to operate a broadcasting network. A four-and-a-half-hour coast-to-coast inaugural broadcast took place on November 15, 1926. The program included Walter Damrosch conducting the New York Symphony Orchestra, with cut-ins from opera singer Mary Garden in Chicago and humorist Will Rogers in Independence, Kansas. The twenty-five stations in the network reached an estimated five million listeners on that occasion. Not until 1927, however, did regular coast-to-coast operations begin.

Starting with the new year in 1927, RCA organized NBC as two semi-independent networks, the Blue and the Red, with the Blue based on WJZ and the old Radio Group network and the Red based on WEAF and the old Telephone Group network.[41] The dual network arose because NBC now had duplicate outlets in New York and other cities, and there would have been no point in merely broadcasting the same programs on two stations in the same service area. As competitive networks developed, however, the dual-network operation took on a more significant character: by tying up not one but two of the best stations in each major city, and by playing one of its networks

---

[40] Quoted in Archer, *op. cit.*, pp. 30–31.
[41] NBC later changed the call letters of WEAF to WNBC.

against the other, NBC had a significant advantage over rival networks.[42]

The second national network followed closely on the heels of NBC. In 1927, the year after NBC began, over seven hundred stations were licensed,[43] with only 7 per cent of the total affiliated with NBC. Stations had trouble finding program material to fill out their schedules. In January, 1927, United Independent Broadcasters was formed to supply program talent on a network basis. Having more ideas than money, the company sought financial backing and received an offer from the Columbia Phonograph Record Company. The record company, interested in publicizing its name and exploring the new field of broadcasting, set up a subsidiary, the Columbia Phonograph Broadcasting System, Inc., to work with UIB. The initial venture failed, and the record company withdrew. UIB, however, retained the subsidiary company, and the present Columbia Broadcasting System's name derives from it.[44] In 1928, William S. Paley became president, bringing with him new financial backing which finally put the firm on a sound basis. Also in 1928, CBS purchased WABC, New York (call letters changed to WCBS in 1946), as its key station there. The company showed a profit by 1929 and soon began to offer NBC competition.

The launching of competing national networks on a commercial basis completed the basic evolution of the original American broadcasting concept. In the few years between 1920 and 1927, a business revolution had taken place. Three major developments had occurred: AT&T, along with its common-carrier concept of broadcasting, had been removed from the field, thereby clearing the atmosphere of confusion about the type of service that broadcasting was to render; the technical facilities and business organization had been developed for successful national syndication of programs by competitive networks; and selling time to advertisers had proved a feasible method of financing.

7.10 / Acceptance of Commercialism

In his 1922 memorandum (Section 7.9) proposing that RCA set up a network company, Sarnoff did not contemplate that broadcasting would be a direct profit-making venture:

---

[42] Coincidentally, RCA had earlier considered a dual-broadcast operation in planning a sister station for WJZ, to be called WJY. RCA planned to operate WJY on a different frequency from WJZ and to dedicate it to classical music. The idea of specialized program services on different frequencies but under the same organization has been adopted in several countries (see Section P.6).

[43] This number would be misleading if one assumed that all licensees were operating on the scale of modern broadcast stations. A great many stations existed more on paper than in fact. For example, the Federal Radio Commission finally cancelled the license of a New Jersey station whose studios consisted of the parlor of the owner's home, whose antenna was a wire on a pole nailed to a shed, and whose signal the Commission's monitors had been unable to pick up in an entire year. [*Technical Radio Laboratory* v. *FRC,* 36 F. (2d) 111 (1929).]

[44] Ironically, CBS bought out the Columbia Phonograph Record Company a decade later.

I feel that with suitable publicity activities, such a company will ultimately be regarded as a public institution of great value in the same sense that a library, for example, is regarded today.[45]

When the National Broadcasting Company became a reality, it seemed expedient to retain George F. McClelland, the key administrative man at WEAF, if he would leave AT&T. When he was offered the vice-presidency, according to General James G. Harbord, then president of RCA, McClelland asked:

. . . what was to be our aim—whether purely a moneymaking affair, or whether we aim to perform a big public service to which the income was somewhat incidental. I reassured him on this point, telling him we had the ambition to give a splendid public service, not unconscious of the fact, however, that if we did it, it would reflect itself to us in profits by that company and increased sales of radio apparatus by our own. He accepted the position without any understanding as to salary.[46]

It is not necessary to conclude that such statements as these—which typify the attitude of many business leaders of the time—were simply hyprocritical eyewash put out by cynical big-business executives who in reality had every intention of exploiting radio broadcasting to the limit.

Within five years all these noble dreams vanished. The dreams were a compound of public relations puffery and good faith; to some extent the dreamers even believed their dreams.[47]

The fact is that men in the position of Sarnoff, Harbord, and McClelland could not themselves fully realize the extent of the social revolution already under way. To them, advertising was indeed a questionable intruder into the sacred privacy of the home. Their ideas of the role of family life in society were still essentially in the nineteenth-century tradition. But this was the "Roaring Twenties." In the aftermath of World War I, Victorian standards of taste and public conduct were rapidly disintegrating. The iconoclastic temper of the times favored radio's commercial trend. A dignified broadcasting service reflecting the hush of a great public library would have been an anachronism.

The advertising men, more sensitive to the jazzed-up tempo of the age, capitalized on the potentiality for new freedoms. Almost before broadcasting executives realized what was happening, the advertising agencies had taken over their programming—and they, rather than the broadcasters, set the commercial tone. Subsequently, broadcasters were severely criticized for surrendering too much responsibility to advertisers. Still later, when they reasserted

---

[45] Quoted in Archer, *op. cit.*, p. 33.

[46] *Ibid.*, p. 281.

[47] Carl Dreher, "How the Wasteland Began; the Early Days of Radio," *The Atlantic*, CCXVII (February, 1966), 57. Reprinted by permission of Collins-Knowlton-Wing, Inc. Copyright © 1966 by The Atlantic Monthly Company, Boston, Mass. Dreher was the first chief engineer at WJZ.

their control over television programming, advertising agencies complained bitterly of their presumption; instead of being taxed with surrendering the program production function to others, the networks came under criticism for exercising too much control by freezing out other program sources.[48]

An accident of history—the fact that commercial radio began simultaneously with the post-World War I breakup of Victorian social attitudes—thus profoundly affected the development of broadcasting in America. RCA's change of heart about advertising has been ascribed to the economic squeeze caused by a combination of the Depression and the out-and-out commercialism of CBS.[49] William Paley, after all, came into broadcasting from the position of advertising manager of his family's cigar company, directly as a result of discovering that radio could sell cigars. These may have been the proximate causes, but underlying them was a more fundamental cause: commercial broadcasting just happened to be uniquely in tune with the times.

Of course, this fact was not immediately obvious. Even after 1927, resistance to the full commercialization of broadcasting continued. At the First Radio Conference in Washington, in 1922, the sentiment against advertising had been almost universal. By the Fourth Conference, in 1925, the idea had been generally accepted, in principle, but the standards to be followed remained in doubt.[50] As late as 1929, the National Association of Broadcasters adopted a code limiting nighttime advertising to dignified identification of sponsors, reserving "direct" advertising for the business hours of the day.[51] In 1930, a United States Senator could still say, "Personally, I think [advertising] is going to be a disappearing part of the service," and the president of NBC could still declare, "I am opposed to direct advertising on the air."[52] Not until advertising agencies began to play a larger part in the control of programming in the 1930's did all-out direct advertising become the generally accepted practice.[53]

---

[48] See House Committee on Interstate and Foreign Commerce, *Television Network Program Procurement,* House Report 281, prepared by FCC Office of Network Study, 88th Cong., 1st Sess. (Washington: Government Printing Office, 1963).

[49] Dreher, *loc. cit.*

[50] The Committee on Advertising and Publicity of the conference declared direct advertising objectionable and recommended goodwill advertising only. [Fourth National Radio Conference, *Proceedings and Recommendations for Regulation of Radio* (Washington: Government Printing Office, 1926), p. 18.]

[51] "Time before 6 P.M. is included in the business day and therefore may be devoted in part, at least, to broadcasting programs of a business nature; while time after 6 P.M. is for recreation and relaxation, and commercial programs should be of the good-will type." [NAB recommendation quoted in Senate Committee on Interstate Commerce, *op. cit.,* p. 1735.]

[52] *Ibid.,* pp. 90, 1705.

[53] In the 1928–1929 season, radio networks had sixty-five nationally sponsored programs. See John W. Spalding, "1928: Radio Becomes a Mass Advertising Medium," *Journal of Broadcasting,* VIII (Winter, 1963–1964), 31–34.

Some never did accept the direction radio took in the 1920's. The pioneer inventor of American broadcasting, Lee de Forest, for example, remained a bitter opponent of commercialism to the end of his life:

As I look back today over the entire history of radio broadcasting since [1907] . . . I . . . am filled with a heartsickness. Throughout my long career I have lost no opportunity to cry out in earnest protest against the crass commercialism, the etheric vandalism of the vulgar hucksters, agencies, advertisers, station owners —all who, lacking awareness of their grand opportunities and moral responsibilities to make of radio an uplifting influence, continue to enslave and sell for quick cash the grandest medium which has yet been given to man to help upward his struggling spirit.[54]

Contemporary critics sometimes say much the same thing about commercial television. Though it inherited intact the commercial patterns and mores developed by radio, television entered the social scene in another post-war period —an era with its own quite different brand of disillusionment and iconoclasm. The type of broadcast commercialism which flourished in response to the social atmosphere between the two world wars no longer harmonized so aptly with the times in the post-World War II era. That kind of commercialism may eventually seem as archaic in the Age of Television as Victorianism seemed in the Roaring Twenties. This possibility will be explored in Section 22.8.

One point of contrast must be mentioned here, however: the fortunes of noncommercial broadcasting. As Table 7.1 indicated, educational institutions operated a substantial proportion of the early AM stations. Some of the very earliest stations, in fact, grew out of experiments in university engineering departments. Yet of over two hundred stations licensed to educational institutions, only thirty-eight remained in operation by 1937.[55] All these stations had been licensed as commercial stations; no special category of noncommercial, or educational, station licenses existed. The success of commercial broadcasting and the shortage of available channels conferred great value on some of the strategically located educational licenses. A few institutions capitalized on the situation and changed from noncommercial to commercial operation. Most, however, had no desire (or legal right) to go into the business of selling advertising, and since they also lacked any strong convictions about the educational value of broadcasting, they put up only token resistance when commercial interests moved to capture their licenses. The few noncommercial AM stations which did continue in operation (mostly at land-grant colleges and universities, where broadcasting could serve an established function in providing extension services to rural listeners) had low power and unfavorable time-sharing arrangements. In effect, therefore, American broadcasting started as an entirely commercial service, without benefit of a leavening alternative.

---

[54] De Forest, *op. cit.,* pp. 442–443.

[55] S. E. Frost, Jr., *Education's Own Stations* (Chicago: University of Chicago Press, 1937), p. 3.

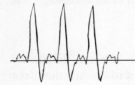

8

ORIGINS OF GOVERNMENT REGULATION OF BROADCASTING

I think this is probably the only industry of the United States that is unanimously in favor of having itself regulated.
SECRETARY OF COMMERCE HERBERT HOOVER (1924)

By their nature, laws tend to lag behind technical development, and the history of radio offers many instances of legal anomalies brought about when novel situations arise which existing laws could not have anticipated.

8.1 / Wire Regulation

Experience with telegraphy provided the precedents for legal regulation of wireless. In most countries, domestic telegraphy became the province of national post-office authorities, which eventually became ministries of posts and telegraphs. At first, international telegraphic messages had to be physically handed across national boundaries and retransmitted on each national system. The first international treaty to secure free flow of telegraphic communication between countries dates from 1849, covering circuits between Berlin and Vienna. This pioneer effort led to the Austro-German Telegraphic Union in 1857, and finally to the first International Telegraphic Convention, drawn up by twenty-five European countries in Paris in 1865. Today's International Telecommunication Union, now a specialized agency of the United Nations Educational, Scientific and Cultural Organization (UNESCO), dates its existence from this meeting.[1] These early national and international efforts at regulating wire communication provided ready-made patterns for regulation of wireless. Thus, today, in Britain as well as many other countries, the Post Office continues to have primary legal responsibility for technical aspects of radio.

The 1857 Austro-German Union created a device so useful that it continues to this day: separation of technical from political regulations in international

---

[1] The ITU celebrated its centenary in 1965 with a handsome and useful history, *From Semaphore to Satellite* (Geneva: The Union, 1965).

154

communications agreements. International diplomacy moves much too slowly to keep up with rapidly changing technology. Political decisions are therefore incorporated in "conventions"—relatively permanent international agreements. Within the broad terms of these agreements, specific regulations can then be freely adopted by technical experts as the needs arise without invoking the cumbersome machinery of international coordination at the highest political level. In America, the present Communications Act compares to the stable international convention, while the Rules and Regulations of the Federal Communications Commission provide the essential day-to-day technical flexibility.

8.2 / Wireless Regulation

The first international conference concerning wireless communication took place in Berlin in 1903. Its main object was to deal with the Marconi Company's refusal to exchange messages with rival commercial systems (Section 6.1)—much as mid-nineteenth-century national telegraphic systems had originally refused to connect up directly to neighboring networks.

Humanitarian considerations soon prevailed, for it was unthinkable that commercial self-interest should long be allowed to come first when human lives were at stake, as in maritime emergencies. The first effective international agreement in the wireless field was reached at the Berlin Convention of 1906, which took steps to ensure that the new medium would be available in times of emergency at sea. The United States did not ratify this agreement until 1912.

Two significant implications can be seen in these early international conventions. Note first that humanitarian considerations provided the initial impetus for establishing legal control of wireless communication. Second, the earliest attempt at regulation was international in scope—a fact indicative of radio's unique ability to transcend political boundaries.

In the United States, Congress amended the Interstate Commerce Act in 1910 to include interstate and foreign wireless as well as wire communication under federal jurisdiction; in the same year the Wireless Ship Act required large passenger vessels to carry radio equipment capable of exchanging messages at a distance of a hundred miles. But the first comprehensive piece of radio legislation in the United States was the Radio Act of 1912, which remained in effect for fifteen years, all through the period of the basic technical and economic evolution of the radio industry.

This law came belatedly (Great Britain had adopted its first radio laws in 1904), as a direct result of the *Titanic* disaster. When the doomed ship sent out the message "We've struck an iceberg. Sinking fast," another ship was only fifteen miles away; but twenty-four-hour wireless watches were not then required, and the other ship's operator had gone off duty fifteen minutes earlier, thereby innocently condemning 1,517 people to freeze to death in the Atlantic. The *Titanic's* own operator died at his transmitter. Later, when the rescue ship *Carpathia* approached the United States with the survivors, radio contact with the mainland was seriously impeded by interference from irrelevant signals.

The *Titanic* disaster gripped the popular imagination, dramatizing as nothing else had done the vital importance of the proper use of radio facilities on ships at sea. It was quickly followed not only by the passage of the Radio Act of 1912 in the United States, but also by another international convention in London in the same year. The United States at last adopted the recommendations of the Berlin Convention of 1906, which provided for the use of the international "SOS" signal, the prevention of unnecessary interference with distress signals, and the interchange of messages without regard to the commercial systems used. The Radio Act empowered the Secretary of Commerce and Labor,[2] among other things, to issue station licenses to United States citizens and to specify the wavelengths to be used (aside from the frequencies between 187 and 500 kc., which were reserved for government use).

In the very year of its passage, however, the Radio Act of 1912 turned out to have a serious technical defect. The Attorney General handed down the opinion that "the Secretary of Commerce and Labor is only authorized to deal with the matter as provided in the act and is given no general regulative power."[3] The Act provided that the Secretary of Commerce and Labor would grant licenses to United States citizens "upon application therefor." It did not provide any grounds on which the Secretary could reject applications. In the light of the limited uses of radio at the time, of course, Congress had no particular reason to anticipate that the Secretary would need to make any choice. Presumably all who wanted to and had a good reason to could be allowed to operate radio stations. Essentially, the Act merely provided a registration procedure, somewhat analogous to the already existing procedure for registering ships.

8.3 / The Radio Act of 1912 Breaks Down

For a decade, this concept of the role of government in relation to radio worked satisfactorily. Existing services needed relatively few transmitters. Aside from amateurs, ships' stations formed the most numerous class; because of their mobility and the intermittent nature of their traffic, they could share a few frequencies without injurious conflict. But when broadcasting, an entirely new class of service, began to demand more and more stations in 1922–1923, a serious problem arose. Analogizing the broadcasting service to the maritime service, the Secretary at first required all broadcast stations to share time on the same frequency. In 1921, 833.3 kc. was assigned to news and entertainment stations, and a second channel, 618.6 kc., to crop and weather report stations. But whereas a ship needs only occasional exchange of specific messages, a broadcast station needs to transmit a continuing program service. The

---

[2] Since 1913 the Secretary of Commerce.

[3] *29 Ops. Atty. Gen.* 579 at 581 (November 22, 1912).

rapid proliferation of broadcast stations soon created intolerable interference. Further increasing the number of frequencies assigned to broadcasting did not solve the problem, for the stations multiplied faster than ever.

To complicate matters, the engineering crudity of many early broadcast stations made them quite incapable of holding closely to an assigned frequency. Worse, some stations were portable and the owners moved them from place to place, completely disrupting any orderly plan of service. An ever-increasing amount of interference resulted. This in turn led some station owners to take matters into their own hands. They began to change frequency, power, times of operation, and location—all in violation of their licenses. Unauthorized changes, of course, merely created worse interference so that a vicious circle was set in motion, and the broadcast service became more and more degraded.

An amusing side light on the kind of problems faced by the Secretary of Commerce in trying to control this obstreperous new medium is revealed by Herbert Hoover, the then Secretary. Aimee Semple McPherson, a phenomenally popular evangelist of the 1920's, operated a pioneer broadcast station from her "Temple" in Los Angeles. The station "wandered all over the wave band," and after repeated warnings a government inspector ordered the station closed down. Secretary Hoover thereupon received the following telegram from Evangelist McPherson:

PLEASE ORDER YOUR MINIONS OF SATAN TO LEAVE MY STATION ALONE. YOU CANNOT EXPECT THE ALMIGHTY TO ABIDE BY YOUR WAVELENGTH NONSENSE. WHEN I OFFER MY PRAYERS TO HIM I MUST FIT INTO HIS WAVE RECEPTION. OPEN THIS STATION AT ONCE.[4]

Clearly, both the number and the operation of stations would have to be controlled in some way; yet under the Radio Act of 1912, the Secretary of Commerce had no choice but to grant licenses to every applicant. In 1923, a court held that "the duty of naming a wave length is mandatory upon the Secretary. The only discretionary act is in selecting a wave length."[5] Unfortunately, there simply were no more usable frequencies for the Secretary to name. Finally, a 1926 court decision completely undermined the Secretary's regulatory power. WJAZ, Chicago (owned by Zenith Radio Corporation), had been licensed to share time with a Denver station. WJAZ had operated at times and

---

[4] Herbert Hoover, *Memoirs* (New York: Macmillan, 1952), II, 142. Miss McPherson was persuaded to engage a competent engineer and allowed to reopen her station.

[5] *Hoover, Secretary of Commerce* v. *Intercity Radio Co., Inc.,* 286 F. 1003 at 1007 (1923). Louis G. Caldwell, the first general counsel of the Federal Radio Commission, later pointed out that this decision "has frequently . . . been given a broader construction than the language of the opinion warrants. It did not hold that the Secretary of Commerce did not have power to restrict the power of a station or its hours of operation or its frequency." [Testimony in Senate Committee on Interstate Commerce, *Commission on Communications,* Hearings on S. 6, 71st Cong., 2d Sess. (Washington: Government Printing Office, 1930), p. 65.]

on frequencies different from those authorized in the license. The Secretary brought suit under the Radio Act of 1912, but the court found in favor of the defendant, stating:

If section 2 [of the Radio Act of 1912] is construed to give to the Secretary of Commerce power to restrict the operation of a station as [the Secretary] contends is done by this license, what is the test or standard established by Congress, by which the discretion of the Secretary is to be controlled? . . . Administrative rulings cannot add to the terms of an act of Congress and make conduct criminal which such laws leave untouched.[6]

The Attorney General followed with an opinion advising Secretary Hoover that there would be no point in pressing the case further—that under the Constitution he was indeed bereft of regulatory power. Said the Attorney General: "It is apparent . . . that the present legislation is inadequate to cover the art of broadcasting which has been almost entirely developed since the passage of the 1912 Act."[7]

A basic American political concept is illuminated by this episode in the history of broadcast regulation. In a "government of laws, not men," the powers entrusted to those in authority must be limited by definition. As the court remarked in the Zenith case, our system does not "leave room for the play and action of purely personal and arbitrary power."

8.4 / Origin of the Radio Act of 1927

In leaving the Secretary's powers undefined, Congress in effect gave him no powers. What little restraint the Secretary had been able to impose on the industry evaporated with the Zenith decision. For three years Secretary Hoover and many of the broadcasters themselves had been urging Congress to bring the Radio Act up to date. Each session of Congress considered bills proposing new legislation. But the nature of broadcasting had not yet been clearly defined, and it was difficult to pass a law to regulate an unknown quantity. The Zenith decision, however, made Congressional action imperative. In the period of less than a year that elapsed between this decision and the passage of the new Radio Act, two hundred new broadcast stations took advantage of the moratorium on regulation and crowded on the air, compounding the bedlam that already existed. By this time it was impossible in most places to receive any kind of consistent broadcast signal. Thirty-eight stations operated in the New York area and forty in the Chicago area. A marked drop in set sales resulted. In his message to Congress in December, 1926, President Coolidge said:

. . . the whole service of this most important public function has drifted into such

---

[6] *U. S.* v. *Zenith Radio Corp.,* 12 F. (2d) 614 at 618 (1926).

[7] 35 *Ops. Atty. Gen.* 126 at 132 (July 8, 1926).

chaos as seems likely, if not remedied, to destroy its great value. I most urgently recommend that this legislation should be speedily enacted.[8]

Finally, on February 23, 1927, a new Radio Act was passed. Despite the urgency of the need for a new law, it can hardly be said that Congress rushed into this piece of legislation. From 1923 on, radio bills had been continually under consideration. Nine Senate or House bills were prepared before a satisfactory measure was agreed on.

The Radio Act of 1927, the first United States legislation to reflect the existence of broadcasting, was to a large extent the product of the radio industry itself. Secretary of Commerce Hoover, an ardent believer in free enterprise, had hoped that the industry would be able to discipline itself without government regulation. To this end he had called a series of National Radio Conferences in Washington in 1922, 1923, 1924, and 1925. In 1922, only twenty-two broadcasters attended; in 1925, the number rose to four hundred. During those four years broadcasting emerged as a recognizably distinct service. Speaking at the Fourth Conference, Hoover said: "Four years ago we were dealing with a scientific toy; today we are dealing with a vital force in American life."[9]

Hoover optimistically called the National Radio Conferences "experiments in industrial self government,"[10] but even at that time he must have suspected the hopelessness of the experiment. He commented repeatedly on the indubitable fact that here was an industry which actually *wanted* government regulation. For example, at the very first National Conference in 1922, he said: "This is one of the few instances that I know of in this country where the public—all of the people interested—are unanimously for an extension of regulatory powers on the part of the Government."[11] From year to year the Radio Conferences grew more explicit in their recommendations for government control. The recommendations of the Fourth Conference (1925) were embodied in a bill (H. R. 5589) which eventually became the Radio Act of 1927. The only basic idea in the Act not already recommended by the Radio Conference was that of a regulatory commission.

The Radio Act of 1927 is essentially the same legislation under which broadcasting and all the other radio services in America operate today, although that Act has since been incorporated in the Communications Act of 1934. The Act brought to an end the era of doubt and confusion concerning the legal status of broadcasting, just as the withdrawal of AT&T from operating broadcast stations in 1926 ended doubt and confusion about the eco-

---

[8] *68th Congressional Record* 32 (1926).

[9] Fourth National Radio Conference, *Proceedings and Recommendations for Regulation of Radio* (Washington: Government Printing Office, 1926), p. 1.

[10] Third National Radio Conference, *Recommendations for Regulation of Radio* (Washington: Government Printing Office, 1924), p. 2.

[11] Department of Commerce, "Minutes of Open Meeting of Department of Commerce Conference on Radio Telephony" (1922, mimeo.), p. 1.

nomic nature of the medium. A number of other circumstances contributed to the significance of this transitional point. The first network company was set up in 1926, the first competitive network operations and regular nationwide network service in 1927. In the same years, a series of technical improvements occurred which encouraged the rapid growth of a mass audience: higher-powered transmitters, improved superheterodyne receiver circuits, the alternating-current power supply (eliminating batteries), the dynamic loudspeaker. We can thus establish the years 1926–1927 as a genuine turning point in the history of broadcasting. After an era of tentative, trial-and-error growth, the new medium entered an era in which it could move forward along a well-defined path of development.

8.5 / Philosophy of the Radio Act

Senator Wallace H. White, who more than any other legislator was responsible for the Radio Act of 1927, summarized its significance for broadcasting by saying:

We have reached the definite conclusion that the right of our people to enjoy this means of communication can be preserved only by the repudiation of the idea underlying the 1912 law that anyone who will may transmit and by the assertion in its stead of the doctrine that the right of the public to service is superior to the right of any individual to use the ether.[12]

The underlying assumptions of the Act may be summarized in the following assertions:

1. *The radio waves or channels belong to the people.* The electromagnetic spectrum is a kind of natural resource of the nation, the value of which could be destroyed by uncontrolled private exploitation. No one has a right to "own" a frequency or channel; it can be used for private purposes only if by such use the public interest also will be served.
2. *Broadcasting is a unique service.* Though similar in some respects to other types of communication services, broadcasting is nevertheless an innovation with unique characteristics which require special recognition.
3. *Service must be equitably distributed.* Since the radio frequencies belong to all the people, all the people have a right to expect to receive benefits from them.
4. *Not everyone is eligible to use a channel.* Licensees must qualify by meeting certain tests, both specific and general.
5. *Broadcasting is a form of expression protected by the First Amendment.* The Constitutional guarantee of freedom of speech and of the press extends to speech or publication through the medium of radio

---

[12] Quoted by Commissioner Robert T. Bartley in FCC mimeo. 1336 (January 29, 1954).

broadcasting, although broadcasting is subject to the special considerations implied by (2) above.

6. *The government has discretionary regulatory powers.* The Act grants certain specific powers of regulation, but since not all situations can be anticipated, the regulatory agency is also granted considerable freedom to use its own discretion. The limit on its discretion is defined by the "public interest, convenience and necessity."

7. *The government's powers are not absolute.* Decisions must be made by due process of law, may not be arbitrary or capricious, and may be appealed to a court of law.

Each of these principles has been tested in the courts and found to be consistent with the Constitution. They remain today as the conceptual foundation of the American system of radio regulation.

The Act contemplated that eventually most of the regulatory power would be vested in the Secretary of Commerce, as it had been under the Radio Act of 1912. It provided for a five-man Federal Radio Commission (FRC) appointed by the President with approval of the Senate. It originally represented five zones of the United States. The FRC was to have been reduced to a lesser role after the first year, but its task proved so much more difficult than Congress had anticipated that the Commission's original powers were extended for another year and then another. Finally it became apparent that the dynamic realm of radio communication would continually raise difficult administrative problems, and the FRC was made a permanent body on December 18, 1929.

8.6 / The FRC Takes Over

The FRC addressed itself to the monumental task before it on March 16, 1927. The task was not made easier by the lack of appropriation for offices, furniture, and staff. The Commission began its work in borrowed quarters with improvised facilities and staff. In its first year, the Commission devoted itself "almost exclusively to clearing up the broadcast situation."[13] Among its first acts were setting the broadcast license period for the time being at sixty days, defining the standard broadcast band as 500–1,500 kc.,[14] standardizing the designation of channels (by frequency rather than wavelength), and eliminating portable broadcast stations. It failed to take really drastic action on the most pressing problem, however—the need to reduce sharply the number of stations in operation. The Commission chipped away at this problem over a number of years. From 1927 to 1932, it reduced the total number of broadcast authorizations only from 681 to 604. However, it did cut back the number

---

[13] FRC, [*First*] *Annual Report* (Washington: Government Printing Office, 1927), p. 1.

[14] The band was extended to its present upper limit of 1,600 kc. in 1937 and to the present lower limit of 540 kc. in 1947.

of stations authorized to operate at night (when sky-wave interference becomes a factor) from 565 to 397.[15] In its second year, the FRC set up the classification system providing for local, regional, and clear channels. Its major project for that year and for some years to come was the effort to equalize the services in the country.

By 1929, the FRC had been challenged on a number of its decisions, particularly those interpreting the phrase "public interest, convenience, and necessity." Defending these decisions in court obliged the Commission to formulate its ideas concretely. Most of the basic concepts in this new area of jurisprudence had their origins in these early cases.[16]

At first, the Commission had issued its rules in the form of sequentially numbered General Orders. By 1931, the number and complexity of its rules had increased to the point where the General Orders became unwieldy. Therefore, the FRC adopted a method of codifying all standing orders in a systematic way as "Rules and Regulations." The first such set of Rules and Regulations became effective on February 1, 1932.

By this time, too, the technology of broadcasting had made many advances. The FRC had had the opportunity to make empirical tests and to collect expert opinion. Propagation theory was beginning to develop. During 1930, broadcasting experienced "almost a complete revolution in the type of equipment used."[17] All this enabled the Commission to adopt more stringent engineering standards aimed at reducing interference and improving signal quality. For example, where formerly stations had been required only to keep within 500 cycles of their assigned frequency, they now had to maintain a 50-cycle tolerance. The FRC issued a detailed set of "Standards of Good Engineering Practice" for the guidance of engineers in carrying out the Rules and Regulations. Stations had to keep logs on both technical operations and programs.

Also in 1930, the Commission adopted the practice of alleviating the pressure of its workload by delegating to Hearing Examiners the authority to conduct initial hearings. These time-consuming procedures resemble court trials, with all parties at interest submitting evidence and arguments with the aid of legal counsel. All these basic practices and procedures, devised during the first five years of the FRC, became a permanent part of the regulatory pattern.

8.7 / The Communications Act of 1934

Even when Congress passed the Radio Act, some Congressmen had wanted to go a step further and place under one federal jurisdiction both wire and wireless communication, both interstate and foreign. By 1929, a bill had

---

[15] FRC, *Sixth Annual Report* (Washington: Government Printing Office, 1932), p. 25.

[16] FRC, *Third Annual Report* (Washington: Government Printing Office, 1929) extracts the pertinent material from the Commission's briefs of that year, pp. 31–43.

[17] FRC, *Fifth Annual Report* (Washington: Government Printing Office, 1931), p. 6.

been introduced to revise the Radio Act by transferring from the Department of Commerce and the Postmaster General their remaining duties in wireless and wire communications and to consolidate all such powers under one law and one regulatory agency. Congressional committees considered several variants of this bill in subsequent years. Finally, in 1934, President Roosevelt forwarded an Interdepartmental Committee recommendation to Congress, explaining:

I have long felt that for the sake of clarity and effectiveness, the relationship of the Federal Government to certain services known as utilities should be divided into three fields: Transportation, power, and communications. The problems of transportation are vested in the Interstate Commerce Commission, and the problems of power . . . in the Federal Power Commission. In the field of Communication, however, there is today no single Government agency charged with broad authority.[18]

This recommendation produced the Communications Act of 1934. This law, still on the books, reenacted the Radio Act of 1927 and added new provisions for jurisdiction over interstate and foreign wire communication. It also added two members to the Commission because of the enlargement of its responsibilities, and its name became the Federal Communications Commission (FCC).

In effect, then, the present law governing radio dates back to 1927. The FCC took over from the FRC with no break in continuity. In every subsequent session of Congress, attempts have been made to amend the Act. Relatively few have become law, and most of those that have concern administration and technicalities. As an example, in the fiscal year 1968, Congress passed four amendments to the Communications Act, only one of which (establishing the Public Broadcasting Corporation) dealt substantively with broadcasting. However, the Commission provided testimony or comment on twenty-four bills affecting its work.[19]

It would appear, therefore, that Congress has been reasonably well satisfied with the working of the federal law governing broadcasting. If any profound dissatisfaction with the 1927 act had existed, Congress would presumably have done more than merely reenact it in 1934. Some credit seems due to the Congressmen of 1927, particularly the late Senator Wallace H. White of Maine, for devising a law in the very infancy of broadcasting which has somehow been able to foster and accommodate the fantastic growth of both wire and wireless communication since that time.

Of course, as we remarked at the outset, the law lags behind technical development. The gap between some of the underlying assumptions of the Act

---

[18] President of the United States, *Federal Communications Commission,* message recommending that Congress create a new agency . . ., Senate Document 144, 73d Cong., 2d Sess. (Washington: Government Printing Office, 1934).

[19] FCC, *Thirty-Fourth Annual Report* (Washington: Government Printing Office, 1969), p. 20.

and the realities of the situation has of necessity become more apparent with time. For example, the 1927 law did not take sufficiently into account the growing influence of networks, so that the Commission has had no way of directly regulating the most powerful force in the broadcasting structure. As Erik Barnouw remarked, the law is "based on a premise that had been obsolete in 1927 and by 1934 was totally invalid: that American broadcasting was a local responsibility exercised by independent station licensees."[20]

Despite such criticism—and a substantial body of opinion holds the Communications Act in even lower esteem—it can be argued that the Act has served its purpose reasonably well, given the realities of American politics and the dynamics of telecommunications development. A more telling case can be made against the way the law has been put to work. The Commission has always been at the focus of intense political pressures. The Executive branch uses its appointive powers politically; Congress uses its confirming, appropriating, and legislative powers politically; and the broadcasters use their lobbying power politically. In consequence, the Commission, whose partisan appointees may be rather compliant to begin with, finds its every move subject to second-guessing from powerful special interests. Often, it seems, the interest of the public, which according to the Communications Act should be paramount, has had the least effective representation, inside the Commission and out. A number of other federal independent regulatory commissions share these same problems, which will be discussed further in Chapter 21.

[20] Erik Barnouw, *The Golden Web: A History of Broadcasting in the United States, 1933–1953* (New York: Oxford University Press, 1968), p. 33.

9

RADIO'S GOLDEN AGE

From the transitional period of 1926–1927 emerged a national broadcasting system characterized by (1) competitive free enterprise and dependence on advertising for economic support; (2) syndication of programs, primarily by means of national networks—without, however, complete sacrifice of local ownership and programming in favor of monopoly ownership or centralized program control; and (3) government regulation, based on a compromise between public and private interests.

These characteristic traits of the American system of broadcasting did not, of course, emerge fully developed in 1927. The techniques of advertising, the functions of networks, and the concept of the dividing line between public and private interests in broadcasting continued to evolve. But radio broadcasting advanced steadily for two decades on the fundamental charter, so to speak, it received in 1926–1927.

This period came to an end in 1948 because of the culmination of a number of developments in television broadcasting. By then sound broadcasting had reached a high-water mark; thereafter it first receded, then found a new level and a new role as it adjusted to the competition of television.

In broad outline, the history of American radio broadcasting in these two decades might be subdivided as follows:

1. 1927–1937. Developmental period in which its characteristic factors—advertising, network operations, and government regulation—settled into a fairly well-defined pattern of interrelationships. Relatively little change in total number of stations (Figure 9.1).

2. 1938–1945. Period of stability in which the medium prospered and even became complacent, with gradual, orderly increase in station and network competition. Increased government surveillance. Artificial stimulation of profits and limitation on competition during World War II.

3. 1946–1948. Period of rapid change. Sudden great increase in number of stations, with resulting sharper competition. FM introduced. Television dominance imminent.

Figure 9.1

Trends in rate of station authorization

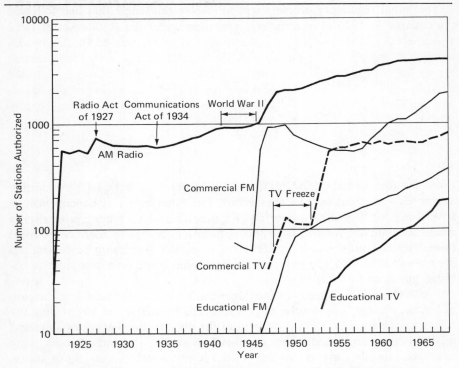

"Authorizations" include Construction Permits, so that their numbers exceed the numbers of stations actually on the air.

Source: FCC, *Thirty-Fourth Annual Report* (Washington: Government Printing Office, 1969).

9.1 / The First Phase

Radio broadcasting's first phase coincided with a severe depression, but this downbeat atmosphere helped rather than hindered the growth of the medium. Erik Barnouw, the radio historian, writes that in the Depression years broadcasting won "a loyalty that seemed almost irrational . . . destitute families that had to give up an icebox or furniture or bedding still clung to the radio as to a last link with humanity."[1] In these years, writes Edward R. Murrow's biographer,

. . . radio came into its own as a form of entertainment and communication, helping alleviate the depressed frame of mind which accompanied the depressed

[1] Erik Barnouw, *The Golden Web: A History of Broadcasting in the United States, 1933–1953* (New York: Oxford University Press, 1968), p. 6.

state of business. Radio was the universal solvent, a forum, a schoolroom, music hall, convalescent ward, companion, and soothsayer.[2]

The initial regulatory problem was to resolve the tangle that had followed the collapse in 1926 of government regulation under the Radio Act of 1912 (Section 8.3). The new law, the Radio Act of 1927, cleared the air by defining the federal government's role in regulating not only broadcasting but all forms of radio communication. By the time the FRC expanded into the FCC in 1934, it had cleared up the original technical confusion of the broadcast industry and had already moved on to the next task—cleaning up programming.

This cleanup was not a matter of interference by the Commission with programming in general. The FRC addressed itself rather to the stations which had succumbed to the temptation—always present in broadcasting and never resisted with entire success—to use the medium to prey on the ills and misfortunes of mankind. Several stations at this time devoted much of their programming to unethical medical advice, astrology, fortune telling, quack psychology, and the like. Some stations built in the earliest days of broadcasting as mouthpieces for the personal idiosyncracies of their owners also survived. The Commission was sustained by the courts in its moves to eliminate specific programming abuses of these kinds.[3]

9.2 / Syndication

Broadcasting consumes talent and program material at an unprecedented rate. The only possible answer to this inexorable demand is syndicating[4] program material and repetitively patterning programs. Early in the history of broadcasting, the need for networks as a means of sharing program expenses became apparent. Programming itself soon began to evolve formats which lent themselves to serialized extension into the indefinite future and which varied according to the cycle of habitual activities in the household. For example, daytime serial dramas ("soap operas") were scheduled daily ("across the board") at times when they could best reach the housewife at home and free from family distractions. Nighttime programming, aimed at the family as a whole, tended toward a weekly scheduling cycle, in formats using the same basic ingredients week after week. Typical were the half-hour comedy-variety programs, with permanent casts and recurring motifs such as Jack Benny's stinginess, Fibber McGee and Molly's overflowing closet, and Bob Hope's "feud" with Bing Crosby.

The need for syndication caused the major stations in the country to affiliate with one of the two national networks, either NBC or CBS. By 1938, 40 per

---

[2] Alexander Kendrick, *Prime Time* (Boston: Little, Brown, 1969), p. 115.

[3] E.g., *Duncan* v. *U. S.*, 48 F. (2d) 128 (1931); *KFKB Broadcasting Assn., Inc.* v. *FRC*, 47 F. (2d) 670 (1931); *Trinity Methodist Church, South* v. *FRC*, 62 F. (2d) 850 (1932).

[4] Technical aspects of syndication are discussed in Chapter 4.

cent of the 660 stations then in operation had become affiliates. However, the importance of networks was much greater than this figure suggests, since the independent (nonaffiliated) stations were mostly in the lower-wattage and part-time class; 98 per cent of the nighttime wattage represented network stations.[5]

Syndication by means of recorded programs and temporary station hookups also started early. In 1928, *Amos 'n' Andy* began distributing episodes of two five-minute recordings each, for which they signed up a group of thirty outlets.[6] When CBS refused further network time to a controversial Catholic priest, Father Charles Coughlin, he formed his own station hookup and in 1932 was heard on twenty-six stations.[7]

Syndication by means of both recordings and live network distribution is vital to music, radio's most fundamental program type. In 1938, music filled over half the schedules of all stations.[8] Broadcasters encountered copyrights almost from the first. The law of copyrights, like that of patents, derives from Article I, Section 8 of the Constitution (Section 5.5). The basic statute now in effect dates back to 1909. It provides for copyrights of twenty-eight years' duration, renewable once; an author surrenders his common-law right to his products when he either publishes his product or copyrights it under the statute. This law left a loophole for broadcasting, since it protected an author only against types of reproduction known in 1909. For instance, novels were protected from reproduction in print, but they could be read on the radio without violating copyright. This loophole was plugged in 1952 by an amendment to the statute.[9]

The novel question posed by radio was: how much should a station or network pay for the right to use copyrighted music? Considering the amount of music used—whether live or recorded, network or local—this was a question of some moment. Since music composers, authors, and music publishers cannot personally keep track of every performance affecting their rights, they formed an organization in 1914 to act for them, the American Society of Composers, Authors, and Publishers (ASCAP). This nonprofit association with thousands of members collects royalties on performances and distributes them to copyright holders. As early as 1922, ASCAP began to demand payment for radio performances of musical works in its catalogue. In fact, so uni-

---

[5] FCC, *Report on Chain Broadcasting* (Washington: Government Printing Office, 1941), p. 31.

[6] Erik Barnouw, *A Tower in Babel: A History of Broadcasting in the United States to 1933* (New York: Oxford University Press, 1966), p. 226.

[7] Barnouw, *The Golden Web*, p. 46.

[8] FCC, *Fourth Annual Report* (Washington: Government Printing Office, 1938), p. 225.

[9] Newer communications technology (*e.g.*, CATV, ETV, computer and microform storage, copying machines) has greatly complicated the problem of copyright law, and as of 1971, Congress, after several years' study, was still debating how best to revise the law to protect copyright holders without unduly restricting the use of modern communication resources.

versal was the problem for broadcasters that they formed their trade association, the National Association of Broadcasters (NAB), in 1923, specifically to
deal with the ASCAP problem. At the Fourth National Radio Conference
(1925), a broadcasters' committee complained that the terms offered by
ASCAP were "prohibitive" and "unstable," and asked for equal treatment for
all stations. Since this problem was covered by existing law, the Conference
took no action on the committee's recommendations.[10]

As radio broadcasting grew, the fees collected by ASCAP amounted to the
major share of the Society's income. When ASCAP proposed another increase
in royalty fees in 1937, the broadcasters finally rebelled. By 1939, they had
formed Broadcast Music, Incorporated (BMI), as their own rival music-
licensing organization, in preparation for a showdown at midnight, December
31, when the old ASCAP contract expired. At about the same time ASCAP
came under attack from the Department of Justice. Under this combined pressure, ASCAP reduced its demands to a point where they became acceptable to
the broadcasters. BMI continued in business, however. All stations are now
licensed by one or more of several music-licensing organizations, for which
they usually pay a percentage of their gross income; this arrangement avoids
the elaborate bookkeeping that per-performance royalties require.[11] Relations
between broadcasters and ASCAP remained uneasy and continue periodically
to flare up into controversy.

9.3 / Broadcast News

News, another important source of broadcast programming depending heavily
on syndication, also caused difficulty in the 1930's. From the first, news had
been a radio staple. It will be recalled (Section 7.2) that the very first broadcast of KDKA had been news of an election. Even in the experimental days,
one of the first practical applications of radiotelegraphy had been to reporting
news of yacht races in 1901 and 1903. The *New York Times* used radiotelegraphy in reporting the Russo-Japanese war (1904–1905).

One of the early discoveries about the use of news-related material in
broadcasting was that the medium lent itself ideally to commentary as well
as to straight news reporting. The pioneer commentator, H. V. Kaltenborn,
started such a series on WEAF in 1923. To his surprise, he found that the
same comments he wrote for his paper, the *Brooklyn Eagle*, without causing
a ripple of concern provoked sharp controversial reaction when spoken on
the radio.[12] He learned also that the executives of a company like AT&T,

---

[10] Fourth National Radio Conference, *Proceedings and Recommendations for Regulation
of Radio* (Washington: Government Printing Office, 1926), pp. 37–38.

[11] See Bruce Robertson, "A New Harmony for an Old Discord," *Broadcasting-Telecasting,* October 25, 1954, pp. 84–87, 103.

[12] See David G. Clark, "H. V. Kaltenborn's First Year on the Air," *Journalism Quarterly,*
XLII (Summer, 1965), 373–381.

the WEAF licensee, were hypersensitive to such reactions—so sensitive, in fact, that after only a few months, WEAF abruptly discontinued Kaltenborn's popular news-commentary program. Nevertheless, news commentary became a radio programming fixture by the late 1930's, when events leading up to the outbreak of World War II called urgently not only for fast reporting but also for interpretation.

Broadcasters distinguished between commentary made by a qualified individual in his own name, such as Kaltenborn, and a station editorial aired in the name of the licensee. An editorial, according to newspaper tradition, represents the *publisher's* point of view. By contrast, both station licensees (the equivalent of publishers) and the regulatory agency questioned the propriety of editorializing by licensees. Moreover, licensees (as in the case of AT&T and the Kaltenborn commentaries) were not prepared to face the adverse reactions controversial opinions inevitably provoke. Yet broadcasting could hardly lay claim to qualifying as a mature news medium as long as licensees declined the responsible role of opinion leadership long accepted by publishers. Not until 1949 did the FCC sanction editorializing by licensees, and only gradually and gingerly did stations take advantage of this right.

Meanwhile, the problem of access to the news had to be solved. Newspapers themselves had exploited each new communications medium to speed up transmission of news. Their interest, however, was in transmission to newspapers, not in transmission directly to the public. This bypassing of the written word seemed to threaten the very life of newspapers. Who would want to buy a paper to read news he had already heard on the radio?

In 1933, the three major American news agencies of that time—Associated Press, United Press, and International News Service—cut off services to radio stations. The networks tried to establish an independent news-gathering agency for broadcasting, but soon gave in to newspaper pressure. The press was even suggesting that Congress intervene with more restrictive legislation—an interesting proposition considering the devotion of the press to the First Amendment and freedom of speech.[13] The established agencies set up the Press-Radio Bureau (1934–1940), permitting stations to broadcast only ten minutes of wire-service news a day, and that only noncommercially and after the news had been published in newspapers. These terms were called "tyrannical and indefensible" by a United States Senator, who likewise criticized the networks for having "surrendered radio's birthright."[14]

This inequitable arrangement, so patently against the public interest, never did work effectively. Only about a third of the stations on the air subscribed to the Press-Radio Bureau service. Since the agreement exempted

---

[13] Llewellyn White, *The American Radio* (Chicago: University of Chicago Press, 1947), p. 46.

[14] Clarence C. Dill, "Radio and the Press: A Contrary View," *Annals of the American Academy of Political and Social Science*, CLXXVII (January, 1935), 170–175. The press side of the controversy is represented in the same publication by E. H. Harris, "Radio and the Press," 163–169.

"commentary," most radio newsmen became "commentators" overnight in order to evade the restrictions.[15] The United Press broke the embargo in 1935, soon to be joined by INS. The Press-Radio Bureau finally expired, unmourned, in 1940. After the press associations began to serve stations it became evident that radio news coverage, despite its ability to beat newspapers on spot news, actually did more to stimulate newspaper reading than to replace it (see the example quoted in Section 11.1). Eventually the wire services acquired even more broadcasters than publishers as customers.

Perhaps because of radio's frustrations in trying to handle news more conventionally, it turned to an unconventional format—dramatized recreation of news events, with actors impersonating the public figures of the day. *The March of Time,* inaugurated by CBS in 1931, had an extraordinary success, despite its questionable mixture of fictional form and factual content.

From the vantage of a later day it would seem wildly irresponsible and even illegal, but at the time it was a glorious game played with bravura by a brilliant company [of performers].[16]

Broadcasters developed radio's potentiality for instantaneous coverage of real-time news from distant points rather more slowly. Sporadic newscasts from overseas started as early as 1930, but not until the last years of the decade, after CBS made Edward R. Murrow its European news director, did overseas broadcast news begin to capitalize on radio's unique advantages. In 1937, when Murrow arrived in Europe, radio news chiefs overseas still spent their time rounding up inconsequential special-event stunts. "Radio was not yet an accepted part of the world of journalism," writes Murrow's biographer, "though it purveyed news of a sort on the periphery of its daily serials and musical programs."[17] The series of political crises that led to World War II soon put an end to the innocuous special-events programs, and Murrow, with others, began organizing complex roundups from capitals all over Europe and reporting "live" from the very fields of battle.

9.4 / Formats and Stars

In another area of radio programming, an accomplishment of the 1930's was the development of special techniques for adapting program materials to the radio medium. Radio introduced relatively little that is new. It turned out to be largely a synthetic or assimilative medium, which took over and adapted the basic communication forms and products of other media. At first, radio

---

[15] Robert R. Smith, "The Origins of Radio Network News Commentary," *Journal of Broadcasting,* IX (Spring, 1965), 113–122.

[16] Barnouw, *A Tower in Babel,* p. 277. The author speculates that the success of this program may have exacerbated the disagreement between broadcasting and the conventional news media.

[17] Kendrick, *op. cit.,* p. 139.

merely reproduced literally the products of the stage, platform, press, pulpit, and concert hall. The first radio dramas, for example, were simply remote broadcasts of unmodified stage performances. Soon producers realized that plays could be much more effective on radio when performed under studio conditions, with carefully coordinated music and sound effects. Loss of the visual element of drama could be offset by using suggestion, appealing to audience imagination, and capitalizing on the intimacy of the medium.

Writers of substance became intrigued by the potentialities of the medium, and in the late 1930's came an extraordinary flowering of radio drama, produced with consummate skill in real time (the networks still banned recordings), featuring such legendary figures as Orson Welles, Norman Corwin, Arch Oboler, Paul Robeson, and Archibald MacLeish. This creative outpouring was made possible by a chance combination of factors: the artistic excitement of exploring a new medium, the idealism and heightened feelings produced by the war psychology, the fat tax-free advertising budgets of wartime industry. It was, says Barnouw, "a byproduct of commercial affluence and had been financed by it, but had been done almost entirely in unsold time, as a result of an executive decision to use that time for more than fill-in purposes."[18] With the end of the war, the resumption of competitive selling, and the fateful diversion of radio-network income to support the infant television industry, this brief, luminous period of creative innovation came to an end.

On the commercial side, light comedy and daytime serials also began to flourish in the 1930's. The daytime serial, aimed at housewives and scheduled Monday through Friday, became especially attractive to sponsors of household products, such as soaps—whence the derisive name "soap opera." This format represented the ultimate refinement of broadcasting's technique for parsimonious consumption of program materials. Each episode carried the story forward by such a small step that plots could inch along for years. The soap opera has been characterized as "the great invention of radio, its single notable contribution to the art of fiction."[19] At their high-water mark, nearly fifty daytime serials could be heard each week, and some proved remarkably long-lived. Not until 1960 did the last of them leave the air, when first NBC and then CBS dropped the few survivors. *Ma Perkins* had endured for 7,065 installments and twenty-seven years![20]

Another distinctive invention of radio with no exact parallel in other media was the "disc jockey" or "DJ" format. This program type capitalizes on the popularity and relatively low cost of recorded music, and on the potentialities for psychological intimacy in the relationship between radio speaker and listener. The DJ projects an audience-pleasing personality while blending

---

[18] Barnouw, *The Golden Web,* p. 88.

[19] Gilbert Seldes, *The Great Audience* (New York: Viking, 1950), p. 113.

[20] Ward Quaal and Leo Martin, *Broadcast Management* (New York: Hastings House, 1968), p. 65.

musical recordings with commercials by means of informal spoken continuity. It is an inexpensive and infinitely flexible format, adaptable to every type of musical taste, to any time of the day or night, and to every class of listener. At first the DJ had rather low caste in the radio-talent hierarchy, but as the quality of recordings improved, so did the DJ's status. The pioneer star of the format, Martin Block, started a DJ program in 1935 which became the famous *Make Believe Ballroom* on WNEW, New York. "Block made disk jockeying pay," as a trade journal put it, "Ted Husing made it respectable, and television made it essential."[21] By the 1940's, top musical stars like Paul Whiteman and Tommy Dorsey were not above presiding over DJ programs. Relaxation of the networks' ban on recorded programs (Section 4.5 and 9.8) gave the final sanction to the DJ format.

When DJ's began to reach beyond the bare essentials of the format—conducting interviews, staging their programs in public places, receiving telephone calls from listeners while on the air—they spun off a whole series of variants. Arthur Godfrey became a network star, first in radio and then in television, by building on a personality and an approach developed in the local-station DJ school. Nighttime DJ's, finding audiences increasingly interested in discussion, began talking more and playing less. In many cases the music element finally disappeared altogether and the DJ was transformed into a radio pundit, a "talk master," who discusses every conceivable topic on the air with in-person guests and telephone callers. Some stations ultimately reached the final stage in this evolutionary process by scheduling *nothing* but discussion programs, twenty-four hours a day.

Radio discovered in the 1930's, as the cinema had discovered years before, that successful syndicated programming on a national scale depends in large measure on certain intangible assets possessed by star performers. These mass-appeal assets justify paying stars salaries which might seem entirely out of proportion to the intrinsic worth of their talents. Radio began to capitalize on the popularity of Hollywood stars in 1930, with *The First Nighter*. Control of talent was from the first an important factor in successful network operations, for which reason both NBC and CBS ran their own talent agencies until the practice was ruled out by the FCC. In the strategy of network competition, the ability of a network to command a lineup of top stars became as important as its ability to muster a lineup of top stations as affiliates.

9.5 / Network Developments

During this period of program evolution, parallel developments in the business operations of national networks had been taking place. Since the FCC limits any one owner to relatively few stations, the basic network-affiliate relationship is contractual rather than proprietary. From the rather loose, informal affiliation agreements in effect when NBC started, this contractual relationship

---

[21] "More than 'Make Believe'," *Broadcasting,* May 25, 1959, p. 116.

had been elaborated, primarily by CBS, into a fairly standardized form. A network offered three basic services to the affiliate: (1) it provided network programs; (2) it arranged for relaying programs from the originating point to the affiliate; (3) it sold some of the affiliate's time in the national market. Exigencies of selling made networks try to control aspects of affiliates' affairs.

In order for the network sales staff to have something definite to sell, affiliates contracted to make certain hours of the day available to the network on an optional basis ("option time"). That meant that the network could count on certain hours being available if it found customers, but was not saddled with the necessity of programming all these hours unless customers for them were found. In return for the network services, the affiliate usually gave a stipulated number of hours to the network free of charge. All income from these free hours went to the network. Income from the other hours optioned to the network was distributed among the affiliates according to agreed-on rates. In the late 1930's, NBC and CBS were distributing about a quarter of their total income among their affiliates.[22]

As a natural outcome of these arrangements, the networks sought to assure themselves of as much stability of coverage as possible. They insisted on access to the affiliate exclusive of other networks; long-term affiliation contracts; optioning all the affiliate's best time; discouraging affiliates from cancelling or rejecting network programs. The power and prestige of the network and the great value of the affiliation made the affiliate particularly susceptible to domination by the network. Yet the licensee of each individual station, network-affiliated or independent, is equally and uniquely responsible under the Communications Act for his own station's programs and conduct.

That CBS- and NBC-affiliated stations were tied to these networks with peculiarly powerful bonds became evident when the Mutual Broadcasting System attempted to expand into a national operation in the late 1930's in competition with the older chains. The latter had tied up all but two of the fifty-two major stations on clear channels and nearly 75 per cent of the powerful stations on regional channels. In 1938, these two networks handled over half the business of the radio industry.[23] At this time there were only 660 stations in operation. Many sizable communities had fewer than four stations. This meant that CBS and NBC (Red and Blue) could effectively prevent competition from Mutual in such communities by means of exclusive affiliation contracts.

Mutual's complaints prompted the FCC to make a thorough investigation of radio-network business practices in 1938. It concluded that the extent of control over the industry hitherto exercised by CBS and NBC was not in the public interest. The Communications Act empowers the FCC to "make special regulations applicable to radio stations engaged in chain [*i.e.,* network] broad-

---

[22] FCC, *Report on Chain Broadcasting*, pp. 41–42.

[23] *Ibid.*, p. 32.

casting."[24] Accordingly, the FCC adopted a set of "Chain Broadcasting Regulations" in 1941, aimed at relaxing the control of radio networks over their affiliates and opening the door to more competition from MBS. NBC and CBS fought the new rules bitterly, predicting that their adoption would mean the end of network broadcasting as it had been known and the negation of the achievements of the two pioneer networks. Not until 1942, four years after the investigation began, did the Supreme Court finally settle the struggle with a verdict in favor of the FCC rules.[25] Later the FCC extended the same rules to network television.

The most tangible outcome of the decision was the end of NBC's dual-network operation. NBC sold the Blue in 1943 to a candy manufacturer, Edward Noble, who changed its name to American Broadcasting Company (ABC) in 1945. The predicted collapse of the network system failed to materialize, though MBS began to expand rapidly.

9.6 / Development of RCA

The *Report on Chain Broadcasting* called attention to the growth of RCA, whose story we left at the point where NBC was founded in 1926. By 1930, two of the co-owners of NBC, General Electric and Westinghouse, had withdrawn, making the network a wholly-owned subsidiary of RCA. In 1932, an antitrust suit caused Westinghouse and General Electric to sell their stock in RCA itself, which thus became entirely independent of its parent companies. Meanwhile, RCA had set up subsidiaries to handle the maritime and point-to-point radio-communications business it had inherited from American Marconi. Radiomarine Corporation of America was incorporated in 1927 and RCA Communications in 1929. The class of business carried on by these subsidiaries, once the major business of RCA, has since come to represent only a minor source of income.

Also in 1929, RCA acquired control of the Victor Talking Machine Company, and in the following year it asserted its growing independence of GE and Westinghouse by going into the manufacture of receivers. RCA's manufacturing activities thereafter expanded into practically all fields of communication and electronics, including phonograph records and players, recording equipment, motion-picture projectors and sound equipment, public-address systems, aviation communication systems, electron microscopes, radio and television broadcast-station facilities, and many others.

---

[24] Section 303 (i). Note that the language of this provision confines the Commission to regulating individual stations, not networks as such. The FCC's only control over networks is thus indirect. Network organizations, as distinguished from stations, are neither licensed nor regulated directly by the FCC.

[25] *CBS* v. *U. S.*, 316 U. S. 407 (1942), and *NBC* v. *U. S.*, 316 U. S. 447 (1942). The Court voted 6 to 3 to uphold the FCC (Section 15.4).

Aside from its own manufacturing activities, RCA had an important influence on manufacturing by others. No salable radio receivers could be built without licenses from RCA for the use of patents it owned or controlled. This near-monopoly had long been a matter of concern to Congress; as early as 1923, the Federal Trade Commission had been directed to investigate the radio-patent situation. Its thorough report[26] had a great deal of influence in subsequent Congressional hearings and even on the Radio Act of 1927. It indirectly brought about the antitrust suits of 1930 and 1932, which led to the withdrawal of GE and Westinghouse from ownership in RCA. The relaxation of RCA's licensing terms resulted in the successful development of a number of rival manufacturers in the 1930's, such as Zenith, Emerson, and Philco. Although paying royalties to RCA for patent rights, these companies were able to compete effectively against RCA, whose great size made it somewhat sluggish compared with the lighter-weight newcomers.[27]

NBC, as a broadcasting network, therefore constitutes only one province in a great communications empire. At the time of the Chain Broadcasting Investigation, that empire even included a talent agency and concert-booking service. But the FCC pointed out that:

As agent for artists, NBC is under a fiduciary duty to procure the best terms possible *for* the artists. As employer of artists, NBC is interested in securing the best terms possible *from* the artists. NBC's dual role necessarily prevents arm's length bargaining and constitutes a serious conflict of interest.[28]

In summarizing the extent of NBC's and RCA's influence, the Commission concluded:

It is significant that these numerous and, for the most part, critically important activities require a capital investment which, in other fields of enterprise, would not be regarded as staggering. The assets of RCA barely exceed $100,000,000; many a railroad, utility, bank, insurance company, or industrial establishment of relatively secondary importance has assets double or treble this amount. This tends to make RCA comparatively independent of the money market.

RCA, like many other giant enterprises today, is a "management corporation." It has nearly 250,000 stockholders. No one owns as much as half of 1 per cent of its stock. In such circumstances, stockholder control is practically nonexistent. RCA's funded debt is small, so there is no substantial creditor influence on the management. As a result, the management is essentially self-perpetuating, and the responsibility of the executives and directors is largely intramural.

In short, RCA occupies a premier position in fields which are profoundly determinative of our way of life. Its diverse activities give it a peculiarly advantageous position in competition with enterprises less widely based. Its policies are

---

[26] FTC, *Report on the Radio Industry* (Washington: Government Printing Office, 1924).

[27] W. Rupert Maclaurin, *Invention and Innovation in the Radio Industry* (New York: Macmillan, 1949), p. 248.

[28] FCC, *Report on Chain Broadcasting,* p. 17. Italics supplied.

determined by a management subject to little restraint other than self-imposed. Whether this ramified and powerful enterprise with its consistent tendency to grow and to expand into new fields at the expense of smaller independent concerns is desirable, is not to be decided here. We have thought it proper, however, to call the attention of Congress and the public to the broader problems raised by this concentration of power in the hands of a single group.[29]

9.7 / Growth of CBS

Though not in the same corporate class with NBC, CBS also came in for a share of criticism in the Chain Broadcasting Investigation. Like NBC, Columbia had its own recording company and its own talent-booking agency. Columbia had taken the lead in evolving the restrictive network-affiliation contracts to which the FCC objected—contracts developed by Columbia in its efforts to compete with NBC. CBS had succeeded so well in these efforts that at the time of the investigation its net income was actually greater than that of NBC, despite the fact that NBC had both the Red and Blue networks.[30] The Blue, however, had been used by NBC more as a foil than as an all-out competitor with CBS. In 1938 the Red stations carried 75 per cent of NBC's commercial programs.[31] The fact is that during the easygoing years of the 1930's there was enough national business and enough high-caliber talent available to support two major networks (regarding NBC as one for the moment) without competition between the two becoming strident.

A new, more competitive era began in the 1940's, however, with four radio networks instead of two competing for the national advertiser's dollar. Moreover, by 1945, over nine hundred stations operated as against fewer than seven hundred in the 1930's (Figure 9.1).

CBS challenged NBC, now shorn of its Blue network, to an all-out battle for the number-one network position. It might seem that in such a battle NBC would have insuperable advantages because of the enormous resources of its parent company, RCA. But just as in the case of the set manufacturers who competed successfully with RCA Victor, Columbia could take advantage of greater maneuverability. One Columbia maneuver was to capture the lead in programming. Another was to delay the coming of television as long as possible in order to give CBS time to develop its own television potentiality.

In 1948, CBS made a celebrated "talent raid" on NBC, buying up many of the top-ranking stars of radio, such as "Amos 'n' Andy," Jack Benny, Burns and Allen, Edgar Bergen, and Bing Crosby. The CBS program strategy was based on (1) recapturing control of network programming and talent from the advertising agencies and (2) building up an overwhelmingly strong radio-talent position. By 1949, CBS was well ahead of NBC in radio time sales and

---

[29] *Ibid.,* p. 20.

[30] *Ibid.,* pp. 17, 24.

[31] *Ibid.,* p. 70.

could claim all ten of the top-rated radio programs. CBS designed these moves to build up radio income for the developmental period during which network radio would have to support network television, as well as to provide a talent pool to draw on as television programming moved out of the experimental into the competitive phase.[32]

9.8 / Mutual and ABC

The Mutual Broadcasting System, whose complaints had precipitated the Chain Broadcasting Investigation, started on a different basis from the other networks. Originally, the two remaining nonnetwork-affiliated major stations on clear channels, WGN, Chicago, and WOR, New York, arranged to sell time jointly with WXYZ, Detroit, and WLW, Cincinnati. The four stations exchanged programs on a network basis. Their chief asset was *The Lone Ranger,* a program started by WXYZ in 1933. Thus MBS was a network owned by stations, rather than a network owning stations. The only way it could expand, of course, was by signing up small stations. Some of the regional networks joined MBS in a body. In the postwar period, the number of small stations increased sharply. By 1948, Mutual had passed the five-hundred mark and advertised itself as "the world's largest network." Of course the number of affiliates in a network is not in itself significant, since one 50,000-w. station on a Clear Channel in a densely populated area has more coverage than scores of 250-w. stations on local channels in rural areas.

The American Broadcasting Company automatically assumed the third rank among the networks when it separated from NBC. The Blue had the advantage of bringing with it a respectable stable of strong affiliates, but it was weak commercially. Like Mutual, ABC had to seek new sources of advertising revenue and new program materials and talent.

ABC and Mutual originated the practice of tapping local advertisers for network revenue, since there were not enough national and regional advertisers to go around. MBS's *Kate Smith Show* was the first major program to be sold cooperatively; instead of one big national sponsor, over two hundred local advertisers shared the bill. The first major nighttime network program sold cooperatively was ABC's *Abbott and Costello,* in 1947.

ABC and Mutual shattered another tradition by using recordings on network programs. In the earliest days of broadcasting, recordings had been frowned on as a fraud on the public. The Department of Commerce actually forbade their use at one time, and one of the earliest rules of the FRC (General Order No. 16, August 9, 1927) required that recordings be clearly announced as such. From the point of view of NBC and CBS, of course, the most valuable asset of networks was bringing major *live-talent* programs to national audiences. The fantastically complex dramatic programs of radio's golden age were all produced live, as were the elaborate wartime news round-

---

[32] See "CBS Steals the Show," *Fortune,* July, 1953, pp. 79–82, 164–166.

ups from dozens of widely separated geographical centers. ABC started using transcribed programs in 1946, quickly followed by MBS. CBS relaxed the long-standing ban for one-time playback of network programs in 1947. Not until 1949, however, did both NBC and CBS permit general use of recordings.[33]

9.9 / Advent of FM

Frequency-modulation (FM) radio introduced another new element to the broadcasting picture of the 1940's. The principle of frequency modulation had long been recognized, the first United States patent on the principle dating back to 1905. But practical application did not become possible until Edwin Armstrong improved the FM technique in 1933 (Section 2.4). Armstrong made his find public at an Institute of Radio Engineers convention in 1935, precipitating the "biggest and bitterest behind-the-scenes fight in radio's career."[34] Armstrong, a man of singular persistence and conviction, fought against the skepticism (not to speak of the outright hostility) of the radio industry. During 1934–1935, he carried out tests, with the cooperation of RCA, from a transmitter site on the Empire State Building. Unfortunately for Armstrong and the cause of FM, RCA had already made deep commitments to the future of television, and it later displaced Armstrong's transmitter in favor of television experiments. In 1937, the inventor built his own transmitter, W2XMN, at Alpine, New Jersey. Armstrong always contended that RCA had deliberately tried to scuttle FM.[35] In 1965, the wheel came full circle with installation of an array of thirty-two FM antennas atop the Empire State Building. Unfortunately Armstrong did not live to see this vindication; he died by his own hand in 1954. The Alpine station later became the Armstrong Field Station for Electronic Research of Columbia University.

The FCC first became interested in the new medium in 1935, and after hearings in 1936, allocated experimental channels to FM. But soon FM again conflicted with television, this time in frequency allocation. In 1939, the FCC allocated nineteen channels to television but only thirteen to FM.

If the Commission and the industry had recognized the future importance of frequency modulation, the FM allocation would have been more generous. For it was

---

[33] On rare occasions, the networks had relaxed the recording ban, for example to broadcast an on-the-spot description of the Hindenburg dirigible fire of 1937, and a BBC eyewitness account of aerial dogfights over the British coast in the opening phases of the Battle of Britain. [Barnouw, *The Golden Web,* p. 109, and Kendrick, *op. cit.,* p. 200.]

[34] "Revolution in Radio," *Fortune,* October, 1939, p. 86.

[35] Testimony of Edwin Armstrong in Senate Committee on Interstate and Foreign Commerce, *Progress of FM Radio: Certain Changes Involving Development of FM Radio and RCA Patent Policies,* Hearings 80th Cong., 2d Sess. (Washington: Government Printing Office, 1948), pp. 11–20 *et passim.* See also Lawrence Lessing, *Man of High Fidelity: Edwin Howard Armstrong* (New York: J. B. Lippincott, 1956), *passim.*

FM rather than television which was on the verge of immediate commercial development. This initial mistake proved difficult to rectify.[36]

In 1940, the FCC moved FM to channels in the 42–50-mc. band and authorized commercial operation. By this time, America was about to plunge into World War II, and a freeze on construction and manufacturing soon halted the free development of FM. Nevertheless, thirty FM stations were on the air by 1942. In 1945, however, because of another extensive hearing and highly controversial engineering evidence, the FCC moved FM up to the 88–108-mc. band (Table 3.2). This was a serious blow, since it outmoded all the receiving sets built originally for the lower band. Most of the major AM stations still felt obliged to take out FM licenses, as insurance against the possibility that FM really would displace AM, as its enthusiasts predicted. FM licenses reached a high-water mark in 1948, when over a thousand were outstanding. But in 1948, television began to expand rapidly, and the number of FM stations began to decline (Figure 9.1). Most FM stations became relatively meaningless satellites of AM stations, merely duplicating AM programs. The few independently operated FM stations, as a group, consistently lost money.

In 1949, 212 commercial FM stations went off the air, and as Figure 9.1 shows, the total authorizations continued to decline year by year. With most FM stations duplicating programs already available on AM and with cheap FM receivers unable to reproduce the full potential range of FM sound, the public had little incentive to invest in FM-equipped receivers.

FM channels are designed to allow incorporation of a variety of subsidiary services by multiplexing (Section 2.6), or in some cases by simplexing (temporary displacement of the regular broadcast service by another service). In the 1940's, broadcast facsimile on FM channels caused a flurry of interest; it was thought a market might be created for newspapers reproduced on home facsimile print-out machines, but the idea failed to catch on. The FCC issues Subsidiary Communications Authorizations to FM stations, permitting them to multiplex a variety of nonbroadcast subscription services in FM channels. These supplementary services, known collectively as "functional FM," include background music for places of business and waiting rooms ("musicasting," "storecasting"), public transportation ("transitcasting"),[37] and the like. Many other more specialized services have been suggested, including even transmission of slow-scan still pictures to accompany radio talks.[38]

---

[36] Maclaurin, *op. cit.,* pp. 229–230. See also testimony of Edwin Armstrong in Senate Committee on Interstate and Foreign Commerce, *op. cit.,* p. 16.

[37] In a suit to enjoin transitcasting as an invasion of privacy, the Supreme Court upheld the right of the broadcasters by a narrow margin. See *Public Utilities Commission of the District of Columbia, et al.* v. *Pollak,* 343 U. S. 451 (1952).

[38] Such experimental services are described in Lorne A. Parker, *SCA: A New Medium* (Madison: University of Wisconsin, 1969).

By 1956, a reverse trend in the number of FM authorizations had set in (Figure 9.1). In 1961, the FCC authorized multiplexing stereophonic sound for a growing audience of "hi-fi" enthusiasts. In 1965, the Commission moved to stop some of the wasteful duplication of programming by commonly-owned AM/FM stations, ruling that in cities of more than a hundred thousand people, at least half the time such FM stations had to be programmed separately. In addition to the factors already cited, the growing popularity of FM can be ascribed to a new market for highly specialized, even esoteric, programming (Section 11.2). By 1970, in some larger cities, where FM flourishes best, as many as three-quarters of the households had FM receivers. An industry committee was even proposing a law to require all radios to be equipped to receive both AM and FM. Such a law would have a precedent in the one requiring all television receivers to be equipped for both UHF and VHF reception (Section 10.4). Armstrong's dream seemed well on the way to coming true at last.[39]

9.10 / The Noncommercial Service

Meanwhile, as indicated at the close of Chapter 7, in sharp contrast to commercial broadcasting, the fortunes of educational, noncommercial stations had been declining during this period. Failure of most educational institutions to defend their original AM assignments against the raids of commercial interests merely confirmed what some had said from the first: a share of the AM frequencies should have been set aside at the outset exclusively for educational use. Educational interests could not reasonably be expected to compete with commercial interests in the open market for the use of radio channels. This point of view revived when Congress began to consider revising the Radio Act of 1927. A proposal to reserve channels for education became a major issue during Congressional debates on the Communications Act of 1934. The only way to have made such reservations, however, would have been to take back assignments already made to commercial operators, since few desirable unused assignments remained. In order not to delay passage of the Act, the supporters of educational reservations agreed to a compromise: a provision in the Act [§ 307(c)] requiring the FCC to report to Congress on the advisability of allocating "fixed percentages of radio broadcasting facilities to particular types or kinds of nonprofit radio programs or to persons identified with particular types or kinds of nonprofit activities."

The FCC duly reported in January, 1935, that in its opinion, existing commercial stations gave ample opportunity for educational programming, so that no special allocation of frequencies for this purpose was needed. In order to bring about the fullest educational use of existing facilities, however, the FCC

---

[39] Overall FM profitability improved, but not as rapidly as the number of authorizations. According to FCC financial data for 1968, FM-only stations as a group still operated in the red, with 433 station reporting a $3.9 million loss.

encouraged the formation of a tripartite industry-government-education committee. Accordingly, the Federal Radio Education Committee (FREC) was set up, comprising over forty leading educators and industry representatives.

In the next few years, the industry and such sources as the Rockefeller Foundation, the Payne Fund, and the Kellogg Fund gave support. The First National Conference on Educational Broadcasting in 1936 was attended by over seven hundred people, twenty-five of them from foreign countries, fifty-nine from the industry. Government officials such as the Secretary of the Interior, the United States Commissioner of Education, and the Chairman of the FCC addressed the Conference. Many high-minded things were said, and everyone agreed that the educational potential of radio was incalculable; in fact, the general atmosphere of enthusiasm and optimism accurately presaged the euphoria surrounding the advent of educational television twenty years later. Even some of the phrases used were identical. Said the FCC Chairman in 1936: "Radio, properly used, can become an even greater instrument of instruction than the printing press."[40] But the high hopes faded and the activities of the FREC dwindled until the 1950's when they ceased altogether, though without any formal announcement of dissolution. Networks gave up their educational showpieces, for example, the CBS daily *American School of the Air* (1930–1948). In practice, the solution proposed by the FCC simply did not work.

Tacitly acknowledging this fact, the FCC in 1945 reversed its previous thinking when the opportunity arose to allocate FM channels.[41] The Commission put twenty FM channels in a special classification exclusively for noncommercial educational broadcasting. In view of the small audience for FM and the limited demand for licenses at the time, this may not seem like a particularly bold gesture, but it did have great significance as a precedent-setting move. The educational FM reservations established the *principle* of withholding a portion of broadcast facilities from commercial use. The later, much more radical, proposal to reserve television channels for education therefore came as less of a shock.

In order to stimulate use of the FM reserved frequencies, the FCC in 1948 liberalized its rules to permit informal operation of very low-power (10 w.) noncommercial stations. Syracuse University, which had cooperated with General Electric in developing low-cost transmission facilities for the 10-w. stations, received the first grant under the revised rules in October, 1948. Many schools which otherwise would not have had sufficient funds for a

---

[40] C. S. Marsh, ed., *Educational Broadcasting, 1936: Proceedings of the First National Conference on Educational Broadcasting* (Chicago: University of Chicago Press, 1937), p. 18.

[41] The first educational FM reservations had been made in 1940, when the FCC made the initial (and abortive) allocation for regular FM operations. At that time five of the forty channels were earmarked for education.

station took advantage of the new rules, and educational FM authorizations have continued to grow (Figure 9.1).[42]

Despite the mild success of educational FM, however, it remained for television to provide the real challenge. FM reservations involved no commercial sacrifice. Television reservations did. With television, the original fervor of educators for broadcasting revived—this time with a difference: this time they prepared to battle uncompromisingly for reserved educational channels.

9.11 / The Eve of Television

The post-World War II era for broadcasting began officially on October 8, 1945, the date on which the FCC returned to peacetime licensing procedures. The years 1937–1944 had been extremely prosperous for the radio industry. The wartime lack of goods to sell had no adverse effect. Indeed, the government's ruling that advertising could be deducted from taxable income as a business expense greatly encouraged large advertising budgets to keep trade names fresh in the public mind. Total annual revenue had more than doubled, and income had risen from twenty cents on the dollar of revenue to thirty-three cents. In 1944 alone, the income of the industry amounted to more than 100 per cent of the value of tangible broadcast property, computed at original cost.[43] Little wonder that the resumption of peace-time licensing found would-be licensees waiting in line to qualify for a share in so lucrative a business. Most of the new licenses were for Class IV or Class II stations located in smaller cities. Whereas at the close of the war only 2 per cent of cities under five thousand people and only 13 per cent of cities of five to ten thousand had stations, within less than two years 16 per cent and 43 per cent of these two classes of communities respectively had radio stations. The total number of radio communities nearly doubled in a sixteen-month period.[44]

Many new stations, located in communities not hitherto served by local stations, opened up sources of local advertising revenue not previously available to radio. As competition grew, they enticed more and more small local businesses into using radio advertising. After all, only a limited number of companies were large enough to use national or regional advertising at the network level; the great unexploited potential lay in the tens of thousands of

---

[42] Nearly four hundred quasi-broadcast educational stations also operate on a campus "wired-wireless basis." They impose a low-level radio signal on the campus electrical-wire network. The signal radiates only a few feet from the wires, so that it does not cause interference but can be picked up by ordinary receivers in dormitories and other on-campus locations. Wired-wireless is not a licensed system, but it must comply with FCC-imposed limits on radiation strength.

[43] FCC, *Public Service Responsibility of Broadcast Licensees* (Washington: Government Printing Office, 1946), pp. 48, 49.

[44] FCC, "An Economic Study of Standard Broadcasting" (FCC mimeo., 1947), p. 1.

small, local merchants. Until 1945, network advertisers (*i.e.,* national and regional advertisers) had contributed the largest share of radio's revenue. In 1947, for the first time, revenue from local advertisers surpassed that from network advertisers (Figure 13.4).

Increased radio competition made itself felt in the program field in forms both good and bad. The emphasis on selling led to an emphasis on program ratings which amounted to a fetish. Reciprocally, a tendency developed toward programs which would "buy" audiences and thereby inflate ratings artificially, *e.g.,* the "giveaway" program, which reached a zenith in 1948. On the local level, the narrow margin of profit of the smaller, independent stations made it difficult to turn down advertising of doubtful ethical standing, and a resurgence of some of the pitchman and patent-medicine-show atmosphere of the earliest days of radio occurred. On the other hand, competition shook the industry out of its complacency and stimulated more imaginative, creative programming. Many stations took the advice that the FCC offered in its 1947 study on the outlook for the industry and began to serve special minority groups which had hitherto not seemed important enough to merit more than passing attention.[45]

By 1948, the history of sound broadcasting in America reached a transition point. Now television began to monopolize public attention. In 1947, Bob Hope scored 30.2 in the Hooper ratings, Jack Benny 27. By 1950, their ratings had tumbled to 2.5 and 5.8. As the "golden age" of radio drew to a close, two of the national radio networks had already taken out insurance against the future by getting a foothold in television. ABC's role was as yet doubtful. Mutual's radio position was precarious, for it depended on small stations, many of which might be expected to suffer as the effects of the television service penetrated more deeply into the country.

Pessimists in 1948 foresaw a bleak future for radio in the face of television's seemingly overwhelming advantages. But already adaptations were beginning, some of which have been pointed out in the present chapter, eventually resulting in a remarkable resurgence of sound broadcasting. In order to view this resurgence in context, however, we will first pick up the thread of television development in the next chapter, postponing comparisons until the succeeding chapter.

---

[45] A *Sponsor* survey in 1955 revealed marked regional preferences for specialized services. For example, 40 per cent of the stations surveyed in New Jersey reported concert music as a specialized service; 48 per cent of Texas stations reported farm programs; 36 per cent of New York stations reported foreign-language programs; 60 per cent of Arizona stations reported Mexican programs; 66 per cent of Alabama stations reported Negro programs; 29 per cent of Georgia stations reported religious programs. [*Sponsor,* July 11, 1955, p. 55.]

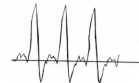

10

TELEVISION:
THE FIRST TWO
DECADES

The de Forest radio transmitter shown in Figure 10.1, first put on the air on August 20, 1920, was put back into operation fifty years later to celebrate the golden anniversary of broadcasting. A receiver built in 1920 to pick up its signals could still pick up the signals of *any* AM broadcast station half a century later. A similar statement could not be made about television receiver-transmitter relationships. Herein lies a significant difference between the technologies of the two media, a difference which delayed the advent of full-scale commercial television service for years. This difference is due to what has been called the "lock-and-key" relationship of the television transmitter and receiver.[1] It will be recalled (Section 3.4) that the television receiver must do more than detect and amplify the television signal. It must also carry out the precisely timed scanning sequence in exact synchronism with the camera. Unless both transmitter and receiver operate on the same line and field frequencies, and unless the receiver is designed to receive and interpret specific synchronizing signals, the key will not fit the lock.

This fact presented the FCC with a problem of timing. The moment that standards for full-scale commercial operation were agreed on, the technology of television might be frozen at that point of its development. Once having bought a large number of receivers, the public obviously acquires a vested interest in the system on which those receivers operate. On the other hand, the longer the FCC delayed permitting full-scale commercial development, the longer the public was denied the television service, the less opportunity manufacturers had to test their products in the market, and the less the free play of competition could contribute to the development of the medium.

---

[1] Testimony of FCC Chairman James Lawrence Fly in Senate Committee on Interstate Commerce, *Development of Television,* Hearings on S. Res. 251 (Washington: Government Printing Office, 1940), p. 7.

Figure 10.1
Detroit's WWJ transmitter in 1920

Fifty years later, WWJ fired up this historic transmitter once more to celebrate radio broadcasting's golden anniversary.

Source: WWJ, Detroit.

10.1 / Evolution of the Television System

Television, as a potentiality, had existed quite as long as radio itself (Figure 5.1). It is rooted, like radio, in the earlier art of wire transmission. Experiments in sending still and moving pictures by wire during the nineteenth century led to development of the wirephoto service. All early attempts at devising a practical television system, however, eventually reached the same impasse: dependence on mechanical moving parts imposed insurmountable limits on the number of lines per picture. As explained in Section 3.1, this meant unsatisfactory picture definition, keeping television in the class of an interesting curiosity. Higher-definition, all-electronic systems were envisaged at the time, but the necessary technology was not yet available.

Most promising of the mechanical devices was the scanning wheel, invented in 1884 by a German, Paul Nipkow. The wheel consisted of a disc pierced by a series of spirally positioned holes. One revolution of the disc scanned a scene in successive lines. As can be seen from the illustration in Figure 10.2,

Figure 10.2
Mechanical television scanning systems

A

B

A. Scanning-disc receiver of 1927. The wheel contains fifty spirally positioned apertures which scan the field with as many lines with each revolution. Note the small image area (the postage-stamp-sized rectangle in the plate at which the viewer gazes) compared with the size of the wheel.

B. Attempted solution of the screen-size problem by Bell Telephone Laboratories, 1927. *Left:* Rear view, showing electric-motor-driven arm which sweeps over twenty-five hundred contacts leading by wire to as many light bulbs, each representing a picture element. *Right:* Viewing screen, with its grid of twenty-five hundred tiny lights, arranged in fifty lines. For an approximation of the resolution capability of such systems, see the fifty-line picture in Figure 3.1.

Source: Bell Telephone Laboratories.

even a relatively large wheel could scan an image not much larger than a postage stamp.

Much effort nevertheless went into attempts to develop and promote mechanical systems in the late 1920's and early 1930's. In America, C. F. Jenkins demonstrated a crude but workable system in 1925 (illustrated in Figure 10.3) and in 1930 started a company to exploit it. In Britain, John Baird obtained an experimental television license in 1926. Despite official skepticism and opposition, Baird and his associates persuaded the British Broadcasting Corporation to start experimental telecasting in 1929 with a mechanical 30-line system. These experiments continued until 1935, with gradual improvements in performance. Meanwhile, British Marconi had joined forces with Electrical and Musical Industries, Ltd. (EMI), to work on a rival electronic system.

Figure 10.3
Charles Jenkins (1867–1934)

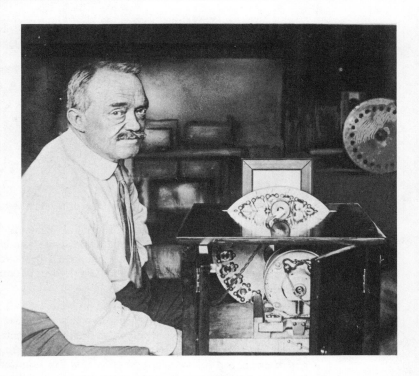

Jenkins demonstrates the mechanical scanning-disc receiver he tried to market in 1925.

Source: National Broadcasting Company.

In 1936, the BBC started regular public telecasting, at first using the Baird and EMI systems side by side. Baird's persistence thus nagged the BBC into establishing the world's first regular television service. But in winning the battle Baird lost the war. Even at the outset, the EMI electronic system, with its 405 lines and 50 fields per second, obtained over three times the definition of Baird's 240 lines and 25 fields per second, and the BBC soon standardized on the EMI apparatus. The BBC paid the penalty of being first, however, for it had settled on too low a line frequency and in 1964 introduced a second system in the UHF band approximating the definition that had meanwhile been adopted in America (Section 3.5 and Table 3.1).

In America, H. E. Ives of AT&T's research laboratories did pioneer work on a complete electronic television system in the 1920's. His primary interest was the problem of picture transmission by wire. Ives sent a closed-circuit television picture of Secretary of Commerce Herbert Hoover from Washington to New York in 1927 in a public demonstration, and in 1929 he even transmitted color pictures. These experiments were important as background for the development of AT&T's coaxial-cable and microwave relay facilities, essential components of a national television system.[2]

Two individual inventors not connected with the major research laboratories also made important contributions—Philo Farnsworth and Allen B. Dumont. Farnsworth's inventions blocked RCA's efforts to obtain patents on a completely independent system, reviving the patent struggle of earlier radio days. When Farnsworth won a long-standing patent suit against RCA in 1941, the contenders compromised by making a cross-licensing agreement. (See Figure 10.4.)

Dumont had early experience in radio and television research through association with Westinghouse and de Forest as a specialist in vacuum-tube design. In 1931, he went into business for himself manufacturing the oscilloscope (cathode-ray) tube, a basic tool of electronic research, essentially similar to the television receiving tube. Demand for these tubes increased rapidly during the 1930's, putting Dumont in a position to capitalize on the television-receiver market when it finally opened up in the 1940's. In fact, Dumont marketed the first American home television receiver as early as 1939.[3] However, mass-produced television receivers were not introduced until after World War II, when RCA began marketing a table model with a 10-inch picture tube. Another pioneer inventor, E. F. W. Alexanderson, famous for the Alexander-

---

[2] In the period 1925–1935, AT&T spent over $2 million in laboratory research on television and coaxial cables—a substantial investment, though representing only about 4 per cent of AT&T's total research bill for the period. [FCC, *Investigation of the Telephone Industry in the United States* (Washington: Government Printing Office, 1939), p. 199.]

[3] Dumont was remarkable for being "one of the very few inventors in the annals of American industry who have made more money from their inventions than anyone else has." Significantly, however, he had to sell a half interest in the Dumont Laboratories to Paramount Pictures in 1938 in order to finance expansion of the firm. See Robert Rice, "The Prudent Pioneer," *The New Yorker*, January 27, 1951, pp. 35–49.

Figure 10.4

Farnsworth's television camera in use

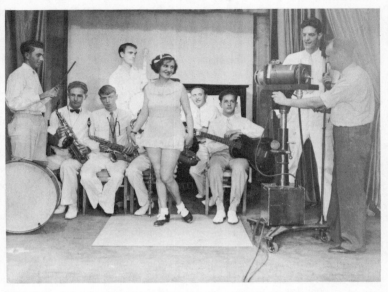

An experimental 1935 production using a single camera without benefit of a viewfinder.

Source: International News Photo.

son alternator (Section 6.6), made experimental television broadcasts in 1928 with a hybrid system over General Electric's Schenectady station.

But the inventor most prominent in the development of electronic television was Vladimir Zworykin, whose interest in the field dated back to his graduate studies in Russia, prior to his emigration to the United States in 1919. Zworykin applied in 1923 for the first patent on an electronic pickup tube, which he called the iconoscope (illustrated in Figure 3.5). In 1930, Zworykin became one of a celebrated team of engineers brought together when General Electric, RCA, and Westinghouse merged their several television research programs at the RCA laboratories in Camden, New Jersey. In addition to Zworykin, the group included Alexanderson, W. W. Engstrom, and about forty other engineers.

The Camden team mounted a systematic attack on all aspects of television development, investigating not only technological problems, but also the subjective question of standards required to win public acceptance of television as a regular service. Up to this point, public interest had been artificially inflated by the curiosity value of television. No one knew for sure how good it had to be to win mass acceptance as a home communications service rather

Figure 10.5
Sarnoff unveiling electronic television at World's Fair

At its first large-scale public demonstration in America in 1939, electronic television approached modern standards.

Source: Radio Corporation of America.

than an occasional novelty. The RCA audience studies made it apparent that higher definition had to be obtained than any existing apparatus could provide. This, in turn, meant concentration on developing an all-electronic system.

During the 1930's, the RCA Camden team tackled and solved all the outstanding problems. In the beginning, they used a hybrid mechanicoelectronic system of 60 lines, producing a picture only 2 inches wide. They gradually improved definition by increasing line and field frequency (Figure 3.1). They increased image size and brightness, eliminated the mechanical feature, adapted their equipment to the VHF frequency band, introduced interlace scanning, started pilot-receiver manufacturing (with a 9-inch picture tube), introduced sets experimentally into homes. This decade of intense, systematic developmental activity culminated in a crucial public demonstration of a 441-line electronic system in 1939 at the World's Fair in New York City (Figure 10.5).[4] There, for the first time, the general American public saw television in action.

---

[4] For further details on the work of the Camden team, see Robert C. Bitting, Jr., "Creating an Industry," *Journal of the Society of Motion Picture and Television Engineers,* LXXIV (November, 1965), 1015–1023.

10.2 / Development of American Television Standards

As far back as 1928, the FRC had made provision for experimental "picture broadcasting."[5] Regular experimental telecasting by NBC's W2XBS began in that year. It took until 1941, however, for the W2XBS successor to receive the first commercial license as WNBT, the NBC flagship station. CBS, which started experimental television broadcasts in 1931 over W2XAB, was authorized to begin commercial operations the same day as WNBT. In 1940, the FCC began hearings on proposals for adopting television standards looking toward full-scale commercial exploitation of the medium. The industry, through the Radio Manufacturers Association (RMA), proposed a 441-line picture at 30 frames per second, using 6-mc. channels. But the companies chiefly concerned—RCA, CBS, Dumont, Zenith, and Philco—were by no means unanimously behind the RMA recommendations. RCA, with the biggest investment in research, was naturally anxious to start capitalizing on its premier patent position as soon as possible. The other companies were less eager. In view of the industry's lack of agreement, the FCC was unwilling to adopt the RMA standards; instead, it tried to compromise by permitting *limited* commercial operation for the sake of further experimentation and field testing, without adopting uniform standards.[6] These new rules, scheduled to go into effect September 1, were announced by the FCC at the end of February, 1940. They would have permitted at least three different and incompatible systems to operate—those proposed by RCA (the RMA standards), Philco, and Dumont.

RCA immediately began an all-out sales campaign to market television receivers. This was precisely what the FCC had tried to avoid in limiting commercial operation. The Commission had hoped that the manufacturers would proceed slowly, without attempting to develop the mass market for receivers before universal standards could be agreed on. Television had been so long delayed and so heavily publicized that vigorous sales campaigns at this time could have eventually resulted in strong pressure to adopt the system used by the company that succeeded in selling the most sets.

The FCC acted decisively. On May 22, it withdrew the February decision and called a new hearing. To many, the Commission's action seemed not only capricious but an attack on free enterprise. A Congressional investigation of the Commission ensued.[7]

To appreciate the pressures at work in this situation, we must recollect that

---

[5] FRC, *Third Annual Report* (Washington: Government Printing Office, 1929), pp. 55–56.

[6] Experimental television licenses had been issued since 1928, but experimental stations could not sell time; their purpose was to experiment with engineering rather than programming. Extensive development of programming necessarily had to wait until time could be sold commercially; by the same token, mass marketing of sets had to wait for programming. By "limited" commercial operation, the FCC intended to open the door to experimentation in programming as well as in engineering.

[7] Senate Committee on Interstate Commerce, *op. cit.*

millions of dollars had already been spent on research on electronic television systems—not to speak of the money that had gone into mechanical systems. RCA alone, in the years 1930–1939, had spent at least $9 million.[8] Many more millions would have to be spent before stations, networks, and manufacturing facilities could be developed to the point where a profit would be made.

To eliminate the possibility that the standards might be influenced by one manufacturer more than another, a new industry-wide committee of engineers, the National Television System Committee (NTSC), was set up to recommend standards. By March, 1941, the NTSC was ready with a new proposal, and finally, in May, 1941, the FCC authorized full commercial operation on these standards on eighteen VHF channels, located between 50 and 294 mc.[9] The NTSC had changed the line standard from 441 to 525, adopted FM rather than AM for the audio component of the signal, and left three different synchronizing methods to compete (RCA's finally won out). CBS pressed for the adoption of color-television standards, but the NTSC believed that not enough was yet known about this art to adopt standards at that time.

Monochrome-television standards as we know them today in the United States date from this FCC decision of 1941. After all the long years of research and experimentation and many false starts, television seemed at last ready to come into its own. But the end of delays had not come yet. Before manufacturers could tool up for mass production, and before new stations could be built and put into operation, the United States entered World War II. On April 22, 1942, all production on such civilian goods as radio and television sets came to a halt. Only six pioneer experimental stations operated during the war years, with only about ten thousand receivers in use.

Nor did the resumption of licensing in 1945 lead to an immediate resumption of television activity. The postwar shortage of materials made it impossible to build stations or manufacture sets immediately. Before the shortages had been overcome, CBS once more raised the issue of color. During the war, much had been learned about the hitherto little-known possibilities of the Ultra-High-Frequency (300–3,000-mc.) band. Previously, the upper limit of the usable radio spectrum had been considered 300 mc.; by the end of the war the limit had been extended to 30,000 mc. This encouraged CBS to contend that television should move into a higher frequency range, where there would be room for the wide channels presumably needed for color. Since the two systems—existing monochrome and proposed CBS color—were incompatible, a choice between them would ultimately have to be made. In the meantime, manufacturers and potential station licensees, unwilling to risk betting on the wrong horse, preferred to wait for clarification of the issue. When the war ended, 158 applications for stations were on file, but half were withdrawn in view of this confused outlook.

---

[8] W. Rupert Maclaurin, *Invention and Innovation in the Radio Industry* (New York: Macmillan, 1949), p. 206.

[9] The number of VHF channels was reduced to thirteen in 1946 and to twelve in 1947.

CBS beat the drum for color with well publicized demonstrations all through the spring and summer of 1946, and in September it petitioned the FCC to authorize commercial operation of the CBS color system in the UHF band. Hearings started in December. On March 18, 1947, the FCC gave its verdict: it considered CBS color not ready for commercial use, and reaffirmed the monochrome standards and the use of VHF channels. Once more television had the go-ahead.

By this time, conditions were more favorable. The image-orthicon camera tube, introduced in 1945, had improved the live pickup capability of the medium; coaxial cables had been developed and installed; wartime shortages were ending. During the summer and fall of 1947, the first television gold rush began.

10.3 / The Turning Point: 1948

Thus, 1948 became a crucial year in the history of American television—the year in which it emerged as a mass medium. For the first time, expansion of the industry could move ahead on a firm technical footing. During 1948, the number of stations on the air increased from seventeen to forty-one, the number of cities served from eight to twenty-three. Set sales increased more than five times over the 1947 level and by 1951 had already surpassed radio-set sales (Figure 10.6). Increased opportunities for viewing in 1948 multiplied the audience in one year by an astonishing 4,000 per cent. Figure 10.7 indicates the steep growth of the television sets-in-use curve; within a decade there were about as many sets in use as families in the United States. Also in 1948, network relay facilities became available in the Midwest as well as on the East Coast; regular network service started, important advertisers began experimenting with the new medium, and large-scale programming began—the national political conventions, Milton Berle's *Texaco Star Theatre,* Ed Sullivan's *Toast of the Town,* a telecast of the Metropolitan Opera's production of Verdi's *Otello.*

By the fall of 1948, however, the FCC became increasingly aware that (1) the current allocation plan, adopted before a great deal was known about VHF propagation, resulted in interference between stations; and (2) the twelve channels then allocated to television were going to be entirely inadequate to take care of the demand for stations. Furthermore, the color question which had clouded the issue all along became more and more pressing as the technology of the medium progressed. Realizing the inadequacy of the existing rules, the FCC stopped processing license applications on September 29, 1948. This started a famous "freeze": it permitted already authorized stations to go ahead with construction but froze all other applications. For nearly four years, until June 1, 1952, the maximum number of stations allowed to operate was arbitrarily limited to the 108 "prefreeze" stations. Even so, during this period television continued to expand phenomenally. The number of sets in use rose from a quarter of a million to over fifteen million. After ini-

Figure 10.6

Radio and television receiver sales, 1950–1968

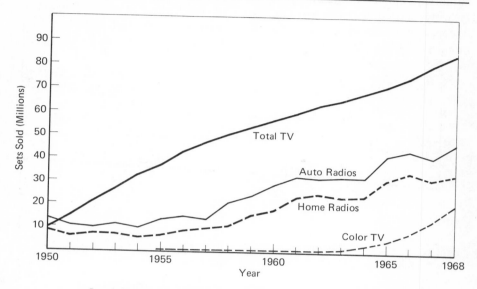

Source: Electrical Industries Association data in *Television Factbook No. 39*, 1969–1970 (published by Television Digest, Inc., Washington, D. C.), pp. 70-a and 78-a.

tial heavy losses, television broadcasters began to earn back their investment rapidly in 1951 (Figure 15.1). The coaxial-cable and microwave network joined the East Coast to the West Coast in 1951, inaugurating national network service which soon reached 60 per cent of all American homes.

Meanwhile, the FCC had been holding a series of hearings to settle the engineering and policy questions which had precipitated the freeze. The long-awaited decision came April 14, 1952, with the FCC's historic "Sixth Report and Order."[10] The new rules provided eighty-two channels—seventy UHF channels in addition to the twelve VHF channels then currently in use by the prefreeze stations. The VHF channels retained the numbers 2–13, the new UHF channels became numbers 14–83 (Table 3.2). A table of 2,053 assignments awarded one or more channels to 1,291 communities, over 66 per cent being UHF assignments. About 10 per cent (242 assignments) were reserved for noncommercial educational use, some in the UHF band and some in the VHF band. The table has been amended from time to time, notably with respect to UHF in 1965–1966. The most significant change was an increase of educational reservations to about 35 per cent of the total.

---

[10] FCC, "Amendment of §3.606 of the Commission's Rules and Regulations, Docket Nos. 8736 and 8975 . . .," 17 *Fed. Reg.* 3905 (1952).

Figure 10.7
Growth of broadcasting audiences

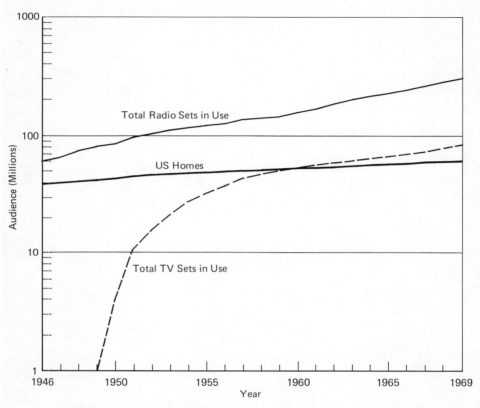

Sources: Radio to 1951, *Broadcasting;* radio since 1952, Radio Advertising Bureau; television, NBC estimates in National Association of Broadcasters, *Dimensions of Television 1968–1969* (Washington: The Association, 1970), p. 8. Used with permission.

Tremendous pressure for new stations had built up during the freeze. Within less than a year, all outstanding uncontested applications had been granted, and then the long drawn-out process of deciding among competing applicants began. The number of stations authorized more than tripled in the first post-freeze year (Figure 9.1).

10.4 / The UHF Dilemma

The advent of UHF stations introduced a complex new problem into the economy of television broadcasting. The FCC intended UHF not merely to supplement the VHF allocations, but to play a vital part in the plan for equitable nationwide distribution of service. The FCC "Sixth Report and Order" had left a number of major markets with no VHF allocations at all. Even after subsequent improvements in the allocation plan, only sixteen markets had enough VHF channels to provide for one independent commercial station in addition to affiliates for each of the three commercial networks (Table 10.1). In setting up the UHF allocations, the FCC established rules about power and antenna height designed to equalize UHF and VHF stations' coverage. In theory, stations on higher frequencies would compensate for their shorter range by using taller towers and higher power than stations on the more favorable lower frequencies. But the technology for the use of very high power

Table 10.1

Commercial VHF channels available in top 100 markets

No. VHF Channels Available	No. Markets in Top 100
4 or more	16
3	47
2	21
1	9
0 (UHF only)	7

Source: Data in FCC, *Thirty-Fifth Annual Report* (Washington: Government Printing Office, 1970), pp. 198–200.

at UHF frequencies had not then been developed. UHF stations, therefore, began at a near-fatal disadvantage.[11] Not only were there no receivers in the hands of the public capable of tuning to the UHF band, but the UHF transmitters were unable to cover as wide an area as their VHF rivals. This made UHF stations in markets already served by VHF an undesirable buy from the advertisers' point of view and hence not attractive as prospective network affiliates. Lacking the attraction of high-prestige network programs, UHF stations had little to induce viewers to buy UHF converters for their receivers. This in turn meant that they had little to offer local advertisers as compared with competitive network-affiliated stations.[12]

To make matters worse, the commercial possibilities of television stations as an investment had been so exaggerated by the artificial competitive situation during the freeze that overeager applicants rushed into UHF without realistically appraising the risks involved. UHF stations as a group lost fortunes

[11] The pioneer commercial UHF station, KPTV, went on the air as the first station in Portland, Oregon, in September, 1952. UHF transmitters not yet being available from manufacturers, KPTV purchased the experimental transmitter with which RCA had been developing UHF since 1949 at KC2XAK in Bridgeport, Connecticut.

[12] Harry M. Plotkin, *Television Network Regulation and the UHF Problem,* memorandum prepared for the Senate Committee on Interstate and Foreign Commerce (Washington: Government Printing Office, 1955).

instead of making them—owing to miscalculation of risks, inept management, and poor local programming, as well as technical limitations. Ironically, after all the years the profitable radio industry had spent castigating the FCC for interfering with the business of broadcasters, the unprofitable UHF television stations now begged for government intervention to pull their chestnuts out of the fire.

These circumstances combined to undermine the allocation plan of the FCC's "Sixth Report and Order," which had not contemplated creating VHF stations as a favored group, with UHF stations occupying a secondary status. UHF reached a high point of 125 stations in 1954 (Figure 10.8). For the next six years the number declined, reaching a low point in 1960, and manufacture of all-channel sets declined almost to the vanishing point.

To save the situation, the FCC obtained belated amendment of the Communications Act in 1962, empowering the Commission to compel manufacturers and importers to equip all new receivers to receive all eighty-two television channels. This requirement became effective on April 30, 1964. Unfortunately, the regulation stopped short of requiring manufacturers to equip UHF tuners with click stops, like the VHF tuners, so that many viewers continued to pass up UHF because of tuning difficulties.[13]

As another element in its effort to put UHF television back in the running, the FCC operated an experimental station in New York in 1961–1962 to obtain conclusive comparative evidence concerning UHF and VHF reception. The test showed that within a twenty-five mile radius, the two systems did equally well. At greater distances, however, VHF came through better. This difference could be overcome only by increased UHF power. Most UHF stations, however, opened at less than maximum authorized power because licensees felt reluctant to make the higher capital investment that maximum power required.[14] Not until the late 1960's did UHF stations begin to use really massive power—up to 5,000,000 w.—and thus to reach parity with VHF competitors.

The FCC's efforts at bolstering UHF had begun to pay off at last, though the ultimate fate of UHF television in a mixed UHF-VHF environment was still not yet certain. As Figure 10.8 shows, after a low point in 1960, UHF stations began a slow but steady climb. In the early 1960's they even showed a profit, as a group. The accelerating growth in number of stations after 1965, however, caused a sharp increase in average loss as new stations came on the air, operating initially at a deficit. The FCC listed 128 commercial UHF stations in operation at the close of 1968, of which 118 reported financial data. Fifty-three of the reporting stations operated at a profit.[15] By that time, the

---

[13] President's Task Force on Communications Policy, *Final Report* (Washington: Government Printing Office, 1968), p. VII-25.

[14] *Ibid.*, p. VII-24.

[15] FCC, *Thirty-Fifth Annual Report* (Washington: Government Printing Office, 1970), pp. 135, 137.

Figure 10.8

Trend in number of commercial UHF television stations and their average earnings

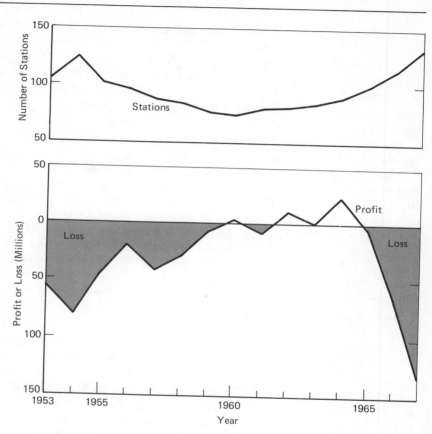

Note: "Profit" or "Loss" before federal tax expressed as average of stations reporting.

Source: FCC data in *Television Factbook No. 40,* 1970–1971 (published by Television Digest, Inc., Washington, D. C.), p. 58-a.

Bureau of the Census estimated that 55 per cent of American households could receive UHF. In the top hundred television markets, however, 27 per cent of the 297 commercial and 49 per cent of the 138 educational UHF allocations still had not been applied for in 1969.[16] Thus the dilemma created by the FCC's intermixture of VHF and UHF television channels persisted into the 1970's.

---

[16] *Ibid.,* p. 200.

10.5 / Color at Last

Meanwhile, as related in Section 10.2, after extensive comparative tests of the rival color systems, the FCC had adopted the CBS-backed standards, effective November 20, 1950. The CBS system appears to have been capable of slightly better color than its chief rival, the RCA system, at the time of the hearings. But the CBS system had two defects which seemed to doom it. First, it depended on a mechanical device for constructing the color signal— a rotating color wheel, which exposed the pickup tube to the primary colors in sequence, field by field. Second, the CBS system was not compatible with existing monochrome standards; it implied the necessity of two separate systems, with separate transmitters and receivers, existing side by side.

The industry generally looked askance at the risk of tooling up for a color system which might eventually be discarded. CBS itself was in a difficult position. For a decade it had been urging adoption of its color system; now that it had won at last, would the triumph turn out to be a Pyrrhic victory? "It would be difficult to find a more negative triumph—a championship dive with no water in the pool," remarked one commentator.[17] Conveniently, however, CBS was saved from the necessity of facing the final test of its color system in the market. First, RCA filed suit against adoption of the new FCC color rules. This delayed matters until the case reached the Supreme Court, which upheld the FCC on May 28, 1951, some six months after its original decision.[18] Next, the Office of Defense Mobilization asked manufacturers not to make color receivers and equipment during the Korean war emergency.

During these delays, a National Television System Committee went to work on an alternative proposal closer to the compatible, all-electronic system advocated by RCA and others. In mid-1953, the NTSC petitioned the FCC to reconsider. RCA, General Electric, Philco, Sylvania, Motorola, and eventually even CBS supported the NTSC proposals. Finally, on December 17, 1953, the FCC adopted new rules for color television based on the NTSC standards.[19] Though CBS had lost, it had in a sense also won. At a crucial stage in television development, it had gained time to prepare itself for television competition with NBC.

Adoption of color standards in 1953 did not produce an immediate changeover. Color receivers cost several times as much as monochrome sets; networks and stations had to make substantial new investments to be able to originate and transmit color programs. Networks, led by NBC (since RCA had the biggest developmental investment at stake), first began gradually to convert prime-time programs, while stations began equipping themselves first to transmit network feeds and films in color.

A dozen years passed before color began to turn the corner. By the end

---

[17] "CBS Steals the Show," *Fortune,* July, 1953, p. 164.

[18] *RCA* v. *U. S.,* 341 U. S. 412 (1951).

[19] FCC, "Amendment of the Commission's Rules Governing Color Television Transmissions," 18 *Fed. Reg.* 8649 (1953).

of 1965, however, nearly all commercial stations could transmit network programs in color—and the networks produced nearly all their prime-time programs in color. At that point, only about 15 per cent of the stations could originate local live color programs, and only about 5 per cent of American homes had color receivers. Late in 1968, however, the boom in color-set sales began (Figure 10.6). Over a quarter of the homes had color sets and purchasing continued at a high level. In October of that year, color sets outsold black-and-white for the first time.

In 1965, American manufacturers had high hopes that the NTSC system would be adopted in Europe, as it had been in Canada and Japan. RCA sent a touring demonstration unit all the way to Moscow. Although the NTSC receiver could be produced more cheaply, the rival SECAM and PAL (Section 3.7) systems won out. BBC, using the latter system, began offering the first European color service in 1967.

10.6 / Commercial-Network Rivalries

Unhampered network competition requires in the first instance that each national network have equal access to all the major markets. This condition exists only when sufficient relay facilities are available for simultaneous transmission of all networks' programs and, at the other end, when there are enough stations of substantially equal power in each market to provide each network with an effective affiliate.

The first intercity relay link able to meet television-frequency band-width requirements became available in 1948, when AT&T linked New York City with Philadelphia. The relay network grew rapidly. On the first coast-to-coast telecast, in 1951, President Truman opened the Japanese Peace Treaty conference in San Francisco. Nevertheless, for several years AT&T could not supply enough circuits for simultaneous transmission, so the networks had to take turns using the available ones.

Even more restrictive, however, was the station-channel ratio. As shown in Table 10.1, relatively few of the major markets have enough VHF channels for all the networks. During the freeze, NBC got an important head start in signing up pioneer VHF stations. CBS also started early but failed to secure the maximum permissible number of owned stations, as NBC had done. CBS corrected this weakness in 1953, when ABC merged with Paramount Theatres. The merger would have given the new company two television stations in Chicago, in violation of the FCC rule against duopoly (Section 15.4). Paramount sold WBKB, one of the pioneer VHF television stations, to CBS, which thereby obtained a coveted owned-and-operated station in another of the most important markets.

By 1953, CBS led NBC in both radio and television audience size. The two networks banked on differing concepts of television programming. CBS followed traditional radio lines—big sponsors, big programs, regular scheduling. NBC, feeling that traditional radio methods did not suit the economics of

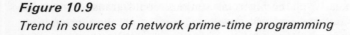

Figure 10.9

Trend in sources of network prime-time programming

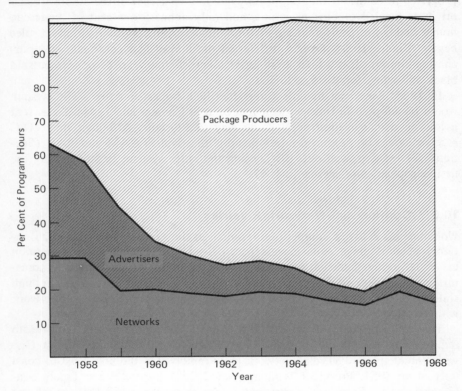

Based on all series regularly scheduled, 6:00–11:00 P.M. The small
residual percentage at the top of the graph represents combinations
of sources.

Source: Data in Arthur D. Little, Inc., "Television Program Production, Procurement,
Distribution and Scheduling" (Cambridge, Mass.: The Corporation, 1969), p. 1.

television, placed emphasis on the "magazine concept" (multiple sponsorship
of big programs like the morning show *Today*), and on "spectaculars" (expensive special programs dropped in only occasionally in place of regularly
scheduled programs).[20]

In both the CBS and NBC planning, the determination to recapture commercial program control from advertising agencies played a significant role.

[20] See Richard A. Smith, "TV: The Coming Showdown," *Fortune*, September, 1954,
pp. 138–139, 164. The pioneer spectacular was the Ford Anniversary Show in June,
1953.

Agencies had created most of the big commercial shows on radio simply because networks and stations had not developed their programming capacity fast enough to fill the need (Section 7.10). Now, in addition to controlling all news and special-events productions, the television networks moved to create their own entertainment programming. As Sylvester Weaver, then President of NBC, put it in 1955, networks "must gamble on shows, on talent, on projects; and we will lose in doing this all too often. But only a great network can afford the risk, and that is essentially why the great network service is so important to this country."[21] As Figure 10.9 shows, advertisers supplied fewer and fewer prime-time programs in the 1960's, but networks also declined somewhat as a program source, leaving the package producers as the main source (though usually with network financial participation).

Mutual was unable to follow the other three radio chains into network television. Dumont provided a weak fourth network service for five years, but dropped out of competition in 1955. ABC entered television late in 1948 but lagged well behind the two older networks until its merger with Paramount Theatres in 1953. Capitalizing on its motion-picture connection, ABC-TV thereupon launched an all-out policy of mass-audience programming based on tried-and-true Hollywood formulas. Many critics felt that the successful example of ABC's assembly-line-movie approach to television programming did much to hasten the end of television's "golden era" of innovation and experimentation.[22] Figure 10.10 shows how drastically ABC cut back on live programming—from 38 per cent of its schedule in 1959 to only 8 per cent in 1969. By the 1960's, ABC began to move up in billings toward the levels of CBS and NBC, and in the 1964–1965 season the television networks found themselves for the first time in a brief three-way tie in average ratings.

Thus, television proved able to support only three commercial national networks, whereas radio had been able to support four (Table 10.2). This reflects differences both in the economics of the two media and in the numbers of stations available for affiliation. As Figure 9.1 shows, after the first few years of expansion following the lifting of the freeze in 1953, the television-station growth curve tended to level off. Yet radio stations continued to multiply substantially, despite television competition. The difference lies, of course, in relative costs, both for capital equipment and for operational expenses (Tables 15.2 and 15.5). The economics of sound radio permit small, localized services in virtually every community. The economics of television, on the other hand, point toward fewer but larger primary transmission sources, with services redistributed by some form of relay to smaller communities. This explains the growth of Community Antenna systems (Sections 4.3 and 11.6),

---

[21] Sylvester L. Weaver, "The Form of the Future," *Broadcasting-Telecasting,* May 30, 1955, p. 56.

[22] See Robert C. Albrook, "TV's Autumn of Reappraisal," *Fortune,* October, 1967, pp. 135–139, 223–230.

Figure 10.10

Trend in television programming by network and mode

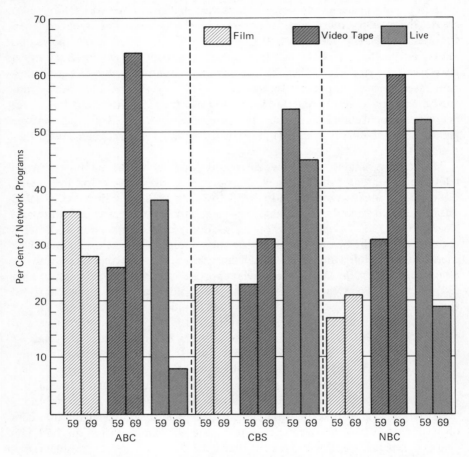

Source: Data in *Broadcasting 1970 Yearbook*, p. 70. Adapted with permission.

whose redistribution facilities give small communities a variety of television services otherwise available only to the largest communities.

In 1955, CBS made a study of television economics which predicted a ceiling of about six hundred commercial stations.[23] With some upward adjustment to take into account general population and economic growth, this estimate seemed valid a dozen years later. On the other hand, substantial growth potential did remain in the field of noncommercial television. The Carnegie

[23] Columbia Broadcasting System, "How Many Stations Can the United States Support Economically?" (October 5, 1955, mimeo).

Table 10.2

Number of commercial-network affiliates

NETWORK	NUMBER OF AFFILIATES	
	Radio	*Television*
ABC	900[1]	159[2]
CBS	246	192
MBS	535[3]	—
NBC	221	213
Total affiliates	1,902	564
Unaffiliated[4]	2,335[5]	108

[1]Aggregate of ABC's four different AM and FM program services.
[2]ABC-TV also has 96 "secondary" affiliates.
[3]Mutual has 47 FM affiliates in addition.
[4]Total stations on the air minus numbers listed as affiliates. An undetermined number of "unaffiliated" stations have partial affiliations with networks.
[5]AM stations only.

Source: Network listings in *Broadcasting 1970 Yearbook.* Used with permission.

Commission on Educational Television predicted in 1966 a need for an increase from 124 to 380 noncommercial stations.[24]

10.7 / Programming Developments

One of the most conspicuous general trends in commercial television programming during its first twenty years was its growing dependence on syndication and recording—more network programming in place of local material on affiliated stations, more film and video-tape programming in place of live production on both networks and stations. Figure 10.5 shows how the proportion of live programming decreased in the course of a decade.

Television networks had originally emphasized live production just as had radio networks in the early days. ABC, however, always depended more on film than the other networks. As we have indicated (Section 10.6), its merger with Paramount Theatres reinforced this policy. In fact, as Figure 10.10 shows, ABC reduced live programming to about the minimum required for news and other timely materials. At the local commercial-station level, these trends toward syndication meant virtual disappearance of live programming except for the simplest formats—typically, local news and a few local public-service programs. An FCC chairman was moved to comment, "Too many local stations operate with one hand on the network switch and the other on a projector loaded with old movies."[25] The problem of the independent (that is, non-

[24] Carnegie Commission on Educational Television, *Public Televison: A Program for Action* (New York: Harper & Row, 1967), p. 75.

[25] Excerpted from *Equal Time: The Private Broadcaster and the Public Interest*, by Newton N. Minow [p. 59]. Edited by Lawrence Laurent. Copyright © 1964 by Newton N. Minow. Reprinted by permission of Atheneum Publishers.

network-affiliated) station can be readily understood; it must work to fill that majority of the schedule which its competitors obtain from their networks with no effort. To do so, it has to compete with the network affiliates for the limited supply of syndicated materials.

Live televison production on a commercially competitive basis, either network or local, is both expensive and inconvenient. Few locally produced programs, cramped as they are by limitations on budget, talent, production facilities, and creative resources, can compete with cheaper syndicated materials for large audiences. At first, however, relatively little usable film was available for commercial programming. Theatrical film producers were chary of releasing their libraries to television, television had not yet started producing its own syndicated films, and video tape had not been introduced. Hence, both stations and networks at first had to depend heavily on live production.

Inevitably, as film and video tape became available, they shouldered live production aside. Film has the important added advantage of being able to go on earning money long after its first showing. This prospect justifies spending much more on the initial production than could be normally afforded for one-time live programs. For example, NBC's *Bonanza,* the first hour-long film series in color made especially for television, cost close to $200 thousand per episode to produce. But it was syndicated in over sixty countries in eight languages in 1966, with an estimated weekly audience of 350 million viewers —for an average production cost per viewer of less than one-tenth of a cent! Filmed entertainment features like these proved immensely popular and increasingly dominated the network prime-time hours.

Meanwhile, the first trickles of feature theatrical films had grown into a flood. In the late 1950's, television was inundated with ex-movie-house entertainment. When some of the later and more prestigious theatrical films finally became available to television, even the networks began scheduling them. Eventually, the wheel came full circle: by 1965, a trend set in for television interests themselves to produce feature films intended for initial television release.

Success of feature films as network offerings suggested a general lengthening of entertainment programs. This trend was reinforced by two other developments: the switch by advertisers from full-program sponsorship to "scatter" purchasing of spots (Section 13.2.) and the competitive strategy of striving to retain audiences once captured. They seemed to like length. In the decade 1957–1968, the fifteen-minute prime-time entertainment program disappeared altogether, and half-hour segments almost tripled in quantity. While in 1957 no two-hour entertainment items at all were scheduled, in 1968 they occupied nearly a fifth of network prime time. Similar trends toward longer segments in news, information, and documentary programming occurred— even to such extremes as documentaries that ran for hours on end.

The trend away from live programming also meant cutbacks in on-the-spot coverage of current events. In 1954, television covered the Congressional Army-McCarthy hearings for thirty-five days. It has been estimated that fifteen years later, preempting that much commercial time would have cost each network an average of $15 million in rebates to advertisers. In the earlier days of television, networks welcomed time-consuming on-the-spot "remotes"—they attracted attention to the medium and provided first-rate drama at a discount. But as advertiser demand, advertising rates, and network competition increased, it became more and more costly to interrupt normal programming with special events. Fred Friendly, Edward R. Murrow's successor as news head at CBS, resigned because the network refused to preempt routine morning programming to cover significant testimony on Vietnam by Ambassador George Kennan before a Senate committee. Friendly blamed not the network officials, but the "system." The preemption would have cost the network a quarter of a million dollars, according to Friendly, and "a system designed to respond to the stock market, which in turn responds to ratings, was governed more by concern for growth and earnings than for news responsibility."[26]

Not without regret did the era of live commercial television programming fade away. Within a decade, pioneers began talking nostalgically about television's "golden age"—the age before the slick, assembly-line, Hollywood type of film production displaced the excitement, the experimentation, and the discovery of live television production. "Despite its relative youth," wrote Murrow's biographer, "the medium has aged prematurely."[27] He considered television's high point to have come as early as 1954: "In drama as well as in news, it was establishing new levels of mass communication and participation, imparting a sense of worthwhileness, originality, above all unpredictability."[28] Film and tape took the unpredictability out of programs, and along with it much of the creative excitement; but the economics of the medium inexorably drove it toward syndication. Nor was this shift solely the product of American commercial competitiveness. The trend was worldwide and also included American educational television.[29]

Yet live programming remains television's unique capability. Piping a feature film from a network headquarters over the relay circuits to several hundred affiliates and radiating it thence to twenty or thirty million homes is a marvelous achievement, but after all a mechanical one. Using the same mechanisms also to give shape and meaning to immediate real events is a feat of higher order. The memorable high points of television programming are of this type—Olympic Games, Congressional Hearings, Great Debates, political con-

---

[26] Fred W. Friendly, *Due to Circumstances Beyond Our Control . . .* (copyright © 1967 by Random House, Inc.), p. 257.

[27] Alexander Kendrick, *Prime Time* (Boston: Little, Brown, 1969), p. 5.

[28] *Ibid.*, p. 70.

[29] Between 1962 and 1968, local production declined from 52 per cent of all ETV programming to 23.4 per cent. [Don H. Coombs, *One Week of Educational Television, No. 5, May 6–12, 1968* (Bloomington, Ind.: National Instructional Television Center, 1969), p. 67.]

ventions, space launchings, moon walks. The most popular programs have all, without exception, had this quality of immediacy and reality.

Of such programs, doubtless television's coverage of the assassination and funeral of President John F. Kennedy in 1963 will always stand out as an unforgettable example. Even those most prone to dismiss commercial television with contempt agreed that on that fateful occasion television lived up to its potentialities fully, with dignity and with extraordinary skill:

During those four fantastic, shocking days, television was as integral a part of the nation's life as food or sleep . . . the greatest escapist medium ever devised made escape impossible.[30]

As proof that television had not yet been reduced to a mere mechanical pipe-line for syndicated films, the networks pooled their resources, set up forty-one cameras in twenty-two Washington locations, and produced an unparallelled living document.

History does not provide high drama for television to feed on every day and every hour. Yet broadcasting goes on, day in and day out, creating a communications demand never before experienced. Between high peaks of achievement like those just mentioned lie the broad valleys—some like to say the "vast wasteland"—of routine programming.[31] When one considers that, in terms of sheer hours of program time to be filled, three television networks could use up a whole year's Hollywood feature-film output plus an entire season of Broadway plays in a few weeks, one gets some concept of the problem that creates the "wasteland." A former FCC Commissioner, Lee Loevinger, asserted that:

All of the good writers who have lived from the time of Shakespeare until today, working as long and as hard as they were able, couldn't turn out enough material to keep American television networks and stations programmed continuously on present schedules with first class materials.[32]

Thus television followed the parsimonious pattern of radio in its basic programming strategies in order to stretch available materials on the Procrustean bed of the daily schedule. This means, as we have said, *syndication*—along with the highly generalized mass appeal it implies. It means repetitive formats, stereotyping and imitation, rapid obsolescence. Many new program series

---

[30] "As 175 Million Americans Watched," *Newsweek,* December 9, 1963, p. 52.

[31] FCC Chairman Newton Minow coined the "vast wasteland" phrase in his first public address after his appointment by President Kennedy, a speech to the NAB in 1961. He challenged broadcasters to sit down and watch television for a full day, assuring them that they would observe a "vast wasteland" of violence, formulas, commercials, and boredom. The phrase immediately caught on and became the rallying cry of television's critics. The speech is reproduced in Minow, *op cit.,* pp. 48–64.

[32] Television Information Office, *Release SM-35,* 1970.

do not last a season.[33] Very few indeed have the substance to last year after year. The stars who have survived longest have learned to ration their appearances. Once caught in the deadly cycle of the weekly grind, even the brightest talents and most luminous ideas lose their luster from overexposure.

In an effort to break out of the routine cycle more often than the accidents of history allow, television developed at least one programming concept different from the radio precedent. Originally called the "spectacular" by its pioneer, one-time NBC president Sylvester Weaver, it represents an occasional special effort to produce something more ambitious and more rewarding than routinely scheduled programs. Spurred on in the early 1960's by the blunt criticism of an unusually articulate FCC chairman, Newton Minow, the networks increased substantially the amount of time and effort devoted to special programs. In the 1964–1965 season, the three commercial networks scheduled 223 hours of prime-time specials; in 1967–1968 they scheduled 434 hours, almost twice as much time.[34] When enough time, money, effort, and creative imagination go into specials, they can outdraw even the most popular routine mass-entertainment programs. *The National Driver's Test,* for example, seen on CBS in 1965 by an estimated 30 million viewers, won a higher rating than the aforementioned top-rated *Bonanza.* But these extraordinary efforts cannot be made routinely, as daily or weekly affairs. The driving-test program introduced a novel idea—giving a nationwide test by television. It took six months to produce and involved elaborate coordination between television production personnel on the one hand and social scientists and traffic experts on the other.[35] As a one-time program it could compete with *Bonanza.* Had it, or something like it, been scheduled week after week against *Bonanza,* however, it would soon have succumbed to the pace. In other words, the bulk of television programming needs extraordinary *staying power* to withstand rapid attrition in audience interest once novelty wears off. This overriding factor reduces routine programming to a level far below the peaks of excellence occasionally reached by "specials."

Actually, variability in quality is not at all unusual in artistic production. Many a prolific poet and novelist is remembered for only a single sonnet or characterization. Broadway produces a dozen failures for every memorable hit. The difference is, of course, that while other creative failures and medi-

---

[33] Melvin Prince applied actuarial statistical tests to network programs and calculated the life expectancy of new network series to be 3.53 years. The longer a program lasts, however, the higher its life expectancy. A series that has already lasted ten years can expect to survive another ten years. ["Life Table Analysis of Prime Time Programs on a Television Network," *American Statistician,* XXI (April, 1967), 21–23.] Of course, mortality is even higher for program *ideas.* It has been estimated that the networks consider some twelve hundred story ideas per year, of which less than 8 per cent even reach the pilot production stage.

[34] Arthur D. Little, Inc., "Television Program Production, Procurement, Distribution and Scheduling" (Cambridge, Mass.: The Corporation, 1969), p. 14.

[35] See Warren V. Bush, "The Test," *Television Quarterly,* IV (Summer, 1965), 21–32.

ocrities lie inconspicuously buried in libraries and museum basements, those of television must be displayed daily in the front window, equally prominently with the successes.

10.8 / Noncommercial Stations

We left educational broadcasting in Section 9.10 still far from being able to offer a genuine alternative to commercial broadcasting, despite the reservation of FM channels exclusively for educational use. Now a third opportunity had come. The small group of pioneers who managed the score of surviving AM educational stations had formed an association, the National Association of Educational Broadcasters (NAEB) in the 1920's. It started informally as an excuse to get together and discuss monotonously consistent common problems: lack of money and lack of appreciation in the upper levels of the educational hierarchy.

In 1949, the NAEB, with financial assistance from the Rockefeller Foundation, conducted a seminar for some of its key members at Allerton House, University of Illinois. This turned out to be one of those germinal occasions from which the participants emerge with a new sense of mission.[36] That mission was nothing less than developing a genuine and dynamic alternative to commercial broadcasting. Financial aid from the Kellogg Foundation, the Fund for Adult Education, and other sources enabled NAEB to set up a permanent headquarters, with a paid staff, first at the University of Illinois, later in Washington, D. C. The Association began a tape radio "network," engaged in research, published reports and studies, awarded fellowships, offered workshops, made grants for program series, and generally injected a new sense of urgency and purpose into the field of educational broadcasting. Among the first fruits of this new era were radio series such as the *Ways of Mankind*,[37] a new breed of educational program. These series, financed by the Fund for Adult Education, broke with the dogged amateurism of traditional educational broadcasting, bringing subject-matter experts and production professionals together—"not into passive presence with each other, but into an active partnership of work for a new kind of product, a fully professional broadcast with an explicitly educational aim."[38]

But of course the NAEB put its main emphasis in the 1950's on television. Educational interests had lagged behind when the FCC produced its first post-World War II table of television assignments in 1948. The Allerton awakening would have come too late had it not been for the freeze, which created a de-

---

[36] Robert B. Hudson, "Allerton House 1949, 1950," *Hollywood Quarterly,* V (Spring, 1951), 237–250; and "Allerton House: Twenty Years After," *Educational Broadcasting Review,* IV (February, 1970), 35–38.

[37] Obtainable on discs from NAEB, 1346 Connecticut Avenue, Washington, D. C.

[38] John W. Powell, *Channels of Learning: The Story of Educational Television* (Washington: Public Affairs Press, 1962), p. 71.

layed opportunity for educators to muster their forces. Iowa State University at Ames, one of the educational radio pioneers, had gained a first television foothold in 1950 with WOI-TV. Although WOI-TV operated commercially, it provided a valuable early proving ground for educational broadcasting.

In 1950, another outcome of the Allerton House seminar, the Joint Committee on Educational Television, set about recruiting and coordinating major educational power groups with a stake in television.[39] The JCET presented the educators' case in the crucial FCC hearings, starting in the fall of 1950 and continuing into 1951. The JCET's formidable battery of some seventy witnesses included prestigious names from the top ranks of the educational establishment, labor, and politics. The industry avoided an all-out battle; with the kind of support marshalled by JCET it would have been like opposing motherhood. Another factor also tended to moderate industry opposition, undermining its usual unanimity in such matters: many existing prefreeze commercial stations welcomed the diversion of channels to education, channels which would otherwise bring commercial competition when the freeze ended.[40] Even so, the JCET counsel felt the educators' case needed some kind of clincher. In the midst of the hearings, the strategists decided to introduce in evidence dramatic proof of commercial television's failure to provide a well-rounded program service. A hastily organized staff made a content analysis of seven days of commercial television programming in New York City. Introduced into the hearing in January, the study[41] had a devastating effect, forcing industry witnesses into taking such untenable positions as asserting that Westerns should be classified as "educational."[42]

When the FCC ended the freeze with its "Sixth Report and Order" in mid-1952, the JCET had won a signal victory: 242 channels (80 VHF and 162 UHF) had been earmarked exclusively for education, representing some 10 per cent of all assignments.[43] In one respect, noncommercial interests still had to defer to commercial interests, however: in the all-important category of VHF channels in major markets, educational television got what was left— if any. It received no VHF reservation in 69 of the top 100 markets, including New York, Philadelphia, Detroit, Cleveland, and Washington. Educational interests finally had to buy a commercial station at a price of more than $6 million to obtain a VHF voice in the vital New York market. As of May 31,

---

[39] The "Committee" of the JCET later became "Council," and still later "Television" became "Telecommunications."

[40] CBS emerged as the chief opponent because the network still lacked television affiliates in several major markets. [Powell, *op. cit.*, p. 67.]

[41] See Dallas W. Smythe, *Three Years of New York Television* (Urbana, Ill.: National Association of Educational Broadcasters, 1953).

[42] Robert A. Carlson, "1951: A Pivotal Year for ETV," *Educational Broadcasting Review*, I (December, 1967), 48–49.

[43] Subsequent revisions of the table of allocations increased the reserved channels to 116 VHF and 516 UHF.

1969, all but one of the VHF and all but 69 of the UHF educational channels in the top markets had been activated or applied for.[44]

Noncommercial educational stations may be licensed only to "nonprofit educational organizations upon a showing that the proposed stations will be used primarily to serve the educational needs of the community; for the advancement of educational programs; and to furnish a nonprofit and noncommercial television broadcast service." Under certain circumstances municipalities also may be licensees. They may transmit "educational, cultural and entertainment programs, and programs designed for use by schools and school systems in connection with regular school courses, as well as routine and administrative material pertaining thereto." Noncommercial stations may not be paid for broadcasting programs; however, they may use "programs produced by or at the expense of or furnished by others than the licensee for which no other consideration than the furnishing of the program is received by the licensee." Programs supplied by a commercial source may be identified as from that source; moreover, "where a sponsor's name or product appears on the visual image during the course of a simultaneous or rebroadcast program either on the backdrop or similar form, the portions of the program showing such information need not be deleted."

Only one station managed to get on the air within the first year following release of the reserved channels: KUHT at the University of Houston opened in May, 1953. The battle for reservations having been won, the longer drawn-out battle to activate them began. The JCET felt a special sense of urgency, for the FCC had not originally committed itself to permanent educational reservations. In the early activation battle, JCET received vital support from the Fund for Adult Education, as it already had in the preliminary struggle for reservations. In the decade 1951–1961, the FAE invested $12 million in helping educational television stations get started and programmed.[45] The Ford Foundation, first through its Fund for Adult Education, later directly, had invested over $120 million in educational television by 1966.[46] Money also came from other foundations, local drives, commercial broadcasting and other industries, school boards and universities, and federal educational research and development funds. Still activation of the precious channels went slowly, while stations already on the air suffered chronic and debilitating budget shortages.

A candid analysis could leave no doubt that in the long run only federal tax monies could provide the level of support, year in and year out, that

---

[44] FCC, *Thirty-Fifth Annual Report* (Washington: Government Printing Office, 1970), p. 200. Note that whereas the FCC set aside 20 of the 100 FM channels *exclusively* for education, in television it reserved not entire channels as such, but only channel assignments in specific localities.

[45] Powell, *op. cit.*, p. 55. This volume, underwritten by the FAE, details its contributions during this ten-year period.

[46] Carnegie Commission on Educational Television, *op. cit.*, p. 27.

noncommercial broadcasting had to have. State and local tax funds already provided almost 60 per cent of the stations' income in 1965–1966.[47] The direct federal contribution was only about 12 per cent, representing part of the matching funds provided by the Educational Television Facilities Act of 1962. This legislation implemented the first direct federal aid to noncommercial broadcasting, though it had previously received indirect federal funds through a variety of educational assistance programs.[48] The ETV Facilities Act of 1962 helped to activate 92 new stations and expand 69 existing stations. By 1968, the close of the period here under review, 156 stations had been activated.

Despite quite remarkable progress, considering the odds, the course of educational television during the 1960's seemed dangerously parallel to that of educational radio—curving downward from a peak of high promise and fervent enthusiasm toward a plateau of mediocrity and neglect. Certainly as a viable alternative service to commercial television the noncommercial service still had a very long way to go. The needed thrust to send the second service into a new and higher orbit came in 1967, with the publication of the report of the Carnegie Commission on Educational Television. Made up of top-level representatives from higher education, the media, business, politics, and the arts, the Commission proposed that Congress establish a "Corporation for Public Broadcasting,"[49] to be financed by a federally imposed manufacturer's excise tax on television sets. It proposed more than doubling the number of noncommercial stations then on the air. The Commission estimated that 337 stations could reach 94 per cent of the population.

Within the year, Congress passed the Public Broadcasting Act of 1967. The Act created the proposed Public Broadcasting Corporation and authorized interim federal funds for its operation. It also extended for three years the ETV Facilities Act of 1962, this time making educational radio as well as television stations eligible for matching grants. But Congress took no action on the key question of long-term, full-scale financing of the system.

10.9 / The "Fourth Network"

Educational television needed money for every aspect of its operations, but for none more than programming. Producing on the cheap had kept the general

---

[47] *Ibid.,* p. 28.

[48] The 1958 National Defense Act provided up to $110 million to "encourage and improve" teaching of certain subjects, and some of this money went into research and experimentation on instructional television.

[49] The Carnegie Commission coined the term "public broadcasting" to disassociate itself from what it regarded as the "somber and static image" projected by the "educational television" service of that time. It also wanted a term that would differentiate between instructional television (ITV), intended for the classroom, and a general service intended for the public at large. The implications of the coinage are discussed further in Section 22.7.

quality of programs low and earned educational television a reputation for pedestrian performance. Educational television, no less than commercial, needs the economic help of syndication to make possible expensive productions (Section 9.2). This meant a network—a centralized procurement and distribution organization to obtain programs for the stations as a group and to arrange for their distribution.

The NAEB's "bicycle tape network" for radio served as a model for a similar interim distribution system for television. It was called the Educational Television and Radio Center and was set up in 1952 at Ann Arbor, Michigan, financed by the Fund for Adult Education. At first it contracted primarily with key member stations as its program producers, thus helping the stations' finances as well as obtaining program series at moderate cost. KQED, San Francisco, and WGBH, Boston, produced some of the first series to have national impact, such as WGBH's *The French Chef* with Julia Child.

In 1959, the network headquarters moved to New York and added the word "National" to its title. Still another change of name occurred in 1963, when NETRC became simple "NET"—National Educational Television. At this point NET supplied ten hours of programming per week, including reruns. In addition to supplying programs, NET also helped activate new stations and performed other nonprogram services for its affiliates.

A new era began in 1964, when the Ford Foundation doubled its previous annual grant to NET on condition that it set higher quality goals for its programs and increase its emphasis on public affairs. The NAEB set up an Educational Television Station division to take over the service functions NET had been performing. NET reduced its weekly output to five hours and completed the devolution of its production contracting from member stations to professional sources. It also began to develop its own production staff, whereas previously it had depended entirely on outside producers. The noncommercial service began to penetrate the national consciousness on a broader scale than ever before as the quality of its programming started to offer a real challenge to the drawing power of commercial televison. To be sure, NET supplies only a few hours per week, but those few hours loomed large in the short schedules of educational television stations.[50]

Still, NET was a network in name only. To become a genuine "fourth network" serving the nation as a whole, the noncommercial service needed interconnection, for as Fred Friendly (who became the Ford Foundation's advisor on public television after his resignation from CBS) put it:

A network without interconnection is not a network at all but only a film syndicate. Aside from the obvious fact that news or special-events programs cannot be syndicated because of the time element, lack of interconnection cripples promotion

---

[50] In 1968, the average ETV station was on the air only fifty-six hours per week, and only about half of the programming was classified as "general" (as opposed to instructional); of the general programming, 45 per cent came from NET. [Coombs, *op. cit.,* pp. 3, 17, and 20.]

and exploitation. . . . In sum, the commercial networks exist thanks to interconnection, and NET is not worthy of the name without it.[51]

At Friendly's suggestion, the Ford Foundation, after a feasibility study, put an imaginative proposal before the FCC in 1966. Why not launch a special-purpose relay satellite to feed *all* networks, with the commercial networks sharing the costs and the noncommercial "fourth network" getting the service free? Why not, moreover, build in a margin above operating costs to realize programming funds for educational broadcasting? The Foundation estimated that initially $30 million per year could be realized in this way, with commercial networks still paying less than they had been paying AT&T for the use of terrestrial circuits.

The Ford Foundation proposal necessarily involved many much larger economic and policy questions about satellite communication. A Congressional committee held hearings,[52] but the FCC took no action. Nevertheless, the daring proposal did have the effect of dramatizing the need and adding a new dimension to the improving public image of educational broadcasting. To prove its point, the Ford Foundation at about the same time allocated funds to defray the cost of experimental live network broadcasts over educational stations. The experiment, a weekly two-hour program, started in late 1967. Meanwhile, in mid-1967, NET represented the entire American broadcasting establishment in a historic globe-circling live broadcast involving fourteen contributing countries. While these developments took place at the national level, a vigorous grass-roots trend toward state and regional networks had been under way, involving 85 per cent of the educational stations by 1968.

Thus, at the end of television's second decade, the outlook seemed favorable for an effective noncommercial "fourth network." The establishment of the Public Broadcasting Corporation under federal auspices promised an eventual solution to the economic problem of noncommercial operation, though financing remained uncertain. The efforts of NET and the Ford Foundation had established that highly professional production and live interconnection give the noncommercial service the audience-pulling power which could justify the high costs of such innovations. And with these and other innovations came a much-needed new image.

The annual convention of the National Association of Educational Broadcasters in 1965 in Washington, D. C., provided a bench mark for the changed situation of educational broadcasting. Over sixteen hundred attended. The Vice-President of the United States, the Secretary of the Interior, and the Chairman of the FCC headed a long list of important guests. Even the commercial sector was impressed:

---

[51] Friendly, *op. cit.,* pp. 306–307.

[52] Senate Commerce Committee, Subcommittee on Communications, *Progress Report on Space Communications, Part 2: The Ford Foundation Proposal for Broadcasters Non-Profit Satellite Service,* Hearings, 89th Cong., 1st Sess. (Washington: Government Printing Office, 1966).

The nation's educational broadcasters had reason to believe last week that they had emerged as a vital force in the broadcasting scene. They not only showed up in record numbers . . . but they attracted an unprecedented number of high government officials.[53]

A dramatic contrast with the unsung early meetings of the NAEB, when a handful of educational radio men would gather in Midwestern college towns to reassert faith in what must often have seemed like a hopeless cause!

---

[53] "Government Brass Glitters at NAEB Meet," *Broadcasting,* November 8, 1965, p. 50.

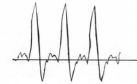

11

INTERMEDIA RELATIONSHIPS: SYMBIOSIS AND CONVERGENCE

Broadcasting as we know it today is obsolete, archaic and doomed.
FORMER FCC CHAIRMAN PAUL A. PORTER

Discussing the development of radio programming in Section 9.4, we pointed out that broadcasting assimilates more than it creates. All the products of man's intelligence and artistic creativity, all of nature and the environment, contribute sustenance to the hungry broadcasting medium. Broadcasters function more as "information middlemen"[1] than as prime producers. The art of broadcasting is an art of popularization—of translating the esoteric language of specialists into the language of everyday life, of imposing syntax on the chaotic imagery of real-life events. Ideally, the popularizer remains true to his source, neither vulgarizing it by sensationalism nor trivializing it by oversimplification; this goal is demanding enough to warrant calling good popularization an art.

11.1 / Media Symbiosis

By drawing on the other media for program materials and at the same time competing with them for audience attention, broadcasting poses a threat but also provides a stimulus. The press when radio news began (Section 9.3) and the cinema when television began (Section 11.3) regarded the newcomers as implacable enemies, threatening their very existence. But they did not die. Instead, they adjusted to the new situation, in the end even benefitting from the change. As it turned out, people did not simply switch off one medium and switch on another. Quite the contrary, interest in one medium stimulated

---

[1] Wilbur Schramm originally used this phrase, but in a more restricted context: *Mass Media and National Development: The Role of Information in the Developing Countries* (Stanford, Cal.: Stanford University Press, 1964), p. 87.

interest in others. One of the first generalizations developed by radio research was that heavy consumers of one medium tend also to be heavy consumers of others.[2] Social commentators gloomily predicted that television would raise a generation of nonreaders, a race of nonparticipators. Yet during television's years of growth, sales of books and recorded music also grew remarkably. Participatory sports (not to speak of participatory politics and social protest) became more popular than ever before.

Relationships among the media, despite fierce competition for advertising dollars and consumer attention, might be described, in biological terms, as symbiotic. They interrelate in complex ways which turn out in the long run to be mutually helpful. They use each other's material and talent; they invest in each other's stock; they benefit from each other's technological developments. Among magazines, *TV Guide* has one of the highest circulations; *Life* publishes books; CBS owns a baseball team; ABC's parent company owns motion-picture theatres; Hollywood makes films for television; television makes films for Hollywood; broadcasting invests in CATV. CBS made millions from an investment of about $360 thousand in the Broadway musical *My Fair Lady;* it sold the film rights for $5.5 million and went on to make much more money in theatre receipts and proceeds from recordings—incidentally greatly stimulating the sales, in paperback, of the play on which the musical was based, Shaw's *Pygmalion.* Volumes could be written about such complex networks of symbiotic relationships among the media, in much of which broadcasting plays a pivotal role.

One of the most striking examples of media symbiosis is the story of the near-demise and subsequent flowering of the phonograph-record industry. It will be recalled (Sections 7.9 and 9.6) that the networks bought out the old-line phonograph companies at a time when radio seemed to have doomed home players to technological obsolescence. From a high of $100 million gross, Victor fell to $10 million in 1932. In the long run, however, radio popularized music and stimulated the urge to buy recordings; at the same time, radio provided technological improvements which reduced the costs of home players and records while tremendously improving their quality. During the 1940's, the traditional big three—Victor, Columbia, and Decca—were supplemented by Capitol, Mercury, MGM, and London (English Decca). With the introduction of long-playing records in 1948, still other, smaller companies sprang up rapidly. The classics achieved a hitherto unheard-of popularity.[3] By 1953,

[2] Paul F. Lazarsfeld and Patricia Kendall, *Radio Listening in America* (New York: Prentice-Hall, 1948), p. 5. During the winter of 1953, an eleven-day strike stopped publication of all major daily newspapers in New York. The radio and television stations redoubled their news coverage, but the strike "resulted in what amounted to almost a physical hunger for the sight of type. The public denuded the newsstands of magazines and paperback books, so intense was its yearning for print." [Ben Gross, *I Looked and I Listened* (New York: Random House, 1954), p. 299.]

[3] See Dero A. Saunders, "Record Industry: The Classics are Hot," *Fortune,* December, 1952, pp. 128–131, 175–182.

record sales had reached $250 million, a quarter of which was in the classical field—a remarkable tribute to both the technological and the aural influence of radio.

11.2 / Whatever Happened to Radio?

Competition flourishes within broadcasting itself: radio competes with television, network stations with independents, VHF *versus* UHF, AM *versus* FM, commercial against noncommercial, network against network. Radio, of course, had to make radical adjustments to survive against television, and within radio, the networks took the first brunt of competition. Not only did television lure away their advertisers and audiences; to compound the loss, network radio had to pay the bill for network television's initial development. Radio's very advertising power was thus turned against itself. Figure 12.1 shows the dramatic rise in television earnings, which moved out of the red in 1951 and shot past radio by 1953; yet the overall earnings of radio did not fall proportionately and in the 1960's actually climbed to new highs. Figure 15.1 reveals part of what happened: though in 1950 networks accounted for a third of all radio time sales, within a decade their share declined to only 6 per cent. Local sales expanded to compensate, accounting for 70 per cent of radio time sales in 1969 as against 43 per cent in 1950. Growth in the number of stations on the air also helped account for radio's expanded income. AM and FM stations on the air almost tripled in number between 1948 and 1968, growing from about two thousand to nearly six thousand (Figure 9.1).

These facts alone cannot account for radio's recovery from what seemed in the early 1950's almost complete submersion by television. In the event, instead of outmoding radio, television forced it to re-examine its premises. Radio had to adopt new strategies, find new sources of appeal, develop new markets. In the process, the medium greatly widened its scope and variety.

Radio, especially in its dominant form, network radio, had been premised on the concept of a family medium—a rounded program service, aimed at a broad spectrum of audience interests, offering a little bit for everybody in the family circle. Pursuit of these goals created a bland, mass-oriented family medium. Television quickly preempted this role. It drove radio out of the living room and into the kitchen, the bedroom, the study, the car. Radio became *personal* and *mobile,* following individual listeners about the house, along the superhighway, to the picnic, onto the beach, over the water, into the streets. Figure 11.1 reflects the trend toward mobility, with home-receiver production dropping since the early 1950's but production of auto, portable, and clock receivers sharply rising. Inexpensive portable sets, helped by development of transistors and miniaturization, showed the highest ratio of gain. Between 1950 and 1970, the United States population increased about a third, but radio set production almost doubled—despite television.

Personalizing radio programming meant becoming more specific in appeal, aiming at a loyal but limited audience in a limited area with a limited service.

Figure 11.1

Trends in radio-receiver production

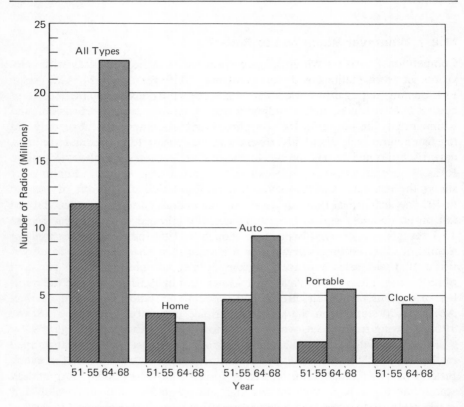

Production was averaged for two five-year periods, 1951–1955 and 1964–1968, to iron out transient annual fluctuations.

Source: Electrical Industries Association data in *Television Factbook No. 39,* 1969–1970 (published by Television Digest, Inc., Washington, D. C.), p. 73-a.

Many a station's audience is too small even to measure by the conventional sampling of rating organizations. Nevertheless, it is there, as special cumulative measurements prove.[4] Typical among the minorities the new radio first cultivated were *age groups*—the teen-ager, the "young marrieds," the mature; *ethnic groups*—particularly the Negroes and Latin-Americans, but varying

[4] Example: the average single half-hour rating for a national radio network in the mid-1960's was found to be only 1.6. In the course of the day, the network reached 12.7 per cent of the potential radio audience, and cumulatively over the period of a week reached a full quarter of the audience. [National Broadcasting Company, *C.R.A.M.: Cumulative Radio Audience Method* (New York: The Company, 1966), p. 47.]

widely according to local circumstances; and *cultural groups*—the opera lover, the jazz buff, the country-and-western fan. Over three hundred stations, as of 1970, programmed to Negroes; over eight hundred carried foreign-language programs, and over a thousand country-and-western music.[5] New stations, finding claims already staked out on the more obvious minority groups, sought out minorities within minorities. Musical tastes, for example, can be almost endlessly subdivided. Eventually, radio supplied something for literally every group with shared interests, even the most esoteric.

Networks had once provided ready-made, distinctive personalities for their affiliates. The then relatively few nonnetwork stations in a community stood out almost automatically, without having to work particularly hard on building an independent image. But with the network stars following the national advertisers into television and new stations cropping up all over the dial, it became difficult for listeners to tell one station from another. Programming "formulas" provided one answer to this problem of identification. A formula specifies in detail the ingredients and the mix that make up a station's characteristic "sound"—a particular type of music, played in prescribed sequence; a characteristic style of vocal delivery; a consistent programming tempo; a rigid patterning of program elements; arresting sound effects; liberal use of slogans and distinctive turns of speech.

In the mid-1950's, the "Top-Forty" formula pioneered this approach with dramatic success. The term referred originally to the forty current best-selling popular records, but it came also to stand for a particular kind of radio formula. Its ingredients included strict confinement to one type of music; stereotyped scheduling of music-voice sequences in very short "takes"; untiring use of echo chambers, voice filters, and assorted beeps, squeals, moans, bangs, whines, roars, and clangs; fast tempo and hysterical vocal style; endless repetition of catch phrases and slogans incorporating call letters and dial number of the station; frequent use of promotional contests and gimmicks. The formula aimed to make the "sound" of the station continuous and instantly recognizable. It succeeded remarkably. Not infrequently a bottom-ranked station would shoot up to the top rank in its market within six months of adopting the Top-Forty formula. An hour's monitoring of such a station during their heyday revealed some dimensions of the formula: 125 program items in the hour; 22 commercials; 73 weather, time, promotional, contest, and other brief announcements; call letters repeated 58 times; "stories" in a three-and-a-half-minute newscast averaged two sentences in length and concerned mostly violence to the person—either assaults or accidents. In short, an aggressive "sound"—loud, brash, fast, hypnotic.

The significance of the Top-Forty formula success story lies as much in its tendency to drive listeners *away* as its ability to attract them. The real secret of its success was its ruthless selectivity in audience appeal. Before the formula

---

[5] *Broadcasting Yearbook* lists stations carrying these major types of minority-appeal programs.

showed the way, few station managers and program directors could quite bring themselves deliberately to alienate some members of the audience for the sake of winning a stronger hold over others. They still clung to the pre-television concept of radio as the bland medium with something for everybody and annoyance for nobody—a fatally mistaken concept for radio in the post-television era.

The formula approach taught the concept of weaving program elements together into a continuous, uninterrupted fabric of sound. Network-dominated radio had emphasized individual programs. But programs, with their definite beginnings and endings, invited dial wandering. Formula radio invited the listener to tune to the *station,* where he could be assured of absolute consistency. At its extreme, this concept produced the "monomorphic" station offering twenty-four hours of the same basic material—the all-news, the all-talk, the all-advertising station. One monomorphic variant to some extent overcomes the one-way nature of broadcasting by inviting listeners to participate on the air via the telephone, at any time of the day or night. Listeners hear both sides of the often heated arguments between telephone caller and station "talk master." Introducing a tape-recorded delay of a few seconds before feeding the program to the transmitter allows the control-room operator to intercept obscenities, libel, or other prohibited matter.

The revival of interest in FM in the 1960's contributed to the increased diversity of the new brand of radio. Small-audience FM-only stations, operated on minimum budgets, became identified with particularly esoteric programming policies, though in some major cities FM stations even challenge AM stations for top-ranking positions. FM became a significant enough market to warrant a place in ABC's 1968 four-way division of its network service into specialized subservices. In recognition of radio's trend toward specialized audience appeals, ABC offers separate "contemporary," "information," "entertainment," and "FM" network services.

Radio networks now offer primarily short-take, interspersed service. CBS, for example, schedules twenty-six program items on weekdays, most only five minutes in length (the longest item is a morning half hour of variety with Arthur Godfrey, the lone survivor from the golden age). The network service totals just over three hours and a half, thinly dispersed over a thirteen-hour broadcast day. News and comment occupy about 70 per cent of the time, with sports, features, variety, and weather filling the rest.

Noncommercial radio found itself even more seriously undermined by television than commercial radio. To be sure, as Figure 9.1 shows, station authorizations continued at a steady rate, but the stations were mostly low power and most of the money and attention were going to the more dramatic and pressing problem of establishing the noncommercial television service. During the hectic years of educational television's evolution outlined in Sections 10.8 and 10.9, radio seemed almost completely neglected. The federal ETV Facilities Act of 1962 provided matching funds for noncommercial television but did not consider radio. However, the Public Broadcasting Act of 1967, which established the Corporation for Public Broadcasting, corrected this omission, both in extending the Facilities Act and in defining the scope of the CPB's responsibilities to include radio.

Accordingly, in 1969, the CPB commissioned a study of educational radio. At the time, the 384 noncommercial FM stations on the air (mostly low power, over half being 10 watters) represented a "mixed bag," the study reported; they lacked any consistent concept of their proper role, most of them having "a real problem of self definition."[6] Only about half subscribed to the National Educational Radio Network of the NAEB, and without subscribing they could not participate at the national level as members of the NAEB's Educational Radio Division. The proliferation of low-power stations had made it physically impossible in some areas to introduce more powerful stations able to offer wide-area services, and the study recommended changes in the FCC rules to correct this unlooked-for allocation problem.[7] In sum, the CPB analysis indicated that noncommercial radio desperately needed money, reorganization at the station level, coordination at the national level, and a more consistent philosophy of goals and service.

11.3 / Big Screen *versus* Little Screen

The motion-picture industry dates back to the early 1890's, well before broadcasting began. Nevertheless, the fortunes of broadcasting and motion pictures were closely intertwined, even before television made its revolutionary impact on the film industry. Radio has been credited with creating a dissatisfaction which ended the era of the silent film:

The illusions of soundless movies had prevailed as entertainment and as art so long as the public was unaccustomed to being stimulated by mechanical music and voice. But as soon as the public's ears were opened by the device of the radio, as they were, during the mid-1920's, to an extent that was profound, and people's minds were stimulated to create images to match what they heard, a vague sense of the lack of aural content in motion pictures began to be felt. A subtle psychological rejection of the incongruity of the silent screen occurred.[8]

As a matter of fact, sound-radio and sound-film technology developed side by side. Sound had been combined with pictures as early as the Edison experiments of the 1890's. But, as in the case of radiotelephony, commercial development of sound had to await the advent of the vacuum-tube amplifier. Lee de Forest himself turned from radio to the new field of sound on film and

---

[6] Samuel C. O. Holt, "The Public Radio Study Report" (New York: Corporation for Public Broadcasting, April, 1969), pp. 47, 55.

[7] *Ibid.,* Exhibit II.

[8] Bosley Crowther, *The Lion's Share: The Story of an Entertainment Empire* (New York: Dutton, 1957), pp. 142–143.

demonstrated his "Phonofilm" method in 1924.[9] This preceded by four years the marketing of Western Electric's sound system and was, moreover, a bona-fide sound-on-film system; Western Electric at first depended on disc recordings. De Forest, however, was unable to persuade the motion-picture interests to risk money for commercial development of his invention. The habit of silence was hard to break: "What stone walls of indifference, stupidity, and solid negativity did we unearth among the dead bones and concrete skulls of motion picture 'magnates'!"[10] Despite many successful demonstrations of his system, de Forest failed to acquire the necessary capital in time to forestall AT&T and RCA.

In 1926, AT&T set up a subsidiary through Western Electric—Electrical Research Products, Incorporated (ERPI)—with a working capital of $40 million to exploit Western Electric's sound system in the motion-picture field. By 1928, after a year's moratorium while the rival sound systems were investigated, all the major film producers had accepted licenses from ERPI. The license terms were calculated to freeze out competition: films made with WE recording equipment could be projected only on WE equipment; WE equipment could be serviced only by WE representatives; WE licensees had to pay a double royalty to project films made with non-WE equipment. In addition to leasing and maintaining the recording and projection equipment and collecting royalties on the use of sound film, ERPI cultivated the market for these services by lending financial assistance through several subsidiaries to film producers. In this way, AT&T found itself once more in show business, a reminder of the WEAF days. In 1937, a court held that the restrictive provisions of the ERPI licenses, though not at first illegal, later became unlawful when competitive sound equipment was available.[11] In the meantime, however, ERPI had modified its practices under the threat of suit from RCA.[12]

AT&T's attempt to gain exclusive control of sound in the film industry was particularly galling to RCA, for part of AT&T's patent resources in the field derived from the cross-licensing agreements between the two companies. In order to assure an outlet for its own products, RCA began purchasing motion-picture company stock in 1927, and by 1932 it held a controlling interest in Radio-Keith-Orpheum (RKO). RKO had an interest in about 150 concerns involved in motion-picture production, distribution, and exhibition. A few years later, after acquiring an assured place in the film-sound business, RCA sold its interest in RKO.

Meanwhile, in 1928, RCA had set up RCA Photophone, Inc., to compete

---

[9] Lee de Forest, *Father of Radio* (Chicago: Wilcox & Follett, 1950), p. 392. De Forest registered seventy-nine patents connected with sound on film.

[10] *Ibid.*, p. 370.

[11] *General Talking Pictures Corp.* v. *AT&T*, 18 F. Supp. 650 (1937).

[12] ERPI's maneuvers in the early days of sound films is traced in FCC, *Investigation of the Telephone Industry in the United States* (Washington: Government Printing Office, 1939), pp. 401–415. The successor to ERPI was Westrex Corporation.

with ERPI. The latter captured an early lead, with installations in 90 per cent of the sound-equipped theatres by the end of 1928. The next year, as the number of theatres capable of exhibiting the new "talkies" rapidly increased, the extent of ERPI's lead fell off sharply. By 1936, resistance to ERPI's highly restrictive contracts had grown to a point where suits amounting to $175 million had accumulated against the company. But ERPI had already begun to relax its contracts under pressure from RCA, and very little in damages was actually collected. Thereafter, RCA and AT&T learned to live side by side competitively in this new field.

Although the introduction of sound in 1927 caused a major upheaval and readjustment in the motion-picture industry, the basic pattern of the industry had already been set by 1920, the time broadcasting began. Even in the nickelodeon days of the early 1900's, it became obvious that the way to make money in motion pictures was (1) to syndicate the product and (2) combine theatres into chains. Syndication in this medium is even more essential than in other mass media. Local production analogous to local live broadcast programming or local news coverage is impossible in the motion-picture field because of the irreducibly high cost of picture production. Entertainment-film production facilities are highly centralized both physically and economically, the aggregate output is relatively small, and the risks are considerable. Intervening between the producer and the exhibitor is the distributor. As the middleman he can exert great pressure on both producer and exhibitor. In order to gain economic efficiency and the strength to bargain effectively with the producer and distributor, the exhibitor tends to build up chains of theatres.

More than in most businesses, the products of the motion-picture business fluctuate wildly in value. No one can predict with certainty whether a film will be a hit or a miss. In order to iron out extreme fluctuations and to hedge against bad guesses, film producers and distributors adopted a selling practice called "block booking." They obliged the exhibitor to contract to rent unproduced films in blocks, or groups, sight unseen. The exhibitor thus found that for every popular money-making picture he was also saddled with a number of second-rate and third-rate releases. Combining the production, distribution, and exhibition functions into one economic unit also helped to iron out the erratic economy of motion-picture production. The producer then had an assured outlet for his product, and the risks of production could be offset by the relative stability of theatre income.

Antitrust suits dragged out for a decade before a Supreme Court decision in 1948 modified these practices.[13] One result was the "divorcement" of the leading companies, known as "The Big Five," by means of consent decrees. In 1950, Paramount Pictures, Inc., split into Paramount Pictures Corporation (production and distribution) and United Paramount Theatres (exhibition). Also in 1950, RKO became RKO Pictures and RKO Theatres, and the next year 20th-Century Fox transferred its 385 theatres to a new company, Na-

---

[13] *U. S.* v. *Paramount Pictures, Inc.,* 334 U. S. 131 (1948).

tional Theatres. In 1953, Warner Brothers became Warner Brothers Pictures and Stanley Warner Corporation (340 theatres). The last of the Big Five to undergo divorcement was Metro-Goldwyn-Mayer, whose theatre interests were assigned to a holding company, Loew's Theatres, Inc., in 1954.

In 1948, the impact of television on movies began to make itself felt, heightening the effect of the Supreme Court decision of the same year against block booking. In the next four years, several thousand marginal theatres closed, box-office receipts fell off alarmingly, production units cut their budgets, studios closed down, and the whole motion-picture industry boiled in a ferment of uncertainty and doubt.[14] The demise of the Embassy Newsreel Theatre in New York was symptomatic. Established in 1929, the first of its kind, the Embassy had capitalized on public interest in pictorial news, particularly sports. Television's first programming success came from on-the-spot coverage of sports events, and the newsreel theatres felt the competition immediately. The Embassy abandoned its news and sports policy on its twentieth anniversary as a newsreel theatre, in November, 1949. An era had ended.

Hollywood reacted to the devastating inroads of television by dusting off some very old film tricks, on the theory that the sheer mechanical superiority of film could beat television at its own game. "Three-D," the first of these gimmicks, had a brief vogue starting in 1952. Three-D achieved the illusion of three dimensions by projecting two slightly overlapping images, photographed through two camera lenses separated like the two eyes of a normal human being. The viewer wore polaroid glasses to merge the two images.

But the sense of depth in human vision does not depend exclusively on binocular vision; one-eyed persons, for example, do not lose all depth perception. In life, a number of different types of "cues" contribute to the perception of the depth dimension.[15] Theoretically, several different cueing devices could be used, singly or in combination, to secure cinematic depth illusion. The most successful system is Cinerama, invented in 1938 by Fred Waller and developed during World War II as a gunnery training device. Cinerama provides a convincing—in fact startling—sense of depth. It uses the cues provided by peripheral vision, that sense of surrounding objects the eye normally receives even when focussed on a particular object directly in the foreground. The ordinary 3-by-4 aspect ratio of television and motion pictures narrows the width of field down to only about one-sixth of the eye's normal arc of vision. Cinerama restores a large part of the scene normally seen out of the corner of the eye on a very wide, deeply curved screen. Three

---

[14] See "Movies: End of an Era," *Fortune*, April, 1949, pp. 98–102; Robert Coughlan, "Now It Is Trouble That Is Supercolossal in Hollywood," *Life*, August 13, 1951, pp. 102–115. Cf. Freeman Lincoln, "The Comeback of the Movies," *Fortune*, February, 1955, pp. 127–131, 155–158.

[15] See Thaddeus R. Murroughs, "Depth Perception with Special Reference to Motion Pictures," *Journal of the Society of Motion Picture and Television Engineers*, LX (June, 1953), 656–670.

projectors with three separate film strips are needed to fill the screen, and the major mechanical problem of the system is to blend and synchronize the three pictures. Cinerama needs a large theatre to seat a small audience; few existing theatres have both the physical dimensions and the necessary audience-turnover potential, and so the system is confined to a relatively small number of showcase locations.

CinemaScope, developed by 20th-Century Fox, is a compromise system adaptable to most theatres. It provides a wide, slightly curved screen filled with a single picture. It uses anamorphic lenses, first in the camera to squeeze an image with about a 3-by-8 aspect ratio down to the 3-by-4 ratio of normal film stock, then in the projector to spread the image out again on a wide screen (Figure 3.3). CinemaScope adds little, if any, depth illusion, but the wide field of view can be impressive. Other wide-screen systems introduced to compete with CinemaScope included VistaVision (Paramount) and Todd-AO (MGM). The latter was the first of the new systems to change the basic 35-mm. film size; it uses double-width film and a 2-by-1 aspect ratio. All the wide-screen systems use multiple sound tracks and speakers to give the illusion that sound is coming from the appropriate sector of the field of view.

These and other technical improvements mean little, however, if the films themselves are not entertaining or artistically sound. Experience soon showed that a simple "flat" black-and-white film could be just as entertaining as one incorporating all the newer gadgets. Even the ordinary 35-mm. films provided a picture scale and a degree of definition television could not duplicate. The really effective answer to television competition turned out to be not technical gimmicks but new approaches to new subject matters. The film industry discovered, just as did radio, that certain of its previous functions had been irrevocably preempted by television. It had to find new ones to take their place. Now television provided most of the bland, family-oriented light entertainment. Movies could still better the economy and the technical resources of the "little screen" with spectacular, large-scale, superstar productions. Movies could also explore the offbeat "adult" subjects taboo on television (just as they had once been taboo on the theatre screen when it was a family-entertainment medium). As usually happens, innovation had both its good and its bad aspects. Release from the prissy standards of the old motion-picture production code helped make possible mature films dealing with the realities of human experience; but it also encouraged shoddy productions frankly aimed at the market for pornography and perverse violence.

Under the impact of television, the monolithic "Big-Five" business structure of classical Hollywood disintegrated. David Selznick, one of the old-style producers, described the traditional Hollywood system:

When I was at Paramount years ago we made fifty-two pictures a year and our executive judgments and prejudices and attitudes were imposed on every one of them. You can't make top pictures that way. You can only make assembly-line pictures. You can't make good pictures by a committee system, filtering them through the minds of half a dozen men. Besides, salaried people are not so likely to come up with big hits.[16]

The vast, centralized production organizations, with their huge studio complexes, stables of star talent on contract, and "assembly-line" methods of year-round feature-film making became a thing of the past. Soon, several times as much footage was being shot in Hollywood for television as for theatre exhibition. The "majors" set up subsidiaries especially to grind out half-hour and hour series for television, Columbia leading the way in 1951 with Screen Gems (incidentally itself a television-station owner). Even more humiliating for traditionalists, newcomers moved in on the Hollywood scene and capitalized on the new television market with huge success. The Lucille Ball-Desi Arnaz combination parlayed a simple television situation-comedy series into a new kind of Hollywood empire. After the success of *I Love Lucy* and a number of other television ventures, Desilu bought out the old RKO-Radio and RKO-Pathé studios.

In any event, the new breed of independent, motion-picture producers which began to emerge in the second half of the 1950's scorned Hollywood make-believe, bypassing the lots with their giant stages, accumulations of properties and costumes, and famous streets of meticulously constructed false-front architecture. Instead, they roamed the country and the world for authentic settings—and for lower overheads.[17] They took their cue from the sudden success of artistically adventurous foreign films. For years, such imports had been shown in tiny "art houses" to little bands of dedicated enthusiasts. Television helped create a mass audience for such fare, much of which could not pass the blandness test as healthy living-room entertainment for the whole family.

Meanwhile, the old-line production companies continued to make money for old-style motion pictures as, one after another, they opened their vaults to television. At first, only pre-1948 films were made available because before that film producers and unions had not anticipated the need for restrictive clauses to control television exhibition. Release of major libraries of the more highly controlled post-1948 films began in the mid-1950's. Feature films thereupon became a major ingredient of television programming (Section 10.7). Eventually, in fact, television created a whole new generation of film fans for pictures made even before they were born. With the six thousand-plus old features on the market beginning to recycle for the nth time and with only a very limited number of new theatre films suitable for broadcast being released each year, television faced a serious shortage of material. Led by NBC with its *World Première* series, the networks escalated the syndicated film-for-television genre into a new film form—the pseudofeature. Running

---

[16] David Selznick, quoted in Richard Dyer MacCann, *Hollywood in Transition* (Boston: Houghton Mifflin, 1962), p. 149.

[17] See MacCann, *op. cit.,* Chapter 4, "Independence with a Vengeance," pp. 50–70.

about as long as standard theatre features and budgeted at $1 million each, these productions successfully filled the growing gap in the television-program spectrum. Not infrequently, pseudofeatures also served another purpose as pilots for possible future syndicated series.

Another symbiotic relationship between Hollywood and broadcasting dates back to the 1930's. Movie studios at first forbade their contract stars even to appear before the microphone, completely misreading radio's promotional value. After overcoming these suspicions, Hollywood became a major contributor to radio programming with such fixtures as *Lux Radio Theatre,* for which Cecil B. DeMille himself was master of ceremonies. Television, too, underwent a period of suspicion, but Hollywood eventually realized that television could be persuaded to give away millions of dollars worth of publicity for upcoming releases for the sake of a few excerpts on the air plus interviews with the stars. The undoubted master of this promotional art was Walt Disney, who broke all Hollywood precedents in 1954 by launching *Disneyland,* a major television series devoted to promoting his own products.

It was not only an exceptionally good TV show, for children and their families. It was also a colossal business parlay, with an air of impudence about it. . . .

The Disney TV show opened ahead of the now famous carnival show place in Anaheim. One of its main functions was to act as a year-long preview advertisement for that wonderful playground. In addition, it was an advertisement for all of the Disney theatrical features. . . . Frequently the whole hour was spent simply "plugging" a forthcoming film.[18]

Again, then, a symbiotic media relationship: television hastened the demise of one motion-picture era but stimulated the rise of another. On balance, the results for films have not been all bad. Movies had a peak year in 1946, just before television took off, when admissions revenue amounted to $1.7 billion (Figure 11.2). With only one brief revival in the mid-1950's, as Figure 11.2 shows, revenue declined sharply until it hit rock bottom at just over $900 million in 1962. Then began a steady recovery that lasted through the decade.

The upturn reflected new patterns not only in methods of production and choice of materials, but in the exhibition and merchandising end of the business. Television's first disastrous onslaught ended forever the age of monstrous baroque movie palaces in downtown areas. But a new market emerged, first for drive-in theatres, then for suburban theatres in the shopping centers, modest in size and discreet in décor, often built as "twins" and even as complexes containing as many as six separate screening areas.

11.4 / Print Media

All the print media—newspapers, magazines, books, comics—have been profoundly influenced by television. Again, as in the cases of radio and films,

---

[18] MacCann, *op. cit.,* p. 14.

Figure 11.2

Trend in domestic motion-picture admissions revenue

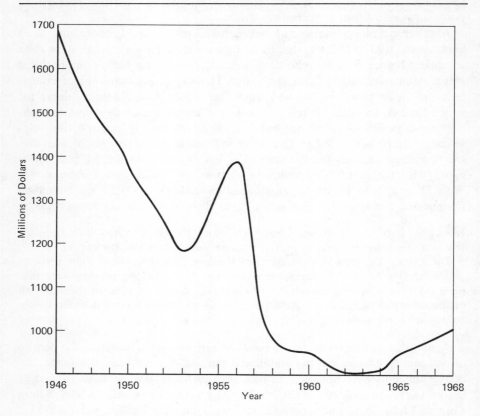

Source: Department of Commerce data in Charles S. Aaronson, ed., *International Motion Picture Almanac, 1970* (New York: Quigley Publications, 1970), p. 56A.

some functions were preempted and corresponding adjustments made. The general-purpose magazine such as the *Saturday Evening Post* disappeared, while more specialized magazines aimed at large specific groups and subcultures grew in numbers and popularity. There appears to have been a certain homogenizing trend in publishing toward a generalized "print medium."[19] Magazines often took on the dimensions of books, some books came out in series at regular intervals like magazines, newspapers featured elaborate "magazine sections."

Far-ranging changes in the newspaper industry antedated radio by many

---

[19] Holt, *op. cit.,* p. 24.

years, however. Ever since the turn of the century, the number of daily newspapers has been shrinking, the circulation of remaining papers rising. In the half century 1920–1970, the number of dailies in the United States decreased 14 per cent, but circulation rose 224 per cent.[20] In the early years of the century over six hundred cities had competing daily papers, but by mid-century the number was less than a hundred.[21] Broadcasting thus permits far more diversification of local sources of news and information than the print media. Although newspaper advertising revenue decreased during the years of radio's emergence (Figure 12.1), not all of the loss could be blamed on the new medium:

There is no evidence . . . that all or even most of radio's spectacular growth came at the expense of newspapers. Radio probably brought much new money into advertising and also took revenues from magazines, farm papers, car cards and the movies.[22]

In Section 9.3, we recounted the short-lived attempt of the press to prevent radio news reporting. The full irony of this opposition became apparent some years later when broadcasting developed into a major source of material for newspapers. The programs, personalities, business dealings, scandals, and regulation of broadcasting constantly make news. A parallel reversal of attitude occurred toward publishing broadcasting program logs. At first, many papers regarded logs simply as advertising for a rival medium.[23] Eventually, however, the broadcast log page, complete with news, gossip, and comment by local and national critics, became an important fixture in newspapers and even evolved in many papers into an elaborate weekly supplement. Yet in spite of such generous coverage in newspapers, the appetite for broadcast news and comment is so insatiable that fourteen million Americans buy the weekly *TV Guide* (started in 1953), as well, in over seventy local editions. Reciprocally, broadcasting has created customers for newspapers and magazine space, ever since the fateful advertisement for Horne's ten-dollar "amateur wireless set" of 1920 (Section 7.2). A 1966 estimate, for example, put newspaper revenue from advertising by broadcasting stations and networks at from $7 million to $10 million per year.

Professional rivalry outlasted business rivalry. Traditional pad-and-pencil newsmen still sometimes resent being shouldered aside by cameras and

---

[20] *Editor and Publisher International Yearbook,* 1970, p. 13.

[21] Raymond B. Nixon, "Trends in Newspaper Ownership since 1945," *Journalism Quarterly,* XXXI (Winter, 1954), 7.

[22] Harvey J. Levin, "Competition Among the Mass Media and the Public Interest," *Public Opinion Quarterly,* XVIII (Spring, 1954), 73.

[23] By 1954, according to an industry survey, in over half the communities reporting, newspapers published program logs without charge, and most of those which did charge were in small communities. [National Association of Radio and Television Broadcasters, "Newspaper Program Listing Practices" (Washington: The Association, 1954, mimeo.).]

microphones; they, along with others, feel that sometimes broadcasting both exploits and is exploited by publicity-seeking figures. In the main, however, broadcast journalists have established their right to equal access to the news along with traditional newsmen. A turning point in this evolution came in 1952 with the "Battle of Abilene," when General Dwight Eisenhower (then the Republican candidate for President) attempted to exclude television newsmen from an important press conference; CBS representatives forced the issue and won the argument.[24] Courts of law provide a conspicuous exception to the equal-access doctrine, however. In accordance with a recommendation of the American Bar Association (Canon 35 of its code of ethics), nearly all states forbid broadcast coverage of court trials.[25] American broadcasting has not yet been allowed to explore another interesting potentiality—live coverage of regular Congressional proceedings—although state legislatures, local school-board meetings, and similar proceedings have been successfully covered by educational stations.

The competition between press and broadcasting, which at first seemed so threatening to the former, provides another example of symbiotic relationships, a sequence of challenge, response, accommodation, and continued mutual stimulation. The same may be said for other facets of the print medium. We have already pointed out how television preempted the role of the general-purpose magazine and stimulated development of special-interest periodicals. Reciprocally, broadcasting discovered one of its own most successful programming strategies in the "magazine format."

Book publishing responded to the challenge with the paperback, which has a long history but exploded as a mass medium only after World War II. Literary classics long available and little bought in the few thousand bookshops of the country became best sellers simply as a result of being marketed inexpensively at far more accessible and homely points of sales numbering in the tens of thousands.

Paper-bound publishers say their market is made up mostly of people who used to read only magazines, who are intimidated by the forbidding air of a bookstore, and who can afford perhaps a small fraction of the price of most new hard-cover books. They buy and read on the move, picking books off a rack or newsstand to read while commuting or traveling or during a frenzied day of changing diapers and making meals. They are impulse buyers who pick books at point of sale, and after reading them throw them away or pass them on to someone else. Few paper-bound buyers, say the publishers, want to keep the books as personal possessions or "furniture."[26]

---

[24] Alexander Kendrick, *Prime Time* (Boston: Little, Brown, 1969) p. 350. In 1954, CBS made the issue of equal access to the news by broadcasters the subject of the first editorial ever broadcast by a national network.

[25] Canon 35 and the power of television to shape events by its very presence are discussed in more detail in Section 24.8.

[26] "The Boom in Paper-Bound Books," *Fortune,* September, 1953, pp. 123–124.

Paperbacks interact symbiotically with other media: a successful television series or motion picture invariably has its counterpart on the bookstands; in fact many authors automatically write for several media simultaneously.

In the "disposable" nature of the books, their adaptation to the tempo of everyday life, their low unit cost, and their method of distribution, we perceive the characteristic features of a mass medium. Their economic success depends on fast turnover; "packaging" aids sales by stressing typical mass appeals. Ludwig Lewisohn's *The Case of Mr. Crump* blossoms forth as *The Tyranny of Sex,* and the back-cover copy on Voltaire's *Candide* tells how "He chased a virtuous maiden through Europe's most bawdy age." If the merchandising methods are not always in keeping with the dignity of the product, it is significant that such titles as Plato's *Dialogues,* St. Augustine's *Confessions,* the *Iliad,* and the *Odyssey* have sold over half a million copies each.[27]

11.5 / Cross-Channel Affiliation

Media symbiosis expresses itself as well in common ownership of two or more enterprises in different media, such as broadcast-station/newspaper combinations. This form of common ownership has been called "cross-channel affiliation"[28] and should be distinguished from "group ownership," which means two or more commonly owned enterprises in the *same* medium. Often, of course, the two types of affiliation coincide.[29] Newspapers were well represented among pioneer broadcast-station owners (Table 7.1), and today most of the best-known names in the newspaper and magazine publishing world have broadcasting affiliations, for example *Time-Life* (KLZ, Denver), *New York Daily News* (WPIX), *Look* (WESH, Orlando), *New York Times* (WQXR), *Newsweek* (WTOP, District of Columbia), *St. Louis Dispatch* (KSD), *Cleveland Press* (WEWS), *Atlanta Constitution* (WSB), *San Francisco Chronicle* (KRON), *Chicago Tribune* (WGN). Most of the corporations represented in these examples control many more stations as well as other cross-channel affiliates. Early in radio history, NBC and CBS linked phonograph-recording and motion-picture interests with broadcasting. The 1953 merger between ABC and United Paramount Theatres produced a combine with assets of $144 million—a respectable size but still small compared to the older network corporations.[30]

---

[27] *Ibid.,* p. 124.

[28] Harvey J. Levin, "Economies in Cross Channel Affiliation of Media," *Journalism Quarterly,* XXXI (Spring, 1954), 167–174.

[29] No specific legal limits to cross-channel affiliation exist except in general antimonopoly laws, but FCC rules limit group ownership of broadcast stations to seven of each type (AM, FM, TV), for a maximum total of twenty-one, only five of which may be VHF television. See Sections 20.3 and 20.4.

[30] In 1967, the FCC agreed to allow a merger between ABC-Paramount and International Telephone and Telegraph Corporation, a huge telecommunications combine. This would have put ABC in a corporate class ahead of CBS, but the Justice Department raised a monopoly question, and after some delay, IT&T withdrew.

During the 1960's, new television-inspired technological resources for teaching and learning led to an interest in combinations of enterprises which came to be called the "knowledge industry."[31] The huge market represented by mass public education had previously been mainly concerned with routine school furnishings and learning aids—desks, blackboards, conventional textbooks. Facilities for motion pictures, slides, and overhead projections—"audiovisual aids"—had remained on the fringe of the market. Television, however, with its peculiarly synergetic force, suddenly brought these and many newer devices into the foreground as part of a systematic application of technology to the learning process. The new learning technology linked up textbooks, television, recordings, motion pictures, teaching machines, libraries, computers. It created a new kind of educational market potentiality.

Many large manufacturers of electronic equipment, like General Electric, Westinghouse, and RCA, set up subsidiaries to explore this new market. Media interests began to diversify their holdings into traditional educational fields such as textbook publishing. During the 1960's, CBS, for instance, purchased Creative Playthings and its subsidiary, the Learning Center; Bailey Films (educational producer-distributor); Holt, Rinehart, & Winston (publisher of textbooks and technical journals); and W. B. Saunders (publisher of medical reference books and texts). CBS later tied these holdings in with another undertaking, Electronic Video Recording (EVR), a new process for playing back recorded pictorial material through home television receivers (Section 4.6 and Figure 4.6). Thus, CBS's Bailey Films provided material for recording on EVR cartridges, while W. B. Saunders provided a textbook to be sold in conjuncton with EVR recordings for a chemistry course.

Media interests conducted such maneuvers in the field of educational technology with the hope of creating a new mass market for their products and services. Some of these hopes may have been overenthusiastic, or at least somewhat in advance of their time. A 1969 government study of the status and future of instructional technology concluded that "technology still touches only a small fraction of instruction" and noted "the discrepancies between the science-fiction myths of instructional technology and the down-to-earth facts."[32] Again, technological capacity outruns readiness for useful application.

11.6 / Community Antenna Television

Community Antenna Television, on the other hand, precipitated a series of cross-affiliation moves in the 1960's to protect old markets rather than to

---

[31] The economic concept of knowledge as an industry was developed by Fritz Machlup in *The Production and Distribution of Knowledge in the United States* (Princeton, N.J.: Princeton University Press, 1962). He defined (p. 7) knowledge production as "discovering, inventing, designing, and planning, but also disseminating and communicating."

[32] Commission on Instructional Technology ("McMurrin Commission"), *To Improve Learning: A Report to the President and the Congress of the United States, House Committee on Education and Labor* (Washington: Government Printing Office, 1970), p. 6.

create new ones. In 1970, broadcasting interests owned over a third of the CATV systems.[33] These owners included manufacturers, stations, networks, and media conglomerates in general. Bartell Media Corporation may be cited to represent the latter. It controls broadcast stations in Milwaukee, San Diego, and New York; *True Confessions, Silver Screen,* and similar popular magazines, with combined circulation of over nine million copies per month; paperback books averaging sales of seven hundred thousand per month; and two CATV systems plus a franchise for another in New York.[34]

Community Antenna Television, technical features of which were discussed in Section 4.3, started modestly in 1949 as a seemingly harmless—one might say benignly parasitic—extension of normal television-station coverage. By 1957, however, broadcasters had begun to wonder whether their initial welcome to CATV had not opened the door to a dangerous predator. The case of UHF television neatly illustrates this reversal of roles; at first, CATV helped UHF by putting its weaker over-the-air signals on an equal footing with VHF signals; later, it hurt UHF by cutting into its already limited audience in ways we shall explore in a moment. CATV's rapid growth in the 1960's included a trend toward larger systems. Although by 1970 the majority of systems still had fewer than five hundred customers, fifty-seven had ten thousand or more subscribers.[35] The trend was both toward larger individual systems and toward whole networks of systems which could eventually rival conventional national television networks in coverage. Similarly, although the majority of systems offered only six to twelve channels, already some had more than twelve, and future systems of twenty and more channels offering a variety of nonbroadcast as well as broadcast (FM radio as well as television) services were in prospect.

As long as CATV merely acted as a neutral relayer within a single market, filling in shadow areas, beefing up the fringes, overcoming local interference on behalf of local stations, it served to make the stations more effective. Some stations found themselves being relayed to subscribers of as many as thirty or forty small cable companies, which substantially improved station coverage. But a CATV operator can provide service to his customers on a dozen or more channels about as easily as he can on only three or four; and the more services he provides, the more customers he can attract. To expand his offering, therefore, he began picking up distant stations well beyond those stations' ordinary over-the-air reception areas. The CATV operator "imported" these distant signals by means of microwave relays, sometimes from markets hundreds of miles away. This growing tendency of CATV to obliterate the fixed market boundaries previously imposed by the physical limitations of over-the-air signals created a wholly novel set of problems for broadcasting.

---

[33] *Television Factbook No. 40,* 1970–1971, p. 66-a.

[34] Data in *Moody's Industrial Manual* (New York: Moody's Investment Services, Inc., July, 1969), p. 1253.

[35] *Television Factbook No. 40,* 1970–1971, p. 67-a.

Assuming no regulatory control, here are just a few of the consequences that might follow if CATV were to obliterate normal television market boundaries:

1. Cable customers in Market A who switched to a channel carrying an imported station's signal from Market B would automatically subtract themselves from the local audience, thereby reducing Market A stations' over-the-air coverage.
2. Worse, a CATV operator might for some reason refuse to carry a local station's signal on the cable, while at the same time importing that station's network programming from a station in a distant market. This substitution would penalize the local station by subtracting the cable clientele from the station's audience for its network programs.
3. Carrying the local station on the cable at the same time as a distant station with the same network affiliation would tend to divide the local station's audience.

Additional problems posed by CATV include:

4. Any nonbroadcast (closed-circuit) programs originated by the CATV operator himself would diminish the audience for broadcast stations.
5. Any advertising sold by the CATV operator for his own programs would diminish the broadcast stations' sources of revenue (by 1969, nearly 200 CATV systems had begun selling commercials).
6. Without having the burden of capital investment and operating overhead of a broadcasting station as such, the CATV operator can originate programs more cheaply than a station; assuming large enough subscription lists and/or CATV operators organized into networks, CATV could afford to outbid broadcasting networks for talent and program materials.
7. Broadcasting stations pay to use copyrighted materials (music licensing fees, author's royalties, etc.). Should CATV operators be held liable for additional copyright-fee payments? If so, how would fees be assessed and collected? Has not a broadcast network already paid for potentially universal coverage? Could further payment be demanded for CATV's coverage increment?
8. What responsibilities does the FCC have in all these matters? CATV is not broadcasting, though most of the time it is interstate by virtue of carrying network programs or other widely syndicated program material. It certainly uses broadcasting and has its own effect on broadcasting. Insofar as CATV installs or uses existing public utility facilities (poles and conduits), to what extent does it also come under the jurisdiction of municipal and state utility authorities?

Such problems as these tend to polarize around three underlying sets of interests: (1) the public's interest in receiving as widely diversified a television service as possible at optimum quality and minimum cost; (2) the television industry's interest in protecting itself from destructive economic competition; (3) the CATV industry's interest in developing an innovative and socially useful business enterprise. In addition, all sorts of subsidiary interests contribute to the stresses of the situation—the telephone companies, which would like to capitalize on CATV's need for microwave relay and cable distribution facilities; manufacturers who supply CATV equipment; "software" suppliers who provide CATV with program materials for closed-circuit originations. It devolved on the FCC to seek a suitable balance among these competing interests.

As late as 1959, however, after CATV had already been in existence for a decade, the FCC still hesitated to assert jurisdiction. The Commission looked to Congress for guidance. Congress debated at length, but no law came forth.[36] Finally, CATV began to reach such large dimensions and to have such serious effects, present and potential, on broadcasting that the Commission was obliged to intervene. For years the FCC had been nurturing UHF television (Section 10.4), yet many UHF stations still lost money or stood at best on shaky financial ground. The losses of revenue threatened by CATV competition could well have pushed many a marginal UHF station into bankruptcy—indeed could even have finally extinguished UHF television altogether. Educational stations, too, seemed particularly vulnerable to CATV audience splitting. Denver ETV interests, for example, opposed import by CATV of ETV signals from the West Coast.[37]

In the long term, a decline in the number of over-the-air television stations caused by CATV would have two serious public-interest consequences: families in thinly populated areas (where distances would make installation of CATV cables too expensive) would be deprived even of such over-the-air television service as conventional broadcasting might supply; and insofar as CATV displaced over-the-air services, it would impose an added financial burden on the viewer, who willy-nilly would have to pay the CATV subscription fee in addition to the cost of buying, maintaining, and operating his television set. The second consideration must be regarded as a key point: the American public invests billions of dollars in broadcast receivers and their operation on the promise and performance of conventional over-the-air broad-

---

[36] *E.g.,* House Committee on Interstate and Foreign Commerce, Subcommittee on Communications and Power, *Regulation of Community Antenna Television,* Hearings on H. R. 7715, 89th Cong., 1st Sess. (Washington: Government Printing Office, 1965); House Committee on Interstate and Foreign Commerce, *Regulation of Community Antenna Television,* Hearings on H. R. 13286 *et al.,* 89th Cong., 1st Sess. (Washington: Government Printing Office, 1966).

[37] Leland Johnson, *The Future of Cable Television: Some Problems of Federal Regulation* (Santa Monica, Cal.: RAND Corporation, 1970), p. 15.

casting services. CATV, as well as any other system (*e.g.*, Subscription Television, Section 11.7) which makes profitable use of this huge investment without having participated in creating it, and which at the same time exacts *additional* charges from the public, can have only one justification: an *augmentation* in service proportionate to the added financial burden it imposes on the public.

The FCC based its first claim of jurisdiction over CATV on the fact that some systems use microwave relays to import the distant signals which threaten hardship for local stations in the CATV's subscription area. In 1962, the Commission accordingly adopted its first two basic rules for CATV: (1) the "carriage rule," which enjoined cable operators from discriminating against a local station by refusing to put it on the cable; (2) the "nonduplication rule," which enjoined them from duplicating a program of a local station by importing that same program from a distant station, except with a reasonable time spread between the two performances of the program.

These rules applied at first only to CATV operators using microwave relays as part of their systems. Three years later, however, the FCC extended them to all CATV systems, whether or not they used radio links. The 1965 rules further restricted the importation of distant signals into the top one hundred television markets of the country. Thus the FCC sought to deal with the problems of competition without unduly restricting the growth of CATV, which it saw as fundamentally a desirable source of program diversity. Indeed, the FCC even required the larger systems to prepare to originate their own services. In 1970, about 17 per cent of the CATV systems provided some local services (news, films, local live programs, etc.), and over 40 per cent offered automated services such as time, weather, and news-ticker read-outs.[38]

One CATV problem lay beyond FCC jurisdiction—the problem of copyright. Insofar as CATV originations involved copyrighted materials, the operators had to pay use fees, of course. However, the Supreme Court ruled in 1968 that under existing copyright laws, CATV systems could not be held liable for paying additional copyright fees for *broadcast* program materials which they merely distributed.[39] The likelihood remained that Congress would close this apparent loophole in the copyright law, with possible serious effects on the future of CATV. Some observers even believed that imposition of use fees for distribution via cable of broadcast material might eventually put the cable systems as presently constituted out of business.[40]

From a business point of view, CATV originally offered a singularly attractive proposition. The key requisite was a local franchise, usually issued by a municipality, in return for a stipulated share of the gross receipts—on the order of 5 to 10 per cent. Municipalities sometimes apportioned different

---

[38] *Television Factbook No. 40,* 1970–1971, p. 77-a.

[39] *Fortnightly Corp.* v. *United Artists Television, Inc.,* 392 U. S. 390 (1968).

[40] H. J. Barnett and E. A. Greenberg, "A Proposal for Wired City Television" (Santa Monica, Cal.: RAND Corporation, 1967), p. 67.

areas to different operators, but each had a CATV monopoly in his own franchise area. Once armed with a franchise, an operator needed only a relatively modest investment in equipment, personnel, and specialized knowledge to get into business. Television stations supplied the actual product entirely free of charge. Even a few hundred subscribers sufficed to make a small CATV operation economically viable. The basic simplicity and profitability of CATV, along with the fact that it served a clearly defined need which people would pay to have satisfied, accounted for its remarkable growth all over the country.

These happy conditions could not last. The organization and conduct of CATV in the 1960's as described here must be regarded as a temporary phase. In a study prepared for the Ford Foundation, the RAND Corporation attempted to foresee likely CATV developments of the 1970's.[41] If CATV continued to expand and to widen the scope of its services, the study concluded that:

Perhaps tens of millions of viewers would be willing to pay subscription fees, perhaps not. Perhaps cable systems are destined to operate largely as extended antennas, as they now are operating, or perhaps they will evolve into full-blown common carrier systems with many new uses in addition to conventional television.[42]

The report went on to recommend adopting liberal growth rules to allow CATV and conventional television to accommodate each other. Competition might well have a "complementary effect"—it might cause a decline in broadcast-television income, but it might also offset this by decreasing television costs through sharing expenses. In short, the predicted mutual effect is again symbiotic.

11.7 / Subscription Television

CATV's unexpected growth distracted attention from another much more glamorous and highly touted supplement to conventional broadcasting, Subscription Television (STV). CATV, in its original conception, merely made existing television programs more accessible. STV proposed to supplement existing programs with entirely different programs, available only to STV subscribers (see Section 4.4 for the technical details).[43] In theory, at least, the subscription system opens up breathtaking financial vistas. It proposes, in a sense, to benefit from the principle of ticketed admission to theatres without having to build and operate theatres or to make and circulate release prints.

---

[41] Johnson, *op. cit.*

[42] *Ibid.,* p. 85.

[43] STV is to be distinguished from a more literal type of box-office system, Theatre Television, which exhibits occasional special events on large screens in conventional theatres and similar public locations.

The public, in buying and maintaining television sets at home, in effect provides the STV operator free theatres, projectors, and release prints. In the version of STV using broadcast stations (rather than cable) as the disseminating medium, even the distribution cost over the air would be minimal, inasmuch as the distributing transmitters would operate much of the time as normal, advertising-supported broadcasting stations. These economies could make even minority programming, on a national scale, highly profitable. Consider some hypothetical yet conservative projections: assume a nationwide STV network, an audience potential of fifty million homes, a program offered at one dollar per home, and a mere 1 per cent of the potential families choosing to subscribe to that particular program. This would mean an audience of five hundred thousand families—hopelessly small for a conventional national-network advertising-supported program. Yet STV would gross from that *one program* half a million dollars. Assume that on the average 1 per cent of the potential families subscribe to an average of only five one-dollar programs per week. In a year, the gross income would amount to $130 million. Yet at no time would the STV program offering have to appeal to more than a very small minority of the potential total audience. This potentiality of STV to satisfy minority tastes with high-quality programs has been attractive to critics of advertising-supported broadcasting who deplore the latter's built-in compulsion always to seek the largest possible audience.[44]

Unfortunately, the validity of these assumptions about STV cannot be fully tested except on a nationwide—or at least on a very broad regional—scale. All experimental STV installations were confined to small areas. They had to aim for relatively large audiences in order to obtain enough subscribers, or else they would have had to set the subscription price too high. Only very wide distribution of the STV offering can make locally small minority audiences potentially large enough in the aggregate to permit paying a high cost for program production and rights, while at the same time keeping the "admission" cost well below the price that would be charged at a theatre, sports arena, or other public place of entertainment or enlightenment.

STV experiments have been conducted since 1950 without overwhelmingly convincing results. Smallness of the experimental systems forced them toward majority-taste programming, so no clear demonstration of STV's potentiality for overcoming advertising-supported television's programming limitations has been forthcoming. Several wired (nonbroadcast) STV systems tested in the 1950's failed to survive. An ambitious California project, Subscription Television, Inc. (led by the imaginative former NBC president, Sylvester Weaver), seemed on the way toward a broad-scale test, but in 1964, the California voters (responsive to the fears of the motion-picture industry) adopted a state law against all forms of subscription television. The California Supreme Court

---

[44] See, for example, R. H. Coase, "The Economics of Broadcasting and Government Policy," *American Economic Review: Papers and Proceedings,* LVI (May, 1966), 440–447.

subsequently voided the act as contrary to the guarantee of free speech,[45] but the sponsors did not revive the project.

Of the dozen STV systems that have been tried, only one survived the vicissitudes of FCC delays, Congressional interference, and theatre interests' propaganda.[46] Zenith's "Phonevision" goes back to laboratory experiments during the earliest days of television. Zenith announced its proposed over-the-air system as early as 1947, but not until 1962 did the FCC finally allow practical experiments to begin. In that year, UHF station WHCT in Hartford, Connecticut, began offering a subscription service under a Zenith franchise. Most of the time, WHCT broadcast normal advertising-supported programming, but for about ten hours per week, it used an "encoder" at the transmitter to scramble picture and sound (Figure 4.3). Only subscribers with decoding attachments for their sets could receive the subscription programs, which consisted mostly of recent feature films not yet available on conventional television and exclusive sports events. Subscribers paid from 50 cents to about $1.50 each for most programs, averaging about $100 per year in "admissions" fees. The subscriber used a key card which, when inserted into the decoding attachment, both activated the decoding mechanism and made a billing record.

The Hartford experiment ran from 1962 to 1969, when Zenith discontinued it because the way finally seemed cleared for STV to move out of the experimental stage. Late in 1969, a Court of Appeals upheld the FCC's authority to receive applications for licensing nationwide STV on a regular basis.[47]

The chief argument against STV by conventional-television interests had been the presumed danger of program "siphoning"—the conversion of the most desirable presently available "free" programming to a subscription status —which could be expected because STV's subscription fees would enable it to outbid advertiser-supported networks for the best talent and program rights. Accordingly, the FCC proposed stringent antisiphoning rules. STV would not be allowed to offer any programs along the lines of the typical television-network and syndicated entertainment series; it would not be allowed to bid against conventional television for the sports features already familiar on television, or to use the older feature films available to conventional television; STV systems would have to provide material other than sports events and feature films at least 10 per cent of the time and would not be allowed to carry commercials. Furthermore, only one STV outlet would be authorized in any one market, and then only in markets which already received four

---

[45] *Weaver v. Jordan,* 64 Cal. (2d) 235 (1966).

[46] A former FCC Chairman remarked that the STV issue "produced one of the biggest paper wars—of press releases, texts of speeches, and nonstop telegrams—that Washington has ever seen." (Exerpted from *Equal Time: The Private Broadcaster and the Public Interest,* by Newton N. Minow [p. 232]. Edited by Lawrence Laurent. Copyright © 1964 by Newton N. Minow. Reprinted by permission of Atheneum Publishers.)

[47] *National Association of Theatre Owners and Joint Committee Against Toll TV v. FCC,* 420 F. (2d) 194 (1969). The Supreme Court refused to review the case.

commercial-station signals (not counting any that might be imported by CATV).[48] Zenith found these restrictions not unduly onerous and made ready to implement agreements by franchising companies which would supply the Phonevision service to a group of large cities aggregating seventeen million people.[49]

11.8 / Convergence

The preceding examples illustrate how television, as the preeminently electronic medium, tends to stimulate convergence of other media technologies into closer and ever more complex relationships. The Carnegie Commission on Educational Television remarked that technological development

. . . makes more visible each day the intimate relationships that link television as a vehicle of information and entertainment with libraries, archives, data processing and data transmission, social development, and social change. The historian of the future may look back upon these latter decades of the twentieth century as the years of a profound revolution in the art and the uses of communication.[50]

In Section 4.7 we discussed some aspects of this convergence—how existing technology could use relay systems to link together all the media in new combinations capable of providing many novel services, as well as performing old services more efficiently.

In 1967, H. J. Barnett and E. A. Greenberg of the RAND Corporation wrote a paper called "A Proposal for Wired City Television" exploring the problem of obtaining more diversified television program services. They examined and rejected as inadequate a half dozen of the conventional proposed solutions, such as the domestic use of satellites and fuller exploitation of UHF, Subscription Television, or Educational Television. All conventional solutions suffered from a common weakness: the low ceiling on the number of television stations imposed by the combined limitations of the electromagnetic spectrum and economic incentive. They concluded that a broad-band cable distribution system, analogous to but more sophisticated than the present CATV systems, could provide an answer. They called their proposed system the "wired city."

The wired-city concept envisions a network of cable connections between homes and switching centers. Twenty channels—or as many more as could be useful—would provide a wide range of program services: conventional

---

[48] FCC, *Fourth Report and Order,* 15 FCC (2d) 466 (1968).

[49] As early as 1949, Zenith had formed Teco, Inc., to promote and develop Phonevision by franchising the system to operating companies to which it would supply the special coding equipment and assistance in management and operations.

[50] Carnegie Commission on Educational Television, *Public Television: A Program for Action* (New York: Harper & Row, 1967), p. 41.

commercial television, subscription television, educational television, instructional television, local closed-circuit originations. The authors estimate that if all twenty channels were put to use an average of ten hours per day in a city with a hundred thousand terminals, use of a channel could be rented for as little as five dollars per hour. Such a channel (or channels) could be made available to all comers on a common-carrier basis. It might be rented by candidates for political office, city officials, advertisers, schools, clubs, churches, and even individuals looking for a personal soap box from which to express private views.

Such applications of the wired-city concept would require no technology not already familiar to CATV operations; they would merely broaden already existing services. Integrating other existing devices would be novel but not technologically difficult. Facsimile, for example, could open up the possibility of receiving mail, documents, magazines and newspapers, photographs, maps, and books in the home. Two-way communication would make possible remote surveillance and alarm systems, a variety of business transactions, and home instruction with direct feedback between student and teacher. Interconnection with computer systems would open up almost endless possibilities for data storage, retrieval, analysis, and other kinds of manipulation.

Science-fiction types of proposals for imaginative new communications devices had been common for a long time. These proposals, however, tended to be long on technological glamor but short on social utility and economic viability. The wired-city concept struck a responsive chord because it achieved a balance of technological innovation, identifiable utilitarian needs, and economic advantage.

The Industrial Electronics Division of the Electronic Industries Association carried the wired-city concept a good deal further under the rubric "broadband communications network" (BCN) in a brief filed with the FCC in 1969.[51] The EIA proposal stressed the important secondary benefits that could accrue from substituting the movement of information over cable networks for the movement of people and documents over road networks. The BCN would enable "pseudo-travel," a logical extension of such existing substitutes for travel as the conference telephone call, by which a small number of individuals separated from each other by perhaps thousands of miles can nevertheless confer as a group; and closed-circuit television, which similarly brings people together for intercommunicating without actually transporting them.

An analysis of mail, for example, shows that 40 per cent of its volume consists of simple business transactions which could easily be consummated without transferring documents from one place to another, exploiting communications devices already in routine use. Many other forms of real travel could be eliminated by pseudo-travel over a broad-band network. The BCN could be used for most banking transactions, for shopping, polling, meter reading. In

---

[51] *The Future of Broadband Communications,* Brief filed with the FCC, October, 1969, in response to Docket 18397, Part V.

fact, it turns out on examination, a surprisingly high proportion of the travelling people do to transact routine business is entirely redundant. The physical transfer of human bodies has no necessary connection with the transfer of most kinds of information. Elimination of all this wasteful physical movement would reduce traffic congestion, cut down on accidents and air pollution, and save immense amounts of money. Most important, it would liberate modern urban man from all the physical and psychic wear of unnecessary routine travel, leaving him that much more time to enjoy meaningful travel for purposes of education and recreation.

The wired-city or BCN concept derives additional support from the fact that it would relieve some of the pressure on the overloaded electromagnetic frequency spectrum (Section 1.8). Ever since the 1950's, one study after another has warned of an approaching spectrum crisis. The President's Office of Telecommunications Management in 1969 reported on the critical insufficiency of spectrum space for land-mobile two-way radio in urban areas; the satellite services' need for more frequencies; "serious congestion in the high frequency part of the spectrum, with no practical solution in sight"; continued use of outmoded equipment which causes "spectrum pollution"; need for "vast expansion" of communication services designed to reduce highway accidents; inadequacy of aviation and navigational communications.[52]

In Section 4.7, we pointed out that the need for equitable distribution of diverse program services motivated the relatively lavish allotment of spectrum space to television. In 1970, the FCC was obliged to take the first steps toward redressing the balance by reallocating some of the UHF television channels at the upper and lower ends of the spectrum for urban land-mobile use. The wired-city mode of program distribution could greatly reduce the number of over-the-air broadcast transmitters needed to provide a varied program service —indeed, could even at the same time *increase* the diversity of program sources. Equitability of distribution would not, however, be solved by the wired city because it would be uneconomical to run cables to homes in remote areas with low population density. Assuming that not everybody will ultimately be jammed into densely populated urban centers, the need for over-the-air distribution in other areas will remain. Nevertheless, the convergence of communication technologies in the last quarter of the twentieth century seemed bound to alter profoundly the familiar shape of the broadcasting system which grew up in its first two quarters.

---

[52] Office of Telecommunications Management, "The Radio Frequency Spectrum: United States Use and Management" (Washington: Executive Office of the President, July, 1969), p. iv.

PART THREE

THE
ECONOMICS OF
BROADCASTING

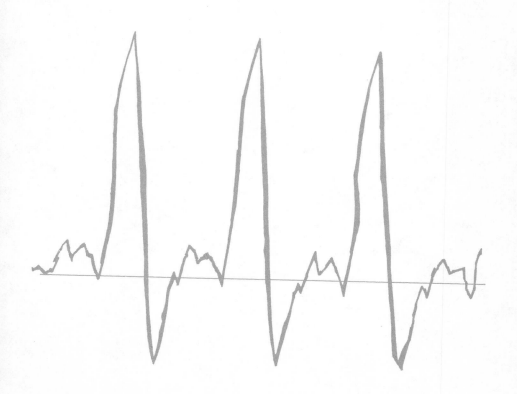

12

THE ECONOMIC ROLE
OF ADVERTISING

We couldn't make a better pickle; so we made a better pickle package.
TELEVISION ADVERTISEMENT

In the United States, advertising is a $20-billion industry, involving in 1968, for example, an expenditure of about $91 per capita. This level far exceeds the per capita expense for advertising in the other leading industrial countries (Table 12.1). Britain spends a third as much, for example, France only a fifth as much. The difference is largely due to the varying intensity with which the mass-consumer market is cultivated, which in turn hinges on the extent to which buying power has been generalized to the population as a whole.

Advertising plays an essential role in the mechanism of mass distribution, as well as a more arguable role in creating appetites for consumer goods. When the housewife stopped making her own soap and buying shoes from the local craftsman, she lost direct contact with the sources of supply. Advertising bridges the gap. In self-service stores, instead of interrogating a human salesman, the shopper consults an index of advertising lore in her head and responds to the stimuli of point-of-sale displays and eye-catching packages. Thus advertising, along with packaging, has to a large degree replaced expensive person-to-person salesmanship.

12.1 / The Advertising Market

About three hundred advertisements of all types impinge on the consciousness of the average American housewife per day.[1] Over thirty thousand branded

---

[1] A highly exaggerated estimate of fifteen hundred exposures per day has been widely quoted. See, for example, Fairfax M. Cone, *With All Its Faults: A Candid Account of Forty Years in Advertising* (Boston: Little, Brown, 1969), p. 9. Advertising agency Batten, Barton, Durstine, and Osborne finally challenged this oft-cited figure, tracing it back to an advertising man's speech in 1957. Their own study, conducted in 1970, indicated an average exposure of 305 messages per day for women, 285 for men. ["A Mere 305 Advertisements Hit Mom Every Day, Not 1,500, BBDO Reports," *Advertising Age,* October 19, 1970, pp. 1, 86.]

Table 12.1
Leading nations in advertising expenditure

RANK	COUNTRY	TOTAL EXPENDITURE (MILLIONS)	EXPENDITURE PER CAPITA
1	United States	$18,350	$91
2	West Germany	2,152	36
3	Great Britain	1,705	31
4	Japan	1,478	15
5	Canada	902	43
6	France	890	18
7	Italy	550	10
8	Sweden	418	52
9	Switzerland	406	68
10	Australia	385	32

Source: 1968 data reprinted with permission from the September 22, 1969, issue of *Advertising Age*, p. 51. Copyright © 1969 by Crain Communications, Inc.

products clamor for attention, with thousands more entering and leaving the marketplace each year.[2] To restimulate flagging consumer attention surfeited by advertising requires great ingenuity and constant effort. Advertising burns up ideas; its work is never done. A successful campaign to launch a new product or lift an old one to new sales levels confers no security, for brand loyalty toward most types of products is notoriously shallow and easily diverted.

Nor is manufacturer-to-consumer advertising the only type. Trade publications thrive on manufacturer or service-supplier advertisements addressed to other manufacturers, services, and dealers. Local retailers, usually with assistance from the manufacturers whose goods they sell, place local advertising for nationally distributed products. Individual companies join forces in associations to promote their particular interests against rival interests, for example private as against public production of electric power or the use of wood in construction as against plastics and metals.

The media of advertising, too, vary widely. It would be hard to find an object or an activity which, at some time or in some way, has not been used as a vehicle for advertising. In addition to the major media, listed in Table 12.2, innumerable minor media can be called upon—matchbook covers, transit posters, skywriting, trade shows and fairs, bumper stickers, lapel buttons, premiums, handbills, shopping bags, blimps. Table 12.2 indicates that among the major media, outdoor advertising is a good deal more conspicuous than

---

[2] In 1968, manufacturers introduced ninety-five hundred new packaged consumer items, of which over 80 per cent failed to catch the public fancy. ["The Great Rush for New Products," *Time,* October 24, 1969, p. 92.]

Table 12.2

U. S. expenditures on major advertising media

MEDIUM	AMOUNT (MILLIONS)	PER CENT OF TOTAL
Newspapers	$5,850	29.9
Television	3,585	18.3
Direct mail	2,680	13.7
Magazines	1,375	7.0
Radio	1,270	6.5
Outdoor	206	1.0
Other	4,805	23.6
Total	$19,565	100.0

Source: Marketing/Communications, February, 1970, p. 55.

its dollar volume would lead one to expect; and probably few people realize that more is spent on direct mail than on both radio and magazine advertising.[3]

The multiplicity of media, each with its own specialized requirements for advertising effectiveness, has produced a boom in the advertising-agency business. Originally simply middlemen in purchasing newspaper and magazine space, agencies have become highly specialized, creative organizations. They not only buy media space and time on behalf of clients, but also write and design advertisements and conduct research on which to base marketing recommendations. Agencies began using scientifically based market-research techniques around 1925.[4]

Broadcasting grew up in this so-called scientific era of advertising practice. Figure 12.1 indicates how television overtook all other media in the period 1950–1964 except newspapers, whose first rank has never been threatened (though television does lead all media including newspapers in *national* advertising). Before television, radio outsold magazines, but by 1953 radio's loss of national advertising to television put magazines ahead once more.

12.2 / Advertising and Promotion As Subsidy

Advertising's usefulness in reducing the cost of information media to the general public must be added to whatever effects it may have in facilitating marketing operations. Advertising revenue defrays about 70 per cent of metropolitan-newspaper and about 60 per cent of general-magazine production

---

[3] The business of renting lists of names alone is said to be a billion-dollar enterprise. Specialized lists of almost every imaginable sort can be rented. See Standard Rate and Data Service, *Direct Mail List Rates and Data* (Skokie, Ill.: The Service, semiannual).

[4] C. H. Sandage, *Advertising: Theory and Practice* (Homewood, Ill.: Richard D. Irwin, 1953), p. 24.

Figure 12.1
Broadcast-advertising growth compared to other media

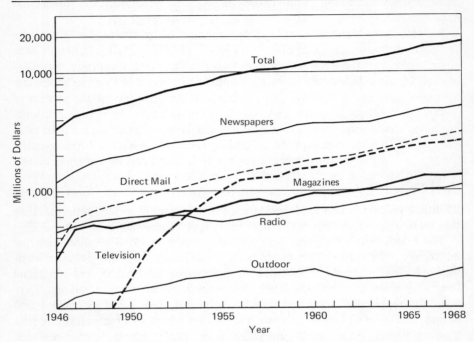

Source: McCann-Erickson, Inc., data in *Television Factbooks* (published by Television Digest, Inc., Washington, D. C.).

costs.[5] Advertising helps keep down the subscription rates of many scientific and learned journals as well as popular magazines and newspapers.

Advertising subsidizes broadcasting somewhat differently. Broadcasters like to speak of their service as being "free" to the consumer, as contrasted with Subscription Television, for example. The radio listener and television viewer do indeed pay no subscription rate or ticket price for programs. However, they do pay a high price for the service as a whole by purchasing, maintaining, and operating receivers. Broadcast audiences, unlike consumers of the other mass media, must make an actual investment *in the medium itself,* for without receivers transmitters are useless. It is almost as though the moviegoer had to own his seat in the theatre, or the reader had to buy his own Teletype machine and subscribe to one of the wire services for news. Advertising does defray the costs of programming commercial stations, but the consumers' investment in receivers outweighs by many times the investment of the industry

---

[5] Department of Commerce, *Statistical Abstract of the United States* (Washington: Government Printing Office, 1969), p. 503.

in transmission facilities.[6] This unique relationship of economic interdependence between producer and consumer in broadcasting needs to be borne in mind whenever making comparisons among and generalizations about the mass media.[7]

Indirect subsidy also derives from promotional use of the media. The terms "publicity," "promotion," "public relations," and "advertising," though usually distinct operationally, in common usage often blend. Generally, advertising can be distinguished by its brief, pointed form, the fact that the advertiser normally pays for it directly, and the explicit identification of the source of payment.[8] Publicity generally seeks to exploit news media. Promotion, according to the dictionary, seeks to "stir up interest in an enterprise"; it might both *use* advertising and *cause* publicity. Public relations implies a broader-scale, long-term campaign aimed at building up an institutional or personal image. A broadcast station uses "promotional announcements" (called simply "promos") to stir up interest in its own forthcoming programs. Since promos involve no payment to an external medium, they are not considered advertisements, though the same announcements published and paid for in a newspaper would be. A news story about an up-coming program printed by a newspaper would be classed as publicity. A press invitation to meet the star of the program at a cocktail party would be a promotional activity; resulting news or feature stories in the paper would be publicity.

A significant amount of broadcast programming is little more than publicity and promotion (see Section 11.3 for the classic case of *Disneyland*). Many shows use as a staple ingredient celebrities or would-be celebrities whose excuse for appearance is promoting their own broadcast programs, night-club appearances, books, films, causes, or points of view. The susceptibility of the medium to promotional uses has also led to abuses in the form of "plugola" and "payola." Unethical performers plant references to commercial products in their programs in exchange for which they themselves, instead of the medium, receive payment. In the field of popular music, plugging songs for pay by disc jockeys became so notorious in the 1950's that Congress investigated the practice and enacted a federal law in 1960 to prevent it (Section 13.5).

---

[6] One estimate placed the public's share of capital investment in broadcasting at 96 per cent, that of the broadcasting industry at 4 per cent. [House Committee on Interstate and Foreign Commerce, *Television Network Program Procurement,* House Report 281, prepared by FCC Office of Network Study, 88th Cong., 1st Sess. (Washington: Government Printing Office, 1963), p. 58.]

[7] The home user of recorded material (sound or picture) must have a playback unit and in that sense also invests in that medium. However, he differs fundamentally from the investor in a broadcast receiver in that he also invests in (or himself creates) the program materials, which he can then use repeatedly and at his own discretion, and he does not pay the additional price of submitting to advertising messages.

[8] Neil H. Borden, *The Economic Effects of Advertising,* 4th ed. (Chicago: Richard D. Irwin, 1947), p. 17. Note that calculated concealment of the source of payment may turn "advertising" into "propaganda." Broadcast advertising must, according to law, identify its source.

12.3 / Advertising and Mass Consumption

Popular writers on advertising like to trace it back to the days of the caveman, or at least to Greece and Rome. It may be true that trade has always included at least a minor element of what we now call advertising—the literal crying of one's wares. More elaborate and persuasive advertising was usually associated with mountebanks and patent-medicine salesmen—an early image that the modern advertising industry has never been able completely to live down, since mountebanks and snake-oil salesmen tend to reappear with slight modifications in every generation. Advertising as an essential element in the distribution system of a society of mass consumers, however, is something novel in human history.

Mass consumption has been made possible by an enormous increase in productivity resulting from technological change, along with a corresponding increase in mass buying power resulting from higher income and consumer credit. For the first time in history, most of a population—not just a tiny minority—has more than enough money for the bare necessities of life. The mass consumer has attained *discretionary* purchasing power—in the aggregate, he has billions of available dollars for free-choice, optional spending.[9] This condition has been variously described by economists as the economy of abundance,[10] the affluent society,[11] and the mass consumption society.[12] One who has never lived in any other environment can hardly conceive of the chasm which separates his modern affluent society from the rest of mankind, for even today, most of the world's population continues to live at or near a bare subsistence level.

In the few fortunate countries where mass consumption has become possible, even luxury products once the symbols of immense wealth have become commonplace, albeit reduced in scale. Yachts, for example: fabulous floating palaces have become an anachronism, but less pretentious mass-produced pleasure craft clog every navigable body of water in America.

Successful mass merchandising of even a marginal and insignificant product brings immense economic rewards. Who would have thought fifty years ago, for example, that a good recipe for fried chicken could make millionaires not just of the man with the recipe, but of literally dozens of people associated with his business? Rosser Reeves invented a "hard-sell" style of television commercial in the 1950's featuring animated diagrams of imaginary physiological processes, such as hammers pounding in an aching head. Within eigh-

---

[9] One estimate projects the United States annual discretionary income as likely to be $280 billion in 1975. [*Fortune* Magazine, *Markets of the Seventies* (New York: Viking, 1968), p. 111.]

[10] David M. Potter, *People of Plenty: Economic Abundance and the American Character* (Chicago: University of Chicago Press, 1945).

[11] John Kenneth Galbraith, *The Affluent Society* (New York: New American Library, 1958).

[12] George Katona, *The Mass Consumption Society* (New York: McGraw Hill, 1964).

teen months after makers of a headache remedy started using this type of commercial, their sales increased $54 million.[13]

Price has nothing to do with such success stories, for price no longer assumes a pivotal role in competitive marketing. After all, since the manufacturers in any established field usually pay pretty much the same rates for such essentials as labor, transportation, raw materials, power, and taxes, prices tend to become stabilized. In any event, the affluent consumer, though not unconcerned about price, need not actually be constrained by it when other criteria seem more important. Competition, therefore,

. . . more often than not centers on peculiar suitability to the user's needs (which producers have studied in detail), on engineering design, durability, low operating and maintenance cost, and scores of other similar considerations usually of more importance to the user's costs than purchase price. Much the same considerations now apply to consumer goods, in which superior packaging, style, color, flavor, durability, weigh heavily in the mind of the customers. It is here that advertising has served such a useful economic function.[14]

Beyond the realm of factual exposition, however, advertising also seeks "to exercise some coercive force upon your judgment, to wheedle it, surprise it, overwhelm it, or at least, persuade it."[15] Even Communist states agree that advertising has a legitimate economic function as a means of disseminating information about products and stimulating consumer demand, but they reject the legitimacy of advertising as a means of persuasion. A nineteenth-century economist, Alfred Marshall, first drew attention to this distinction between factual and persuasive advertising in the context of theoretical economics. Marshall could find no justification for persuasive advertising.[16] A major study of advertising's economic effects reached the conclusion that "it all depends" —in some situations advertising did appear wasteful, in others beneficial, though on the whole it appeared to be an economic asset.[17] A Canadian economist reviewing the evidence on behalf of his government identified forty-three alleged advantages and thirty-three alleged disadvantages of advertising, which led him to conclude that "there is hardly any other area of economic activity where the gulf between speaking well and speaking ill of an industry is as wide as in the case of advertising."[18]

In the mass-consumption society, advertising not only seeks to persuade but has taken on a new and even more controversial role as a generator of con-

---

[13] Thomas Whiteside, "The Man from Iron City," *The New Yorker,* April 27, 1969, pp. 54, 57.

[14] David E. Lilienthal, *Big Business: A New Era* (New York: Harper & Bros., 1953), p. 52.

[15] Max Radin, *The Lawful Pursuit of Gain* (Boston: Houghton Mifflin, 1931), p. 57.

[16] Alfred Marshall, *Principles of Economics* (New York: Macmillan, 1961).

[17] Borden, *op. cit.*

[18] O. J. Firestone, *Economic Implications of Advertising* (Toronto: Methuen, 1967), p. 21.

sumer desires—a "synthesizer of wants," to use Galbraith's phrase. Mass advertising can stimulate demand for objects of which consumers never heard before and for which they never felt any previous need. Only because mass advertising creates markets overnight where none already existed can manufacturers bring out the thousands of new products—or new versions of old products—each year to keep the economy continually expanding.

Broadcasting proved uniquely adaptable to this role of educating for consumption, of creating new consumer needs, new standards, new tastes. Broadcasting can dramatize marginal differentiation among products. It can enter into the home, follow the housewife as she goes about her tasks, accompany the wage earner in his car, provide a constant background for the teenager as he studies and plays. Broadcast advertising thus capitalizes on discretionary purchasing power more effectively than any other medium.

12.4 / The Case Against Advertising

The New York Historical Society once gave an exhibition called "Eat, Drink, and Be Wary—a Backward Glance at Foods, Drugs, and Cosmetics Before the Protective Acts of 50 Years Ago." Among the exhibits was this preradio "word from our sponsor":

The
Matchless Sanative
Invented by the Immortal

LOUIS OFFON GOELICKE, M.D.,
of Germany, Europe,

IS astonishing the WORLD with its mighty victories over many FEAR-FUL DISEASES, which have been pronounced INCURABLE by physicans in every age, being the most

VALUABLE MEDICINE

and the most unaccountable in its operations of any ever prepared by human hands; a medicine obtained EQUALLY from the ANIMAL, MINERAL AND VEGETABLE KINGDOMS, thus possessing a

THREE-FOLD POWER;

a medicine, of more value to mankind than the united treasures of our globe, and for which we have abundant cause to bless the beneficent hands of a kind Providence; a medicine, which begins to be valued by PHYSICIANS, who have heretofore opposed it, who are daily witnessing its astonishing cures of many whom they had assigned to the grasp of the   INSATIABLE GRAVE!!   a precious and powerful medicine, which has thoroughly filled the *great vacuum in the Materia Medica;* and thereby proved itself TO BE THE

CONQUEROR OF PHYSICIANS

Commercials for some of the remedies still advertised on radio and television today may incline critics to think that only the medium, not the message, has changed, despite modern legal restraints.

To be sure, in the earliest days of radio the medical nostrums, quack doctors, fortune tellers, and real-estate swindlers were beginning to find it hard to place their advertising in the print media. They discovered in broadcasting a new, even more persuasive medium. The pioneer radio critic, Ben Gross, recalls:

Tailors, preachers, loan sharks, swamis, and physical-culture men, merchants, nostrum dispensers and frenzied advocates of odd ideas, such as Colonel Henderson of Shreveport, Louisiana, who combined primitive theology with hatred of chain stores, indulged in a saturnalia of "free speech." . . . In a steady procession, there came before the microphones newscasters who merely read word-for-word items from the daily papers, owners of diploma mills, crystal-gazing fortunetellers, installment furniture men, conductors of matrimonial bureaus, fakers, nuts and dreamers making merry carnival.[19]

Other evidence is quoted in Section 19.8. As the medium matured, however, most outright quackery disappeared, though the records of the Federal Trade Commission show that an element of misrepresentation certainly persists. The combination of legal restraints, industry self-regulation, the individual integrity of advertisers and media managers, and public pressure can be counted on to keep advertising chicanery and deception within bounds in the long run. Some critics, however, have a much more fundamental concern: the stimulation of new consumer wants by advertising. Arnold Toynbee, the most influential critic of this school, accuses advertising-promoted affluence and materialism of betraying the high ideals of the American social revolution:

. . . there is a limit, and a narrow one, to the quantity of goods that can be effectively possessed, in the sense of being genuinely enjoyed, by a single human being in a single lifetime. . . . The true end of Man is not to possess the maximum amount of consumer goods per head. When we are considering the demand for consumer goods, we have to distinguish between three things: our needs, our wants, and the unwanted demand, in excess of our genuine wants, that we allow the advertising trade to bully us into demanding if we are both rich enough and foolish enough to let ourselves be influenced by advertising.[20]

Toynbee asserts that short of disarmament, elimination of "bogus wants" offers the best source of increased public funds for social improvement.

In this Toynbee echoes an economist, John Kenneth Galbraith, who has become the leading theoretical opponent of mass advertising. Production, instead of being guided by "spontaneous" consumer wants, "synthesizes" arti-

---

[19] Ben Gross, *I Looked and I Listened* (copyright 1954 by Random House, Inc.), pp. 68–69.

[20] Arnold Toynbee, *America and the World Revolution and Other Lectures* (New York: Oxford University Press, 1962), pp. 131, 144.

ficial wants for him, says Galbraith.[21] A serious consequence of this reversal, in Galbraith's view, is an overemphasis on producing private consumer goods and services as the key to economic well-being, to the neglect of the essential public services on which those very private goods make ever more urgent demands.

Advertising operates exclusively . . . on behalf of privately produced goods and service. . . . The engines of mass communication, in their highest state of development, assail the eyes and ears of the community on behalf of more beer but not more schools. . . . Every corner of the public psyche is canvassed by some of the nation's most talented citizens to see if the desire for some merchantable product can be cultivated. No similar process operates on behalf of the nonmerchantable services of the state.[22]

The result, Galbraith tells us, is deterioration of our environment and the condition of public life. Increased consumption of automobiles, for example, creates the need for more highways, more traffic police, more antipollution measures, more junk-disposal facilities. Advertising persuades consumers that they need a second or third car, or a more stylish, better-equipped car; but advertising makes no corresponding effort to persuade consumers to vote for the tax measures needed to pay for the additional social services that the increase in vehicles inevitably requires. The result: more traffic congestion; more safety violations; more smog, death and injury; more junk blighting the landscape.[23]

Potter, though fundamentally more sympathetic to advertising then Galbraith, comes to about the same conclusion by a different route:

. . . advertising has in its dynamics no motivation to seek the improvement of the individual or to impart qualities of social usefulness, unless conformity to material values may be so characterized. . . . It is this lack of institutional responsibility, this lack of inherent social purpose to balance social power, which, I would argue, is a basic cause for concern about the role of advertising.[24]

12.5 / For the Defense

Allegations of synthesized consumer wants, economic waste, diversion of attention from needful public services to private consumption, and social irresponsibility have been built into a powerful indictment of the economic role

---

[21] Galbraith, *op. cit.*, p. 125.

[22] *Ibid.*, p. 205.

[23] In fact, the Advertising Council, a cooperative effort by media and creative advertising personnel, does provide just the top-quality free advertising for "nonmerchantable services" which Galbraith advocates. According to the Council's Annual Report for 1969, in that year the value of its contributions amounted to $463 million. Galbraith would doubtless argue, however, that an amount equal to only about 2 per cent of commercial advertising hardly constitutes a fair distribution of resources between the two sectors.

[24] Potter, *op. cit.*, p. 177.

of advertising. Defendants of the system generally lack the academic prestige of Toynbee and Galbraith, but what they lack in theoretical sophistication they perhaps make up in practical knowledge.

Academic commentators tend to take it for granted that advertising possesses almost unlimited powers of persuasion. Potter, for example, declares that

. . . advertising now compares with such long-standing institutions as the school and the church in the magnitude of its social influence. It dominates the media, it has vast power in the shaping of popular standards, and it is really one of the very limited group of institutions which exercise social control.[25]

Those who work in the media often find themselves wishing it were only so! The previously cited failure of 80 per cent of the new packaged consumer products introduced annually hardly supports the allegation that industry simply manufactures consumer wants at will. Of course, these failures may simply reflect lack of skill in synthesizing wants. But the leading case on record of such a failure certainly cannot be explained on these grounds.

The classic case is the Edsel automobile, marketed by the Ford Motor Company in 1957 after the most prodigious and expensive campaign of promotion, publicity, and advertising ever staged to introduce a new product.

Advertising, together with a vast program of publicity . . . brought three million people into showrooms across the country when the drumbeating was loudest and the car was introduced. There, completely unmoved, they turned thumbs down on it. Why, no one exactly knows.[26]

The company employed top people in each specialized field of public communication and gave them unstinted budgets. Two-page spreads in *Life* kicked off the final consumer campaign. Ed Sullivan was preempted and his prime-time television hour filled with a highly successful musical special featuring Bing Crosby, Frank Sinatra, and Rosemary Clooney. A gala three-day, all-expenses-paid press preview for 250 reporters and wives ended with 71 reporters driving brand-new Edsels back to their home towns, where they delivered them to local Edsel dealers. Ford paid $90 thousand for the preview, but this was a trifle. By the time the Edsel finally went out of production nearly three years later, it had cost the Ford Motor Company and the Edsel dealers on the order of $400 million—"the greatest tragedy in American manufacturing history," says Cone, who points out:

---

[25] *Ibid.,* p. 167.

[26] Cone, *op. cit.,* p. 5. Cone's agency, Foote, Cone and Belding, handled the Edsel advertising account. For a more complete narrative, see John Brooks, *The Fate of the Edsel and Other Business Adventures* (New York: Harper & Row, 1963). Other such cases are reviewed by Thomas L. Berg in *Mismarketing: Case Histories of Marketing Misfires* (Garden City, N. Y.: Doubleday, 1970). He concludes (p. 2) that "failure is a pervasive characteristic of modern marketing."

If publicity and advertising could have made any difference, they would have made the new car a success . . . the buildup for the Edsel was the most intensive in the history of the automobile business.[27]

Many reasons for the Edsel's spectacular failure have been advanced, among them the allegation that it illustrated what happens when too much dependence is put on market research.[28] However, no explanation stands up to analysis—except acknowledgement that the public has a mind of its own after all. Despite the most favorable sales climate, despite the most skillful marshalling of all the arts of publicity and persuasion, the Edsel failed to create a want.[29]

The Edsel case dramatizes a common marketing experience—not every advertising campaign succeeds. Transfer of brand loyalty, a well-recognized market phenomenon, indicates that advertising cannot always succeed even in maintaining existing wants. Such experiences suggest that creating wants must be somewhat more complicated than simple manipulation of passive consumers by marketeers. Fairfax Cone, after forty years and billions of dollars worth of practical advertising experience, concluded:

Most of the viewers who fear advertising as an evil force give it too much credit. About all it can do under the most skillful direction (and by skillful direction I don't mean either hidden or otherwise undue persuasion) is to exploit a given interest, predilection, disposition, prejudice or bias and bring this to bear on a buying decision.[30]

In *The Mass Consumption Society,* Katona suggests that an accurate description of want creation would give the consumer the primary role:

Under what conditions are the "persuaders" successful? Quite simply, when they swim with the current . . . if and when advertising conforms with trends in consumer wants, it exerts some influence.[31]

Research on the persuasive powers of the communications media (reviewed in Chapter 23) bears out this conclusion: the media succeed best when reinforcing existing attitudes; they succeed least when running counter to established opinions, prejudices, and values. As Katona puts it, "the influence of advertising, just as of any other mass medium, decreases in proportion to the

---

[27] Cone, *op. cit.,* pp. 251, 255–256.

[28] S. I. Hayakawa, "Why the Edsel Laid an Egg," *ETC.: A Review of General Semantics,* XV (Spring, 1958), 217–221.

[29] Further evidence of the limitations of advertising may possibly be found in the fact that the second year's Edsel model, with some changes in horsepower and dimensions, began to sell a little better (though still far below the break-even point) *without* benefit of heavy advertising. [Brooks, *op. cit.,* pp. 67–68.]

[30] Cone, *op. cit.,* p. 8.

[31] Katona, *op. cit.,* p. 61.

importance the consumer attaches to the matter."[32] He points out that in fact consumers do not take seriously the marginal product differentiations advertising exploits. That explains why consumer loyalty is fickle. Profound beliefs about matters people consider consequential, however, tenaciously resist change. They are as likely to be strengthened as weakened by media attempts at conversion. Galbraith agrees, although in support of a different argument:

The fact that wants can be synthesized by advertising, catalyzed by salesmanship, and shaped by the discreet manipulations of the persuaders shows that they are not very urgent. A man who is hungry need never be told of his need for food.[33]

This very superficiality of most consumer wants is what troubles Toynbee. He looks at creature comforts from an ascetic, even downright puritanical, point of view: "The major religions agree in denigrating material things"— the kind of things that satisfy "bogus" wants created by advertising. In times past, when the major religious doctrines took shape, the masses of their adherents could not possibly have hoped to possess more than the bare minimum of material things. Understandably, religious leaders denigrated what they could not confer. Any other preachment would have been futile, if not suicidal. Popular religions *had* to find ways to make the immemorial poverty and deprivation of the mass of mankind easier to bear. Revolutionary economic and social changes (in some parts of the world at least) have removed these ancient barriers to material progress. Deprivation of the masses is no longer a necessity. Need it still be regarded as a virtue?

A subsistence peasant farmer feels no "spontaneous" wants for such luxuries as a tractor, fertilizer, and improved hybrid seeds; his wife feels no innate urge for piped water, power-milled flour, and detergents. Such people may not articulate wants for life-saving and pain-relieving drugs. These hypothetical examples, though extreme, are not merely straw men. Consumers generally, even those living in a technologically advanced environment, lack the imagination and specialized knowledge even to conceive of specific new products. Their wants take more generalized forms. They want good health, offspring, comfort, pleasant surroundings, variety, recreation, status, entertainment, personal attractiveness. The consumer cannot be expected to invent the specific products and services which may satisfy these general wants. This innovative role belongs to the producer. The housewife may not have wanted instant mashed potatoes—the possibility of such a preparation probably never occurred to her—but she *does* want her work load lightened, and if instant mashed potatoes help satisfy that want without at the same time frustrating the want for tasty food, who is to begrudge her? "Before a new product reaches the market," as Katona puts it, "before the consumer is told by the producer what is available, wants do not take a form specific enough to serve

---

[32] *Ibid.*, p. 58.

[33] Galbraith, *op. cit.*, p. 128.

as a guide for industry."[34] He reminds us, moreover, that psychological wants can be just as real as physical wants. To equate legitimate wants strictly with necessities like food is to ignore an equally vital area of human needs.

David Ogilvy quotes the father of the labor movement in England as saying, "The tragedy of the working class is the poverty of their desires." "I make no apology," says Ogilvy, "for inciting the working class to desire less Spartan lives." He goes on:

If you don't think people need deodorants, you are at liberty to criticize advertising for having persuaded 87 per cent of American women and 66 per cent of American men to use them. . . . If you disapprove of social mobility, creature comforts, and foreign travel, you are right to blame advertising for encouraging such wickedness. If you dislike affluent society you are right to blame advertising for inciting the masses to pursue it. If you are this kind of Puritan, I cannot reason with you.[35]

12.6 / "On the Other Hand . . ."

The foregoing argument in defense of mass advertising concerns underlying assumptions about its economic and moral justification. Whichever view we take on these fundamental issues, advertising continues as a fact of life in advanced economies and has to be reckoned with on a pragmatic level. On this level, even advertising's best friends will admit that all is not well. Outright dishonesty, as we have said, no longer constitutes a major problem, though curbing it requires constant government surveillance and industry self-discipline.

David Ogilvy, the agency head quoted earlier in defense of advertising, also makes this indictment:

It is television advertising which has made Madison Avenue the arch-symbol of tasteless materialism. If governments do not soon set up machinery for the regulation of television, I feel that the majority of thoughtful men will come to agree with Toynbee. . . . I have a vested interest in the survival of Madison Avenue, and I doubt whether it can survive without drastic reform.[36]

Few in the industry go so far as Ogilvy in calling for government intervention. Instead, they call for better self-discipline within the industry. A broadcasting trade journal, after commenting on seven years of investigation and litigation to halt allegedly false radio advertising of a medicinal product, editorialized:

What gives us pause is that the questionable advertising was accepted—after a final decision by the Appellate Court—by so many radio stations. This fact will

---

[34] Katona, *op. cit.,* p. 56.

[35] David Ogilvy, *Confessions of An Advertising Man* (New York: Dell, 1964), p. 196.

[36] *Ibid.,* pp. 201–202.

not embellish radio's record. . . . The radio system of America was built upon higher principles than those of the wandering medicine show.[37]

We have already cited (Section 12.1) the problem of quantity—the huge number of advertising messages to which the consumer is exposed. Katona sees this rising din as a major threat to the future of advertising:

The problem of too much advertising plagues us today and threatens us to a much larger extent in the future. The economy is growing and with it the number of advertised products and the funds available for advertising. But the amount of time the individual has to read or hear messages remains unchanged . . . advertising might do well to lean less heavily on persuasion and testimonials and more on technical information and explanations of the purposes best served by the products it desires to sell.[38]

Obtrusiveness causes problems primarily in the broadcast media. The eye can skip about at will in space media, but the viewer/listener cannot as easily bridge interruptions in the time media. The industry has been gradually edging the length and frequency of commercials upward (Section 13.3). According to an FCC Commissioner, the number of network commercials doubled in the years 1964–1970; the number of all television commercials (network and local) rose 41 per cent in the period 1966–1970.[39] Commercial interruptions have long been one of the most frequently criticized aspects of broadcasting.[40] Nevertheless, consumers could be counted on to remain relatively passive as long as they had no alternative other than not listening or watching at all. One of the expected benefits from noncommercial broadcasting, as it widens its coverage and its programming appeal, is that it may make audiences less tolerant toward the deterioration of commercial programming caused by excessive fragmentation and dilution by advertising messages.

---

[37] "Bitter Pill," *Broadcasting-Telecasting,* December 24, 1956, p. 86.

[38] Katona, *op. cit.,* p. 296. Galbraith (*op. cit.,* p. 161) ironically envisions the future: "On some not distant day the voice of each individual seller may well be lost in the collective roar . . . advertising will beat helplessly on ears that have been conditioned by previous assault to utter immunity. . . . Silence, interrupted perhaps by brief, demoniacal outbursts of salesmanship, will ensue."

[39] Robert E. Lee, "Don't Kill the Goose!" Address to Association of National Advertisers, April 13, 1970 (mimeo.), pp. 5–6.

[40] See Gary A. Steiner, *The People Look at Television: A Study of Audience Attitudes* (New York: Alfred A. Knopf, 1963), Chapter 7, and the discussion in Section 13.3 below.

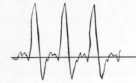

13

BROADCAST-ADVERTISING PRACTICE

Advertising practice had, of course, been well established in print and other media by the time broadcasting appeared. Broadcasting introduced novel elements, notably the shift in concept from space or position to *time* as the advertising container. The existing framework of advertising practice in the print media nevertheless provided a general model for broadcasting, although increasing complexity of production in each medium eventually required more and more specialization by advertising practitioners.

13.1 / Integration of Advertising in the Program Structure

Segmentation into discrete programs or program items provides the most elementary structural feature of broadcast programming. The need to conform to audience habits and to maintain internal coordination obliges these elements, in turn, to be governed by clock time. Practical considerations of audience availability and receptivity dictate the best times of day for each type of program, depending on local life styles. In highly industrialized areas, people are awake and available as potential audience members at night, for example, while in rural areas, farmers go to bed earlier and "prime time" takes on a different meaning. Coordination of networks with affiliates and even of operations within a single organization requires adherence to a relatively inflexible clock schedule. Contractual obligations to advertisers, where they exist, again compel programs to follow predictable time patterns. Critics sometimes complained about this arbitrary chopping of program time into predetermined lengths and the enforced pruning of content to fit. Yet even educational broadcasting (which has no obligations to advertisers), as well as broadcasters in underdeveloped countries (where audiences have no highly developed time sense), have found it expedient to structure their program scheduling fairly rigidly according to the clock.

Insofar as advertising does enter into a service, provision must be made for incorporating it systematically into the overall program structure at predictable intervals. Deciding on these intervals automatically creates a degree of tension between those responsible for advertising and those responsible for programming. From the programmer's point of view, advertising disturbs the ideally smooth flow of material; research confirms what common sense suggests—advertising interruptions cause a drop in audience attention.[1] But from the seller's point of view, advertising should be placed at points of maximum exposure and highest interest, integrated so cunningly that avoidance is difficult or impossible. As an advertising medium, broadcasting gains an advantage from being time-bound rather than space-bound: the eye can more easily evade advertising by choosing selectively from a page or other spatial configuration than can either the eye or ear dodge commercials by choosing selectively from a time continuum.

Policy must determine, then, the balance struck between these opposing viewpoints. Some broadcasting systems maintain an absolute demarcation between commercials and other program material, segregating all advertising in special commercial periods analogous to a classified-advertisement section or an advertising supplement in newspapers. Other systems permit scattering commercials throughout the day's programming, dropping them in between programs or within programs at natural internal breaks. This method approximates display advertising in space media, where advertisements are closely associated with nonadvertising matter throughout the publication, but differences in typography (and even the word "advertisement" if its format might mislead the reader into confusing it with editorial matter) maintain a clear differentiation. In broadcasting, Britain's Independent Television Authority follows an analogous practice, in accordance with the Television Act of 1964, § 7(6):

No advertisement may include anything that states, suggests or implies, or could reasonably be taken to state, suggest or imply, that any part of any programme broadcast by the Authority has been supplied or suggested by any advertiser.[2]

American broadcasting follows the still more liberal policy of allowing close association between advertiser and program, both in explicit sponsorship of programs by advertisers and in close integration of advertising with program content. American broadcasting departs, therefore, from the general practice of the print media; they normally neither allow advertisers to control (or provide) nonadvertising content, nor permit integration of advertising with editorial content to the degree common in broadcasting. To pursue the print analogy to its conclusion, the equivalent of the sneakily integrated commercial which takes the listener/viewer unawares would be a commercial paragraph in the midst of a news story, introduced without change of type style or other visual separation of commercial from editorial matter.

---

[1] Viewer drop-off during television commercials increased during the 1960's, averaging 27 per cent by 1970, according to Edward H. Meyer in "Is the Golden Goose Beginning to Lay Leaden Eggs?" (New York: Grey Advertising, Inc., April 12, 1970, mimeo.), p. 8.

[2] Quoted in Independent Television Authority, *ITV 1969: A Guide to Independent Television* (London: The Authority, 1969), p. 217.

13.2 / Sponsors and Spots

Radio advertising began, however, on a much more tentative basis. When WEAF began to sell time in 1922, the first purchaser bought a ten-minute segment. H. M. Blackwell, a representative of the Queensboro Corporation, used the ten minutes for an institutional talk about Hawthorne Courts, a cooperative apartment development in Jackson Heights, N. Y. Blackwell mentioned the Queensboro Corporation only once and dealt chiefly with the healthfulness of living in the suburbs. He closed on a mild note of urgency, to be sure, but with no mention of price or other commercial details: "Let me close by urging you to hurry to the apartment house near the green fields . . . the community life and friendly environment that Hawthorne advocated."[3] Indeed, Blackwell talked more about Hawthorne the writer than about Hawthorne the homesite.

Station policy of that period forbade direct selling. Licensees regarded radio as a public-relations medium—a means of creating goodwill, not a direct means of making sales. The art of public relations has been defined as 90 per cent doing good and 10 per cent talking about it, and one obvious way of doing good on the radio is to present an attractive program. In the early 1920's, however, stations handled programming rather haphazardly. Norman Brokenshire, describing his experiences at WJZ in 1924, says: "If people dropped into the studio and could perform in any way, we had a program to put on the air; if no one dropped in, we were stuck." One day when no one dropped in and Brokenshire was improvising program material to fill one schedule blank after another, he finally resorted to hanging the microphone out the studio window to broadcast "the sounds of New York."[4]

These circumstances invited advertisers to capitalize on the public hunger for professionally competent entertainment by assuming responsibility for programs as well as for advertising. Program sponsorship resulted, operating on the theory that the advertiser may subject the audience to a small amount of advertising in return for a dividend in good entertainment. Accordingly, most of the major users of early network-radio advertising were sponsors who needed—and could afford—to spend money on institutional or general goodwill advertising. In 1927, the leading product group on network radio was naturally that of the radio manufacturers themselves, who had everything to gain from improved programming. Radio manufacturers became less important after 1929, by which time the burden had been taken up by other sponsors; but history repeated itself in 1948 when the manufacturers primed the television pump by sponsoring the kind of programming which would sell television sets. The second-largest radio-network sponsor group in 1927 comprised insurance and finance companies—large corporations which at that

---

[3] Gleason L. Archer, *History of Radio to 1926* (New York: The American Historical Company, 1938), pp. 397–399.

[4] Norman Brokenshire, *This is Norman Brokenshire* (New York: David McKay, 1954), pp. 53–54.

Figure 13.1

"The Cliquot Club Eskimos"

A musical group featured on one of radio's first sponsored programs. The announcer is Graham McNamee.

Source: Brown Brothers.

time used primarily dignified institutional advertising. Their number decreased in favor of such product groups as foods and drugs after radio began to be used for direct selling.

Restrictions on direct salesmanship on radio relaxed slowly and unevenly. The earliest network advertisers evaded rules against repeated mention of the sponsor's name by attaching it to the performers. Browning King's *Wednesday Night Dance* featured the "Browning King Orchestra," which of course had to be identified by name before each selection was played. Audiences of the 1920's heard the "Clicquot Club Eskimos," the "A & P Gypsies," the "Ipana Troubadours," and so on (Figure 13.1). Here is an example of an opening "billboard" from this period:

Relax and smile, for Goldy and Dusty, the Gold Dust Twins, are *here* to send their *songs there,* and "brighten the corner where you are." The Gold Dust Corporation, manufacturer of Gold Dust Powder, engages the facilities of station WEAF, New York, WJAR, Providence, WCAE, Pittsburgh, WGR, Buffalo, WEEI, Boston, WFI, Philadelphia, and WEAR, Cleveland, so that the listeners-in may have the opportunity to chuckle and laugh with Goldy and Dusty. Let those Gold Dust Twins into your hearts and homes tonight, and you'll never regret it, for they *do* brighten the dull spots.[5]

As early as 1926, the La France Company (laundry aids) used commercial announcements not much different in length and content (though stilted in style) from those which later became common. Nevertheless, the networks retained the ban against mentioning price until 1932.

Sponsorship entails a double expense for the advertiser: he pays not only for time on the station or network, but also for talent and other program ingredients. Not all advertisers want or can afford such expense. The immediate alternative was to schedule isolated commercial announcements, disassociated from programs. The transition from the end of one program to the start of the next made a natural break into which extra, free-floating announcements could be inserted. The legal requirement of periodically announcing call letters and location (station identification, or "ID") also provided ready-made interstices in the programming sequence. Thus developed the station-break "spot" announcement. Network affiliates "cut away" from the network for thirty seconds (increased in 1960 to forty seconds for television affiliates) at the close of each network program to insert local commercials and station identification. A tradition grew up in radio that station-break announcements should be limited to one spot plus a brief commercial "service" announcement, such as a time signal. The radio industry's 1948 code stipulated:

The placement of more than one commercial announcement between two commercial programs should not be permitted except in those instances when one of the two announcements is a sponsored time signal, weather report, station promotion or location announcement of not to exceed a total of ten seconds in length.[6]

Under pressure to find openings for more spots, stations evolved a third device for integrating commercials into programming—the *participation* (or participating) program. The station rather than an individual sponsor provided the program; it then sold "participations" to several advertisers, who became in effect co-sponsors. This device justified spotting announcements *within* programs, even though they were not sponsored in the original sense.

Stations developed the participating format as a device for selling local advertisers and local programming. Later, as radio-network competition increased, the networks also adopted the format. Typically, radio networks sold daytime shows in quarter-hour participations. The high cost of television encouraged this trend—to the point, in fact, where full-program sponsorship be-

---

[5] Quoted in William P. Banning, *Commercial Broadcasting Pioneer: The WEAF Experiment 1922–1926* (Cambridge, Mass.: Harvard University Press, 1946), p. 262.

[6] National Association of Radio and Television Broadcasters, *Standards of Practice for American Broadcasters* (Washington: The Association, 1948), p. 7.

came more the exception than the rule in network television in the 1960's. Reluctant to risk their entire budgets on single-program series which might or might not pay off in the long run, most national advertisers began to spread their bets over a number of programs. This stratagem came to be called "scatter buying." Table 13.1 indicates its growth. Of prime-time network spot-buying advertisers, about half in 1957 and over 70 per cent in 1967 spent less than enough to sponsor fully a single half-hour series.[7]

Table 13.1

Trend toward multiple sponsorship of major network programs

No. Sponsors Per Program Series	% of Program Series	
	1957	*1967*
1	44.1	3.7
2	41.5	6.2
3 or more	9.3	90.1
15 or more	0.0	63.0

Based on regularly scheduled entertainment series of all networks, 6:00–11:00 P.M.

Source: Data in Arthur D. Little, Inc., "Television Program Production, Procurement, Distribution and Scheduling" (Cambridge, Mass.: The Corporation, 1969), p. 21.

To recapitulate, American broadcasting integrates commercials with the program service in three principal ways: (1) within sponsored programs, which the sponsor designs to accommodate commercial announcements at strategic intervals; (2) in the transitional periods between programs (station breaks); (3) within participation programs, which the station (or network) designs to accommodate commercial announcements from varied clients at strategic intervals.

As minor advertising modes, two other techniques may be mentioned: the "pitch" and the "announcement program." The word "pitch" originally meant the place where a street hawker set up a temporary stand; in broadcasting it means an extended, high-pressure sales talk which may run on for many minutes—even fifteen or thirty. The very term "announcement," however, implies brevity, and by tacit agreement one minute came to be considered the maximum normal length. Typically, the pitchman advertises a product for sale by mail, often grossly overpriced. In the early days of television, stations accepted a wave of pitch advertising, creating an atmosphere of carnival fakery in broadcasting which damaged its image as an ethical advertising

---

[7] Arthur D. Little, Inc., "Television Program Production, Procurement, Distribution and Scheduling" (Cambridge, Mass.: The Corporation, 1969), p. 34.

medium.[8] The NAB Television Code rules out pitch advertising on the grounds that it is "inconsistent with good broadcast practice and generally damages the reputation of the industry."[9]

The announcement program crowds an almost uninterrupted series of commercial announcements into a single time segment under the guise of a "shopping guide" or some similar service. "Classified advertisements of the air" represents a more straightforward name for this all-advertising format.

Commercially supported programs (sponsored and participating) do not necessarily fill the whole broadcast schedule, so stations and networks must usually maintain some programs on a noncommercial basis. Broadcasters invented the term "sustaining" for such programs. Some program material by its very nature cannot be commercialized—occasions of state, such as Presidential addresses, for example. Beyond that, however, the FCC at one time looked upon sustaining programs as having an important "balance-wheel" function. Commercial motivations tend to narrow down the choice of programs likely to be sponsored; sustaining programs, the FCC reasoned, should provide opportunities for material less likely to find sponsors, such as that serving the interests of minorities, nonprofit organizations, and program experimentation.[10]

The disillusioning experience of education in trying to use commercial facilities (Section 9.10) indicates that this ideal failed to work out in practice. Broadcasters naturally tended to design sustaining programs with ultimate sale in mind, so that the very same program might be sustaining one day, commercial the next. When a sustaining program went commercial it immediately acquired a larger audience. Evidently listeners had the feeling that anything not attractive to an advertiser could not be very good in the first place—or conversely, that anything for which an advertiser was willing to pay had to have some merit.[11] Alternatively, stations tended to skimp on expenses of programs destined to remain sustaining, so that to be a "sustainer" was a mark of inferiority in the public mind.

In 1960, after an inquiry into program practices, the Commission discon-

---

[8] In 1954, 70 per cent of the country's television stations were said to be accepting pitch advertising. See John Osbon, "The Pitchman in the Parlor," *Broadcasting-Telecasting,* August 9, 1954, p. 80. In the early 1950's, a cosmetics manufacturer was spending $8 million annually on television pitch advertising which the FTC alleged made false claims. [FTC, *Annual Report, 1954* (Washington: Government Printing Office, 1955), p. 32.]

[9] National Association of Broadcasters, Code Authority, *The Television Code,* 14th ed. (Washington: The Association, September, 1969), p. 23.

[10] FCC, *Public Service Responsibility of Broadcast Licensees* (Washington: Government Printing Office, 1946), pp. 12–35.

[11] Radio news commentator Raymond Gram Swing acquired White Owls as sponsor and "was puzzled to find that even friends thought more of him now he had his cigar sponsor." [Erik Barnouw, *The Golden Web: A History of Broadcasting in the United States, 1933–1953* (New York: Oxford University Press, 1968), p. 81.]

tinued consideration of sustaining programs as a significant element in fulfilling public-interest requirements, saying:

Our own observations and the testimony of this inquiry have persuaded us that
there is no public interest basis for distinguishing between sustaining and commercially sponsored programs in evaluating station performance. . . .

Sponsorship of public affairs, and other similar programs may very well encourage broadcasters to greater efforts in these vital areas . . . sponsorship fosters
rather than diminishes the availability of important public affairs and "cultural"
programs.[12]

13.3 / Salience of Commercial Content

Policy determines not only placement of commercial material within the program structure but also the degree of salience allowed. Salience is partly a
function of the content and style of the commercials themselves—whether
argumentative or factual, aggressive or "soft sell," imaginative or dull, whis-
pered or shouted (the FCC conducted a two-year study of the relative loudness of commercials and issued a policy statement in 1965).[13]

More objectively, salience also depends on easily measurable quantities—
the length of individual advertisements, the number scheduled consecutively,
their cumulative length and frequency per hour. Herein broadcasting differs
significantly from the space media: space is expandable, time is not. If a
newspaper's advertising load increases, it can accept it by simply adding
pages, without penalizing editorial space. A broadcasting station, however, has
an absolute maximum of twenty-four hours per day for program and advertising content, and in only some of those hours are audiences optimally available. Increasing one type of content necessarily decreases the other.

A newspaper or magazine can increase its news pages and advertising. But the
television station manager, who has only a certain number of hours a day to sell,
can only reap more profits by raising rates, selling more commercials, holding
program costs down and giving up no more time to network unscheduled news
events than his budget for this contingency allows. Therefore, a decision to pre-
empt a whole day for Churchill's funeral, or to cancel all nighttime programs when
the Gemini VIII astronauts lost control after their docking operation, affect local
revenues so much that station managers complained that their monthly earnings
had sagged because of a decision made in New York. In contrast, the newspaper
that adds four to eight pages for an important story loses little or nothing in advertising revenue.[14]

---

[12] FCC, "Report and Statement of Policy re: Commission en banc Programming Inquiry," 25 *Fed. Reg.* 7291 at 7295 (1960).

[13] FCC, *Thirty-First Annual Report* (Washington: Government Printing Office, 1966),
pp. 92 ff.

[14] Fred Friendly, *Due to Circumstances Beyond Our Control* . . . (copyright © 1967
by Random House, Inc.), p. 276.

Thus daily newspapers can devote an average of about 60 per cent of their space to advertising without prejudice to the editorial content, whereas if broadcasters used 60 per cent of their time for advertising they would stand a good chance of losing their licenses.

The FCC has always considered the relative prominence of commercial material in the programming structure as having a public-interest significance. In its 1946 essay on public-service responsibilities of stations, the "Blue Book," the Commission cited a number of cases of advertising "excess." For example, it criticized a station for averaging 16.7 spots per hour, another for running 6 spots consecutively, and others for interrupting newscasts with middle commercials. In its 1960 updating of its programming-standards statement, the Commission warned that licensees must "avoid abuses with respect to the total amount of time devoted to advertising continuity as well as frequency with which regular programs are interrupted for advertising messages."[15]

Applicants for new licenses must describe the commercial policies they propose to follow. Operating stations must keep logs showing the length, position, and classification of all announcements (see log-keeping rules quoted in Section 18.2). Data from these logs may be used as evidence if a renewal application is designated for hearing. Yet the FCC has never set up fixed quantitative standards for advertising content. In general, it asks stations to justify commercials in excess of the maximums in the voluntary codes of self-regulation adopted by the National Association of Broadcasters (Table 13.2). At one point the FCC proposed to adopt the NAB standards as its own and make them into law. Broadcasters lobbied vigorously against official adoption of their own trade-association standards, inspiring a bill in Congress to forbid any such action on the part of the FCC. At the ensuing Congressional hearings, testimony of the FCC Chairman explained one reason for the opposition: an FCC study of station logs indicated that 40 per cent of the stations exceeded NAB time-limitation standards.[16] Early in 1964, the FCC terminated its "overcommercialization" investigation and dropped the proposal to impose fixed standards in favor of "closer scrutiny" of how well stations lived up to their application promises. It continued its case-by-case approach, which leaves room for wide variations according to local circumstances. Indeed, in 1966 the Commission even authorized an FM station in Los Angeles to broadcast experimentally a service consisting entirely of classified advertisements.

Even in its 1946 study the FCC had already commented on the "progressive relaxation in standards."[17] That relaxation has continued. The NAB's 1937

---

[15] FCC, *Public Service Responsibility of Broadcast Licensees,* pp. 40–47; FCC, "Report and Statement of Policy re: Commission en banc Programming Inquiry," at 7295.

[16] House Committee on Interstate and Foreign Commerce, Subcommittee on Communications and Power, *Broadcast Advertisements,* Hearings on H.R. 8316 *et al.,* 88th Cong., 1st Sess. (Washington: Government Printing Office, 1963), p. 38.

[17] FCC, *Public Service Responsibility of Broadcast Licensees,* p. 42.

Radio Code allowed, as basic maxima, nine minutes of commercial material in a one-hour daytime program and six minutes in a nighttime hour. The 1970 Radio Code permits *double* the early daytime standard—eighteen minutes per hour, day or night. Television continues the day/night (or prime-time/non-prime-time) distinction.[18] The first NAB Television Code (adopted on March 1, 1952) allowed six and seven minutes of commercial time per hour for nonprime time and prime time respectively. By 1970, in the fourteenth edition of the Code, these limits had increased to ten minutes and sixteen minutes—the latter representing more than a 225 per cent increase. Similar increases have occurred in the number of announcements run "back to back," that is, consecutively at one time. We noted in Section 13.1 that originally at station breaks, one announcement plus a service announcement seemed sufficient. The 1970 Television Code allowed four consecutive station-break commercials. Exceptions and escape clauses make the present NAB codes considerably less restrictive than the bare recital of "normal" numerical limits suggest. Table 13.2 summarizes both the limits and the exceptions. As an example, despite the maximum limitations of sixteen minutes of "nonprogram material" and eight program interruptions in sixty minutes, an advertising-agency head could complain of being able to count *thirty-seven* separate "messages" in only seven minutes of television viewing.[19]

Monitoring a television-network half-hour prime-time news program in mid-1970 produced the following log:

ITEM			LENGTH	ELAPSED TIME
1.	News:	Opening credits	0:23	00:23
2.	*News:*	*Segment 1*	5:52	06:15
3.	Commercial 1:	Cigarette	0:30	06:45
4.	Commercial 2:	Paint	0:30	07:15
5.	*News:*	*Segment 2*	6:15	13:30
6.	Commercial 3:	Financial service	1:00	14:30
7.	*News:*	*Segment 3*	3:20	17:50
8.	Commercial 4:	Dental care	0:30	18:20
9.	Commercial 5:	Dental care	0:30	18:50
10.	*News:*	*Segment 4*	3:59	22:49
11.	Commercial 6:	Paint	0:30	23:19
12.	Commercial 7:	Cigarette	0:30	23:49
13.	*News:*	*Segment 5*	3:35	27:24
14.	Commercial 8:	Toilet preparation	0:30	27:54
15.	Commercial 9:	Toilet preparation	0:30	28:24
16.	News:	Closing credits	0:36	29:00
17.	Network promo		0:20	29:20
18.	Local commercial		0:20	29:40

---

[18] This distinction goes back to the concept that advertising belonged to business hours, not to the evening hours after work (Section 7.10).

[19] Meyer, *op. cit.*, p. 8.

Table 13.2

Summary of NAB Television Code commercial-salience standards

Commercial[1] Salience as Measured by	Maximum Allowed		Special Provisions and Exceptional Cases
	In Prime[2] Time	*In Other Time*	
Cumulative length per time period	10 in 60[3]	16 in 60	"Reasonable use" of names of prize donors, guest identifications, name on set or properties Shopping guides
Frequency of interruption per program	4 in 60 2 in 30 2 in 15 2 in 10	8 in 60 4 in 30 2 in 15 2 in 10	News, weather, sports, and special events Variety programs (allowed 3 in 30 and 5 in 60 in prime time) Shopping guides
Number of consecutive commercial announcements			
within programs	4	4	Shopping guides Single-sponsor programs (if result is fewer interruptions) Ads for multiple products treated as one announcement
at station breaks	3	3	Ads for multiple products treated as one announcement

[1]The Code Authority uses the phrase "non-program materials." The following items are counted as program material: public-service announcements; program promotional announcements for the same program; program credits if no longer than 30 seconds.

[2]Prime time = any consecutive three hours between 6:00 P.M. and midnight.

[3]Read as follows: A maximum of 10 minutes may be devoted to commercial announcements in any consecutive prime-time 60-minute period, except as noted in right-hand column.

Source: Material in National Association of Broadcasters, Code Authority, *The Television Code,* 14th ed. (Washington: The Association, September, 1969), pp. 20–22.

ITEM	LENGTH	ELAPSED TIME
19. Local commercial	0:15	29:55
20. Local promo	0:05	30:00
21. Next program opening		

Station-break time is always deducted from nominal program length. In this instance, forty seconds must be allowed for the station break, the period between network programs when the local station cuts away from the network line and inserts its own locally originated announcements. In the nominal half-hour news program, actual news (broken into five segments) occupied just over twenty-three minutes.[20] Twelve announcements (nine of them commercials, which interrupted the news four times) occupied the rest of the news period. Between the last segment of news and the start of the next network program, seven consecutive announcements occurred. How do these figures square with the NAB Television Code's prime-time maxima of (1) only two interruptions per half hour of program material; (2) cumulative length of ten minutes per hour for nonprogram material; (3) three station-break announcements? Table 13.2 provides the answers: (1) news programs are an exception to the limitation on number of program interruptions; (2) credit and promotional announcements do not count as commercials, leaving only five minutes of countable announcements; (3) only the three announcements *after* Item 17, the network promo, count as station-break announcements.

Thus, despite seemingly rather conservative limits on commercial salience imposed by the letter of the NAB codes, in practice the final impression created for the listener/viewer is one of "clutter." An interruption interrupts, after all. Hair-splitting technicalities about what kinds of interruptions qualify as commercials and what kinds qualify as something else do not lessen the clutter. Listener/viewers can hardly be expected to welcome more interruptions in one kind of program than in another kind simply because some formats (*e.g.,* news) lend themselves more readily to fragmentation, or to consider two commercials only one merely because they come from the same company and one is called a "piggyback" by the Code Board.[21] Nor do the NAB codes address themselves at all to such irritating deceptions as persuading the audience to wait through several commercials for "more to come"—when it consists of nothing but a closing announcement.[22]

---

[20] Acceptance of such extreme fragmentation of news contrasts with the earlier concept of even *one* interruption in a fifteen-minute radio newscast being an intolerable breech of journalistic decorum. Raymond Gram Swing lost his cigar sponsor (Section 13.2) in the 1930's because he would not agree to a commercial in the middle of his program. [Barnouw, *op. cit.,* p. 148.]

[21] See "Code Board Acts to Cut Clutter," *Broadcasting,* June 1, 1970, p. 19. The discovery by researchers in the late 1960's that thirty-second spots yielded higher commercial value proportionate to their cost than one-minute spots contributed greatly to increased clutter.

[22] The time standards form only part—actually a minor part—of the NAB codes, which are discussed at length in Section 22.2.

Not surprisingly, when asked to agree or disagree with statements about the number, taste, loudness, and content of commercials, most people (80 per cent) agreed that "there are far too many commercials on television."[23] In another major survey, when asked what they disliked most about television commercials, nearly half the respondents mentioned content and an equal number mentioned timing (length, frequency, placement). Respondents' attitudes toward "programming yielded . . . nothing approaching widespread dissatisfaction," but the author concluded that "commercials undeniably qualified on this score."[24]

13.4 / Bases of Advertising Rates

Broadcasting stations sell "time" to advertisers. Station time has meaning, however, only insofar as it represents audience time, which in turn has significance only insofar as it represents audience attention. In 1949, the FCC attempted to give this view legal validity when it tried to rule out "giveaway" programs, on the ground that the programs constituted lotteries, which are illegal in broadcasting (Section 17.11). The law defines a lottery as "a chance for a prize for a price." Does the listener/viewer's time represent a consideration? Does he pay a price merely by paying attention? The FCC thought so, but the courts thought otherwise.[25]

Nevertheless, advertisers obviously do pay in the final analysis to engage the attention of audiences, not merely to occupy time on broadcast facilities. In consequence, stations set a value on their time in terms of their physical ability to reach people and to motivate them to tune in. The methods used for measuring these variables are discussed in Chapter 14. Suffice it here to point out that normally any station's theoretical audience potentiality has to be fragmented several ways before its actual audience at any particular time can be defined. Its ultimate potentiality is represented by the number of receivers in working order in its signal-coverage area. This is likely to be close to 100 per cent for radios, and from 85 to 95 per cent for television sets. However, only some sets will be turned on at a given moment; of those turned on, only some will be tuned to Station X. If Station X competes with twenty other radio and television stations in its market area, the audience must be divided into as many fractions. In this highly competitive situation, programming provides the all-important variable.

A station's rates, then, depend first on its power and frequency, which determine its physical reach; second, on the number of people with sets within

---

[23] Burns W. Roper, *A Ten-Year View of Public Attitudes Toward Television and Other Mass Media, 1959–1968* (New York: Television Information Office, 1969), p. 24. On the whole, however, the majority attitude toward commercials was favorable, according to the Roper surveys.

[24] Gary A. Steiner, *The People Look at Television: A Study of Audience Attitudes* (New York: Alfred A. Knopf, 1963), p. 209.

[25] *ABC* v. *U. S.,* 110 F. Supp. 374 (1953). Affirmed *FCC* v. *ABC,* 374 U. S. 284 (1954).

its signal area; third, on the ability of its programming to attract audiences. All of this can be roughly reduced to a single comparison statistic—cost per thousand (CPM), the cost to an advertiser of reaching a thousand people or homes (Section 14.8). This statistic enables direct comparison of rates between stations or between broadcasting and other media.

However, CPM takes into account only quantitative aspects of media reach. Calculating the less measurable and tangible qualitative aspects of media worth makes time and space buying more of an art than an exercise in arithmetic. For example, consideration must be given to the consumer interests and purchasing power of the audience itself. A station serving a high-income suburb would reach more prospective Cadillac customers, presumably, than a station serving a depressed rural or inner-city area. Demographic data and economic indices provide an assessment of this audience variable. Still less tangible are such factors as the degree to which the prestige and authority of a medium or a particular representative of a medium add to its effectiveness as an advertising vehicle.

Taking all these variables into consideration, stations eventually arrive at a price tag for the use of their facilities, usually with differing rates for the three basic types of advertising insertions discussed in Section 13.2—station-break spots, participating announcements, and sponsorship. Among television stations, the highest one-time rate for a sixty-second announcement can vary from over $1,000 in the top market to under $35 in the smallest markets.

Television networks generally base their rates on varying percentages of an hourly rate for each affiliate. This time rate, in turn, is based on a formula which takes into consideration each affiliate's coverage, circulation, overlap with other affiliates, and other factors affecting its audience-pulling power. Base hourly station rates for purposes of calculating network charges varied in 1970 from about $75 per hour for stations in the smallest markets (not counting a few "bonus" stations, which are thrown in free, and noninterconnected stations) to $10,000 in the top markets. Finally, the actual charges to the television-network advertiser are calculated on a percentage of the sums of these hourly rates, varying from 7 to 45 per cent, depending on the quantity of time bought, the season, and the time of day. The national radio networks place their emphasis on spots and participations. In 1970, top one-minute spots on ABC's four networks cost from $650 to $1250, Mutual's $1,200, and NBC's $1,450. CBS asked $5,200 for a ten-minute participation segment in the Arthur Godfrey program, which allowed for two minutes of commercial time.[26]

13.5 / Rate Differentials

Variations in the value of time—audience availability at different times of the day and geographical relevance to the advertiser's trading area—complicate

---

[26] Rates as quoted in Standard Rate and Data Service, *Network Rates and Data* (Skokie, Ill.: The Service, June 10, 1970).

the broadcasting-rate structure. Figure 13.2 indicates how the audience changes from hour to hour. The value of station time to advertisers changes correspondingly, of course. For this reason, most stations sell time in two or more classes (usually labelled "A", "B", "C", etc.). Many television stations even vary their rate hour by hour throughout the day, as the audience potential changes. Prime time, the period of maximum audience availability, varies from one market to another, generally falling between 6:00 and 11:00 P. M. A narrow fringe on each side of the prime-time segment offers an intermediate audience potential; daytime hours constitute a third level; and early-morning/late-night hours a fourth. Radio listening tends to follow an opposite and much flatter curve, as indicated in Figure 13.2. Some radio stations consider "traffic time" as their prime time, though the flattening out of radio listening throughout the day and evening has caused a trend toward a single time classification for radio. Discounts for the lesser time classes vary, with a general trend as

Figure 13.2
Relation of audience size to time of day

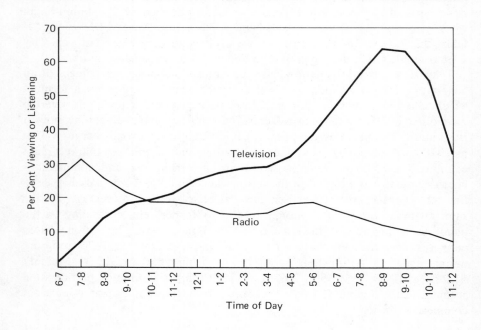

The two curves are not directly comparable: radio's is based on individual adult listening, television's on homes tuned in per average minute.

Sources: Television, A. C. Nielsen Co. data; radio, Radio Advertising Bureau data in *Broadcasting 1970 Yearbook,* p. A126. Adapted with permission.

follows: Class A time (prime), full rate (100 per cent); Class B, 65 per cent of A; Class C, 50 per cent; Class D, 35 per cent. Since audiences tend to be larger in winter than in seasons when more out-of-home activity takes place, some stations also make seasonal rate changes.

Variations in program popularity must be considered as well as changes in audience potential according to time of day or season. Most stations therefore set special rates for participations in established programs, adjusted according to research data on audience size. Networks similarly vary the cost of spots on television series. In 1971, NBC-TV charged $41,000 for a thirty-second spot in its most popular prime-time show, but only $23,000 for a spot in its lowest-rated program.

Rates vary also because advertisers' trading areas vary. Broadcasting inherited from newspapers the custom of recognizing this fact by setting a lower rate for local (or retail) than for general (or national) advertising. A purely local advertiser, such as a retail shop keeper, receives no benefit from advertising which reaches beyond the neighborhood from which he draws his customers. Large stations, however, cover relatively wide metropolitan or urban areas combining a number of neighborhood marketing zones. A nationally distributed product such as a gasoline can benefit from this wider reach, since customers can find the product in all neighborhoods. Another justification for a rate markup for national advertising is that it usually involves two commissions, one to the medium's national sales representative (Section 13.7) and one to the client's advertising agency (Section 13.8). Local rates vary from about 20 to 50 per cent less than national advertising rates, though some stations maintain a single rate.

Quantity discounts contribute another source of rate variability. Price reductions for quantity buyers are, of course, standard business practice. It costs money to negotiate and write contracts, draw up advertising schedules, change the details in program logs, alter billings. The more stable the advertising orders, the less money and time a station wastes on paperwork. But broadcasters have another compelling reason for encouraging quantity buying: under most circumstances an isolated commercial announcement would be of doubtful value. Broadcast advertising relies heavily on repetition for its effectiveness. It operates on the principle of cumulative exposure over a period of time and capitalizes on the mnemonic power of repetition. Any single announcement will normally reach relatively few people; of those few, fewer still will respond to the first impression. But a series of announcements scheduled at staggered times of the day and week and spread over a period of months may gradually reach and drive itself home to virtually the entire audience.

Broadcasters usually base quantity discounts on frequency of insertion and amount of time bought per unit. Practices vary widely, but the rate cards reproduced in Figure 13.3 are representative of moderate-size stations. The television station in Figure 13.3 charges a hundred dollars for a Class AA time, single-insertion, sixty-second announcement; but the price drops to only sixty dollars if the client contracts for fifty announcements in a month—a 40-per-cent discount. In amount of time per unit, a half-minute spot costs seventy dollars, but a full minute costs not twice that much but only a hundred dollars; a five-minute program costs fifty dollars, but a full hour program costs not twelve times fifty dollars but only four hundred. The radio station in Figure 13.3 offers a special type of quantity discount in the form of "package plans." Some stations offer quantity discounts only with such plans.

Television has found it useful also to discount for "preemptibility." On most stations, the advertiser pays a premium price for an assured, fixed position in the programming. A preemptible order can be changed either on short notice or without notice to a different position. Preemptibility helps the station even out its commercial load, making it easier to sell the less desirable positions and providing temporary fillers for the more desirable positions pending their sale at higher rates. A related device allows for the sale of preemptible thirty-second announcements in positions normally planned for twenty-second announcements, pending finding a customer for the shorter period. The preemptible customer gets thirty seconds at the price of twenty seconds, for allowing himself to be moved or cancelled at any time without notice.

One form of discount never appears in a rate card—rates set below the published level in under-the-table deals. Prejudicial as this practice is to the integrity of the medium, rate cutting seems to be endemic in the broadcasting industry. It assumes many guises. The advertiser may pay full rates for time, for example, but not have to pay fully for talent, facilities, or other extra expenses; he may be given elaborate merchandising services gratis, the cost of which would normally be added to the bill; he may pay full rates for a series of spots but then get additional spots free as a "bonus." Cut-rate selling tends to be self-defeating, since it is impossible to keep such deals confidential. Eventually everyone demands the same discount, so the station might just as well have published a new and lower rate in the first place. In the meantime, competing stations are under pressure to cut their rates, too. The problem emerged early in broadcasting. Writing in 1933, the pioneer student of broadcast advertising noted:

With regard to commercial practices, the principal problem affecting the future development of radio broadcast advertising is the maintenance of rates. . . . If this is not done, the progress of the industry will be greatly impeded. Since price-cutting brings with it the temptation to cut the quality of the program and to accept business of doubtful value, it tends to cheapen the entire industry and to cause broadcast advertising to lose prestige. Since advertising is founded upon respect for and confidence in the advertiser and the medium, such a tendency would do tremendous harm to the development of broadcasting.[27]

---

[27] Herman S. Hettinger, *A Decade of Radio Advertising* (Chicago: University of Chicago Press, 1933), p. 316.

A rate-evading device known as "per inquiry" (PI) in effect puts payment for broadcast advertising on a commission basis. In a PI deal, the station receives payment not for time devoted to commercials but for the number of inquiries received or items sold in response to the commercials. Often the station itself handles the transaction by telephone and mail, retaining its share of the purchase price, which may be as high as 50 per cent. The product is usually a low-cost item of doubtful intrinsic value: patent medicines, how-to-do-it books, religious articles, household gadgets, and the like.

Unbilled advertising slipped into programs by performers ("payola," "plugola") can be considered as another form of rate evasion. Disc jockeys and others responsible for recorded-music programs exercise significant power over the exposure and hence the success of popular music. "Song plugging" has a long history, but broadcasting gave it a new dimension. The rapidity with which broadcasting and the modern disc and tape recording industry disseminate compositions, the overwhelming number of new pieces released, and the high returns brought in by hit songs all conspire to put great pressure on the leading disc jockeys, whose approval can lift a new song out of anonymity. "Payola" began innocently enough, with record companies merely supplying stations with free samples of their new pressings. But the expanding industry poured out such an avalanche of new pressings that even potential hits could be buried and forgotten. This situation led record distributors to use bribery to secure favored treatment for particular tunes. A Congressional investigation uncovered a wide range of direct and indirect forms of such payola. Congress amended the Communications Act in 1960 in an effort to stop payola, but the results seem to have been questionable.[28]

A number of stations indignantly fired disc jockeys, and the jittery record companies became far more prudent. But the American Broadcasting Company made it plain it would not dismiss the star of its teenage dance hour, Dick Clark, despite revelations that he pushed songs published by companies in which he had a financial interest.[29]

Clark denied any wrongdoing and saw no inconsistency in the fact that he was involved in the ownership of a maze of thirty-three companies dealing in music while he hosted a highly successful television program featuring popular music.[30] That payola survived the 1960 publicity and legal proscription seems indicated by the necessity of another FCC inquiry in 1964.

[28] House Committee on Interstate and Foreign Commerce, Subcommittee on Legislative Oversight, *Responsibilities of Broadcast Licensees and Station Personnel* (*Payola and Other Deceptive Practices in the Broadcast Field*), Hearings in 2 parts, 86th Cong., 2d Sess., (Washington: Government Printing Office, 1960).

[29] Stan Opotowsky, *TV—The Big Picture* (New York: Collier Books, 1962), p. 255.

[30] Meyer Weinberg, *TV and America: The Morality of Hard Cash* (New York: Ballantine Books, 1962), p. 207. Weinberg discusses the payola case at length on pages 197–213.

Plugola involves the seemingly gratuitous mention or showing of a commercial product in an entertainment program for which the entertainer (rather than the medium) gets compensation. It has long been an established business in the film industry; unmotivated but conspicuous display of brand-name merchandise in a motion picture invariably suggests that plugola is at work. A legendary radio pioneer of the late 1920's, "Uncle Don" Carney, is said to have been the first broadcaster "to accept loot night after night in exchange for favors and plugs for products."[31] Plugola violates § 317(a) of the Communications Act, which requires disclosure of the source of advertising.

The law makes payola and plugola, as particular forms of rate-card evasion, illegal. Similarly, an FCC regulation (§ 73.124) proscribes methods of billing which inflate the prices actually paid for time or which otherwise misrepresent transactions. But there is no law against rate cutting as such.

Although not necessarily a rate-evading expedient, bartering should be mentioned as another anomalous business practice affecting rates. Exchange of goods and services instead of money for radio time became a common practice in 1929 and during the following Depression years. Many a station in those difficult days set up its studio in a hotel, equipped its officers, fed its employees, and used automobiles on due bills for radio time.[32] During the 1960's, a resurgence of bartering on a more sophisticated level occurred, with such deals as feature films and syndicated television programs being offered to stations in exchange for presold participating announcements within the programs. The stations sold the remaining participations to local or national spot advertisers.

13.6 / Rate Cards

Stations publish rate cards as the formal price tag on their time. It would be impracticable for national advertising agencies to keep an up-to-date file of the separate individual rate cards of over seven thousand stations. A commercial firm, Standard Rate and Data Service (SRDS), supplies such information for network and national spot radio and television, as well as other media, in a series of monthly rate catalogues.

Figure 13.3 reproduces sample entries from the SRDS *Spot Television* and *Spot Radio* series. In order to keep these catalogues down to reasonable size, SRDS identifies most of the standardized entries by code numbers. For example, in Paragraph 5 of the television rate card in Figure 13.3, the code number "40a" after "Basic Rates" means "rates subject to change without notice"; the code number "41b" means "basic rates quoted do not include special facilities (studio, film, remote charges) or talent, announcers, directors,

---

31 Bill Treadwell, *Head, Heart and Heel* (New York: Mayfair Books, 1958), pp. 49, 130.

32 Erik Barnouw, *A Tower in Babel: A History of Broadcasting in the United States to 1933* (New York: Oxford University Press, 1966), pp. 235–237.

Figure 13.3
Sample rate-card listings in SRDS publications

A. Radio

W J T N
1924

American Entertainment Ntwk

 RAB

Subscriber to the NAB Radio Code
Media Code 4 233 3550 4.00
James Broadcasting Co., Hotel Jamestown, Jamestown, N. Y. 14701. Phone 716-487-1151.

STATION'S PROGRAMMING DESCRIPTION
WJTN: Programmed for adult audience.
Talk and middle-of-the-road music predominant sound. NEWS: 5 min newscasts on hour and half hour with 15 min at 7:30 am, noon, 6 pm & 11 pm containing both national and local items. Sportscasts and play-by-play local and national sports featured. Country and western music worked into format, and also musical programs for Swedish, Italian, and Puerto Rican population in area. Contact Representative for further details. Rec'd 7/31/68.
1. PERSONNEL
Pres. & Gen'l Mgr.—Simon Goldman.
Vice-Pres. & Mgr.—J. Carl Willems.
Sales Manager—Merrill Rosen.
2. REPRESENTATIVES
Alan Torbet Associates, Inc.
Boston—Eckels & Queen, Inc.
Regional Reps Corp.
3. FACILITIES
500 w. days, 250 w. nights; 1240 kc.
Non-directional.
Operating schedule: 5:15-1 am. CST.
4. AGENCY COMMISSION
15% on net time charges; no cash discount.
5. GENERAL ADVERTISING See ended regulations.
General: 1a, 3a, 4a, 4d, 5, 6a, 7a, 8.
Rate Protection: 15b, 16.
Basic Rates: 20b, 21a, 21b, 21d, 22b, 23a, 24a, 24o, 24c, 26, 28a, 28c, 29a
Contracts: 40a, 41, 42a, 44a, 44b, 46, 47a, 49, 51a.
Comb.: Cont. Discounts: 60b, 60d, 60g, 60i, 61a, 62d.
Cancellation: 70b, 70e, 71a, 73b.
Prod. Services: 80, 82.
Affiliated with KBS.
Affiliated with American Entertainment Network.
Member: Goldman Group; Northeast Radio Network.
National AgRadio Groups, Inc.
TIME RATES
Eff 12/1/68—Rec'd 11/7/68.
6. SPOT ANNOUNCEMENTS

	1x	13x	26x	52x	104x	156x	260x
1 min.	11.00	10.45	9.90	9.35	8.80	8.25	7.70
20/30 sec.	8.80	8.35	7.90	7.50	7.05	6.60	6.15
10 sec.	5.50	5.25	4.95	4.70	4.40	4.15	3.85

7. PACKAGE PLANS

PER WK:	5 ti	10 ti	15 ti	20 ti	30 ti
1 min.	8.80	8.25	7.70	7.15	6.60
20/30 sec	7.05	6.60	6.15	5.70	5.30
10 sec.	4.40	4.15	3.85	3.60	3.30

All spots may be combined for discounts.
8. PROGRAM TIME RATES

	1x	13x	26x	52x	104x	156x	260x
1/2 hr.	49.50	45.85	43.45	41.05	38.60	35.95	33.85
1/4 hr.	33.00	30.60	28.95	27.40	25.75	24.00	22.55
10 min.	25.30	23.55	22.30	21.05	19.80	18.45	17.35
5 min.	16.50	15.70	14.85	14.05	13.20	12.40	11.55

9. PARTICIPATING PROGRAMS
The Dunigans—12:35 pm & 5:05 pm Mon thru Fri.
Flat 11.00
Melva Webber Show—1:20 pm Mon thru Fri. Flat 11.00.
Jim Roselle Show—7-9 am Mon thru Sat. Flat 11.00.
WJTN Farmer—5:30-7 am Mon thru Sat. Flat 11.00.

B. Television

K T V W-TV
TACOMA
(Airdate August 2, 1953)
Media Code 6 249 0300 1.00
KTVW, Box 7067, 5544 N. 35th St., Tacoma, Wash. 98407. Phone 206-752-3544.
Sales Office: Financial News Center-Sales Office Suite 2500 Northern Life Tower, Seattle, Wash. 98101.
1. PERSONNEL
Owner and Operator—Estate of J. Elroy McCaw.
General Manager—Don Courtnay.
Operations Manager—Jim Turpinat.
Program Director—Tom Rogstad.
Chie. Engineer—Ray Swalley.
2. REPRESENTATIVES
Jack Masla & Co., Inc.
3. FACILITIES
Video 316.000 w., audio 158.000 w.; ch 13.
Antenna ht.: 784 ft. above average terrain.
Operating schedule: 24 hours Mon thru Fri; 11-6 am Sat; 11-1:30 am Sun.
4. AGENCY COMMISSION
15% to recognized agencies on all time, studio, and talent charges unless otherwise specified; no cash discounts.
5. GENERAL ADVERTISING See ended regulations
Rate Protection: 10f, 11f, 12f, 13f, 14f.
Contracts: 20a, 22c, 24a.
Basic Rates: 40a, 41a, 41b, 43a.
Cancellation: 70a, 70e, 71.
Prod. Services: 87a, 87b.
6. TIME RATES
Eff ....Rec'd 9/18/69.
7. SPOT ANNOUNCEMENTS
AA—3:30-7 pm.
A—12:30-3.30 pm & 7-11 pm.
B—Sat & Sun.

CLASS AA

PER WK:	PER MO:	PER YR:		60 sec	30/20
1 ti				100.00	70.00
5 ti				100.00	70.00
10 ti	10 ti			95.00	63.00
15 ti	15 ti			90.00	59.50
20 ti	20 ti	200 x		80.00	56.00
30 ti	30 ti	300 x		75.00	52.50
40 ti	40 ti	400 x		70.00	49.00
50 ti	50 ti	500 x		65.00	45.50
10 sec—50% of 60 sec				60.00	42.00

CLASS A

1 ti				80.00	56.00
5 ti	5 ti			75.00	52.50
10 ti	10 ti			70.00	49.00
15 ti	15 ti			65.00	45.50
20 ti	20 ti	200 x		60.00	42.00
30 ti	30 ti	300 x		55.00	38.50
40 ti	40 ti	400 x		50.00	35.00
50 ti	50 ti	500 x		45.00	31.50
10 sec—50% of 60 sec.					

CLASS B

1 ti				40.00	28.00
5 ti	5 ti			35.00	24.50
10 ti	10 ti			30.00	21.00
15 ti	15 ti			25.00	17.50
20 ti	20 ti			20.00	14.00

10. PROGRAM RATES

	1 hr	1/2 hr	1/4 hr	5 min
1 x	400	250	125	50

Subject to availability, plus production costs.
DISCOUNTS
13 wk—10%   26 wk—20%   52 wk—40%
11. SPECIAL FEATURES
STOCK MARKET AND BUSINESS NEWS
These rates apply to all telecasts between 7 am and 1 pm Mon thru Fri.
ANNOUNCEMENTS:

PER WK:	Open	5 ti	10 ti	15 ti	20 ti	25 ti	30 ti
1 min	40	38	36	34	32	30	28
30 sec	30	28	26	24	22	20	18
20 sec	26	24	22	20	18	16	14

Any spot less than 20 seconds will carry a 20 second rate.

DISCOUNTS ON ANNOUNCEMENTS
13 wk—5%   26 wk—10%   39 wk—15%   52 wk—20%
PROGRAMS:

PER WK:	Open	2 ti	3 ti	4 ti	5 ti
1/4 hr.	166	162	158	154	150
10 min.	136	132	128	124	120
5 min	76	73	70	67	64

COLOR
Schedules network color.
Equipped with low band VTR.

Video tape recording facilities available.
12. SERVICE FACILITIES
Operations Desk: See address at beginning of listing.
2 film projectors (16mm).
Slides
2 slide projectors.
2 x 2 tape mounted (do not send metal).
Must be 35mm only.
Safe viewing area 3/4" x 1".
13. CLOSING TIME
48 hours prior film, slides, artwork and programs.
Failure on part of advertiser to comply relieves station of obligations to adhere to schedule. Station will endeavor to make emergency changes up to air time but without guarantee of performance. Materials for Sunday and Monday should arrive by previous Friday.

Source: Standard Rate and Data Service, *Spot Radio Rates and Data* (Skokie, Ill.: The Service, July 1, 1970), p. 615; *Spot Television Rates and Data* (Skokie, Ill.: The Service, July 15, 1970), p. 483. Used by permission.

props, sets, art work, slides, station-identification cards, special technical facilities, or extra camera rehearsal time."

Following are some of the major topics in addition to rates themselves covered in rate cards:

Commission. Stations allow 15 per cent commission to "recognized" advertising agencies; most limit commissionable charges to those for time, but some allow commission on such additional charges as talent fees and studio rehearsal fees.

Acceptability. Stations often have special rules on acceptability of certain categories of advertising and programs, notably liquor advertising, and political, religious, and foreign-language programming.

Rate inclusions. Normally the basic rates cover time on the transmitter plus the minimum studio facilities required to air the simplest form of recorded advertisement. Some stations make additional charges for the use of various types of facilities, music performing-rights fees, live-talent fees, and so on.

Rate protection. Since stations change their rates often, clients with existing contracts need some assurance of stability. Protection from the effects of rate changes to existing contracts runs from a minimum of about a month to a maximum of a year.

Product protection. Clients want to be protected from the adjacent scheduling of competitive-product advertising. Stations usually promise a minimum of about fifteen minutes' separation between advertisements for like products.

Spot length. Some stations have discontinued one-minute spots altogether and offer thirty-second spots as the maximum acceptable length.

Combinability of discounts. Usually stations place limitations on the extent to which clients can add together more than one contract or different types of contracts, such as contracts for participations and sponsorships, in order to earn quantity discounts.

13.7 / Local, Network, and National Spot Advertising

In Section 13.5, we alluded to differences in the geographical scope of trading areas—a local merchant needs to reach only the contiguous area from which he draws his clientele, whereas a national or regional distributor can benefit from advertising which covers more than a single trading area or market. The very nature of broadcast signals limits the coverage of any given station to one relatively limited contiguous geographical area.[33] A broadcast-

---

[33] We exclude from consideration in the present context the distant services provided by sky waves and shortwaves, though some countries do use shortwave broadcasting commercially. Note also that CATV can extend the normal market boundaries of stations (Section 11.6).

ing station therefore constitutes by definition a single-market, or local, advertising medium—albeit with a rather wide range from the smallest to the largest class of station. In this respect broadcasting compares with most American newspapers, which despite special regional editions and nationally syndicated supplements, nevertheless remain identified with a particular city of publication. Magazines, on the other hand, provide advertisers with a unitary medium of regional and national circulation.

The need to provide a similar multiple-market broadcast-advertising service was one of the compelling commercial motives for combining stations into networks. Networks transformed a local into a national medium, giving national advertisers a valuable new mechanism not duplicated by any existing advertising vehicle. Like magazines, networks enable advertisers to reach all markets in the country in a single transaction with identical advertising messages controlled and supervised from a convenient central point. Unlike magazines, networks have the advantages of circulating *daily,* rather than weekly or monthly, and of working through *local* media, since all stations are by definition local. This paradoxical character of network broadcast advertising of being at once local and national, as well as its flexibility in timing, accounts in large part for network television becoming the leading medium for national advertising.

Networks, as we pointed out in Section 9.5, perform three main functions for their affiliates: they provide programs, arrange interconnection facilities for distributing the programs, and sell affiliates' time in the national market. Because of limitations on multiple-station ownership, most affiliates have a contractual rather than a proprietary relationship with their network (Section 15.3). A network headquarters organization reflects its triple function. The several networks are variously organized, but they generally include under the *sales* function departments to handle research, advertising, promotion, and national spot sales for "O&O" (network-owned and -operated) stations; under the program *distribution* function, departments of engineering, station relations, and traffic; under the *program* function, departments for production, production services, continuity acceptance, news, and public affairs, as well as programs in general. These functions are supported by the activities common to any large business enterprise—administration, finance and accounting, purchasing, labor relations and personnel, and legal matters. The O&O stations operate independently under a separate administrative department. The headquarters offices of the networks are in New York, with major production centers also located in Hollywood. Offices are also maintained in other major cities, notably Chicago and Washington.

The number of stations affiliated with each network (Table 10.2) does not necessarily indicate the number carrying any given network program. To the degree possible without weakening the continuity of its service, a network responds to the specific needs of advertisers by offering varying combinations of stations, formerly built around a minimum billing or a "must-buy" minimum group of affiliates.[34] Another source of variability in station lineup comes from the problem of securing affiliate "clearance." Under the FCC's Chain Broadcasting Regulations (Section 15.4), affiliates have the right to reject network offerings, in which case they are said to fail to "clear" time for the network. Affiliates sometimes reject programs whose subjects or treatments they fear will offend local sensibilities. However, more program rejections fall in the category of network public-affairs programming offered on a sustaining basis. Local television stations find it hard to resist the temptation to substitute saleable syndicated film material for such offerings. Thus, the significance of network lists of prestige-laden public-service programs must be assessed by asking, "How many affiliates carried them"?

Major national advertisers of certain types find the network mode of coverage ideally suited to their needs. For example, only networks could provide the prestigious showcase demanded by some of the great corporations such as AT&T and Dupont for their institutional advertising. At the other end of the spectrum, network advertising works wonders for such mass-consumption items as cosmetics and proprietary drugs. Many national and regional advertisers, however, have more narrowly defined coverage needs—whether in geographical or demographic terms—which the relatively inflexible station lineup of networks cannot ideally satisfy. Though a network arranges varying groups of affiliates according to advertiser needs, still it provides only one particular outlet in each market, usually one of the largest and most expensive stations. That particular station may not be the best one for the advertiser's purpose. An advertiser of farm machinery, for example, would want to concentrate his coverage in rural areas and to choose stations with established farm audiences. The large urban network affiliates might not be the ideal ones. The third category of broadcast advertising, national spot, satisfies such specialized needs.

The national spot advertiser can "spot" his advertising anywhere on the map, selecting the precise combination of markets and station types to suit his campaign. He can use any kind of program except network programs as a vehicle, or he can use any kind of participating or station-break spot-announcement schedule he chooses. He may find it effective to capitalize on local talent—a popular newscaster, sports commentator, women's-show host, or disc jockey with an established following in the community. Networks cannot duplicate this kind of hometown association, which the advertiser may regard as a valuable adjunct to his advertising message.

To aid in the sale of national spot advertising, a special class of middlemen

---

[34] "Must-buy" requirements were criticized as being analogous to block booking in film rentals (Section 11.3), and during the 1960's the networks voluntarily dropped them. See House Committee on Interstate and Foreign Commerce, Subcommittee on Transportation and Communications, *Network Broadcasting*, Report of the FCC Network Study Staff ("Barrow Report"), House Report 1297, 85th Cong., 1st Sess., (Washington: Government Printing Office, 1958), pp. 469–527.

Table 13.3

Relative importance of local, network, and spot advertising in broadcasting

MEDIUM	SOURCE OF ADVERTISING REVENUE (%)		
	Local	*Network*	*Spot*
Radio (AM and FM)	65	4	31
Television	22	30	48

Source: FCC, *Thirty-Fifth Annual Report* (Washington: Government Printing Office, 1970), pp. 134, 145.

emerged in the early 1930's—the station representatives. The national "rep" maintains offices in the principal business centers, functioning as sales agent for a string of local stations which otherwise would have no direct access to the main offices of national advertisers and their agencies. He receives a commission on sales, varying from 5 to 15 per cent.

A network affiliate thus has three sales forces at work for it: its own local sales-department staff, its network sales department, and its national representative. An independent station, of course, relies entirely on its local sales force and its national representative. As Table 13.3 shows, television depends most on national-spot revenue, whereas local advertising supplies most of radio's revenue. It was not always so. In the early 1940's, radio too derived most of its revenue from networks, as Figure 13.4 indicates. But a decline in the proportion of radio-network advertising had already set in before television began to compete. Radio's shift toward local advertising was due in the first instance to the growth in numbers of stations. Nothing illustrates more sharply the difference in the economies of the two media than the contrast between the two charts in Figure 13.4. While network business has declined almost to a vanishing point in radio, it has actually grown to a new high in television.

13.8 / Advertising Agencies

Virtually all modern businesses of any size include money for advertising in their annual budgets, often pegged to the previous year's actual or the next year's anticipated sales level. Relative to sales volume, makers of perfume, cosmetics, and other toilet preparations spend the most on advertising (on the order of 15 per cent), followed by makers of proprietary drugs (about 11 per cent). Other businesses that spend relatively high amounts on advertising in proportion to sales are beverages and motion-picture theatres.[35]

How to spend the money budgeted for advertising effectively poses complex problems when large sums are involved, as in the case of the top advertisers

---

[35] S. Watson Dunn, *Advertising: Its Role in Modern Marketing* (New York: Holt, Rinehart and Winston, 1969), p. 257.

Figure 13.4
Trends in network, national-spot, and local advertising

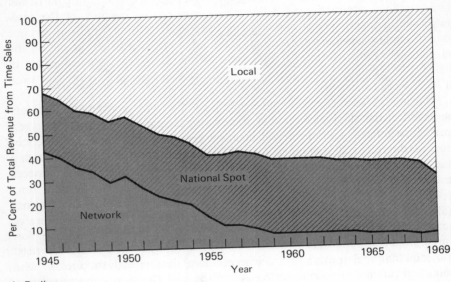

A. Radio

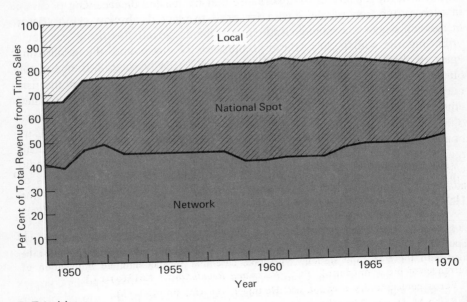

B. Television

Source: FCC, *Annual Reports* (Washington: Government Printing Office, annually).

listed in Table 13.4. Which media to use, to what extent to use each (note the variety of media mixes used by similar products in Table 13.4), what kinds of advertising vehicles to employ—such decisions require highly specialized expertise. Similarly, preparing the advertising itself, selecting particular media outlets, contracting with the media, supervising conduct of the campaign—all demand specialized skills and experience. Enter Madison Avenue —that much-glamorized, criticized, admired, and mistrusted home of the advertising agency (although only two of the top ten agencies listed in Table 13.5 actually have offices on Madison Avenue and two are not even in New York).

Forerunners of these veritable symbols of the mass-consumption society were rather shabby nineteenth-century newspaper-space brokers. They bought space in wholesale lots and resold it at whatever markup they could get. In the last quarter of the century the outlines of the agency as known today evolved, with standardization of space rates and payment for agency services in the form of commissions. In the early days of commercial radio, time brokers emerged once more as intermediaries between national advertisers and individual radio stations. Ben Gross relates a story which tells something of the atmosphere of early commercial radio. In 1922, a would-be time broker bought time for resale from WEAF. The station, however, became alarmed at so much commercialism and refused to continue dealing with the broker, who thereupon purchased time from WAAM, Newark. The station owner was so doubtful of the legality of the procedure that he insisted on receiving payment in cash rather than by check and arranged to meet the broker clandestinely in a hotel, where the money could change hands secretly.[36]

During the mid-1930's, station-representative firms and the advertising agencies absorbed the time broker's functions.[37] N. W. Ayer & Son, one of the oldest advertising agencies in the print media, claims to have been the first major agency to take radio seriously as an advertising medium.[38] Ayer handled advertising for an optical company on WEAF as early as 1922 and introduced one of the most popular early network-sponsored programs, the National Carbon Company's *Eveready Hour,* in December, 1923. By 1928, Ayer had already set up a separate radio department. Another pioneer agency in radio was Lord and Thomas, whose Albert Lasker (one of the legendary figures of advertising history) placed nearly half of NBC's national advertising in the 1927–1928 season.[39] Lasker overcame NBC's reluctance to use direct adver-

---

[36] Ben Gross, *I Looked and I Listened* (New York: Random House, 1954), pp. 66–67. Few stations now sell time on a brokerage basis. Time-brokerage contracts must be filed with the FCC and stations must take care that they contain no implication of surrender of program control. [FCC, *Rules and Regulations* § 1.613(6)(c).]

[37] For a contemporary account, see Hettinger, *op. cit.,* pp. 160–172.

[38] Ralph M. Hower, *The History of an Advertising Agency: N. W. Ayer & Son at Work, 1869–1949,* rev. ed. (Cambridge, Mass.: Harvard University Press, 1949), p. 132.

[39] John Gunther, *Taken at the Flood: The Story of Albert J. Lasker* (New York: Harper & Bros., 1960), p. 194.

Table 13.4

Top ten U. S. advertisers and media used

RANK	ADVERTISER	EXPENDITURE	PER CENT OF TOTAL ALLOTTED TO							
			Spot TV	Netw. TV	Spot Radio	Netw. Radio	News-papers	Genl. Mags.	Farm/ Bus. Mags.	Out-door
1	Proctor & Gamble Co.	$187,641,834	29.7	63.2	0.2	—	1.0	5.4	0.5	—
2	General Motors Corp.	159,518,366	7.9	25.7	15.9	2.2	14.5	25.0	4.1	4.6
3	Bristol-Myers Co.	109,500,318	16.7	53.6	4.3	1.0	1.8	18.0	4.5	—
4	General Foods Corp.	105,276,943	36.6	47.2	2.7	0.3	6.8	6.0	0.3	0.2
5	Ford Motor Co.	99,799,112	8.0	30.7	16.6	3.4	10.7	22.3	4.1	4.3
6	Colgate-Palmolive Co.	99,270,345	29.2	54.1	7.6	3.0	2.7	3.3	0.1	0.1
7	American Home Products (drugs and cosmetics)	86,349,917	23.4	48.8	14.6	2.4	3.1	6.9	0.6	0.3
8	R. J. Reynolds Tobacco Co.	78,852,535	15.6	64.4	5.9	1.0	2.6	9.8	0.6	0.1
9	Sterling Drug, Inc.	66,576,501	15.8	57.4	4.5	4.2	2.2	15.0	1.0	—
10	American Brands (tobacco)	65,956,189	15.0	56.5	1.1	—	8.3	17.8	0.3	0.9

Note: Includes only "measured" media. Total expenditures are higher when point-of-purchase promotion and other advertising and promotion expenditures are included. In terms of total advertising expenditure, Proctor & Gamble spent $275 million.

Source: 1969 data reprinted with permission from the August 24, 1970, issue of *Advertising Age*, pp. 24–25. Copyright © 1970 by Crain Communications, Inc.

Table 13.5

Ten largest U. S. advertising agencies (by gross world billings)

RANK	AGENCY	BILLING (MILLIONS)		
		U. S.	*Foreign*	*Total*
1	J. Walter Thompson Co.	$444.0	$292.0	$736.0
2	Young & Rubicam	371.2	151.6	522.8
3	McCann-Erickson, Inc.	253.3	257.8	511.1
4	Ted Bates & Co., Inc.	229.9	145.2	375.1
5	Batten, Barton, Durstine & Osborne, Inc.	336.4	19.8	356.2
6	Leo Burnett Co., Inc.	288.2	67.7	355.9
7	Doyle Dane Bernbach, Inc.	234.7	35.2	269.9
8	Foote, Cone & Belding Advertising, Inc.	202.7	62.8	265.5
9	Ogilvy & Mather, Inc.	152.8	77.0	229.8
10	Grey Advertising, Inc.	183.8	44.3	228.1

Source: 1969 data reprinted with permission from the February 23, 1970, issue of *Advertising Age*, p. 40. Copyright © 1970 by Crain Communications, Inc.

tising, insisting on using commercials modelled closely on the established copywriting style familiar in space media.

Agencies now maintain elaborate specialized departments to handle broadcast advertising. For example, J. Walter Thompson Co., the largest American advertising agency (Table 13.5), has a broadcasting department under a senior vice-president staffed by two associate directors, an administrator, a manager of network buying, a manager of spot buying, nine broadcast supervisors, and nearly forty buyers.[40]

Reduced to its simplest terms, the advertising agency functions as a specialized extension of the client's own advertising department for planning and executing campaigns. The agency contracts with the medium on behalf of the client, pays the net bill after subtracting its own commission, and passes the gross billing on to the client. This system puts the agency in a curious position: its commission comes from the medium (in the form of agency discount on time or space), yet the money ultimately comes from the advertiser (who is not entitled to the agency discount, although some large corporations have their own "house agencies" which are recognized as legitimate advertising agencies by the media). The American Association of Advertising Agencies comments:

It is important to note that the agency contracts with media in its own name, as an individual contractor. In its relations with media it is not legally the agent of its client, and the word "agent" or "agency" is, in a legal sense, a misnomer.[41]

---

[40] *Broadcasting 1970 Yearbook,* p. E53.

[41] The American Association of Advertising Agencies, *The Structure of the Advertising Agency Business* (New York: The Association, 1954), p. 19.

Traditionally, agency compensation has been 15 per cent of the media charges, usually not counting production and other additional "noncommissionable" expenses. In the 1950's, the American Association of Advertising Agencies tried to regularize and police the agency business by setting up standards of recognition and fixing compensation at a 15 per cent commission. However, the Justice Department viewed enforcement of such rules as restraint of trade, and in 1956 the AAAA entered a consent decree by which it agreed to refrain from fixing commissions, setting up standards of approval for agencies, and other measures that had been proposed for policing the industry.

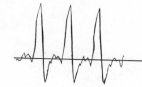

14

TESTS AND MEASUREMENTS

Investors in stations and messages alike demand practical information on ways to prepare program materials to achieve desired effects; on the extent to which these materials, once broadcast, actually reach the desired audiences; and on the extent to which audiences, once reached, respond with desired behaviors. Research seeks empirical answers to such questions. Researchers pretest program materials; estimate size and composition of audiences for programs, stations, and networks; and analyze such behavioral responses as brand-name recollection, purchasing, and acquiring attitudes, skills, or information. This chapter deals mainly with this kind of research and mainly with one type of measurement within this kind—ratings. More basic communication research aimed at developing a theory of mass communication, solving long-term problems, and analyzing broad social effects will be discussed in Chapter 23.

14.1 / The Special Need for Broadcasting Research

Despite its pragmatic and commercial orientation, audience research plays an important role in noncommercial broadcasting as well as in advertising-supported systems. Indeed, an explicitly educational program needs objective data on audiences and program effectiveness even more urgently than programs whose goal is simpler forms of response such as purchasing. The first demands for audience research by the British Broadcasting Corporation came from producers concerned with teaching programs.[1] If noncommercial broadcasters use less research than commercial stations, it is because they cannot afford more.[2]

---

[1] Asa Briggs, *The History of Broadcasting in the United Kingdom,* II (London: Oxford University Press, 1965), 257. See also Section P.4 for discussion of audience research in relation to policy.

[2] The foundation-supported Children's Television Workshop, producer of the children's series *Sesame Street,* took a whole year to pretest every element of the program, making it perhaps "the most researched, tested and studied program in television history." [Edward L. Palmer, "Research at the Children's Workshop," *Educational Broadcasting Review,* III (October, 1969), 43–48.]

Users of all mass media regard scientifically based research as an essential management tool, but it has a particularly important function in broadcasting. The intangibility of the broadcast product makes research data the only evidence of consumption. In terms of measuring results, however, all media share a common problem: communication is a chain of events, one of whose links cannot be directly observed. This inaccessible link connects message with behavior. Messages can be measured and behavior can be measured, but a causal connection between the two, being subjective, must usually be inferred. It is difficult to demonstrate conclusively that Behavior A resulted directly and solely from Message X.

Broadcasting's special need for research and the special difficulty of obtaining satisfactory consumption data help account both for the industry's heavy dependence on ratings and for deficiencies in the rating system. Despite drawbacks and problems, however, research is so essential that stations, networks, agencies, and advertisers all continue to spend millions of dollars annually on it and to base on it decisions involving expenditure of many more millions.

Volunteer letters from radio listeners provided the earliest form of audience information. Listeners eagerly sent in comments and reports of reception in the early days, when radio was still a novelty. After the novelty wore off, stations began offering gifts and prizes to stimulate listeners to write. Broadcasters still use audience mail to some extent to demonstrate program "pull" and to construct "mail maps" illustrating station coverage; but they recognize that writers-in are unlikely to represent the general audience. Mail is not therefore regarded as a reliable tool for most research purposes.

In 1927, a baking-powder sponsor underwrote the first national radio survey using formal research methods. This pioneer study led in 1930 to establishment of a continuing rating service, The Cooperative Analysis of Broadcasting.[3] The CAB, which used telephone-recall data to produce "Crossley Ratings," was supported cooperatively by advertising interests. The CAB discontinued its service in 1946 when commercial sources began offering comparable services. In that year, another cooperative research venture started, the Broadcast Measurement Bureau, supported by radio stations themselves. BMB used mailed postcard questionnaires to produce not ratings but nationwide, county-by-county station-circulation information. BMB issued two radio reports, one in 1946 and one in 1949, before going out of business in 1950 for lack of station support.

The BMB represented a broadcasting-industry attempt to set up a service somewhat like the Audit Bureau of Circulation, which since 1914 has produced impartially audited and universally accepted reports on the paid circulation of print media. However, broadcasting offers no such simple, clear-

---

[3] Archibald Crossley, "The Advertiser Looks at Radio—1930," in Advertising Research Foundation, *Milestones in Media Research* (New York: The Foundation, 1963), pp. 4–5. One of the findings of the 1927 study was that some local stations were deleting the network's baking-powder commercials and substituting locally sold commercials.

cut basis of measurement as the sale of countable physical entities like newspapers or magazines. A publication is a unitary physical object, even though it contains a variety of items which attract varying degrees of reader attention. Broadcasting content cannot be treated in such unitary terms. It spreads out over a time and evaporates as fast as it is "published." In consequence, no single universally acceptable way of measuring broadcast consumption has evolved. Instead, a number of research companies using rival research methods compete in the audience-measurement field.

14.2 / Preliminary Market Data

Most market research builds on a platform of market information already available for the asking. Government agencies pour forth quantities of basic demographic and economic data. The chief source is the Department of Commerce, in particular its Bureau of the Census; but virtually every government office makes its own contribution to the statistical flood, as do trade associations and other private sources. If each market-research project had to start *ab ovo* without benefit of these free preliminary data, most such projects would be prohibitively expensive. Even with free help, the machinery of market research may seem elaborate and expensive enough. For example, the "audimeter," a device for recording set tuning, is said to have cost $9 million just to develop.[4]

Market-research studies usually begin, therefore, with relevant facts from existing sources—already available data concerning populations and the economy. Before even starting to gather original data, the researcher can thus learn about such population characteristics as geographical distribution, occupation, income, age, education, race, and sex, and about such economic indicators as retail-sales volume, auto registrations, house ownership, power consumption, agricultural and manufacturing production. Spared the task of collecting essential background information each time he undertakes a project, the market researcher can concentrate most of his efforts on acquiring the specific new information the client wants.

Let us consider as an example one of the favorite devices of market research —the trial run in test markets. Preliminarily, it should be understood that we use the term "market" in two ways. Up to this point we have been using it in the general sense of the total marketplace, the whole arena of buying and selling. The "test market" introduces the more specific concept of a single, unified physical trading area within the total arena. The media define their markets variously, in accordance with their own distribution and their users' consumption patterns. Television generally uses a set of about two hundred markets as defined by the American Research Bureau, a commercial research firm which introduced the concept of television "areas of dominant influence"

---

[4] Arthur C. Nielsen, *Evolution of Factual Techniques in Market Research* (New York: A. C. Nielsen Co., 1952), p. 18.

Table 14.1

Radio and television penetration in U. S.

HOMES	NUMBER	PENETRATION (%)
Total in U. S.	61,460,446	—
with radio	60,600,000	98.6
with television	58,500,000	95.3
with color television	22,200,000	37.5

Source: Television, 1969 estimates by A. C. Nielsen Co.; radio, 1969 Radio Advertising Bureau data in *Broadcasting 1970 Yearbook*, p. A125. Adapted with permission.

(ADI's) in 1966.[5] A test market, then, is exactly such a well-defined trading area.

Effectiveness of two different versions of new advertising copy, for example, may be compared by running each in different but "matching" test markets. The markets have to be matched in population and economic characteristics to ensure that differences in results can be ascribed to the advertising itself and not simply to preexisting differences in the markets. Available data make it relatively easy for the researcher to locate suitable test markets that match. It would be difficult and almost prohibitively costly to measure all characteristics afresh before even beginning the tests.[6]

For broadcasting, the basic market datum is the number of receivers in working order in each market. The ratio between the total households in the market and the number equipped with receivers gives a relative measure called *penetration* or set *saturation*. Table 14.1 shows national radio and television saturation. So many households in the United States have radio and television sets that for practical purposes the potential broadcast audience can be considered as virtually identical with the population itself. However, specific markets vary, especially in television saturation. Projected local television saturation by county for 1970 ranged from a low of 74 per cent of homes (*e.g.*, in Apache County, Arizona) to a high of 98 per cent (*e.g.*, Fairfax County, Virginia).[7]

---

[5] See *Broadcasting Yearbooks, Television Factbooks,* Standard Rate and Data Service publications, and other marketing serials for market tables. Another frequently used market concept is the "Standard Metropolitan Statistical Area" ("Metro" for short), defined by the Bureau of the Census as a cluster of counties including one or more cities of at least fifty thousand people. The Bureau has enumerated 230 such areas, covering about three-quarters of all the families in the United States.

[6] For more detailed examples of how existing data can be employed, see Department of Commerce, *Measuring Markets: A Guide to the Use of Federal and State Statistical Data* (Washington: Government Printing Office, 1966), and Dick Twedt, "How to Use the Survey to Select and Evaluate Test Markets," in *Sales Management 1969 Survey of Buying Power,* pp. A31–35.

[7] American Research Bureau, *Revised Estimate of United States Television Households, 1969* (Beltsville, Md.: The Bureau, 1969).

14.3 / Coverage and Circulation

The number of receivers physically located in a market tells us nothing about actual communication. Sets become significant only when people turn them on and attend to messages. Nevertheless, it is important initially to define the maximum audience potential of a station, the number of homes that physically *could* be reached if all conditions were absolutely ideal. This statistic is referred to in audience research as *coverage*.[8] A station's coverage depends on (1) the geographical distribution of receivers relative to the transmitter's location and (2) the contours of the station's signal area. In Section 2.2, we saw how stations' signal-radiation patterns vary in both reach and shape. Measurements of signal strength in the field, supplemented by reports of reception on home receivers, determine a station's coverage area. Once the geographical limits of signal coverage have been established, the number of receivers present within that area constitutes the station's total audience potential. In practice, coverage area is usually defined in terms of counties.

In order to reach the full potential of its coverage, a station would have to broadcast a program irresistibly compelling to every family in its coverage area; all families would have to be at home and awake; all sets would have to be in working order and tuned to that one station. These conditions, obviously, can never be met in practice, and so another statistic, *circulation,* is used to denote an estimate of audience reached. The term is borrowed from newspapers, but as we have already pointed out, broadcasting content cannot logically be treated in unitary terms, like issues of a newspaper. What is the logical "circulation unit" of broadcasting? Is it one program, a single day's service, a week's, a month's? Is it the product of a single station or a whole network of stations?

Typically, circulation is reported in terms of (1) one complete week's service (thus covering the full range of program types, which tend to vary with time of day and day of week) and (2) tuning to the station or network at least *once* during the week by each reported audience member (or household, whichever base is used). Broadcast circulation thus reflects the generalized pulling power of a station or network, rather than the pull of any single unit of programming.

Circulation again gives us a measure of potential audience rather than the actual audience for any particular program. But whereas the coverage figure gives us no assurance that *anyone* in the coverage area actually tunes to the station in question, circulation data at least indicate that a specified number of people in the potential audience actually do sometimes tune to that station.

Coverage and circulation measurements may seem almost too vague and theoretical to have much value. They do have essential usefulness, however, in providing a basis for computing rates for station and network time sales.

---

[8] Research terms used in this chapter conform to definitions in National Association of Broadcasters, *Standard Definitions of Broadcast Research Terms* (Washington: The Association, 1967).

They also give advertising-agency time buyers essential comparative information in advance of purchase. Among several stations or networks available for a given advertising campaign, which ones can probably best cover the target audience? If the product is aimed at urban rather than rural dwellers, for example, there is no point in buying extensive coverage in rural areas.

Coverage and circulation data thus help decision making in the planning stage of advertising campaigns. After the decision has been made, after the outlets have been selected and the broadcasts started, the next question is "How much of the potential circulation was actually reached"? This question is crucial, for the single readily manipulable variable in the equation is programming (including, of course, commercials). Coverage and circulation re-remain relatively stable, but programming is dynamic. One program or programming format is a hit, another a dud. Today's brilliant success becomes tomorrow's trite failure. When researchers attempt to measure this volatile dimension of individual program popularity, trouble begins. This is the realm of the controversial "ratings" which dominate commercial broadcasting.

14.4 / Program Ratings

A program rating provides an estimate of relative audience size—"relative" because it is based on a percentage.[9] It can be viewed as an estimate of relative *popularity* in the sense that people tune to one program in preference to other competing programs available at the same time (as well as in preference to doing something other than watching or listening). The base on which the percentage is calculated is the *total potential* audience, *i.e.,* all the sets or people with access to sets in the area measured. As was previously pointed out (Section 14.3), no program reaches this total potential in actual practice. The most popular network-television programs generally earn ratings in the 20's.[10]

Program ratings can be calculated in several ways, depending on the time dimension. For example, an *instantaneous* rating reports an estimate of audience size at one particular moment; an *average* rating reports an estimate of the audience size when the audience for such moments are averaged, without duplication, over a fixed period of time such as thirty minutes; a *cumulative* rating ("cume") gives an estimate of audience size based on the sum of the audiences, without duplication, for two or more periods of time. Repetition

---

[9] The per-cent symbol (%) is dropped in expressing a rating, as is the decimal point for the first *two* places in the original calculation. Example: if the base number (*e.g.,* total television households) divided into the number of households tuned to Program A yields .065, this means that 6.5 per cent of the households were tuned to Program A, or that the rating of Program A is 6.5.

[10] Nielsen reported an average rating of 18.9 for all 1969 network prime-time television programs. As of January, 1970, the highest recorded by Nielsen for a regularly scheduled network program was a "total audience" rating of 32.4 and an "average audience" rating of 27.3 for an NBC *Bob Hope Christmas Show*. [Nielsen Marketing Service release (New York: A. C. Nielsen Co., February 6, 1970).]

is a central feature of broadcast-advertising strategy (Section 13.5); but a rating based on an individual program or a single week of programs fails to reflect cumulative reach over a longer period of time during which the same commercials recur. Researchers usually use four weeks as the time base for calculating a cume. A four-week cume gives an estimate of the unduplicated, or net, audience reached during the four weeks. An individual who tuned each week to a particular weekly program would be counted as one, even though he tuned in four times; on the other hand, four *different* individuals, each of whom tuned in to only one of the four weekly programs, would be counted as four. Cumes are especially valuable in planning or appraising spot-advertising campaigns.

The sum of all program ratings for a given time period provides an estimate of the total audience for all stations in the market during that period. This statistic, called a "households-using-television" or "households-using-radio" rating,[11] can be used to find the "share of audience" rating, which uses the actual rather than the potential audience total as its numerical base. See Figure 14.1 for a graphic description of several types of ratings.

It should be evident from the foregoing that a rating is not a simple, uniform measurement. In order to interpret the term "rating" in any given context, we need first to ask at least five questions about how it was derived: (1) What criterion was used for counting an audience unit either in or out of this particular audience? (2) What was counted as an audience unit—a whole household or an individual, and if an individual, were any age limits imposed? (3) The audience for what broadcasting entity was measured—a station, a network, a group of stations, a program, a group of programs? (4) Were audience members outside of homes counted as well as those in homes? (5) What time base was used—instantaneous, average, or cumulative?

14.5 / Measurement from Samples

Ratings attempt to measure highly volatile behavior patterns. Broadcast audiences fluctuate constantly—from minute to minute throughout the day, from day to day, from season to season, and from place to place. Picture a time-lapse film of the sped-up comings and goings of the members of any family in their television viewing area. This is the kind of complex activity ratings try to measure. It would be clearly impossible to tabulate all this coming and going by millions of people tuning millions of sets to thousands of stations scattered from one end of the country to the other—and at that, mostly in privacy where behavior cannot even be observed. Drastic simplifications are obviously essential for any kind of empirical measurement.

One simplification is to ignore the varying levels of attention and types of motivation which characterize listening/viewing. The researcher cannot take

---

[11] Formerly called "sets-in-use" rating. This term proved misleading after multiple-set homes became common. It now refers to individual sets rather than to households.

Figure 14.1
Rating terminology

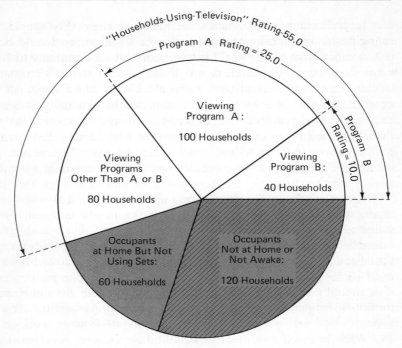

Sample: 400 Television Households
Universe: All Television Households in the Market

The pie represents a hypothetical probability sample of 400 television households, drawn from the 100,000 television households in the market being surveyed. Note that the rating is derived from a percentage based on the *total* sample (400), not just that part of the sample viewing programs at the time.

In the example the universe (= 100 per cent of the population being measured) is defined as all television households in the market. The universe could also be defined in other ways, for example, as *all households* in the market; this would lower the ratings (assuming that fewer than 100 per cent of the households are television households). The rating based on a universe defined as all households using receivers at the time is called a "share-of-audience" rating. In this case, there are 220 such households in the sample, and the share of audience of Program A would be 100/220, or .454, expressed as a rating of 45.4.

The sum of all ratings at the time (= the total *actual* audience) is called the "households-using-television" rating. To *project* the rating of 25.0 for an estimate of the total number of households tuned to Program A, take 25 per cent of 100,000 (= 25,000 households). This figure might then be multiplied by the average household size of the community to find the estimated audience of Program A in terms of individual viewers.

time to probe into such variables; he must use some very simple, uniform, clear-cut item of behavior to test whether or not a person should be counted as a member of an audience. This test reduces itself essentially to *set tuning:* is (or was) the set turned off or on? If on, to what station? This simple set-use test leaves out a good deal we would like to know about an audience member. It does not even tell us for sure that he actually was an audience member, since a receiver could be turned on in an empty room. People sometimes leave sets on to deter burglars or entertain the dog. Even with people present, we do not learn how much attention they paid to the program; whether the individual listener/viewer's attitude was favorable, indifferent, or hostile; whether he chose the program after considering all the alternative programs available at the moment, or merely left the dial wherever it happened to be set; whether one member of the family imposed his program choice on all the rest, etc.[12]

A second simplification used in audience research takes advantage of the repetitious patterns of programming. Most programs ("specials" excepted) occur in series, scheduled in daily or weekly cycles. The relative popularity of individual programs in a series tends to remain stable, for audiences develop habitual listening and viewing patterns and program loyalties. To measure audiences for every program every day of the week every week of the year would involve much unnecessary labor. Rating research therefore depends on samples of program time—a test week every few weeks is adequate for most purposes. Network programming is rated daily, but only by geographical sample—a few cities of "equal network opportunity." For the more stable parameters, such as circulation levels, measurement need be made only every few months or at even longer intervals.

The third and most controversial type of simplification used in audience research reduces the audience itself to the dimensions of a small sample. Of all the research procedures, audience sampling causes the most skepticism. To the lay observer, it seems like a denial of plain common sense to claim that a tiny sample of a few hundred could provide a remotely adequate basis on which to ascertain the program preferences of two hundred million people. Yet sampling passes unchallenged in untold numbers of other situations which affect human well-being—for example in establishing the useability of medicinal drugs.

Statisticians can demonstrate that within definable limits of accuracy, it is indeed possible to get reliable estimates from small samples—provided always that the subjects of measurement and the methods used conform to the requirements of sampling theory. In the most commonly used type of sampling,

---

[12] A technique designed to penetrate the privacy of the viewing situation actually did use time-lapse photography of family viewing areas. Photographic studies of ninety-five families, involving 358 individual viewers, showed no audience at all 19 per cent of the time sets were on; 21 per cent of the time viewers were present but inattentive. [Charles L. Allen, "Photographing the TV Audience," *Journal of Advertising Research,* V (March, 1965), 2–8.]

the chief requirement is that each member of an entire population must have an equal chance of being selected as a member of the sample. Selection of all sample members ("sampling units") must be governed by chance. Only in this way can the mathematical laws of probability apply. Simple as this requirement may seem, in practice it is usually difficult and often literally impossible to arrange matters so that each member of a large population actually does have an equal chance of being selected as a sample member.[13] Compromises on the ideal sampling procedure which undermine reliability thus begin at the outset.

Nevertheless, investigators in every branch of inquiry routinely use sampling as a measurement technique. Most social surveys of the entire population of the United States successfully use samples of two thousand to five thousand individuals. Innumerable measurement situations other than broadcasting occur in which a complete census would be impossible. Moreover, the incidental errors that occur in the handling of many million bits of information can easily make a complete census less accurate than a well-conducted sample survey. In many situations, either sampling must be used or rational judgment must give way to guesswork. If, as former NBC president Pat Weaver remarked, audience research is "just one step from the entrails of the chicken," even one step in the direction of objectivity is preferable to sheer superstition.

The Committee on Nationwide Television Audience Measurements (CONTAM) demonstrated the feasibility of using small samples specifically to obtain broadcast rating measurements for the benefit of a Congressional investigating committee. CONTAM drew a large series of samples from a television audience whose actual program preferences were already known. The known "population" consisted of completed viewing diaries from over 56,000 homes. These diaries had been collected by a commercial research firm, the American Research Bureau, in the course of a national survey of television-station circulation, and tabulated so that the actual rating of each program by that particular population had been established.

For the demonstration, CONTAM selected 10 programs of varying types and levels of popularity, then estimated the rating of each program for samples of varying sizes. Samples of 25, 50, 100, 500, 1,000, 1,500, and 2,500 diaries were used. One hundred samples of each size were chosen. This meant 800 samples (that is, groups, not just individuals) for each of the 10 programs, or a grand total of 8,000 samples, involving selection at random of over 5 million sampling units. Of course, the selected diaries (the sampling units) were returned to the pool after each sample had been tabulated so that the population remained absolutely the same for the drawing of each sample.

Figure 14.2 shows some of the results for one program. Results for the other 9 programs were similar. The distribution of estimated values above and below the true rating follows the pattern predicted by statistical theory. The

---

[13] In practice, a *known* though unequal chance also fulfills the requirement, since compensation can be made for a known inequality.

Figure 14.2

Effect of sample size on accuracy of rating estimate

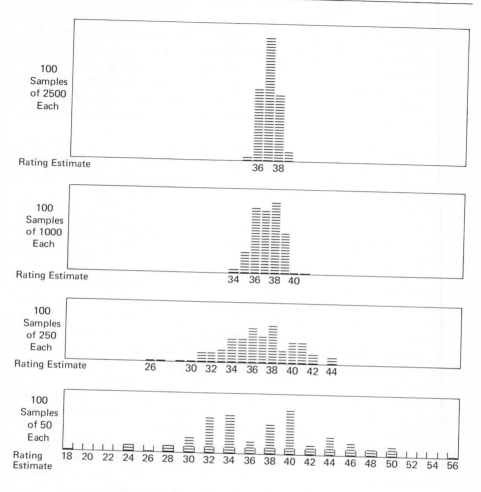

How program-rating estimates based on samples of various sizes compare with the known rating based on an actual census of the entire population. The program was *Dr. Kildare,* the population some 56,000 completed viewer diaries. The actual rating was 37. Each horizontal bar in the columns represents one complete sample of the designated size. One hundred samples of each size were drawn.

Read as follows: When 100 samples, each of 50 diaries, were drawn from a population of 56,000 diaries, one sample of 50 yielded an estimated rating for *Dr. Kildare* as low as 18 and one sample of 50 yielded a rating as high as 56; however, most of the sample estimates were within a few rating points of the correct rating of 37.

Source: Data of Committee on Nationwide Television Audience Measurements in House Committee on Interstate and Foreign Commerce, Special Subcommittee on Investigations, *Broadcast Ratings: The Methodology, Accuracy, and Use of Ratings in Broadcasting,* Hearings, Part 4 (Washington: Government Printing Office, 1965), p. 1848.

smallest-size sample shown in the figure is 50—much smaller than samples normally used in actual rating surveys. Rating estimates based on samples of that small size varied considerably from the true rating of 37—as far off as 18 on the low side and 56 on the high side. Even so, only 4 of the 100 samples erred to this extreme. Indeed, 63 of the 100 estimates fell within 5 rating points of the true figure. Thus, even a sample of admittedly inadequate size yields estimates which in the majority of cases come reasonably close to the truth.

Increasing sample size to 250 produced a marked improvement in reliability. Now the estimates began to cluster tightly around the true figure, with fewer extreme misses. At the next level, all the samples of 1,000 fell within 3 rating points of the true figure. Further increase in sample size did not yield a proportional increase in reliability, however. Samples of 2,500, though 2.5 times larger, did not produce estimates 2.5 times more accurate than samples of 1,000. A point of diminishing returns sets in after which larger samples produce such small gains in reliability that they become too costly to be worthwhile.

This demonstration with actual audience data showed that with proper sampling procedures, relatively small samples can be used to estimate program ratings with reasonable accuracy. Of course, "proper sampling procedures" present no problem with a static "population" of diaries, which can be manipulated at will. Real-life populations are far less stable and accessible, and real-life field work introduces all sorts of human errors not encountered in the demonstration.

The CONTAM demonstration shows why no sample-based rating is anything more than an *estimate,* no matter how careful the procedure or how large the sample. A sample-based estimate entitles one to say no more than that the obtained figure is *probably* correct within certain limits. Notice that the statistician uses not one, but two escape clauses: not only must we accept that the estimated value may fall above or below the true value by a certain amount; even this assurance is given us only as a probability, not a certainty.

The degree of confidence we can assume in an estimated rating not varying above or below its true value by more than a specified amount can be determined mathematically. Using the example in Figure 14.2 of rating estimates based on samples of 1,000, with a true value of 37, probability theory predicts that with a 95-per-cent level of confidence (*i.e.,* 95 chances out of 100), the estimates will differ from the true rating value by *no more* than 3.1 rating points. In other words, at least 95 per cent of the time samples of 1,000 should provide estimates falling within the range 40.1 to 33.9 when the true value is 37 (*i.e.,* 37 plus or minus 3.1). In the CONTAM demonstration, as shown in Figure 14.2, 98 per cent of the 100 estimates fell within these limits.[14]

---

[14] A table of probable deviation limits for samples of varying sizes can be found in National Association of Broadcasters, *A Broadcast Research Primer* (Washington: The Association, 1966), p. 19.

Realization that ratings based on sampling amount to no more than esti-mates, with a known chance of being somewhat above or below the true value, makes it evident that small differences in ratings should not be regarded as significant. In the context of the above sample, if Program A received a rating of 37 and Program B a rating of 36, the difference would be insignif-icantly small and we would have no statistical justification for asserting that the ratings proved one program had a larger audience than the other.

14.6 / Rating-Data Collection

Data on which to base ratings can be obtained by asking either sample mem-bers or their receiving sets to report on listening/viewing behavior. Receiving sets equipped with tuning recorders "tell" about their owners' behavior. The metering device in most general use, trade-named the "audimeter," is the product of A. C. Nielsen Co., which uses it for national television-rating serv-ices. The audimeter keeps a continuous timed record on a film strip, reporting receiver "on" periods and tuning from station to station. The company at-taches an audimeter to every receiver in each sample home. Even portable battery sets which may be moved about the house can be monitored with a remote signalling device. For national ratings, Nielsen uses a sample of about twelve hundred homes, selected on the basis of a sophisticated national sam-pling design. Since it is expensive to secure the cooperation of designated sam-ple members and to equip their sets with audimeters, Nielsen retains the same sample permanently, replacing drop-outs as required. The audimeter's con-tinuous, minute-by-minute record of tuning by station enables reconstructing a detailed picture of audience flow, both throughout the course of a program and from one program to another. "Instantaneous audimeters" deliver their information by wire directly to a central collecting point, instead of recording it on film for later analysis.[15]

The audimeter tells about sets, only indirectly about people. Audiences can be asked to testify directly about their own listening/viewing behavior, either orally or in writing. Door-to-door interviewing can be used but is a relatively costly and cumbersome method compared to telephone interviewing. In-person interviewers often show the respondent a list of programs that were on during the time period in question ("roster" or "aided" recall). "Coincidental tele-phone" interviews avoid errors due to memory lapses by asking respondents what they are listening to or viewing at the moment—the listening/viewing and the question *coincide*. However, since it is not practicable to call people late at night or early in the morning, interviewers do ask respondents to recall their listening/viewing activities for these time periods at later, more con-venient times.

---

[15] American Research Bureau's "ARBitron" system also reports instantaneously, and in 1970 a device was put into operation which senses channel settings in CATV-served receivers and relays the information back to a central computer.

Written testimony of audience behavior takes the form of diaries filled out by sample members at the time of listening/viewing. Figure 14.3 shows the form of such a diary. Respondents receive a small reward for mailing in their completed diaries at the end of 'the week. American Research Bureau uses diaries for both local and national ratings. Nielsen supplements and validates audimeter set-tuning data periodically with diary data, using another and simpler recording device, the "recordimeter," in conjunction with the diary. The recordimeter keeps a simple log of set-use time but not of tuning. Every half hour while the set is on, the recordimeter gives viewers an audible and visual reminder to make a diary entry.

Each method of collecting data has its own advantages and disadvantages. The set-metering device necessitates a relatively very small, permanent sample. Nielsen claims to have spent $200 thousand to set up a national "master sample" of potential audimeter homes from which the actual national sample of about twelve hundred is drawn.[16] With such a small sample, a few discrepancies or irregularities could seriously affect results. The coincidental telephone method uses much larger samples, for only a tiny bit of information is gleaned from each respondent. Telephone directories make it relatively easy to draw samples—though always within the restriction that not everybody has a listed telephone and therefore not everybody has a chance of being chosen as a sample member. Diaries cost little compared with the meters and samples can therefore be larger, but cooperation tends to be low and the researcher depends heavily on respondents to fill out diaries intelligently and accurately and return them promptly.

The companies supplying rating services issue periodic reports to subscribers throughout the year. The reports contain quantities of information beyond the basic rating or circulation data. For example, American Research Bureau's local-market reports consist of nearly sixty columns of figures. In addition to ratings, the client gets such information for each time segment as a breakdown of the estimated audience by age groups and sex and estimates of audience consumption of such products as soaps, drugs, beverages, and gasolines.

14.7 / Ratings Under Fire

During the late 1940's and the 1950's, several factors combined to place extraordinary stress on the rating system. These were years of broadcast-industry expansion, encouraged by the phenomenal profitability of the more favorably placed stations. In fact, a relatively high proportion of stations lost money, despite the economic well-being of the industry as a whole. The combination of high stakes on the one hand and high losses on the other put managements under pressure to seek larger audiences at the very time when the increased number of stations tended to break down audiences into ever-smaller frac-

---

[16] A. C. Nielsen Co., "Designing and Constructing Nielsen's Master Sample" (New York: The Company, n.d.), p. 7.

Figure 14.3
Viewer diary

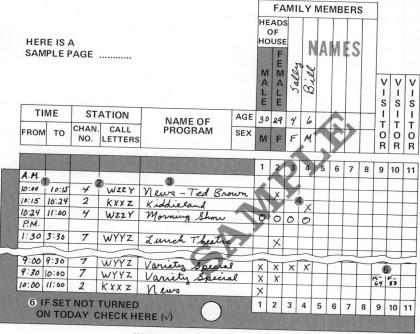

HERE IS A SAMPLE PAGE ....

WHEN TO FILL IN THE DIARY —

—Each time the set is turned on
—Then, immediately after each program

—When there is a change in the people watching
—Each time the set is turned off

Instruction page from week-long diary. In addition to a separate page on viewing for each day of the week, the respondent is asked to fill out two supplemental pages about his family's product consumption.

Source: American Research Bureau.

tions. At the network level, ABC-TV adopted an intensely competitive programming strategy which finally brought it within sight of the ratings enjoyed by CBS and NBC (Section 10.6). In 1964–1965, the network-television rating race resulted for the first time in a three-way tie, though ABC subsequently dropped back again.

Meanwhile, radio had been so completely transformed that the older methods of radio-audience measurement no longer had relevance. Instead of perhaps five or six stations, urban radio audiences now often had twenty or thirty to choose from, including not only AM but also FM and television. Most radio-station ratings had become miniscule—on the order of only one, two, or three rating points. Multiple-set (both radio and television) homes had become commonplace, and a large proportion of all radio listening took place outside the home. The older methods of radio-audience measurement had been based on the concept of radio as a home medium, listened to by the family seated in a group around a console set in the parlor. These conditions had long since ceased to exist.

Intense competition, overdependence on ratings as the primary guide to programming, long-standing doubts about the reliability and relevance of research techniques, failure of research to keep pace with changing times—all contributed to a crisis of confidence in the whole rating system in the early 1960's. Rating pressures were widely believed to have motivated the rigging of quiz programs which caused such a scandal in the late 1950's (Section 16.3). A Federal Trade Commission investigation in 1962 resulted in Cease and Desist Orders alleging misrepresentation by three major rating companies. A full-dress Congressional investigation in 1963–1964 revealed not only carelessness and ineptitude by research companies, but even extensive doctoring of data and outright deception.[17] These revelations vindicated some of the criticisms which had originated within the industry as well as outside. Criticisms had tended to fall into the three main categories suggested by the title of the Congressional committee's report: *methodology, accuracy,* and *use.*

On the score of methodology, the main questions concerned (1) the reliability of audience sampling; (2) the contradictory results issued by competing rating services; and (3) the effects of noncooperation by designated sample members on the representativeness of samples. We have already discussed the theoretical justification of sampling. A committee of the American Statistical Association, employed by the Congressional committee to evaluate rating methods, concluded that critics had been placing undue emphasis on sample size and should worry more about methodological inadequacies and lack of basic research on the effects of such factors as noncooperation of sample

---

[17] House Committee on Interstate and Foreign Commerce, Special Subcommittee on Investigations, *Broadcasting Ratings: The Methodology, Accuracy, and Use of Ratings in Broadcasting,* Hearings, Parts 1–3, 88th Cong., 1st Sess.; Part 4, 88th Cong., 1st and 2d Sess. (Washington: Government Printing Office, 1963, 1964, and 1965).

members and interviewer bias. The statisticians recommended that rating services make more complete disclosures of their methods and the significance of their results.[18]

Contradictory results obtained by different commercial research organizations measuring the same audiences had always been a source of much irritation in the industry. At best some differences must be expected because sampling produces estimates; other apparent discrepancies in results can arise from lack of standardized definitions. However, it was hard to explain away discrepancies even within the same company's results. For example, the investigation turned up an extraordinary case of two estimates of audience size for a single program by the same rating service: the audience of only five stations was estimated to be over 118 thousand homes, while the national audience for a network of 179 stations carrying the same program was estimated to consist of only 99 thousand homes![19]

Noncooperation of sample members was much discussed at the hearings because it compromises sample design. It will be recalled from our previous discussion of sampling theory (Section 14.5) that each member of a population being investigated should have an equal or known chance of being selected as a sample member. Careful sample design, including planned operational procedures for sample selection, fulfills this requirement. In dealing with human populations, however, the researcher rarely succeeds in actually reaching every designated sample member. Some may be on vacation, sick, or even dead. Many may be available but unwilling to cooperate. When asked if they would be willing to keep viewing diaries, for example, half or more of the people designated in the sample design usually either refuse outright or are unable to cooperate because of language difficulty. Of those who agree to keep the diaries, some will fail to do so; others will misunderstand the instructions and their diaries will have to be discarded.[20] The researcher thus bases his measurements on a faulty sample, one not true to the original sample design. This discrepancy may or may not matter, depending on whether noncooperators, as a group, tend to differ significantly in their listening/viewing habits from cooperators.

The FTC issued Cease and Desist Orders against three major companies, calling on them to stop misrepresenting the accuracy and reliability of their figures. Among the practices proscribed by the FTC were use of hearsay information, failure to account for nonresponding members of samples, mislead-

---

[18] William G. Madow, *et al., Evaluation of Statistical Methods Used in Obtaining Broadcast Ratings,* House Report 193, 87th Cong., 1st Sess. (Washington: Government Printing Office, 1961).

[19] House Committee on Interstate and Foreign Commerce, *op. cit.,* p. 236.

[20] The Madow committee reported that about 70 per cent of homes designated in sample designs accepted audimeter placement. An average of about 5 per cent of the audimeter readouts had to be discarded for mechanical faults and 15 to 20 per cent of the sample families had to be replaced each year. [Madow, *et al., op. cit.,* p. 73.]

ing claims about the nature of samples, improper combining of data from incompatible sources, and the use of arbitrary "adjustments" on research findings.[21]

The rating services had evaded outside appraisal of their methods by failing to make full and candid disclosures in their reports and by refusing to respond constructively to inquiries. One station executive testified to the subcommittee:

Never, during the years I have discussed rating services with people selling them, have I been able to get clear cut, documented answers to four very simple questions. What was the exact size of the sample used to produce the ratings? Exactly how was the sample drawn? What was the exact manner in which data was obtained from the sample? And, finally, what was the geographic distribution of the sample?[22]

Stations made their own contribution to rating deception by "hypo-ing." Knowing in advance the week in which a survey was scheduled in their service area, stations would lay on vigorous audience-building campaigns using heavy advertising, promotional stunts with contest prizes, or special feature films, much above the run-of-the-mill programming of the station. These efforts caused temporary increases in stations' audience shares and hence artificially inflated ratings.

14.8 / Misuse of Ratings

Assuming impeccable research procedures and high statistical reliability of ratings—what then? Many critics base their objection to the system not so much on the ratings themselves as on the way the industry uses them. They see programming judgment reduced to the rule of arithmetic, even the meaningless arithmetic of insignificant differences as small as a fraction of a rating point.

This surrender has been periodically dramatized when a network has cancelled a quality program with respectable though moderate ratings, over the objections of loyal followers and sponsor alike. Fierce television-network competition in the limited prime-time hours requires, in general, that each program capture a 30-per-cent share of the audience or better. Advertisers could easily be found for a lesser share, but the "audience-flow" concept dominates programming strategy. Once a large share of the audience has been captured, it must be held at all costs. A temporary drop in audience share caused by a lower-rated program coming between two high-rated programs can never be fully recovered—part of the potential audience for the ensuing high-rated program has been permanently lost to another network or another activity. A CBS official appearing before a Senate investigating committee gave as an

---

[21] House Committee on Interstate and Foreign Commerce, *op. cit.*, pp. 141–152.

[22] *Ibid.*, p. 196.

example a program called *Stage 7,* which drew a 32.1 share-of-audience rating when preceded by *Fred Waring,* whose share was 32.8. When *GE Theatre,* with a rating of 54.6, was moved into the *Waring* slot, the *Stage 7* share jumped 40 per cent, to a rating of 45.1.[23]

Little wonder that prime time is dominated by programs aimed at the lowest common denominator of popular taste. Sylvester Weaver, a former NBC president, in testimony before the House committee investigating ratings, cited a *Variety* headline:

GODFREY AND LUCY CLOBBER CULTURE

The two entertainers had drawn an estimated audience of thirty-eight million, while a competing ballet performance drew only thirty million.[24] Audiences of even five or six million could be considered eminently satisfactory for high-quality programs of specialized interest, but they could also be considered disasters in a sequence of prime-time competitive network programming.

Networks at least occasionally go against the mechanical dictates of rating rules for the sake of public service, but spot advertising has no such obligation. "Spot buying is rating buying, nothing else," Weaver told the committee.[25] He was referring to the fact that spot buyers translate ratings into "cost per thousand" (CPM), a relative measure of a medium's efficiency in reaching prospective buyers, obtained by dividing advertising costs by the number of thousands of homes reached. Ratings supply the divisors for this formula. For example, a representative of Colgate-Palmolive told the committee that its CPM for television advertising ranged from $3.80 to $4.20.[26]

Time buyers may even ask for a "rating guarantee"; if a station's ratings fall behind the level reported just prior to the time buyer's purchase, the station makes up the difference in CPM by giving extra spots. Another measure used in spot buying is "cost per gross rating point." A trade publication supplies a table of such costs for 170 radio markets, based on a five-times-a-week order on the second-most expensive station in each market for twenty-second an-

---

[23] House Committee on the Judiciary, Antitrust Subcommittee, *Monopoly Problems in Regulated Agencies, Part 2: Television,* 4 vols., 84th Cong., 2d Sess., (Washington: Government Printing Office, 1957), pp. 5185–5187. The classic cancellation case was *The Voice of Firestone,* a middle-brow music program, cancelled by NBC over the vigorous objections of the company and many fans after twenty-five years of prime-time sponsorship by the tire company. Harvey Firestone, Jr., wrote: "The reason given by the network . . . was that it did not have a high rating. The network pointed out that although our program was of outstanding quality, the program preceding us had a higher rating than our show. . . ." [*Ibid.,* Part 1, p. 20.]

[24] House Committee on Interstate and Foreign Commerce, *op. cit.,* p. 172.

[25] *Ibid.,* p. 178.

[26] *Ibid.,* p. 378.

nouncements in prime time. In 1969, Los Angeles, for example, had a cost per gross rating point of $153 and Nashville a cost of $11.[27]

Industry witnesses before the Congressional investigating committee defended the rating system by insisting that they based their programming judgments on a variety of considerations—that ratings were only one consideration among many. When pressed, however, witnesses were vague about the nature of these other considerations. The operative order of priorities might be the one suggested (much later) by Fred Friendly, one-time president of CBS News:

1. The ratings . . .
2. The effect of these ratings on advertisers.
3. The effect of these ratings on the company's expected earnings, and their effect on the stock market.
4. The company's corporate image as reflected in the press, by the leadership of the community and at the FCC—in that order.
5. Responsibility for true public service and personal taste in entertainment and cultural programs.[28]

Friendly goes on to say that CBS and NBC had once ranked these priorities in reverse order, but ABC's challenge for ratings leadership forced them into a more hard-nosed competitive policy.

14.9 / Methodological Studies and Innovations

The House investigating-committee hearings revealed conditions in the rating field which could not be brushed aside. The industry moved promptly to correct obvious abuses and to undertake the kind of basic methodological research recommended by the Madow committee. Before the hearings were over, a Broadcasting Rating Council had been formed by the industry to set up minimum standards and to accredit rating firms after independent audits. The Council concerns itself only with research on audience size and composition. Its auditors spot check such elements as sample design, field work, computerization accuracy, and form of reporting. The fact that preliminary audits of applicant services invariably show deficiencies that have to be corrected before accreditation is granted indicates the effectiveness of the Council—though it must be kept in mind that application for accreditation is voluntary.[29]

The Committee on Nationwide Television Audience Measurements, set

---

[27] *Broadcasting 1970 Yearbook,* pp. 64–66.

[28] Fred W. Friendly, *Due to Circumstances Beyond Our Control* . . . (copyright © 1967 by Random House, Inc.), p. 272.

[29] At the start of 1970, four companies had received accreditation: American Research Bureau for five of its radio and television services, A. C. Nielsen for four television services, Pulse for a radio service, and a Honolulu company for its traffic radio audit.

up by the National Association of Broadcasters and the networks in 1963, immediately embarked on a program of basic research. We have already described CONTAM's first study, on the feasibility of using small samples (Section 14.5). The second tackled the question of the significance of differences in rating methods, comparing prime-time ratings reported by Nielsen (meters) and American Research Bureau (diaries). Nielsen used a fixed national sample of about 1,000 homes, while ARB used a one-time sample of about 55,000 homes. CONTAM hypothesized that major deficiencies in either method would cause significant differences in their results (since the two methods and their procedures differ so markedly, it seemed unlikely that both would err by the same amount in the same direction). In the CONTAM comparison, the two services coincided in their ranking of programs 94 per cent of the time, a reasonably high level of agreement.[30]

CONTAM next turned its attention to the oldest way of obtaining systematic rating data, the coincidental telephone method. There had always been some doubt about what assumption to make when no one answers the telephone after a stipulated number of rings. CONTAM set out to learn what it could about the real meaning of "no answers," and at the same time to see what effect the interviewer herself might have on results. The test group consisted of a national sample of 4,000 telephone listings. Interviewers were given special intensive training. One group of interviewers placed calls under close supervision and monitoring; another group placed calls from their homes without supervision.

On the first try, interviewers successfully completed 60 per cent of their attempted calls; they tabulated 19 per cent as "no answer" after two dialings of eight rings each—about twice the amount of effort normally applied in such surveys. Persistent follow-up for two more days eventually reached more than 90 per cent of the "no answers"—or established that the telephones were disconnected even though they "rang." About 5 per cent of the "no answers" were deliberate—people had been home, but for a variety of reasons refused to answer the telephone. Data obtained from this persistent follow-up made a difference in the "homes-using-television" rating: one dialing of five rings produced a rating of 52.5, but two dialings of eight rings each, plus follow-up as needed in the next two days, produced a rating of 57.5. The usual assumption that "no answer" should be interpreted as "not at home" and therefore "not watching television" apparently leads to systematic underestimation of audience size.

Comparing the results obtained by the closely supervised interviewers with those obtained by interviewers who worked on their own at home indicated a significantly greater variability in the unsupervised interviewers' results. Previously, interviewer bias had not been given much thought in the seemingly simple, highly standardized operation of the coincidental telephone call. The study indicated that conducting research reliably by the coincidental tele-

---

[30] House Committee on Interstate and Foreign Commerce, *op. cit.*, pp. 1855–1860.

Table 14.2

Characteristics of survey noncooperators

CHARACTERISTIC	PEOPLE ASKED TO KEEP VIEWING DIARY (%)	
	Cooperators	*Noncooperators*
5 or more viewing hours per day	53	46
2 or less viewing hours per day	16	11
4 or more in household	50	41
Less than 40 years old	33	26
60 or older	17	23
Some college	33	26
Less than high-school graduation	23	29

Read as follows: Of people who cooperated in keeping a rating-survey diary, 53 per cent said they watched television 5 or more hours per day, but of people who refused to cooperate, only 46 per cent said they watched that much, etc.

Source: Data in House Committee on Interstate and Foreign Commerce, Subcommittee on Investigations, *Report on Broadcast Ratings*, House Report 1212, 89th Cong., 2d Sess. (Washington: Government Printing Office, 1966), pp. 15–16.

phone method requires a good deal more time, money, and effort than had been supposed.[31]

All methods have in common the problem of noncooperation—people who according to the sample design should serve as sample members but who refuse to participate or fail in some way to do their part. Another industry study sought out noncooperators who had been identified in an ARB national diary survey involving a designed sample of nearly two hundred thousand. Comparing cooperators with noncooperators indicated that cooperators as a group watched more television, had larger households, were younger and better educated (Table 14.2).[32] The differences were not as marked as some critics of ratings expected. Their main practical effect is slight overestimation of audience size. An ARB study of noncooperation obtained similar results. It compared diary cooperators and noncooperators in twenty-four markets. The two groups agreed on seventy-one program ratings; they differed on only six programs, with cooperators rating five programs significantly higher and one program significantly lower than noncooperators.[33]

Radio interests, too, participated in the drive to improve research. The "All-Radio Methodology Study" ("ARMS"), organized in 1963 by the National Association of Broadcasters and the Radio Advertising Bureau, spent nearly

---

[31] Committee on Nationwide Television Audience Measurements, *How Good Are Television Ratings? (Continued)*, 1969 (distributed by Television Information Office, New York).

[32] House Committee on Interstate and Foreign Commerce, Special Subcommittee on Investigations, *Report on Broadcast Ratings*, House Report 1212, 89th Cong., 2d Sess. (Washington: Government Printing Office, 1966), pp. 15–16.

[33] American Research Bureau, *The Influence of Non-Cooperation in the Diary Method of Television Audience Measurement* (Beltsville, Md.: The Bureau, 1963).

a third of a million dollars studying variations on standard data-gathering methods. According to ARMS, the study represents "the most comprehensive evaluation of its type ever undertaken in communications research."[34] ARMS employed an independent research firm, Audits and Surveys, to compare three methods of data collection, along with variants within each method. Preliminarily, the researchers established that the coincidental telephone method is the most accurate yardstick. Part of the preliminary investigation also established that 91 per cent of the interviewees correctly identified the radio station they were listening to at the time of the interview. Incorrect identifications were randomly scattered and so did not introduce bias. Using a coincidental telephone survey in Philadelphia, supplemented by an auto-traffic survey by means of stoplight interviews and set-use meters installed in autos, the researchers established a reference level of radio use in the area as a standard against which to measure other methods. They then made eleven more surveys, using as many methodological variants. Table 14.3 summarizes the results. They indicate that diary results can be too low, too high, or about right, depending on which particular variant of the method is used. Placing the diaries in sample homes by means of in-person interviews and picking up the diaries personally (rather than doing these things by telephone and mail) seem to have favorably affected diary-keeping accuracy. All four variants of the telephone recall method produced low estimates, but the two variants of the in-person roster-recall method both yielded relatively accurate measurements. The evidence of the ARMS study is said to have convinced American Research Bureau that it should discontinue the multimedia diary approach (Variant 3 under "Diary" in Table 14.3).

Two research projects attempted to make more sophisticated estimates of network-radio audiences than had hitherto been available. NBC, in response to the dilemma presented by conflicting data on radio audiences provided by existing research, undertook a three-year series of studies of cumulative radio-audience measurements, with special attention to the effect of sample non-cooperation.[35] NBC used the "augmented coincidental" technique, which involved interviewing by telephone not just one but *every* member of sample families thirteen years old or over and following up "not at homes" to account for out-of-home listening by recall. Those who still could not be contacted or interviewed were resurveyed at a later date to obtain noncooperator information. A second part of the C.R.A.M. project used daily telephone calls to the same sample for seven consecutive days. This method was adopted as a substitute for the weekly diary because of the high rate of noncooperation experienced in diary placement. Sixty-three per cent of the designed telephone

---

[34] All-Radio Methodology Study, *ARMS: What It Shows, How It Has Changed Radio Measurement* (Washington: National Association of Broadcasters, n. d.), p. 3; Audits and Surveys, Inc., *All-Radio Methodological Study*, 2 vol. (New York: The Corporation, 1966).

[35] National Broadcasting Company, *C.R.A.M.: Cumulative Radio Audience Method* (New York: The Company, 1966).

Table 14.3
Effect of variations in rating-research methods

Method	Variants	Compared with "Standard" Estimate of "Individuals-Using-Radio" Rating		
		Low	About Right	High
Diary	1. Sample homes recruited by telephone, radio only, daily mail return			X
	2. Same as 1, except weekly return			X
	3. Same as 2, except multimedia	X		
	4. Sample homes recruited by personal visit, radio-only diary, daily mail return			X
	5. Same as 4, but diaries picked up weekly		X	
Telephone recall	1. Radio only, "today" recall	X		
	2. Radio only, "yesterday" recall	X		
	3. Multimedia, "today" recall	X		
	4. Multimedia, "yesterday" recall	X		
In-person roster-recall interview	1. Radio only, "today" recall		X	
	2. Radio only, "yesterday" recall		X	

Read as follows: The diary method, when sample members were recruited by telephone and asked to keep a diary of radio listening for one week and mail the diary in at the end of the week, yielded a *higher* estimate of listenership than the probable actual level of listenership, etc.

Source: Material in All-Radio Methodology Study, *ARMS: What It Shows, How It Shows, How It has Changed Radio Measurement* (Washington: National Association of Broadcasters, n. d.).

sample cooperated in the seven-day coincidental survey, and follow-ups later overcame enough noncooperator resistance to obtain at least some information from 71 per cent of the sample. Analyzing noncooperators indicated that the more emphatic their refusal to cooperate the less they listened to radio. NBC used data on noncooperation to construct a weighting factor which it then applied in estimating the total audience. Cumulative measurements indicated that three-quarters of the adult population used radio in the course of a single day; in the course of a week, the cumulative total reached above 90 per cent. The comparable figures for the combined networks were about 39 per cent for one day and about 60 per cent for a week.

The four radio networks cooperate in the continuing "Radio's All-Dimension Audience Research" (RADAR) project, which employs a technique similar to the "augmented recall" of C.R.A.M.[36] Instead of interviewing every family member, however, RADAR first lists individually all family members associated with the telephone households in the sample, then draws a sample of specific individuals to interview. RADAR achieves over 80 per cent cooperation, and like C.R.A.M. feeds back information on noncooperator characteristics as a corrective in arriving at final listening-level estimates. RADAR also arrived at similar results to C.R.A.M.'s, estimating that radio reaches about 70 per cent of the population in one day and cumulatively over 93 per cent in seven days.

The Congressional investigation could not, of course, change the order of priorities in programming judgments of commercial broadcasters, but it did precipitate improvement in rating practice. Serious research on methodology has made the industry more aware of the real limitations on rating precision. The rating-service reports now make full disclosure of their methods and levels of reliability. Confusion and inconsistencies have been reduced by research standardization.[37] The Federal Communications Commission regards evidence of "hypo-ing" and other rating abuses by stations as unfavorable to the licensee at renewal time, and the House Committee on Interstate and Foreign Commerce has followed up its original investigation with periodic progress reports.

14.10 / Other Types of Research

Ratings receive so much notoriety that they tend to obscure the fact that a great deal of less conspicuous broadcast market research goes on in the background. At the beginning of this chapter, we pointed out that research is used in preparing program materials and following up evaluations of results, as well

---

[36] Brand Rating Research, Inc., *Radio's All-Dimension Audience Research* (New York: The Company, *seriatim*).

[37] National Association of Broadcasters, *Standard Definitions of Broadcast Research Terms* (Washington: The Association, 1967), and *Recommended Standards for the Preparation of Statistical Reports in Broadcast Audience Measurement Research* (Washington: The Association, 1969).

Figure 14.4
Program-analyzer audience profile

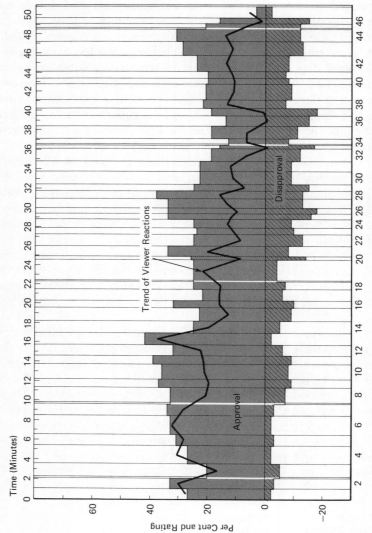

Chart from a test of a pilot drama film showing generally unfavorable reaction. In practice, the program series lived up to this prediction: it failed. Each vertical bar represents a particular program unit of varying length. The superimposed curve depicting the reaction trend is based on a special formula for combining "like," "don't like," and "indifferent" votes into a single value.

Source: Columbia Broadcasting System.

as in estimating audience size and composition. David Ogilvy, a leading advertising-agency head, has said:

The most important word in the vocabulary of advertising is TEST. If you pre-test your product with consumers, and pre-test your advertising, you will do well in the market place. . . . Test your promise. Test your media. Test your headlines and your illustrations. Test the size of your advertisements. Test your frequency. Test your level of expenditure. Test your commercials. Never stop testing. . . .[38]

Researchers use many methods for testing, ranging from random interviews on the streets and in stores to systematic probes of carefully designed samples in panel groups. One of the more interesting techniques uses a device for registering audience reaction at the push of a button.[39] CBS has a Program Analysis Unit which invites people in groups of from a dozen to thirty to a special studio to preview program material. Each panel member has a pair of buttons to record either "like" or "dislike." Reactions are recorded on both IBM cards and visual-display devices (polygraphs). From the latter, the session director gets an immediate picture of each panel member's reactions. After viewing, panel members fill out a questionnaire and then discuss their reactions with the session director. Profile charts are made up later to show minute-by-minute composite reactions (Figure 14.4). CBS uses the technique for testing audience reactions to pilot programs, casting alternatives, effect of color, and the like.

As we have said (Section 14.1), noncommercial broadcasting also needs and benefits from research. In the future, we should be hearing more, for example, about advance-planning studies undertaken to guide producers in the most effective way to develop informational programs. The case of *Sesame Street* was mentioned in Section 14.1. Such studies have long been routine at the BBC.[40] For example, when planning a series on mental health, the Corporation first conducted a survey to find out about existing attitudes toward mental-health problems, the kinds of ideas people had that needed to be either corrected or reinforced, how to avoid making the series too upsetting to listeners, the kinds of information on mental health that people lacked but needed. With this kind of background about their "market," obviously the producers could do a better job. Nor do the research principles involved differ fundamentally from those employed in commercial market research. In either case, effective communication is the goal.

---

[38] David Ogilvy, *Confessions of an Advertising Man* (New York: Dell, 1964), pp. 107–108.

[39] Tore Holonquist and Edward Suchman, "Listening to the Listener: Experiences with the Lazarsfeld-Stanton Program Analyzer," in Paul F. Lazarsfeld and Frank N. Stanton, *Radio Research 1942–1943* (New York: Duell, Sloan & Pearce, 1944), pp. 265–334.

[40] See W. A. Belsen, *The Impact of Television: Methods and Findings in Program Research* (Hamden, Conn.: Archon Books, 1967).

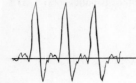

15

FINANCIAL ORGANIZATION OF BROADCASTING

By ordinary economic yardsticks, commercial broadcasting hardly qualifies as big business. Table 15.1 indicates its modest size in terms of national income relative to other selected industries. However, the role of broadcasting as a communication medium lends it social importance out of proportion to its direct economic importance. Its full significance even in economic terms must, moreover, take into account the secondary economic activities broadcasting creates or supports—receiver and equipment manufacturing, sales, and servicing; electric-power consumption; trade and consumer publications; advertising, talent, market-research, legal, and engineering services. The annual cost of repairing radio and television receivers alone amounts to as much as the entire earnings of the broadcasting industry. Yearbooks list talent agents and managers, program production and distribution firms, commercial producers, television film-processing laboratories, consultants, news services, public-relations and promotional services, station brokers, national representatives, schools—all dependent in whole or in part on the existence of broadcasting.[1]

Table 15.1

Trend in national income, selected industries

INDUSTRY	INCOME (MILLIONS)		% GROWTH[1]
	1953	*1968*	
Automobile	$7,698	$17,435	226
Telephone and telegraph	4,118	12,690	308
Printing and publishing	4,389	10,597	241
Amusement and recreation services	958	2,778	290
Broadcasting	481	1,506	313
Motion pictures	835	1,418	170
Tobacco products	615	1,395	227

[1]No allowance made for decline in value of the dollar.

Source: Department of Commerce data in *World Almanac and Book of Facts* (New York: Newspaper Enterprises Association, 1955 and 1970 editions).

---

[1] *Broadcasting 1970 Yearbook* lists over three thousand such satellite businesses.

Table 15.2

Investment in tangible broadcast property

SERVICE	NUMBER OF STATIONS	ORIGINAL COST	AVERAGE COST PER STATION
VHF television	488[1]	$896,061,000	$1,836,188
UHF television	154	154,174,000	1,001,129
Radio	4,141[2]	670,134,000	161,829

[1]Excludes 15 network-owned stations.
[2]Excludes 20 network-owned stations.

Source: Data in FCC, *Thirty-Fifth Annual Report* (Washington: Government Printing Office, 1970), pp. 138, 147.

15.1 / Investment, Revenue, and Income

Television caused a significant shift in broadcasting toward larger economic entities. In the 1940's, the entire outlay for starting a small radio station need not have exceeded the cost of a single color-television camera in the 1970's. Construction cost of even the average radio station just after World War II was well below $100 thousand.[2] Television made such sums seem inconsequential. Table 15.2 indicates that by 1969 the average capital cost for VHF stations had exceeded $1.8 million—about eleven times as much as the average for radio stations. Moreover, given the shortage of VHF channel allocations, the market value of favorably located television stations exceeds by many times their capital costs. The first television station to be sold went in 1949 for a third of a million dollars. In 1964, a Pittsburgh VHF station brought $20.5 million, an amount said to have been over five times the value of its tangible assets.

Broadcasting properties figured often in the trend toward "conglomerate" mergers in the 1960's. This increased identification of broadcasting with the country's major corporate power structures (intensifying a characteristic present from the beginning, as shown in Chapter 7) had significant economic implications for the nature of the service: restriction of ownership to fewer potential investors, with a trend toward corporate rather than individual entrepreneurship; altered managerial outlook with larger stakes involved; emphasis on large-market investments and consequent concentration in areas of dense population; more syndication to provide programs capable of drawing larger and larger audiences. Radio proved adaptable to severe market limitations. Indeed, most AM stations are located outside metropolitan areas.[3] But television offers no equivalent for Class II or Class IV AM "coffee-pot" or FM "underground" stations. Market size affects every aspect of the television enterprise: the larger the market the higher the salaries, the larger the staffs,

---

[2] FCC, "An Economic Study of Standard Broadcasting" (1947, mimeo.), pp. 44, 49.

[3] FCC, *Thirty-Fifth Annual Report* (Washington: Government Printing Office, 1970), p. 148. See the definition of "standard metropolitan statistical area" in Section 14.2.

Table 15.3

Broadcast income (before federal taxes)

SERVICE	NATIONAL NETWORKS		NETWORK O&O STATIONS		OTHER STATIONS		TOTAL (MILLIONS)
	No.	Amt. (*Millions*)	No.	Amt. (*Millions*)	No.	Amt. (*Millions*)	
Radio	4[1]	$(6.0)[2]	20	$ .8	4,141	$122.5	$117.3
Television	3	56.4	15	122.4	627	316.0	494.8
Industry total	7	$50.4	35	$123.2	4,768	$438.5	$612.1
% of industry total	8		20		72		100

[1]Counting ABC's four specialized services as one network.
[2]Loss.

Source: 1968 data in FCC, *Thirty-Fifth Annual Report* (Washington: Government Printing Office, 1970), pp. 133, 146.

the longer the program day, the greater the number of network programs carried, the more remote programs originated—and, of course, the more lucrative the station.

Table 15.3, analyzing industry income, indicates the importance of network owned-and-operated stations to the networks' economic position: the relatively few O&O stations (15 television and 20 radio) realized a fifth of the entire industry income, bringing the network organizations' total share up to 28 per cent. The 4,768 remaining stations divided somewhat less than three-quarters of the industry's aggregate income. Taken as a whole, this represented a healthy profit, as shown in Table 15.4—in one year, radio earned back 30 per cent of its depreciated capital investment and television 70 per cent. In some years, earnings even surpassed capital investment. Figure 15.1 shows the spectacular growth of television earnings, from a loss in 1950 to more than radio in 1953 and an almost unbroken advance thereafter. This rise depressed radio's earnings for a decade, but in 1962 they, too, began a slow upward trend. However, it must be borne in mind that these increased

Table 15.4

Broadcast investment-to-income ratios

SERVICE	INCOME[1] (MILLIONS)	DEPRECIATED INVESTMENT (MILLIONS)	INVESTMENT/INCOME RATIO
Radio	$117.3	$368.7	.31
Television	494.8	706.9	.70

[1]Before federal taxes.

Source: 1968 data in FCC, *Thirty-Fifth Annual Report* (Washington: Government Printing Office, 1970), pp. 135, 138, 146, 147.

Figure 15.1

Trends in broadcast earnings (before federal taxes)

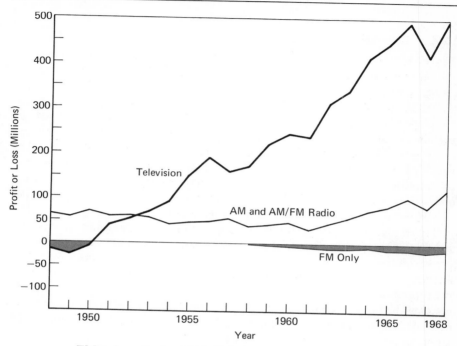

FM-only radio for 1948–1961 included in AM-FM radio.

Source: Television Factbook No. 40, 1970–1971 (published by Television Digest, Inc., Washington, D. C.), pp. 58-a and 69-a; FCC, *Thirty-Fifth Annual Report* (Washington: Government Printing Office, 1970), pp. 48-a, 57-a.

radio earnings had to be shared out among ever-increasing numbers of stations, whereas television's station growth went much more slowly (Figure 9.1).

These industry-wide totals and averages, however, conceal the fact that a relatively large number of individual stations lose money. In fiscal 1968, over 14 per cent of the reporting VHF television stations and over 55 per cent of the reporting UHF stations claimed losses for the year.[4] These losses amounted to $36 million—almost twice as much as *all* television stations paid to their owners out of current earnings.[5] Twenty-eight per cent of the AM and AM-FM stations and 78 per cent of the FM-only stations reported losses.[6]

---

[4] *Ibid.,* p. 136.

[5] *Ibid.,* p. 139. Significance of the loss figure is somewhat lessened by the fact that nearly half of it consisted of charges to depreciation.

[6] *Ibid.,* pp. 149, 156.

In short, the oft-quoted saying that the profitability of broadcasting equates a station license with "a license to steal" applies only to the more fortunate licensees.

15.2 / Operating Expenses

The FCC's standard reporting formula requires breakdown of commercial-station expenses into four categories: general and administrative, technical, selling, and program. These classes of expense reflect the functional departmentalization of operations. Table 15.5 shows that on a national average, radio spends the most for general and administrative expenses, while television spends the most for programs. Television stations cost on the average over seven times as much as radio stations to operate. Analysis by market reveals that program costs tend to rise with size of market, general and administrative to decrease; this trend is more marked in television than in radio.[7] Salaries and wages represent the largest single operating-expense item, taking over half of radio's budget and over a third of television's.

The broadcasting labor force of under a hundred thousand is relatively small—much smaller than that for printing and publishing, banking, or real estate, for example. The great majority of radio stations have very small staffs, and employment has even been declining in recent years as more stations automate production functions and computerize bookkeeping, billing, and traffic systems. In 1969, less than 20 per cent of the AM and FM stations employed over twenty full-time staff members; 40 per cent of the FM stations got along with five or less employees. Television's median number of employees was about forty-five per station.[8] These figures refer to full-time staff employees. They do not include "talent" hired for particular jobs on temporary assignments. Staff employees also often function in "talent" roles, usually receiving compensation in the form of talent fees above their staff salaries. The free-lance entrepreneur usually sells his services here and there according to demand. Most such artists do not identify exclusively with broadcasting but market their services in several media.

Some forty unions and labor organizations operate in the broadcast field, divided broadly into technical and creative categories. Unionization of talent has been more complete than of staff employees. Union activity is intense at the network level and in the major production centers, where demand for the specialized creative and craft jobs is concentrated. At the local-station level, only the technicians and the announcing staffs are likely to be unionized, except in the largest metropolitan stations. The American Federation of Musicians at one time set up a system of quotas, forcing radio stations willy-nilly

---

[7] National Association of Broadcasters, "Television Financial Report, 1969" and "Radio Financial Report, 1969" (Washington: The Association, 1969), *passim*. Program costs averaged 49 per cent of all station expenses in the top ten markets, only 29 per cent in the bottom fifty markets.

[8] *Broadcasting 1970 Yearbook,* p. B294.

Table 15.5

Average commercial broadcast-station annual expenses

CLASS OF EXPENSE	AVERAGE PER STATION			
	RADIO[1]		TELEVISION[2]	
	Amount (Thousands)	*Per Cent*	*Amount (Thousands)*	*Per Cent*
Sales	$ 38	19	$ 183	11
Technical	21	11	232	16
General and administrative	76	39	513	32
Program	61	31	652	41
Total	$196	100	$1,580	100

[1] 4,029 AM stations, excluding 20 network O&O stations.
[2] 551 TV stations, excluding 15 network O&O stations.

Source: 1968 data in FCC, *Thirty-Fifth Annual Report* (Washington: Government Printing Office, 1970), pp. 137, 147.

to employ musical groups, but this practice stopped in 1946, when Congress passed the Lea Act outlawing featherbedding and related coercive practices in broadcasting (§ 506 of the Communications Act).

The first successful strike against a radio station may have been that organized in 1926 against a CBS station in St. Louis by the International Brotherhood of Electrical Workers, a technicians' union started in the late nineteenth century by telephone linemen.[9] The IBEW later obtained a network contract with CBS. In 1953, NBC technicians formed a separate association of their own which ultimately became the National Association of Broadcast Engineers and Technicians (NABET), the first purely broadcasting union. Later the word "Engineers" was changed to "Employees" to broaden the union's scope. Rivalry between NABET and IBEW has produced many disputes. A third technical union, an old rival of IBEW, entered the television scene from the motion-picture industry. Its impossibly long name, the International Alliance of Theatrical Stage Employees and Moving Picture Machine Operators of the United States and Canada is mercifully abbreviated to the acronym "IATSE" (pronounced "eye-at-see").

The only other unions formed entirely for broadcast employees are the American Federation of Television and Radio Artists, started first in radio in 1937, and the black National Association of Television and Radio Announcers. The rival Screen Actors Guild fought AFTRA for control of talent used in video recording, but AFTRA won the dispute on the grounds that video recording is more analogous to live television than to film. Other major unionized creative groups include the American Guild of Variety Artists, Directors' Guild of America, and Writers' Guild of America.

---

[9] Allen E. Koenig, ed., *Broadcasting and Bargaining: Labor Relations in Radio and Television* (Madison: University of Wisconsin Press, 1970), p. 22.

15.3 / Economics of Networking

National networks, more than any other single factor, made possible the rapid growth in America first of radio and then of television into virtually universal national media. A network affiliation is almost the *sine qua non* of television-station profitability. In fact, some of the most intense intramural industry competition has centered around the demand for affiliation.[10] Yet a network affiliate realizes only a minor proportion of its revenue in the form of compensation for network time. Networks pass on about a third of their gross revenue from network time sales to their affiliates.[11] Although Table 13.3 indicates that 30 per cent of the *total* television-industry revenue came from network time sales, only 15 per cent of *affiliates'* revenue (excluding O&O stations) came from network sales.[12]

Networks pay affiliates for the use of their time on the basis of a compensation formula, agreed to in the network/affiliate contract. In addition to the previously mentioned discount on time sales, contracts usually provide for the affiliate to receive sustaining programs free and in turn to contribute a stipulated number of free hours to the network. The free hours provide an indirect incentive to the affiliate to *clear* network programs. Clearance (that is, making requested time available for network programs) is vital to network operations, since clients would soon become dissatisfied if networks could not in fact deliver their affiliates when ordered. Taking into account the commercial value of the free time contributed to the network by the affiliate, it can be shown that the more hours the affiliate clears for network programs, the higher the percentage of gross time billing the affiliate receives in compensation from the network.[13]

Why do television stations find network affiliation so important if they derive so little revenue from network time sales? Basically because only network programming can maximize circulation: audiences and audiences alone

---

[10] In fiscal 1968, 13 per cent of network-affiliated VHF stations and 32 per cent of affiliated UHF stations lost money; the figures for losing independents were VHF, 32 per cent; UHF, 97 per cent. [FCC, "TV Broadcast Financial Data, 1968," News Release 35922, August 6, 1969.] The contrast is somewhat exaggerated because the independents were, in the main, latecomers which had to accept the less profitable locations and less desirable facilities, and which have had less time to establish their businesses.

[11] In fiscal 1968, of network time sales of $633.7 million, the networks retained 62 per cent and passed on 6 per cent to their O&O stations and 32 per cent to other affiliates. [FCC, *Thirty-Fifth Annual Report,* p. 153.]

[12] *Ibid.,* pp. 133, 135.

[13] One study indicated that with the amount of free hours held constant, a station which cleared thirty hours would receive only 6.6 per cent of its gross network billing, whereas one that cleared two hundred hours would receive 29.3 per cent. [House Committee on Interstate and Foreign Commerce, Subcommittee on Transportation and Communications, *Network Broadcasting,* Report of the FCC Network Study Staff ("Barrow Report"), House Report 1297, 85th Cong., 1st Sess. (Washington: Government Printing Office, 1958), p. 464.]

enable stations to sell local and national spot advertising, their major source of revenue. In addition, of course, network-program time frees the affiliated station's programming and production staff to concentrate its energies on producing only a limited number of local programs and buying rights to only a limited number of nonnetwork-syndicated programs to fill out the broadcast schedule. By contrast, the independent station must compete not only with other nonnetwork stations but also with the networks and their affiliates for the rights to the limited amount of available syndicated program materials, and it must work under the gruelling pressure of local responsibility for production every minute of the broadcast day. The FCC encourages independent production of nonnetwork-syndicated television programming by "package producers" to promote program diversity, prevent undue network dominance of the programming field, and expand the resources available to independent stations.

Although a market for independently produced and syndicated program material certainly exists, the fact remains that the network system of syndication (regardless of who actually produces the individual items in the network's schedule) has unique features other systems of syndication cannot match. These features include the structuring of programming into consistent and attractive patterns; the cultivation of a distinct institutional personality; the timeliness of interconnected distribution; the opportunities for promotion and planned audience building; and the incorporation into the schedule of prestige programming items at a loss or with reduced profit. It is not generally realized, for example, that the major share of network *gross revenue* actually comes not from time sales but from sale of talent and services. But the latter are sold at close to cost or even at a loss in order to build up the network's programming strength, so that the networks depend on time sales for *net income*.[14] In fiscal 1968, the national television networks grossed $633.7 million from the sale of network time and $722.1 million from the sale of talent, programs, and other sources; time sales thus accounted for only 47 per cent of gross revenue.[15]

Table 15.6, showing average program costs, makes a case in point: whereas entertainment types averaged a little more than $4 thousand per rating point, public-affairs programs averaged over $12 thousand per rating point. Obviously, independent syndicators have no economic incentive to produce anything but the most popular types of entertainment shows. Networks have the same incentives economically, but as networks and as station licensees they also work under noneconomic compulsions which in practice do result in a leavening of public-affairs programs, whatever problems remain in the relative amount and quality of such alternatives.

In any event, the overriding fact about programs is their extraordinarily and increasingly high costs. In 1968, an hour-long *Bonanza* cost $188 thousand

---

[14] *Ibid.*, pp. 401–406.

[15] FCC, *Thirty-Fifth Annual Report*, p. 133.

Table 15.6

Average prime-time television-program costs by type and rating

PROGRAM TYPE	NUMBER ON AIR	AVERAGE COST PER HALF-HOUR	AVERAGE RATING	COST PER RATING POINT
Comedy	36	$67,100	16.9	$ 3,970
Variety	13	69,000	16.6	4,157
Westerns	12	69,300	17.2	4,029
Feature films	4	75,600	16.3	4,638
Public affairs	2	78,500	6.4	12,265

Source: Data in John A. Dimling, *et al.*, *Identification and Analysis of the Alternatives for Achieving Greater Television Program Diversity in the United States* (Report 226), prepared for President's Task Force on Communications Policy (Lexington, Ky.: Spindletop Research, July 26, 1968), p. III-10.

plus $360 thousand for air time; *Bewitched* (situation comedy), $85 thousand plus $80 thousand for a half-hour of air time; *Ed Sullivan Show* (variety), $195 thousand plus $340 thousand for an hour's air time; *Walter Cronkite* (news), $150 thousand per half-hour plus $90 thousand air time; and a single participation in the *Lawrence Welk Show* (musical variety), $38 thousand.[16]

Independent stations rely basically on three sources of syndicated program material: feature films, package-produced series (the type referred to in the trade specifically as "syndicated programs"), and off-network series (programs originally released as network offerings, subsequently sold in the same manner as "syndicated" material). Prices per showing vary according to market size. First-run rentals of thirty-minute syndicated episodes ranged in 1968 from $32 to $445, off-network episodes $42 to $471.[17]

15.4 / Network-Affiliation Contracts

FCC regulations permit commercial networks to own outright relatively few of their affiliates (seven each in the AM, FM, and TV services, with only five of the latter in the VHF band). These owned-and-operated stations play a more important role than their number suggests, for their great profitability gives the networks a stable financial underpinning. In 1968, for example, as mentioned in Section 15.3, the fifteen network-television O&O stations received an average of $2.7 million each in network sales revenue, while 627 remaining television stations received an average of about a third of a million dollars each.[18] The President of CBS told a Congressional committee that

---

[16] Roy Danish, "The Shaping of the Television Medium" (New York: Television Information Office, June 1, 1968), p. 5.

[17] Arthur D. Little, Inc., "Television Program Production, Procurement, Distribution and Scheduling" (Cambridge, Mass. The Corporation, 1969), p. 115.

[18] Based on data in FCC, *Thirty-Fifth Annual Report,* p. 133.

"without some owned and operated stations, the network is just not a profitable piece of business."[19] The O&O's also provide the networks with a voice in the major markets; and they confer legal status on the networks as station owners vis-à-vis the FCC, which has jurisdiction only over stations, not over networks as such.

Thus, the great majority of "network" stations have only a contractual relationship with networks. The economic compulsions of the network/affiliate relationship naturally lead toward contractual terms favorable to the stronger of the two parties. From the network's point of view, it would be ideal to have exclusive and immediate access to all of its affiliates' time all of the time. However, such an extreme degree of network control would paralyze the affiliate's ability to obtain local and national spot business, leaving it completely dependent on the network. This kind of overcentralization the FCC sought to prevent. In Section 9.5, we reviewed the historical circumstances leading to the FCC's "Chain Broadcasting Investigation" in 1938. NBC and CBS bitterly opposed the curbs on network/affiliate contracts proposed by the FCC. Even after wringing some concessions from the Commission, they carried their case to the Supreme Court, which upheld the FCC in 1943 in a landmark decision, the so-called "Network Case."[20] In 1955, Congress authorized the Commission to launch an investigation of television networks, which led to establishing a permanent Office of Network Study in the Commission and some further evolvement of the Chain Broadcasting Regulations as they affected television.[21]

Since the Communications Act makes no provision for regulating networks as such, the Chain Broadcasting Regulations addressed themselves to the affiliation contracts between stations and networks. These agreements remained closed to public scrutiny until the FCC ruled that they must be opened for inspection in 1969. The regulations governing contracts follow in summary:[22]

1. *Exclusivity of affiliation.* Contracts may not prevent an affiliate from accepting programs made available to it by a rival network.

---

[19] House Committee on Interstate and Foreign Commerce, Subcommittee on the FCC, *Investigation of Radio and Television Programs,* Hearings on H. R. 278, 82d Cong., 2d Sess. (Washington: Government Printing Office, 1952), p. 310.

[20] *NBC* v. *U. S.,* 316 U. S. 447 (1942). The investigation itself is detailed in FCC, *Report on Chain Broadcasting* (Washington: Government Printing Office, 1941)—one of the primary documents of American broadcasting history.

[21] The first response to the Congressional study directive (popularly known as the "Barrow Report," after Roscoe Barrow, Director of the special Study Staff) is House Committee on Interstate and Foreign Commerce, *Network Broadcasting.* . . . The first reports by the permanent FCC Network Study group appeared in the same Committee's *Television Network Program Procurement,* House Report 281, 88th Cong., 1st Sess. (Washington: Government Printing Office, 1963).

[22] FCC, *Rules and Regulations* for AM, § 73.131–138; FM, § 73.231–238; TV, § 73.658(a)–(i).

2. *Territorial exclusivity.* Contracts may not prevent a network from releasing a program to a station other than its own affiliate in a market where its own affiliate declines to carry the program. This type of exclusivity had previously been practiced in return for exclusivity of affiliation. The purpose of these two rules is to prevent "dog-in-the-manger" competitive tactics which prevent the showing of programs and thereby deprive the public of benefitting from them.

3. *Term of contract.* Affiliation contracts may not run for longer than two years, renewable six months before expiration. Before this regulation went into effect, both NBC and CBS contracts bound their radio affiliates for five years but themselves for only one.

4. *Option time.* Contracts with AM and FM affiliates may not require them to option more than a limited amount of time to their networks, or to make option time available on less than fifty-six days' notice. TV affiliation contracts may not provide at all for option time. An invention of CBS, option time had come to be regarded as the very heart of the affiliation contract, the device whereby networks made certain their affiliates' most desirable broadcast hours were available on call. This arrangement gave the network salesmen assurance that they could deliver these times to advertisers, without returning to each affiliate to secure clearance before making sales commitments. The network assumed no obligation to program unsold option time, however, and so the affiliates labored under the disadvantage of having to sell network option time locally or to national spot advertisers only on a short-notice, preemptible basis—and preemptibility lowers the value of time (Section 13.5). The Commission's proposal to eliminate option time altogether in the new radio rules was finally withdrawn in the face of such predictions as:

. . . competition among competently managed networks would be replaced by an unwholesome conglomeration of opportunistic "time brokers" catering to an aggregation of local monopolies in the various towns and cities of the nation.[23]

Instead, the Commission inserted the fifty-six-day notice clause and limited optionable time to a maximum of three hours in each of four day-parts. While retaining limited option-time provisions in the radio rules, the Commission later eliminated it altogether from the television rules. The predicted collapse of the American system of broadcasting did not take place, presumably because television stations need network affiliation so badly they usually clear time for network programs without the compulsion of a contractual obligation.[24]

---

[23] FCC, *Report on Chain Broadcasting,* p. 116.

[24] The "Barrow Report" found that clearance by affiliates for television networks varied from program to program, from no refusals to requested stations to refusal by as high as 67 per cent of the requested stations. The average level of refusal for one network was 18 per cent. [House Committee on Interstate and Foreign Commerce, *Network Broadcasting . . . ,* pp. 310–326. See also Section 13.7 on the subject of network clearance.]

5. *Right to reject programs.* Contracts may not prevent affiliates from rejecting network-offered programs, even in option time. This rule provides three broad bases for such refusals: (1) programs the affiliate "reasonably believes to be unsatisfactory or unsuitable"; (2) programs "contrary to the public interest" in the opinion of the affiliate; (3) in order to substitute "a program of outstanding local or national importance." This regulation reflects the doctrine that the licensee has ultimate legal responsibility for his station's programming, which may not be delegated to the network or anyone else. Except in the case of known controversial programs, however, the licensee obviously does leave much of the programming responsibility for his station to the network—an argument advanced by those who favor the licensing of networks as well as stations. In practice, affiliates tend to reject two types of network programs: those which do not make money and those which cause trouble (Section 13.7).

6. *"Duopoly."* An AM network may not own more than one station covering the same service area. This regulation affected NBC's ownership of key stations in its Red and Blue networks in each of four major markets. In the FM and television rules this restriction applies to network ownership of a station where the existing stations "are so few or of such unequal desirability . . . that competition would be substantially restrained."

7. *Dual networks.* A network organization may not operate two or more networks covering the same territory at the same time—again a rule aimed at the NBC Red-Blue radio-network combination.

8. *Control of rates.* Contracts may not allow networks to influence affiliates' rates for nonnetwork time. Networks set rates for network time, by agreement with affiliates, on the basis of formulas that seek to ensure relative equity in accordance with the audience-drawing power of each affiliate. If the affiliates' national-spot rates get far out of line with the network rates, however, the network sales staff runs into difficulties. Therefore, networks have a strong interest in the level of nonnetwork rates of their affiliates.

9. *Representation.* In the television rules only, contracts are forbidden with network organizations which act as national sales representatives for stations other than their O&O stations. The rule reflects the direct competition between station sales representatives (Section 13.7) and network sales for national advertising accounts.

Despite these curbs on commercial-network economic dominance of affiliates, concern about the oligopoly power of the television chains revived as television grew. In the 1960's, this concern centered around the chains' economic influence on program production. It will be recalled that in the early days of network radio (Section 7.10), advertising agencies assumed a major role as program producers. When television arrived, the networks moved to prevent similar abdication of their own role in production. In addition to originating more of their own productions, they also made it a policy to acquire joint rights over programs bought from package producers. These rights gave the networks a share of the income from subsequent off-network syndication in the United States and from first-run syndication abroad.

The FCC took the view that the independent producer found himself in an adverse bargaining position if he had to yield some of the rights in his production to the networks in order to market it to the networks. The networks, after all, also produce programs in direct competition with package producers. The Commission felt that the increased control of networks over programming worked against the principle of program diversity. It found that between 7:30 and 10:30 P.M., affiliates carried less than two hours of nonnetwork programming *per week,* and even that small amount of time was filled mostly by "off-net" (network "rerun") programs. First-run syndicated material (packaged nonnetwork programs) had practically disappeared from the market. Network evening hours had been one-third occupied by independently produced and controlled programs in 1957; by 1968 less than 4 per cent of the time was so occupied.[25]

In 1970, following extensive hearings on rules first proposed in 1965, the Commission further restricted the commercial television networks, ruling that (1) they may no longer acquire subsidiary rights in programs bought for network showing from independent package producers; (2) networks may not syndicate programs (that is, distribute for nonnetwork, local showing), except for sale of their own programs overseas; (3) in the top fifty markets where three or more commercial television stations operate, networks may not program their affiliates for more than three hours in the prime-time segment, 7:00–11:00 P.M. Anticipating that affiliates would take the easy way out in filling this time, the Commission also ruled that the nonnetwork time may not be filled with off-network or feature-film reruns. These rules, it was hoped, would create a market for new package-produced programs.

15.5 / Economics of Noncommercial Broadcasting

We left noncommercial television in Sections 10.8 and 10.9 on the verge of takeoff but still not undergirded by adequate permanent funding. As far back as the early 1930's, some advocates of noncommercial broadcasting had proposed that the new Communications Act should provide for *nonprofit* rather than noncommercial stations, entitled to sell enough time to defray operating costs. The proposal came up again during the JCET strategy meetings leading up to the 1951 FCC hearings which resulted in the reservation of educational television channels. Some of the educational broadcasters (remembering their years of economic frustration as educational radio-station managers) urged that JCET hold out for nonprofit rather than noncommercial channels, but

---

[25] FCC, "Report and Order," 35 *Fed. Reg.* 7417 (1970).

Table 15.7

Trends in ETV-station financial support

SOURCE OF FUNDS	PER CENT OF TOTAL EXPENDITURES		
	Cumulative Through 1966	*1955–1966*	*1968–1969*
Taxes			
State (nonuniversity)	22.3	27.1	29.0
Local	23.2	18.9	23.8
State university	11.0	11.2	6.1
Federal	5.2	11.8	6.8
Total, tax sources	61.7	69.0	65.7
Nontax sources			
Foundations	13.4	14.4	7.7
Subscribers	8.6	5.5	6.8
Program grants	4.1	—	NR
Business	6.7	3.5	2.6
Underwritten programs	1.4	1.9	3.0
Other	4.1	5.7	8.9
Total, nontax sources	38.3	31.0	29.0
Mixed tax, nontax sources (CPB, NET, etc.)	NR	NR	5.3
Total, all sources	100.0	100.0	100.0

Sources: Cumulative and 1955–1966, Carnegie Commission on Educational Television, *Public Television: A Program for Action* (New York: Harper & Row, 1967), pp. 243, 250; 1968–1969, National Association of Educational Broadcasters, *The Financial Status of Public Broadcasting Stations in the United States, July 1968–June 1969* (Washington: The Association, 1970), p. 14.

the Council decided that realistically, their only hope for reservations lay in complete disassociation from commercialization.[26]

Occasional and volunteer sources of funds helped get noncommercial stations started but proved completely inadequate either to meet all current costs or to provide any long-term fiscal security. These sources included foundation grants (the major component), gifts from business firms (including both cash and equipment from commercial stations), viewer subscriptions, annual public fund drives, underwritten programs, and production contracts. The noncommercial character of the stations does not prevent certain limited uses of advertising, such as crediting a commercial source for "underwriting" the costs of production or selling goods by auction and crediting donors (who are usually businessmen). However, as Table 15.7 indicates, such

---

[26] Nevertheless, two institutions—the University of Missouri and Bob Jones University—individually proposed nonprofit commercial operations. The FCC replied that it viewed the goal of reserved channels as "establishment of a genuinely educational type of service," and this goal "would not be furthered by permitting educational institutions to operate in substantially the same manner as commercial applicants. . . ." [FCC, "Sixth Report and Order," 17 *Fed. Reg.* 3905 at 3911 (1952).]

sources never provided substantial support. Taxes have always supplied more than 60 per cent of operating costs, and the trend was toward a still higher tax proportion. At the close of fiscal 1969, 80 per cent of the 185 stations on the air were licensed to public educational (*i.e.,* primarily tax-supported) entities—state systems, universities, or local school boards.[27]

Obviously, financial support of noncommercial broadcasting had to become both more stable and more generous. Several expedients were suggested, not all based on taxation. The Carnegie Commission considered set license fees, Subscription Television, CATV, a tax on commercial-station revenue, and earmarking federal income taxes on commercial television enterprises. The Ford Foundation's broadcast-network relay-satellite proposal (Section 10.9) would have turned the profits of the commercial aspect of the system over to educational broadcasting. The Carnegie Commission finally opted for proposing a form of indirect taxation on viewers, an excise tax on television-receiver sales. Congress passed over this element of the Carnegie Commission plan when it enacted the Public Broadcasting Act of 1967 (Section 17.9). It did set up the Public Broadcasting Corporation, but on interim funds voted year by year.

The Carnegie Commission estimated the median operating budget of existing educational television stations in 1966 at just over a quarter of a million dollars. By 1969 it had increased to nearly $400 thousand. Comparison with commercial-station data in Table 15.5 shows that this still amounted to only about one-quarter of the average commercial-station operating expense—far short of being competitive, even after adjusting for the omission of selling expense and for the short operating schedule of the educational stations (in 1969 their median was only sixty-nine hours per week during the school year, half that during school vacation.[28] By having to go dark on weekends and holidays, educational stations lost one of their major opportunities to build audiences.

Employment levels provide another significant comparison, with median full-time employees per station about forty-five in commercial, little more than half that in noncommercial television.[29] Expenditures for programs make still another revealing contrast. Table 15.6 provides some estimates of high commercial programming costs; subtracting producer's profit, one can generalize by saying that nationally distributed commercial programming costs on the order of $100,000 per hour. The Carnegie Commission found NET, the educational-station network, averaging only $20,000 per hour—again a five-to-one

---

[27] FCC, *Thirty-Fifth Annual Report,* p. 37.

[28] National Association of Educational Broadcasters, *The Financial Status of Public Broadcasting Stations in the United States, July 1968–June 1969* (Washington: The Association, 1970), p. 10.

[29] *Broadcasting 1970 Yearbook,* p. B-294; Carnegie Commission on Educational Television, *Public Television: A Program for Action* (New York: Harper & Row, 1967), p. 246.

ratio. Granted that noncommercial broadcasting should depend less on high-salary superstar talent, the Commission estimated that the median budgets for noncommercial program production should nevertheless reach about $45,000 per hour. The Commission foresaw three levels of production: major series contracted out to professional producers ($29,000 to $100,000 per hour); nationally distributed programs produced by key stations in the network ($30,000 per hour); local programs and station-to-station exchange programs ($3,300 per hour).[30]

These financial comparisons provide a rough measure of the distance the noncommercial service still had to go to function as a full-scale and mean-ingful alternative. Not every educational-television critic agreed that it should. Some feared that emphasis on competition, audience promotion, and program ratings would destroy the educational essence of the noncommercial service (see Section 22.6 for fuller discussion of divergent philosophies of the service). The Carnegie Commission, more realistically, based its recom-mendations on an economic "criterion of feasibility." In order to be economi-cally justifiable, the Commission estimated, a noncommercial station should give substantially reliable service to a minimum of seventy thousand people, unduplicated by another noncommercial station. According to American Re-search Bureau audience estimates, only a dozen of the existing stations at the time of the Carnegie Commission studies fulfilled this criterion in their weekly circulation (viewing at least once in a week) and only three in average daily circulation.[31]

---

[30] *Ibid.,* pp. 188, 190–191.

[31] *Ibid.,* pp. 136, 253. The Commission's recommendation was based on projected U. S. population estimates for 1980.

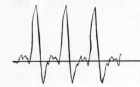

16

ECONOMIC
CONSTRAINTS ON
PROGRAMMING

Our intention is to examine the major influences which have shaped American broadcasting, to answer the question "What makes broadcasting in America the way it is?" At this halfway point, we pause to recollect that Part One dealt with ways in which the physical nature of the medium imposes its own limitations; Part Two dealt with the part played by accidents of timing and historical context in shaping the medium. Now at the close of Part Three, we turn to ways in which economic influences affect its output.

Part Four will go on to deal with social influences—the law's compulsions and the weight of public opinion. In making this division, we recognize a certain artificiality: economic processes operate in a social context. Still, for purposes of exposition and organizational clarity, it may be helpful to consider primarily economic influences at this point, before considering primarily social influences.

16.1 / The Luxury of Integrity : Marginal Stations

It would be an oversimplification to regard the profit motive as reducing commercial broadcasting to a case of pure economic determinism. Any two station or network managers equally influenced by the profit motive may arrive at quite different decisions from the same set of facts. Stations and networks turn down large amounts of business for a variety of reasons—mainly, perhaps, because of foreseen adverse economic consequences, but also for reasons of taste, ethical integrity, and social responsibility. Yet broadcasting stations, as business enterprises, have two peculiarities which affect their ability to withstand adverse economic conditions without serious deterioration of standards: (1) Declining income cannot be countered by equivalent reductions in expenses, as it can in many other businesses; as a licensed medium, broadcasting has to comply with minimal engineering standards, maintain a minimum schedule of operations, and otherwise meet externally imposed standards not required of nonregulated businesses. (2) A losing station is slow to die: a broadcast license represents in a sense a kind of lottery ticket—success may always be just around the corner, if only the right formula can be found. Therefore, failing stations tend to hang on long past the point of no return; someone nearly always turns up to risk investing just a little more money or time on the chance that the license will finally pay off.[1] In their desperation, operators of such stations tend to abandon all programming standards, to resort to all the undesirable, borderline commercial practices—rate cutting, accepting questionable advertising, overloading programs with bargain commercials, double billing.

The problem of the marginal station has received judicial recognition. Application for a new station in an already saturated market gives rise to opposition from the existing station (or stations) on the grounds of economic injury. The Appeals Court has held that the Commission must give existing stations an opportunity to present proof of such alleged injury—not because the FCC has a duty to protect the commercial interests of licensees, but because it must consider whether increased competition will "spell diminution or destruction of service," to the detriment of the public interest.[2]

The general level of commercial broadcasting could be much improved were it possible, without creating even more undesirable consequences in the process, simply to kill off, quickly and painlessly, many marginal stations whose income cannot support a reasonable standard of program service and advertising integrity. For the damage they do spreads far wider than their own meager coverage. The stronger, more ethically operated stations in their area find themselves under great pressure to lower their standards, too. Gresham's famous law, that bad money drives out good, so often applied to broadcast programming, applies equally to all broadcast standards.

Maintaining high standards implies some degree of economic freedom to make appropriate decisions; a manager must be free to say "No" without going bankrupt.

It is almost impossible to explain to an advertiser why his particular program, which he is convinced is selling his product, is not acceptable to you, and yet unless this explanation is undertaken and followed by rejection, it is not long before the whole program standard of the station is lost, and your entire schedule becomes a heterogeneous hodgepodge of good, bad, and indifferent material . . .[3]

---

[1] For statistics on the number of stations reporting operation at a loss, see Section 15.1. An elementary example of marginal station standards: the owner of two small AM stations pleaded "press of the immediate necessities of operation and meeting the stations' payrolls with insufficient staff to deal with regulatory matters" as an excuse for not responding to FCC reminders that he had failed to submit renewal applications. One station had six employees, the other seven; the owner managed both and acted as the only salesman. ["N. C. AM Owner Explains Why He Ignored FCC," *Broadcasting,* November 9, 1970, pp. 51–52.]

[2] *Carroll Broadcasting Co.* v. *FCC,* 258 F. (2d) 440 (1958). See Section 18.7 for further discussion of the economic-injury issue.

[3] Robert D. Swezey, "Television and the Dirty Look" (Washington: National Association of Radio and Television Broadcasters, 1954, mimeo.), p. 3.

The degrees of economic freedom among stations cover a tremendous range. The management of a station on a good channel in a rich market without excessive competition can afford the luxury of integrity. It can afford to turn down questionable advertising, refuse to make under-the-table rate-cutting deals, discriminate in selecting program material, adhere conscientiously to advertising and program codes, produce good local public-service features, and risk reprisals from interests adversely affected by courageous editorials. The management of a marginal station, unsure of being able to meet its payroll at the end of the week, can ill afford such luxuries.

Though there appears to be no complete answer to the problem of the adverse effects of the economically marginal commercial station, harsher application of FCC rules and regulations might help. By and large, the Commission appears to have leaned over backwards in making sympathetic allowances for the business problems of economically weak licensees. Stations have often accumulated extraordinarily long lists of violations before finally being brought to book (Section 18.8).

16.2 / Service to Minorities

A broadcasting system dependent on advertising for financial support—and which moreover allows the advertiser and his agents extensive influences over program production and selection—must inevitably reflect the point of view of the business community. Regarded primarily as vehicles for advertising, programs function as means, not ends. This view of their function diverts attention from their intrinsic content and quality as programs, accentuating the "vast-wasteland" image—proven formulas, stereotypes, blandness, mass appeal.

The implications of advertiser influence go beyond the merely negative sense of lost opportunities—the screening-out and levelling-down process of syndication to achieve mass-appeal entertainment. Commercially oriented programming tends also to draw a certain picture of the world, a picture reflecting established majoritarian values—the materialism and the life style of the economically dominant culture group. Commercial broadcasters necessarily live and breathe in the atmosphere of the business and political power structure of their respective communities. They can hardly be expected to understand—much less program sensitively for—the viewpoint, tastes, and needs of the ghetto, the disaffected, and other minorities. This media bias is one of the most widely quoted findings of the Kerner Commission on Civil Disorders, which analyzed the urban riots of 1967:

The media report and write from the standpoint of a white man's world. The ills of the ghetto, the differences of life there, the Negro's burning sense of grievance, are seldom conveyed. Slights and indignities are part of the Negro's daily life, and many of them come from what he now calls "the white press"—a press that repeatedly, if unconsciously, reflects the biases, the paternalism, the indifference of white America. . . .[4]

Similarly, a federally sponsored study of violence pointed to the socioeconomic bias of the media: "The outstanding characteristics of ideas that have difficulty gaining access [to the mass media] are that they are new, that their proponents lack prominence, and that they threaten the values of the social group to which the broadcaster or publisher belongs."[5]

One of the ironies, if not indeed the dangers, of media bias is that ghetto dwellers are among the heaviest consumers of broadcasting. It would be surprising if the contrast between the glossy, affluent world of most broadcast programming and advertising and the real world of the ghetto did not create tensions. Yet not until violence had indeed begun was any serious attention paid to the fact that broadcasting, often overtly as well as merely by implication, had systematically reinforced local racial, economic, and cultural prejudices.

For a decade broadcasting has been the focal point of a mounting concern on the part of minorities over mass communication's failure to portray sympathetically the values, attitudes and behavior of blacks, Indians, Spanish-surnamed Americans, orientals, Jews and similar groups.

Broadcast advertising and programming are often insensitive to people's needs and desires. Television and radio can be peculiarly vicious in trampling on the dignity of minority citizens who are at the bottom of the economic heap and not greatly valued as consumers. Broadcasting has glorified material standards and creature comforts and has raised the expectations of the poor, but has done little to help poor people achieve the prospects it dangles before them so alluringly.[6]

It is no accident, perhaps, that the most phenomenally popular broadcast series of all time in America was radio's *Amos 'n' Andy,* regarded by those affected as a systematic libel on black Americans:

In retrospect it is easy—at the time it was less easy—to see the stories and *Amos 'n' Andy* as part of the ghetto system. All of it was more readily accepted and maintained if one could hold onto this: "they" were lovely people, essentially happy people, ignorant and somewhat shiftless and lazy in a lovable, quaint way. . . . The nation needed the fantasy. It was a wall buttressed by decades of jokes, vaudeville sketches, cartoons, and joke books. . . . So ingrained was all this that

---

[4] National Advisory Commission on Civil Disorders ("Kerner Commission"), *Report* (New York: Bantam Books, 1968), p. 366.

[5] Robert K. Baker and Sandra J. Ball, *Mass Media and Violence,* Vol. IX, A Report to National Commission on Causes and Prevention of Violence (Washington: Government Printing Office, 1969), pp. 67–68.

[6] Office of Communication, United Church of Christ, "Racial Justice in Broadcasting" (New York: The Church, 1970), p. 3.

the idea of Negro objections to *Amos 'n' Andy* was at first received with disbelief. Was it not known that Negroes loved *Amos 'n' Andy?*[7]

In the 1950's a score of NBC affiliates refused to clear time for *Tosca* because it featured Leontyne Price, and as recently as 1968 the sponsor of an NBC special tried to edit out a moment when singer Petula Clark touched Harry Belafonte.[8]

Broadcasting did, it is true, discover a Negro radio market, which is exploited by over three hundred stations. In many cases "exploit" applies in the worst sense:

Most such stations are not licensed to blacks. More often than not they regard blacks as consumers who are fair game for exploitation by unscrupulous advertisers. Black-oriented stations often callously refuse to broadcast news concerning black activities and interests. They permit loan sharks, furniture sharks and other exploiters of the poor to advertise at will. They disregard the educational needs of their listeners. They present few programs that air controversial issues of concern to blacks. . . . Other ethnic-oriented stations are said to engage in similar deceptive practices.[9]

Neglect of the ethnic minority interests provides a highly visible and dramatic case in point. However, it would be a serious misconception to define the problem of commercial broadcasting *vis-à-vis* service to minority interests in ethnic terms alone. The underlying problem is that in truth, the entire public is made up of minorities. As the President's Task Force on Communications Policy said in 1968: "Ours is a pluralistic society, in culture as well as in ethnic origins and life-styles of its people. A medium of expression as pervasive as television should reflect and enrich this cultural pluralism."[10] Interests vary infinitely, and most individuals form linkages with many groupings—neighborhood, social clubs, school class, church, hobby, political party, occupation, sports, and so on. Most of these associations, taken singly, represent minority-group interests.

Some of our tastes and needs we share with virtually everybody; but most—and they are often those which engage us most intensely—we share with different minorities. A service which caters only for majorities can never satisfy all, or even most, of the needs of any individual. It cannot, therefore, satisfy all the needs of the public.[11]

---

[7] Erik Barnouw, *A Tower in Babel: A History of Broadcasting in the United States to 1933* (New York: Oxford University Press, 1966), p. 230.

[8] Allen E. Koenig, ed., *Broadcasting and Bargaining: Labor Relations in Radio and Television* (Madison: University of Wisconsin Press, 1970), pp. 208, 214.

[9] Office of Communication, United Church of Christ, *op. cit.,* p. 15.

[10] President's Task Force on Communications Policy, *Final Report* (Washington: Government Printing Office, 1968), p. VII-3.

[11] Great Britain, Committee on Broadcasting ("Pilkington Committee"), *Report, 1960,* Cmnd. 1753 (London: Her Majesty's Stationery Office, 1962), p. 16.

16.3 / The Quiz Scandals

The search for innocuous but nevertheless immensely popular programming has repeatedly edged commercial broadcasting into types of entertainment which systematically capitalize on such human weaknesses as cupidity and morbidity. In the early 1950's, a craze for merchandise "giveaway" programs swept television. The critic Ben Gross characterized them as "not entertainment, but incitements to human cupidity." A trade journal editorialized:

We are opposed to money and prize giveaway programs as parasitic and undesirable. We believe they are used artificially to stimulate audience and ratings. We believe, moreover, that as long as manufacturers can get free air credits by donating merchandise, they won't buy time. We believe these programs violate the commercial time limitations of the radio and TV codes.[12]

Giveaways like *Strike It Rich,* on which contestants told heartrending stories of poverty and suffering, were singled out for attack from many quarters. *Life* editorialized that such programs "have sunk about as low as it is possible to sink," and John Crosby called them "the shame of television." But from the purely commercial point of view they were good programs—they drew large audiences.

The fact that the program commands an audience of commercially significant size is both a criticism of the morbidness that afflicts too many people and of the network and sponsor that pander to it. *Strike It Rich* exists only because it engages in that most depressing of all ways to make a buck—exploitation of human suffering. . . . The program is a classic example of pseudo-humanitarianism without excuse or merit.[13]

The giveaways in turn gave way to a flood of quiz contests later in the 1950's—*The Sixty-Four Thousand Dollar Question, Twenty-One, The Big Surprise,* and countless imitations. Five new quiz shows appeared on the air in a single day. In dramatic confrontations between chorus-girl experts on astronomy, minister experts on love stories, shoemaker experts on opera, college-teacher experts on everything, contestants won and lost hundreds of thousands of dollars in a single night before the television cameras. Authenticity and drama were heightened by contestants caged in "isolation booths," armed guards and bank vice-presidents opening strong boxes on camera to remove sealed envelopes containing the golden questions, a Northwestern University English professor who "supervised" their preparation. Enboothed contestants raised the tension still higher with lip-biting, brow-wrinkling, eye-rolling histrionics. There was only one catch: the contests were rigged. Con-

---

[12] "High Court Looks at 'Giveaways'," *Broadcasting-Telecasting,* October 19, 1953, p. 130.

[13] "In Review," *Broadcasting-Telecasting,* August 31, 1953, p. 16. For a spirited defense of *Strike It Rich,* see Max Wylie, *Clear Channels: Television and the American People* (New York: Funk & Wagnalls, 1955), pp. 7–10, 227–235.

testants often knew in advance what to expect, they won or lost in accordance with carefully laid plans to maximize suspense, producers coached them how to act out agonized brain-racking to best effect.

As early as 1956, hints of quiz "fixing" began to surface. In 1957, a feature *Time* article mentioned that producers "may be taking great risks" to whip up flagging ratings; "the producers of many shows control the outcome as closely as they dare," wrote *Time*, carefully adding "—without collusion with contestants."[14]

Collusion was in fact the name of the game. In the midst of pious disclaimers all around from package producers and network officials, the New York District Attorney started an investigation in the fall of 1958. Ultimately, ten persons pleaded guilty to having perjured themselves in denying complicity in quiz rigging. The first official confirmation of fraud did not come out until July, 1959, and by that time the quiz craze had already run its course, after earning many millions for drug and cosmetic sponsors.[15]

The year 1959 became known as the "year of the scandal" for television. A report by the Attorney General to the President, Congressional hearings,[16] and an FCC investigation brought out much latent hostility toward television and renewed attacks by its long-standing critics and even by its friends. Strong measures were advocated, and Congress considered a bill empowering the FCC to license networks and to impose license suspensions and heavy fines for violation of regulations. By the time the bill reached the President for signature its teeth had been blunted. The maximum penalty had been reduced to a wrist-slapping $10 thousand maximum fine and/or one year in jail, and the network-licensing proposal had been dropped.

The significance of the quiz scandals, in the present context, is that they dramatized divergent points of view of what broadcasting is all about. The Communications Act, as well as most serious observers of the social scene, regarded broadcasting as an important means of communication fraught with serious social responsibilities. Advertisers, their agents, and many broadcast officials, on the other hand, regarded broadcasting as just another branch of show business. On the one side, the quiz deceptions seemed like a massive betrayal of public confidence, a symptom of widespread moral decay; on the other side, they seemed no more fraudulent than a stage pistol that fires blanks instead of lethal bullets. Many of those directly involved seemed genuinely amazed that the simulated spontaneity and rigged outcomes should be regarded as any more seriously misleading than stage makeup. The public apparently shared their ambivalence. Opinion surveys soon after the dis-

---

[14] "The $60 Million Question," *Time,* April 22, 1957, pp. 78–82.

[15] Meyer Weinberg, *TV and America: The Morality of Hard Cash* (New York: Ballantine Books, 1962), pp. 46 ff. Revlon, a major quiz sponsor, experienced an increase in average net profit from $1.2 million to $11 million in four years.

[16] House Committee on Interstate and Foreign Commerce, Special Subcommittee on Legislative Oversight, *Investigation of Television Quiz Shows,* Hearings in 2 parts, 86th Cong., 1st Sess. (Washington: Government Printing Office, 1960).

closure indicated that though many people felt outraged at having been so egregiously taken in, many others still approved of the quizzes and a quarter of the respondents saw nothing wrong with the deception.[17]

Ambivalence about the nature and responsibility of broadcasting and broadcasters goes back to their very beginnings. David Sarnoff's original vision equated the first national network-to-be with "a public institution of great value in the same sense that a public library, for example, is regarded today" (Section 7.10). The advertising-agency men who later took charge of most of radio's network commercial programming equated it with advertising copy. The attitude which made the quiz rigging possible had always been part of broadcasting; it just happened that the extraordinary notoriety of the quiz programs made people pay attention to something they had not hitherto seriously considered. Bill Stern, a pioneer radio sports announcer, ingenuously volunteered a perfect illustration of the "show-biz" rationale in explaining why much of the "reporting" on his popular *Colgate Sports Newsreel* consisted of sheer fabrication:

I am certain that no harm was done to anyone through our recounting of these admittedly dramatized stories, which were aimed solely at entertaining those who listened to my show. . . . I was living in the make-believe world of the theatre and the license I took was basically harmless. Diversion was my stock in trade and I thrived, rightly or not, on the same fanciful principles used by other communications media which lift audiences out of a humdrum, monotonous existence of mundane fact and insipid incident.[18]

16.4 / Vulnerability to Pressure

If the advertising viewpoint tends to encourage escapist programming, by the same token it tends actively to discourage more substantial programming. Every program topic of any substance stimulates the partisan emotions of one group or another. Controversy is inevitable and ordinarily healthy. In commercial broadcasting, however, controversy can have an unhealthy, debilitating effect on programming when advertisers overrespond to relatively inconsequential or ill-founded opposition. Hypersensitivity of sponsors affected programming from the early days of broadcasting. One of the notable personalities of the 1930's on radio was Alexander Woollcott, whose *Town Crier* was sponsored by Cream of Wheat. The sponsor asked Woollcott to stop criticizing Adolf Hitler. When Woollcott declined, the company cancelled its sponsorship.[19] Three decades later, the sponsor of a *Playhouse 90* drama about the

---

[17] Alexander Kendrick, *Prime Time* (Boston: Little, Brown, 1969), p. 130; Weinberg, *op. cit.,* pp. 238–242.

[18] Bill Stern, *The Taste of Ashes: An Autobiography* (New York: Henry Holt, 1959), p. 105.

[19] Erik Barnouw, *The Golden Web: A History of Broadcasting in the United States, 1933–1953* (New York: Oxford University Press, 1968), p. 35.

Nuremberg trials of Nazi war criminals deleted a reference to killing in gas chambers. The sponsor: the natural-gas industry.[20]

Time and again, sponsors have caved in to pressures without daring to take the time and trouble to establish their bona fides. The Xerox Corporation, a rare exception, followed up attacks on a series of specials about the United Nations sponsored by the Corporation. Bernard Rubin relates how the John Birch Society urged subscribers to its bulletin to attack Xerox for lending support to the United Nations, that "instrument of Soviet Communist conspiracy."[21] On cue, 61,000 anti-U.N. letters arrived. This would have been much more than enough to persuade most advertisers to drop the project instanter. But instead of tamely accepting the letter attack at its face value, Xerox did some analyzing. On closer examination, it appeared that the 61,000 letters had actually been written by only about 16,000 different people. Waiting a little longer, the Corporation eventually received about 14,500 letters of more spontaneous origin approving their program choice. Xerox went still further, employing the Elmo Roper research firm to survey public reaction objectively. The result: the public voted ten to one in favor of the programs.

Most advertisers, however, have neither the time nor the money—even if they do have the will—to stand up to pressure groups long enough to find out whether they represent any responsible and significant segment of public opinion. The more usual attitude of advertisers is represented by the following statement of Proctor and Gamble's one-time television script policy, as cited by former FCC Chairman Newton Minow:

There will be no material that may give offence, either directly, or by inference, to any organized minority group, lodge, or other organizations, institutions, residents of any State or any section of the country, or a commercial organization of any sort. This will be taken to include political organizations, fraternal organizations, college and school groups, labor groups, industrial, business and professional organizations, religious orders, civic clubs, memorial and patriotic societies, philanthropic and reform societies . . . athletic organizations, women's groups, etc., which are in good standing.[22]

Mere "flyspecks," said a network president in rebuttal to complaints by writers about such restrictions. Minow's response: "Some flies. Some specks."[23]

A more sinister potentiality of commercial broadcasting's vulnerability to pressure emerged during the late 1940's and early 1950's—the systematic practice of blacklisting performers, writers, directors, and others in the creative

---

[20] Newton N. Minow, *Equal Time: The Private Broadcaster and the Public Interest* (New York: Atheneum, 1964), p. 14.

[21] Bernard Rubin, *Political Television* (Belmont, Cal.: Wadsworth, 1967), p. 5.

[22] Excerpted from *Equal Time: The Private Broadcaster and the Public Interest,* by Newton N. Minow [p. 18]. Edited by Lawrence Laurent. Copyright © 1964 by Newton N. Minow. Reprinted by permission of Atheneum Publishers.

[23] Minow, *loc. cit.*

aspect of broadcasting to punish them for alleged political views. The most publicized case was that of Jean Muir, an actress in a television series sponsored by General Foods. On the strength of a few complaints about Miss Muir's politics (estimates varied from twenty to two hundred), the company summarily cancelled the actress's contract at a cost to itself of $10 thousand. Among the subversive activities charged against Miss Muir was sending a telegram congratulating the Moscow Art Theatre on its fiftieth anniversary.

A few cases of such dismissals received wide publicity in the period 1949–1951; then, according to a study of blacklisting commissioned by the Fund for the Republic, the networks and major agencies "institutionalized" advance screening procedures to avoid the kind of publicity the Muir case provoked.[24] Top-ranking broadcasting executives were assigned to devote their full energies to combing through published lists and compiling their own "black," "gray," and "white" lists, negotiating with self-appointed "experts" on Communist infiltration, hearing appeals from victims, and issuing "clearances." Scores of writers, performers, newsmen, and other creative people in broadcasting suddenly found themselves dismissed, like Jean Muir, or else mysteriously unable to find work. Careers of many innocent people were permanently damaged. A few even committed suicide.

Among those who benefitted from this extraordinary usurpation of power were the publishers of such newsletters as *Counterattack: The Newsletter of Facts of Communism,* which produced the most notorious of the blacklists in 1950, entitled *Red Channels: The Report of Communist Infiltration in Radio and Television.* Even the flimsiest connection with a suspect benefit performance or meeting or movement was enough to earn one's name a place on such lists. Proving that listings were completely false (as many of the accused did), showing that the circumstances were entirely innocent (as many did), or disclaiming any Communist leanings (as many tried to do) did not avail to "clear" names once clouded. Mere innocence did not suffice. The private anti-Communist "investigators," "experts," and "consultants" demanded that suspects undergo a grovelling purge of "dangerous neutralism." AWARE, Inc., published *The Road Back: Self Clearance,* in which it stipulated that in order to clear their names, those guilty of having been accused should actively "support anti-Communist persons, groups, and organizations" and "subscribe to anti-Communist magazines, read anti-Communist books, government reports and other literature." It even suggested that religious conversion would be regarded as a favorable sign of political redemption.[25]

The broadcasting industry knuckled under to this reign of intimidation with scarcely a murmur of public protest, while secretly disbelieving in the mummery. Of industry members responding to a survey commissioned by the Fund for the Republic, only 11 per cent considered the blacklisters as "sincere and

---

[24] John Cogley, *Report on Blacklisting II: Radio-Television* (New York: Fund for the Republic, 1956), pp. 23, 42.

[25] Quoted in Cogley, *op. cit.,* p. 136.

patriotic." Others referred to them variously as "misguided," "crazy," "prof-
iteers," and "pathological." Sixty-seven per cent of the industry members interviewed believed the blacklisters were motivated by professional jealousy.
But no one wanted to be quoted by name.[26]

Not many had been as blunt as the playright, Elmer Rice, who publicly
charged that "crass commercial cowardice has become more important than
standing up for principles of liberty. I hope the various actors' unions will
start taking definite stands."[27] Only Actors' Equity did take an antiblacklist-
ing stand. The American Federation of Television and Radio Artists was almost torn apart by controversy. A problacklist group of officers proved to
represent only a minority, but AFTRA still failed to come to the aid of its
accused members, who were facing the most serious crises in their professional
careers.

One of these was John Henry Faulk, a successful radio personality on CBS,
who helped organize an antiblacklist but anti-Communist ticket for AFTRA
and was elected second vice-president of the New York local. The problacklist faction included several officers of AWARE, Inc., one of the private Com-
munist-hunting organizations of the period. Following the defeat of its slate
in the AFTRA election, AWARE published a report accusing Faulk of seven
instances of association with activities it considered politically suspect. Some
time later, CBS discharged Faulk while he was out of the country on vacation
and he found his professional career abruptly and totally at an end.[28]

In 1956, Faulk brought suit against AWARE, Vincent Hartnett (one of its
founders), and Lawrence Johnson, a Syracuse supermarket operator active
in the vigilante-style movement, alleging a malicious conspiracy to defame.
Six years later Faulk finally won his case. The trial devastatingly exposed the
malicious, self-serving, and specious character of the blacklisters. Every one
of the seven charges against Faulk was proved false. The peculiar viciousness
of the libel so impressed the jury that, of its own motion, it awarded more
damages than the suit asked—a total of $3.5 million. "This unprecedented
award," said the presiding judge, "was evidently intended to express the conscience of the community, represented by this jury . . . concerning a matter
of fundamental rights. . . ."[29] On an appeal, the defendants received another
stinging rebuff when a five-man New York appellate court unanimously upheld the guilty verdict, remarking that "the acts of the defendants were proved
to be as malicious as they were vicious." However, the court did reduce the
damages to a more reasonable $550 thousand.[30]

---

[26] *Ibid.,* p. 242.

[27] *Ibid.,* p. 39.

[28] See John H. Faulk, *Fear on Trial* (New York: Simon and Schuster, 1964), and
Koenig, *op. cit.,* pp. 244–245.

[29] Louis Nizer, *The Jury Returns* (Garden City, N. Y.: Doubleday, 1966), p. 459.

[30] *John H. Faulk* v. *AWARE, Inc., et al.,* 19 A. D. (2d) 464 (1963).

With the benefit of hindsight, one can find a number of indications to suggest that their sense of economic vulnerability made advertisers, networks, and agencies give in to a tyranny which would have collapsed in the face of a firm commitment to normal American standards of evidence, due process, and fair play. The Faulk verdict came too late to be of practical help to the chief victims. But it did expose in retrospect the incredible flimsiness of the professional blacklisters' ramshackle guilt-by-association edifice. Louis Nizer, Faulk's lawyer, concluded his story of the case by saying, "One lone man had challenged the monstrously powerful forces of vigilantism cloaked in super patriotism. . . ."[31] Yet Nizer's own masterful dissection of the defendants' motives and methods proved not their power but their pitiful weakness. What made them seem monstrously powerful was the response of men in the advertising companies, agencies, networks, and stations, who simply surrendered to pressure without firing a shot.

There were honorable exceptions. Chet Huntley, for example, then a Los Angeles news broadcaster sponsored by a coffee company, was threatened with a boycott of his sponsor's product because he spoke favorably of UNESCO and unfavorably of Senator Joseph McCarthy of Wisconsin. Huntley's supporters organized a counterboycott and the coffee sponsor stood firm. Gypsy Rose Lee, attacked for alleged association with four subversive groups, produced a list of about three hundred benefits she had performed and asked how she could possibly have investigated the political complexion of every one; ABC refused to act without more substantial evidence, and none was forthcoming.[32] One of Faulk's libellers, the chain-store operator, in concert with a Syracuse American Legion post, managed to terrorize Madison Avenue with threats of boycotts; yet the local Syracuse broadcasters simply decided to ignore any such charges unless substantiated with more compelling evidence than the blacklisters usually brought forth.[33] Even in the Muir case, despite its extraordinary notoriety, evidence indicates that had General Foods merely ignored the charges against her, economic repercussions on the company would have been minimal. In the midst of all the publicity, General Foods itself commissioned a Gallup opinion survey which indicated that less than 40 per cent of the sample had even heard of the case, and of those who had heard of it, less than 3 per cent could tie it in with the correct sponsor.[34]

In rebuttal, the advertiser may well ask what rule of business requires him to take even a slight risk of this sort. His position was expressed in the Fund for the Republic study by the president of the American Tobacco Company:

---

[31] Nizer, *op. cit.*, pp. 464–465.

[32] Cogley, *op. cit.*, pp. 88, 24.

[33] *Ibid.*, pp. 107–108.

[34] Merle Miller, *The Judges and the Judged* (Garden City, N. Y.: Doubleday, 1952), p. 46.

When a company such as ours uses its corporate funds to sponsor a program on television or radio, it does so with but one purpose—to reach the largest possible number of the public as its audience, and to present its products to that audience in the most favorable light . . . we would be wasting shareholders' funds were we to employ artists or other persons who, under company auspices, are likely to offend the public.[35]

The problem may be precisely that broadcasting is not merely business. We return once more to ambivalent concepts of the broadcast medium and its responsibilities. Do business motivations, on the record, provide adequate moral basis for the conduct of a broadcasting service? James Cogley concluded the Fund for the Republic study of blacklisting by pointing out that when broadcasters took on the role of judging political guilt and innocence they extended themselves well beyond the realm of economics:

If the American businesses which together comprise the radio-tv industry are to assume the burdens of government, they must also assume responsibility for dispensing justice. They cannot have it both ways. They cannot argue on the one hand that economic considerations come before all else, and, on the other, speak glowingly of the contribution "business statesmanship" is making to a business-oriented democratic society.[36]

16.5 / Affiliate Clearance of Network Programs

We turn now to "clearance" in a different sense, the process of making an affiliate's time available to its network for scheduling network programs (Section 15.3). Attention tends to focus on the ways economic constraints work at the center. They also work on networks from the edges, through affiliates, in terms of clearance. Ironically, affiliates usually invoke their right to reject network programs, guaranteed in the Chain Broadcasting Regulations (Section 15.3), for reasons quite different from those the FCC had in mind. The intent of the rule was to ensure the licensee's right to use his judgment in rejecting network programs as "unsatisfactory," "unsuitable," "contrary to the public interest," or in conflict with more important programs of the moment. In practice, affiliates more often invoke the rule in order either to cater to local prejudice or to make more money from a substitute program of lesser quality. In the case of noncommercial stations, of course, only the former applies (Section 16.7). Sometimes commercial stations evade the onus of noncarriage by recording network public-service programs and playing them back at otherwise useless hours, such as 1:00 A.M. Their clearance record looks good until one checks on the actual times of broadcast.

An FCC Chairman proposed at one time to require affiliates to report, with reasons, on rejections of network public-affairs programs:

---

[35] Cogley, *op. cit.*, p. 101.

[36] *Ibid.*, p. 209.

The networks produce some magnificent informative programing. The need for this kind of programing is both urgent and obvious: it deals with many critical issues arising in our troubled times. . . . Yet often over half the networks' affiliates won't carry these programs. Instead, they substitute a commercial program designed to get a better rating.[37]

Edward R. Murrow's biographer estimates that on the average only about 45 per cent of CBS's affiliates cleared time for Murrow's news documentaries, which almost invariably stimulated controversy. He pictures the networks caught in the middle between reciprocating economic pressures:

The demand of the affiliates for more mass-appeal programs, with the threat of replacing network offerings by their own canned fare, forms one of the arms of the pincers within which network programmers operate, the other arm being the demand of the stockholders for more dividends.[38]

Though it would be unthinkable for the FCC to compel affiliates to carry specific network programs, the Commission could well raise the question whether an affiliate's general pattern of network clearances over a period of time reflected a lack of sensitivity to public need. Certainly the Commission showed concern on this subject in its 1946 "Blue Book," which devoted a long and critical section to data on affiliate rejection of network sustaining features in order to substitute local commercial programs.[39] The Commission has also looked with favor on an agreement between a station and organized citizens' groups which were challenging its renewal that the station would not reject programs of interest to local audiences without first consulting the interested groups (Section 18.5).

Without some such countervailing pressures on affiliates from forces other than economic, to expect any far-reaching reform of network programming policies seems highly unrealistic. In the final analysis, the affiliates hold the trump cards. Edward Murrow's successor as news head for CBS concluded:

The real paradox of television is that if by some miracle the network shareholders and officers suddenly determined to use only good taste, good judgment and their conscience, to guide their choice of programming, the power of the local stations would overrule them. Moreover, a network operating with an unbridled sense of responsibility would soon see its affiliates seceding to another network, perhaps even a new one, that traveled the low road to ratings and revenues. The harsh fact is that most affiliates are too profitable under present circumstances; mining

---

[37] Excerpted from *Equal Time: The Private Broadcaster and the Public Interest,* by Newton N. Minow, [p. 75]. Edited by Lawrence Laurent. Copyright © 1964 by Newton N. Minow. Reprinted by permission of Atheneum Publishers.

[38] Kendrick, *op. cit.,* p. 17.

[39] FCC, *Public Service Responsibility of Broadcast Licensees* (Washington: Government Printing Office, 1946), pp. 18–36.

gold from the ether as they are, they have no incentive to tamper with the magic results of "giving the people what they want."[40]

"Giving the people what they want"—after "public interest, convenience, and necessity" the most-discussed phrase in the literature of broadcasting—requires more detailed examination.

16.6 / Economics of "Cultural Democracy"

The time-honored rejoinder of spokesmen for commercial broadcasting, whenever the quality of its programming comes under attack, has been to shift responsibility to the audience. The argument runs: we broadcasters cannot compel people to listen or watch; they cast their vote democratically with the tuning dial; we simply give them what they want. This process is described as cultural democracy—free exercise of the franchise, popular choice, majority rule.

Research does seem to bear out the contention that people generally like what they are being given. On the one hand, program ratings evidence huge audiences for existing program fare. On the other hand, inquiries as to whether people would rather have something different usually produce evidence of satisfaction by the majority with what is already available. Roper Research Associates asked a national audience sample:

How do you personally feel about the balance between news and public affairs versus entertainment—would you like to see more news and public affairs on television, or more entertainment, or do you like the balance that now exists?

The majority (59 per cent) expressed itself satisfied with the existing balance; 23 per cent wanted more news and public affairs, and 11 per cent wanted more entertainment. The researchers concluded that these answers "suggest that in this respect television is doing a good job of fulfilling its charge to serve all groups and the diverse interests of the entire public."[41] Similar results came from a question about the balance between light entertainment and more serious, cultural programming: 41 per cent liked the present balance, 31 per cent wanted more serious programming, 21 per cent wanted more light programming.[42] When these responses were broken down by educational level, it became evident that the higher the respondent's education the less satisfied he felt with the present balance: 48 per cent of those with grade-school level education felt satisfied, but only 27 per cent of those who had gone to college; only 18 per cent of the former wanted more serious programs, as against 59 per cent of the college-level respondents.

---

[40] Fred W. Friendly, *Due to Circumstances Beyond Our Control* . . . (copyright © 1967 by Random House, Inc.), pp. 274–275.

[41] Burns W. Roper, *A Ten-Year View of Public Attitudes Toward Television and Other Mass Media, 1959–1968* (New York: Television Information Office, 1969), pp. 19–20.

[42] *Ibid.*, pp. 21–22.

However, such data must be qualified by the oft-remarked fact that people apparently tend to say one thing and do another. In his major study of audience attitudes, Steiner asked people to categorize their favorite programming in terms of light and heavy entertainment, news, and information and public events; he compared the results with their actual viewing and found, for example, that although 23 per cent of the more highly educated named information and public events as their favorite, only 8 per cent actually watched such programs during the test period. Steiner concluded that "those groups in the population who stress the need for more information, as well as the public in general, usually fail to select today's information fare over today's entertainment."[43]

When they do try to please the better educated, therefore, practical broadcasters often find themselves disillusioned. Cancelling routine entertainment to broadcast important public-affairs programs invariably brings a deluge of complaints from people who want what they have been getting and bitterly resent having it taken away, even though the substitute may be as unique as man's first walk on the moon. When "better" alternatives are regularly available, audiences still choose lighter entertainment. Introduction of commercial television into Britain, alongside the BBC noncommercial service, provided a revealing case in point:

Studies carried out in England in 1955, 1956, and 1960 showed clearly how exposure to more demanding and "better" programs is avoided once there is a choice . . . crime and detective series, panel games, Westerns, drama, and variety remained high, while information programs and documentaries lost two-thirds to three-quarters of their viewers. Five years later, the trend had become even more marked.[44]

Limited experience with Subscription Television also suggested that viewers preferred in that medium precisely the same types of sports and entertainment programs already available on conventional television.[45]

In short, much in the practical experience of commercial broadcasters encourages "giving the public what it wants" and justifying this course as cultural democracy in action. Their argument, in effect, holds that economic incentives suffice to control the nature of the broadcast-program service. The listener/viewer occupies the driver's seat because he can turn off the set, and if enough people turn off the set they effectively turn off the money, too. Many

---

[43] Gary A. Steiner, *The People Look at Television: A Study of Audience Attitudes* (New York: Alfred A. Knopf, 1963), pp. 126, 188.

[44] Hilde T. Himmelweit, "An Experimental Study of Taste Development in Children," in Leon Arons and Mark A. May, eds., *Television and Human Behavior: Tomorrow's Research in Mass Communication* (New York: Appleton-Century-Crofts, 1963), pp. 46–47.

[45] David M. Blank, "The Quest for Quality and Diversity in Television Programming," *American Economic Review: Papers and Proceedings,* LVI (May, 1966), 448–456. However, see Section 11.7 regarding the limitations of small-scale STV.

a practical businessman/broadcaster sees this down-to-earth faith in consumer sovereignty as the adequate determiner of programming in the same light as his cherished beliefs in American free enterprise, free speech, and free competition. He sees no reason why he should apologize to those who would impose program standards enunciated by some voice other than the *vox populi*.

In keeping with this reasoning, the industry adopted the position that any additional control over programs exerted by the FCC or other extramural forces was unnecessary, unwise, and legally unjustifiable. This philosophy crystallized around the radio networks' unyielding opposition to the FCC's Chain Broadcasting Regulations, which, as we have seen (Section 9.5), the industry fought all the way to the Supreme Court in 1943. The high point in resistance came during the period when Judge Justin Miller was President of the National Association of Broadcasters (1945–1951). Judge Miller was the admitted architect of a well-documented and systematic ideological attack on all FCC controls save those over purely technical matters of frequency, power, signal quality, and the like. The broadcasters' case received its fullest and most vehement airing at hearings of a Senate committee in 1947.[46] At this hearing Judge Miller and a number of other broadcasting executives joined forces in a frontal attack on the power of the FCC to exercise discretionary control over programming. Again and again members of the Senate subcommittee pinpointed the issue:

SENATOR McFARLAND: Would the effect of your language be to prohibit the Federal Communications Commission from refusing to renew a license, no matter how poor the programs may have been over that station?

MR. MILLER: If it is merely a matter of poor programming, it would; yes.

THE CHAIRMAN [Senator Wallace H. White]: I would like to have your view as to whether, in reaching a conclusion as to the public service or the want of public service being rendered, the regulatory body has a right to look at the programs and has any control whatsoever over the programs sent out.

MR. MILLER: I think it has not.

THE CHAIRMAN: So you would say that the quality of the program has nothing to do with the question of whether a public service is being rendered or is not being rendered.

MR. MILLER: I do . . .

THE CHAIRMAN: . . . Why, it seems to me that the quality of the program and the character of the program is the outstanding factor in determining whether the station is performing a public service or is not.[47]

Perhaps the word "quality" provides the key. The economic "cultural-democracy" argument rests on sheer numbers. It regards programs—and indeed in the final analysis, people—as means to an end, not ends in themselves.

---

[46] Senate Committee on Interstate and Foreign Commerce, *To Amend the Communications Act of 1934,* Hearings on S. 1333, 80th Cong., 1st Sess. (Washington: Government Printing Office, 1947).

[47] *Ibid.,* pp. 119 ff.

Even in the marketplace of physical goods (as contrasted with the market-place of ideas), willing buyers for a product do not necessarily justify the sale of the product. When the NAB president told a Senate committee he believed that economic competition should be the "controlling force" over program-ming, the Chairman of the committee replied:

Now, if you say the economic thing should be controlling . . . most of the people of the country like to gamble, we will say, and the radio people say because of that fact they listen to our gambling programs. Supposing that a great many people like things that border on the obscene. Should radio companies put on that kind of a program? If they are going to be governed simply by the economics of the thing, that is what would happen.[48]

Putting it another way, what people *want* does not necessarily coincide with what they need. Given the special circumstances of broadcasting—first, the limits on the channels available, with the consequent conferral of local mo-nopolies on licensees; second, the fact that it deals in ideas, not merchandise merely—it is questionable whether catering only to the wants and ignoring the needs of society can be justified.

In any event, the "give-people-what-they-want" formula grossly oversimpli-fies the real situation. How does one find out what people want? By audience research—but as shown in Section 14.5, research deals not with wants but with tuning behavior, from which wants must be inferred. Whatever signifi-cance attaches to tuning behavior, it tells us in any event only about the past. People do not go on wanting exactly the same thing in the same form forever. Someone has to take the next step into the future—someone innovative and venturesome, not someone shackled to last month's statistics on what the au-dience "wanted" in the past.

In Section 12.5 we argued that the mass consumer cannot be expected to have the technical knowledge, imagination, and creative flair to articulate de-mands for specific new and improved products. The producer, not the con-sumer, must play the innovator role. Broadcast programming presents an analogous producer-consumer relationship. The listener/viewer cannot be ex-pected to have the creative imagination necessary to foresee what new and better programs might be invented. In this sense, questions in audience sur-veys about what kinds of programs people want, such as those reported earlier in this section, are an exercise in futility. Of course respondents say they are satisfied with present programming—they cannot really imagine alternatives. For lack of inventiveness and innovative imagination, people generally accept and learn to like what they get, as long as it offers some positive satisfaction —and as long as no one offers any more satisfying alternative. As an adver-tising executive put it to some of his colleagues, programming guided by the results of past research leads nowhere:

---

[48] Senate Committee on Interstate Commerce, *To Amend the Communications Act of 1934,* Hearings on S. 814, 78th Cong., 1st Sess. (Washington: Government Printing Office, 1944), p. 194.

It is the great mass of people who stand by, chanting that the horseless carriage will never replace the horse, and that if God intended man to fly He would have given him wings. . . . If Christopher Columbus, the well-known sailor from Genoa, had applied modern advertising research methods to his proposed voyage, a consumer jury test would have told him in advance that the world was flat, depth interviews with expert seamen would have revealed the impressive monsters that awaited him hungrily at the end of the sea; motivational studies among his crew would have shown that they were only interested in money; Ferdinand and Isabella would have cancelled the appropriation; America would never have been discovered, and *you* would all be *Indians.*[49]

The political analogy—the "voting-with-the-dial" concept of cultural democracy—is also simplistic. In democratic elections the ballot does not decide everything; the voters expect representatives, once elected, to use responsible judgment on the issues that come before them, not merely to hold a plebiscite every time a decision must be made. The losing side does not lose its rights; minorities continue to be served. Governance of broadcast programming by the quantitative criteria of audience research "votes," however, ignores the rights of minorities, reduces programming decisions to the simple "yes-no" of the plebiscite, and produces the bland, lowest-common-denominator type of programming that earned the "vast wasteland" epithet.

16.7 / Economic Constraints on Noncommercial Programming

For an overview of the economic determinants of the commercial service, let us summarize at this point the types of influence and their effects discussed in this chapter. The following should be read as a rather arbitrary and broad generalization, leaving ample room for exceptions.

MOTIVATION	POSSIBLE EFFECTS ON PROGRAMMING
	On the Part of the Medium
Economic survival under marginal conditions	Overcommercialization Tolerance for unethical advertising General deterioration in program quality Adverse effect on practices of competing stations
Maximization of profits	Imbalance in favor of commercially salable program types Exploitative program types (*e.g.,* giveaway, quiz) Rejection of good but unprofitable network offerings

---

[49] Charles H. Brower, "The Growing Pains of Advertising," *Broadcasting-Telecasting,* January 17, 1955, p. 37

| Identification with community economic power structure as source of revenue | Avoidance of subjects or treatments threatening to dominant local economic and social interests
Absence of programs serving minority interests |

On the Part of the Advertiser

Avoid offending potential customers	Avoidance of controversial subject matter and treatment Emphasis on escapism, irrelevance, blandness Vulnerability to pressure groups
Avoid undue risks in advertising investments; get most for money	Imitative, follow-the-leader stereotypes: formula programming Aim at lowest common denominator of popular taste; neglect of minority tastes Overdependence on audience research
Avoid aiding competition and downgrading own products	Interference in details of program content and treatment

Edward R. Murrow had as much experience as anyone with programs which defied these economic influences. During the 1950's his *See It Now* series of documentary reports and exposés almost invariably created intense controversy. Murrow was fortunate in having, to a unique degree, the confidence of both the top management of his network, CBS, and his sponsor, Alcoa, which supported the series for four years. Murrow himself had great faith in and hopes for the American commercial system. His biographer writes:

He knew that most of the money that paid for radio and television came from a small number of American corporations, and that therefore the thinking of their executives was bound to have an effect on the nation's thinking, in terms of the kinds of programs they sponsored. Murrow proposed that better broadcasting be induced through these men, from the top. However much it could be criticized, he felt that the commercial system of broadcasting was still the better alternative to state-operated and government-financed communications. This was his ingrained approach to the deficiencies of the medium. . . .[50]

The Murrow programs could be cited as a powerful rebuttal to all that has been alleged about the restrictive effects of economics on programming, were it not for the fact that Murrow himself finally lost faith in the system. In the end he withdrew, disillusioned, from commercial broadcasting. His successor at CBS, Fred Friendly, did the same and turned his energies to the noncommercial field.

---

[50] Kendrick, *op. cit.,* p. 402.

Simply eliminating the advertiser does not, however, eliminate economics. It still costs a lot of money to build and run a television station, and to isolate the recipient of large amounts of money from the influence of the source is notoriously difficult. Whether the funds come from advertisers, subscribers, local or federal taxes, foundations, auction sales, or program-production contracts, economic influence flows from the source, even though the degree and kinds of influence may vary widely.

For example, the foundations which, next to tax sources, have provided the largest share of educational broadcasting support have well-defined goals in mind. Naturally, they do not hesitate to influence recipients of grants to further those goals. During the critical first years of educational television, its chief foundation support came from the Fund for Adult Education (Section 10.8). The Fund's "areas of concern"—the American heritage, social anthropology, international understanding, and community self-development—automatically became educational televison's areas of concern.[51] A Fund-sponsored survey of this period declares:

Out of the Fund's own philosophy of adult education arose a requirement . . . that a reasonable proportion of the programming should be in the area of *adult education in the liberal arts and sciences.* The [Educational Radio and Television] Center was given the corresponding mandate, that this should be the area of its program production for the stations; and in a high proportion of cases the only "liberal education" that the stations offered in their early years was that furnished by the Center.

* * * * *

. . . the fate of ETV in the late '60's is in large part bound up with the question whether school and college broadcasting will take it over. The adult beachhead fortunately was the first one established; and its survival, and extension farther into the field of battle, will be essential in preserving ETV as a social force rather than merely a visual aid.[52]

In short, the economic power of the Fund played a key role in determining the very nature of educational broadcasting.

In 1963, the Ford Foundation announced a major increase in its funding of NET, the educational television-network center.

With the grant, the Foundation asked the Center, and the Center agreed, to reduce its package [of network programming] to five hours of *new* programming a week, at least half of which would be in the area of public affairs, and to devote its resources to a television program service of high quality.[53]

Naturally, NET complied with this requirement.

---

[51] John W. Powell, *Channels of Learning: The Story of Educational Television* (Washington: Public Affairs Press, 1962), p. 70.

[52] *Ibid.,* pp. 89, 61.

[53] Fritz Jauch, "A Brief History of Educational Television in the United States" (New York: National Educational Television Network, n.d., mimeo.), p. 11.

In Section 16.5, we pointed out how the desires to substitute more salable programs and to conform to local prejudices often cause commercial affiliates to reject their networks' public-affairs program offerings. Though salability does not enter into noncommerical broadcasting calculations, conformity sometimes does. The president of NET complained that an American educational station refused to run an episode of the highly praised, internationally distributed *Forsyte Saga* series because a character "commits rape upon his own wife in a brief scene that is crucial to an understanding of the characters. . . ." More than half the educational stations refused to clear time for a documentary about Cuba's Fidel Castro.[54] Five educational stations rejected a program on American participation in past wars.[55] The first program released to NET by the Public Broadcasting Laboratory, most of which concerned racial problems, was carried by only one of thirty-four Southern educational stations.[56] The entire Alabama state educational television network of eight stations was accused of refusing clearance for such NET programs as *Soul, Black Journal,* and *On Being Black.* The network alleged that they contained "lewd, vulgar, obscene, profane or repulsive" material. The FCC turned down a protest against renewal of the stations' licenses on the grounds that it could not interfere with licensee judgment in the choice of particular programs.[57] Evidently commercial broadcasting holds no monopoly on timidity and conservatism when it comes to scheduling programs which might stir up adverse local reaction.

Whether or not noncommercial, educational stations *should* deal in provocative programming raises another issue, mentioned in Section 22.7. In the present context, it suffices to make the point that economic constraints affect noncommercial as well as advertising-supported broadcasting. Educational stations, though free from the kinds of direct advertiser pressure summarized at the beginning of the section, nevertheless usually depend for financial support on a power structure identical in most respects to the relationship between commercial broadcasting's owners and advertiser clients. That identity tends to be closest for educational stations licensed to local school boards and state educational systems (42 per cent in 1969), less close for stations licensed to broadly based community foundations representing a wide range of interests and deriving financial support from a variety of sources.

Because television requires a relatively large investment in capital equipment and annual operating expenses, it has a "high profile" economically. Its involvement with rather large sums of money adds to its inherent conspicu-

---

[54] James Day, "The Social Responsibility of Public Broadcasting," *Educational Broadcasting Review,* III (Special Issue, 1969), 12.

[55] "Even ETV Has Its Censors," *Broadcasting,* February 23, 1970, p. 65.

[56] Dave Berkman, "Inner City," *Educational Television,* February, 1970, p. 33. The program is reviewed in *Educational Broadcasting Review,* I (December, 1967), 70–74.

[57] "Ala. ETV Upheld on Right to Reject," *Broadcasting,* July 6, 1970, p. 34. See the comment in Section 16.5 on the FCC's concern with this subject.

ousness as a communications medium. This economic characteristic of the medium, we suggest, almost automatically imposes programming constraints. One would be hard put to find a television equivalent, for example, of the Pacifica Foundation stations, a group of noncommercial listener and foundation supported FM radio outlets noted for their provocative programming policies. These policies have repeatedly brought the stations into conflict with elements within their communities and even occasioned a Congressional investigation.[58] The FCC's statement on renewal of the Pacifica licenses in 1964, after it had considered complaints against the stations' programming, has been called "probably the strongest ever issued by the Commission to that time defending the right of a station to air provocative programs."[59] In dismissing complaints against Pacifica, the FCC relied on a subsection of the Communications Act charging the Commission with "promoting the larger and more effective use of radio in the public interest [§ 303(g)]." Said the Commission:

We recognize that . . . such provocative programing as here involved may offend some listeners. But this does not mean that those offended have the right, through the Commission's licensing power, to rule such programing off the air-waves. Were this the case, only the wholly inoffensive, the bland, could gain access to the radio microphone or the TV camera.[60]

It is difficult to imagine a noncommercial television station hazarding the risks undertaken by the Pacifica stations. Television stations simply have too much at stake—the livelihood of too many employees; the investment of time and money by too many influential community leaders; linkages to too many local, regional, and national political institutions. Sheer economic size, in short, tends to involve even noncommercial television with the power structure and hence to constrain its programming policies along acceptably uncontroversial lines.

This is not by any means to write off the noncommercial service as incapable of offering a distinguishable alternative to the commercial service. The lesson of the experiences mentioned in this section seems to be that vigilance will be needed to make sure that the noncommercial service does not succumb to the same types of economic constraints that limit the scope of the commercial service. In recommending a Corporation for Public Broadcasting, the Carnegie Commission was at pains also to recommend a system of financing (an excise tax on television receivers) calculated to be as free as possible from such economic constraints (Section 10.8). Congress chose not to launch the Corporation with that degree of fiscal autonomy, electing instead

---

[58] See Senate Committee on the Judiciary, Subcommittee to Investigate Administration of Internal Security Act, *Pacifica Foundation*, Hearings in 3 parts, 88th Cong., 1st Sess. (Washington: Government Printing Office, 1963).

[59] Gene R. Stebbins, "Pacifica's Battle for Free Expression," *Educational Broadcasting Review*, IV (June, 1970), 22.

[60] *In Re Pacifica Foundation*, 36 FCC 147 at 149 (1964).

to start with annual appropriations. This method of financing does not encourage risk taking. As MIT economist Sidney Alexander has remarked:

It is said that nothing is so timid as a million dollars, but I would guess that a bureaucrat dependent on a Congressional appropriation can offer a million dollars a lesson in timidity. How far a Public Television Corporation can be insulated from this timidity is a question of fact for political science. The best way to find out is to try.[61]

---

[61] "Public Television and the 'Ought' of Public Policy," *Washington University Law Quarterly,* Winter, 1968, p. 63.

PART FOUR

SOCIAL
CONTROL OF
BROADCASTING

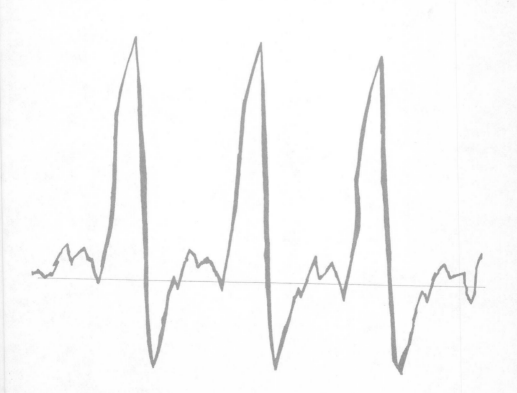

17

THE LAW OF
BROADCASTING

In the previous chapter, we touched on one of the enduring issues in the arena of broadcasting-policy debate: the extent to which economic influences should be left alone to determine, through processes of commercial competition and free consumer choice, the nature of the program service. In Section P.2, however, we also drew attention to the fact that broadcasting inevitably involves larger considerations of national policy and international coordination. At the very minimum, rules are needed to control the physical aspects of radio use—frequencies, channels, power, types of emissions, geographical locations, times of operation. Without such rules, as American broadcasters discovered in the early 1920's (Section 8.3), interference between stations simply renders the whole system useless. But since in addition radio communication has vital significance for national defense and the dissemination of essential public information, no government—even the most permissive—stops short with merely regulating the physical aspects of radio use.

And so, despite the argument for economic determinism by American commercial broadcasters and their appeal to the First Amendment to protect them from government concern with programs, social as well as economic constraints help to shape the program service which eventually reaches the American public. Society exerts its own controls most explicitly and directly through legal sanctions. Almost equally powerful sanctions of social approval/disapproval operate through the medium of public opinion. The law controls only a small fraction of all the possible social situations and behaviors. Moreover, it evolves more slowly than events. Much of it is archaic, much only belatedly catching up with current needs. In short, we must look not only at the law but also beyond the formal legal machinery to appreciate the full scope of social control over broadcasting. Therefore, in the last chapter of this part, we will go on from the law to consider other agents of social control, such as self-regulatory, educational, and consumer organizations.

17.1 / The Communications Act

We traced the early development of government regulation of radio in Chapter 8, bringing it to the point where the Communications Act of 1934 went into effect, creating the Federal Communications Commission, the federal agency responsible for regulating broadcasting. The Act limits the Commission's jurisdiction to nongovernmental uses of radio; yet governmental uses account for 42 per cent of the spectrum in the 30–10,000-mc. range, and another 26 per cent is shared by government and private users.[1] Section 305 of the Act gives the President, instead of the FCC, frequency-assignment and other regulatory powers over government stations. This divided responsibility creates a spectrum-management problem which was the subject of a series of studies over a period of two decades. In 1970, a new Office of Telecommunications Policy was set up in the Executive branch, with responsibility for advising the President on overall communications policies, spectrum management, international agreements, and federal research and development activities. It directs assignment of government spectrum allocations, maintaining an advisory relationship with the FCC. The sharing of allocations continues to be coordinated through the Interdepartmental Radio Advisory Committee, which was founded in 1922.

The Communications Act is incorporated into the organized body of federal law as Title 47 of the United States Code, "Telegraphs, Telephones and Radio Telegraphs."[2] This organic law of radio derives ultimately from the authority of the Constitution. Congress asserts control over radio communication by virtue of the "Commerce Clause," the Constitutional delegation to Congress of jurisdiction over "Commerce with foreign Nations, among the several States, and with the Indian tribes [§ 8(3)]." Another major Constitutional provision, the First Amendment, prohibits Congress from making any law "abridging the freedom of speech, or of the press." The Communications Act specifically classifies broadcasting as a form of communication protected by this language. Several other basic Constitutional issues arise in the course of administering the Communications Act, among them questions concerning lawful delegation of legislative powers, taking of private property for public use, due process of law, and state *versus* federal jurisdiction.

Congress wrote the Communications Act, for the most part, in general terms. The Federal Communications Commission makes the specific applications, so that in practice broadcasters generally encounter the law in the form of FCC Rules and Regulations. Every regulation promulgated by the FCC must, of course, have a justification in the Communications Act, from which the FCC derives its authority; therefore the Rules and Regulations have the force of federal law, even though not directly enacted by Congress.

---

[1] Office of Telecommunications Management, "The Radio Frequency Spectrum: United States Use and Management" (Washington: Executive Office of the President, July, 1969), p. D-7.

[2] Citations of the Communications Act in this Chapter refer to the law as it appeared in *United States Code Annotated* (St. Paul, Minn.: West), updated through the 1970 Cumulative Pocket Part. See Bibliographical Notes for explanation of legal sources and the citation system used in this and following chapters.

Frequently, the FCC makes decisions in disputes among those who come before it. These decisions, though not quite the same as court decisions (since the FCC is not actually a judicial tribunal), tend to establish precedents[3] and provide a commentary by the FCC on the Communications Act and its own regulations.

The legality of both the rule making and the decision making of the FCC may be challenged in the courts. Appeal may be made to establish whether the Commission acted within the limits placed on it by the Communications Act and other applicable federal laws. Such right of appeal is, of course, a basic concept of American government; no law may give an official or group of officials unlimited power or undefined discretion. The absence of limitation on the discretion of the Secretary of Commerce in the Radio Act of 1912 brought about its downfall (Section 8.3). Congress carefully avoided that pitfall in writing the Radio Act of 1927. Court decisions—whether supporting or reversing the FCC—contribute to the corpus of radio law by establishing legal precedents. Those few disputes which reach the Supreme Court become the leading cases.

Stations cannot be subjected to both federal and state controls in matters covered by the Communications Act. This does not remove stations entirely from state jurisdiction, however; for example, state rather than federal laws cover libel and slander. Similarly, the Communications Act does not interfere with the application of relevant federal laws not a part of the Act, such as copyright, obscenity, labor, and lottery laws.

The body of American domestic radio law is grouped into six subchapters of Title 47 in the *United States Code*: (1) general provisions, (2) common carriers, (3) radio (in two parts—the first general, the second concerning shipboard radio), (4) procedure and administration, (5) penalties, and (6) miscellaneous. Section numbers conform to these groupings; for example, sections dealing with radio are numbered in the 300's. We are primarily concerned here with the general provisions which set up the Federal Communications Commission, the radio provisions, and some of the provisions governing administration and procedure. We will outline the essential content of the Act, organizing the material in terms of the underlying principles mentioned in Chapter 8. The practical application of these principles and the controversies they stimulate will be considered in succeeding chapters.

17.2 / Functions of the FCC

The purpose of the chapter on wire or radio communication is set forth as follows:

For the purpose of regulating interstate and foreign commerce in communication by wire and radio so as to make available, so far as possible, to all the people

---

[3] Technically speaking, *stare decisis,* the rule of legal precedent, does not apply to administrative decisions.

of the United States a rapid, efficient Nation-wide, and world-wide wire and radio communication service with adequate facilities at reasonable charges, for the purpose of the national defense, for the purpose of promoting safety of life and property through the use of wire and radio communication, and for the purpose of securing a more effective execution of this policy by centralizing authority heretofore granted by law to several agencies and by granting additional authority with respect to interstate and foreign commerce in wire and radio communication, there is hereby created a commission to be known as the "Federal Communications Commission," which shall be constituted as hereinafter provided, and which shall execute and enforce the provisions of this chapter. [§ 151]

This section reminds us that the purpose of repealing the Radio Act of 1927 and substituting the present Act was to centralize authority; the 1934 legislation reenacted the 1927 radio laws with only minor changes. The jurisdiction of the FCC extends to (1) both wire and radio communications, insofar as they are (2) either interstate or foreign.

Section 151 provides for a Commission to execute and enforce the Act. Section 154 describes the Commission. Its seven members are appointed by the President with the advice and consent of the Senate, one member being designated by the President as chairman. Commissioners must be citizens, may not have a financial interest in any type of communications business, must devote full time to the job. No more than four of the seven commissioners may be of the same political party. Amendments to the Act deleted a provision allowing Commissioners to accept fees for papers and publications and added a rule forbidding any Commissioner who resigns before expiration of his full seven-year term from representing clients before the Commission within one year of his resignation.

Congress thus sought to prevent economic and political bias on the part of the Commission. The term of seven years, contrasted with the presidential term of four years, makes it impossible for an incoming President to change the personnel of the Commission abruptly (the terms of the Commissioners are staggered so that only one expires each year). On the other hand, a new President can to some extent immediately implement his administration's policies through exercising his right to appoint the chairman.

The Act empowers the Commission to "perform any and all acts, make such rules and regulations, and issue such orders, not inconsistent with this chapter, as may be necessary in the execution of its functions [§ 154(i)]." In only a few instances did Congress tie the Commission's hands with highly specific regulations. For example, it placed a specific upper limit of three years on the term of broadcast licenses—though even here the Commission may use its discretion in issuing licenses for *shorter* periods. Most provisions of the Act give the Commission wide latitude in applying its judgment to the particular set of facts of each case. Nevertheless, the new law would have met the same fate as the Radio Act of 1912 if the Commission had been given unqualified discretionary latitude. It was essential somehow to limit the Commission's powers in every case. Congress met this problem by using a phrase long familiar in the public-utility field—"public interest, convenience, and [sometimes "or"] necessity."

17.3 / The "Public Interest, Convenience, and Necessity" Standard

Congress created the FCC as its agent to carry out general Congressional intent. Wherever the legislature did not wish to be specific, it left the Commission free to use its own judgment—subject always to the test of public interest, convenience, and necessity. For example, the following instructions appear in the law with regard to the Commission's licensing power (italics supplied):

The Commission, *if public convenience, interest, or necessity will be served thereby*, subject to the limitations of this chapter, shall grant to any applicant therefor a station license provided for by this chapter. [§ 307(a)]

* * * * *

. . . Upon the expiration of any license, upon application therefor, a renewal of such license may be granted from time to time for a term of not to exceed three years in the case of broadcasting licenses, and not to exceed five years in the case of other licenses, *if the Commission finds that public interest, convenience, and necessity would be served thereby*. . . . [§ 307(d)]

* * * * *

. . . *if* the Commission, upon examination of such application [for construction permit, license, or modification or renewal thereof] *shall find that public interest, convenience, and necessity would be served* by the granting thereof, it shall grant such application. [§ 309(a)]

* * * * *

No construction permit or station license, or any rights thereunder, shall be transferred, assigned, or disposed of in any manner, voluntarily or involuntarily, directly or indirectly, or by transfer of control of any corporation holding such permit or license, to any person *except* upon application to the Commission and *upon finding by the Commission that the public interest, convenience, and necessity will be served thereby*. . . . [§ 310(b)]

* * * * *

Any station license or construction permit may be modified by the Commission either for a limited time or for the duration of the term thereof, *if* in the judgment of the Commission *such action will promote the public interest, convenience, and necessity*. . . . [§ 316(a)]

* * * * *

. . . changes in the frequencies, authorized power, or in the times of operation of any station, shall not be made without the consent of the station licensee *unless*, after a public hearing, the Commission shall determine that *such changes will promote public convenience or interest or will serve public necessity*. . . . [§ 303(f)]

Thus the Commission must consult the public interest, convenience, and necessity in making every major decision about licensing.

Section 303 of the Act lists a number of rather specific powers of the FCC, including the powers to (a) classify stations, (b) prescribe the nature of the service to be rendered, (c) assign frequencies, (d) determine station location, (e) regulate the kind of apparatus used, (f) prevent interference, (g) study new uses for radio and provide for experimental uses of frequencies, (i) make special regulations for network stations, (j) require the keeping of records, (l) prescribe qualifications for station operators and issue them licenses, (o) designate call letters, (p) publish necessary information, and (s) require UHF tuners in television sets. This entire list, however, is preceded by the admonition to do these things *as public convenience, interest or necessity requires.*

Few significant provisions fail to leave the door open for the exercise of FCC discretion. The phrase "public interest, convenience, and necessity" or any variant thereof therefore takes on critical importance; in effect, it determines the practical results of applying the generalities contained in the law. The function of the public-interest concept has been well summarized in a District of Columbia Appeals Court decision:

The Congress of the United States, which has plenary power to regulate the radio industry, has designated the Commission as its administrative agent, because it is desired to have the regulatory work done by technically trained experts, skilled and experienced in the technical duties of radio regulation. The Congress defined the scope of the authority of its agent or, as is sometimes said, it established the standard according to which the agent should act. The broad scope of authority, or standard of action, established by the Communications Act is that public interest, convenience and necessity must be served. Within that framework the administrative agent is free to exercise its expert judgment; it cannot act unconstitutionally, for neither could its principal, the Congress, and the stream cannot rise higher than the source; it must proceed within the scope of the authority granted to it, that is to say, it must observe the standard established; and it cannot act arbitrarily or capriciously. . . . The doctrine is that the act of the administrative agent is the act of Congress itself; as long as the agent stays within the boundaries of the standard and does not act arbitrarily or capriciously. . . . It would be difficult, if not impossible, to formulate a precise and comprehensive definition of the term "public interest, convenience, or necessity," and it has been said often and properly by the courts that the facts of each case must be examined and must govern its determination.[4]

17.4 / Rights to Hearings and Appeals

As the Court remarked, the Commission may not act arbitrarily or capriciously in its decisions or rule making. In the first place, it cannot take any

[4] *WOKO, Inc.* v. *FCC*, 153 F. (2d) 623 at 628–629 (1946). See Section 19.8.

important action involving opposing interests without first holding a hearing and considering the points of view of the persons involved. If the Commission decides not to grant a license request, it must advise the applicant and others concerned of its objections; the applicant then has an opportunity to reply, and if the Commission still decides against the applicant, it must set the matter for hearing, "specifying with particularity the matters and things in issue [§ 309(e)]." If the Commission proposes to change a station's power, frequency, or time of operation, the licensee is automatically entitled to a hearing [§ 303(f) and § 316].

On the other hand, if the Commission grants an application *without* a hearing, the grant remains for thirty days subject to protest from "any party in interest"; if the protest shows the protestant to be a real party in interest raising specific issues, the Commission must hold a hearing on the matter and postpone the effective date of its decision [§ 309(d)].

After hearings are held, the hearing officers (either Commissioners or hearing examiners delegated for the purpose) must file an initial or tentative decision [§ 409]. Exceptions may then be filed by the parties involved, pointing out objections to the conclusions reached in the decision. If requested, the Commission must then consider oral arguments on the exceptions before issuing a final decision or order [§ 409(b)]. If the Commission wishes to revoke a license or issue a Cease and Desist Order, it must first invite the licensee to appear at a hearing to show cause why such action should not be taken [§ 312(c)]. In all these proceedings the Commission is governed by the Administrative Procedures Act, which applies in general to agencies of the federal government. Finally, a "person aggrieved or whose interests are adversely affected" by a decision or order which grows out of a hearing may also petition for a rehearing, although the Commission may use its own discretion in granting such requests [§ 405].

Although the FCC is only quasi-judicial (*i.e.,* is not strictly speaking a court of law), its procedures must conform in general to judicial standards and it must, of course, observe the safeguards provided by the Constitution. On occasion judges have reminded the FCC of these obligations:

. . . it will be helpful to spell out the process which a commission properly follows in reaching a decision. The process necessarily includes at least four parts: (1) Evidence must be taken and weighed, both as to its accuracy and credibility; (2) from attentive consideration of this evidence a determination of facts of a basic or underlying nature must be reached; (3) from these basic facts the ultimate facts, usually in the language of statute, are to be inferred, or not, as the case may be; (4) from this finding the decision will follow by the application of the statutory criterion.

*　　*　　*　　*　　*

Administrative orders, quasi-judicial in character, are void, if a hearing was denied, if that granted was inadequate or manifestly unfair, if the finding is contrary to the indisputable character of the evidence, or if the facts found do not as a matter of law support the order made. The commission may not capriciously make findings by administrative fiat. Such authority, however beneficently exercised in one case, could be injuriously exercised in another, is inconsistent with rational justice, and comes within the Constitution's condemnation of all arbitrary exercise of power.[5]

Even after all the safeguards of hearings, rehearings, initial decision, exceptions, and oral arguments have been exhausted, a person adversely affected by Commission rules or decisions still has a further recourse. Section 402 provides for appeals to the courts to enjoin, set aside, annul, or suspend Commission actions. Appeals go initially to the United States Court of Appeals for the District of Columbia. If the Court of Appeals fails to satisfy a litigant, he can petition the Supreme Court of the United States to review the decision of the lower court. The Supreme Court is not bound to accept the case if in its opinion it involves no substantial federal question.

All the materials developed at hearings and the other procedures prior to an appeal become part of the record for consideration by the courts. Generally speaking, the courts have taken the position that they should not substitute their judgment for that of the FCC, the body set up by Congress for the purpose of bringing expert judgment to bear on regulatory problems. The court usually confines its actions to determining whether the Commission has followed proper procedure, whether it has acted within its lawful powers, and whether it has been arbitrary or capricious in its conclusions. Supreme Court Justice Frankfurter explained:

Congress has charged the courts with the responsibility of saying whether the Commission has fairly exercised its discretion within the vaguish, penumbral bounds expressed by the standard of "public interest." It is our responsibility to say whether the Commission has been guided by proper considerations in bringing the deposit of its experience, the disciplined feel of the expert, to bear on applications for licenses in the public interest.[6]

17.5 / "Ownership" of Radio Frequencies

All the powers of the Commission, as indeed the effectiveness of the Act itself, revolve around the licensing power.[7] This in turn derives from the fundamental assertion of the Communications Act—that electromagnetic frequencies used for communication cannot be privately "owned":

---

[5] *Saginaw Broadcasting Co.* v. *FCC*, 96 F. (2d) 554 at 559 (1938); *White* v. *FRC*, 29 F. (2d) 113 at 115 (1928).

[6] *FCC* v. *RCA Communications, Inc.*, 346 U. S. 86 at 91 (1953).

[7] The reference here is to the licensing of *stations*. The Act also empowers the FCC to license *operators* of transmitters to ensure proper technical operation; such licenses (like station licenses) can be issued only to United States citizens [§ 318; § 303(1), (m)]. The FCC has set up several kinds of operators' licenses, classed according to the type of equipment for which the operator is to be responsible. FCC regional offices give examinations and issue licenses. The law requires licensed operators in attendance at certain classes of transmitters, but not in studios for the handling of studio equipment.

It is the purpose of this chapter, among other things, to maintain the control of the United States over all the channels of interstate and foreign radio transmission; and to provide for the use of such channels, but not the ownership thereof, by persons for limited periods of time, under licenses granted by Federal authority, and no such license shall be construed to create any right beyond the terms, conditions, and periods of the license. No person shall use or operate any apparatus for the transmission of energy or communications or signals by radio . . . except under and in accordance with this chapter and with a license in that behalf granted under the provisions of this chapter. [§ 301]

Congress emphasized this point requiring that a licensee sign a waiver "of any claim to the use of any particular frequency or of the ether as against the regulatory power of the United States because of the previous use of the same [§ 304]." Furthermore, although the FCC may determine the form of the licenses it issues, a license *must* include the condition that it "shall not vest in the licensee any right to operate the station nor any right in the use of the frequencies designated in the license beyond the term thereof nor in any other manner than authorized therein [§ 309 (h), (l)]."

This emphasis reflects the experience of the period prior to 1927, when regulation broke down because the law did not give the government unequivocal control of the broadcast frequencies. Congress foresaw, moreover, that introducing effective control was bound to encounter the claim that prior use of frequencies had conferred a kind of squatter's right on pioneer broadcasters.

The Act further safeguards the licensing power by providing that a license cannot even be issued until after a station has been constructed and tested; it can then be determined empirically that its signal does in fact conform to the requirements of the license. Hence the first step toward acquiring a broadcast license is to obtain a CP. The application for a CP requires all the information which will be requested in the license itself.

Upon the completion of any station for the construction . . . of which a permit has been granted, and upon it being made to appear to the Commission that all the terms, conditions, and obligations set forth in the application and permit have been fully met, and that no cause or circumstance arising or first coming to the knowledge of the Commission since the granting of the permit would, in the judgment of the Commission, make the operation of such a station against the public interest, the Commission shall issue a license to the lawful holder of said permit for the operation of said station. . . . [§ 319(c)]

Thus Congress made plain its intention of taking no chances on any misinterpretation: the radio frequencies are public property and accordingly must be operated in the public interest. The government may decide not only who shall be licensed to use this property, but whether a licensee shall be entitled to continue to use it after the first grant is made—for license renewals are not automatic but are subject to the discretion of the FCC [§ 307(d)]; moreover, a license can be revoked before the expiration of its term [§ 312]. This circumstance places broadcasting in the position of being less free of government control than nonlicensed businesses, and yet more free than public utilities or common carriers.

A basic Constitutional question raised by the establishment of federal control is whether radio communication is (1) interstate and (2) commerce. It must qualify in both these respects in order to be subject to federal control under the Interstate Commerce Clause of the Constitution. These questions were settled relatively early by the courts:

It does not seem to be open to question that radio transmission and reception among the states are interstate commerce. To be sure it is a new species of commerce. Nothing visible and tangible is transported. . . . The joint action of the transmitter owned by one person and the receiver owned by another is essential to the result. But that result is the transmission of intelligence, ideas, and entertainment. It is intercourse and that intercourse is commerce. . . . The suggestion that broadcasting which is not for profit is not commerce may be put aside as imposing an unwarranted limitation upon the power of Congress.[8]

Even though the intended service area of a given station lies entirely within a state, broadcasting may be regarded as interstate in scope, for there is no way of controlling the interference area of a signal.

Revoking licenses or deleting stations has been challenged as violating the Fifth Amendment by taking private property for government use and taking property without due process of law, but the courts have consistently upheld the power of the government to control the frequencies:

That the Congress had the power to give this authority to delete stations, in view of the limited radio facilities available and the confusion that would result from interferences, is not open to question. Those who operated broadcasting stations had no right superior to the exercise of this power of regulation. They necessarily made their investments and their contracts in the light of, and subject to, this paramount authority. This Court has had frequent occasion to observe that the power of Congress in the regulation of interstate commerce is not fettered by the necessity of maintaining existing arrangements which would conflict with the execution of its policy, as such a restriction would place the regulation in the hands of private individuals and withdraw from the control of Congress so much of the field as they might choose by prophetic discernment to bring within the range of their enterprises.[9]

This does not mean that the private enterprise based on the use of this public property, the radio frequencies, loses all claim to security. Only when a conflict of interest occurs—when the broadcaster's private interest conflicts with the public interest in the effective use of the electromagnetic spectrum— must the private interest give way. The classic instance of this kind of conflict arises when an existing licensee resists allowing another station in his

---

[8] *U.S.* v. *American Bond & Mortgage Co.,* 31 F. (2d) 448 at 454 (1929).

[9] *FRC* v. *Nelson Bros. Bond & Mortgage Co.,* 289 U. S. 266 at 282 (1933).

area on the ground that there is not enough business to support two stations. This "economic-injury" issue was adjudicated by the Supreme Court in *Sanders Brothers,* one of the most frequently cited of all broadcast cases:

Plainly it is not the purpose of the Act to protect a licensee against competition but to protect the public. Congress intended to leave competition in the business of broadcasting where it found it, to permit a licensee who was not interfering electrically with other broadcasters to survive or succumb according to his ability to make his programs attractive to the public.[10]

Even temporary licensed use of a frequency allocation is not open to all comers. Licensees must meet criteria of eligibility:

All applications for station licenses, or modifications or renewals thereof, shall set forth such facts as the Commission by regulation may prescribe as to citizenship, character, and financial, technical, and other qualifications of the applicant to operate the station; the ownership and location of the proposed station . . . the frequencies and the power desired to be used; the hours of the day or other periods of time during which it is proposed to operate the station; the purposes for which the station is to be used; and such other information as it may require. . . . [§ 308(b)]

Of these, the citizenship qualification is the most specific, since § 310(a) goes on to deny licenses to aliens. An applicant's financial qualification can be expressed quantitatively; he is expected to have enough money at his disposal not only to build a proposed station but to operate it at a loss for a time. Character qualifications are revealed by past and present conduct; on the negative side, for example, prior conviction of a crime or misrepresentation of facts to the Commission would be very damaging. Technical qualifications include knowledge and understanding of the law of broadcasting, station operations, programming, and engineering. The applicant is not expected to be a lawyer, a program director, or an engineer; but he must show that he has expert counsel in those matters in which he is not himself an expert.

A license or CP may be transferred to another operator only if the Commission finds that the transfer would serve public interest, convenience, and necessity; such a finding must be based on the transferee meeting the same conditions as an original applicant [§ 310(b)]. The intrinsic value of CP's and licenses led to "trafficking"—some investors obtained them merely to resell at a quick profit (Section 18.9). Congress thought the FCC unduly restrictive in its efforts to combat trafficking and amended § 310(b) by adding that in acting on applications for transfer, "the Commission may not consider whether the public interest, convenience, and necessity might be served by transfer to a person *other than the proposed* transferee or assignee [italics supplied]."

---

[10] *FCC* v. *Sanders Bros. Radio Station,* 309 U. S. 470 at 475 (1940).

Despite the fact that commercial broadcast licenses confer on their recipients an opportunity to profit—often very greatly—the Communications Act made no provision for payment by licensees for use of the spectrum, though the Fourth Radio Conference in 1925 had in fact suggested license fees ranging from $25 to $5 thousand. This omission seems the more surprising when one considers that the federal treasury bears the considerable cost (about $20 million in fiscal 1969) of administering the Act. As a result of a Congressional resolution of 1952 urging administrative agencies to become self-supporting, the FCC finally began charging nominal "filing fees" in 1964. The Appeals Court upheld the move and the Supreme Court refused to review the decision.[11] In 1970, the Commission proposed a new scale of both filing and grant fees which would realize enough revenue to cover its budget.[12]

17.6 / Uniqueness of Broadcasting

In Chapter 7 we saw how radically broadcasting departed from previous forms of communication enterprise. The Communications Act recognizes that peculiar and separate character by three interlocking definitions:

"Radio communication" or "communication by radio" means the transmission by radio of writing, signs, signals, pictures, and sounds of all kinds, including all instrumentalities, facilities, apparatus, and services . . . incidental to such transmissions. [§ 153(b)]

*   *   *   *   *

"Common carrier" or "carrier" means any person engaged as a common carrier for hire, in interstate or foreign communication by wire or radio or in interstate or foreign radio transmission of energy, except where reference is made to common carriers not subject to this chapter; but a person engaged in radio broadcasting shall not, insofar as such person is so engaged, be deemed a common carrier. [§ 153(h)]

*   *   *   *   *

"Broadcasting" means dissemination of radio communications intended to be received by the public, directly or by the intermediary of relay stations. [§ 153(o)]

Preliminarily, it should be observed that the legal definition includes television as well as sound transmission under the term "broadcasting." The most significant element in this series of definitions, however, is exclusion of broadcasting from the "common-carrier" category. This distinction is vital. The common-carrier concept (which extends to transportation systems such as railroads as well as to communication systems) applies to business enter-

---

[11] *Aeronautical Radio, Inc., et al.* v. *U. S. and FCC*, 335 F. (2d) 304 (1964).

[12] FCC, "Notice of Proposed Rule Making . . . Relating to Schedule of Fees," 35 *Fed. Reg.* 3815 (1970).

prises of such character that public policy requires their services to be made available equally to all. The Interstate Commerce Act makes it unlawful for a carrier subject to that Act to give "any undue or unreasonable preference or advantage" to one user of a carrier over another, or to subject any user to "any undue or unreasonable prejudice or disadvantage [Ch. I, § 3(1)]."

Carriers occupy a position of limited monopoly, since public policy forbids duplicate services where deterioration of service might result. One cannot build a railroad, start a bus line, inaugurate an air route, or install a telephone system for public hire without a license from either a state or a federal agency, depending on whether the proposed service is intrastate or interstate in scope. Such a license carries with it protection from competition, in return for which the licensee accepts close supervision of his business by the licensing agency.

Consider what would have been the consequences of applying the common-carrier concept to broadcasting: a station licensee would have had to accept all buyers of time on a first-come, first-served basis. The licensee could not have concerned himself with what the purchasers of time did with that time, so long as nothing unlawful was done. Licensees would have had no control whatever over what was said or shown on their facilities and hence could not have been held responsible for the character of the broadcasting service rendered.

All this would completely reverse the primary emphasis of broadcasting, which is on the interests of the *recipients* of the messages, not the *senders*. "It is the right of the viewers and listeners, not the right of the broadcasters, which is paramount," wrote the Supreme Court's Mr. Justice White.[13] This emphasis is appropriate because the senders are using a facility (*i.e.,* the electromagnetic spectrum) belonging to the recipients. Those who profit economically from the commercial broadcasting service—licensees and advertisers—do so only in consideration of a service rendered to the general public.

One further point about the definition of broadcasting: it is a form of communication *intended* to be received by the public. This phrase automatically excludes all forms of communication which, though perhaps *receivable* by the public, aim at specific recipients—for example, direct communication to individuals in the audience by broadcast performers. Such a communication is a common-carrier use of broadcasting. The FCC does not make an issue of the casual "hellos," waves of the hand, anniversary greetings, etc., which frequently occur. However, direct communications have been more substantial in some cases. For example, a station received license renewal only after discontinuing programs of direct personal advice by an astrologer and a "spiritual psychologist." The Commission remarked:

. . . their practices involved the transmissions of point-to-point or individual messages that could not reasonably be said to have any general interest for the public. Broadcasting is by definition and essential characteristics a service for the general public. The use of a broadcast station for point-to-point delivery of messages is

---

[13] *Red Lion Broadcasting Co.* v. *FCC; U. S.* v. *Radio Television News Directors Association,* 395 U. S. 367 at 390 (1969).

inconsistent with the terms of the station license and the regulations under which licenses are issued.[14]

An illustration of the practical significance of the definition of broadcasting is found in the case of "functional" FM operation, *i.e.,* providing special programs for stores, busses, and other locations (Section 9.9). The FCC found this type of service to be nonbroadcast in character and provides a special class of license—a Subsidiary Communications Authorization—to permit FM stations to offer this service.

. . . in so far as the programming is directed to the special interests of the industrial, mercantile, transportation, or other subscribers and is not primarily intended for reception by the general public, [functional FM] must be characterized *predominantly* non-broadcast in nature. The fact that a large portion of these transmissions—including most of the program material—may be received by the general public on home receivers as an incidental by-product of the primary intent of the transmission does not change this rationale.[15]

Since transmissions under a Subsidiary Communications Authorization are not broadcasting, they come under the protection of § 605 of the Communications Act, which forbids the unauthorized divulgence or publication of communications subject to the Act. Broadcasting is, necessarily, made an exception to this rule. The applicability of § 605 to functional FM stations, however, empowers the stations to prevent unauthorized persons from installing receivers to take advantage of their service. As long as the service was "broadcasting" they could not prevent this form of piracy.

17.7 / Equitable Distribution of Service

The principle of public ownership of the frequencies and the definition of broadcasting entitle *all* the people to service. Section 151 of the Act, it will be recalled (Section 17.2), speaks of "all the people of the United States." With more specific reference to broadcasting:

In considering applications for licenses, and modifications and renewals thereof, when and insofar as there is demand for the same, the Commission shall make such distribution of licenses, frequencies, hours of operation, and of power among the several States and communities as to provide a fair, efficient, and equitable distribution of radio service to each of the same. [§ 307(b)]

---

[14] *In re Scroggin & Co. Bank (KFEQ),* 1 FCC 194 at 196 (1935). Other similar cases have involved programs of financial advice, horse-racing information, and medical advice. The concept of broadcasting as "a service for the public" does not rule out the special-interest station which aims the bulk of its programming to a particular public, such as a specific ethnic or cultural group. Educational broadcasting is excepted from the rule.

[15] FCC, "Amendment of Parts 2 and 3 of the Commission's Rules and Regulations . . . ," 20 *Fed. Reg.* 1821 (1955).

Since the Commission is limited by the element of "demand" (from would-be licensees), it cannot arrive at an ideal distribution of facilities. The demand will naturally tend to exceed the supply in areas of highly concentrated population and commercial activity. By setting up a nationwide allocation table of television channels in advance of authorizing the service, the Commission prevented inequalities which would undoubtedly have arisen if television allocations had been governed entirely by uncontrolled economic demands.

"Fair, efficient, and equitable distribution of radio services" has been interpreted to mean more than simply providing a local program service for the benefit of listeners and viewers. Both the FRC and the FCC considered it vital to provide local *access* to broadcast facilities for the benefit of originators of communications other than licensees, as well as for the benefit of receivers of communications. This interpretation has been supported by the Supreme Court: "Fairness to communities is furthered by a recognition of local needs for a community radio mouthpiece."[16] Local access means an opportunity for local businesses to use the medium for advertising, for local candidates to appeal for political support, for local public-service agencies to promote their objectives, for representatives of local controversial issues to air their points of view, for local governments to inform the electorate, for local educational and cultural institutions to broaden their community service, for local newsmen to report on community happenings, for local talent to have an outlet, and so on. Ideally, a station serves its area as a means of community self-expression, giving it a broadcast voice as well as a broadcast ear.

The requirement of equitable distribution of service, combined with the interpretation that the Act means by this *local* stations, has had a profound effect on the nature of the broadcasting service. From the point of view of sheer efficiency (note that § 307(b) speaks of a "fair, *efficient,* and equitable distribution of radio service") it would be better to use far fewer but much more powerful stations. That way, distributing service could in fact be fairer, more efficient, and more equitable. The FRC and FCC preferred to sacrifice efficiency in order to preserve localness. The President's Task Force on Communications Policy corroborated this view in 1968:

No aspect of communications policy is more important than measures or arrangements which would permit or encourage the growth of communications of all kinds within localities: the discussion of local issues; contact with local or regional political leaders; tapping local talents; the use of local resources in education, technology, sports, and expression of all sorts of local interests.[17]

To encourage more local involvement in FCC proceedings, Congress amended the Communications Act to require local public notice of the filing of broadcast applications and the designation of hearings on such applica-

---

[16] *FCC* v. *Allentown Broadcasting Corp.,* 349 U. S. 358 at 363 (1955).

[17] President's Task Force on Communications Policy, *Final Report* (Washington: Government Printing Office, 1968), pp. VII–5–6.

tions. Congress also expects the Commission to consider whether public interest, convenience, or necessity would be served by holding such hearings in the locale of the proposed station rather than in Washington, D. C. [§ 311].

17.8 / Program Regulation and the First Amendment

Congress explicitly classified broadcasting as a form of communication covered by the word "speech" in the First Amendment:

Nothing in this chapter shall be understood or construed to give the Commission the power of censorship over the radio communications or signals transmitted by any radio station, and no regulation or condition shall be promulgated or fixed by the Commission which shall interfere with the right of free speech by means of radio communication. [§ 326]

Yet Congress evidently also recognized that the uniqueness of broadcasting (Section 17.4 above) entitled it to special treatment, different from the conventional "press." For it went on to include in the Act provisions restricting the freedom of broadcast-station owners to say whatever they wanted to on the air. Most substantial and controversial of these restrictions concerns the broadcast rights of candidates for public office—the "equal-time" provision:

(a) If any licensee shall permit any person who is a legally qualified candidate for any public office to use a broadcasting station, he shall afford equal opportunities to all other such candidates for that office in the use of such broadcasting station: *Provided,* That such licensee shall have no power of censorship over the material broadcast under the provisions of this section. No obligation is hereby imposed upon any licensee to allow the use of its station by any such candidate. [§ 315]

Congress amended § 315 on two occasions. The amendments aimed at stopping broadcasters from making higher than normal charges to political candidates and at preventing claimants for equal time from exploiting normal news coverage of rival political candidates' activities. Section 315(a) now continues:

Appearance by a legally qualified candidate on any—

(1) bona fide newscast,

(2) bona fide news interview,

(3) bona fide news documentary (if the appearance of the candidate is incidental to the presentation of the subject or subjects covered by the news documentary), or

(4) on-the-spot coverage of bona fide news events (including but not limited to political conventions and activities incidental thereto),

shall not be deemed to be use of a broadcasting station within the meaning of this subsection. Nothing in the foregoing sentence shall be construed as relieving broadcasters, in connection with the presentation of newscasts, news interviews, news documentaries, and on-the-spot coverage of news events, from the obligation imposed upon them under this chapter to operate in the public interest and to afford reasonable opportunity for the discussion of conflicting views on issues of public importance.

(b) The charges made for the use of any broadcasting station for any of the purposes set forth in this section shall not exceed the charges made for comparable use of such station for other purposes.

The first sentence of § 315(a) creates a dilemma for licensees which tends to defeat the purpose of the law: if, say, a national network wanted to donate time to the presidential candidates of the major national parties, it would open itself up to demands for "equal time" from a swarm of insignificant though legally qualified candidates representing miniscule constituencies. As a result, appearances of the major political candidates have usually been limited to paid time periods. In 1960, as an experiment, Congress temporarily suspended this part of § 315 for that year's candidates for President and Vice President of the United States only. This suspension enabled the networks to stage the "Great Debate" series between Presidential candidates Kennedy and Nixon (Section 24.3). Without the suspension, § 315 would have entitled *fourteen* minor candidates to equal free time. Congress decided not to continue the suspension in effect.

Congress added a related proviso on political broadcasts in the Public Broadcasting Act of 1967. Section 399 provides that noncommercial educational stations may not editorialize or support candidates for political office. A different kind of political exclusion appears in § 397, providing that nothing in the public-broadcasting sections shall be deemed "to authorize any department, agency, officer, or employee of the United States to exert any direction, supervision, or control over educational television broadcasting or over the curriculum, program of instruction, or personnel of any educational institution, school system, or educational broadcasting station or system."

The proviso against censorship in § 315(a) caused still another dilemma for broadcasters. Though forbidden by federal law to censor political candidates' scripts, they could at the same time be held responsible for libel in such scripts under state laws. The Supreme Court resolved the conflict in 1959. In exempting stations from suit under § 315(a), the Court said: "We have not hesitated to abrogate state law where satisfied that its enforcement would stand 'as an obstacle in the accomplishment and execution of the full purposes and objectives of Congress.' "[18]

The last sentence in § 315(a), concerning "reasonable opportunity for discussion of conflicting views," is considered of key importance as statutory confirmation of the FCC's emphasis on the "fairness doctrine" (Section 20.9) as an element in meeting the public-interest requirements of licensees.

Aside from these § 315 regulations, the Act contains relatively few specific rules regarding programs. Section 317 requires that anything broadcast for which payment is made (whether in cash or in kind) must be announced as

---

[18] *Farmers Educational and Cooperative Union of America* v. *WDAY, Inc.,* 360 U. S. 525 at 535 (1959).

paid for or furnished by the person responsible. An exception is made for
the use of stage properties and the like. This regulation links up with § 508,
requiring disclosure of payola-plugola types of payments, which Congress
added to the Act after investigating these practices. Section 509, another
amendment, prohibits rigging the outcome of contests. Federal law forbids
obscenity, lotteries, and fraud on radio, but as part of the Criminal Code
rather than the Communications Act (Section 17.11).

Although the Act thus gives the FCC little explicit control over programs,
it does grant wide latitude indirectly and by implication. Operation in accordance with "the public interest, convenience, and necessity," as required by
the Act, can be judged only in the light of a station's performance. A station's
performance consists, of course, of a program service. The Commission takes
the position—supported by the courts—that the licensee alone must assume
direct responsibility for programs; but the FCC in turn must hold the licensee
responsible for programming to satisfy the public interest, convenience, and
necessity. The Commission will not substitute its judgment for that of the
licensee on individual program decisions, but it may review the *overall* performance of the licensee—its program plans and promises and their ful-
fillment.

Thus the Commission, despite the prohibition against censorship in § 326
of the Act, does exert influence over the general shape of programming—to
an extent that would certainly not be tolerated in the print media. The justification lies in viewing broadcasting as a distinctively different medium. The
Supreme Court has repeatedly expressed this distinction. For example:

Although broadcasting is clearly a medium affected by a First Amendment interest
. . . differences in the characters of the new media justify differences in the First
Amendment standards applied to them.[19]

17.9 / Comsat and Public Broadcasting

In 1962, Congress passed the Communications Satellite Act, which appears
as §§ 701–744 of Title 47. The Act sets up a combination government-
private corporation responsible for operating an international satellite relay
system (Comsat). It represents the United States in the International Telecommunications Satellite Consortium (Intelsat), which it also manages. Intelsat
had sixty-eight member countries by 1969. The FCC shares responsibility
for the system with the President and the National Aeronautics and Space
Administration (NASA). The latter provides the launch facilities for Comsat's stations. The FCC's role includes ensuring equal access to the system by
competing carriers—which in turn requires technical compatibility between

---

[19] *Red Lion Broadcasting Co.* v. *FCC; U. S.* v. *Radio Television News Directors Association,* at 386.

the satellites and existing systems—and authorizing the construction of earth stations, of which there were twenty-one worldwide in 1969.[20]

Comsat is fully subject to the common-carrier provisions of the Communications Act. It is known as "the carrier's carrier," its chief customers being the existing terrestrial common-carrier systems. In 1968, Comsat charged $650 for the first ten minutes and $17 for each additional minute to transmit television (both sound and picture) between the United States and Europe. By the end of 1967, the Corporation had begun to show a profit.

Also in 1962, Congress passed the Educational TV Facilities Act, the first explicit expression of federal responsibility for noncommercial broadcasting. The Act authorized $32 million over a five-year period in matching funds, to be awarded by the Department of Health, Education, and Welfare, for constructing educational-television stations. The Public Broadcasting Act of 1967 renewed the facilities-aid arrangement for another three years, authorizing $38 million and extending the grants to educational radio as well as television.

The 1967 Act also established a Corporation for Public Broadcasting. As a matter of policy, Congress declared:

. . . it is necessary and appropriate for the Federal Government to complement, assist, and support a national policy that will most effectively make noncommercial educational radio and television service available to all citizens of the United States. . . . [§ 396(a)(5)]

The Corporation, which "will not be an agency or establishment of the United States Government [§ 396(b)]," is governed by a fifteen-man board of directors appointed by the President with the advice and consent of the Senate. Among the purposes and activities of the Corporation, § 396 of the Act lists:

Facilitating "full development of educational broadcasting in which programs of high quality, obtained from diverse sources, will be made available to noncommercial educational television or radio broadcast stations, with strict adherence to objectivity and balance in all programs or series of programs of a controversial nature"

Assisting in setting up network interconnection so that all stations "that wish to may broadcast the programs at times chosen by the stations"; common carriers are authorized to give free service or reduced rates to such networks, subject to FCC approval

Carrying out its work "in ways that will most effectively assure maximum freedom from interference with or control of program content or other activities"

Making contracts and grants for production of programs

---

[20] FCC, *Thirty-Fifth Annual Report* (Washington: Government Printing Office, 1970), pp. 73–77.

Establishing and maintaining a library and archives

Encouraging development of new stations

Conducting research and training

In carrying out these functions, the Corporation may not own any facilities itself. Congress authorized $9 million to support the CPB for fiscal 1967–1968.

The third item in the Public Broadcasting Act authorized a half million dollars for the Secretary of Health, Education, and Welfare to make

. . . a comprehensive study of instructional television and radio (including broadcast, closed circuit, community antenna television, and instructional television fixed services and two-way communication of data links and computers) and their relationship to each other and to instructional materials such as videotapes, films, discs, computers, and other educational materials and devices, and such other aspects thereof as may be of assistance in determining whether and what Federal aid should be provided for instructional radio and television and the form that aid should take. . . . [§ 301]

This document was duly published in March, 1970.[21]

17.10 / Enforcement Provisions

The FCC has at its disposal measures for enforcing the Communications Act and its own Rules and Regulations at six different levels of urgency. The mildest action consists simply of a letter stating the FCC's views, usually in response to a complaint against a licensee from a third party. These letters normally take the form of a request for the station's side of the story, but recipients often read implied threats into them. Stations

. . . soon learned that the easiest way to dispose of the matter without incurring substantial legal fees was to apologize for the isolated lapse of judgment, promising to take corrective measures. Thus the FCC letter was usually regarded as less of an enquiry than a request for corrective action.[22]

This informal method, along with individual public statements Commissioners often make, has been called the "raised-eyebrow" technique of regulation—a threat of punitive action, stated or implied, which often secures compliance as effectively as action itself.

In 1952, Congress amended the Act to authorize the mildest formal enforcement procedure, the Cease and Desist Order [§ 312(b)]. The FCC

---

[21] Commission on Instructional Technology ("McMurrin Commission"), *To Improve Learning: A Report to the President and the Congress of the United States,* House Committee on Education and Labor (Washington: Government Printing Office, 1970).

[22] Gene R. Stebbins, "Pacifica's Battle for Free Expression," *Educational Broadcasting Review,* IV (June, 1970), 21.

itself requested this change, feeling it needed an enforcement instrument less final than loss of license:

The record of the Commission shows that there are very few revocations and very few denials of licenses since it does not wish to impose this harsh remedy. The Commission is of the opinion that the Broadcasting industry believes it can get away with almost anything because the Commission will not revoke their licenses or deny an application for renewal.[23]

To effectuate a Cease and Desist Order, the FCC must first issue a "show-cause" order, giving the alleged offender an opportunity to give reasons why the Order should not be issued. The Cease and Desist Order seems to be unduly cumbersome in relation to its severity as a penalty. Accordingly, in 1960, still another amendment provided for "forfeitures" (in effect fines) of up to $1 thousand per day of violation, with a maximum of $10 thousand [§ 503(b)].

The most severe penalties directly affect licenses. In ascending order of gravity, they are short-term renewals [§ 307(d)], denial of renewal at the expiration of a license period [§ 307(d)], and revocation [§ 312(a)]. In practice, the most common enforcement procedure affecting licenses is "designation for hearing" at license-renewal time. This procedure enables the Commission and interested third parties to raise questions about whether the public interest, convenience, and necessity would be served by the proposed renewal. Until 1969, interested third parties were confined to other *licensees* claiming either economic injury or signal interference. In that year, the Appeals Court reconfirmed an earlier decision asserting the right of the *public* affected by a station's service to have legal standing to intervene in a renewal hearing.

The case dated back to 1955, with the beginning of a series of complaints against WLBT, a Jackson, Mississippi, television station, alleging overcommercialization, unfair treatment of news, and discrimination against the Negro population, which amounted to nearly half the residents within the station's viewing area. The Commission renewed WLBT's license in 1958 on finding that the instances of unfairness had been "isolated" cases. The alleged unfairness continued. When WLBT's 1964 renewal time came around, the United Church of Christ, through its Office of Communication, sought to intervene on behalf of the viewers alleged to have been discriminated against. The Commission denied the petition to intervene, stating that the petitioners "can assert no greater interest or claim of injury than members of the general public." The Commission argued that the right to intervene had to be predicated on "a legally protected interest or an injury which is direct and substantial."[24] Considering that the station's programming adversely affected

---

[23] Testimony of Wayne Coy, FCC Chairman, in House Committee on Interstate and Foreign Commerce, *Amending Communications Act of 1934,* Hearings on S. 658, 88th Cong., 1st Sess. (Washington: Government Printing Office, 1951), p. 137.

[24] *Office of Communication of the United Church of Christ* v. *FCC,* 359 F. (2d) 994 at 999 (1966).

nearly half of the potential audience, the injury seemed to qualify as both direct and substantial. Nevertheless, the Commission, without a hearing, once more renewed WLBT, though this time on one year's probation. The United Church of Christ appealed the decision, and the Court reversed the FCC, requiring it to withdraw the license extension, set hearings on renewal, and to allow public intervention at the hearings.[25]

An idea of the frequency with which the FCC invokes the more serious sanctions can be gained from the record for fiscal 1969:

Forfeitures. Two hundred and eighteen cases (as against only twenty-three in 1964, when the fines were introduced), ranging in amount from $25 to the maximum, $10 thousand. Examples: fraudulent billing, broadcasting lottery information, engineering-rule violations.

Short-term renewals. Five cases. Example: "failure to meet licensee responsibilities in making claims as to size of an audience."

Revocations and renewal denials. Final action on five cases. Example: renewal denied a Newark, N. J., station "on issues which include misrepresentation to the Commission, inadequate licensee control over operation of station, failure to identify sponsorship of broadcast matter, and failure to file time-broker contracts."[26]

17.11 / Other Laws Affecting Broadcasting

The Communications Act expressly charges the FCC with carrying out the provisions of international treaties [*e.g.,* § 303(r)]. Those of most immediate concern involve neighboring countries—Canada, Mexico, and the offshore islands. The North American Regional Broadcast Agreement (NARBA), last renewed in 1960, controls AM regional broadcasting-channel allocations (see Table 2.2). Supplemental agreements cover FM and television.

Broader international coordination takes place through the International Telecommunication Union, whose origins were traced in Section 8.1. Over 130 countries belong to the ITU. The Union's radio division, the International Radio Consultative Committee (CCIR), has fourteen study groups dealing with specialized radio problems such as propagation, relay systems, vocabulary, and space communication. The ITU's International Frequency Registration Board receives and publishes notifications of frequency usage from member countries and endeavors to minimize interference by obtaining compliance with international agreements on frequency allocations. The FCC acts for both government and nongovernment services in dealing with the IFRB on behalf of the United States.[27]

---

[25] *Office of Communication of the United Church of Christ* v. *FCC,* 16 R. R. 2095 (1969).

[26] FCC, *Thirty-Fifth Annual Report,* pp. 53–55.

[27] *Ibid.,* pp. 98–100.

The ITU assigns initial letters to be used for radio call signs throughout the world. The letters "K", "N," and "W" and part of the "A" series have been assigned to the United States. Section 303(o) of the Communications Act empowers the FCC to designate station call letters to American non-government stations. American broadcasting stations use four-letter call signs, beginning with "K" if located west of the Mississippi, with "W" if located east. A few pioneer stations (KDKA, Pittsburgh; KOA, Denver) have been allowed to retain call signs of different patterns, authorized before the present rules were adopted. New stations may select their own call-letter combination in accordance with the rules.

Prohibitions against obscenity, fraud, and lotteries on radio, once part of the Communications Act, were recodified as part of Title 18 of the Civil Code. Of these, the antilottery statute comes most frequently into play because of the widespread use of contests in promoting stations and advertised products. In fact, the NAB has issued a guide to assist licensees in evaluating the legality of contests.[28]

A number of federal agencies take an interest in controlling broadcast advertising. Chief among these, the Federal Trade Commission, is concerned, among other things, with "the use of false and misleading advertising concerning, and the misbranding of, commodities, respecting the materials and ingredients of which they are composed, their quality, purity, origin, source, attributes, or properties or nature of manufacture, and selling them under such name and circumstances as to deceive the public." As an aspect of fair trade, the FTC also has jurisdiction over making "false and disparaging statements respecting a competitor's products and business." The FTC examines samples of radio and television continuities as well as other advertising.

Most allegations of illegal advertising by the FTC are settled by "stipulation," *i.e.,* the advertiser changes the questionable practice voluntarily. If the advertiser chooses not to accede, the FTC can issue a Cease and Desist Order and secure compliance through the courts. FTC complaints have not been confined to the fly-by-night advertisers of unethical products and services; a great many of the well-known major advertisers have been cited as well.

As carriers of unfair advertising, stations are relatively immune from legal punishment other than FCC action. Under the Wheeler-Lea Act of 1938 (amending the FTC Act) a station is held responsible for fraudulent advertising only if it prepares the broadcast material itself; if it did not prepare the material it can absolve itself by naming the source. Licensees are responsible, however, for violations of the Food and Drug Administration standards, and the Post Office Department can bar the use of the mails to stations engaged in fraudulent advertising. A "fraud by radio" provision of the United States Criminal Code enables the Department of Justice to attack the source

---

[28] National Association of Broadcasters, "Broadcasting and the Lottery Laws," 4th ed. (Washington: The Association, April, 1962).

of advertising directly; the broadcaster is at fault only insofar as he "know-ingly permits" transmission of the material.

Insofar as broadcasting functions as a news medium it is generally subject to the body of statutes and precedents known informally as the "law of the press." Gillmor and Barron, in their authoritative casebook, *Mass Communication Law,* remark that "one of the startling realities of the law of broadcasting as compared to the law of the press is that the legal framework of broadcasting is altogether different from that of the press."[29] Broadcasting operates within an elaborate statutory framework, the Communications Act, whereas the conventional press relies on a framework of tradition and precedent built up over the years by case law. And, as we have had repeated occasion to point out (*e.g.,* Section 17.5), broadcasting has unique features which set it apart from other media, even with respect to the applicability of the First Amendment. Nevertheless, the list of press-law topics selected for discussion by Gillmor and Barron obviously has relevance to broadcasting: libel, obscenity, fair trial, freedom of access to information, freedom to travel, right of privacy, lobbying, antitrust laws, labor laws, advertising, copyright.

Virtually every press-law issue involves—in the background if not in the forefront as the pivot of the argument—the Constitutional question of free speech. Moreover, this question is fundamental to the whole structure of broadcast regulation. We will devote special chapters to it, but first, let us see how the FCC puts into practical effect the organic law of broadcasting outlined in the present chapter.

---

[29] Donald M. Gillmor and Jerome A. Barron, *Mass Communication Law: Cases and Comment* (St. Paul, Minn.: West, 1969), p. 641.

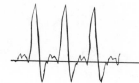

18

ADMINISTRATION OF THE LAW: THE FCC AT WORK

Starting with the Interstate Commerce Commission in 1887, Congress set up a whole series of independent regulatory federal agencies to supervise private activities in commerce, utilities, transportation, labor, finance, communication, and other such dynamic fields. As one of these agencies, the Federal Communications Commission plays a hybrid role which blurs the traditional lines of demarcation among the Legislative, Executive, and Judicial branches of American government. The FCC functions as an arm of Congress (Section 17.1), but most of its work is executive in character—carrying out laws enacted by the Legislature. Insofar as it interprets these laws and adjudicates applications and appeals, its function verges on the judicial. When it makes rules and regulations, it acts in a quasi-legislative capacity.

This mixed responsibility is reflected in the way the Commission is set up. Congress created the FCC and defined its scope of operation. On the other hand, the President appoints the Commissioners, though his choice must be approved by the Senate. Sometimes the Senate holds extensive hearings on appointments, effectively reminding appointees of their responsibility to Congress.[1] Moreover, Congress constantly looks over the shoulder of the Commission. Every major question that comes before it is likely to be looked into by the Senate Interstate Commerce Committee, the House Interstate and Foreign Commerce Committee, a special committee, or occasionally one of the other standing committees of Congress. Finally, Congress always has the last word, since it approves the FCC budget and has the power to change the Communications Act itself.

---

[1] For an example, see Senate Committee on Interstate Commerce, *Confirmation of the Members of the Federal Communications Commission,* Hearings (Washington: Government Printing Office, 1935). These hearings concerned six of the original appointees: Thad H. Brown and Eugene O. Sykes, previously members of the FRC; Norman Case, former Governor of Rhode Island; George H. Payne, an editor; Irvin Stewart, formerly a communications specialist with the Department of State; and Paul Walker, formerly a state utilities commissioner.

Figure 18.1
FCC Broadcast Bureau organization chart

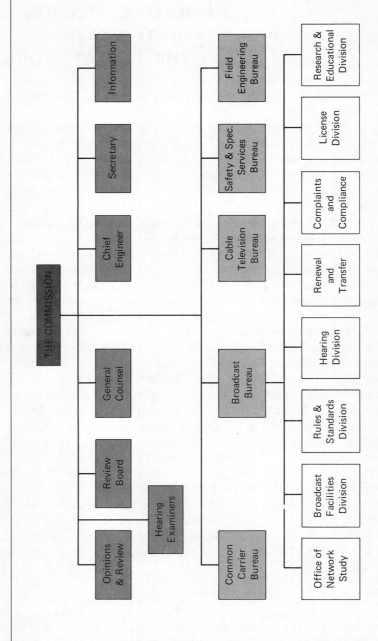

Source: Data in FCC, *Thirty-Fifth Annual Report* (Washington: Government Printing Office, 1970), p. 228.

18.1 / Organization of the FCC

As indicated in Figure 18.1, the FCC divides its operations into five functional bureaus (CATV was elevated to bureau status in 1970). About 1,500 employees staff the Washington headquarters and forty-eight field offices and monitoring stations. The Commission's fiscal 1969 budget amounted to $20.7 million. Filing fees earned back less than a quarter of this expense, but increases in fees were planned to cover the full expense of operations in the future (Section 17.5).

Although common-carrier and safety-special services involve many more licenses than broadcasting (Table 1.2), the Broadcast Bureau deals generally with more controversial questions and carries a heavier load of decision making and litigation. A few statistics from the Commission's *Thirty-Fifth Annual Report* will give an idea of its overall work load. During fiscal 1969, the Commission handled:

39,398	engineering-infraction notices
2,352	unlicensed-station detections
14,475	station inspections
20,978	interference complaints
40	international conferences
100	equipment-type approvals
208	broadcast hearings
58,000	public complaints, comments, and inquiries about broadcasting
902,500	applications
16	comments or appearances concerning Congressional bills
120	court proceedings

18.2 / FCC Rules and Regulations

The origin of the FCC Rules and Regulations has been previously described (Section 8.6). New rules appear first in the form of proposals, so that interested parties may have an opportunity to comment. On complex matters (such as, for example, the rules governing chain broadcasting or color television), extensive hearings or fact-gathering investigations may be conducted. When finally adopted, rules go into official effect after publication in the *Federal Register*.[2]

An example comparing the sparseness of the Communications Act with the elaborateness of the corresponding FCC rules will show the relationship between the two. The Communications Act provides as follows:

§ 303. Except as otherwise provided in this Act, the Commission from time to time, as public convenience, interest, or necessity requires shall—

* * * * *

---

[2] See Bibliographical Notes.

(j) Have authority to make general rules and regulations requiring stations to keep such records of programs, transmissions of energy, communications, or signals as it may deem desirable.

In practice, the Commission requires broadcast stations to keep two types of records: one covering the technical operation of transmitters, the other covering the content of programming. The rules for the latter follow, in part:

§ 73.670 *Program Log.*   (a) The following entries shall be made in the program log:

(1) *For each program.*   (i) An entry identifying the program by name or title.

(ii) An entry of the time each program begins and ends. If programs are broadcast during which separately identifiable program units of a different type or source are presented, and if the licensee wishes to count such units separately, the beginning and ending time for the longer program need be entered only once for the entire program. The program units which the licensee wishes to count separately shall be entered underneath the entry for a longer program, with the beginning and ending time of each such unit, and with the entry indented or otherwise distinguished so as to make it clear that the program unit referred to was broadcast within the longer program.

(iii) An entry classifying each program as to type, using the definitions set forth in Note 1 at the end of this section.

(iv) An entry classifying each program as to source, using the definitions set forth in Note 2 at the end of this section. (For network programs, also give name or initials of network, *e.g.,* ABC, CBS, NBC.)

(v) An entry for each program presenting a political candidate, showing the name and political affiliation of such candidate.

(2) *For commercial matter.*   (i) An entry identifying (*a*) the sponsor(s) of the program; (*b*) the person(s) who paid for the announcement, or (*c*) the person(s) who furnished materials or services referred to in § 73.654(d). If the title of a sponsored program includes the name of the sponsor, *e.g.,* XYZ News, a separate entry for the sponsor is not required. See Note 3 at the end of this section for definition of commercial matter.

(ii) An entry or entries showing the total duration of commercial matter in each hourly time segment (beginning on the hour) or the duration of each commercial message (commercial continuity in sponsored programs, or commercial announcement) in each hour. See Note 5 at the end of this section for statement as to computation of commercial time.

(iii) An entry showing that the appropriate announcement(s) (sponsorship, furnishing material or services, etc.) have been made as required by section 317 of the Communications Act and § 73.654. A check mark ($\sqrt{}$) will suffice but shall be made in such a way as to indicate the matter to which it relates.

(3) *For public service announcements.*   (i) An entry showing that a public service announcement (PSA) has been broadcast together with the name of the organization or interest on whose behalf it is made. See Note 4 at the end of this section for definition of a public service announcement.

(4) *For other announcements.*   (i) An entry of the time that each required

station identification announcement is made (call letters and licensed location; see § 73.652).

(ii) An entry for each announcement presenting a political candidate, showing the name and political affiliation of such candidate.

(iii) An entry for each announcement made pursuant to the local notice requirements of §§ 1.580 (pregrant) and 1.594 (designation for hearing) of this chapter, showing the time it was broadcast.

(iv) An entry showing that a mechanical reproduction announcement has been made in accordance with the provisions of § 73.653.

(b) Program log entries may be made either at the time of or prior to broadcast. A station broadcasting the programs of a national network which will supply it with all information as to such programs, commercial matter and other announcements for the composite week need not log such data but shall record in its log the time when it joined the network, the name of each network program broadcast, the time it leaves the network, and any nonnetwork matter broadcast required to be logged. The information supplied by the network, for the composite week which the station will use in its renewal application, shall be retained with the program logs and associated with the log pages to which it relates.

*   *   *   *   *

NOTE 1. *Program type definitions.* The definitions of the first eight types of programs (a) through (h) are intended not to overlap each other and will normally include all the various programs broadcast. Definitions (i) through (k) are subcategories and the programs classified thereunder will also be classified under one of the appropriate first eight types. There may also be further duplication within types (i) through (k); (*e.g.*, a program presenting a candidate for public office, prepared by an educational institution, would be classified as Public Affairs (PA), Political (POL), and Educational Institution (ED)).

(a) *Agricultural programs* (A) include market reports, farming, or other information specifically addressed, or primarily of interest, to the agricultural population.

(b) *Entertainment programs* (E) include all programs intended primarily as entertainment, such as music, drama, variety, comedy, quiz, etc.

(c) *News programs* (N) include reports dealing with current local, national, and international events, including weather and stock market reports; and when an integral part of a news program, commentary, analysis, and sports news.

(d) *Public affairs programs* (PA) include talks, commentaries, discussions, speeches, editorials, political programs, documentaries, forums, panels, round tables, and similar programs primarily concerning local, national, and international public affairs.

(e) *Religious programs* (R) include sermons or devotionals; religious news; and music, drama, and other types of programs designed primarily for religious purposes.

(f) *Instructional programs* (I) include programs (other than those classified under Agricultural, News, Public Affairs, Religious or Sports) involving the discussion of, or primarily designed to further an appreciation or understanding of, literature, music, fine arts, history, geography, and the natural and social sciences;

and programs devoted to occupational and vocational instruction, instruction with respect to hobbies, and similar programs intended primarily to instruct.

(g) *Sports programs* (S) include play-by-play and pre- or post-game related activities and separate programs of sports instruction, news or information (*e.g.,* fishing opportunities, golfing instructions, etc.).

(h) *Other programs* (O) include all programs not falling within definitions (a) through (g).

(i) *Editorials* (EDIT) include programs presented for the purpose of stating opinions of the licensee.

(j) *Political programs* (POL) include those which present candidates for public office or which give expressions (other than in station editorials) to views on such candidates or on issues subject to public ballot.

(k) *Educational Institution programs* (ED) include any program prepared by, in behalf of, or in cooperation with, educational institutions, educational organizations, libraries, museums, PTA's or similar organizations. Sports programs shall not be included.

NOTE 2. *Program source definitions.* (a) *A local program* (L) is any program originated or produced by the station, or for the production of which the station is substantially responsible, and employing live talent more than 50 per cent of the time. Such a program, taped, recorded, or filmed for later broadcast shall be classified by the station as local. A local program fed to a network shall be classified by the originating station as local. All nonnetwork news programs may be classified as local. Programs primarily featuring syndicated or feature films or other non-locally recorded programs shall be classified as "Recorded" (REC) even though a station personality appears in connection with such material. However, identifiable units of such programs which are live and separately logged as such may be classified as local (*e.g.,* if during the course of a feature film program, a nonnetwork 2-minute news report is given and logged as a news program, the report may be classified as local).

(b) *A network program* (NET) is any program furnished to the station by a network (national, regional, or special). Delayed broadcasts of programs originated by networks are classified as network.

(c) *A recorded program* (REC) is any program not defined in (a), (b), (c) above, including without limitation, syndicated programs, taped or transcribed programs, and feature films.

NOTE 3. *Definition of commercial matter* (CM) includes commercial continuity (network and nonnetwork) and commercial announcements (network and non-network) as follows: (Distinction between continuity and announcements is made only for definition purposes. There is no need to distinguish between the two types of commercial matters when logging.)

(a) *Commercial continuity* (CC) is the advertising message of a program sponsor.

(b) A commercial announcement (CA) is any other advertising message for which a charge is made or other consideration is received.

(1) Included are (i) "bonus spots"; (ii) trade-out spots, and (iii) promotional announcements of a future program where consideration is received for such an announcement or where such announcement identifies the sponsor of a future

program beyond mention of the sponsor's name as an integral part of the title of the program. (*E.g.,* where the agreement for the sale of time provides that the sponsor will receive promotional announcements, or when the promotional announcement contains a statement such as "LISTEN TOMORROW FOR THE—[NAME OF PROGRAM]—BROUGHT TO YOU BY—[SPONSOR'S NAME]—.")

(2) Other announcements including but not limited to the following are not commercial announcements:

(i) Promotional announcements, except as heretofore defined in paragraph (b) of this Note.

(ii) Station identification announcements for which no charge is made.

(iii) Mechanical reproduction announcements.

(iv) Public service announcements.

(v) Announcements made pursuant to § 73.654(d) that materials or services have been furnished as an inducement to broadcast a political program or a program involving the discussion of controversial public issues.

(vi) Announcements made pursuant to the local notice requirements of §§ 1.580 (pregrant) and 1.594 (designation for hearing) of this chapter.

NOTE 4. *Definition of a public service announcement.* A public service announcement is an announcement for which no charge is made and which promotes programs, activities, or services of Federal, State or local Governments (*e.g.,* recruiting, sales of bonds, etc.) or the programs, activities or services of nonprofit organizations (*e.g.,* UGF, Red Cross Blood Donations, etc.), and other announcements regarded as serving community interests, excluding time signals, routine weather announcements and promotional announcements.

NOTE 5. *Computation of commercial time.* Duration of commercial matter shall be as close an approximation to the time consumed as possible. The amount of commercial time scheduled will usually be sufficient. It is not necessary, for example, to correct an entry of a 1-minute commercial to accommodate varying reading speeds even though the actual time consumed might be a few seconds more or less than the scheduled time. However, it is incumbent upon the licensee to ensure that the entry represents as close an approximation of the time actually consumed as possible.[3]

To clarify particularly knotty problems the Commission sometimes gathers together material from its own Rules and Regulations, decisions, and letters to licensees, along with supporting material from court findings and dicta. These "primers," as they have been called, cover such subjects as the Fairness Doctrine (Section 20.9) and how a license applicant should evaluate community needs (Section 18.5).

When decision making requires formal hearings—for example in connection with enforcement (Section 17.10) or mutually exclusive applications (Section 18.3)—a Hearing Examiner conducts adversary proceedings, resembling a court trial. The Examiner makes an initial decision which goes to either a

---

[3] § 73.670

Review Board or a panel of Commissioners for analysis. The Commission may finally affirm, modify, or reverse an initial decision, after which the Office of Opinions and Review writes up the supporting arguments.

18.3 / Mutually Exclusive Applications

An application for a new license is likely to be contested by one or more rival applicants. Such "mutually exclusive" applications provide the most revealing test of the FCC's interpretation of the public interest, convenience, and necessity standard. Each applicant usually meets the bare statutory requirements for a license; therefore the Commission must fall back on estimating which will best serve the public interest.

The specific statutory requirements are relatively simple: a licensee must be a citizen of the United States, must have a good character, and must possess adequate financial and technical qualifications. Most applicants meet these requirements on an equal footing, with the help of competent advice on technical requirements.

The applicant (or, more accurately, his legal counsel) combs through prior decisions and statements of the FCC to find additional grounds on which to claim superiority. A survey of the FCC's first year of decisions, for example, reveals that it considered the following facts favorably:

1. Commercial support for the station shown to be probable (1 FCC 267)
2. Local talent and program material shown to be available (1 FCC 259)
3. Previous experience in broadcasting indicated applicant able to render a meritorious service (1 FCC 253)
4. Applicant had engaged an experienced staff (1 FCC 244)
5. Programs proposed shown to suit local needs and to constitute a complete and diversified service (1 FCC 212)

Over the years a set of "comparative criteria" has evolved which the FCC summarized in a policy statement in 1965.[4] These fall into two groups of factors, (1) programming plans (Section 18.4) and (2) facts of ownership (Section 18.6). These correspond to the FCC's avowed objectives of ensuring the best possible programming in terms of the actual needs of the particular community served; and of ensuring diversification of media control, so that the public can rely on competing sources of information to correct each other's biasses and errors.

Nevertheless, choosing among applicants still remained difficult, especially during the 1950's when major television grants were being contested. Competition became so intense in some cases that applicants attempted to affect decisions by bringing pressure to bear on Commissioners through Congress-

---

[4] FCC, "Policy Statement on Comparative Broadcasting Hearings," 30 *Fed. Reg.* 9660 (1965).

men and other people of influence. Some of these *ex parte* interventions reached such flagrant proportions that the applicants were disqualified outright and more than one Commissioner resigned (Section 21.3).

"Strike applications" and "pay-offs" were other by-products of the intense rivalry in mutually exclusive application cases. Some applicants intervened merely for the sake of putting roadblocks in the way of legitimate would-be licensees, who would then be asked to buy off the strike applicants in order to avoid further costly litigation and loss of time. An amendment to the Communications Act [§ 311(c)] now forbids an applicant to withdraw from a comparative hearing without FCC approval and limits payment by a remaining applicant to the actual out-of-pocket costs of the withdrawing applicant.[5]

18.4 / Program Criteria

For almost two decades, applicants wanting to know what program criteria they should meet had to make *ad hoc* deductions from past decisions of the FRC and FCC. Finally, in 1946, the FCC issued its first comprehensive, reasoned statement on the subject, the so-called "Blue Book." It was superseded in 1960 by a much briefer statement of policy.[6] In the intervening fourteen years, the Commission had softened its tone considerably. The "Blue Book" devoted much attention to "commercial excesses" and to specific failures of specific stations to live up to their program promises. It emphasized a need for sustaining programs, which the new policy statement explicitly rejected (Section 13.2). According to the 1960 statement, the "major elements usually necessary to meet the public interest, needs and desires of the community" include:

1. Opportunity for local self-expression (Section 18.5)
2. Development and use of local talent (Section 18.5)
3. Programs for children
4. Religious programs
5. Educational programs
6. Public-affairs programs
7. Editorializing by licensees (Section 20.7)

---

[5] Congress investigated a case in which the AVC Corporation bought five UHF television Construction Permits from the Overmeyer Corporation, paying an amount alleged to be equivalent to $4 million, although Overmeyer's out-of-pocket expense was estimated at only $1.3 million. [House Committee on Interstate and Foreign Commerce, Special Subcommittee on Investigations, *Trafficking in Broadcast Station Licenses and Construction Permits,* Hearings in 2 parts, 90th Cong., 1st and 2d Sess. (Washington: Government Printing Office, 1969).]

[6] FCC, "Report and Statement of Policy re: Commission en banc Programming Inquiry," 25 *Fed. Reg.* 7291 (1960); FCC, *Public Service Responsibility of Broadcast Licensees* (Washington: Government Printing Office, 1946).

8. Political broadcasts (Section 20.8)
9. Agricultural programs
10. News programs
11. Weather and market reports
12. Sports programs
13. Service to minority groups (Section 16.2)
14. Entertainment programs

This program-type breakdown, it should be noted, is followed closely by the log-keeping rules quoted in Section 18.3, in which the program types are defined.

In view of the actual content of commercial broadcasting, it might come as a surprise to many to learn that entertainment is only one of fourteen elements of program content considered important by the FCC. However, the Commission sets up no quantitative standards, pointing out that these "usually necessary elements" should not be regarded as a "rigid mold or fixed formula."[7]

On the subject of advertising, the policy statement warns:

. . . the licensee has the additional responsibility to take all reasonable measures to eliminate any false, misleading, or deceptive matter and to avoid abuses with respect to total amount of time devoted to advertising continuity as well as the frequency with which regular programs are interrupted for advertising messages. This duty is personal to the licensee and may not be delegated.[8]

As to what constitutes an "abuse" in total amount of advertising, the station application form (FCC Form 301) provides a clue. It asks applicants to break down broadcast hours into four categories by the number of minutes devoted to commercial matter: hours containing up to ten minutes of advertising; ten to fourteen minutes; fourteen to eighteen; above eighteen. Additional information must be given on hours in the last category—a strong hint that it may be approaching the "abuse" level.

The FCC Rules and Regulations permit educational broadcasting stations to offer "educational, cultural and entertainment programs, and programs designed for use by schools and school systems in connection with regular school courses, as well as routine and administrative material pertaining thereto [§ 73.621(c)]." When Congress passed the Public Broadcasting Act of 1967 it accepted the FCC's prior definition, merely stating that "educational programs" means those "primarily designed for educational or cultural purposes."

---

[7] In 1971, however, the FCC proposed to set up quantitative standards for television local, news, and public-affairs programming. See FCC, "Notice of Inquiry: Formulation of Policies Relating to Broadcast Renewal Applicant, Stemming from Comparative Hearing Process," FCC 71–159 (February 23, 1971).

[8] FCC, "Report and Statement . . . ," p. 7295.

It should be noted that though on the one hand educational stations may broadcast entertainment programs, on the other hand commercial stations are not relieved of the general responsibility to include educational programming in their schedules, as shown by its inclusion in the fourteen major elements listed earlier.

18.5 / Meeting Community Needs: "Localness"

Several of the elements mentioned in the FCC program-policy statement refer explicitly to local relevance—local self-expression, local talent, service to minority groups. In addition, the usefulness of religious, educational, public-affairs, editorial, political, agriculture, news, and weather programs depends largely on their relevance to the local situation. In fact, the Commission said flatly:

. . . the *principal ingredient* of the licensee's obligation to operate his station in the public interest is the diligent, positive, and continuing effort by the licensee to discover and fulfill the tastes, needs, and desires of his community or service area, for broadcast service.[9]

This emphasis on "localness" stems, as we have said (Section 17.7), in part from § 307(b) of the Communications Act, which directs the Commission to allocate facilities so as to provide "a fair, efficient, and equitable distribution of radio service" to all the states and communities.

Though originally Congress may have intended little more in this provision than to prevent regional favoritism in assigning stations, over the years the Commissions coupled the idea of "localness" with "public interest, convenience, and necessity" to make it one of the chief criteria for evaluating program proposals. We have already cited instances of how the FCC used the localness test in its earliest decisions (Section 18.3). In 1948, the Court of Appeals upheld the FCC in denying an application for improved facilities based on the licensee's proposal to act as a "mere relay station" for network programs.[10] In 1962, it upheld the FCC in refusing an applicant for an FM license in Elizabeth, New Jersey, because he proposed a schedule identical with programs on stations in Illinois and California, with no effort to discover whether it met the actual needs of Elizabeth.[11] The most emphatic judicial recognition of the importance of localness in determining operation in the public interest came from the Supreme Court in the *Red Lion* case, where the Court emphasized the primacy of audience rights over broadcaster rights, as pointed out in Section 17.7.[12]

---

[9] *Ibid.*, p. 7294. Italics supplied.

[10] *Simmons* v. *FCC*, 169 F. (2d) 670 (1948).

[11] *Patrick Henry, et al.* v. *FCC*, 302 F. (2d) 191 (1962).

[12] *Red Lion Broadcasting Co., Inc.*, v. *FCC*, 395 U. S. 367 (1969).

Although of such long standing, the localness requirement failed to achieve practical effects commensurate with its importance in the eyes of the FCC and the courts. A built-in centripetal force drives broadcasting toward program syndication, the very opposite of localness. Syndicated recorded material is cheaper, easier to handle, more popular, and more profitable than most local material. Economic factors all conspire against local programming.

Recognizing the need for more effective countervailing incentives, the FCC revised its application forms in 1966 to put more pressure on genuine "ascertainment of community needs" and planning of relevant programming. Section IV-A of Form 301 requires the renewal or new-station applicant to:

1. Describe methods used to ascertain the "needs and interests of the public served by the station," identifying "groups, interests and organizations" consulted and areas to be served
2. Describe "significant needs and interests of the public" he proposes to serve
3. List typical programs planned to satisfy the needs and interests so identified[13]

18.6 / Ownership Criteria

Emphasis on availability of local broadcast facilities for reception and use naturally leads to consideration of ownership factors. An applicant has an advantage if he can demonstrate that he has participated actively and personally in the life of the community. A past history of service in charitable drives, social-welfare organizations, community-betterment enterprises, and similar projects argues that he will be likely to understand and serve the needs of the locality.

Similarly, an applicant who can show that he plans to participate directly and personally in station management has an advantage over one who plans merely to sit back and collect profits earned by hired hands. Integration of ownership and management tends to assure the Commission that the professed objectives of the owner will be carried out conscientiously in day-to-day operation. A corporate applicant gains an advantage if it can show that its stockholders are local residents and represent diversified interests in the community. Local residence suggests that the licensee will have a real, personal stake in the community it proposes to serve.

Diversification of media ownership also enters into the comparative-merits formula. In keeping with the First Amendment ideal of maximizing "diverse and antagonistic sources" of information, the FCC counts it as a favorable point if a licensee does not already own media facilities, particularly facilities serving the same area as the proposed station. However, the negative influence of multiple-station ownership or multimedia ownership can be offset by an

---

[13] See Section 21.6 on the extent to which this device succeeded. See also FCC, "Primer on Ascertainment of Community Problems," FCC 71–176 (February 23, 1971).

outstanding record of past achievement. An experienced media owner can point to demonstrable achievements while the newcomer to the field can only theorize. Further implications of group ownership are discussed in Sections 20.3 through 20.5.

18.7 / Obtaining a License

An applicant's first step is finding an available frequency. If he is applying for an AM channel, he must arrange for his own engineering investigation to establish a proposed location, frequency, and class of station which will not cause objectionable interference. Naturally, the most desirable locations have long since been occupied, so the applicant would probably try to buy an existing station rather than start a new one. The applicant for an FM or television channel can consult the allocation tables to determine which frequencies remain unoccupied in which localities.

Having settled on an available frequency, the applicant next asks for a Construction Permit and gives local public notice of his intentions so that interested parties in the proposed service area can interpose if they have cause. The FCC holds applications for thirty days to give time for such interventions.

In the event of contention, either from others seeking the same facilities or from persons claiming adverse effects from the proposed grant, the application will be designated for hearing. An existing licensee can claim that the service area cannot support another commercial station. He may not base his objection merely on prospective loss of business to himself; but he may allege deterioration of service to the community—an adverse effect on the public interest—as a result of inadequate financial support.[14] In holding that the FCC must consider allegations of prospective financial injury, the Appeals Court pointed out:

> . . . economic injury to an existing station, while not in and of itself a matter of moment, becomes important when on the facts it spells diminution or destruction of service. At that point the private element of injury ceases to be a matter of purely private concern.[15]

An existing station may also claim loss of coverage due to signal interference from a proposed new station or a change in an existing station's facilities. This argument has produced more litigation and legal quibbling than any other single issue in broadcasting law. The classic example, the KOA case, resulted in seventeen judges writing ten different opinions, five on one side, five on the other. KOA, a Class I-A Clear-Channel AM station in Denver, was once owned by NBC. The Commission, by a bare majority, proposed to grant a modification of license for WHDH on the same channel in Boston, changing it from 1 kw. daytime to 5 kw. unlimited time. This move was fought with particular

---

[14] *FCC v. Sanders Bros. Radio Station,* 309 U. S. 470 (1940) is the leading case.
[15] *Carroll Broadcasting Co. v. FCC,* 258 F. (2d) 440 at 443 (1958).

tenacity, despite the wide separation of the two stations, because it represented an encroachment on the Clear-Channel principle. The Commission was finally allowed to make the change and subsequently even granted WHDH 50 kw.[16]

Hearings usually cost a great deal of money. Not only must the applicant employ specialized legal counsel, he must also pay for engineering and other consultants, preparing and duplicating elaborate exhibits (sometimes stacks of documents five or six feet high), purchasing hearing transcripts, transport and maintenance of witnesses in Washington, and the like. Costs of prosecuting a competitive application for a major television facility run into hundreds of thousands of dollars.[17] Initial decisions, exceptions, oral arguments before the Commission, and appeals can stretch out into years, during which the applicant's investment is tied up. In addition, the applicant must be prepared to operate initially at a substantial loss while the station establishes itself in the market. In short, broadcasting has a high cost of entry, which places significant limits on the opportunities to own broadcasting stations and provides strong incentives to earn rapid profits once the license is won.

Assuming the applicant survives all the hazards along the way and receives a Construction Permit, he can finally start building his proposed physical plant. Only after construction has been completed can he apply for a license and for permission to begin conducting program tests.

18.8 / Keeping a License

Once licensed and in regular operation, the station owner normally experiences relatively little official supervision or monitoring to check up on whether he is serving the public interest. The licensing procedure has already established his good character and his good intentions to operate in the public interest. Program plans and policy statements in his application provide a blueprint for responsible operation.

The FCC's field staff usually monitors and inspects stations for technical rather than programming violations. The technical and program logs (Section 18.2) provide a running record of operations in case any checkup is required. Questions about programming usually come to the FCC's attention through complaints lodged against the licensee by individuals or organizations. In fiscal 1970, for example, the Commission received about twenty-six thousand complaints about programming (Table 18.1).[18]

---

[16] *In re Matheson Radio Co. (WHDH)*, 8 FCC 397 (1940); *NBC* v. *FCC,* 132 F. (2d) 545 (1942); *FCC* v. *NBC,* 319 U. S. 239 (1943).

[17] Senate Committee on Interstate Commerce, *Workload of the Federal Communications Commission,* Hearing, 83d Cong., 1st Sess. (Washington: Government Printing Office, 1953). The hearing procedure and its problems are discussed in detail on pp. 13–35.

[18] That year there was a marked increase in complaints about alleged distortion or suppression of news; "un-American" programs; obscenity, profanity, and indecency; and unfairness. [FCC, Public Notice 53229, July 30, 1970.]

Table 18.1

Public complaints received by FCC

Subject of Complaint	Number Received	
Programming		
Distortion or suppression of news	5,139	
Fairness Doctrine and "equal time"	2,722	
Contests and promotions	2,677	
Advertising	1,829	
Specific programs	1,195	
Crime, violence, horror	1,147	
Un-American, Communistic, etc.	1,008	
Miscellaneous	4,228	
Total programming complaints		19,945
Other		5,975
Grand total		25,920

Source: FCC tabulation.

The FCC has to discard most complaints, either because they have no substance or because they ask the Commission to overstep its jurisdiction by interfering with licensees' legitimate exercise of programming responsibility. Chairman Newton Minow tells of a letter he received from an "extremely conscientious broadcaster":

His letter was in reply to a complaint from a female radio listener objecting to a commercial for an automobile dealer which featured the football slogan, "I'm too pooped to punt"! The lady objected to the word "pooped"; and after reading his exhaustive—and exhausting—reply, I simply wrote to him, "I'm too pooped to comment"![19]

When follow-up is warranted, the FCC writes a letter of inquiry to the licensee (Section 17.10) and the correspondence goes into the licensee's file for review at license-renewal time.

Licenses come up for renewal in groups by states. Normally the FCC renews them routinely as a group, but occasionally a third-party challenge to renewal necessitates a hearing. Sometimes the licensee's file will contain an accumulation of unfavorable material justifying the Commission itself in designating the renewal for hearing. This material might include audience complaints, citations for technical or other violations of the Rules and Regulations, records of Cease and Desist Orders and forfeitures (see Section 17.10 regarding enforcement of rules), or records of actions by other jurisdictions, such as the Federal Trade Commission.

---

[19] Excerpted from *Equal Time: The Private Broadcaster and the Public Interest,* by Newton N. Minow [p. 7]. Edited by Lawrence Laurent. Copyright © 1964 by Newton N. Minow. Reprinted by permission of Atheneum Publishers.

Following are some examples of infractions which led to renewal hearings:

RENEWAL GRANTED	RENEWAL DENIED
Inspector found transmitter being operated by unlicensed operator (2 FCC 51)	Licensee had surrendered control over programming; programs included objectionable one by a marriage broker; technical equipment was in very poor repair; management's financial affairs were in very poor condition; station had engaged in unethical business practice (2 FCC 209)
Station discontinued objectionable programs, in one of which analyses of dreams and advice on love, marriage, business, and various other subjects were given; technical flaws had been due to transmitter repairs; evidence of failure to identify transcription according to rule was conflicting (4 FCC 125)	
	Station's service had been interrupted owing to faulty equipment; time brokerage was permitted; misrepresentation in advertising was condoned (4 FCC 521)
Broadcasting alleged lottery advertising discontinued after few days (4 FCC 186)	
Station had been cited a number of times for violation of technical rules and failure to keep log properly; it had briefly carried a program by an astrologer (7 FCC 219)	Licensee transferred control of station in violation of law, made false representations to the Commission, was not financially qualified to continue operation (8 FCC 434)

See also Section 17.10 for other data on renewal denials.

In rare cases of notorious misconduct, licenses have been revoked even before renewal time. Statutory grounds for license revocation include false statements in applications, "willful or repeated failure to operate substantially as set forth in the license," violations of Cease and Desist Orders, "conditions coming to the attention of the Commission which would warrant refusing to grant a license or permit on an original application," and violation of the statutes against fraud, obscenity, and lotteries (§ 312). The Commission bears the burden of proof in a revocation proceeding. Refusing renewals, on the other hand, requires only a finding that the refusal would serve public interest, convenience, and necessity [§ 307(d)]. Administratively, the Commission thus finds it easier simply to fail to renew than to revoke.

Table 18.2 analyzes the reasons cited by the FCC for revoking or denying renewal of seventy-eight licenses in the years 1934–1969. Deletions averaged less than three per year. Indeed, if one discounts the stations which apparently surrendered their licenses voluntarily by failing to stay on the air or to prosecute their renewal applications, the total involuntary deletions amount to only fifty-eight stations in a span of thirty-six years. It is noteworthy that of these only one station was charged with false advertising, one with overcommercialization, and one with departing from program promises.

Table 18.2

Reasons for license deletions

Reasons Cited by FCC[1]	Frequency Cited In		
	Revocations *(N=32)*	*Denials* *(N=46)*	*Total* *(N=78)*[2]
Misrepresentation to FCC	20	20	40
Unauthorized transfer of control	9	19	28
Technical violations	8	19	27
Abandonment, failure to prosecute renewal	8	12	20
Character of licensee	4	11	15
Financial incapacity of licensee	3	3	6
Fraudulent contests on station	1	1	2
False advertising on station	0	1	1
Indecent program materials	0	1	1
Overcommercialization	0	1	1
Departure from promised programming	1	0	1
Miscellaneous	7	10	17
Totals	61	98	159

[1] Most cases involved more than one reason; hence not each of these reasons would necessarily suffice by itself.

[2] The five most recent cases were still on appeal when the study was made.

Source: Data in John A. Abel, Charles Clift III, and Fredric A. Weiss, "Station License Revocations and Denials of Renewal, 1934–1969," *Journal of Broadcasting,* XIV (Fall, 1970), 411–421.

18.9 / Transferring a License

Since a licensee may not own a license, what happens if he wants to sell his station?[20] A station as a successful going concern is worth much more than the aggregate value of its individual parts; the actual sale prices of stations often amount to many times the value of the physical property involved (Section 15.1). Part of the difference may be chargeable to "goodwill," but most of it is due to the value of the license itself—or, more accurately, the temporary right to use a particular broadcast channel which the license confers.

The fact that licenses have cash value on the market, even though they do not represent "ownership" of a broadcast channel, has led to applications for CP's and erection of stations as pure business speculations—"for sale, not for service." This "trafficking in licenses" directly contravenes the theory of the Communications Act. The Act assumes that an applicant for a broadcast license wants to render a public service, not merely build a station for the sake of a quick and profitable sale, with no real intention of serving the public.

The trafficking problem was pointed up by a hearing on the transfer of WLW, Cincinnati, to the Aviation Corporation (Avco). WLW was licensed

---

[20] In fiscal 1969, the Commission received 1,066 applications for transfers of ownership. [FCC, *Thirty-Fifth Annual Report* (Washington: Government Printing Office, 1970), pp. 129–131.]

to the Crosley Corporation, an old-line electronics-manufacturing concern. Avco, a holding company with many subsidiaries, was buying the Crosley Corporation, and the broadcast properties of Crosley were mere incidentals in the $22-million transaction. The transfer was approved by a bare majority of the FCC, which took occasion to remark that more than 50 per cent of the existing licensees at that time (1945) had been selected not by the Commission but by transferors.

The FCC minority dissent pointed out that Avco's officers demonstrated serene and unblushing ignorance of the most elementary facts about broadcasting, the Communications Act, and the obligations they were proposing to undertake; the Commissioners added that even an applicant for the lowest grade of operator's license has to pass a test to show that he understands his duties and responsibilities under the Act.

Programming is the essence of broadcasting and yet not a single witness for the transferee demonstrated more than the vaguest idea about the kind of program service which would be rendered, the availability of program talent and sources, the needs of the people in WLW's service area, or even about the type of program service being rendered under the previous management. They did not even know how much they were paying for the broadcasting facilities being purchased.[21]

This case prompted the FCC to adopt the "Avco Rule," which required owners to solicit competitive bids for stations offered for sale. The FCC could then choose the best-qualified applicant. In the four years of the Avco Rule, few competing bids were entered and usually the original applicant was approved anyway. In 1949, the Commission repealed the rule.

In 1958, Congress amended § 310(b) of the Communications Act, forbidding the FCC from considering any transferee other than the one to whom the licensee wished to sell. The Commission attempts to discourage trafficking by requiring a hearing on any proposed transfer of control within three years of the original grant. Any earlier attempt to sell creates a presumption of trafficking.[22]

18.10 / Advertising Regulation

"Puffery" in advertising has long been legally recognized in common law as distinct from deception. The law assumed that the normal person recognizes that the advertiser will put his best foot forward and makes allowances accordingly. Borden surveyed consumers' reactions to magazine advertising and concluded:

---

[21] *In re Powel Crosley, Jr.,* 11 FCC 3 at 37 (1945).

[22] *In re KORD, Inc.,* 31 FCC 85 (1961). In *Crowder* v. *FCC,* 399 F. (2d) 569 (1969), the Appeals Court upheld a license revocation based on trafficking; the Supreme Court declined to review the case.

Examination of the data suggests that consumers have a considerable tolerance for exaggeration and puffery in advertising. Apparently they do not expect advertisements to be absolutely honest documents, just as absolute honesty is not expected in connection with most human activities. They undoubtedly expect advertisements to be biased and to present merchandise in an attractive light.[23]

With the growth of persuasive advertising, however, a more protective policy toward the gullible and uninformed was adopted. The psychological impact of broadcasting and its accessibility to the illiterate and near-illiterate make it an efficient means of capitalizing on the gullibility of the uninformed or uneducated listener/viewer. Thus broadcasting is in a position to exploit those who are economically least able to afford exploitation and intellectually least able to defend themselves.

In the early days of radio, fraudulent health "experts" flocked to the new medium. The advertising of a man purporting to be an astrologer-psychologist-doctor-scientist and that of another billed as a "world famed spiritual psychologist" dealt with

. . . questions purporting to come from their audience, these selections usually including a wide variety of material with a liberal allowance of matter bordering on indelicacy and scandalousness, if not actually scandalous. Even a cursory examination of the discussions broadcast would seem to have been enough to convince the management of the station that they were intended to exploit and victimize the credulous, to capitalize the troubles and distress of questioners and in some instances even to draw upon the public by appeal to religious instincts.[24]

License renewals of five stations were set for hearing because of advertising containing such continuity as the following:

Here is good news for all those people who are sick or in ill health. The Alhambra Electronic Institute has installed the latest Scientific Invention—the Electron-o-meter—a machine that shows you definitely the cause of your illness, the condition of your internal organs, the severity of the ailment, and how to correct the faulty condition.[25]

This miraculous instrument was made available at one dollar per examination, although the announcement went on fraudulently to claim that ten dollars was the regular fee, with the one-dollar fee available only to the first ten applicants.

The licensees' slight sense of responsibility led them to argue that it was not their job to evaluate advertising, to which the FCC replied: "The contention that licensees should not have the duty of examining into the propriety

---

[23] Neil H. Borden, *The Economic Effects of Advertising,* 4th ed. (Chicago: Richard D. Irwin, 1947), p. 760.

[24] *In re Scroggin & Co. Bank (KFEQ),* 1 FCC 194 at 196 (1935). The station's license was renewed.

[25] *In re Ben S. McGlashan (KGFJ) et al.,* 2 FCC 145 at 149 (1935). All five licenses were renewed.

of advertising to be broadcast is manifestly contrary to the law."[26] Nor does the FCC accept the evasive excuse that other stations have carried the same advertising: licensees "have the positive unqualified responsibility of serving the public interest as a matter of law, and it will not avail one licensee that some other station . . . has placed upon others the responsibility which is his, as licensee of a station."[27]

By 1940, the Commission had eliminated such extreme types of exploitative advertising from broadcasting. Exploitation continued in somewhat less obvious forms—bait-switch advertising,[28] shoddy per-inquiry merchandise, exaggerated and misleading claims (especially for patent medicines). Television introduced a new form of deception, the "simulated" demonstration.

In its first ruling on deceptive television advertising, the famous "sandpaper case," the Supreme Court upheld the Federal Trade Commission after a four-year battle to stop the use of deceptive methods of "proving" advertising claims visually on television. The FTC objected to a visual demonstration of a shaving cream's alleged efficacy in "shaving" sandpaper. In fact, the sandpaper had to be soaked in the cream for eighty minutes before it could be "shaved"; moreover, the commercial used a plexiglass mockup for the demonstration instead of real sandpaper. The Appeals Court reversed the Commission twice before the Supreme Court finally settled the question. By that time, it had been conceded that the orginal sandpaper claim could not be proved; the Supreme Court focussed on whether it was unlawful to use substitute "props" to simulate demonstrations in television advertising. The Court upheld the FTC in its contention that it is deceptive to offer the viewer "proof" of a claim by means of a simulated visual demonstration.[29]

This ruling failed to end questionable demonstrations, however, for in 1970 the FTC still found occasion to issue complaints against ten major companies. One case concerned marbles in the bottom of a soup bowl which forced the solids in the soup to the top, making it look richer than it actually was. In another case, a real astronaut was used to introduce two huge plastic balloons attached to the exhausts of automobiles. This demonstration purported to prove that the advertised brand of fuel caused less air pollution than its competitors. Sure enough, the "other" fuel blackened its balloon, while the advertised brand's balloon remained perfectly clear. The commercial omitted to mention, however, that some of the most dangerous pollutants generated by internal-combusion engines remain invisible and so could not in any event be revealed by the "balloon test."

---

[26] *Ibid.,* p. 147.

[27] *In re The Farmers & Bankers Life Ins. Co. (KFBI),* 2 FCC 455 at 459 (1936).

[28] Advertising which draws customers in with offers of very low price; but when they ask about the low-priced article, the advertiser tries to switch them to a higher-priced item by various stratagems, such as running down the low-priced item.

[29] *FTC* v. *Colgate-Palmolive Co.,* 330 U. S. 374 (1965). The ruling does not prevent the use of substitutes (*e.g.,* for ice cream, which melts too fast under the lights) when not used to prove a claim.

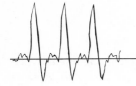

19

REGULATION:
ENEMY OF FREEDOM

We move on now from pragmatic rules and regulations to the larger principle which looms in the background of most significant issues about the regulation of broadcasting in America—freedom of speech.

19.1 / The Dangerous Experiment

In adopting their Constitution, Americans embarked on a dangerous experiment. Contrary to conventional wisdom of the past, they acted on the hypothesis that ordinary people could govern themselves. They saw no need for a specially ordained or peculiarly gifted governing family, class, or caste. In order to be fit for self-government, people must have unhampered access to the knowledge necessary for making political judgments. Universal education and the free exchange of information follow logically from this proposition. It assumes that the utmost freedom of expression will in the long run be best both for the individual and for society, for truth will ultimately prevail over falsehood if given the opportunity to be heard.

Thomas Jefferson's faith in an uncensored press never wavered, despite his being pilloried by the newspapers of his time with a viciousness unknown today:

No experiment can be more interesting than that we are now trying, which we trust will end in establishing the fact that man may be governed by reason and truth. Our first object should therefore be to leave open to him all the avenues to truth. The most effectual hitherto found is the freedom of the press.

*   *   *   *   *

I have lent myself willingly as the subject of a great experiment, which was to prove that an administration, conducting itself with integrity and common understanding, cannot be battered down, even by the falsehoods of a licentious press. . . . This experiment was wanting for the world to demonstrate the falsehood of the pretext that freedom of the press is incompatible with orderly government.[1]

---

[1] Letter to Judge Tyler, 1804; letter to Thomas Seymour, 1807. Quoted in Saul K. Padover, ed., *Thomas Jefferson on Democracy* (New York: New American Library, 1946), pp. 95–96.

The First Amendment to the Constitution protects four fundamental private rights which governments in all ages have been most prone to violate: freedom of religion, freedom of speech and press, freedom of assembly, and freedom to petition the government for redress of grievances. In the present context, reference to the First Amendment means specifically freedom of speech and press. "Speech" or "utterance" will be used, according to convention, interchangeably with "press"; and "publish" may mean "broadcast" or "exhibit."

The Amendment itself covers the all-important subject of free speech in only ten words (italics supplied):

Congress shall make no law respecting an establishment of religion, or prohibiting the free exercise thereof; *or abridging the freedom of speech, or of the press;* or the right of the people peaceably to assemble, and to petition the Government for a redress of grievances.[2]

The First Amendment occupies a preferred position in the Bill of Rights which gives it "a sanctity and a sanction not permitting dubious intrusions."[3] As Justice Holmes put it, "if there is any principle of the Constitution that more imperatively calls for attachment than any other it is the principle of free thought—not free thought for those who agree with us but freedom for the thought we hate."[4]

Mr. Justice Douglas, in an eloquently argued dissent, restated the rationale of the First Amendment:

Free speech has occupied an exalted position because of the high service it has given our society. Its protection is essential to the very existence of a democracy. The airing of ideas releases pressures which otherwise might become destructive. When ideas compete in the market for acceptance, full and free discussion exposes the false and they gain few adherents. Full and free discussion even of ideas we hate encourages the testing of our own prejudices and preconceptions. Full and free discussion keeps a society from becoming stagnant and unprepared for the stresses and strains that work to tear all civilizations apart.

Full and free discussion has indeed been the first article of our faith. We have founded our political system on it. It has been the safeguard of every religious, political, philosophical, economic, and racial group amongst us. We have counted on it to keep us from embracing what is cheap and false; we have trusted the common sense of our people to choose the doctrine true to our genius and to reject the rest. This has been the one single outstanding tenet that has made our institutions the symbol of freedom and equality. We have deemed it more costly to liberty to suppress a despised minority than to let them vent their spleen. We

---

[2] The First Amendment restricts only the federal government, but the Fourteenth Amendment extends the prohibitions of the federal Constitution to the state governments. In addition, all the state constitutions contain provisions similar to those of the First Amendment.

[3] *Thomas* v. *Collins,* 323 U. S. 516 at 530 (1945).

[4] *U. S.* v. *Schwimmer,* 279 U. S. 644 at 654–655 (1929).

have above all else feared the political censor. We have wanted a land where our people can be exposed to all the diverse creeds and cultures of the world.[5]

The English philosopher John Stuart Mill gave the libertarian philosophy its classic expression in 1859. "If all mankind minus one," he wrote, "were of one opinion, and only one person were of the contrary opinion, mankind would be no more justified in silencing that one person, than he, if he had the power, would be justified in silencing mankind." He goes on:

. . . the peculiar evil of silencing the expression of an opinion is, that it is robbing the human race; posterity as well as the existing generation; those who dissent from the opinion, still more than those who hold it. If the opinion is right, they are deprived of the opportunity of exchanging error for truth: if wrong, they lose, what is almost as great a benefit, the clearer perception and livelier impression of truth, produced by its collision with error.[6]

Not an easy ideal to practice, for although no one has difficulty in recognizing the importance of freedom for himself, it requires an unusual measure of self-restraint and tolerance always to grant the importance of that same freedom to those with whom we violently disagree. "The last acquisition of civilized man," Justice Learned Hand remarked, "is forbearance in judgment and to it is necessary one of the highest efforts of the will."[7] We tend to assume that we have already arrived at our destination, to "think that new truths may have been desirable once, but that we have had enough of them now."[8] From this conviction arises obsessive attachment to the *status quo* and the fatal delusion that it is possible to attain total security. But, as Justice Holmes said, "all life is an experiment":

. . . when men have realized that time has upset many fighting faiths, they may come to believe even more than they believe the very foundations of their own conduct that the ultimate good desired is better reached by free trade in ideas—that the best test of truth is the power of the thought to get itself accepted in the competition of the market, and that truth is the only ground upon which their wishes safely can be carried out. That at any rate is the theory of the Constitution. It is an experiment, as all life is an experiment.[9]

So much does the theory of the Constitution remain an experiment that even after two centuries it still seems too dangerous for the majority to accept. At

---

[5] *Dennis* v. *U. S.,* 341 U. S. 494 at 584–585 (1951).

[6] John Stuart Mill, *On Liberty* (Oxford: Basil Blackwell, 1946), pp. 14–15.

[7] Learned Hand, *The Spirit of Liberty* (New York: Alfred A. Knopf, 1952), p. 27.

[8] Mill, *op. cit.,* p. 24.

[9] *Abrams* v. *U. S.,* 250 U. S. 616 at 630 (1919). The phrase "competition of the market" should be noted for future reference. In the next chapter we discuss how changing conditions have given a new significance to the traditional libertarian concept of a "marketplace of ideas."

fairly frequent intervals an editor or researcher gets the idea of asking a cross-section of American citizens what they think of the Declaration of Independence, the Preamble to the Constitution, or the Bill of Rights. Invariably a large proportion of the respondents recoil from these articles of faith—often mistaking them for Communist-inspired propaganda.

Who could possibly quarrel with the basic freedoms guaranteed by the U. S. Constitution? Most Americans, according to a poll conducted by CBS News. A majority of 1,136 people polled in a representative sampling of Americans in effect do not now support five of the ten protections of the Bill of Rights.[10]

Three-quarters of the respondents answering a question aimed at testing whether they accepted the fundamental thesis of the First Amendment said "No." Like results have invariably been obtained from similar surveys.

In other words, the profound meaning and value of the Bill of Rights are not so obvious that they can be appreciated without effort. To begin with, some sense of history and of world politics is indispensable if one is to realize fully the unpleasant alternatives to these freedoms, despite their dangers. Moreover, the front-line legal battles are usually fought by obscure little men with funny names and uncomfortably radical or obsessive ideas. To such anti-heroes the average citizen owes the preservation of freedoms that would otherwise gradually erode away. Rarely does the clean-cut, all-American suburbanite turn up in the Supreme Court as the protagonist in a key First Amendment case.

19.2 / Censorable Matter: Obscenity in Print

The Constitutional prohibition mentions no exceptions: "Congress shall make *no* law. . . ." The admonition is absolute. Yet we know that in practice there must be exceptions. We do have laws to penalize those who commit slander and libel. Fraudulent utterances are punishable. The freedom to disclose trade as well as state secrets is abridged. We are not at liberty to plagiarize with impunity, to publish obscene materials, or to incite an insurrection.

"The hermit is free to sing but not to sing in a chorus or opera."[11] Freedom of speech takes on meaning only in an organized society. By the same token, organized society requires protection from patently harmful speech.

The very utterance of such words is considered to inflict a *present* injury upon listeners, readers, or those defamed, or else to render highly probable an immediate breach of the peace. This is a very different matter from punishing words because they express ideas which are thought to cause a *future* danger to the State.[12]

---

[10] "Soundings on the Right," *Time,* April 27, 1970, p. 19.

[11] William Ernest Hocking, *Freedom of the Press: A Framework of Principle* (Chicago: University of Chicago Press, 1947), p. 67.

[12] Zechariah Chafee, Jr., *Free Speech in the United States* (Cambridge, Mass.: Harvard University Press, 1942), p. 149. Italics supplied.

Yet concepts of what is injurious change. The practical limits of freedom constantly shift with the times. Take the social injuries alleged to be caused by utterances called "obscenity." Until a series of decisions starting in 1933 with the vindication of James Joyce's classic, *Ulysses,* the nineteenth-century Comstock law severely curtailed circulation of literature in America. Suppression by local and state boards and police authorities was supplemented by the Postmaster General, who personally exercised almost unchecked administrative censorship over printed matter through his control over what could be mailed and over low-rate mailing privileges.

We start from the Victorian view that everything has to be fit for even the youngest and most susceptible eyes and ears. A complete book could be suppressed for minor, isolated passages that censors considered potentially harmful to a child or emotionally immature person. Here are the highlights of changing standards:

1933—"Ulysses." James Joyce's novel, long circulated clandestinely, finally became legally available when a New York court judged it not on isolated passages but on its general effect as a *complete* work on a *normal* reader, and in the light of the author's *artistic intention.* [*U. S.* v. *One Book Called "Ulysses,"* 5 F. Supp. 182.]

1953—"Esquire." The Postmaster General suspended the second-class mailing permit of *Esquire* magazine, alleging that parts of it consisted recurrently of obscene material. In affirming a lower court's reversal of the Postmaster's action, the Supreme Court remarked that "a requirement that literature or art conform to some norm prescribed by an official smacks of an ideology foreign to our system." This case effectively discouraged reckless use of the postal authorities' power to suppress. [*Hannegan* v. *Esquire, Inc.,* 327 U. S. 146.]

1957—Roth. Ironically, this pivotal Supreme Court decision upheld the conviction of Roth for mailing indecent books, but at the same time firmly established new and more liberal obscenity criteria. The test of obscenity became sixfold: "whether to (1) the *average* person, applying (2) *contemporary* standards, the (3) *dominant* theme of the material, (4) taken *as a whole* appeals to (5) *prurient* [lascivious, lustful] interest in sex," and (6) is *utterly without redeeming social value.* Mr. Justice Brennan, for the majority, wrote: "All ideas having even the slightest redeeming social importance—unorthodox ideas, controversial ideas, even ideas hateful to the prevailing climate of opinion—have the full protection [of the First Amendment], unless excluded because they encroach upon the limited area of more important interests. But implicit in the history of the First Amendment is the rejection of obscenity as utterly without redeeming social importance." [*Roth* v. *U. S.,* 354 U. S. 476.]

1964—"Tropic of Cancer." Like *Ulysses,* Henry Miller's book had long been clandestinely circulated. It became "the most litigated book in the history of literature,"[13] the subject of more than sixty suits with conflicting outcomes. Finally the Supreme Court reversed a Florida conviction, establishing a new precedent: the "community standards" of *Roth* must be generalized *national* standards, not the provincial standards of a particular locality. This concept has interesting implications regarding refusal of local stations to carry national network programs which meet general national standards but offend local or regional customs (Section 16.5). [*Grove Press* v. *Gerstein*, 378 U. S. 577.]

1966—"Fanny Hill," Ginzburg, and Mishkin. The earliest American obscenity case dates back to 1821, when a pornographic eighteenth-century novel about a prostitute, popularly known as *Fanny Hill*, was suppressed. One hundred forty-five years later the Supreme Court lifted the ban, by a vote of six to three, finding that the novel had some redeeming social value after all. The majority opinion made the point that the three major criteria—prurient appeal, community standards, and social value—had to be applied *separately* and *independently*. Despite judging the book to fail the first two tests, the Court protected it on the strength of the third. On the same day the Court handed down decisions against *Eros* and other publications of Ralph Ginzburg, and against frankly hard-core pornography aimed at deviant sexual interests ("too sickening to be prurient") published by Edward Mishkin. Altogether the justices wrote fourteen different opinions on these three cases—a symptom of the continuing difficulty of reaching agreement on obscenity issues. *Ginzburg* was interesting for its emphasis on a relatively new concept: guilt hinged not on the publications themselves but in the *advertising* for them, which was judged to pander to prurient interests; if the publisher himself characterized his works as obscene, the Court was willing to take his word for it. [*A Book Named "John Cleland's Memoirs of a Woman of Pleasure"* v. *Attorney General of the Commonwealth of Massachusetts*, 383 U. S. 413; *Ginzburg* v. *U. S.*, 383 U. S. 463; *Mishkin* v. *State of New York*, 383 U. S. 502.]

Obscenity cases in broadcasting have been rare, and the statute (18 U. S. C. 1464) has never been tested. However, with increasing freedom in print and entertainment and with changing community standards, obscenity charges against broadcasters can be expected to increase. In 1970, the FCC imposed a token fine on a Philadelphia educational FM station for airing indecent words, in an effort to precipitate a test case.[14] New grounds for censorship

---

[13] Donald M. Gillmor and Jerome A. Barron, *Mass Communication Law: Cases and Comment* (St. Paul, Minn.: West, 1969), p. 311.

[14] The Appeals Court upheld the FCC's denial of renewal in a case growing out of allegations of the use of suggestive language on the air by a performer, but the case hinged on licensee misrepresentation and the Court did not directly adjudicate the censorship issue. [*In re Palmetto Broadcasting Co. (WDKD)*, 33 FCC 265 (1961) and 33 FCC 250 (1962); *E. G. Robinson* v. *FCC*, 334 F. (2d) 534 (1964).]

seem to be emerging with the new media. A ban against broadcast cigarette advertising seemed especially significant because it singled out broadcasting for treatment different from other media. Similarly, proposals to limit the amount of violence depicted on television suggest emergence of a new dimension of censorable forms of expression in one particular medium.

19.3 / The "Social-Value" Test

The foregoing review suggests that obscenity falls outside the protection of the First Amendment because, by definition, it has adverse social effects. If, however, a work taken as a whole has social value, this positive value may "redeem" obscenity by outweighing its negative consequences. Or, to put it around the other way, the dangers to society of suppressing material of social value may outweigh the dangers to society of not suppressing obscene material.

Suppose, however, there were nothing to redeem? Suppose the assumption that obscenity is socially harmful *per se* has no substantial foundation in fact? Mr. Justice Harlan raised this question in the *Roth* case:

There is a large school of thought, particularly in the scientific community, which denies any causal connection between the reading of pornography and immorality, crime or delinquency.[15]

This school of thought later received strong support from the federal Commission on Obscenity and Pornography. After two years of study and research, the majority reported: "The Commission cannot conclude that exposure to erotic materials is a factor in the causation of sex crime or sex delinquency." Similar commissions in European countries "all concluded that consensual exposure of adults to explicit sexual materials causes no demonstrable damaging individual or social effects."[16]

The Supreme Court seems to have vacillated somewhat on the underlying question of social value as a prerequisite for First Amendment protection in other contexts. In a landmark press-freedom decision, the *Near* case, the Court protected a scandalmongering Minneapolis newspaper, saying, "The fact that the liberty of the press may be abused by miscreant purveyors of scandal does not make any the less necessary the immunity of the press from previous restraints in dealing with official misconduct." The Court went on to quote the well-known words of Madison:

---

[15] *Roth* v. *United States,* 354 U. S. 476 at 501 (1957).

[16] Commission on Obscenity and Pornography, *Report* (New York: Bantam Books, 1970), pp. 32, 50. These majority conclusions came from twelve of the eighteen Commissioners. Three Commissioners filed a vigorous dissent in which, among other things, they accused the majority of relying on "shoddy" scholarship (p. 456) and misrepresenting the law (p. 490); asserted that society's interest in suppressing obscenity is "the prevention of moral corruption, and *not* to prevention [*sic*] of overt criminal acts" (p. 457); and characterized the social-value test as "pernicious" (p. 497) and the cause of a flood of pornographic films and publications (p. 499).

Some degree of abuse is inseparable from the proper use of everything, and in no instance is this more true than in that of the press. It has accordingly been decided by the practice of the States, that is better to leave a few of its noxious branches to their luxurious growth, than by pruning them away, to injure the vigour of those yielding the proper fruits.[17]

Again, in a case involving fictional material of questionable merit, the Court declared: "Though we can see nothing of any possible value to society in these magazines, they are as much entitled to the protection of free speech as the best of literature."[18] In reversing the FCC's attempt to rule out give-away programs on the grounds that they are lotteries, a lower court rejected the lottery charge and went on to say the "fact that radio and television 'giveaway' programs might have little possible value to society does not deprive the producers of such programs of their constitutional protections of free speech."[19]

Yet, in the *Chrestensen* case, the Supreme Court took the view that advertising matter of a purely commercial and private nature does not merit First Amendment protection. When prevented by a New York City ordinance from distributing a leaflet on the streets advertising a submarine he was exhibiting in New York Harbor, Chrestensen sought to overcome the objection by printing on the other side of the handbill a protest against the City Dock Department. The Supreme Court found against the would-be advertiser, holding that the expression of opinion on the reverse side of advertising was motivated merely by the desire to evade the ordinance. Said the Court, "If that evasion were successful, every merchant who desires to broadcast advertising leaflets in the streets need only append a civic appeal, or a moral platitude, to achieve immunity from the law's command."[20]

Some years later, however, Mr. Justice Douglas (who had participated in the decision) remarked that the doctrine of *Chrestensen* "has not survived reflection." The First Amendment is not, he said, "confined to discourse of a particular kind or nature. . . . The profit motive should make no difference, for that is an element inherent in the very conception of a press under our system of free enterprise."[21]

Certainly advertising appears entitled to First Amendment protection when it deals with matters not purely private and selfish. The commercial company which the New York City Transit Authority retained to sell subway advertising refused to accept posters opposing the Vietnam war as "too controversial," even though advertising had been accepted for such causes as the

---

[17] *Near* v. *Minnesota,* 283 U. S. 697 at 718 (1931).

[18] *Winters* v. *New York,* 333 U. S. 507 at 510 (1948).

[19] *ABC* v. *U. S.,* 110 F. Supp. 374 at 375 (1953).

[20] *Valentine* v. *Chrestensen,* 316 U. S. 52 at 55 (1942).

[21] *Cammarano* v. *U. S.,* 358 U. S. 498 at 514 (1959).

USO, Radio Free Europe, and the *Muhammed Speaks* newspaper. The Court found the company's claim that the posters might cause "serious disturbances, disorder and vandalism" insufficient, pointing out that one of the very functions of free speech is to "invite dispute."[22]

19.4 / Libel and "The Right to Defame"

Libel and slander undoubtedly do have adverse effects on individuals, but again a doctrine analogous to the "redeeming social-value" test applies when the press and public officials are involved. Libel (or slander, the spoken form of libel) has as many jurisdictions as there are states. In brief and in general it means using words which defame, exposing their object to public hatred, shame, contempt, ostracism, and the like. It can cause loss of employment (see the Faulk blacklisting case in Section 16.4 above) as well as mental anguish. In most jurisdictions, truth is an absolute defense against libel. News media, however, can in addition plead various types of privilege on the "redeeming social-value" principle—the value to society of free and fair comment by news media outweighs risk of damage to individuals due to incorrectness of the facts, as long as no deliberate malice is involved.

The best way to test whether or not genuine freedom of speech exists is to criticize those in power—if necessary, to criticize them harshly and vociferously. Is an officeholder believed to be dishonest, incompetent, ignorant, lazy, unprincipled? If so, there must be an opportunity for publicly exposing him. Even if the accusations are mistaken, there should at least be an opportunity to bring them into the light and test them. The first act of a dictator on seizing power is forcibly to suppress freedom of the opposition to criticize his régime. But in a democratic system, "the right to censure is the *right to defame*."[23]

During a period of racial disturbances connected with a bus boycott in Montgomery, Alabama, supporters of the boycott bought a full-page advertisement in the *New York Times*. The advertisement criticized Montgomery officials. Sullivan, one of the officials, brought suit for libel and won a half-million-dollar judgment, affirmed by the State Supreme Court. The United States Supreme Court, however, unanimously reversed the verdict, holding that even if the allegations were untrue (and many facts stated in the advertisement were incorrect), they would constitute libel only if published with malice or reckless disregard for the facts.

The constitutional guarantees require, we think, a federal rule that prohibits a public official from recovering damages for a defamatory falsehood relating to his

---

[22] *Kissinger* v. *New York City Transit Authority*, 274 F. Supp. 438 (1967).

[23] Louis G. Caldwell, "Freedom of Speech and Radio Broadcasting," *Annals of the American Academy of Political and Social Science*, CLXXVII (January, 1935), 183.

official conduct unless he proves that the statement was made with "actual malice" —that is, with knowledge that it was false or with reckless disregard of whether it was false or not.[24]

We cannot, after all, expect polite and gracious refinement in the midst of intense controversy, for "debate on public issues should be uninhibited, robust, and . . . may well include vehement, caustic, and sometimes unpleasantly sharp attacks on government and public officials."[25]

The Court extended the risks inherent in being a public official to "public figures" when it reversed an award of damages to a retired general, Edwin Walker. The Associated Press reported that Walker assumed a leading role in fomenting and personally leading violent opposition to the admission of James Meredith to the University of Mississippi. Walker was no longer on active duty with the Army and had no official capacity in connection with the events at the University, but the Court held that he had injected himself into the controversy in such a way as to become a self-appointed "public figure."[26] As such, he had to expect the consequences in terms of criticism of his conduct.

19.5 / "Clear and Present Danger" to the State

Restrictions on free speech based on obscenity and libel laws, though not to be dismissed lightly, do after all affect only a limited range of utterances. Laws designed to protect the state itself from imminent danger affect a much wider range. Sedition and treason threaten not just some activities (publishing), not just some individuals (persons libelled), but all activities and the entire population. Not surprisingly, the most intense and intractable opposition to free speech arises when such threats seem imminent. Under what circumstances can the higher claims for safety of the state remove the protective shield of the First Amendment? Some of the best thinking of legal minds has been addressed to this key First Amendment issue.

Justices Holmes and Brandeis developed one answer in a series of notable Supreme Court cases following World War I, the "clear-and-present-danger" principle. It first appeared in an opinion written by Holmes in 1919. The case involved a wartime attempt to obstruct the military draft by means of a circular intended to incite direct resistance. Said Holmes:

We admit that in many places and in ordinary times the defendants in saying all that was said in the circular would have been within their constitutional rights. But the character of every act depends upon the circumstances in which it is done. . . . The question in every case is whether the words used are used in such circumstances and are of such a nature as to create a clear and present danger

---

[24] *New York Times Co.* v. *Sullivan*, 376 U. S. 254 at 279 (1964).

[25] *Ibid.,* at 270.

[26] *Associated Press* v. *Walker*, 388 U. S. 130 (1967).

that they will bring about the substantive evils that Congress has a right to prevent. It is a question of proximity and degree.[27]

In subsequent cases Holmes and Brandeis elaborated on this principle, emphasizing repeatedly that in order to justify suppression a danger must be both very apparent and very immediate. In 1927, Brandeis expressed it this way:

Those who won our independence by revolution were not cowards. They did not fear political change. They did not exalt order at the cost of liberty. To courageous, self-reliant men, with confidence in the power of free and fearless reasoning applied through the processes of popular government, no danger flowing from speech can be deemed clear and present, *unless the incidence of the evil apprehended is so imminent that it may befall before there is opportunity for full discussion.* If there be time to expose through discussion the falsehood and fallacies, to avert the evil by the processes of education, the remedy to be applied is more speech, not enforced silence.[28]

The "clear-and-present-danger" theory gained ground until after World War II. The security-conscious, fear-ridden atmosphere of the subsequent "cold-war" period, however, was not hospitable to this interpretation of the First Amendment. Many Americans grew less confident of the outcome of full discussion, more apprehensive that evil would befall before discussion could take place. An important Supreme Court decision in 1951 seemed to retreat from the Holmes-Brandeis position. In the *Dennis* case, the Court upheld the Smith Anti-Subversive Act, under which Communist party leaders in this country have been jailed.[29] Justices Black and Douglas wrote vigorous dissents to the majority opinion.

The *Dennis* case brought into sharp focus the outstanding political problem of the times—how can democracy combat communism without sacrificing the very things it seeks to preserve? The freedom-of-speech issue in this case was whether the accused could be found guilty on the basis of things said which did not represent a clear and present danger to the country, as this phrase had been generally understood, but instead an indirect and relatively remote danger. Mr. Justice Douglas remarked that the tendency of the majority opinion was "to make freedom of speech turn not on *what is said,* but on the *intent* with which it is said. Once we start down that road we enter territory dangerous to the liberties of every citizen."[30] Mr. Justice Black said flatly: "No matter how it is worded, this is a virulent form of prior censorship of speech and press, which I believe the First Amendment forbids . . . the only

---

[27] *Schenck* v. *U. S.,* 249 U. S. 47 at 52 (1919).

[28] *Whitney* v. *California,* 274 U. S. 357 at 377 (1927). Italics supplied.

[29] *Dennis* v. *U. S.,* 341 U. S. 494 (1951).

[30] *Ibid.,* at 583.

way to affirm these convictions is to repudiate directly or indirectly the established 'clear and present danger' rule."[31]

In keeping with this comment, a less stringent test began to appear in decisions of the late 1950's, the "balancing" test. In *Barenblatt*, the Supreme
Court upheld the conviction of a graduate student for refusing to answer
questions about political affiliations in a House Un-American Activities Committee hearing. He relied on the First Amendment to protect him; but the
Court said that a decision between the right of the government to interrogate
and the right of the individual to be silent "involves a balancing by the courts
of the competing private and public interests at stake in the particular circumstances shown."[32] Again Black dissented with a vigorous assertion of the
libertarian position. Such a balancing of interests, he said,

. . . completely leaves out the real interest in Barenblatt's silence, the interest of
the people as a whole in being able to join organizations, advocate causes and
make political "mistakes" without later being subjected to governmental penalties
for having dared to think for themselves. . . . For no number of laws against
communism can have as much effect as the personal conviction which comes from
having heard its arguments and rejected them, or from having once accepted its
tenets and later recognized their worthlessness.[33]

19.6 / The Inalienable Right to Speak

The issue resolves itself into one of principle *versus* expediency. On the one
side stand those who feel that some concession has to be made to public
sentiment of the moment, especially in time of crisis. On the other side stand
those who feel that the First Amendment grants *inalienable* rights which must
be preserved at all costs. Mr. Justice Black spoke for inalienability:

I believe that the First Amendment, made applicable to the States by the Fourteenth, protects every person from having a State or the Federal Government fine,
imprison, or assess damages against him when he has been guilty of no conduct
. . . other than expressing an opinion, even though others may believe that his
views are unwholesome, unpatriotic, stupid or dangerous.[34]

Alexander Meiklejohn upheld this position by distinguishing between forms
of speech which serve purely personal and selfish purposes and those which
serve the needs of a self-governing society.[35] The former he included under the
"liberty" mentioned in the Fifth Amendment rather than in the First. The

---

[31] *Ibid.*, at 579–580. Justice Frankfurter, in a separate opinion concurring with the
majority, gives a scholarly analysis of the origin and history of the clear-and-present-
danger principle.

[32] *Barenblatt* v. *U. S.*, 360 U. S. 109 at 126 (1959).

[33] *Ibid.*, at 144.

[34] *Garrison* v. *Louisiana*, 379 U. S. 64 at 79 (1964).

[35] Alexander Meiklejohn, *Free Speech and Its Relation to Self Government* (New
York: Harper & Bros., 1948).

Fifth Amendment prohibits the government from depriving any person of life, liberty, or property without due process of law; "liberty" in this context has been interpreted to include the liberties enumerated in the First Amendment.

The difference between the two amendments is an emphatic one and readily apparent. Deprivation of a liberty not embraced by the First Amendment, as for example the liberty of contract, is qualified by the phrase "without due process of law"; but those liberties enumerated in the First Amendment are guaranteed without qualification, the object and effect of which is to put them in a category apart and make them *incapable of abridgement by any process of law.*[36]

Meiklejohn contends that speech which serves private ends can be legally censored in accordance with due process; only that speech which serves public ends qualifies for the protection of the First Amendment. The latter is the kind of utterance which has to do with the individual's functions *as a citizen.* In Meiklejohn's view there are two sets of civil liberties: one may be abridged by due process of law; the other is beyond the reach of the law, belonging to those inalienable rights" to life, liberty, and the pursuit of happiness expressed in the Declaration of Independence.

19.7 / New Media and "The Press"

The modern mass media have introduced means and types of expression not contemplated by the authors of the Constitution. At first there was doubt whether motion pictures should be considered a form of "the press" and therefore entitled to the protection of the First Amendment. In 1915, the Supreme Court upheld an Ohio court which held motion pictures to be mere "spectacles," saying:

It cannot be put out of view that the exhibition of moving pictures is a business pure and simple, originated and conducted for profit, like other spectacles, not to be regarded, nor intended to be regarded by the Ohio constitution, we think, as part of the press of the country or as organs of public opinion.[37]

This opinion coincided with the release of the first motion picture to deal with a social question, *The Birth of a Nation,* whose ideological content produces controversy down to this day.

The *Mutual Film* case left motion pictures vulnerable to government censorship. Attempts to enact federal film-censorship laws failed, but a number of states and many municipalities adopted local censorship measures.[38] In 1952,

---

[36] *Associated Press* v. *National Labor Relations Board,* 301 U. S. 103 at 135 (1937). Italics supplied.

[37] *Mutual Film Corp.* v. *Industrial Commission of Ohio,* 236 U. S. 230 at 244 (1915).

[38] Pennsylvania had the earliest state censorship law, passed in 1908. An attempt under the Pennsylvania law to censor films shown over television was overthrown on the grounds that broadcasting is interstate commerce. The provision of the Communications Act forbidding censorship (§ 326) was interpreted as removing this subject from state jurisdiction. [*Allen B. Dumont Laboratories* v. *Carroll,* 184 F (2d) 153 (1950).]

however, in the *Miracle* case, the Supreme Court reversed its position of 1915. *The Miracle,* an Italian film which many Catholics found offensive (although the Catholic church did not proscribe the film in Italy), was banned in New York under a statute permitting state censorship on the grounds of sacrilege. The Supreme Court ruled against that part of the statute, holding: "It is not the business of government in our nation to suppress real or imagined attacks upon a particular religious doctrine, whether they appear in publications, speeches, or motion pictures."[39] The *Miracle* case was decided on the narrow grounds of the adequacy of "sacrilege" as a basis for censorship and did not therefore rule out existing state and local censorship laws; it did, however, establish that the term "press" in the First Amendment includes films. Shortly thereafter followed Supreme Court reversals of instances of censorship based on "immorality," "harmfulness," and "contribution to racial misunderstanding."[40]

The Supreme Court affirmed that New York violated the First Amendment in banning the film *Lady Chatterly's Lover* (based on the D. H. Lawrence classic). The State made no obscenity charge, but held that the picture as a whole was immoral because it implied that adultery is "a desirable, acceptable and proper pattern of behavior."[41] The Supreme Court pointed out that "the First Amendment's basic guarantee is of freedom to advocate ideas. The State, quite simply, has struck at the very heart of constitutionally protected liberty." It is not the business of the Court to uphold any one set of moral standards or religious precepts; rather it is to uphold the right to advocate all shades of opinion. For the First Amendment's guarantee of liberty to speak

. . . is not confined to the expression of ideas that are conventional or shared by a majority. It protects advocacy of the opinion that adultery may sometimes be proper, no less than advocacy of socialism or the single tax. And in the realm of ideas it protects expression which is eloquent no less than that which is unconvincing.[42]

The *Jacobellis* case extended the *Tropic of Cancer* doctrine (Section 19.2) to the film medium. Films, like books, must be judged by generalized standards, not merely local ones: "It is, after all, a national Constitution we are expounding."[43]

---

[39] *Joseph Burstyn, Inc.* v. *Wilson, Commissioner of Education of New York,* 343 U. S. 495 at 505 (1952).

[40] *Commercial Pictures Corp.* v. *Regents of New York* and *Superior Films* v. *Ohio Department of Education,* 346 U. S. 587 (1954). The films involved were *La Ronde, M,* and *Native Son.*

[41] *Kingsley International Pictures* v. *Regents of New York,* 360 U. S. 648 at 685 (1959).

[42] *Ibid.,* at 689. Compare this dictum with the Motion Picture Code's rule, "Illicit sex relationships shall not be justified" and the NAB Television Code's, "Illicit sex relations are not treated as commendable." See, however, the FCC's comments on the difference between broadcasting and other media at the end of this section.

[43] *Jacobellis* v. *Ohio,* 378 U. S. 184 at 195 (1964). The Ohio Supreme Court had upheld the conviction of Jacobellis for showing *The Lovers.*

Freedman tested the Constitutionality of the Maryland motion-picture licensing law by refusing to submit an admittedly harmless film to the State censors for the "prior restraint" of licensing for exhibition. The Maryland Court of Appeals upheld the statute, but the Supreme Court unanimously reversed, holding that, even if it did not directly censor, the statute could achieve censorship indirectly, merely by procrastinating in the award of a license or in the hearing of an appeal. The Supreme Court held that the censor must either issue a license promptly or else go to court without delay to obtain a restraining order. Moreover, the burden of proof must be on the censor to convince the court that the proscribed film violates the law, rather than on the exhibitor to prove the opposite. The element of prior restraint in licensing statutes, the Court pointed out, automatically raises a "presumption against constitutional validity." The Court thus recognized the Constitutionality of licensing statutes, but only when hedged about by particularly stringent procedural safeguards against unlawful restraints.[44]

A student of press freedom summarized the status of films in relation to the First Amendment in the late 1960's as follows:

The Court was still struggling with the problem of establishing a clear and workable definition of obscenity; but aside from obscenity, the day appears to be past when a motion picture can be pre-censored because it propounds a viewpoint that some person or persons consider to be immoral, blasphemous, or against public interest.[45]

As for broadcasting, the Radio Act of 1927 explicitly gave the new medium First Amendment status (Section 17.8). This means, in accordance with the foregoing discussion of First Amendment interpretation, that the government (specifically the FCC) is positively forbidden to interfere with the freedom of broadcasters to say anything they like over their stations, with only a few exceptions. These exceptions permit the government (as long as it does not act arbitrarily or capriciously) to prohibit or modify (1) certain specific types of intrinsically injurious broadcast material, such as obscenity; (2) broadcast materials presenting a clear and present danger to the safety of the state.

In actual practice, government regulation goes a long way beyond these limits. As the previous chapters have indicated, the FCC asserts the right to review the whole program service of stations and to take the character of that service into consideration when deciding on license renewals. Moreover, the FCC sets standards of public interest, convenience, and necessity in dictating specific types of programs and the balance among the various types (Section 18.4).

Had government regulation of broadcast programming under the FRC and FCC been applied to newspapers instead of broadcast stations, it could never

---

[44] *Freedman* v. *State of Maryland,* 380 U. S. 51 (1965).

[45] William A. Hachten, *The Supreme Court on Freedom of the Press: Decisions and Dissents* (Ames: Iowa State University Press, 1968), p. 249.

have been successfully defended in the courts. It would certainly have been found unconstitutional at many points. Broadcasters have lost their licenses for programs far less intemperate and scandalous than the articles in the Minneapolis newspaper granted a cloak of immunity by the Supreme Court in the *Near* case.[46] But, as the FCC has pointed out (with frequent concurrence by the courts), broadcasting must be considered in its own context:

. . . radio and TV programs enter the home and are readily available not only to the average normal adult but also to children and the emotionally immature. . . . Thus, for example, while a nudist magazine may be within the protection of the First Amendment . . . the televising of nudes might well raise a serious question of programming contrary to [the obscenity statute]. . . . Similarly, regardless of whether the "four letter words" and sexual descriptions, set forth in "Lady Chatterly's Lover" (when considered in the context of the whole book) make the book obscene for mailability purposes, the utterance of such words or the depiction of such sexual activity on radio or TV would raise similar public interest and [obscenity statute] questions.[47]

19.8 / The Public-Interest Concept and the First Amendment

Broadcasting thus has special social responsibility not quite like that of any other medium. This responsibility is implied in the Communications Act by the phrase "public interest, convenience, and necessity." Neither the term nor the concept originated with broadcasting legislation. The term was borrowed from public-utilities law—a fact which explains the words "convenience" and "necessity." A water supply for fighting fires is a public necessity; considerations of public convenience may dictate the route a transportation line should take. The word "interest" applies most aptly to the broadcasting situation.

The concept of public interest cropped up almost from the very beginning of discussions of the nature of broadcasting. At the First Radio Conference, in 1922, Herbert Hoover remarked that "this large mass of subscribers need protection as to the noises which fill their instruments [*i.e.,* radio receivers]."[48] Two years later, Hoover testified at a Congressional hearing:

Radio communication is not to be considered as merely a business carried on for private gain, for private advertisement, or for entertainment of the curious. It is a public concern impressed with the public trust and to be considered primarily from the standpoint of public interest to the same extent and upon the basis of the same general principles as our other public utilities.[49]

---

[46] Caldwell, *op. cit.,* p. 203.

[47] FCC, "Report and Statement of Policy re: Commission en banc Programming Inquiry," 25 *Fed. Reg.* 7291 at 7292 (1960).

[48] Department of Commerce, "Minutes of Open Meeting of Department of Commerce Conference on Radiotelephony" (1922, mimeo.), p. 3.

[49] Testimony of Herbert Hoover in House Committee on Merchant Marine and Fisheries, *To Regulate Radio Communication,* Hearings on H. R. 7357, 68th Cong. (Washington: Government Printing Office, 1924), p. 10.

At the Fourth Conference, in 1925, the National Association of Broadcasters presented a resolution recommending that a law should be enacted making public "convenience and necessity" the basis of choice among competing applications; a Committee on Operating Regulations mentioned "public interest" as a guide.[50] At that conference, Hoover remarked: "We can surely agree that no one can raise a cry of deprivation of free speech if he is compelled to prove that there is something more than naked commercial selfishness in his purpose."[51] The legislative history of the Radio Act of 1927 makes it apparent that Congress adopted essentially the same point of view. In answer to the NAB's later contention that the Commission was created merely to regulate technical aspects rather than program aspects of broadcasting, Senator Burton K. Wheeler replied:

Well, I was on the committee that considered the matter at that time, and I do not agree with you that that was the entire idea, just to regulate the physical aspects of radio broadcasting stations. That was not the intention of the Senate. I went through all those hearings at that time, sat as a member of the committee, and it was not the intention of the committee, nor of the Senate, just to regulate these physical things.[52]

From the outset, the FRC assumed that its supervisory duty definitely included consideration of program service:

The radio act specifies that the commission shall exercise no censorship over programs. Nevertheless, the kind of service rendered by a station must be a means of appraising its relative standing and must be considered by the commission in making assignments.[53]

Some examples of the specific requirements of the Commission concerning programming which have been challenged as violations of the First Amendment but upheld in the courts will illustrate.

Requirement of balance between commercial and sustaining time. Bay State Beacon, Inc., lost in a competitive hearing for a Brockton, Massachusetts, radio channel because, among other things, it proposed to devote less time to sustaining programs than the successful applicant. Bay State proposed to make 80 per cent of its time available for regular commercial sponsorship, 15 per cent for "institutional sponsorship" (public-service agencies charged at half-rates), and only 5 per cent for sustaining programs.[54]

---

[50] Fourth National Radio Conference, *Proceedings and Recommendations for Regulation of Radio* (Washington: Government Printing Office, 1926), pp. 10, 23.

[51] *Ibid.*, p. 7.

[52] Testimony of Senator Burton K. Wheeler in Senate Committee on Interstate Commerce, *To Amend the Communications Act of 1934,* Hearings on S. 814, 78th Cong., 1st Sess. (Washington: Government Printing Office, 1944), p. 238.

[53] FRC, *Third Annual Report* (Washington: Government Printing Office, 1929), p. 3.

[54] 12 FCC 567 at 569 (1948). Affirmed 171 F. (2d) 826 (1948).

Requirement that licensee affirmatively seek out discussions of controversial public issues. Johnston Broadcasting Company and a rival applicant for a radio channel in Birmingham, Ala., were substantially equal except that Johnston did not show that "an affirmative effort" to encourage programs dealing with controversial issues would be made, whereas the opposing applicant provided for "positive action" on this score. Johnston lost primarily on this ground.[55] On appeal, the Commission was sustained on this point (though reversed on other grounds). The court remarked that

. . . in a comparative consideration, it is well recognized that comparative service to the listening public is the vital element, and programs are the essence of that service. So, while the Commission cannot prescribe any type of program (except for prohibitions against obscenity, profanity, etc.), it can make a comparison on the basis of public interest and, therefore, of public service. Such a comparison of proposals is not a form of censorship within the meaning of the statute.[56]

Requirement that programming be tailored to the local community. Allen T. Simmons (WADC) and another station each applied for a mutually exclusive change to a more desirable frequency and higher power. The Simmons application was rejected because it proposed to carry nothing but network programs from 8:00 A.M. to 11:00 P.M. This, said the Commission,

. . . is not only tantamount to a voluntary abdication to the network of the duty and responsibility of a broadcast station licensee to determine for itself the nature and character of a program service which will best meet the needs of listeners in its area, but is an abdication to an organization which makes no pretense to scheduling its programs with the particular needs and desires of any one service area in mind.[57]

Requirement that certain network business practices affecting programs must be changed. This followed from the FCC's investigation of chain broadcasting, which has been previously cited in several different connections, notably in Section 9.5. The Supreme Court decision affirming the right of the FCC to regulate contracts between networks and affiliates is the leading case in point and therefore is quoted at length:

The Regulations, even if valid in all other respects, must fall because they abridge, say the appellants, their right of free speech. If that be so, it would follow that every person whose application for a license to operate a station is denied by the Commission is thereby denied his constitutional right of free speech. Freedom of utterance is abridged to many who wish to use the limited facilities of radio. *Unlike other modes of expression, radio inherently is not available to all. That is its unique characteristic, and that is why, unlike other modes of expression, it is subject to governmental regulation.* Because it cannot be used by all, some who wish

---

[55] 12 FCC 517 at 524 (1947).

[56] *Johnston Broadcasting Co.* v. *FCC,* 175 F. (2d) 351 at 359 (1949).

[57] 12 FCC 1160 at 1173 (1947). Affirmed 169 F. (2d) 670 (1948).

to use it must be denied. But Congress did not authorize the Commission to choose among applicants upon the basis of their political, economic or social views, or upon any other capricious basis. If it did, or if the Commission by these regulations proposed a choice among applicants upon some such basis, the issue before us would be wholly different. The question here is simply whether the Commission, by announcing that it will refuse licenses to persons who engage in specified network practices (a basis for choice which we hold is comprehended within the statutory criterion of "public interest"), is thereby denying such persons the constitutional right of free speech. The right of free speech does not include, however, the right to use the facilities of radio without a license. The licensing system established by Congress in the Communications Act of 1934 was a proper exercise of its power over commerce. The standard it provided for the licensing of stations was the "public interest, convenience or necessity." Denial of a station license on that ground, if valid under the Act, is not a denial of free speech.[58]

*   *   *   *   *

The [Communications] Act itself establishes that the Commission's powers are not limited to the engineering and technical aspects of regulation of radio communication. Yet we are asked to regard the Commission as a kind of traffic officer, policing the wave lengths to prevent stations from interfering with each other. *But the Act does not restrict the Commission merely to supervision of the traffic. It puts upon the Commission the burden of determining the composition of that traffic.* The facilities of radio are not large enough to accommodate all who wish to use them. Methods must be devised for choosing from among the many who apply. And since Congress itself could not do this, it committed the task to the commission.[59]

In most cases, as we have already pointed out (Section 18.8), when the Commission cites a given program or practice as contrary to the public interest, the accused station voluntarily changes the program or practice and continues in operation. Two cases in which programs were directly responsible for loss of license may be regarded as significant tests of the Commission's powers. In each case the Commission was upheld by the Court of Appeals and the Supreme Court refused to review the lower court's decision.

KFKB in Milford, Kansas, was owned by one Dr. J. R. Brinkley, who won national notoriety for a "goat-gland" operation which purported to restore flagging male vitality. Brinkley used the station to advertise his hospital and certain drugs which he packaged and retailed through hundreds of outlets. Three daily half-hours on the station were devoted to a "Medical Question Box" program on which Brinkley would diagnose the ailments of correspondents and prescribe his packaged remedies. Excerpts from actual broadcasts illustrate the technique:

Here's one from Tillie. She says she had an operation, had some trouble 10 years ago. I think the operation was unnecessary, and it isn't very good sense to have an

---

[58] *NBC* v. *U. S.*, 319 U. S. 190 at 226–227 (1943). Italics supplied.

[59] *Ibid.*, at 215–216. Italics supplied.

ovary removed with the expectation of motherhood resulting therefrom. My advice to you is to use Women's Tonic No. 50, 67, and 61. This combination will do for you what you desire if any combination will, after three months persistent use.

*   *   *   *   *

Sunflower State, from Dresden, Kansas. Probably he has gallstones. No, I don't mean that, I mean kidney stones. My advice to you is to put him on Prescription No. 80 and 50 for men, also 64. I think that he will be a whole lot better. Also drink a lot of water.[60]

The last prescription is interesting in view of the fact that the drugs prescribed were medicaments for *both* kidney stones and gallstones. The unethical procedure of diagnosing aliments and prescribing medicines on the basis of letters from patients embroiled Brinkley with the American Medical Association, which found that he possessed no recognized medical degree. The FRC refused to renew his license. In upholding the FRC the Court remarked: "In considering the question whether the public interest, convenience or necessity will be served by a renewal of appellant's license, the commission has merely exercised its undoubted right to take note of appellant's past conduct, which is not censorship."[61]

The second case involved a different class of objectionable programs. KGEF was licensed to the Trinity Methodist Church, South, in Los Angeles, but in fact was owned by one Reverend Dr. Shuler. Many local residents protested the renewal of KGEF's license, with some ninety witnesses appearing at the FRC hearing. Shuler had used the station for highly personal attacks and had twice been convicted of using it to obstruct the orderly administration of justice.

On one occasion he announced over the radio that he had certain damaging information against a prominent unnamed man which, unless a contribution (presumably to the church) of a hundred dollars was forthcoming, he would disclose. As a result, he received contributions from several persons. He freely spoke of "pimps" and prostitutes. He alluded slightingly to the Jews as a race, and made frequent and bitter attacks on the Roman Catholic religion and its relations to government.[62]

In upholding the FRC's decision not to renew the license, the Appeals Court said:

Appellant [Shuler] may continue to indulge his strictures upon the characters of men in public office. He may just as freely as ever criticize religious practices of which he does not approve. He may even indulge private malice or personal slander—subject, of course, to be required to answer for the abuse thereof—but he

---

[60] *KFKB Broadcasting Association, Inc.* v. *FRC,* 47 F. (2) 670 at 671 (1931).

[61] *Ibid.,* at 672. Brinkley almost succeeded in becoming Governor of Kansas, being one of the first to use radio effectively in a political campaign.

[62] *Trinity Methodist Church, South* v. *FRC,* 62 F. (2d) 850 at 852 (1932).

may not, as we think, demand, of right, the continued use of an instrumentality of commerce for such purposes, or any other, except in subordination to all reasonable rules and regulations Congress, acting through the Commission, may prescribe.[63]

These early cases make it clear that (1) those who choose to become broadcast licensees thereby voluntarily subject themselves to certain restrictions of their freedom of utterance, and (2) although the First Amendment applies to broadcasting, it does not apply in exactly the same way or to exactly the same degree that it does to the medium of print.

---

[63] *Ibid.,* at 853.

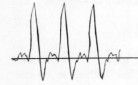

20

REGULATION: ALLY OF FREEDOM

The disposition of mankind, whether as rulers or as fellow-citizens, to impose their own opinions and inclinations as a rule of conduct on others, is so energetically supported by some of the best and by some of the worst feelings incident to human nature, that it is hardly ever kept under restraint by anything but want of power.

JOHN STUART MILL

20.1 / The Marketplace of Ideas

Fear of the absolute power of government dominated the thinking of the statesmen who "brought forth a new nation" in 1776. All political experience had taught that the state, unless held in check, inevitably uses its collective force to restrict the individual liberties of its citizens. The state's coercive resources of law, police, and military force prevail against the puny strength of the private individual. The Constitution, and in particular the Bill of Rights (the first ten amendments being essentially a part of the original document), arms the individual citizen with a counterbalancing power. The First Amendment therefore views the *government* as the source of power from which suppression of freedoms may be expected, and hence forbids *Congress* to abridge those freedoms.

Suppression, however, can likewise come from private, nongovernmental sources of power. Mill warned of the "despotism of custom" and the intolerance of majorities. Protection against the government is not enough:

There needs protection also against the tyranny of the prevailing opinion and feeling; against the tendency of society to impose, by other means than civil penalties, its own ideas and practices as rules of conduct on those who dissent from them; to fetter the development, and, if possible, prevent the formation, of any individuality not in harmony with its ways, and compels all characters to fashion themselves upon the model of its own. There is a limit to the legitimate interference of collective opinion with individual independence: and to find that limit, and maintain it against encroachment, is as indispensable to a good condition of human affairs, as protection against political despotism.[1]

---

[1] John Stuart Mill, *On Liberty* (Oxford: Basil Blackwell, 1946), p. 4.

Closely linked to the despotic potentialities of "prevailing opinion and feeling" is the coercive power of large economic concentrations. The technological revolution of the nineteenth century and its twentieth-century economic consequences have given rise to private domestic empires far more powerful than any conceivable by the eighteenth-century standards of the Constitution's authors.

According to the eighteenth-century doctrine of *laissez faire,* unrestricted economic competition will *automatically and inevitably* result in the greatest social good for the greatest number. Then-prevailing conditions of communication, transportation, merchandising, purchasing power, and business organization tended to keep domestic industries localized and to impose limits on growth. But under modern conditions of distribution and growth potential, competition can produce results quite opposite to those predicted by the *laissez faire* theory. The passage in 1890 of the Sherman Act, the first United States antitrust law, reflected the fact that under modern conditions an unregulated economic system is not necessarily self-perpetuating.

The libertarian philosophers based their faith on a theory of free exchange of ideas analogous to the *laissez faire* theory of economics. The analogy continues to be used today:

It is the purpose of the First Amendment to preserve an uninhibited marketplace of ideas in which truth will ultimately prevail, rather than to countenance monopolization of the market . . .[2]

The goods retailed in the eighteenth-century "marketplace of ideas" came from small traders competing on relatively equal terms. The marketplace consisted of leisurely face-to-face discussions, town meetings, pamphlets, small newspapers counting their circulation in the hundreds. Virtually anyone with something to say could make his voice heard.

20.2 / Preservation of Competition in Ideas

In the modern marketplace, however, giant corporations retail ideas through the media of print, film, and broadcasting to millions on a national scale. The number of separate marketing entities shrinks as corporate conglomerates grow. Syndication turns outlets into mere transmission belts for centrally manufactured materials. Economic factors favor some classes of ideas over others, as shown in Chapter 16. Limited variety of ideas combines with inequality of entry into the marketplace to impede competition and the "self-righting" process. The very speed with which national media can saturate the whole country with a given idea raises the question whether there is enough time for the hypothesized sorting-out process to take place, even if other conditions are favorable. Increasingly, therefore, students of the subject have come to doubt the validity of the unsupervised-marketplace concept, although

---

[2] *Red Lion Broadcasting Co., Inc.* v. *FCC,* 395 U. S. 367 at 390 (1969).

the courts continue to rely on it, as shown by the quotation from *Red Lion* above. Baker and Ball, in their study of violence in the mass media, speak of "the marketplace myth":

Under the traditional view of the First Amendment, the role of the gatekeeper and the right of the owner to choose, are plenary. . . . The nation's broadcasters, publishers, and editors decide who shall have the opportunity to be heard—an understandable and pragmatically necessary process. But, with the present structure of the communication business, it results in a marketplace far different from the 18th century concept of a marketplace for ideas.[3]

Jerome Barron, a specialist in communications law, regards the marketplace concept as a romantic fallacy:

Our constitutional theory is in the grip of a romantic conception of free expression, a belief that the "marketplace of ideas" is freely accessible. But if there ever were a self-operating marketplace of ideas, it has long since ceased to exist. . . . To those who can obtain access to the media of mass communications First Amendment case law furnishes considerable help. But what of those whose ideas are too unacceptable to secure access to the media? To them the mass communications industry replies: The First Amendment guarantees our freedom to do as we choose with our media. Thus the constitutional imperative of free expression becomes a rationale for repressing competing ideas.[4]

The media constantly appeal to the letter of the First Amendment to gain protection from government interference in business practices violating the spirit of the amendment. The Associated Press, for example, provided a leading case when it contended that restraining it from using monopolistic business practices amounted to interference by the government with freedom of the press. But the Supreme Court replied:

It would be strange indeed . . . if the grave concern for freedom of the press which prompted adoption of the First Amendment should be read as a command that the government was without power to protect that freedom. . . . Surely a command that the government itself shall not impede the free flow of ideas does not afford non-governmental combinations a refuge if they impose restraints upon that constitutionally guaranteed freedom. . . . Freedom of the press from governmental interference under the First Amendment does not sanction repression of that freedom by private interests.[5]

---

[3] Robert K. Baker and Sandra J. Ball, *Violence and the Media,* Vol. IX, A Report to National Commission on Causes and Prevention of Violence (Washington: Government Printing Office, 1969), p. 69.

[4] Jerome A. Barron, "Access to the Press—A New First Amendment Right," *Harvard Law Review,* LXXX (1967), 1641–1642, reprinted in Donald M. Gillmor and Jerome A. Barron, *Mass Communication Law: Cases and Comment* (St. Paul, Minn.: West, 1969), pp. 117–141.

[5] *Associated Press* v. *U. S.,* 326 U. S. 1 at 20 (1945).

Thus, under modern conditions of communication, the government emerges sometimes as the *ally* of freedom as well as the enemy. Just as changed conditions in the literal marketplace of goods call for measures to preserve competition, so changed conditions in the figurative marketplace of ideas seem to call for some comparable intervention.

In broadcasting, two major impediments to the self-righting process can be discerned: monopolistic concentrations of control, or oligopolies, which reduce the diversity of communications sources; and unfair practices in operating the media which distort or selectively screen the material that does get through. We can summarize the chief manifestations of these impediments as follows:

A. Monopolistic concentrations of control through
   (1) Patents on media technology
   (2) Facilities (superior frequencies, power)
   (3) Group ownership of media and other enterprises
   (4) Overcentralization of program production (see Section 15.4)

B. Unfairness resulting from
   (1) Private censorship; intentional distortion of factual matter
   (2) Avoidance of serious or provocative program content
   (3) One-sided presentation of controversial opinions

Let us now review how government, through the FCC and the courts, has sought, as an ally of freedom, to interpose the First Amendment as a protection against these restraints from private sources.

20.3 / Monopolistic Media Concentrations

Having decided in 1920 not to keep radio a government monopoly (Section 7.4), Congress was almost immediately faced with the possibility that it would become a private monopoly. The Federal Trade Commission, after an extensive study, published a report in 1923 indicating that a monopolistic patent situation existed in radio.[6] This report influenced Congress to include antimonopoly provisions in subsequent radio legislation. Antitrust suits eventually eliminated a variety of coercive practices whereby the Radio Group capitalized on its patent monopoly, forcing release of essential patents to rival manufacturers on reasonable royalty terms. The evolution of technology continues to create monopoly-prone situations. Under modern conditions, a different kind of patent-monopoly threat has emerged—collusion among competitors to suppress or postpone technological improvements in consumer goods that threaten to outmode current products.

Broadcasting itself is quasi monopolistic by nature. A license confers a monopoly, within a limited area, on the use of a particular channel; limits on

[6] FTC, *Report on the Radio Industry* (Washington: Government Printing Office, 1924).

the number of channels useable in a given area without interference impose like limits on the total amount of competition in that area.

The potentialities for aggravating this inherent monopolistic tendency by granting unusually favorable technical advantages was illustrated by an experiment with "superpower" in 1934. The FRC granted WLW, Cincinnati, a Special Temporary Authorization to operate at half a million watts—ten times the prevailing maximum power. In 1927, when the FRC had begun, the maximum obtainable power had been only about 30,000 w. By 1931, 50,000 had been reached, and now "superpower" became possible. The tenfold increase gave WLW an overwhelming competitive advantage. According to an official survey, WLW became the station of first choice among the listeners of thirteen states.[7] The outcry from WLW's competitors stimulated a "sense of the Senate" resolution that 50,000 w. should be the maximum power allowed.[8] The FCC reduced WLW's power accordingly, and ever since, 50,000 w. has remained the maximum power allowed domestic AM stations.

Nevertheless, the very physical nature of radio precludes licensee equality. Physical factors (favorable frequency, good propagation conditions) combine with historical factors (for example, obtaining a license prior to the television freeze) and economic factors (obtaining a channel in a rich market) to make some licenses immensely more valuable than others. These inherent inequalities may be exaggerated when more than one station comes under common control, or when common ownership combines stations with other media. This monopolistic tendency could take several forms:

(1) Ownership of two or more stations covering the *same service area*. The FCC rules out this form of monopoly on stations of the same type (AM, FM, or TV) by its "duopoly" rule (Section 15.4). AM-FM-TV combinations in the same area are common, however.[9]

(2) Ownership of two or more stations located in *different areas*. The FCC limits such multiple ownership to seven stations of each type, with a ceiling of five VHF television stations.[10]

(3) Ownership of both stations and other communications media in the same service area. An applicant who already owns the only local news-

---

[7] FCC, *Second Annual Report* (Washington: Government Printing Office, 1936), p. 61.

[8] S. Res. 294, 75th Cong. (June 13, 1938). The Senate may also have been influenced by the antilabor policies of WLW's owner, Paul Crosley, Jr., which he imposed on the news operation of his station. See Erik Barnouw, *The Golden Web: A History of Broadcasting in the United States, 1933–1953* (New York: Oxford University Press, 1968), pp. 130–133.

[9] The Commission proposed limiting new licensees to only one class of station per market (the "one-to-a-customer" policy); however, the usual "grandfather" clause prevented disturbing existing multiple ownerships—which made the proposed rule relatively meaningless. [FCC, "First Report and Order on Multiple Ownership of Standard, FM, and Television Broadcast Stations," 35 *Fed. Reg.* 5948 (1970).]

[10] Educational broadcasting is exempted from these limits in order to allow full development of state educational networks.

paper, for example, would (other things being equal) suffer a disadvantage competing with an applicant without such a monopoly potential (but see the discussion on FCC inconsistency on this point in Section 21.6).

(4) Ownership of both stations and other communications media in different service areas. Most of the larger corporate media enterprises discussed in Section 11.5 tend this way.

(5) Ownership of stations by conglomerate corporations.

The FCC considers *diversification* of media control an important—but not overwhelmingly important—factor in making comparative decisions. Practical experience and an outstanding past record could be points in favor of an applicant who already owns a station or a newspaper, as against an applicant without any prior experience in the media (Section 18.6).

Multiple ownership does have arguments in its favor. As in other businesses, large size has economic advantages enabling better service to the public from a group of stations than any one of the group might be able to render independently. The multiple owner can realize savings in overhead, employ high-caliber supervisory personnel, bargain effectively with networks and other sources of supply, take advantage of shared experience and know-how from one market to the next.

On the other hand, it seems more important to ensure the viability of the small, local broadcasting firm than of other types of enterprise. Standardization of consumer goods has no socially detrimental effects, whereas standardization of ideas does. Whether toothpaste is manufactured locally or shipped from the other end of the country makes no difference, since there is no need for local flavor in toothpaste; but there is need for local flavor in ideas, opinions, and information.

Actual evidence of the practical effects, good or bad, of the several kinds of multiple ownership has not been overwhelmingly on one side or the other. A study financed by the National Association of Broadcasters compared single-owner and multiple-owner stations in three matched markets, obtaining data from interviews with media personnel and "business and community leaders." Among the conclusions: multiple-owner stations (1) have larger news staffs, more news programs; (2) tend to hire more professionally oriented managers; (3) depend less on short-term profit making; (4) resort to fewer undesirable business practices.[11] The methods used in this research have been challenged.[12] Harvey Levin has specialized in the study of multiple

---

[11] George H. Litwin and William H. Wroth, *The Effects of Common Ownership on Media Content and Influence: A Research Evaluation of Media Ownership and Public Interest* (Washington: National Association of Broadcasters, 1969).

[12] Cf. book review in *Educational Broadcasting Review*, III (December, 1969), 69–76; and James N. Rosse, Bruce M. Owen, and David L. Grey, "Economic Issues in the Joint Ownership of Newspaper Media," *Studies in the Economics of Mass Communication*, Memorandum No. 97 (Stanford University Research Center in Economic Growth, May, 1970).

ownership and concluded that its effects are, on the whole, undesirable.[13] On the other hand, Peter Steiner, who has also given special attention to the economics of media ownership, concluded after reviewing Levin's book that the evidence is thin: "It is not clear that the basic character of U. S. broadcasting [is] significantly influenced by the degree of joint ownership or that [it] would be appreciably altered by a vigorous drive for diversification."[14]

20.4 / Cross-Channel Affiliation and Conglomerates

More complex issues arise when multiple ownership combines broadcasting with other media ("cross-channel affiliation") and other types of business enterprise ("conglomerates"). In 1969, the FCC announced an inquiry into ownership of broadcasting stations by conglomerate corporations.[15] Among the topics to be investigated the Commission listed: fairness and freedom in presenting program material; lack of supervision by top officials; siphoning broadcast profits to serve other units in the corporate group; undue competitive "leverage"; possible impediments to technical development.

We have already referred to the merger once planned between the American Broadcasting Company and the International Telephone and Telegraph Company (Section 10.6). Had this merger gone through, ABC would have become part of a conglomeration of over four hundred boards of directors with holdings in some forty foreign countries, interests in consumer finance, life insurance, investment funds, loan companies, car rentals, book publishing, and American defense and space contracts. "The mere awareness" of these high-level involvements, wrote FCC Commissioner Nicholas Johnson, would have made it impossible for news staffs to cover stories affecting them objectively.[16]

20.5 / Newspaper-Broadcasting Combinations

Newspaper/broadcast-station combinations created one of the most intricate and controversial problems in ownership regulation.[17] The underlying dilemma again comes from conflicting public-interest claims: which matters more, diversification of media ownership or quality of program service? Every li-

---

[13] Harvey J. Levin, *Broadcast Regulation and Joint Ownership of Media* (New York: New York University Press, 1960).

[14] Peter O. Steiner, Review of Levin, *op. cit.,* in *American Economic Review,* LI (June, 1961), 472.

[15] FCC, "Notice of Inquiry into the Ownership of Broadcast Stations by Persons or Entities with Other Business Interests," 34 *Fed. Reg.* 2151 (1969).

[16] Nicholas Johnson, *How to Talk Back to Your Television Set* (Boston: Little, Brown, 1970), "The Media Barons," pp. 45–78.

[17] In 1970, publishing companies owned 394 AM, 245 FM, and 189 TV stations, according to *Broadcasting 1970 Yearbook,* p. 15. See also Section 11.4 regarding this ownership trend.

cense granted to a publisher automatically reduces diversification. On the other hand, an established publisher may well appear to be the best qualified applicant by virtue of experience, knowledge of the community, financial resources, and proven record of service.

In 1941, the Commission initiated an inquiry looking toward possible exclusion of newspaper owners from broadcast-station ownership. Politically powerful newspaper interests strongly opposed this move, and the FCC eventually gave up its original intention "in view of the grave legal and political questions involved."[18] Instead, the Commission continued to consider newspaper ownership as one of the several criteria in comparative hearings. The courts confirmed the legality of using this criterion. In the 1951 *Scripps Howard* case, the Appeals Court supported the FCC's reliance on diversification as the reason for denying a Construction Permit to a newspaper-owned applicant. The Court cited the *Associated Press* case (Section 20.2), where the Supreme Court had emphasized the role of the First Amendment in encouraging "the widest possible dissemination of information from diverse and antagonistic sources":

In considering the public interest the Commission is well within the law when, in choosing between two applications, it attaches significance to the fact that one, in contrast with the other, is disassociated from existing media of mass communication in the area affected.[19]

In the *Mansfield Journal* case the Court supported the Commission's use as disqualifying evidence the fact that the newspaper applicant had allegedly used unfair competitive practices:

. . . whether Mansfield's competitive practices were legal or illegal, in the strict sense, is not conclusive here. Monopoly in the mass communication of news and advertising is contrary to the public interest, even if not in terms proscribed by the antitrust laws.[20]

Again the Court went back to the *Associated Press* case to stress the duty of government to prevent private enterprise from frustrating the objectives of the First Amendment:

Just as the First Amendment does not provide the press with immunity from the commands of the antitrust laws, so a newspaper, when it stands as an applicant for

---

[18] FCC, "Newspaper Ownership of Radio Stations," 9 *Fed. Reg.* 702 (1944). Prodded by the Justice Department, the FCC reopened the question in 1970. See FCC, "Amendment of . . . the Commission's Rules in Relation to Standard, FM, and Television Multiple Station Ownership," 35 *Fed. Reg.* 5963 (1970).

[19] *Scripps Howard Radio, Inc.* v. *FCC,* 189 F. (2d) 677 at 683 (1951). The Supreme Court refused to review the decision, 342 U. S. 830 (1951).

[20] *Mansfield Journal Co.* v. *FCC,* 180 F. (2d) 28 at 33 (1950).

a radio license, may not rely on the First Amendment to compel the Federal Communications Commission to disregard public interest in considering its application.[21]

20.6 / Private Censorship

In a 1969 address, the Vice-President of the United States made an unprecedented (for a high government official) public attack on network-television news, accusing the leading networks of one-sidedness, monopoly, and (by implication) conspiracy to misrepresent the national administration. Said Agnew:

I'm not asking for Government censorship or any other kind of censorship. I'm asking whether a form of censorship already exists when the news that 40 million Americans receive each night is determined by a handful of men responsible only to their corporate employers and is filtered through a handful of commentators who admit to their own set of biases.[22]

The answer to the Vice-President's question is "No." A handful of men filtering news through a handful of commentators who admit to biasses does not constitute censorship in any meaningful sense. Some distinction has to be made between censorship and the essential journalistic functions of selecting, editing, and commenting on news. Without such a distinction, every reporter, every editor, every station manager becomes a censor, which makes the word so broad it becomes meaningless. Licensees of broadcasting stations have undelegatable responsibility for programming their stations to serve the public interest. This responsibility involves blue pencilling some programs and some parts of programs; yet it would be patently absurd to call this exercise of legally imposed responsibility "censorship."

If we look to past experience for clues to the essential elements of censorship, we find that throughout most of history (and to this day in many countries) they include (1) systematic suppression *before* publication (2) by a government official (3) backed by the coercive powers of the state (4) of material allegedly harmful to the state, to religion, or to public morals. The classic common-law exegesis was given by Blackstone:

The liberty of the press is indeed essential to the nature of a free state; but this consists in laying no previous restraints upon publications, and not in freedom from censure for criminal matter when published. Every freeman has an undoubted right to lay what sentiments he pleases before the public; to forbid this is to destroy the freedom of the press, but if he publishes what is improper, mischievous, or illegal, he must take the consequences of his own temerity.[23]

---

[21] *Ibid.*, at 35.

[22] The speech and a reply by Frank Stanton, President of CBS, are reproduced in *Educational Broadcasting Review*, IV (February, 1970), 12–22.

[23] Quoted in William A. Hachten, *"The Supreme Court on Freedom of the Press: Decisions and Dissents* (Ames: Iowa State University Press, 1968), pp. 41–42. The FCC

Modern libertarianism has broadened this concept of "previous restraint" in two directions. Restraint need not always be "previous" in the sense of requiring submission of copy for clearance or licensing prior to publication; the imminent *threat* of harassment or punishment can have a deadening effect, for "it is not merely the sporadic abuse of power by the censor but the pervasive threat inherent in its very existence that constitutes the danger to freedom of discussion."[24] Secondly, as indicated in previous sections, it is now recognized that under modern conditions, *private* agencies as distinguished from government may attain enough power to impose illegal restraints on freedom of speech. The Vice-President undoubtedly had in mind this kind of private power on the part of television networks.

This definition implies systematic and deliberate *omission* ("restraint"), guided by a particular aim. It leaves room for mistakes—not only honest ones, but even careless or ignorant ones. It leaves room for normal journalistic selection and editing, as long as it does not systematically suppress material to a particular end. It leaves room for inevitable personal bias—for according to contemporary opinion, absolute journalistic objectivity is probably neither possible nor desirable. Elmer Davis, for example, said that objectivity, "a necessary and useful ideal in its day, has been carried so far that it leans over backward and often obscures the truth instead of revealing it."[25]

The network newsmen may have used bad editorial judgment, but their "corporate employers" (the alleged censors) were guilty, if at all, of granting them too much *freedom* to select and comment, rather than of imposing *restraints* on their journalistic judgment. At worst, the networks could be accused of *unfairness* in the exercise of their power over a medium of communication. The unfairness concept, to which we return in following sections, helps make an extremely useful and important distinction between censorship as such and a whole range of lesser encroachments on free communication. Censorship remains primarily a government-inspired form of coercion. To confuse it either with journalistic editing or with simple unfairness in the operation of the media is to obscure a vital distinction, not merely a semantic one.

Authentic cases of news censorship have not often come to light in broadcasting. In the 1948 *Richards* case, the licensee of stations in Detroit, Cleveland, and Los Angeles was accused by professional newsmen of trying to force them systematically to slant news in keeping with his personal political beliefs—a clear case of censorship by a private agent. Hearings on the charges

---

is at great pains never to give the appearance of prejudging programs in a way that could open it to the charge of using "previous restraint."

[24] *Near v. Minnesota,* 283 U. S. 697 at 713 (1931).

[25] Elmer Davis, "The Need for Interpretive Reporting," in Ralph D. Casey, *The Press in Perspective* (Baton Rouge: Louisiana State University Press, 1963), p. 63. For discussion of practical aspects of this question in broadcasting, see Fred W. Friendly, *Due to Circumstances Beyond Our Control . . .* (New York: Random House, 1967), pp. 197–204.

went on for seven months and Richards is said to have spent nearly a million dollars defending himself. He died in 1951, before the case was decided, and the FCC dropped the investigation upon receiving assurances that the alleged censorship would be discontinued by those who succeeded to the licenses.

More frequent in broadcasting are cases of program editing or cancellation by licensees, better considered under the rubric of "fairness" than censorship. Allegations of censorship by entertainers when words are "bleeped" out of tapes or when programs are cancelled have to be considered in the light of the licensee's legal responsibilities. The broadcaster not only has the right but, as we have said, the nondelegatable duty to determine which spokesman should discuss which issues at which times on his facilities. It is the height of naïveté for comedians, singers, and other entertainers to cry "Censor!" when a station or network declines to accept self-appointed and inappropriate spokesmen who unilaterally choose inappropriate times to discuss controversial subjects. This is not to say that the broadcaster is never wrong. He may well misjudge the appropriateness of the spokesman, the time, or the subject, in which case he may be guilty of the lesser charge of unfairness.

20.7 / Editorializing by Licensees

An FCC policy turnabout with regard to editorializing by licensees illustrates a trend toward placing heavier emphasis on the licensee's obligation to provide serious program content as an aspect of fairness. About 1940, a Boston radio station, WAAB, adopted a policy of "editorializing," *i.e.,* expressing views on political candidacies and other controversial public questions in the name of the station itself.[26] In the ensuing "Mayflower" decision the Commission took the view that such editorializing was not in the public interest, holding that "a truly free radio cannot be used to advocate the causes of the licensee. It cannot be used to support the candidacies of his friends. It cannot be devoted to the support of principles he happens to regard most favorably. In brief, the broadcaster cannot be an advocate."[27] The licensee submitted affidavits showing that it had discontinued its editorializing practices and would never revive them in the future, in consideration of which the Commission renewed the license. That "the broadcaster cannot be an advocate" became, in effect, the law without having been challenged.

The Mayflower decision caused much adverse comment among thoughtful

---

[26] As distinguished from opinions expressed by news commentators in their own name, long a common practice (see Section 9.3). At one time editorializing by *sponsors* aroused concern. Ford's *Sunday Evening Hour* on radio, for example, featured intermission talks attacking such New Deal measures as unemployment insurance. See Barnouw, *op cit.,* p. 34; and FCC, *Public Service Responsibility of Broadcast Licensees* (Washington: Government Printing Office, 1946), pp. 46–47.

[27] *In re The Yankee Network, Inc.,* 8 FCC 333 at 340 (1941). The decision derives its popular name from the Mayflower Broadcasting Corp., which applied for the channel occupied by WAAB. The Mayflower application was rejected on other grounds.

critics. In 1949, after eight days of hearings, the FCC reversed itself. The new opinion acknowledged the inconsistency of regulating broadcasting in the interests of free speech and at the same time denying that freedom to those who happened to be broadcast licensees, even though stations "should not be used for the private interest, whims, or caprices of the particular persons who have been granted licenses."[28] Editorializing, the FCC now thought, could be regarded as part and parcel of that "affirmative duty" of the licensee to provide coverage of controversial issues of public importance—not so much in the interest of the licensee's right to speak as in the interest of the public's right to hear:

It is the right of the public to be informed rather than any right on the part of the Government, any broadcast licensee or any individual member of the public to broadcast his own particular views on any matter, which is the foundation stone of the American system of broadcasting.[29]

Open editorializing, the Commission reasoned, would put the licensee on record, and "the public has less to fear from the open partisan than from the covert propagandist."

The newly granted right to editorialize carried with it the obligation to present contrary views. This obligation gave broadcasters pause, even though they had advocated reversal of the Mayflower decision. Few took immediate advantage of the opportunity. In the 1960's, however, with considerable urging by Commission Chairman Newton Minow,[30] substantial numbers of stations began to editorialize. According to a 1963 survey, fears about opening up a Pandora's box of counterclaims for time appeared unfounded: responding stations reported that less than 6 per cent of their editorials stimulated valid requests for reply.[31] By 1969, it was estimated that about half the stations editorialized at least occasionally, but still relatively few did so on a regular daily or weekly basis.[32]

20.8 / "Equal Time" for Political Candidates

Section 315 of the Communications Act, it will be recalled (Section 17.8), requires licensees to afford candidates for public office "equal opportunities"

---

[28] FCC, "Editorializing by Broadcast Licensees," 14 *Fed. Reg.* 3055 (1949). Note that the 1967 Public Broadcasting Act forbids editorializing by educational stations (Section 17.9).

[29] *Ibid.*, at 1249.

[30] See Newton N. Minow, *Equal Time: The Private Broadcaster and the Public Interest*, (New York: Atheneum, 1964), Chapter 7, "Editorializing: The Second Mayflower," pp. 146–159.

[31] John E. McMillin, "New Voices in a Democracy," *Television Quarterly*, III (Summer, 1964), 44–45.

[32] *Broadcasting 1970 Yearbook*, p. 22.

at rates no higher than those charged to others for comparable time periods. It should be noted that § 315 applies specifically and exclusively to legally qualified candidates for political office.

In practice, broadcasters find that applying this seemingly straightforward regulation raises many practical problems. For example, although according to the statute "no obligation is imposed upon any licensee to allow the use of its station for any such candidate," the Commission struck down an announced policy of not cancelling any regularly scheduled commercial programs for paid political programs. WDSU, New Orleans, had such a policy, concerning which the FCC declared:

This statement of policy reflects such a complete failure on the part of [the licensees] to appreciate their obligations as station licensees (to operate in the public interest) as to require severe censure of such policy . . . a station licensee has both the right and the duty to cancel such previously scheduled programs as may be necessary in order to clear time for broadcasts of programs in the public interest.[33]

In 1967, President Johnson broadcast an end-of-the-year network interview, a tradition started five years previously. Senator Eugene McCarthy, a candidate for President, claimed the right to equal time. The FCC rejected this claim on the grounds that Johnson, although "legally qualified" (in the words of the statute), had not actually announced his candidacy. McCarthy pointed out that Johnson, by merely withholding formal announcement, could effectively deny opponents the protection of the equal-time rule; nevertheless, the Appeals Court upheld the FCC.[34]

The Commission received so many requests for interpretation of § 315 that it issued an "Equal Time Primer."[35] Here are some of the situations it covers:

Q. Does the rule apply to spokesmen for candidates?
A. No, only to candidates in person.
Q. If a candidate speaks in some capacity other than his capacity as a candidate, must his opponents still be given equal time?
A. Yes.
Q. A television weathercaster, not identified by name on his weather programs, ran for the Texas legislature. Must his opponents be given time equal to the weathercasts?
A. No.

---

[33] *In re Stephens Broadcasting Co. (WDSU)*, 11 FCC 61 at 65 (1945). Cf. *In re Homer P. Rainey*, 11 FCC 898 (1947).

[34] *McCarthy* v. *FCC*, 390 F. (2d) 471 (1968). In the event, Johnson did not run, thereby justifying the decision.

[35] FCC, "The Use of Broadcast Facilities by Candidates for Public Office," 31 *Fed. Reg.* 660 (1966).

Q. One candidate was nominated by three parties, A, B, and C; he was opposed by a candidate nominated by Party D. Does the first candidate have the right to claim equal time for *each* of the three parties he represents as against the candidate for Party D?

A. No.

Q. Does § 315 apply to supporters and opponents of public questions to be voted on in public elections?

A. No, it applies only to candidates for political office.

The equal-time rule has been widely misinterpreted as applying to controversial situations other than political campaigns—for example, licensee editorials, personal attacks, or speeches by incumbent public officials at times when no political campaign is in progress.[36] Although all such situations obviously share a common element, the cases are quite distinct. Section 315 has from the outset conferred on legally qualified candidates for public office a special status shared by no other users of broadcast facilities. Their right is statutory; the rights of others are a matter of administrative interpretation by the FCC under the Fairness Doctrine.

20.9 / The Fairness Doctrine

In 1931, a pioneer CBS foreign correspondent managed to get George Bernard Shaw to speak by radio to the United States—at the price of agreeing not to censor his words. "Hello, America! . . . How are all you dear old boobs who have been telling one another for a month that I have gone dotty about Russia"? Shaw went on at length in fulsome praise of Communism. Not all American listeners could see the humor of it, and CBS gave a clergyman time to reply to that "licensed charlatan of English letters."[37] This kind of "right of reply" had long been informally invoked by broadcasters and expected by the FCC. It figured prominently in the FCC's 1946 statement of public-service responsibilities, the "Blue Book":

The problems involved in making time available for the discussion of public issues are admittedly complex. Any vigorous presentation of a point of view will of necessity annoy or offend at least some listeners. There may be a temptation, accordingly, for broadcasters to avoid as much as possible any discussion over their stations, and to limit their broadcasts to entertainment programs which offend no one.

To operate in this manner, obviously, is to thwart the effectiveness of broadcasting in a democracy.

*   *   *   *   *

---

[36] Even station managers were confused on this point according to a 1966 NAB survey. [National Association of Broadcasters, "Radio and Television Editorializing: Management Attitudes, Station Practices, and Public Reactions" (Washington: The Association, n.d.).]

[37] Erik Barnouw, *A Tower in Babel: A History of Broadcasting in the United States to 1933* (New York: Oxford University Press, 1966), pp. 248–249.

The carrying of any particular public discussion, of course, is a problem for the individual broadcaster. But the public interest clearly requires that an adequate amount of time be made available for the discussion of public issues.[38]

At one time the NAB recommended a policy of refusing to sell time for soliciting memberships, discussing controversial subjects (including race, religion, politics), or airing programs on a number of other emotionally charged topics. On its face, this policy left room, of course, for giving free time for such subjects; in practice, however, the policy appears to have been used to screen out program material which might annoy advertisers or create uncomfortable public relations. The UAW-CIO challenged this policy when it petitioned the FCC not to renew the license of WHKC, Columbus, alleging discrimination and censorship. The FCC in effect ruled out the NAB policy, saying that it is the

. . . duty of each station licensee to be sensitive to the problems of public concern in the community and to make sufficient time available, on a nondiscriminatory basis, for full discussion thereof, without any type of censorship which would undertake to impose the views of the licensee upon the material to be broadcast . . . the operation of any station under the extreme principles that no time shall be sold for the discussion of controversial public issues and that only charitable organizations and certain commercial interests may solicit memberships is inconsistent with the concept of public interest established by the Communications Act as the criterion of radio regulations.[39]

Fairness assumed the status of an official doctrine in 1949 with the Commission's report on editorializing (Section 20.7). In that report the Commission spoke of the

. . . affirmative responsibility on the part of broadcast licensees to provide a reasonable amount of time for the presentation over their facilities of programs devoted to the discussion and consideration of public issues. . . . And the Commission has made it clear that in such presentation of news and comment the public interest requires that the licensee must operate on a basis of overall fairness. . . .[40]

Originally purely an administrative interpretation of the public-interest principle, the Fairness Doctrine appeared to receive Congressional blessing in the 1959 amendment to § 315 of the Communications Act, which, after enumerating the types of bona-fide news appearances which need not be considered as equal-time appearances, went on:

Nothing in the foregoing sentence shall be construed as relieving broadcasters, in connection with the presentation of newscasts, news interviews, news documen-

---

[38] FCC, *Public Service Responsibility of Broadcast Licensees,* p. 40.

[39] *In re United Broadcasting Co. (WHKC),* 10 FCC 515 at 517–518 (1945). The station agreed to modify the objectionable policy and the petition was accordingly dropped.

[40] FCC, "Editorializing by Broadcast Licensees," at 3056.

taries, and on-the-spot coverage of news events [the four previously enumerated exceptions], from the obligation imposed upon them under this chapter to operate in the public interest *and to afford reasonable opportunity for the discussion of conflicting views on issues of public importance.* [Italics supplied.]

This provision the FCC regards as statutory confirmation of its interpretation that the licensee has an "affirmative duty" to schedule programs dealing with public issues.[41]

The fairness concept brings to the forefront the special responsibility of the broadcast licensee as a trustee of the public interest. The requirements of being fair to the ultimate owners of the frequency spectrum may impose restraints on the licensee to say (or refrain from saying) what he would like.

There is nothing in the First Amendment which prevents the Government from requiring a licensee to share his frequency with others and to conduct himself as a proxy or fiduciary with obligations to present those views and voices which are representative of his community.[42]

Thus, the tendency to avoid serious and provocative program content (discussed in Chapter 16) may be viewed as an unfair use of broadcast facilities. The licensee may not justify excluding significant and relevant program material by his own personal fears, prejudices, or indifference.

As the problems incidental to the Fairness Doctrine began to mount in the 1960's, the Commission issued another of its "primers" on the subject.[43] Here are some examples of rulings found in the primer:

When is an issue an issue? A station broadcast a number of anti-Pay-TV statements but gave no time to the other side because it regarded the Pay-TV issue as primarily national, not important locally. *Ruling:* The station thought it sufficiently important locally to allow one side to be presented. Why not the other? "A licensee cannot excuse a one-sided presentation on the basis that the subject matter was not controversial in its service area."

Controversy concealed in noncontroversial program format. A program called "Living Should Be Fun" ostensibly dealt objectively with nutrition but actually contained attacks on fluoridization of water, defense of a controversial drug, and the like. *Ruling:* Licensees have "the obligation to know what is being broadcast over their facilities." Anyone who actually listened to the program could recognize that it contained controversial material despite its title.

Alleged absence of support for the other side. A program called "Communist Encirclement" espoused such views as "Socialist forms of government [are]

[41] FCC, "Report and Statement of Policy re: Commission en banc Programming Inquiry," 25 *Fed. Reg.* 7291 at 7294 (1960).

[42] *Red Lion Broadcasting Co., Inc.* v. *FCC,* at 389.

[43] FCC, "Applicability of the Fairness Doctrine in the Handling of Controversial Issues of Public Importance," 29 *Fed. Reg.* 10416 (1964).

transitory forms of government leading eventually to Communism." The licensee claimed that only Communists could represent the other side and he knew of none in the community. *Ruling:* "There are responsible contrasting viewpoints on the most effective methods of combatting Communist infiltration."

Affirmative responsibility to seek out the other side. A station replied to allegations of one-sidedness that it was ready to make time available for opposing views "on request." *Ruling:* Licensees must play a "conscious and positive role in bringing about balanced presentation," not merely wait for requests.

"Equal time" to reply not required. A spokesman for one view complained that the air minutes allowed his view amounted to less than the time allowed the opposing view. *Ruling:* The Fairness Doctrine requires a "reasonable opportunity" to present contrasting views, not equal time.

May the station choose the spokesman for the other side? Ruling: Yes and no. The licensee may exercise good-faith discretion in choosing a spokesman, except that personal attacks entitle the individual attacked to the right of personal reply.

Despite efforts at clarification, application of the Fairness Doctrine generated many dilemmas for broadcasters and FCC alike. Claims and counterclaims for reply time mounted year by year. In a relatively early instance, Senator Joseph McCarthy demanded time to reply to a highly incidental allusion to himself in a speech by former President Harry Truman. Later that year, Edward R. Murrow volunteered rebuttal time following a program critical of the Senator on the CBS *See It Now* series. A leading trade magazine called the Senator's rebuttal performance "irresponsible" and argued that the fairness principle would not work "by simply handing out facilities and time without retaining the right of editorial judgment."[44] On the other hand, some critics felt that whatever the merits of the two cases, McCarthy had in fact been treated unfairly. His ineptly produced reply stood little chance against the expert Murrow production, which had been months in preparation.[45]

No one could have foreseen at that time the ultimate extension of the Fairness Doctrine even to advertising. In 1967, John Banzhaf III complained to the FCC that WCBS-TV in New York violated the Fairness Doctrine in refusing time for rebuttal of cigarette advertising on television. CBS contended that by carrying a number of programs on the health hazards of smoking it had already fulfilled its obligation. The FCC rejected Banzhaf's claim for "roughly approximate" time for reply but did agree the licensee must give "a significant" amount of time to the anticigarette argument. The Appeals

---

[44] "Is the Sky the Limit?" *Broadcasting-Telecasting,* April 12, 1954, p. 134. For other *See It Now* fairness problems, see Fred W. Friendly, *op. cit., passim.*

[45] Gilbert Seldes, *The Public Arts* (New York: Simon & Schuster, 1956), Chapter 24, "The Situations of Edward R. Murrow," pp. 212–228.

Court upheld the FCC.[46] The Court pointed out that where one side has a compelling economic interest as well as large financial resources, it may be necessary to "redress the balance." Said the Court: "Not all free speakers have equally loud voices, and success in the marketplace of ideas may go to the advocate who can shout the loudest or most often."[47]

20.10 / *Red Lion:* Fairness Affirmed

In 1967, the FCC added two further regulations under the Fairness Doctrine: (1) in the case of personal attacks, the station must send a notice to the person attacked within one week, along with a tape or transcript, and offer time for reply; (2) in the case of licensee editorials endorsing or opposing candidates for political office, similar steps must be taken within twenty-four hours. While the Commission thus continued to build a complex framework of fairness rulings, doubts persisted as to the underlying legality of the doctrine.

Finally, in 1969, a decisive Supreme Court test came in the *RTNDA* and *Red Lion* cases, decided simultaneously. The first grew out of the FCC's just-mentioned special fairness rules on personal attacks and candidate endorsements. The Radio Television News Directors Association challenged these rules as unconstitutional. The Appeals Court upheld the RTNDA, but the Supreme Court unanimously reversed.[48]

The *Red Lion* case arose out of the refusal of WGCB-AM-FM, of Red Lion, Pennsylvania, to give time to Fred J. Cook for reply to a personal attack (the case originated in 1964, well before the special FCC rules on personal attacks had been promulgated). Cook, author of a book critical of one-time Presidential candidate Barry Goldwater, had been charged with Communist affiliations by Rev. Billy James Hargis in a right-wing syndicated radio-program series, *The Christian Crusade.* When Cook requested time to reply, WGCB demanded that he either pay for the time or offer proof that he could neither find a sponsor nor afford to pay for the time himself. The FCC ruled that the Fairness Doctrine required a station to make time available for reply to a personal attack, if necessary gratis.

WGCB appealed, but the Appeals Court upheld the FCC's decision.[49] The Supreme Court unanimously supported the lower court, providing a landmark affirmation of the FCC's Fairness Doctrine. The decision gives unmistakable priority to listener/viewer rights as against broadcaster rights:

---

[46] FCC, "Letter to WCBS-TV" (FCC 67–641), June 2, 1967; *Banzhaf* v. *FCC,* 405 F. (2d) 1082 (1968). The FCC emphasized that its ruling was limited to cigarette advertising and based on Congressional intent expressed in the Cigarette Labeling and Advertising Act.

[47] *Ibid.,* at 1102–1103.

[48] *RTNDA* v. *FCC,* 400 F. (2d) 1002 (1968); *U. S.* v. *RTNDA,* 395 U. S. 367 (1969).

[49] *Red Lion Broadcasting Co., Inc.* v. *FCC,* 381 F. (2d) 908 (1967).

. . . the people as a whole retain their interest in free speech by radio and their collective right to have the medium function consistently with the ends and purposes of the First Amendment. It is the right of the viewers and listeners, not the right of the broadcasters, which is paramount. . . . It is the right of the public to receive suitable access to social, political, esthetic, moral, and other ideas and experiences which is crucial here.[50]

20.11 / The Right to Media Access

The Fairness Doctrine may be stated in other terms as the right of people who do not own broadcasting stations nevertheless to use them to express ideas and opinions. Jerome Barron has called this "an emerging First Amendment right of access to the media."[51] This is one corrective proposed for the inadequacy of the self-righting principle in the free marketplace of ideas, discussed at the outset of this chapter. "We are on the verge," says Barron, "of a more comprehensive and sensitive idea of what freedom of expression should mean in a technological age."[52]

What we have in *Red Lion* is the burial of a First Amendment theory which equated freedom of speech solely with freedom of the men who control the media. *Red Lion* marks the rise of a First Amendment view which is oriented to the need of the fragments of our public for access for their ideas.[53]

The Commission for Freedom of the Press explored the media-access concept in depth during the 1940's:

. . . since freedom is for action, and action is for an end, the positive kernel of freedom lies in the ability to achieve the end; to be free means to be free *for* some accomplishment. This implies command of the means to achieve the end.[54]

---

[50] *Red Lion Broadcasting Co., Inc.* v. *FCC,* 395 U. S. 367 at 390.

[51] Jerome A. Barron, "An Emerging First Amendment Right of Access to the Media?" *George Washington Law Review,* XXXVII (1969), 487–509. Note that the term "access" occurs in two other contexts in broadcasting literature: the right of newsmen to gain access to news sources, and the idea of broadcasting as a "limited-access medium." The latter refers to spectrum limitations on accommodation of stations and is sometimes advanced as the theoretical justification for the Fairness Doctrine. Some commentators suggest that spectrum limitations on access to broadcasting either no longer exist or are on their way out. However, even if some technological breakthrough removed *all* physical limitations on the number of stations that can take to the air, station operators would still be using the publicly owned spectrum and would still be subject to economic constraints. The *Red Lion* opinion relies on the limited-access argument and is at pains to dismiss the counterarguments. [*Red Lion Broadcasting Co., Inc.* v. *FCC,* 395 U. S. 367 at 396.]

[52] Barron, "An Emerging First Amendment Right . . . ," p. 509.

[53] Jerome A. Barron, "The Meaning and Future of Red Lion," *Educational Broadcasting Review,* III (December, 1969), 10.

[54] William Ernest Hocking, *Freedom of the Press: A Framework of Principle* (Chicago: University of Chicago Press, 1947), p. 54.

Or, in the FCC's words, "Freedom of speech can be as effectively denied by denying access to the public means of making expression effective—whether public streets, parks, meeting halls, or the radio—as by legal restraints or punishment of the speaker."[55] Against this view, it may be argued that no one forces a newspaper publisher to open his editorial columns to those who do not happen to have a newspaper at their disposal as a personal organ of expression. However, the FCC here refers to *public* means of expression, placing broadcasting in the same context as public streets and parks.

Access to broadcasting facilities cannot be extended to everyone on demand. In *Red Lion,* the Court pointed out that half the entire population might listen and half speak in simultaneous face-to-face communication; half might publish and half might read; "but only a tiny fraction . . . can hope to communicate by radio at the same time." A nice question is therefore raised as to which subjects and persons shall be granted or denied access. This question arose in 1946 when Scott, an atheist, petitioned the FCC not to renew the licenses of three California stations because they had refused to give him an opportunity to reply to attacks on atheism contained in religious programs. The Commission dismissed Scott's petition, leaving the burden of responsibility for implementing fairness on the stations. In doing so, however, the Commission apparently feared that its decision might be misinterpreted as giving stations carte blanche to prevent the broadcasting of all minority points of view. "If freedom of speech is to have meaning," the FCC pointed out, "it cannot be predicated on the mere popularity or public acceptance of the ideas sought to be advanced. It must be extended as readily to ideas which we disapprove or abhor as to ideas which we approve."[56] At the same time the Commission recognized the quandary in which the licensee finds himself:

In making a selection with fairness, the licensee must, of course, consider the extent of the interest of the people in his service area in a particular subject to be discussed, as well as the qualifications of the person selected to discuss it. Every idea does not rise to the dignity of a "public controversy," and every organization, regardless of membership or the seriousness of its purpose, is not per se entitled to time on the air. But an organization or idea may be projected into the realm of controversy by virtue of being attacked. The holders of a belief should not be denied the right to answer attacks upon them or their belief solely because they are few in number.[57]

---

[55] *In re Robert Harold Scott,* 11 FCC 372 at 374 (1946). Essentially the same position is adopted in the Mayflower decision (Section 20.7).

[56] *Loc. cit.*

[57] *Ibid.,* at 376. Despite the fact that the FCC rejected Scott's petition, using the occasion merely to restate the traditional libertarian position on freedom of speech, the decision has been severely attacked. The President of the NAB called it a "masterpiece of confused thinking" and quoted a House Select Committee's opinion that "the Commission in the Scott decision demonstrated a dangerous and unwarranted policy of 'thought policing' that has no basis in law." [House Committee on Interstate and Foreign Commerce, *Amending Communications Act of 1934,* Hearings on S. 658, 88th Cong., 1st Sess. (Washington: Government Printing Office, 1951), p. 375.]

The Commission's reasoning in this opinion clearly echoes Mill, but the FCC retreats somewhat from Mill's militant individualism. If in fact "all mankind minus one were of one opinion," in such a case the majority must surely prevail as far as broadcasting is concerned; the lone dissident could not reasonably expect to use broadcasting facilities to argue his case. Again we encounter a circumstance peculiar to broadcasting which requires special consideration. Broadcasting is a mass medium and as such normally deals in program material adapted to the needs and interests of at least *relatively* large numbers of people (though not necessarily the majority). Mill's lonely one-man minority might talk on a street corner, circulate pamphlets, make a documentary film, or use many other private avenues of expression; but he could not reasonably assert a right to use the public facilities of broadcasting—unless, perhaps, because of someone else's initiative in subjecting him to personal attack.

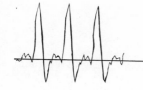

21

REGULATION AND THE PUBLIC INTEREST: FACTS AND FICTIONS

So great, in truth, is the gap between the theory of the regulatory agency and the operation of such an agency in practice that the entire regulatory process today is founded upon a series of basic fictions. BERNARD SCHWARTZ[1]

21.1 / Defects of the Regulatory Agencies

The independent regulatory agency—that administrative device which Congress adopted first in 1887 with the Interstate Commerce Commission—has proved seriously defective as a means of protecting the public interest. The older agencies, such as the ICC and the Federal Trade Commission (started in 1914), aimed originally at protecting businessmen from each other; but in the present century came recognition that the consumer needed protection as well. An amendment in 1935 extended the FTC's responsibility to consumer protection, and the Adminisrative Procedures Act of 1946 attempted to modernize all the regulatory agencies and to involve the public more than previously.[2] Still, they remained relatively unresponsive to public need as contrasted with the needs of the businesses they are charged with regulating. Ralph Nader was quoted as saying:

"The regulatory agencies have failed by the most modest of standards," in great part because their top men are too cozy with the industries that they oversee and often use their Government jobs as stepping stones to lucrative private careers in the same field. By his count, 75% of the former commissioners of the Federal Communications Commission are employed or retained by the communications industry. This, he charges, amounts to a "deferred bribe."[3]

---

[1] Bernard Schwartz, *The Professor and the Commissions* (New York: Alfred A. Knopf, 1959), p. 114.

[2] Louis M. Kohlmeier, *The Regulators: Watchdog Agencies and the Public Interest* (New York: Harper & Row, 1969), p. 268.

[3] "The U. S.'s Toughest Customer," *Time,* December 12, 1969, p. 90.

In mid-twentieth century, "consumerism" had a significant place in a ground swell of public impatience with the defeatist attitude implicit in the old cliché, "You can't fight city hall." More and more people seemed to believe that citizen activism could actually do something to bring promise and practice in American political and commercial life closer together. An untypical FTC Commissioner declared:

We must institutionalize the means whereby the public may be aware of, and participate in, political and governmental processes that affect the quality of all our lives. We must open wide the doors and windows of government agencies, so that the public may see for itself what is or is not being done, and demand an accounting from those in charge.[4]

These comments are especially interesting in the light of the many roadblocks the FTC Chairman is alleged to have put in the way of the public investigators of the FTC organized by Ralph Nader,[5] and refusal of the FCC Commissioners to answer a questionnnaire from a Congressional investigating committee about their finances (Section 21.2).

The Interstate Commerce Commission is notorious for its subservience to railroad interests, its red tape, and its nitpicking harassment of the trucking industry. The story is told of a trucker who, becoming fed up with ICC tariff (rate) schedule red tape, submitted a fake schedule of rates for transporting an imaginary commodity, yak fat. The railroads protested the schedule, submitting evidence "proving" that the trucker must be competing unfairly by transporting yak fat at a loss. An ICC rate-schedules board duly met and solemnly voted to investigate the trucker's threat to railroad profitability.[6]

The Federal Communications Commission and the Federal Trade Commission have been among the most frequently analyzed and adversely criticized of the regulatory agencies. As one analyst remarked, the FCC "has had a rather long turn at the whipping post,"[7] dating back to its earliest days. Both official investigations and private studies have regularly concluded with charges of (1) endless red tape, which causes unconscionable delays in Commission decisions; (2) inconsistency and vacillation in decisions, which impugn the validity of the Commission's standards of judgment; (3) *ex parte* interventions and fraternization with the industry, which throw doubt on the impartiality of the Commission; (4) appointment of Commissioners with no outstanding qualifications, who are prone to accept high-paying jobs from the industry they have been regulating after they resign or their terms of office expire.

---

[4] Philip Elman, "The Regulatory Process: A Personal View," Address to American Bar Association Antitrust Section, August 11, 1970 (mimeo.), p. 22.

[5] Edward F. Cox, *et. al., "The Nader Report" on the Federal Trade Commission* (New York: Richard W. Baron, 1969).

[6] Kohlmeier, *op. cit.,* pp. 193–195.

[7] Henry J. Friendly, *The Federal Administrative Agencies: The Need for Better Definition of Standards* (Cambridge, Mass.: Harvard University Press, 1962), p. 53.

21.2 / Delays and Decisional Inconsistency

One-time Chairman Newton Minow described the FCC as working "in a jungle of procedural red tape that flowers wildly out of the quicksands of constantly changing public policy."[8] Judge James Landis, in an official report to President-elect Kennedy, said the Commission "has drifted, vacillated, and stalled in almost every major area."[9] Many important cases drag on for years without settlement. A conspicuous instance was the *WLBT* case (Section 17.10), which dated back to 1964 and still was not settled in 1970, despite sharp criticism from the Court of Appeals, which declared that the "administrative conduct reflected in this record is beyond repair." Much delay, to be sure, comes from appeals by the parties involved, but observers both inside and outside the Commission believe that procedures could be streamlined and delays much reduced.

FCC Chairman Newton Minow, in his letter of resignation to President Kennedy, called the Commission's decision making an "unpredictable, crazy-quilt pattern."[10] Judge Landis saw little relation between decisions and putative standards: "The anonymous opinion writers for the Commission pick from a collection of standards those that will support whatsoever decision the Commission chooses to make."[11]

The writer alludes here to the fact that, unlike judges, the Commissioners do not write their own opinions. Instead, they hand their decision on to the Office of Opinions and Review (see FCC organization chart, Figure 18.1). One investigator reports that the Office of Opinions once dutifully wrote up a hundred-page opinion justifying a competitive television grant, only to have the Commission change its mind and award the license to another applicant. The Office went back to work and came up with another hundred pages, equally convincing in reaching an opposite conclusion. The investigator echoes Judge Landis: "The Commission juggles its criteria in particular cases so as to reach almost any decision it wishes and then orders its staff to draw up reasons to support the decision."[12]

21.3 / Lobbying and *Ex Parte* Interventions

"The agencies," says Kohlmeier, "have institutionalized industrial protectionism. They are umpires not of the consumer interest versus business but of com-

---

[8] Excerpted from *Equal Time: The Private Broadcaster and the Public Interest,* by Newton N. Minow [p. 8]. Edited by Lawrence Laurent. Copyright © 1964 by Newton N. Minow. Reprinted by permission of Atheneum Publishers.

[9] James M. Landis, *Report on Regulatory Agencies to the President-Elect,* submitted by the Chairman of the Subcommittee on Administrative Practices and Procedures for the use of the Senate Committee on the Judiciary, 86th Cong., 2d Sess. (Washington: Government Printing Office, 1960), p. 53.

[10] Minow, *op. cit.,* p. 282.

[11] Landis, *loc. cit.*

[12] Schwartz, *op. cit.,* pp. 191, 151.

peting business interests."[13] The Commissioners work in a milieu permeated by those who are regulated—their legal counsels, public-relations men, lobbyists, often-compliant Congressmen. Judge Landis reported to the President-elect that the FCC appeared to have been more susceptible to *ex parte* influences than any other agency—though there surely must have been rivals for this dubious distinction.[14] Many *ex parte* approaches come from lawyers, according to Landis:

. . . indeed, one of the worst phases of this situation is the existence of groups of lawyers, concentrated in Washington itself, who implicitly hold out to clients that they have means of access to various regulatory agencies off the record that they are more important than those that can be made on the record. These lawyers have generally previously held positions of more or less importance in the Government.[15]

Another study led to the conclusion that "the inter-relationships of the regulated, the regulator, Congress and the White House are known to all concerned and the lobbyists' hospitality and contributions are part of the mortar of the politics of regulation."[16]

Occasionally, investigations give fleeting glimpses into this Washington jungle. In 1957, for example, the House Interstate and Foreign Commerce Committee hired a young university-professor expert on government administrative agencies to head the investigative staff of its Special Subcommittee on Legislative Oversight. The professor, Dr. Bernard Schwartz of New York University, understood that the Subcommittee intended to check up on the sort of job the independent administrative agencies were doing. As soon as he began to uncover evidence of misconduct in the agencies, however, he learned that the parent Commerce Committee and its chairman, Rep. Oren Harris of Arkansas, had no such intention. Schwartz then realized that he had been hired as a "harmless, academic type" who could be counted on to confine himself to ivory-tower legal theory without delving realistically into embarrassing practical matters.[17]

Refusing to be overawed and unwilling to connive at suppressing the damaging information he had unearthed, Schwartz went to the newspapers with his story and forced a public hearing. The Committee managed to get rid of him early in 1958, after seven months. In that relatively short time, however, and despite harassment and sabotage from the Commerce Committee and its stooges on his own staff, Schwartz managed to uncover enough evidence of misconduct to lead eventually to the forced resignations of two FCC Commissioners and a high-ranking White House official.

---

[13] Kohlmeier, *op. cit.,* pp. 93–95.

[14] Landis, *op. cit.,* p. 53. *Ex parte* communications are unethical private contacts with judges designed to influence their actions on pending cases (see Section 18.3).

[15] *Ibid.,* pp. 13–14.

[16] Kohlmeier, *op. cit.,* p. 77.

[17] Schwartz, *op. cit.,* p. 3.

Schwartz drew back the curtain briefly on a scene characterized by an "all-pervasive system of personal fraternization between commissioners and those whom they regulated."[18] They refused to respond to a Committee questionnaire on their financial involvements. Schwartz uncovered evidence suggesting reasons for this reluctance. Commissioners made trips all over the country to inspect stations at the expense of licensees. Some accepted color-television sets and free-maintenance contracts, luxury-vacation trips, and similar favors from regulated companies. They not only accepted payment of expenses for these trips from the companies, but sometimes also submitted duplicate expense vouchers to the government and collected a second time. In one instance, Schwartz was able to show that FCC Chairman John C. Doerfer had collected *three* times for part of a trip on which he had attended both a station dedication in Oklahoma and an NAB meeting on the West Coast.

The accused Commissioners and their Congressional apologists on the Subcommittee pooh-poohed such peccadilloes—much as so many in broadcasting had lightly dismissed the rigging of the quiz programs (Section 16.3). The taxpayer outside the mutual-benefit circle might wonder, however, what else must be going on if so much questionable activity could be uncovered in a short time by a relatively inexperienced investigator, working with an unsympathetic staff and over the opposition of his employers. He might well question what opportunity the public had constantly to remind the Commissioners of *its* interests with gifts and lavish entertainment. "When Chairman Doerfer defended his attendance at broadcasting conventions as part of his duty to know the problems of broadcasters, a congressman asked coldly, 'Where do you go to learn the problems of the public?' "[19]

In the course of his truncated investigation, Schwartz unravelled the classic *ex parte* scandal, the Miami *Channel 10* case—one of a series of such scandals which occurred during the intense battles in the late 1950's for the few remaining VHF channels in major markets, each worth many millions of dollars. The FCC's Hearing Examiner, after prolonged hearings and delays, had finally awarded Channel 10 to Frank Katzentine, owner of a Miami Beach radio station, who scored high in terms of local ownership, integration of management with ownership, and experience. To everyone's amazement (except those who knew what was going on backstage), the Commission reversed the Examiner. It awarded the grant to National Airlines, which had been rated *lowest* of the four contestants by the Examiner.

Katzentine cried "Foul," alleging that a recently appointed Commissioner from Florida, Richard A. Mack, had pledged his vote in advance to the airline. Schwartz's investigation showed that Mack had received a number of checks

---

[18] *Ibid.*, p. 77.

[19] Excerpted from background essay by Lawrence Laurent in *Equal Time: The Private Broadcaster and the Public Interest,* by Newton N. Minow [p. 278]. Edited by Lawrence Laurent. Copyright © 1964 by Newton N. Minow. Reprinted by permission of Atheneum Publishers.

as well as highly profitable business favors from a Miami lawyer who had been retained by the airline only because of his long-standing friendship with the Commissioner.[20] These links formed part of a maze of interlocking business and political relationships stretching between Florida and Washington. Ultimately, three of the four contestants were disqualified for *ex parte* activities involving a number of prominent senators as well as FCC members. Mack resigned under pressure, as did the FCC Chairman some time later.

21.4 / The Commissioners — Before and After

The *Channel 10* case raised the question of the quality of appointments to the Commission. Much of the time the White House used its appointive power to the regulatory commissions simply as a means of paying off minor political debts. Despite the tremendous powers commissioners wield over commercially valuable rights and vital aspects of national life, the positions do not rank high in the Washington pecking order, so that few outstandingly able and ambitious men would be satisfied with a commissioner career. Yet the underlying theory of the regulatory agencies is precisely that they will be manned by career men especially qualified by virtue of long experience and expertise in the highly technical activities they oversee.

In point of fact, few Federal Communications Commissioners have significant background in the field of communications, nor do most of them stay in office long enough to develop a high level of expertise. They usually come from other government administrative jobs or the legal profession. No scholar or student of communications, as such, has ever been appointed. A study of Commissioners of the years 1927–1961 indicated that none had come *from* high-level broadcasting management, though six went *to* such jobs; fourteen went into law practice—mostly communications law. One Commissioner, Sam Pickard (1927–1929), became a CBS vice-president and also part owner of a radio station in reward for helping it obtain network affiliation. The station later lost its license because his part in its ownership was concealed.[21] Commissioner Charles Denny (1945–1947) resigned, not long after some FCC decisions highly valuable to RCA, to become an NBC vice-president. "The move, like earlier metamorphoses of this sort, caused a hue and cry. When had the subject of a network executive first been hinted?"[22] Commissioner Frederick Ford (1957–1965) became president of the National Community Antenna Association at more than double his government salary. Even that critical gadfly, Chairman Newton Minow, became a CBS counsel following his

---

[20] *Ibid.,* p. 198.

[21] Lawrence W. Lichty, "Members of the Federal Radio Commission and the Federal Communications Commission, 1927–1961," *Journal of Broadcasting,* VI (Winter, 1961–1962), 23–24. See also *FCC* v. *WOKO,* 329 U. S. 223 (1946).

[22] Erik Barnouw, *The Golden Web: A History of Broadcasting in the United States, 1933–1953* (New York: Oxford University Press, 1968), pp. 243–244.

resignation, thus finding himself "paid to defend the same practices he had latterly been criticizing."[23]

Intense political and lobbying pressures have generally tended to force Commissioners into one of two extreme camps—the apologists for unrestrained business control of broadcasting, or the crusading do-gooders allegedly bent on destroying the American system of free broadcasting. Commissioners George McConnaughey (1954–1957), Robert E. Lee (1953–   ), and Rosel Hyde (1946–1969) are often cited as leading examples of the "hands-off" school of regulation. Men like these were so outspoken in their opposition to government interference with commercial broadcasters that they inspired the description "a system of regulation by anti-regulators."[24] Commissioners James Fly (1939–1944), Newton Minow (1961–1963), and Nicholas Johnson (1966–   ) may be cited as representatives of the crusading type. Fly was a Roosevelt appointee, former general counsel for the TVA:

He was a disturbing phenomenon. No other FCC chairman had even faintly resembled him. He put a certain passion into his FCC work. When NAB adjourned a meeting at which he was attacked before he could reply he later said it reminded him of a "dead mackerel in the moonlight—it both shines and stinks."[25]

Fly created such intense opposition that Representative Eugene Cox of Georgia tried to get him impeached. Not until another liberal Commissioner, Clifford Durr, came up with documentary evidence that Cox had been paid to help get a license for a Georgia station (a criminal offense) did Cox relinquish his vendetta against the crusading Commissioner. Newton Minow was another Democratic appointee (President Kennedy) and another phrase maker (the "vast wasteland"; Section 10.7). Nicholas Johnson was the most outspoken critic of the FCC itself, a frequent and pungently vocal dissenter to many FCC decisions.

21.5 / Congressional and Executive Intervention

In extenuation of Commission vacillation and weakness, it must be conceded that it operates at the center of a storm system of intense pressures—from Congress, the Executive branch, and the industry. Commission decisions must often be made "under pressures that would not be tolerated in a traffic court."[26]

Congress gave the Commission the Communications Act as its mandate and turned it loose to carry out that mandate independently. The continuing role of

---

[23] Alexander Kendrick, *Prime Time* (Boston: Little, Brown, 1969), p. 477. Minow later became Board Chairman of the RAND Corporation.

[24] Robert Bendiner, "FCC: Who Will Regulate the Regulators?" *The Reporter*, September 19, 1957, p. 26.

[25] Barnouw, *op. cit.*, p. 174.

[26] Bendiner, *op. cit.*, p. 29.

Congress, theoretically, is to pass on the President's appointments for the Commission, oversee its budget, and occasionally check up on its performance (as the Special Committee on Legislative Oversight was supposed to do). In practice, Congress second-guesses the Commission on virtually every issue that gets publicity, large and small. Congress has kept the Commission under constant inquisition ever since the pioneering days of the FRC.[27] Newton Minow said that when he was FCC Chairman he "heard from Congress about as frequently as television commercials flash across the screen."[28]

An FCC member may be admonished one day by the Chairman of the Senate Commerce Committee for being too aloof from members of the broadcasting industry. He will be told that he cannot regulate effectively unless he understands the problems faced by radio and television station operators. . . . In the very next session the same FCC member may be advised by the very same congressman that he has gotten too close to the broadcasting industry.[29]

Since Congressmen depend heavily on broadcasting both in electioneering and for keeping themselves before the electorate between campaigns, they tend to be highly responsive to requests from their home-state station owners. The trade press fosters the myth that broadcasters live in fear and trembling of an all-powerful FCC. But the industry's success in neutralizing the more activist of the Commissioners and lobbying out of existence the more sweeping reforms proposed in Congress belies the myth. An economist has remarked that FCC regulation resembles a wrestling match: "The grunts and groans resound through the land, but no permanent injury seems to result."[30] Lawrence Laurent, a Washington newspaper commentator on broadcast matters, writes:

There has rarely been any fear . . . of the federal regulators. This lack of fear comes from the broad political power that goes with ownership of a radio or television station. A broadcaster gets a respectful hearing when he talks with a congressman.[31]

[27] Walter Emery, *Broadcasting and Government* (East Lansing: Michigan State University Press, 1961), pp. 294–301.

[28] Excerpted from *Equal Time: The Private Broadcaster and the Public Interest,* by Newton N. Minow [p. 36]. Edited by Lawrence Laurent. Copyright © 1964 by Newton N. Minow. Reprinted by permission of Atheneum Publishers.

[29] Excerpted from background essay by Lawrence Laurent in *Equal Time: The Private Broadcaster and the Public Interest,* by Newton N. Minow [pp. 277–278]. Edited by Lawrence Laurent. Copyright © 1964 by Newton N. Minow. Reprinted by permission of Atheneum Publishers.

[30] R. H. Coase, "The Economics of Broadcasting and Government Policy," *American Economic Review: Papers and Proceedings,* LVI (May, 1966), p. 442.

[31] Excerpted from background essay by Lawrence Laurent in *Equal Time: The Private Broadcaster and the Public Interest,* by Newton N. Minow [p. 46]. Edited by Lawrence Laurent. Copyright © 1964 by Newton N. Minow. Reprinted by permission of Atheneum Publishers.

The FCC cannot fail to be acutely aware of the broadcasting interests of Congressmen and members of the Executive branch (reaching all the way to the top during the Johnson administration). No improper conduct, no *ex parte* intervention, need take place for powerful figures in the political hierarchy to secure "courtesies" from the Commission. Thus the ownership of broadcast properties by politicians—especially those directly concerned with overseeing the Commission—raises serious conflict-of-interest questions.

During the period when Schwartz was employed by the Special Legislative Oversight Committee, it came to his attention that Rep. Oren Harris, Chairman of the parent House Commerce Committee—chief Congressional watchdog of the FCC—had received a quarter interest in a television station for a mere $500 plus a promissory note for $4,500. Shortly thereafter, according to Schwartz, the FCC, which had previously turned down a similar request, granted the station a major increase in power.[32] It is safe to assume that the Congressman never said a word about favorable treatment to the Commissioners.

21.6 / The Mythology of Regulation

With surprising frequency, commentators on the federal regulatory agencies use words like "myth," "fiction," "formality," and "ritual" to describe their operations. Judge Landis called their methods "Alice-in-Wonderland procedures."[33] After analyzing sixty contested television decisions, Schwartz concluded that the adversary hearings had turned into a "ritual" that has no necessary connection with the "real process of administrative decision."[34] Another commentator called the hearing procedure "ritualistic, formalistic, wasteful and inefficient; it's an antipoverty program for very affluent Washington lawyers."[35] It has even been alleged that license applications are "boiler-plate affairs drawn up by professionals, sometimes used over and over again with different names."[36]

By tacit agreement, all parties—the Commission, the lawyers, the applicants—appear to go through a prescribed set of expensive motions without for a moment believing in what they are doing. Certainly the numerous instances of licensees who fail to live up to the promises in their applications or to conduct their stations according to the theoretical requirements of public interest testify to the truth of this description. Let us consider briefly a few of the major public-interest tenets which ostensibly govern FCC decisions but which in practice often seem ignored.

---

[32] Schwartz, *op. cit.,* p. 96. Egged on by Schwartz, the press asked Rep. Harris so many embarrassing questions about the deal that he soon sold his interest.

[33] Landis, *op. cit.,* p. 54.

[34] Schwartz, *op. cit.,* p. 169.

[35] H. H. Goldin, "Discussion of 'Evaluation of Public Policy Relating to Radio and Television . . .'," *Land Economics,* XLI (May, 1965), 168.

[36] Bendiner, *op. cit.,* p. 27.

COMPARATIVE CRITERIA

When two or more applicants apply for the same facility, the FCC chooses a winner according to their respective merits as measured by a set of comparative criteria (Section 18.3). Much of this elaborate exercise is rendered meaningless because most television stations become network affiliates:

With rare exceptions . . . the work in deciding which of twelve contenders should win the license has really settled very little. Whichever contender was victorious—Tweedledum or Tweedledee—he will plug in the same equipment to the same network TV programs. His personal and professional qualifications for being awarded the channel dwindle down to a few independent decisions in a few open hours, usually hours viewed by the smallest number of people.[37]

UNLICENSED NETWORKS AND PROGRAM RESPONSIBILITY

Licensees have nondelegatable responsibility for their programming. Yet networks, which are not licensed, in practice assume most of the responsibility for most of their affiliates' television programming. The FCC itself used the familiar word "fiction" concerning this situation:

If we are to have network sales and programming [the] responsibility of the licensee to choose and select programs must primarily remain a legal fiction and a virtual practical impossibility with respect to network programs. The indulgence of any fiction cannot help but spread its mockery to other areas of the law, with the result that respect tends to break down all along the line.[38]

PROGRAM PROMISES AND LICENSE RENEWALS

Every licensee, whether in an original application or a renewal application, makes specific program commitments to prove his ability and his intention to operate in the public interest. The Communications Act limits the term of a broadcast license to three years, in part so that the Commission will automatically have periodic opportunities to consider whether the licensee has in fact been operating in the public interest. In practice, every investigation has shown that large numbers of licensees flagrantly disregard their promises as soon as they get on the air, and the Commission merely rubber-stamps most renewals.[39] Said two of its members, "the Commission is making virtually no use of the information that it is now receiving from licensees in the renewal forms."[40]

---

[37] Excerpted from *Equal Time: The Private Broadcaster and the Public Interest,* by Newton N. Minow [p. 300]. Edited by Lawrence Laurent. Copyright © 1964 by Newton N. Minow. Reprinted by permission of Atheneum Publishers.

[38] FCC, Office of Network Study, "Responsibility for Broadcast Matter," Docket No. 12782 (1960, mimeo.), p. 109.

[39] In fiscal 1969, the FCC approved 2,757 broadcast-station renewal applications; dismissed, denied, or returned 50; designated 16 for hearing. [FCC, *Thirty-Fifth Annual Report* (Washington: Government Printing Office, 1970), pp. 129–131.]

[40] *Broadcasting in America and the FCC's License Renewal Process: An Oklahoma Case Study,* 14 FCC (2d) 1 at 4 (1968).

From time to time, individual Commissioners have become disturbed at this abdication of regulatory responsibility. For example, the "Blue Book" investigation in 1946 was launched for just this reason:

. . . the licensee asks for a three-year renewal and the record clearly shows that he has not fulfilled the promises made to the Commission when he received the original grant. The Commission in the past has, for a variety of reasons, including limitations of staff, automatically renewed these licenses even in cases where there was a vast disparity between promises and performance.[41]

Fifteen years later, in 1961, according to the then FCC Chairman:

. . . we informed every broadcaster of a change in the Commission's renewal policy. In the past we granted renewals even though there had been a substantial failure to live up to the programming representations, where the applicant "up-graded" his proposals and gave reliable assurances that these proposals would be carried out. This will no longer be the case.[42]

A decade later, another Commissioner could say:

The typical station's license renewal proceeding goes like this. The FCC gathers at ringside and offers to referee. At the sound of the bell the licensee jumps into the ring and begins shadow boxing. At the end of three minutes he is proclaimed the winner by the FCC majority, found to have been serving the public interest and his community, and given a three-year license renewal.[43]

LOCALNESS

In Section 18.5, we discussed the heavy emphasis placed by the Commission and the courts on the element of "localness" in program plans. Applicants dutifully interview local "community leaders," consult educational and public-service institutions, and promise substantial local programming. Often such program plans are impracticable on their face. The FCC's 1946 study revealed the most cynical disregard for such pledges, even in some cases after licensees had been warned of their dereliction. Every subsequent study of local-programming promise and performance has turned up similar evidence. For example, after a detailed analysis in 1968 of all stations in one state, Commissioners Cox and Johnson concluded that in practice, "the concept of local service is largely a myth." Their analysis indicated that "with a few exceptions, Oklahoma stations provide almost literally no programming that can meaningfully be described as local expression."[44]

---

[41] FCC, *Public Service Responsibility of Broadcast Licensees* (Washington: Government Printing Office, 1946), p. 3.

[42] Excerpted from *Equal Time: The Private Broadcaster and the Public Interest,* by Newton N. Minow [p. 93]. Edited by Lawrence Laurent. Copyright © 1964 by Newton N. Minow. Reprinted by permission of Atheneum Publishers.

[43] Nicholas Johnson, *How to Talk Back to Your Television Set* (Boston: Little, Brown, 1970), pp. 176–177.

[44] *Broadcasting in America and the FCC's License Renewal Process: An Oklahoma Case Study,* at 12.

Even after the FCC revised its station-application form to require reports on specific efforts made to ascertain community needs (Section 18.5), apparently licensees still failed to grasp what the FCC was after, for in 1969 it proposed a "primer" explaining in even more elementary terms.[45] One finds it hard to believe that so much coaching would really be required if licensees in fact made the expected "diligent effort, in good faith" to provide for local needs and interests.

A study of the "community-needs" exhibits in over two hundred applications on file with the Commission revealed that only 30 per cent of the applicants had made an actual canvass of the general public, as required by the Commission. Many used unsound methods of research and biassed methods of selecting "community leaders" to give them guidance. Some applicants revealed complete incomprehension of what they were supposed to do, and few showed any evidence of relating the community needs they did identify to program proposals designed to answer those needs.[46] Some forty years of licensing nominally based squarely on an obligation to ascertain and satisfy local community needs had apparently not sufficed to build up an understanding either of what this obligation means or of a *modus operandi* for meeting it.

Although the FCC does not require educational stations to make the survey of local needs required of commercial stations, one of the advantages claimed for noncommercial broadcasting has always been its potentiality for fuller development of local programming. In practice, localness in noncommercial operations has too often been used as an excuse to evade provocative NET programming and to justify mediocrity; in this respect, said the president of NET, "the record of public television leaves much to be desired—both in boldness and imagination."[47]

LICENSEE AS TRUSTEE OF PUBLIC INTEREST

The Communications Act, the Rules and Regulations of the FCC, and innumerable court decisions make it clear that the licensee has no property right in the frequency spectrum, that his use of a channel is justified only insofar as he serves the public interest, that his personal gain is secondary to the public benefit. This theory appears to be regarded with complete cynicism by many a businessman/licensee. He apparently finds it impossible to conceive that voluntary investment and risk taking do not entitle him to unrestricted freedom to seek profit. Chairman Newton Minow concluded that

---

[45] FCC, "Primer on . . . Ascertainment of Community Problems . . . ," 34 *Fed. Reg.* 20282 (1969). The FCC exempts educational stations from these requirements.

[46] Thomas F. Baldwin and Stuart H. Surlin, "A Study of Broadcast Station License Application Exhibits on Ascertainment of Community Needs," *Journal of Broadcasting,* XIV (Spring, 1970), 157–170.

[47] James Day, "The Social Responsibility of Public Broadcasting," *Educational Broadcasting Review,* III (Special Issue, 1969), 13.

. . . far too many licensees do not regard themselves as "trustees of the public." The frequency is regarded as "theirs," not the public's, and the license is seen to be not one to operate in the public interest but rather to get the greatest financial returns possible out of their investment.[48]

Judge Burger of the District of Columbia Appellate Court (later Chief Justice of the Supreme Court) put it even more bluntly:

After nearly five decades of operation the broadcast industry does not seem to have grasped the simple fact that a broadcast license is a public trust subject to termination for breach of duty.[49]

TRAFFICKING IN LICENSES

In its 1958 amendment to § 310(b) of the Communications Act, Congress appears to have deliberately encouraged trafficking in licenses by tying the FCC's hands. The amendment prevents the FCC from adopting measures such as the Avco Rule (Section 18.9) to ensure that a new owner will be as carefully scrutinized in terms of the public interest as was the original owner. This produced what one legal commentator has called

. . . the absurd spectacle wherein a considered selection of the applicant who can best serve the public interest, made after much travail and expense [by the FCC], can be rendered nugatory by private arrangements among the very persons who have submitted themselves to the Commission's determination.[50]

EXCESSIVE FCC LENIENCE

In Section 16.1 we pointed out that marginal commercial stations with insufficient income to operate ethically tend to linger on, often dragging down the standards of other stations in their area with them. One reason for continued existence of such stations has been the Commission's extreme reluctance to apply its own rules with vigor. Typically, the stations cited in the "Blue Book" for a variety of substandard practices all received renewals. A Commissioner cited the refusal of the Commission majority to revoke the license of an operator accused of "not paying his employees, stealing news, ordering his engineer to make fraudulent entries in the station's logbook, operating with an improperly licensed engineer and 87 other technical violations over a three-year period."[51]

One reason for the FCC's reluctance to enforce its own rules vigorously is the almost certain knowledge that any move to do so will provide immediate repercussions in Congress. An example was the "Pastore Bill," introduced in

---

[48] Excerpted from *Equal Time: The Private Broadcaster and the Public Interest,* by Newton N. Minow [pp. 91–92]. Edited by Lawrence Laurent. Copyright © 1964 by Newton N. Minow. Reprinted by permission of Atheneum Publishers.

[49] *Office of Communication of the United Church of Christ v. FCC,* 359 F. (2d) 994 at 1003 (1966).

[50] H. J. Friendly, *op. cit.,* p. 72.

[51] Nicholas Johnson, "No, We Don't," *The New Republic,* December 6, 1969, p. 17.

identical form by dozens of Congressmen in an obvious response to an industry lobbying campaign, aimed at preventing the FCC from questioning license renewals except in extreme cases of improper conduct.[52]

DIVERSIFICATION

In forty-four single-newspaper towns the paper also owns the only television station. Over half the commercial television stations in 1968 belonged to multiple owners. An FCC Commissioner pointed out in 1969 that in the eleven largest cities in the United States, every network-affiliated VHF station belonged to a multistation owner or newspaper-broadcasting combine. A special FCC study of stations in Oklahoma revealed that though seventy-three different firms owned stations in the state, the four top companies took in 88 per cent of the broadcast income.[53] The extraordinary profitability of the national network O&O-station groups has already been noted (Section 15.3).

Such concentrations of control have come about despite the fact that a major underlying assumption of the American system holds that media ownership and control should be as diversified as possible, and despite the fact that the FCC counts diversification as one of the major criteria in comparative hearings. The Commission has given the appearance of glaring inconsistency in the application of this criterion. "The most vexing problem in the diversification area," says Judge Friendly, "has been the award of radio and television licenses to newspaper publishers." He ascribes the failure of the FCC to adopt a hard-and-fast policy with regard to newspaper-owner applicants to Congressional pressures.[54]

In the *McClatchy* case, for example, the FCC Hearing Examiner's initial decision preferred the Sacramento, California, television application of a company with numerous newspaper and broadcasting holdings over a contestant with no such media involvements; the Examiner, relying on a previous FCC decision, based his preference for McClatchy on its wide experience and the fact that it had never shown any monopolistic tendencies. The Commission reversed its Examiner, preferring McClatchy's rival on the diversification issue. The Appeals Court upheld the Commission.[55] But in the *WHDH* case the Commission reached the opposite conclusion, awarding an extremely valuable Boston channel to the publishers of a major daily newspaper and owner of a major AM radio station in the same city.[56] This time the Appeals Court re-

---

[52] Cf. "Making the FCC's Mission Impossible," *Consumer Reports,* February, 1970, pp. 109–111.

[53] *Broadcasting in America and the FCC's License Renewal Process: An Oklahoma Case Study,* at 14.

[54] H. J. Friendly, *op. cit.,* p. 65.

[55] *McClatchy Broadcasting Co.* v. *FCC,* 239 F. (2d) 15 (1957).

[56] *Memorandum Opinion and Order. In re application of WHDH, Inc., et al.,* 22 FCC 761 (1957).

manded the case to the Commission for further hearing. After a dozen years of litigation, the FCC reversed itself, threw out its latest hearing examiner's decision, and awarded the grant to a competing applicant—a unique instance of license denial on comparative criteria to a station which had already been in actual successful operation for twelve years.[57]

The rules limiting single owners to seven of each class of station is another case of lip service. The limitation makes little sense if the intention is really to prevent undue concentration of control or gross inequalities among licensees. Owning twenty-one maximum-facility stations in the top seven markets would give a single licensee tremendous power in terms of audience impact; on the other hand, twenty-one minimum-facility stations in minor markets could reach no more than the audience of a single one of the first licensee's major-market stations. If ownership of more than one station can be justified at all, logically the limitation should be based on coverage rather than on numbers of stations regardless of power, frequency, and location. Apparently the Commission adopted the latter method to avoid having to require networks to dispose of their O&O stations.

MONOPOLY

The Communications Act explicitly instructs the FCC to prevent monopoly. "In a number of cases," according to Schwartz "it has simply refused to take account of relevant antitrust considerations." The Commission apparently did not consider it important, for example, in the WHDH case that the company had been found guilty of violating antitrust laws. The FCC's patent advisor of many years told Schwartz that the FCC majority voted a hands-off policy with regard to allegations of patent monopolies on the part of licensees.[58]

21.7 / Proposals for Reform

The practices outlined in the previous section indicate that to a large extent the Communications Act serves as no more than a façade of pious theories. Expediency and crass cynicism rule events behind the façade. No serious investigator of the FCC has offered a favorable diagnosis; all agree on the need for drastic reforms. Perhaps the Commission system itself is unworkable. That is the conclusion of economist R. H. Coase:

. . . we cannot expect a regulatory commission to act in the public interest, particularly if we have regard to its actions over a long period. . . . However fluid an organization may be in its beginning, it must inevitably adopt certain policies and organizational forms which condition its thinking and limit the range of its policies.

---

[57] *WHDH, Inc., et al.,* 16 FCC (2d) 1 (1969). This intricate case was complicated by charges of *ex parte* intervention, concealment of ownership, antitrust violations, and the death of one of the principals in the course of the years. The 1969 FCC decision was still not final, as the Court had retained jurisdiction.

[58] Schwartz, *op. cit.,* pp. 130–133.

Within limits, the regulatory commission may search for what is in the public interest, but it is not likely to find acceptable any solutions which implv fundamental changes in its settled policies. The observation that a regulatory commission tends to be captured by the industry it regulates is I think a reflection of this, rather than, in general, the result of sinister influences. It is difficult to operate closely with an industry without coming to look at its problems in industry terms . . .[59]

Newton Minow, in his letter of resignation to President Kennedy in 1963, after a little more than two years as Chairman of the FCC, cited three different official studies with whose recommendations for reform he agreed. The summary below includes these and other reforms that have been suggested by both private and official investigators.

Single administrator. Regulation by commission "produces a dangerous depersonalization and invisibility of agency activity," according to Philip Elman.[60] A single administrator could be an outstanding man, with clearcut authority, able to act quickly and decisively, accountable for consistency in decisions.

Separation of judicial and administrative functions. There should be a special and separate court to adjudicate cases, with judges expert in the law of communication who would have to think through and write their own decisions.

Insulation from Executive branch. If the commission form is retained, the Chairman should no longer be appointed by the President nor should the chief employees be subject to the political-spoils system.

Insulation from Legislative branch. The Commission should be given some insulation from petty Congressional pressures, especially from Congressmen who have financial interests at stake. The chief watchdog committees should be manned by Congressmen without broadcasting interests.

Quality of Commissioners. Commissioners should be chosen for their expertise and ability, not for political reasons. A single-administrator system would make it easier to find just the right man—and to pay him enough to justify a career in the office. Some have suggested lifetime appointment to eliminate rapid turnover and susceptibility to political pressures. A longer delay (three years has been suggested) between termination of service as a Commissioner and appearance before the Commission representing clients would lessen the temptation to start forming industry alliances while still in government service.

More realistic licensing and renewal policies. The empty rituals described in Section 21.6 should be replaced by realistic procedures and standards, rigorously enforced. Among the changes that would help in this direction: requiring licensees to pass a test demonstrating a minimum degree of expertise in the theory of broadcasting law and the principles of the public-interest concept; adopting definite and stringent rules limiting multiple ownership and

---

[59] Coase, *op. cit.,* pp. 441–442.

[60] Elman, *op. cit.,* p. 12.

cross-channel affiliation; systematic cross-checking of performance with promise on renewals; more rigorous enforcement of rules and much higher penalties for infractions, perhaps adjusted to ability to pay; licenses for networks; when stations are sold, open application to all who meet the minimum acceptable financial offer; assurance of more sensitivity to the local program needs of the entire population in the service area.

Better representation of public interest. Ensure that the public obtains enough presence and representation before the Commission to balance out the public-relations and lobbying activities of the industry. This proposal is discussed at more length in Section 22.8.

Sell the right to use channels to highest bidder. Perhaps the most radical proposed reform, this idea has been put forward by economists who find it hard to justify a commercial system which operates entirely outside normal pricing mechanisms. The licensee gets an extremely valuable right for virtually nothing (neither the filing fee nor the grant fee amounts to more than a token payment); yet he can turn around and sell that right at great profit. The President's Office of Telecommunications Management has proposed harnessing economic incentives to improve efficiency in spectrum use:

Regulatory pressures alone, as we have applied them, are not enough to bring about the introduction and use of equipment designed to higher standards to conserve spectrum or to make extensive changes to benefit another user in the interests of efficient use of the spectrum. . . . Regulatory pressure will never match the rewards that could come from self-motivated research stimulated by direct economic benefit.[61]

The returns to the federal government could be substantial. The Telecommunications Management Office, extrapolating from somewhat limited known data, estimated that the actual annual income from spectrum use by commercial interests amounts to something on the order of $100 *billion.*[62]

21.8 / The Federal Trade Commission

Another of the federal regulatory agencies with important broadcasting responsibilities, the Federal Trade Commission (Section 17.11), has also been charged with abysmal failure to protect the public interest. A committee appointed by the American Bar Association to study the performance of the FTC reported in 1969 that the agency had been pronounced inadequate by a series of investigations stretching back half a century. The committee concluded that unless far-reaching changes are made, the FTC might just as well

---

[61] Office of Telecommunications Management, "The Radio Frequency Spectrum: United States Use and Management" (Washington: Executive Office of the President, July, 1969), p. A–9. See also Harvey J. Levin, *Broadcast Regulation and Joint Ownership of Media* (New York: New York University Press, 1960), p. 175; and Coase, *op. cit.*

[62] Office of Telecommunications Management, *op. cit.,* p. F–8.

go out of business. Among the derelictions listed by the committee were mismanagement of resources, incompetence of personnel, waiting for complaints to come from the outside, preoccupation with inconsequential matters, and extraordinary delays.[63]

An even more devastating indictment came the same year from a group of investigators organized by Ralph Nader, the consumer-protection activist. The Nader study group confirmed the faults noted by the Bar Association committee, adding that the FTC is "itself one of the most serious and blatant perpetrators of deceptive advertising in America."[64] They noted that the FTC failed even to protect businessmen. Like the marginal-station operator, the unethical businessman infects his competitors: "Under the present régime at the FTC, a businessman who suffers because of a competitor's unethical practices must either adopt the same practices or commit economic suicide."[65]

The FTC has a remarkable record for long drawn-out cases. The Cox study group found that the average case took four years to settle, and some took as many as twenty. The *Carter* case, for example, took sixteen years. In 1943, the FTC held 149 hearings regarding claims of a heavily advertised patent medicine, "Carter's Little Liver Pills." The pills contained two chemicals known as "irritative laxatives" but were advertised as affording treatment for a "vast array of common human ailments."[66] According to the FTC Hearing Examiner, this misrepresentation had been going on for *seventy* years. The case accumulated over two thousand exhibits and fifteen hundred pages of record. It went all the way to the Supreme Court, back down to the FTC, and up to the Supreme Court again before the misrepresentation was finally stopped.

One reason for delays is that the FTC can take no definitive legal action by itself but must refer cases to the Justice Department for prosecution. According to news reports of charges made by the FTC in 1970, the Justice Department often delayed prosecutions unduly and even assumed the prerogative of deciding which FTC cases warranted follow-up. The FTC's main enforcement weapon, the Cease and Desist Order, can be appealed at length, as in the *Carter* case. Meanwhile, the advertising the FTC believes to be false continues to be used unless a court explicitly enjoins it, and the Commission has been reluctant to request injunctions. Many a nostrum crash-merchandised on radio and television has earned millions for its promoters, run its course, and dropped out of the market before the FTC could belatedly slam the barn door.

To avoid such delays, the FTC relies heavily on informal methods of

---

[63] American Bar Association, Commission to Study the Federal Trade Commission, *Report* (Chicago: The Commission, 1969), pp. 1–2. Miles W. Kirkpatrick, Chairman of the ABA Commission, was appointed FTC chairman in 1970.

[64] Cox, *et. al., op. cit.,* p. 38.

[65] *Loc. cit.*

[66] *Carter Products, Inc.* v. *FTC,* 268 F. (2d) 461 at 470 (1959). Cert. den. 361 U. S. 884 (1959).

obtaining compliance: "industry guides," "advisory opinions," and voluntary-compliance agreements. None of these has the force of law, none imposes any penalty for bilking the public. Voluntary compliance involves no admission of guilt; the accused advertiser merely agrees to discontinue the objectionable practice, without admitting any wrongdoing or making any restitution.

Experts have recommended reforms of the FTC's organization, personnel, and procedures similar to those recommended for the FCC. Among additional proposals for the FTC are using injunctive powers to suspend all allegedly illegal advertising, pending settlement; requiring advertisers found guilty of using illegal advertising to *make public corrections* in their subsequent advertising; encouraging "class actions," whereby suits can be brought on behalf of the unnamed consumers who may, as a group, have been affected by illegal advertising; assessing damages for illegal advertising. Only aggressive punitive measures like these seem likely to have any deterrent effect. The FTC's traditional methods, even when successful, impose no stigma, for many of the "best" companies and advertising agencies constantly provoke FTC charges of misleading advertising.

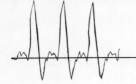

22

BEYOND THE FCC: NONREGULATORY SOCIAL CONTROLS

In the preceding chapters we discussed government regulation as a form of social control over broadcasting. We turn now to consider other forms of social control exerted by such agents as public opinion, standards of professional conduct, the competitive example of noncommercial broadcasting, and consumer activism.

22.1 / Origin of Institutionalized Self-Regulation

Broadcasters must, if they are to succeed, become especially sensitive to the changing winds of public opinion. Every department head at every level of broadcasting constantly makes decisions reflecting his personal assessment of what public opinion will welcome, tolerate, or condemn. The smallest stations cannot afford to assign this decision-making role to a specialized unit or officer; but in larger enterprises it becomes a major and highly technical activity. A national television network needs a department of fifty or more people to handle "continuity acceptance" (the euphemistic title developed by radio), at a cost of more than a half million dollars per year.[1] Such a department clears twenty-five to thirty-five thousand commercials annually, not to speak of program screening. Networks operate under pressure from every conceivable special interest, each of which can find objectionable allusions in the most unlikely places. According to a network continuity-acceptance chief:

We are looked to for fair treatment of and consideration for the gas interests (if a death was caused by same), the meat interests (if a high cost of living reference or adlib suggests that rising prices pertain only to lamb chops), florists (if a line admonishes "Please omit flowers"), the bowling and billiard people (if gangsters are depicted as collecting only in poolrooms), the warehouse interests (if clichéd writing suggests that night watchmen are invariably eighty years old, invariably sleepy, invariably assigned to dirty and abandoned warehouses in the worst section of towns where murders invariably occur). Some of our duties out

[1] Bruce A. Linton, *Self-Regulation in Broadcasting: A Three-Part College Level Study Guide* (Washington: National Association of Broadcasters, 1967), p. 25.

of context seem amusing, but we find ourselves taking them just as seriously as we do problems everybody admits are important.[2]

As a natural outcome of this activity, broadcasting organizations sought common solutions to common problems and at the same time strength in numbers. Thence came institutionalized interpretation of public opinion—self-regulatory codes for the industry as a whole.

Most self-regulation by businesses and industries arises from the need to cultivate good public relations and to forestall official regulation by government. It does not necessarily follow that self-regulation always remains at this level. The very mental discipline of developing a well-thought-out code as an explicit statement of principles, objectives, and standards can have a long-term self-educating effect. Unconsciously, the members of an industry may begin to acquire in fact and practice a sense of responsibility to which at first they may have paid mere lip service.[3]

Self-regulation of broadcasting finds its precedent and archetype in the motion-picture production code. The content of films, the advertising of films, and the conduct of people associated with films came under increasingly severe criticism during the early 1920's, accelerating a trend toward official censorship by municipalities and states. In 1922, the major producing companies set up an organization, later called the Motion Picture Production Association of America, to repair the industry's reputation. Will H. Hays resigned as United States Postmaster General to become the first head of the MPAA, which became popularly known as the Hays Office. Hays's salary of $100 thousand indicated how seriously producers regarded their problem.[4]

By 1930, the Hays Office had evolved a formal production code to govern the details of motion-picture content. At first the code had relatively little practical effect, but in 1934 the Catholic Legion of Decency organized a nationwide movement to boycott objectionable films. This box-office threat resulted in an enforcement mechanism, the Production Code Administration, with provisions for issuing official certificates of approval.

The original MPAA code leaned heavily on moralizing precepts and didactic theology. Its elaborate series of "don't's" and "be careful's," taken literally,

---

[2] Letter from Stockton Helffrich, then NBC's Continuity Acceptance Department Manager, Washington, May 24, 1955.

[3] When the National Association of Broadcasters first asked radio stations for copies of their local policy statements as a basis for drawing up the NAB Radio Code, few licensees had gone to the trouble of thinking through a statement of policy and reducing it to writing. [Testimony of NAB President Neville Miller in Senate Committee on Interstate Commerce, *To Amend the Communications Act of 1934,* Hearings on S. 814, 78th Cong., 1st Sess. (Washington: Government Printing Office, 1944), p. 176.]

[4] He was succeeded in 1945 by Eric Johnson, previously president of the Chamber of Commerce of the United States. In 1966 Jack Valenti, formerly an aide to President Johnson, became MPAA president at a salary of $175 thousand.

would have turned all pictures into tracts and parables, preventing films from reflecting life itself with any degree of realism. Critics complained that the code foreclosed the use of the film medium in America for genuine artistic, creative expression. A series of Supreme Court decisions undercutting censorship in the late 1950's and the 1960's (Section 19.7), along with the general trend toward permissiveness in society, ultimately brought revolutionary changes in the code.

In 1966, the MPAA adopted a system long used in most other countries of classifying films in terms of their suitability for minors. With all films equally open to minors, the tendency had been to reduce all productions to the level of children. A 1970 revision of the code stipulated four categories: "G" for general audiences of all ages; "GP" for all ages, but with parental guidance suggested: "R," restricted to persons over seventeen unless accompanied by parent or adult guardian; and "X," restricted to persons over seventeen (older in some areas).[5] An idea of the nature of the change in the tone of the "don't's" and "be careful's" retained in the new code may be deduced from these comparisons:

1930 MPAA CODE (REVISED TO 1954)	1970 MPAA CODE
Sex perversion or any inference of it is forbidden.	Restraint and care should be exercised in presentations dealing with sex aberrations.
Pointed profanity and every other profane or vulgar expression, however used, are forbidden.	Undue profanity shall not be permitted.

22.2 / NAB Codes

Broadcasters formed their own trade association, the National Association of Broadcasters, in 1923 (Section 9.2).[6] Membership is voluntary, and as of 1970 about half the radio stations and 86 per cent of the television stations belonged to the Association (Table 22.1). The NAB's major function is to lobby for commercial broadcasting interests in Washington, but it also performs many direct services for its members as well, including code making and administering.

The NAB adopted its first Radio Code in 1929. That and several subsequent revisions proved ineffectual. An attempt to secure a "pledge of ad-

---

[5] "The Motion Picture Code and Rating System," Motion Picture Association of America, 522 Fifth Avenue, New York (January, 1970). An adverse outcome of introducing the rating system was a rash of films deliberately made and advertised to exploit the "X" rating.

[6] Called National Association of Radio and Television Broadcasters (NARTB) from 1951 to 1957.

herence" to implement a new code in 1958 obtained signatures from only 14 per cent of the radio stations on the air.[7] Finally, in 1960–1961, with the imposition of fees for setting up a Code Authority with a permanent staff and enforcement procedures, the NAB Radio Code began to have practical effect.

The Television Code, adopted in 1952, drew on the MPAA production and NAB Radio Codes for its substantive provisions. However, both the broadcasting codes avoided the dogmatism of the original MPAA code, with its emphasis on such concepts as "sin," "evil," "criminal classes," and "baser emotions." Like the Radio Code, that for television remained virtually dormant until the NAB's 1960–1961 moves setting up an authority to oversee implementation of both codes, at a cost of over half a million dollars per year. Stations may belong to the NAB without subscribing to the codes, and a higher proportion of both radio and television stations subscribe to the Association than subscribe to the codes (Table 22.1).

Table 22.1

NAB membership and Code subscribership

	AM/FM		TELEVISION	
	Number	*Per Cent*	*Number*	*Per Cent*
Total stations on air	6,364	100	630	100
members of NAB	3,286	51	529	86
Code subscribers	2,382	34	410	65

Source: Letter from National Association of Broadcasters, Code Authority, August 20, 1970.

The Radio and Television Codes differ in detail but cover essentially the same ground in two main divisions—program standards and advertising standards. The former pay special attention to programs dealing with education and culture, children, news, controversial public issues, politics, and religion. The advertising division, in addition to time standards (reviewed in Section 13.3 and Table 13.2), has special provisions covering advertising medical products, contests, and premiums and other offers. The degree of proscriptiveness varies from item to item. At one extreme, some rules simply reiterate binding legal requirements, such as the federal prohibition against advertising lotteries. At the other extreme, items such as a recommendation against charges to churches for television time leave a choice open to the subscriber. Most items consist of "should's" and "not acceptable's." Examples:

Under "General Program Standards":

"Suicide as an acceptable solution for human problems is prohibited."

---

[7] Linton, *op. cit.,* pp. 11–14.

Under "Treatment of News and Public Events":

"Commentary and analysis should be clearly identified as such."

Under "General Advertising Standards":

"The advertising of hard liquor (distilled spirits) is not acceptable."

Under "Presentation of Advertising":

"Advertising should offer a product or service on its positive merits and refrain by identification or other means from discrediting, disparaging or unfairly attacking competitors, competing products, other industries, professions or institutions."[8]

As one of its functions, the Code Authority deals with interpreting the codes' provisions—often a difficult task in itself, considering the infinite subtleties of expression at the command of producers and the inexhaustible ingenuity of advertising agencies. The Code Authority reviews some two thousand new commercials per year, including advertisers' documentation of any claims they may put forward. These research reports often involve highly technical data, for analysis of which the Authority uses a Medical and Science Advisory Panel of some forty specialists. When efforts to secure compliance in preparation of new commercials fail, the Authority alerts subscriber stations to the release of the noncompliant commercials. Although the networks assume the major responsibility for clearing their own program materials, the Code Authority also reviews eight to nine hundred network programs per year, of which about 6 per cent require negotiation.[9]

Other functions of the Code Authority include maintaining liaison with over twenty Washington bureaucracies concerned with advertising; monitoring stations; following up complaints; and finally, carrying out enforcement procedures. In the last lies the second major weakness of the self-regulatory system (the first is that not all stations subscribe). Both subscription and compliance are voluntary. An erring subscriber loses at most his right to display the code seal and to advertise himself as a subscriber. These losses hardly amount to compelling sanctions; yet antitrust laws prevent trade associations from exercising coercive control over their membership, even in a good cause. Compare the case of the AAAA's attempt to police advertising agencies, mentioned in Section 13.8.

Self-regulation thus has its limitations, in both what it sets out to do and what it accomplishes even at that level. A one-time director of the NAB Code Authority admitted:

Even if our entire [NAB] membership conforms religiously to the spirit and letter of the Radio Code, such a substantial part of the industry is completely outside the jurisdiction of self-regulation that it is virtually impossible for us to maintain industry standards in any practical sense. The public is still being victimized by the

---

[8] Quotations from National Association of Broadcasters, Code Authority, *The Television Code,* 14th ed. (Washington: The Association, September, 1969).

[9] Data in this paragraph supplied in a letter from Stockton Helffrich, Director of the NAB Code Authority, Washington, June 3, 1970.

poor programming and shoddy practices of a large segment of the industry which has no interest in standards and feels no compulsion to observe them.[10]

The marginal economic existence of many stations accounts for this indictment from an industry member. By their own confession, they simply cannot afford to adhere even to the mild standards set up by the industry itself. As we pointed out in Section 16.1, the example of these marginal stations tends to undermine standards of the industry as a whole.

Nevertheless, the broadcasting codes must be counted as exerting a constraining influence, despite limitations on their scope and enforcement. Even though self-regulation originates *within* the commercial medium, we regard it in the present context as a form of social rather than economic constraint. The observation that the codes tend to follow rather than lead public opinion justifies this interpretation. The broad principles announced in the Radio Code's "Creed" and the Television Code's "Preamble" give ample warrant for seeking out and correcting abuses before they become notorious. In practice, however, the "thou shalt not's" of the codes usually appear only after adverse publicity has already called attention to the need. They thus represent an industry assessment of the constraints necessitated by the force of public opinion.

22.3 / Professionalism : Individualized Self-Regulation

Professionalizing broadcasting occupations has often been suggested as a way to secure better social control of the medium without unduly enlarging the role of government regulation.[11] The NAB codes, as we have said, represent *institutionalized* self-regulation. The NAB itself consists of an association of enterprises, rather than an association of individual workers in the field. A curious fact of broadcasting in America is that though a technician has to pass a formal test and earn an FCC license in order to operate even a very small transmitter, a licensee can own and manage a string of multimillion-dollar broadcasting stations without having to demonstrate any special knowledge whatever of either broadcasting in general or the special responsibilities of licensees in particular (see the *Avco* case, for example: Section 18.9).

In the practical terms of day-to-day operations, the private conscience and sense of responsibility of the individual worker—writer, salesman, air personality, control operator, editor—govern what goes out over the air. The multitude of their small decisions determines the actual quality of the broadcast service. Legal regulation and institutionalized self-regulation can govern only a small proportion of these decisions; most remain personal. Lewis Hill, originator of the unique "listener-sponsored" Pacifica Foundation stations,

---

[10] Robert Swezey, quoted in *Equal Time: The Private Broadcaster and the Public Interest,* by Newton N. Minow [pp. 169–170]. Edited by Lawrence Laurent. Copyright © 1964 by Newton N. Minow. Reprinted by permission of Atheneum Publishers.

[11] See, for example, Nicholas Johnson, *How to Talk Back to Your Television Set* (Boston: Little, Brown, 1970), pp. 183–184.

based his programming philosophy on the concept of the individual worker's responsibility:

Even if someone else has decided why there should be a broadcast and what should be in it, these are the people who make it. Yet we never hear these people mentioned in any serious social or moral criticism of American radio. They do not appear in the demonologies of the advertiser and the mass. They constitute most of the radio industry, but are perhaps the last people we would think of in trying to place final responsibility for what radio does.[12]

Each individual worker thus bears—at least in theory—a special and compelling public responsibility. Full understanding of this responsibility would certainly require specialized study and training, yet none is required. Commissioner Nicholas Johnson contrasted this complete absence of required preparation for broadcasters with the credentials required of an applicant for the post of third-grade teacher:

The applicant may have to have a college degree from a school of education. She must be qualified under standards established by the state for a teacher's certificate. She must meet the standards of the local school board. She probably must have spent some time as a supervised practice teacher . . . she must meet these standards because she is going to spend time with a group of perhaps twenty-five children for several months out of the year. . . .

Contrast these concerns and standards, if you will, with those we associate with broadcasters, with their access to millions of young minds for far more hours every year.[13]

Professionalism implies individual self-regulation—the voluntary adoption of high standards of ethical personal conduct in the pursuit of an occupation fraught with social responsibility. The state may step in to administer and enforce standards, but they originate within the profession itself. Only the practitioners are presumed to have the necessary specialized training and knowledge to set appropriate standards for licensing.

"What are the distinctive marks of a skill group that deserves to be called a profession"? asked Harold Lasswell. He answered in terms of the paramountcy of the public interest over private interest:

The essential mark is not only the acquisition of skills, not only the development of literate theories of these skills, but the demand to serve the public interest.

The mark of a profession from this point of view is whether its members will turn down jobs. A rough-and-ready way to decide whether you have a profession is to find out if people will turn down jobs in the field because the jobs would be against the public interest.[14]

---

[12] Eleanor McKinney, ed., *The Exacting Ear: The Story of Listener-Sponsored Radio* (New York: Random House, 1966), p. 20.

[13] Johnson, *op. cit.,* pp. 183–184.

[14] Harold Lasswell, "Educational Broadcasters as Social Scientists." Reprinted from *The Quarterly of Film, Radio, and Television,* VII (Winter, 1952), published by the University of California Press. Pp. 160–161.

We have pointed out (Section 16.1) that broadcasters do in fact turn down business, but more on an institutional than on an individual level. Professionalized personnel would, as individuals, refuse to participate in broadcasting material judged not in the public interest, as defined by their own application of their own professional code of ethics.

Perhaps the Radio Television News Directors Association comes closest to meeting this test of professionalism as a broadcast employee group. Its Code of Broadcast News Ethics includes, as Article Six:

Broadcast newsmen shall seek actively to present all news the knowledge of which will serve the public interest, no matter what selfish, uninformed or corrupt efforts to color it, withhold it or prevent its presentation.

However, the code takes no stand on such problems as overclose identification of news with advertising, which at one time troubled the consciences of radio newsmen. Nor does there seem to be any record to indicate the effectiveness of the code in terms of "turning down jobs." On this point, the RTNDA president stated: "This matter of ethics is a highly personal thing and we have found very few members who have been willing to admit that they ever had real confrontations with management in regard to the code. This is particularly true where newsmen resign positions on grounds of conscience."[15]

Bruce Linton, after an exhaustive study of professionalism and its implications for broadcasting, concluded that although there had been "a tremendous growth of professional spirit" in broadcasting during the 1960's, at best it could still be considered only a "quasi-profession."[16]

22.4 / Education for Broadcasting

One prerequisite for developing a profession certainly is a recognized, communicable body of knowledge essential to the occupation. Such a body of knowledge has been evolving along with broadcasting itself. A 1969–1970 survey indicated that at least 174 colleges and universities offered degrees in broadcasting and had over ten thousand students as candidates for such degrees (counting only third- and fourth-year undergraduate students).[17]

However, the academic community has been uncertain about how to classify and structure broadcasting as a subject for academic study and research. Although fairly consistent nationwide curriculum patterns have now emerged, institutions still differ widely in their emphases and ways of incorporating broadcasting into the larger academic framework.[18] For example, nearly half

---

[15] Letter from J. W. Roberts, Washington, September 2, 1970.

[16] Linton, *op. cit.,* pp. 17, 3.

[17] Harold Niven, "Twelfth Survey of Colleges and Universities Offering Courses in Broadcasting, 1969–1970," *Journal of Broadcasting,* XIV (Summer, 1970), 337–376.

[18] See Association for Professional Broadcasting Education, *Organizational Patterns of Broadcast Instructional Programs in American Colleges and Universities* (Washington: National Association of Broadcasters, 1970).

the broadcasting curricula in the previously mentioned survey fall under speech-oriented academic units, about a fifth under "communications," and about 10 per cent under journalism. Only a quarter fall under independent broadcasting (sometimes broadcasting and film) units.

The dominance of speech stems from the fact that the earliest courses in broadcasting (coming long before television, of course) tended to be courses in announcing. This early linkage of broadcasting education with performance skills was unfortunate, since performance is only the tip of the iceberg. It tended to underemphasize the economic, social, and technical aspects of the medium. Most radio-station managers regarded their announcers as salesmen and were baffled by graduates of early radio curricula who thought of announcing as a form of dramatic art.

The implication that performance was the heart of broadcast study also impeded orderly development of broadcasting curricula by arousing suspicions that broadcasting was too vocational to merit academic status. The fact that broadcasting impinges on so many different existing disciplines also caused difficulties. It has links with speech, drama, journalism, advertising, public relations, marketing, management, economics, law, engineering, creative writing, psychology, sociology, education, art, music. This complex pattern of kinships sometimes caused jurisdictional disputes and poorly balanced broadcasting curricula.

Some institutions answered the dilemma with an interdisciplinary approach to broadcast teaching. Another and stronger trend has been the "communications" approach emphasizing the common principles underlying methods of mass communication. This is a promising concept, but it has definitional problems. Some institutions use the term "communications" merely as an administrative convenience, an excuse to lump a group of not necessarily compatible studies under a single title, rather than as a dynamic analytical concept for exploring the nature of a group of related communications media. Symptomatic of this state of affairs is a type of textbook which purports to take a "communications" or "mass-media" approach but turns out on examination to be merely a collection of essays by narrowly disciplined specialists in journalism, broadcasting, films, social psychology, advertising, and the like, each pursuing his separate way.

In 1955, in an effort to deal systematically with some of these problems, a group of college teachers of broadcasting formed the Association for Professional Broadcasting Education, in cooperation with the National Association of Broadcasters.[19] The National Association of Educational Broadcasters and several other academic groups already existed, but their focus was on educational-station operation and the use of broadcasting as an educational tool. The APBE struck a new note with its emphasis on education *for* broadcasting. In

---

[19] The APBE was successor to an earlier attempt to form a broadcasting curriculum-accrediting organization. See Sydney W. Head and Leo Martin, "Broadcasting and Higher Education: A New Era," *Journal of Broadcasting,* I (Winter, 1956–1957), 39–46.

the long run, it was hoped, the Association might make an important contribution to the improvement of American broadcasting—both commercial and educational—by helping to develop that "body of communicable knowledge" essential for professionalizing broadcasting occupations. The APBE's first accomplishment was founding a professional publication, the *Journal of Broadcasting,* which became a valued source of information for teachers of broadcasting and other specialists in mass communication.

22.5 / Professional Criticism of Broadcasting

Traditionally, professional critics of the arts exert a certain amount of social control by interpreting and in some degree influencing public opinion. Broadcasting critics, however, suffer from the peculiar disadvantage of having to deal almost always in the past tense. Jackie Gleason defined television critics as men who report traffic accidents to eyewitnesses.[20] Broadcast programs do not remain available over a period of time like books, plays, motion pictures, or art works. The broadcast critic cannot influence future attendance. He therefore loses his main—if not his sole—source of leverage with producers.[21]

The assimilative nature of broadcasting creates another problem for the critic. A theatre or cinema critic deals with a particular art form; book reviewers specialize according to their field of expertise; but a broadcast critic reviews not only drama but also news, editorials, documentaries, biographies, music, sports, hobbies, games, science, medicine, children's programs—in fact, programs involving the whole range of human interests and activities. Jack Gould, the *New York Times* critic, remarked that the "basic flaw of TV criticism is the critic's presumption that he is equipped to review anything and everything."[22]

In fact, most broadcast critics spread themselves even more thinly by attempting to cover many aspects of the medium *other* than programs. Again, this tendency seems to set broadcast criticism apart. Book reviewers do not usually involve themselves in the corporate structure of the publishing industry, nor do theatre reviewers need to worry about government regulation or backstage technology. According to Lawrence Laurent, a broadcast critic

. . . must be something of an electronics engineer, an expert on our governmental processes, and an esthetician. He must have a grasp of advertising and marketing

---

[20] Lawrence Laurent, "Wanted: The Complete Television Critic," in Robert L. Shayon, *et al., The Eighth Art* (New York: Holt, Rinehart and Winston, 1962), p. 155.

[21] Sometimes critics see programs before air time, and program series can be reviewed *qua* series. The fact remains, however, that the broadcast reviewer cannot influence "attendance" over a period of time as can reviewers of other media.

[22] Quoted in Solomon Simonson, *Crisis in Television: A Study of the Private Judgment and the Public Interest* (New York: Living Books, 1966), p. 147.

principles. He should be able to evaluate all of the art forms; to comprehend each of the messages conveyed, on every subject under the sun through television . . . [to] stand above the boiling turmoil while he plunges into every controversy as a social critic and guardian of standards.[23]

Laurent concludes that such an ideal critic does not exist.

In practice, broadcast critics appear to devote relatively little space to program reviews. A content study of newspaper columns by three well-known critics broke their subject matter down into fourteen categories.[24] Only one critic, Jack Gould, devoted most of his attention to reviews (just over half). Hal Humphrey of the *Los Angeles Times* stressed personalities (40 per cent), while Larry Wolters of the *Chicago Tribune* devoted the largest proportion of his space (31 per cent) to advance information on programs. Each of these critics felt that one of his major functions was "to serve as a catalyst for better programming and the full use of the potential of the television medium." Thus critics *see* themselves, at least, as playing an active role in the social control of the medium.

22.6 / The Control Function of Educational Broadcasting

We have chosen to treat educational broadcasting as an aspect of social control in this chapter because (1) it offers an alternative to the dominant private, commercially supported service, and (2) its policies as a primarily public, tax-supported service represent a conscious effort at social control, a calculated counterpoise to the biases of the commercial service. However, as we shall see, the appropriateness of this social role has not been universally acclaimed.

Before discussing the issues, some definitions may be in order. Perhaps only the United Nations exceeds educational broadcasting in fondness for acronyms. The following brief dictionary may prevent subsequent confusion:

ETV = Educational Television. The generic name, used by the FCC ("noncommercial, educational television"). Includes *both* ITV and PTV, *q.v.*

ITV = Instructional Television. Broadcast (open-circuit) courses of formal instruction for in-school consumption, as distinguished from public-affairs, news and information, cultural, entertainment, and adult educational programs on ETV stations.

CPB = Corporation for Public Broadcasting. Federally sponsored organization recommended by the Carnegie Commission (Section 10.9) to lift ETV into a higher orbit, created by the Public Broadcasting Act of 1967 (Section 17.9).

PTV = Public Television. Term invented by the Carnegie Commission to

---

[23] Laurent, *op. cit.,* p. 156.
[24] Peter E. Mayeux, "Three Television Critics: Stated vs. Manifest Functions," *Journal of Broadcasting,* XIV (Winter, 1969–1970), 25–36.

stand for all ETV programs *other* than ITV; also, by implication, to stand for the higher level of programming expected under CPB auspices. Congress accepted the term in titling the Public Television Act of 1967.

CCTV = Closed-Circuit Television. Nonbroadcast wire-distributed television. Hagerstown, Maryland, has the most widely celebrated educational CCTV system (see Section 4.4).

ITFS = Instructional-Television Fixed Services. A group of channels outside the broadcast band set aside by the FCC especially for the relay of educational (ITV and administrative) material (see Section 4.4).

NET = National Educational Television. Formerly NETRC (see Section 10.9). The independent nonprofit corporation responsible for producing PTV programs for national distribution to ETV stations. It does not handle the actual distribution. In 1970, NET merged with WNDT, New York's ETV station, which then became WNET.

NAEB = National Association of Educational Broadcasters. Originally primarily an association of educational radio-station managers (Section 10.8), but seeks now to serve as an umbrella organization representing ETV, ITV, and PTV interests, both institutional and individual. It publishes *Educational Broadcasting Review.*

In Section 10.9 we saw how traditional educational-radio interests, represented by the NAEB, joined hands with representatives of the powerful educational establishment to form the Joint Council on Educational Television, which won the battle for channel reservations. Almost at once, a deep philosophical rift began to appear on the basic questions "What should 'educational television' mean? What should be its goals?" One side saw ETV as a broadly inclusive cultural and informational service; the other saw it in the much narrower framework of service to formal public education. At the risk of some oversimplification, we may refer to these two orientations as the PTV and the ITV approaches.

Officially, the FCC left a good deal of definitional latitude. In the order establishing the reserved channels, it noted that it had taken into consideration evidence of "the potential of educational television both for in-school and adult education, *and as an alternative to commercial programming.*"[25] The Commission's operating rules explicitly authorize ETV stations to carry "educational, cultural and entertainment programs [§ 73.621(c)]." Clearly, the Commission had no intention of limiting "educational" programming to ITV. Nor did the pioneer NAEB radio veterans. But the JCET, by bringing the national public-education interests into the picture (along with their tremendous financial resources), also brought in the concept of ETV as primarily a new and improved audio-visual teaching device.

Initially, however, ETV-station activation depended almost completely on

---

[25] FCC, "Sixth Report and Order," 17 *Fed. Reg.* 3905 at 3909 (1952). Italics supplied.

the support of the Fund for Adult Education. And, as we pointed out in Section 16.7, the Fund linked its millions of support dollars firmly to the PTV philosophy of programming for the general public, thereby preserving ETV as "a social force rather than merely a visual aid."

The Carnegie Commission and Congress carried forward this concept in establishing the CPB. In the meantime, however, in actual practice ETV stations had developed distinct ownership groups with differing motives and philosophies—universities (31 per cent of the stations in 1969), community foundations (28 per cent), state networks (29 per cent), and public schools (12 per cent). The community foundations represented a wide spectrum of educational and cultural interests; although they usually depended financially on contracts with schools to provide ITV services, they primarily subscribed to the PTV philosophy. ITV, on the other hand, gave public-school and state network stations almost their sole justification for using school tax funds. University stations tended to vary according to the type of institution and its relation with state networks.

22.7 / ITV-PTV Dichotomy

The ITV-PTV issue tended to color the entire operational approach to the programming of the two types of stations. The difference went deeper than merely whether programs should be aimed primarily at (and tailored for) in-school or general audiences. The Carnegie Commission talked about its philosophy of the PTV program service in such terms as these:

It should show us our community as it really is . . . a forum for debate and controversy . . . bring into the home meetings, now generally untelevised, where major public decisions are hammered out, and occasions where people of the community express their hopes, their protests, their enthusiasms, their will . . . provide a voice for groups in the community that may otherwise be unheard.

*   *   *   *   *

[PTV] can increase our understanding of the world, of other nations and cultures, of the whole commonwealth of man . . . should have the means to be daring, to break away from narrow conventions, to be human and earthy . . . should be an innovative laboratory for the analysis of the intellectual, artistic, and social substance of our culture.[26]

Thus, PTV sees itself as a dynamic social force. An ITV proponent summed up the opposing view by asserting that the CPB's approach "indicates a questionable bureaucratic concern with directing social change rather than in promoting the development of educational broadcasting."[27] Similarly, in a little-

[26] Carnegie Commission on Educational Television, *Public Television: A Program for Action* (New York: Harper & Row, 1967), pp. 92–96.

[27] Vernon Bronson, "When Educational Television Goes Public," *Educational Broadcasting Review,* III (December, 1969), p. 13.

noted dissent to the Public Television Act of 1967, a Congressional committee minority scoffingly concluded:

An oversimplified definition would call [PTV] "cultural uplift." It is visualized by
its most enthusiastic supporters as the great and overshadowing element in noncommercial broadcasting. It will be the highbrow answer to mundane commercialism. It will sparkle, it will soar, it will also sear and singe. It will be a force for
social good (as Mr. Friendly and his fellow enthusiasts see the social good). It
will bite at the broad problems of national policy and make timid men (such as
Presidents, Governors, and legislators) cringe. It could, and in the opinion of
some witnesses, should and will crusade.

We know we are not alone in feeling some misgivings about creating a mechanism for the kind of broadcasting which might result from ambitions such as
these.[28]

ITV proponents thought more in terms of the captive audience of the classroom than in terms of programming to attract free-choice audiences large
enough to justify using open-circuit broadcast facilities. Some even felt that
active competition with commercial broadcasting for audience attention would
somehow drag ETV down to the commercial level. This detached attitude
profoundly affected the ITV philosophy of ETV programming and production.

The Carnegie Commission had recognized that one of the important functions of an effective national PTV network would be transcending local standards of programs and production: "There must be a system-wide process of
exerting *upward pressure* on standards of taste and performance."[29] The ITV
philosophy, influenced by the localism of public education, tended to resist
this "upward pressure." One by-product was the rather frequent rejection of
NET offerings by ITV-oriented stations (Section 16.7).

The ITV philosophy could also be held responsible for a variety of regulatory provisions which tend to insulate ETV from some types of programming
involvement. For example, the Public Broadcasting Act itself forbids ETV
stations to editorialize. The FCC does not require ETV stations to survey the
television needs of their communities and to program accordingly. Some states
have placed additional restrictions on ETV of doubtful legality. In the first
court test of such restrictions, the Maine Supreme Court overturned an
onerous regulation in the statute establishing that state's ETV network. The
statute had made it a criminal offense for the state's ETV stations to carry
broadcasts "for the promotion, advertisement or advancement of any political
candidate . . . or opposing any specific program, existing or proposed, of
governmental action."[30]

---

[28] 1967 *Cong. and Admin. News* 1772 at 1831–1832.

[29] Carnegie Commission on Educational Television, *op. cit.*, p. 36. Italics supplied.

[30] John R. Morison and Donald R. McNeil, "State Supreme Court Rules Political Programming May Not Be Restricted," *Educational Broadcasting Review*, IV (August,
1970), 7–14.

ITV turned out to be less than a universal success, despite ample evidence that teaching by television *can* be done efficiently (Section 23.6) and despite a number of conspicuous exceptions to the general rule. In the late 1960's, ITV critics freely used such terms as "disaster" and "enormous failure." The Commission on Instructional Technology, created by the Public Broadcasting Act of 1967 (Section 17.9), reported to the federal government:

In most school television the screen time is filled with the face of the studio teacher, who is almost certain not to be one of the great minds working on the frontiers of the subject matter being presented . . . the dream of shared resources and widespread exposure to a corps of real master teachers has not been fulfilled. Moreover, the large number of local production units have led to a dissipation of talent and dollars.[31]

The Commission concluded that "one-shot injections of a single technological medium are ineffective."[32]

Enthusiasts had oversold ITV initially as a money saver and panacea. Its effective use, it turned out, required more radical organizational changes and more systematic support from related technology than its enthusiasts realized, or were willing to admit. Vested interests, tradition-minded administrators, and insecure teachers resisted the fundamental pedagogical changes required for ITV success. Reliance on local talent for ITV materials meant that "the medium displayed in public what had heretofore gone on behind too many closed classroom doors—uninspired teaching."[33] The commitment of public education to local control blinded those responsible for ITV to the essentiality of syndication in television. Thus, a survey of 150 elementary ITV series found 70 per cent submarginal in quality and less than 10 per cent really fit to use.[34] Though in particular situations ITV worked exceedingly well, the experience of pilot programs, instead of inspiring widespread imitation, turned out to be "not readily transportable."

For these and other reasons it became clear that the PTV and ITV concepts make an incompatible marriage:

The ties to the schools and universities have brought additional problems of financing and bureaucracy which make many former advocates now believe that instructional broadcasting should be separated in some way from public broadcasting.[35]

---

[31] Commission on Instructional Technology ("McMurrin Commission"), *To Improve Learning: A Report to the President and the Congress of the United States,* House Committee on Education and Labor (Washington: Government Printing Office, 1970), p. 69.

[32] *Ibid.,* p. 7.

[33] Judith Murphy and Ronald Gross, *Learning by Television* (New York: Fund for Advancement of Education, 1966), p. 10.

[34] *Ibid.,* p. 62.

[35] Michael B. Grossman, "The Quasi Nongovernmental Organization in Public Broadcasting," *Educational Broadcasting Review,* III (December, 1969), 29. Grossman draws

In the long run, for most ITV applications broadcast (open-circuit) television offers too little flexibility while at the same time wasting valuable spectrum space. Most educational situations call for more individualized instruction than open-circuit television can furnish. CCTV systems, interconnected by ITFS relay networks and integrated with other types of learning aids such as libraries of recorded material randomly accessible to individual students on demand ("dial access"), make more sense educationally. In the words of the Carnegie Commission, such integrated systems "promise to return to the classroom the flexibility that the present use of open-circuit broadcasting denies it."[36]

For those familiar with broadcasting history, the incompatibility of ITV and PTV came as no surprise. The situation closely paralleled previous experience: the FCC had turned down the proposal to reserve AM radio channels for education (Section 9.10), arguing that commercial broadcasting could supply all the air time needed. In practice, however, the needs and goals of the two types of broadcasting urged them in opposite directions.

22.8 / Broadcasting and Consumerism

We have dealt hitherto in this chapter with varying classes of indirect spokesmen, or surrogates, for the ultimate consumer of broadcasting. We consider next the more direct ways consumers can share in controlling the medium.

One of the ironies of the affluent society is that as the consumer's buying power went up, his ability to protect himself went down. The more numerous and complex consumer goods became, the less the consumer could understand their qualities, their hazards, and their upkeep. Reforms came slowly, partly because often the most vocal consumer spokesmen blamed the system itself rather than its abuses. This made it easy for opponents to use accusations of disloyalty to the "American system" as a red herring to distract attention from real consumer grievances. By mid-century, however, the problems of the mass consumer in a technologically complex society could no longer be brushed off in the name of free enterprise. A United States Senator could write: "The economic issues of consumer protection . . . are so outrageous and explosive that they can be ignored only with serious threat to the fiber of society."[37]

Caveat emptor may have made sense in an age when buyer and maker were neighbors and equally expert in judging the quality and worth of goods. But the twentieth-century "amateur, part-time buyer" faces a "professional, full-

---

an interesting analogy between PTV's struggle for autonomy within a tax-supported framework and the similar struggle of universities.

[36] Carnegie Commission on Educational Television, *op. cit.*, p. 82.

[37] Warren Magnuson and Jean Carper, *The Dark Side of the Market Place* (Englewood Cliffs, N. J.: Prentice-Hall, 1968), p. xiv.

time seller" of goods fabricated in some far-off computerized factory.[38] The consumer cannot possibly "be wary" of the infinite varieties of harm and deception that may lurk in the modern array of consumer goods. He depends of necessity on the aid of such consumer protections as Pure Food and Drug, Truth in Packaging and Labelling, and Truth in Lending laws.

As to broadcasting, a Commissioner said flatly, "The FCC has demonstrated conclusively, for all to see, its inability to serve the public interest without active participation of public groups."[39] As we saw in Section 21.3, the Commissioners work in an atmosphere saturated with licensee influences. That vague abstraction "the public" cannot, like licensees, drop in for friendly chats in Commissioners' offices. It cannot invite them to attend dedications of additions to the living room and in other ways keep them constantly aware of its bonhomie, generosity, and power. The problem resolves itself, therefore, into inventing a machinery for transforming an abstraction, "the public interest," into a flesh-and-blood presence.

For most of broadcasting's history anyone who presumed to speak for the public against commercial interests found himself branded by the trade press and convention orators as an enemy of the American way of life at worst, at best as a muddle-headed do-gooder. Unfortunately, it was often true that special-interest groups with an axe to grind were the only ones with sufficient zeal to organize and make themselves heard. In the 1960's, however, riding on the wave of new "consumerism," the broader public interest began to find more effective spokesmen than before:

In the past criticism of television was pretty much the property of the "intellectual" few. Those who carped were reminiscent of the old definition of a critic as "the legless man who teaches running." And about as effective! But not any more. In today's climate where criticism of our institutions has become a way of life, the vociferous new breed of consumer critics of TV is not only getting plenty of exposure, but demonstrating surprising political muscle, too.[40]

In an unprecedented "how-to-do-it" book, an FCC Commissioner himself took the lead in advising the public on ways of developing "political muscle." In *How to Talk Back to Your Television Set,* Nicholas Johnson advocated a more sophisticated approach to broadcast consumerism than the traditional letters from the audience. His formula:

. . . in order to get relief from legal institutions (Congress, courts, agencies) one must assert, first, the factual basis for the grievance and the specific parties involved; second, the legal principle that indicates relief is due (constitutional provisions, statute, regulation, court or agency decision); and third, the precise

---

[38] "The U. S.'s Toughest Customer," *Time,* December 12, 1969, pp. 89–98.

[39] Nicholas Johnson, "No, We Don't," *The New Republic,* December 6, 1969, p. 19.

[40] Edward H. Meyer, "Is the Golden Goose Beginning to Lay Leaden Eggs?" (New York: Grey Advertising, Inc., April 12, 1970, mimeo), p. 4.

remedy sought (new legislation or regulations, license revocation, fines, or an order changing practices).[41]

This formula was applied in the landmark *WLBT* case described in Section 17.10. It established that responsible local citizens' organizations have legal standing to intervene in license renewal proceedings as a matter of right. A rash of renewal interventions followed—not all well founded, to be sure, but significant as a move away from consumer docility and FCC "neutrality on the side of the licensee."

The newly established power of consumer groups to intervene in renewals led to a constructive innovation—settlement of consumer grievances by negotiation and formal agreement. The *KTAL* case paved the way for this new consumer-protection mechanism. A coalition of citizen groups intervened in the renewal application of KTAL-TV, a Texarkana, Arkansas, station. After negotiations, the station agreed to a thirteen-point policy statement, acknowledging local needs brought to its attention by the viewer groups and agreeing to specific measures to meet those needs. For example, although licensed to Texarkana, the station's main studios and offices are in Shreveport, Louisiana —seventy miles distant, in another state. The station agreed to provide toll-free telephone service from Texarkana to its Shreveport studios; to improve equipment in the Texarkana studio; and to improve local news coverage in Texarkana. The station obligated itself "to discuss programming regularly with all segments of the public" and to announce its readiness to do so regularly over the air in prime time. These promises were more than mere window dressing, for in renewing the license the FCC advised the licensee:

. . . your performance . . . will be carefully examined at the end of the license period to determine whether you have made an affirmative and diligent effort to serve the needs and interests of the city to which KTAL-TV is licensed.[42]

Several national organizations assist citizens' groups in such efforts to "reify" the public interest. Examples:

The Office of Communication of the United Church of Christ, which played a key role in the *WLBT* case, published a citizens' guide, "How to Protect

---

[41] Johnson, *How to Talk Back to Your Television Set,* p. 202.

[42] Office of Communication, United Church of Christ, "Racial Justice in Broadcasting" (New York: The Church, 1970), p. 9. Terms of the agreement are reproduced in Ralph M. Jennings, "How to Protect Citizen Rights in Television and Radio" (New York: Office of Communication, United Church of Christ, 1969), pp. 17–18. In 1965, the FCC had helped set the stage for more consumer participation by requiring easier public access to official information about stations. Previously, the general public could not readily get at essential information such as the promises stations made in applications and the scheduling of renewal hearings. Now stations must keep all significant documents on file locally and available for public inspection and must publicize all major license-related actions.

Citizen Rights in Television and Radio" by Ralph M. Jennings, and offers direct local assistance.

The Citizen's Communications Center of Washington, D. C., provides legal and other professional services.

The Institute for American Democracy publishes a newsletter and a citizens' handbook on how to implement the Fairness Doctrine, with particular reference to broadcast propaganda of the far right and the far left.[43]

The American Council for Better Broadcasts, founded in 1953, encourages systematic evaluation of programs by the general public. Working with parent, student, and other local groups, the Council supplies a newsletter, study kits, lists of articles, and program evaluation cards. The Council tabulates the results of annual listener evaluations and distributes them to advertisers, the broadcasting industry, and government officials concerned.

Several other stratagems for personifying the public interest have been suggested, among them:

Citizens' council. From the early beginnings of radio, repeated proposals and efforts have been made to establish a high-level national advisory council or commission to monitor the performance of broadcasters and the Commission on behalf of the public. Commissioner Johnson included such a recommendation in his "how-to-do-it" manual. His proposed commission would analyze and evaluate broadcasting practices, programming standards, FCC activities, and the like; conduct research; have the power to publicize its findings, obtain government data, and appear as an advocate on behalf of the public.[44]

Legal counsel. The Justice Department has a Community Relations Service which helps citizens who lack legal resources to obtain their rights. The FTC provides free legal counsel for aggrieved citizens unable to spend the time and money to come to Washington to appear before the Commission to follow up their cases. It has been suggested that a similar representative or "ombudsman" should function within the FCC as the legal watchdog of the public interest.

---

[43] Charles R. Baker, "How to Combat Air Pollution: A Manual on the FCC's Fairness Doctrine" (Washington: Institute for American Democracy, 1969).

[44] Johnson, *How to Talk Back to Your Television Set,* pp. 190–198.

PART FIVE

ASSESSMENT: THE INFLUENCE OF BROADCASTING

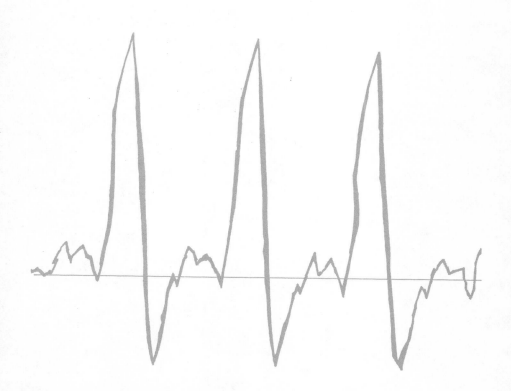

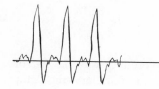

23

MASS-MEDIA EFFECTS: RESEARCH AND THEORY

Teachers, preachers, parents, and legislators have asked [researchers] a thousand times over these past fifteen years whether violence in the media produces delinquency, whether the escapist nature of much of the fare does not blind people to reality, and just what the media can do to the political persuasions of their audiences. To these questions we have not only failed to provide definitive answers, but we have done something worse: we have provided evidence in partial support of every hue of every view.[1]

JOSEPH T. KLAPPER

Broadcasting exists—and causes enough concern for people to write and read books about it—for one reason only: it has effects. Some kinds of effects are self-evident—the purchase of sets, the sale of advertising, the devotion of time to watching and listening. Other kinds of effects cannot be measured directly. They must be inferred from indirect and often inconclusive evidence. Yet society needs to understand such effects, as best it can, in order to exercise rational control over broadcasting. So society has intensely practical reasons for being interested in mass-media research.

23.1 / Development of Media Research

Development of mass-communication study as a scientific discipline paralleled the development of broadcasting. Mass propaganda was widely used for the first time in World War I. Following the war, people were shocked by disclosure of ways propaganda had been used to manipulate their emotions, whipping up intense war hysteria. It seemed as if this sinister new weapon might become all-powerful, capable of "manufacturing consent" of the masses to almost any excess, at the will of unscrupulous propaganda masters. This concern stimulated social scientists in the 1920's to begin analyzing the social and

---

[1] Joseph T. Klapper, *The Effects of Mass Communication* (New York: Free Press, 1960), p. 2.

psychological dynamics of mass persuasion. One by-product was the list of propaganda tricks with which every school child became familiar—the "glittering generalization," "name calling," the "bandwagon effect," "card stacking," and the like.

As behavioral scientists dug deeper into the subject, however, they found increasing evidence that the powers of propaganda had been overestimated. The process of mass communication turned out to be more complex than isolated World War I propaganda campaigns suggested, operating as they did within a highly limited framework. Instead of a simple, rather mechanistic one-for-one causal relationship between message and effect, researchers identified a whole range of "intervening variables"—nonobservable factors *other than the message itself* which play a role in determining what effects a message will have, if any. The longer researchers studied the media the more of these variables turned up, and the more complex the mass-communication process appeared.

Harold Lasswell epitomized the essential questions that can be asked when analyzing the communication process in a well known formula: Who says what, through what channel, to whom, with what effect?[2] One can thus subdivide media study by focussing attention on communicators, on the media they use, on their target audiences, or on the effects the messages have on audiences. Each of these elements constitutes a variable in itself, and all interact with each other.

The communicator starts with a certain subjective intention, but his character, motivations, communications skills, and other variables modify the intended message even before he launches it on its way. The channel, or medium of communication, through which he transmits the message has its own limitations and exerts its own influences. The recipient's interpretation may be affected by the reception environment; moreover, his perception of the message will be affected by his personal emotional state, his established attitudes, his customery framework of beliefs and expectations, and many other possible social and psychological variables. After all this, the message *may,* perhaps, have some effect.

An effect need not be a directly observable outcome. Again, Lasswell contributed a useful formulation by pointing out that responses to communications can be considered as occurring at five different stages or levels.[3] First must come *attention,* of course; but attention quickly wanes if a higher level of effect is not reached. The next stage is *comprehension,* followed by *enjoyment* (like-dislike, etc.), *evaluation* (approve-disapprove, etc.), and finally overt *action.* Responses at each level can be measured, though at the first four levels only inferential measurements can usually be made, inasmuch as most such

---

[2] Adapted from Bruce L. Smith, Harold D. Lasswell, and Ralph D. Casey, *Propaganda, Communication, and Public Opinion* (Princeton, N. J.: Princeton University Press, 1946), p. 121.

[3] *Ibid.,* p. 80.

responses are subjective. For example, evaluation responses can be measured by questionnaire tests for attitude change after exposure to a persuasive argument.

Even at the final level of observable action, valid measurement remains difficult, for in practice most communications aim at post-exposure rather than immediate responses. Many other stimuli may impinge on the subject between the time he receives the stimulus of the message and the time he finally takes action. A person exposed to a television advertisement, for instance, may some time later purchase the advertised product—but was his act of purchasing motivated solely by the television advertisement? Or did he respond to other influences, such as a friend's recommendation, advertising in other media, some obscure point-of-sale impulse—or a combination of these?

23.2 / Noncontent Influences on Effects

So complex is the interaction of intervening variables in communications that researchers have begun to think it misleading to talk about "effects" as such at all. The word implies a straight-line causal sequence which does not seem to describe what usually happens in the actual communication process. Rather, they say, communication should be regarded in terms of a *field* of forces, or a *system* of interacting components—models which indicate the influence of engineering and electronic information theory.

One may group the noncontent factors contributing to the effects messages will have in terms of (1) the channel or medium used, (2) the personality of the recipient, and (3) situational factors at the time of reception.[4] Any communication medium assumes a status position in the eyes of consumers. This status in turn affects how they evaluate the messages it conveys. For example, people have no difficulty in assigning relative degrees of prestige and credibility to each of the media they use.

In 1946 and again in 1948, the National Association of Broadcasters commissioned the National Opinion Research Center to survey public attitudes toward radio.[5] These pioneer national surveys served as models for many subsequent media "image" studies. They indicated among other things that people generally held radio in high esteem, believing that it was doing a "better job" than newspapers, local governments, and even schools.

Later, Roper Research Associates conducted a similar series of studies for the broadcasters on the public's image of television.[6] The researchers inter-

---

[4] Franklin Fearing, "Social Impact of the Mass Media of Communication," in National Society for the Study of Education, *Fifty-Third Yearbook, Part II: Mass Media and Education* (Chicago: University of Chicago Press, 1954), pp. 165–191.

[5] Paul F. Lazarsfeld and Harry N. Field, *The People Look at Radio* (Chapel Hill: University of North Carolina, 1946); Paul F. Lazarsfeld and Patricia L. Kendall, *Radio Listening in America* (New York: Prentice-Hall, 1948).

[6] Burns W. Roper, *A Ten-Year View of Public Attitudes Toward Television and Other Mass Media, 1959–1968* (New York: Television Information Center, 1969).

viewed a national sample six times between 1959 and 1968, repeating some questions each time, but also introducing new ones. The public image of television seemed to remain relatively stable throughout the decade, but with a steady trend toward heightened approval and acceptance. In answer to a question about believability—which public medium would be considered most believable in case of conflicting news reports—29 per cent of the 1959 sample mentioned television, 32 per cent mentioned newspapers; by 1968, the choice had been reversed, with 44 per cent mentioning television as the most believable and only 21 per cent newspapers.[7]

Personality factors in the recipients of messages affect the ways they perceive what they see and hear. The media deliver identical messages, so the stimulus remains constant for all recipients; but it stimulates different people to "see" or "hear" different things. Listeners and viewers do not, in other words, passively soak up communications; they *interact* with the messages they receive:

. . . the individual reacts *on* the stimulus material (content) rather than passively responding *to* it . . . the perceiver structures the situation (stimulus material, content) in a manner which makes it meaningful to him. . . . In general, we want to be disturbed as little as possible and to continue to perceive the world in ways that confirm our existing frame of reference. We become skillful in avoiding stimulus material (for example, communications content), which is likely to seriously challenge our established value systems.[8]

The "boomerang effect" is an example of a practical result of this interaction between recipient and message. Experiments have shown that highly prejudiced people tend to misinterpret messages containing evidence against their prejudices; they distort the evidence to reinforce their existing attitude, instead of allowing it to reduce their hostile feelings. Thus propaganda can "boomerang," producing exactly the opposite of the intended effect.[9]

Even in the absence of prejudice, people under emotional stress may have difficulty in accepting evidence which contradicts their existing mind set. The most striking authenticated instance of direct mass-media effects at the level of overt action occurred when Orson Welles broadcast a dramatization of an H. G. Wells science-fiction story, *The War of the Worlds*. Many listeners mistook the on-the-spot-news style dramatization for reports of a real invasion by "Martians." Analysis of the ensuing panic provided significant case studies

---

[7] *Ibid.*, p. 4. Marshall McLuhan, in *Understanding Media: The Extensions of Man* (New York: McGraw-Hill, 1965) and other works, declares that the medium *is* the message, by which he apparently means to say that the most important effect broadcasting can have is to alter our entire way of perceiving the world.

[8] Fearing, *op. cit.*, p. 173.

[9] Eunice Cooper and Marie Jahoda, "The Evasion of Propaganda: How Prejudiced People Respond to Antiprejudice Propaganda," *Journal of Psychology,* XXIII (January, 1947), 15–25.

of mass-media effects.[10] For example, some of the subjects tried to check on the authenticity of the broadcast; but when presented with evidence of its fictitiousness, they turned it around to support their conviction that the invasion was real:

"I looked out of the window and everything looked the same as usual *so I thought it hadn't reached our section yet.*"

"We looked out of the window and Wyoming Avenue was black with cars. *People were rushing away, I figured.*"

"My husband tried to calm me and said, 'If this were really so, it would be on all stations' and he turned to one of the other stations and there was music. *I retorted, 'Nero fiddled while Rome burned.'* "[11]

The individual audience member also brings to the communication experience the particular sociophysical situation in which he is immersed—not only his immediate social and physical circumstances, but also the wider situation of his entire social background. Such mundane factors as the degree of comfort or the competing visual and audible stimuli in the immediate environment affect perception. A small audience in a large auditorium reacts differently from a large audience. The individual also reacts in terms of the "internalized" social environment he carries with him wherever he goes—the standards and attitudes of his primary group.

We can conclude from the foregoing that any communication may become profoundly altered in the course of transmission, reception, and interpretation. The mass media, moreover, operate at a special disadvantage because the sender has no immediate way of knowing when or how his message goes astray. In face-to-face communication, visual and auditory cues tell the speaker about audience reactions. The speaker can adjust what he says and how he says it from moment to moment, in accordance with how the audience responds. This sensitive interaction between communicator and audience is often referred to in communications research as *feedback,* again a term drawn from engineering.

Feedback, in the engineering sense, means "the control of a system by reinserting into the system the result of its performance."[12] An air conditioner's thermostatic control provides a familiar example: it senses the changes in temperature it causes in the environment; it relies on this information to "tell" itself when to turn off and on, in accordance with programmed temperature limits. Feedback thus has a *circular* and *continuous* character. In communica-

---

[10] Hadley Cantril, *The Invasion from Mars: A Study in the Psychology of Panic* (Princeton, N. J.: Princeton University Press, 1947).

[11] Statements of participants in the panic, quoted in Cantril, *op. cit.,* pp. 93–94 *passim.*

[12] Norbert Wiener, *The Human Use of Human Beings* (Boston: Houghton Mifflin, 1950), p. 71.

tion, feedback is not merely information "fed back" from the audience. It includes (1) information which comes back to the sender about how his audience is reacting to his message, and (2) his modifications of subsequent communications in response to that information. For mass media, the first element consists of program ratings, audience letters, and other types of reported responses; the second consists of necessarily delayed corrections and adjustments in subsequent programs.

23.3 / Opinion Leaders and the "Two-Step Flow"

Some of the basic concepts about how mass-media persuasion works emerged from a major study of voting behavior by Lazarsfeld and his associates in the 1940's[13] They made an intensive study of how people in Erie, Pennsylvania, made up their minds about voting in a national election. Although the media influenced some people directly, they influenced many more only indirectly, through intervenors whom the researchers called "opinion leaders"—respected family members or acquaintances whose personal views carry special weight with others. The researchers called this process the "two-step flow" of influence—step one from media to opinion leaders, step two from opinion leaders to others.

However, the media did not influence even the opinion leaders in direct proportion to the amount or persuasiveness of media content available on each candidate. Media consumers tend to be *selective* in their consumption—paying attention to communications that fit well with their already established opinions and attitudes, avoiding communications which challenge or contradict them. Because of selective exposure, media generally tend to reinforce people's existing viewpoints rather than to convert them to new viewpoints.

Katz and Lazarsfeld followed up the Erie study with a more refined and detailed investigation of the two-step flow concept.[14] They painstakingly tracked down decisions people had made about movie going, food buying, dress, and public issues, ascertaining whether the media or other people had been more influential. Again, personal influence played a more prominent role in each type of decision than the influence of radio, newspapers, magazines, and books. Many other experiments and field investigations tended to confirm and refine the hypotheses developed in these well-known studies.

Summarizing the implications of research on mass-communication effects as a whole in 1960, Klapper put forward five tentative conclusions about what the research seemed to say. He called them "emerging generalizations," emphasizing their tentative nature:

---

[13] Paul Lazarsfeld, Bernard Berelson, and Hazel Gaudet, *The People's Choice: How the Voter Makes Up His Mind in a Presidential Campaign* (New York: Duell, Sloan & Pearce, 1944).

[14] Elihu Katz and Paul F. Lazarsfeld, *Personal Influence: The Part Played by People in the Flow of Mass Communications* (Glencoe, Ill.: Free Press, 1955).

1. "Mass communication *ordinarily* does not serve as a necessary and sufficient cause of audience effects, but rather functions among and through a nexus of mediating factors and influences."
2. "Mediating factors" generally tend to cause the media to *reinforce* rather than *change* existing conditions.
3. When the media do cause change, they are likely to do so because the "mediating factors" either are absent in that particular case or themselves favor change.
4. In some situations, the media seem to have direct effects or to serve immediate needs of audiences.
5. The status of a medium and the current reception situation (including such factors as the general climate of opinion) help determine how effective the medium will be.[15]

23.4 / Conditions for Effectiveness

Research tells us, then, that effective mass communication will *usually* conform to the existing needs and value system of its target audience. Messages that contradict existing attitudes, opinions, beliefs, prejudices are likely to be evaded, ignored or misinterpreted. In sum, "the efficacy of mass communication in influencing opinions and attitudes is inversely correlated with degree of change."[16]

Mass advertising produces desired effects, as we pointed out in Section 12.5, because it capitalizes on existing predispositions. The conspicuous success of advertising in securing results has led to the assumption that the same techniques could be applied with equal efficacy to totally different objectives. Advertising executive Arthur E. Meyerhoff, for example, proposed restructuring the United States Information Agency along the lines of an advertising agency and using commercial merchandising methods to fight a propaganda war with the USSR.[17]

Doubtless mass-commodity advertising techniques can be effective for some propaganda purposes. Communication research indicates, however, that they could probably solve only a small proportion of the manifold tasks faced by a national propaganda agency. Lazarsfeld and Merton suggest that advertising can do no more than act as a guide:

. . . the leap from the efficacy of advertising to the assumed efficacy of propaganda aimed at deep-rooted attitudes and ego-involved behavior is as unwarranted as it is dangerous. Advertising is typically directed toward canalizing preexisting behavior patterns and attitudes.[18]

---

[15] Klapper, *op. cit.*, pp. 7–8.

[16] *Ibid.*, p. 15.

[17] Arthur E. Meyerhoff, *The Strategy of Persuasion: The Use of Advertising Skills in Fighting the Cold War* (New York: Coward-McCann, 1965).

[18] Paul F. Lazarsfeld and Robert K. Merton, "Mass Communication, Popular Taste and Organized Social Action," in Lyman Bryson, ed., *The Communication of Ideas* (New York: Harper & Bros., 1948), p. 114.

Wiebe studied actual cases of effective mass-communication campaigns dealing with ideological rather than commercial goals.[19] The campaigns had such objectives as the sale of war bonds, reducing juvenile delinquency, and encouraging voluntary civil-defense mobilization. The author concluded that advertising techniques do indeed work for social objectives, if the communications meet certain "minimum conditions." These he defined as:

1. *Force.* The communication must provide forceful motivation, capable of triggering an existing predisposition in the direction of the desired action.
2. *Direction.* The communication must include a practical "how-to-do-it" component concerning the desired course of action.
3. *Mechanism.* Some convenient implementing social mechanism for carrying out the action must exist, such as the local retail shop in the case of a nationally advertised commodity.
4. *Adequacy and compatibility.* The implementing social mechanism must be adequate to the job and compatible with the motivation.
5. *Distance.* The implementing social mechanism must be easy to use—both literally (physically accessible) and psychologically (pleasant to use; not intimidating).

One of the campaigns Wiebe studied fulfilled all conditions ideally and realized a stunning success—a radio campaign to sell war bonds staged by Kate Smith.[20] Wartime emotions provided strong existing motivations on which Miss Smith could build her persuasive strategy; the action called for was simplicity itself—"telephone the station you are listening to and make a pledge." The implementing mechanism was completely compatible and adequate, involving minimum effort for the respondent.

Another campaign, an effort to persuade people to volunteer for civil-defense work, succeeded *too* well: so many people volunteered that the program series had to be cancelled. This case illustrated inadequacy of the implementing mechanism: not enough training facilities had been planned. A third example, a radio documentary on juvenile delinquency, illustrated what happens in the absence of the "how-to-do-it" element. Although the program generated high motivation among listeners, it gave them no practical guidance on how to go about solving the problem and so accomplished nothing despite being more than adequate as a message.

Sometimes, it is true, the mass media bypass these mechanisms to stimulate more direct action—as Klapper acknowledged in his generalizations listed at the close of Section 23.3. This happens in times of acute social crisis, when instability and confusion shatter all familiar frames of reference. Under such abnormal conditions the listener or viewer cannot turn to opinion leaders for

---

[19] Gerhart D. Wiebe, "Merchandising Commodities and Citizenship on Television," *Public Opinion Quarterly,* XV (Winter, 1951), 679–691.

[20] Analyzed by Robert K. Merton in *Mass Persuasion: The Social Psychology of a War Bond Drive* (New York: Harper & Bros., 1946).

guidance or rely on his own familiar modes of reaction. The panic caused by the Orson Welles broadcast (Section 23.2) provided an example: no established rules existed for dealing with invaders from Mars.

The leader of a political or military coup invariably makes seizure of public communications facilities a top-priority target. During the time of crisis the media become the sole sources of reassurance and guidance in a topsy-turvy world. Characteristically, though, once order has been restored and stable social conditions again prevail, even absolute control of the media and unremitting propaganda cannot snuff out the spirit of opposition. For this reason, the clever dictator deliberately fosters an atmosphere of chronic uncertainty and incipient crisis in order to maintain his audience's susceptibility to propaganda.

23.5 / Cultural-Effects Analysis

In Section 23.1, we pointed out how concern about World War I propaganda stimulated interest in the study of mass communciation. This research orientation emphasized persuasive communications and the role of the media in political processes—an emphasis that continues, restimulated by increased political use of television. Following World War II, interest in another class of effects also became prominent: "fear of cultural debilitation, which had increased through the Thirties and Forties, emerged as an equally important concern in the Fifties."[21]

The researchers we have been discussing use the empirical methods of behavioral science, whereas the group concerned about cultural effects leans more on the critical methods of history, literature, and the arts. Their point of view arises from their concept of the "mass society" produced by modern socioeconomic conditions. Mass society has spawned "mass culture," which differs significantly from both the "high culture" and the "folk culture" of the past.

In the mass society, according to this school of thought, class differences and fixed status positions have disintegrated, undermining aristocratic, elitist standards. Social and physical mobility has disturbed settled patterns; the masses have lost the feeling of identity and stability once conferred by strong family ties, sense of place, and participation in tradition. Restless and dissatisfied, they suffer from a kind of rootlessness called *anomie*. The mass media cater to this undisciplined mass society, with appalling effects on the higher arts and the consumers of the media:

The entertainment industry is confronted with gargantuan appetites, and since its wares disappear in consumption, it must constantly offer new commodities. In this predicament, those who produce for the mass media ransack the entire range of past and present culture in the hope of finding suitable material. This material,

---

[21] D. A. Hansen and J. H. Parsons, *Mass Communications: A Research Bibliography* (Berkeley, Cal.: Glendessary Press, 1968), p. ii.

however, cannot be offered as it is; it must be prepared and altered in order to become entertaining; it cannot be consumed as it is.[22]

The process of adaptation for the mass media inevitably debases "high culture" without producing anything worthwhile in its place. Dwight MacDonald describes the process in these rather typical terms:

. . . Mass Culture is a dynamic, revolutionary force, breaking down the old barriers of class, tradition, taste, and dissolving all cultural distinctions. It mixes and scrambles everything together, producing what might be called homogenized culture. . . . It thus destroys all values, since value judgments imply discrimination.

* * * * *

There are theoretical reasons why Mass Culture is not and can never be any good. I take it as axiomatic that culture can only be produced by and for human beings. But in so far as people are organized (more strictly, disorganized) as masses, they lose their human identity and quality.[23]

Concern about the effects of popular art date as far back as the invention of printing. Some Gutenberg contemporaries deplored printing as a vulgar and debasing substitute for calligraphy—just as some conservers of tradition objected to putting the Metropolitan Opera on radio in the 1920's. The issue began to come to the foreground when writing emerged as an independent profession in the eighteenth century. At that time, a commercial book market among middle-class readers came into being. Previously writers had depended almost entirely on subsidies from patrons.[24]

Broadcasting, however, undoubtedly introduced a unique element: never before had the *whole people* of countries been showered with such deferential attention as the mass media provide. Popularization of the arts on an unprecedented scale created the need for a new framework of evaluation. It makes little sense to apply the traditional yardsticks to the new media.

Critics who were trained to talk about pictures in frames, and books in private libraries or in school classrooms, and music made by visible and present musicians, trained to describe situations which still exist and are more than ever important but which have little to do with mass communications, have done the arts great disservice by chatter about what they call popular arts without knowing in any precise way what they are talking about.[25]

---

[22] Hannah Arendt, "Society and Culture," in Norman Jacobs, ed., *Culture for the Millions? Mass Media in Modern Society* (Boston: Beacon Press, 1964), p. 48.

[23] Dwight MacDonald, "Theory of Mass Culture," *Diogenes,* III (Summer, 1953), 5, 13–14. Reprinted in part in Alan Casty, ed., *Mass Media and Mass Man* (New York: Holt, Rinehart and Winston, 1968), pp. 15, 23.

[24] Leo Lowenthal, "An Historical Preface to the Popular Culture Debate," in Jacobs, *op. cit.,* pp. 28–42.

[25] Lyman Bryson, *The Next America: Prophecy and Faith* (New York: Harper & Bros., 1952), p. 134.

As Bryson points out, such critics condemn broadcasting as a whole, rather than selecting for appraisal those items of content which merit critical attention. Book reviewers never make such sweeping judgments about "print" or art critics about "paint." "The new art is carelessly judged as a whole; the old arts are carefully judged by only parts of their performance good enough to demand judgment."[26] One cannot reasonably expect to be able to turn on the radio or television set at any time, night or day, to find immediately a program suited to a particular taste.[27] No more would one expect to be satisfied with the first book that came to hand on the shelf in a bookstore or library.

Behind some of the cultural criticism of the mass media and the resentment at their profane encroachments on the arts seems to lurk a political and moral judgment: it seems morally wrong for people to waste their time with the trashy output of mass media when they could be doing something more beneficial and constructive. As Paul Lazarsfeld put it, social reformers "fought for several generations to give people three more hours of free time each day. Now that their old battle is won, they find that people spend this time listening . . . to radio programs."[28]

23.6 / Effects of Teaching by Television

A third strain of research emphasis developed with the emergence of educational television in the 1950's. Some investigations had already been made into the effectiveness of films and radio as teaching media, but now came an unprecedented outpouring of federal funds for research on the "new media." In practice, this meant primarily television.

The basic question, of course, was whether or not a teacher using television had the same effect on learning as a teacher in the conventional classroom. However, the research has ranged over innumerable subsidiary questions such as the effects of varying techniques of presentation, varying conditions of reception, and ways of securing reverse communication from students to teacher.

Chu and Schramm, after analyzing the great accumulation of research data, concluded that it proved beyond all reasonable doubt that television can be effective in teaching *any* subject "where one-way communication will contribute to learning."[29] They tabulated results from 207 studies involving 421 comparisons between conventional and television teaching and found no significant difference in the great majority (308, or 73 per cent) of the cases.

---

[26] *Ibid.*, p. 135.

[27] Note, however, that cable and cassette television (Sections 4.3 and 4.6) may one day emancipate broadcasting from the clock, giving audiences the same freedom of timing they have in choosing reading matter. See the comment on this point in the Afterword.

[28] Lazarsfeld and Kendall, *op. cit.*, p. 85.

[29] Godwin C. Chu and Wilbur Schramm, *Learning from Television: What the Research Says* (Washington: National Association of Educational Broadcasters, 1956), p. 8.

In 83 cases television teaching proved significantly superior, in only 55 cases significantly inferior.

The authors derived sixty rules expressing in brief form "what the research says." Examples:

Rule 7. There is no evidence to suggest that either visual magnification or large-size screen will improve learning from television in general [p. 23].

Rule 14. There is insufficient evidence to suggest that dramatic presentation will result in more learning than will expository presentation in instructional television [p. 30].

Rule 30. Learning from television by the students does not seem necessarily to be handicapped by the lack of prompt feedback to the instructor [p. 49].

Rule 58. The use of visual images will improve learning of manual tasks, as well as other learning where visual images can facilitate the association process. Otherwise, visual images may cause distraction and interfere with learning [p. 90].

Chu and Schramm concluded that the effectiveness of television teaching depends heavily on the circumstances of reception: "the amount of learning from television depends at least as much on what happens *at the receiving end*" as what happens at the sending end.[30] They refer here to such factors as the way the classroom teacher or monitor prepares the students for the television lessons, supervises the lesson reception, and follows up the reception, as well as the physical conditions of reception. This finding appears to confirm the conclusions of earlier research (Section 23.2) about the role of recipient personality and situational factors in determining the effect of mass communications.

"What-the-research-says" analyses like the Chu and Schramm study of research on television teaching serve the extremely useful purpose of providing a meeting ground between theory and practice. Usually research defines problems narrowly and reaches conclusions thornily hedged about with exceptions and stipulations. The communication practitioner has insufficient time and patience to penetrate these thickets, assess quantities of research reports, and deduce operational rules. Practitioners tend to rely on rule of thumb and intuition, while the possibly useful message of research lies buried in the learned journals. Similarly, most people arrive at conclusions about the effects of the media on the basis of unsystematic observation and common-sense conclusions. These pragmatic assessments form the main subject of the next chapter.

---

[30] *Ibid.,* p. 14.

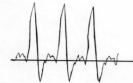

24

EFFECTS OF BROADCASTING: PRAGMATIC ASSESSMENTS

Every time a new medium appears on the scene, we seem to expect revolutionary changes. The optimists stress its potential for education, the pessimists the possibility of abuse. For every expectation, so it appears, there is an equal and opposite expectation. Exorbitant claims are balanced by dire predictions, but most commentators agree that things will never be the same again.[1]

KURT AND GLADYS LANG

Whatever the research may say, people in general act on the common-sense conviction that broadcasting has a wide range of highly specific effects. Pragmatically, they behave as if predicted effects actually do take place; therefore these putative effects have an influence, whether or not they all occur in fact.

24.1 / Varieties of Broadcasting Effects

In this concluding chapter we look at some of the chief effects popularly ascribed to broadcasting. They range over a wide field and stimulate opinion and comment from every conceivable source. Marshall McLuhan tells us the media "are so pervasive in their personal, political, economic, aesthetic, psychological, moral, and social consequences that they leave no part of us untouched, unaffected, unaltered."[2] Not everyone grants the media such all-encompassing powers, but everyone does seem to feel they affect his interests in one way or another.

We usually think of effects in terms of what media do to *audiences*. However, a more complete inventory must also include effects of media on their *users* and on their *subjects*. As media users, for example, American political parties have altered the staging of their conventions to make them more amenable to effective television coverage. So, too, have individual politicians altered

---

[1] Kurt and Gladys Lang, *Politics and Television* (Chicago: Quadrangle Books, 1968), p. 14.

[2] Marshall McLuhan and Quentin Fiore, *The Medium is the Massage: An Inventory of Effects* (New York: Bantam Books, 1967), p. 26.

traditional methods of campaigning to take advantage of broadcasting. In many news situations, the presence of microphones and cameras affects the subjects of coverage, so that (consciously or unconsciously) they behave differently because of being covered.

In Table 24.1, we have listed types of alleged broadcasting effects which cause the most concern and discussion. The table is offered as a convenience in surveying in main outline the scope of the subject matter, not as a complete and scientific system of classification. Other ways of ordering the topics could be used with equal or superior logic. Many more effects could be added. In most areas, it will be noted, contradictory conclusions as to effects can be reached, as suggested by the quotation at the head of this chapter.

Several classes of the effects of broadcasting in Table 24.1 have already been discussed—effects on goods consumption and production, on other media, and on minority groups. In the pages that follow we will discuss only a few of the more controversial and significant of the remaining classes of effects listed in the table.

24.2 / Social Processes : Change and Conformity

As one of its major functions, public communication facilitates social change. This function underlies the high priority the American system of government gives to freedom of speech (Section 19.1). Change being inevitable, society needs mechanisms for accomplishing it peacefully. Without free exchange of ideas and arguments, conflicting bottled-up pressures may mount to the point of exploding into violence and tearing society apart. "Unless the communication process allows us to maintain a certain consensus on how we want . . . change to take place and to identify the goals of social change, we have a complete breakdown of social organization."[3]

The extent to which broadcasting either facilitates or obstructs peaceful social change remains one of the larger unsettled controversies about the medium. In Chapter 16 we discussed economic constraints which, even in noncommercial broadcasting, tend to cause overrepresentation of majoritarian views, underrepresentation of dissenting minority views. According to the Kerner Commission on Civil Disorders, the news media contributed to violent social confrontations in the 1960's by failing to report the buildup of explosive pressures in the nation's ghettos: "The communications media, ironically, have failed to communicate."[4]

---

[3] John E. Ivey, Jr., "Communications as a Social Instrument," in University of Illinois Institute for Communications Research, *Communications in Modern Society* (Urbana: University of Illinois Press, 1948), p. 148.

[4] National Advisory Commission on Civil Disorders ("Kerner Commission"), *Report* (New York: Bantam Books, 1968), p. 383. Note that this lack of communication must be blamed not on repression of free speech, but on failure to make full use of existing freedom. In other words, speech freedom serves as a means, not as an end in itself. The theory works only if people are willing to use the tools it supplies.

Mass-media conservatism and avoidance of controversial or unpopular ideas automatically reinforce the social and economic status quo: "By leading toward conformism and providing little basis for a critical appraisal of society, the commercially sponsored mass media indirectly but effectively restrain cogent development of a genuinely critical outlook."[5] According to economist Herbert Schiller:

Communications, which could be a vigorous mechanism of social change, have become instead, a major obstacle to national reconstruction. They have been seized by the commanding interests in the market economy, to promote narrow national and international objectives while simultaneously making alternate paths seem either undesirable or preventing their existence from becoming known.[6]

Conservative status quo values mean not so much the values by which society actually governs itself as the values of tradition, which often command merely lip service from their most enthusiastic supporters:

The curse of modern mass culture seems to be its adherence to the almost unchanged ideology of early middle-class society, whereas the lives of its consumers are completely out of phase with this ideology. This is probably the reason for the gap between the overt and the hidden "message" of modern popular art. Although on the overt level the traditional values of English Puritan middle-class society are promulgated, the hidden message aims at a frame of mind which is no longer bound by these values.[7]

Until the late 1960's, most entertainment programming pretended Negroes existed, if at all, only as menials or happy-go-lucky musicians. Erik Barnouw, the broadcast historian, observed:

Radio had been close to lily-white, but implicitly. Television was explicitly and glaringly white. A seeming mirror of the world, it told the Negro continually he did not exist. . . . It is perhaps not a coincidence that the beginnings of the Negro revolt—the rise of the "invisible man"—coincided with the spread and penetration of television.[8]

The fact that broadcasting is not all of a piece complicates making a fair evaluation of these views of its overall performance in the service of change. In

---

[5] Paul F. Lazarsfeld and Robert K. Merton, "Mass Communication, Popular Taste and Organized Social Action," in Lyman Bryson, ed., *The Communication of Ideas* (New York: Harper & Bros., 1948), p. 107.

[6] Herbert I. Schiller, *Mass Communications and American Empire* (New York: Augustus M. Kelley, 1969), p. 29.

[7] T. W. Adorno, "How to Look at Television." Reprinted from *The Quarterly of Film, Radio, and Television,* VII (Spring, 1954), published by the University of California Press. P. 219.

[8] Erik Barnouw, *The Golden Web: A History of Broadcasting in the United States, 1933–1953* (New York: Oxford University Press, 1968), p. 297.

Table 24.1
Informal inventory of broadcasting effects

SUBJECT MATTER AFFECTED	EXAMPLES OF ALLEGED EFFECTS	
	"Good"	*"Bad"*
SOCIAL PROCESSES AND INSTITUTIONS		
Sociopolitical change	Facilitates peaceful evolution	Reinforces status quo
Socialization	Helps extend experience vicariously	Provides misleading models
Family life	Draws members together in common home experiences	Inhibits intrafamily communication, active cooperation
Political campaigns	Informs and involves electorate	Merchandises candidates, emphasizes personalities at expense of issues
Political power balance	—	Builds up Executive at expense of Legislative branch
News dissemination	Makes people better informed	Manufactures pseudo-events, oversimplifies
Legal proceedings	Educates public	Denies defendants due-process rights
INDIVIDUAL BEHAVIOR		
Aggression and violence	Provides harmless catharsis for aggressive impulses	Teaches and encourages delinquency, crime
Consumption of goods	Provides information on new and improved products	Encourages unnecessary emulative consumption
Participatory activity	Widens interests, stimulates participation	Encourages passivity

Individual perceptions, attitudes, values

Acquisition of knowledge	Extends knowledge of world beyond horizon	Oversimplifies and distorts reality
Values	Teaches socially accepted values	Teaches materialism, ends justify means
Racial attitudes	——	Stereotypes denigrate minority groups
Perception of economic inequality	Motivates ambition, upward striving	Reinforces resentment, envy

Individual psychological needs

Companionship	Provides therapeutic substitute	Induces apathy, withdrawal
Recreation	Provides useful release from boredom	Displaces more active, useful, constructive activities
Retaliation against authority	Relief of tension through fantasy	——

The economy

Sales of goods and services	Encourages productivity by expanding market	Consumer goods produced at expense of needed public services
Standard of living	Goods cheaper because mass produced	Cost of advertising adds to consumer's burden

Other media

Fine arts	Makes available to wider audience than ever before	Debases, homogenizes, trivializes
Print	Stimulates interest in reading about new subjects	Displaces reading
Spectator sports	Intensifies interest, popularizes new types	Overcommercializes, discourages attendance
Motion pictures	Stimulates more creative film making	Encourages production of X-rated films not releaseable on television

fairness, one must concede that broadcasting includes at least occasional courageous treatment of controversial social issues on the frontiers of change, as well as widely syndicated hatemongering programs opposing every constructive social development. Honest artistic achievements sometimes occur as well as meretricious "show-biz" banalities. Though television's bias may have exacerbated the racial confrontation in the first place, it later helped to hasten change. The same might be said of the ways American broadcasting made the country aware of arguments against the Vietnam war, the extent of ecological vandalism, the breadth of the generation gap, the smoldering resentment of the "silent majority."

Nevertheless, after duly allowing for exceptional cases, one must conclude that the mass media address themselves to genuinely new ideas and artistic forms only belatedly. They fail to attract the most innovative thinkers and creators. By their very nature, mass media demand group enterprise, teamwork, a high degree of mechanical and administrative coordination. They *institutionalize* creativity. The germinal artist and thinker, working out a private vision, needs a degree of autonomy the mass media simply cannot provide. An original artistic or intellectual insight loses its cutting edge through too much handling as it passes through the media mill. A characteristic blandness and slickness results—a mechanical surface perfection often strangely at odds with the banality of content.

24.3 / Broadcasting's Socializing Role

A second and related broad social question concerns the extent (and the ways) broadcasting acts as an agent of socialization, the process by which human beings learn the extraordinarily complex interpersonal rituals and the value systems of their own culture. In the past, the child learned this behavior from parents, peer group, formal education, and rites of initiation. Now, the media generally and television especially also share in this function.

Television is a primary source of socialization for low-income teenagers. In the absence of family, peer, and school relationships, television becomes the most compatibile substitute for real-life experiences.[9]

This change in the agents of socialization may have profound significance. Always in the past—and today in the less developed cultures—the processes of socialization have been rigidly specified and jealously guarded. For the first time in human history, part of this vital function has been surrendered to forces outside the traditional hierarchy of controls.[10]

Klapper points out the difficulty of isolating the effect of the media from

---

[9] National Commission on the Causes and Prevention of Violence, *To Establish Justice, To Insure Domestic Tranquility,* Final Report (New York: Bantam Books, 1970), p. 162.

[10] See Section 24.9 for comment on another possible role of television in the process of socialization.

more traditional socializing influences;[11] but this difficulty disappears where traditional influences become attenuated, as usually happens in the ghetto situation. Children begin absorbing television impressions in infancy. Later they may spend most of their waking hours with the set as "baby-sitter." They tend to accept everything they see—news, drama, cartoons, comedy—uncritically as equally valid and equally true to life.[12] Presumably radio, too has similar socializing effects, especially on adolescents and in terms of music. Some observers believe that the lyrics of popular songs which, openly or cryptically, treat the use of narcotics as normal and desirable, have such an effect.[13]

Another subhypothesis has been suggested by Charles A. Reich—that the child receives a traumatic shock when he discovers at length that the myth world of television bears little resemblance to the real world, for

. . . when the television child finally encounters the real world, he does not find families like those on "Father Knows Best" and "My Three Sons." He finds not the clean suburbs of television but the sordid slums of reality. He finds not the perpetual smiles and the effervescent high spirits of a Coke ad but anxieties and monotony. And when he stops believing in this mythic world, the breach in his credulity is total.[14]

24.4 / Social Institutions : Political Campaigns

Effects of broadcasting on politics have been studied more exhaustively than any other category of media influence. Types of effects range from the measurable, such as amounts spent by candidates on station time, to the inferential, such as the effect of given broadcasts on the outcome of a close election. The costliness of broadcast time appears to give the rich (or richly supported) candidate an insuperable advantage—except that in a number of instances media expenditures in excess of $1 million for a single state office have not sufficed to win the election.[15] Merchandising techniques to sell candidates appear to give the man with the cleverest media advisors and advertising agency

---

[11] Joseph T. Klapper, *The Effects of Mass Communication* (New York: Free Press, 1960), p. 255.

[12] Robert K. Baker and Sandra J. Ball, *Mass Media and Violence*, Vol. IX, A Report to National Commission on Causes and Prevention of Violence (Washington: Government Printing Office, 1969), p. 242.

[13] Advertising also is alleged implicitly to encourage the "drug culture" with its message that pills and potions offer acceptable solutions to social and psychological problems.

[14] Charles A. Reich, *The Greening of America* (New York: Random House, 1970), p. 205.

[15] Expenditures for radio and television time in the 1968 campaign totalled nearly $60 million, of which about 63 per cent went to television. Political broadcast expenditures increased fourfold between the general campaigns of 1956 and 1968. These figures do not include costs of production and promotion, estimated to amount to about $20 million. [FCC, *Thirty-Fifth Annual Report* (Washington: Government Printing Office, 1970), pp. 178, 180.]

the edge—except that many observers believe that television tends to unmask the "real" man in spite of makeup and all the arts of salesmanship. Some critics feel that broadcasting turns political campaigns into personality contests, at the expense of issues; others believe that politicians have always depended more on such superficial emotional appeals than on appeals soberly confined to the intellect.

Politics and broadcasting have been closely linked from the very beginning, starting even before the historic KDKA report of the 1920 Harding-Cox election results (Section 7.2). In the early days of radio, political commentators predicted that the new medium would demand more issue-oriented discourse from candidates. Instead, radio lent itself effectively to rabble-rousers and demagogues. Identical hopes were later held out for television, with like results. Coolidge made the first election-eve address on a radio network in 1924, and Roosevelt began using radio as a personal political weapon in 1933 with his "fireside chats." In the same year, politics first capitalized on the merchandising skills of advertising agencies, when Lord and Thomas helped the Republicans defeat Upton Sinclair for governor of California.[16] Contemporary Madison Avenue techniques came much later, in the presidential campaign of 1952, when Rosser Reeves of Ted Bates and Company, master of the hard-sell commercial, designed spots used in a saturation campaign for General Eisenhower. The trend toward candidate packaging culminated in 1968 with the comeback of Richard Nixon from political limbo in a media campaign orchestrated to an extent never before attempted.

Nixon was no stranger to the power of television. In the 1952 Eisenhower campaign, when Nixon ran for vice-president, disclosure of his use of funds collected by California supporters precipitated a crisis of confidence. The Republicans had been sanctimoniously deploring the "corruption in Washington" tolerated by their opponents; now the news media had revealed the Republicans' own candidate as the recipient of undisclosed financial favors. When Eisenhower failed to come promptly to his running mate's defense, Nixon's candidacy seemed doomed. In a do-or-die effort, Nixon appeared on national television to deliver the now historic "Checkers" speech which "not only saved his place on the ticket, but also transformed him from a sudden campaign liability into a campaign asset." Sophisticated political observers may have regarded the speech as unscrupulously calculating in its sentimentality and crass in its appeals, but its effectiveness with the voters showed what skillful political use of television in a controlled situation could accomplish.[17]

---

[16] Barnouw, *op. cit.*, pp. 15–16. The motion-picture industry foreshadowed television political spots by staging anti-Sinclair "interviews" for incorporation into newsreels. See Upton Sinclair, *I, Candidate for Governor, and How I Got Licked* (New York: Farrar & Rinehart, 1935), pp. 150–156.

[17] Bernard Rubin, *Political Television* (Belmont, Cal.: Wadsworth, 1967), p. 35. Checkers was the name of Nixon's dog, which he satirically mentioned as a gift he dared to keep.

In a subsequent campaign, another key broadcasting experience may have proved Nixon's undoing—the unique "Great Debates" of the 1960 Kennedy-Nixon contest. The two candidates clashed in four hour-long network television programs shortly before the election.[18] Although this series of programs resulted in the "largest number of studies of a single public event . . . in the history of opinion and attitude research"[19] to that date, the effect on the outcome of the campaign remained arguable. The consensus seems to be that on balance the debates probably damaged Nixon; the actual vote was so close even a slight loss could have been crucial.

These experiences must have influenced Nixon's sophisticated use of television in the 1968 campaign, which Joe McGinniss documented with an unprecedented inside view of electronic campaign strategies.[20] McGinniss observed the whole candidate-merchandising process firsthand. He relates how the candidate's advertising staff meticulously organized seemingly spontaneous televised question-and-answer sessions for which it selected the audience and questioners with infinite care, planning and cueing audience responses for desired effects. According to McGinniss, Nixon's campaign themes, in terms of words, consisted of endlessly repeated clichés; but clever blending of words with arresting pictures resulted in television commercials that gave these tired themes an illusion of freshness, originality, and verve. McGinniss concluded:

With the coming of television, and the knowledge of how it could be used to seduce voters, the old political values disappeared. Something new, murky, and undefined started to rise from the mists.

* * * * *

Style becomes substance. The medium is the massage and the masseur gets the votes.[21]

McGinniss believes that television's alleged ability to expose the inner man may operate in uncontrived situations; but his firsthand observation of the Nixon campaign convinced him that the camera's candid eye can be completely deceived if the subject controls the medium by using his own professional planners, writers, makeup men, producers, and cameramen.

---

[18] Temporary suspension of § 315 of the Communications Act made this possible (see Section 17.8). Actually, the opponents did not literally debate; they answered, in turn, questions posed by network newsmen.

[19] Rubin, *op. cit.*, p. 19. See Sidney Kraus, ed., *The Great Debates: Background, Perspective, Effects* (Bloomington: Indiana University Press, 1962); includes texts of telecasts and summary of thirty-one studies.

[20] Joe McGinniss, *The Selling of the President, 1968* (New York: Trident Press, 1969).

[21] *Ibid.*, pp. 28, 30. McGinniss depicts Nixon as somewhat reluctantly bowing to the contrivances of his staff, rather than as an enthusiastic participant in the artifices of image building.

24.5 / Politics and Pseudo-Events

Once in office, an American president has unexcelled opportunities to capital-ize on the media for obtaining favorable coverage of his policies and actions. Kennedy started the tradition of live Presidential press conferences, and Nixon first dramatized a Presidential veto by signing it in public on television. Aside from the influence of such formal public occasions, however, the media affect the conduct of political life in thousands of small, hidden ways. Daniel Boorstin has explored the strategies of news timing, leaks, trial balloons, back-ground briefings, and the like. He calls these techniques of news manipulation "pseudo-events."[22]

Some observers believe that the growing dominance of the Executive branch over the Legislative branch of American government can be ascribed in part to easy Presidential access to the media. Concentration of the whole of the im-mense power and prestige of the Executive branch in a single image and a single voice allows the President and his staff to manipulate pseudo-events with great efficiency and to maximize the benefits of publicity. The other branches of government, not having a unitary image, voice, or point of view, operate at a great disadvantage in this arena. Congress has perhaps added to this inherent disadvantage by refusing to allow its sessions to be broadcast.

Televised Congressional *hearings,* however, have produced some high mo-ments of political drama—though still with ambiguous final effects. The most celebrated case, the 1954 Army-McCarthy Hearings, holds particular interest because it *could* be interpreted as a case of poetic justice—"the media that create personalities can destroy personalities."[23] Though tempting, this inter-pretation has not been conclusively proved.

Senator Joseph McCarthy had skillfully exploited the media to build him-self up in the early 1950's as a crusader against alleged Communist subver-sion in government—to the extent that he lent his name permanently to a whole era and to a set of demagogic strategies. According to Boorstin, he built his career "almost entirely on pseudo-events." A favorite McCarthy pseudo-event was a morning news conference called merely to announce an afternoon news conference. Often nothing came forth in the afternoon session, either, but McCarthy would feed the reporters vague hints about missing witnesses and the like from which they happily manufactured pseudo-event head-lines.[24]

The nationally televised hearings, held before the Senate Permanent Sub-committee on Investigations, concerned a dispute between McCarthy and the Army, but the subject of dispute soon receded into the background as the spectacular grandstanding of the participants ran on for a full month.

---

[22] Daniel J. Boorstin, *The Image: A Guide to Pseudo-Events in America* (New York: Harper & Row, 1961).

[23] Rubin, *op. cit.,* p. 14.

[24] Boorstin, *op. cit.,* pp. 21–22.

[McCarthy] led the way in abandoning almost all pretense of objectivity and began to lash out wildly at everyone who bothered him. In doing this he played almost exclusively to the unseen audience. Soon, every newly made television personality at the hearings was doing the same thing.[25]

In the eyes of his already persuaded enemies, television's dissection of McCarthy's methods in closeup seemed completely devastating. To them, television clearly destroyed McCarthy by exposing him. But were his ardent supporters similarly affected? The Langs thought not; they could find no evidence that McCarthy's position began to erode until later, when the Senate moved to censure him.[26] The ability of television to debunk personalities seems not to work when it encounters strongly held contrary convictions (Section 23.2).

24.6 / Behavioral Effects: Violence

Concern about the prevalence of violence in television entertainment and its possible influence on real-life aggressive behavior began in the early days of television as a mass medium. Congress held hearings on the subject in 1955, 1961, and 1964. The National Commission on the Causes and Prevention of Violence (appointed in 1968 by the President, following assassination of Senator Robert Kennedy and Dr. Martin Luther King) reported that it "received from the general public more suggestions, strong recommendations and often bitter complaints about violence in television than about any other single issue."[27] A Commission study of public opinion found that three quarters of a national sample of adults believed it "likely or possible" that violence in television plays a part in making America a violent society, 86 per cent that it "triggers violent acts from people who are maladjusted or mentally unstable."[28]

Content analyses invariably show that entertainment television programs, in particular cartoons and action dramas that attract children, depict extraordinarily large amounts of violent and criminal behavior. The Violence Commission Task Force made yet another content study, covering children's watching hours (4:00–10:00 P.M. weekdays and Saturday and Sunday mornings) for a week in 1967 and a week in 1968. The average number of violent incidents per hour declined from 7.5 to 6.7 in the intervening year, apparently as a result of the industry's campaign to reduce violence.

However, the context in which these acts took place concerned the Commission even more. Violence occurred in the mythical world of television mostly between strangers, whereas in the real world it occurs mostly between

---

[25] Rubin, *op. cit.*, p. 15.

[26] Lang and Lang, *op. cit.*, p. 30.

[27] National Commission on the Causes and Prevention of Violence, *op. cit.*, p. 170.

[28] Baker and Ball, *op. cit.*, p. 379.

relatives and acquaintances. Heroes initiated it as frequently as villains; witnesses usually remained passive; neither legal consequences nor suffering usually followed. By a curious reversal, such prohibitions in the Television Code as that against "use of visual or aural effects which would shock or alarm the viewer, and the detailed presentation of brutality or physical agony" may actually be a disservice. The Violence Commission believed that "the painful consequences of violence are underplayed and de-emphasized by the 'sanitized' way in which much of it is presented." Such "deference to public taste," said the Commission, ". . . results in an essentially cosmetic approach to the portrayal of violence which does not get to the heart of the problem."[29]

Klapper's analysis of the available empirical evidence led him to relatively conservative conclusions. The findings, he said, "strongly suggest that crime and violence in the media are not likely to be prime movers toward delinquency."[30] In keeping with the general message of media-effects research (Section 23.2), specific research on the influence of violence in the media suggested that the media at most accentuate tendencies already present. A violent episode in a program might "trigger" a person already prone to violence or crime, but would not be likely to precipitate such acts by individuals not already inclined toward antisocial behavior as the result of influences other than the media.

Klapper's conservative conclusions were perhaps oversimplified by apologists for the television industry, who tended to use them to support a contention either of "no effect" or at least "no proven effect." They overlooked Klapper's conscientious reminder that research "has in a sense evaded the socially important question of whether [violence in the media] is in an overall sense socially harmful or socially innocuous."[31]

Many parents and some child psychologists and psychiatrists had long been convinced of a direct link between media violence and child behavior. This view gained strength during the 1960's. The alarming rise in real-life criminal violence—assassinations, street crimes, riots, bombings—demanded explanation. The fact that television constantly offers models of violent behavior—and most constantly to the very people most likely to be already violence-prone for other reasons—provided a ready-made explanation which common sense found hard to ignore. Even the apparent growth of indifference to violence—the standers-by and the passers-by who witness violent crimes without lifting a hand to help the victims—seemed attributable to the surfeit of media violence. Perhaps people had become "desensitized" because of constant exposure to meaningless, consequence-free violence in the media.

Research developed since Klapper's survey gave the Commission some ammunition but still provided insufficient evidence for a firm conclusion. The

---

[29] National Commission on the Causes and Prevention of Violence, *op. cit.*, pp. 166, 171.
[30] Klapper, *op. cit.*, p. 165.
[31] *Ibid.*, p. 158.

Commission staff, relying on probabilities and common-sense arguments, concluded:

For the present, we know that the mass media and mass media entertainment are significant aspects of the daily lives of most Americans. While the evidence is incomplete, we can also assert the probability that mass media portrayals of violence are one major contributory factor which *must* be considered in attempts to explain the many forms of violent behavior that mark American society today.[32]

The research evidence, as Klapper agreed, does indicate that media content may encourage behavior already present as a potentiality. The Commission staff pointed to the existence of significantly large groups of potentially violent persons:

. . . our cities contain increasing numbers of people with violent attitudes and habits, smouldering grievances, and easy access to targets of hostility. To televise violence into [*sic*] such an audience without expecting to arouse violent behavior seems sharply inconsistent with the belief that broadcasting cigarette commercials for an audience that includes smokers can increase sales.[33]

The intervening variables which empirical media research has stressed as the alternative (or essential correlative) causes of media effects may have been losing their potency with these types of people. Ironically, contemporary social conditions may have weakened the effectiveness of these intervening variables: "Society has been moving closer to being the way we once thought it was, while we have been abandoning that once inappropriate image of it."[34]

The major research-based defense of violence in the media rests on the classical "catharsis" theory—the belief that an audience's vicarious experience of violent emotions in an empathic fictional setting tends harmlessly to purge the audience of similar emotions. After reviewing research on the catharsis effect, one specialist on the Violence Commission staff concluded:

. . . the results of all the studies of emotional catharsis through vicarious participation in observed aggression provide little support for any simple conception of the aggression catharsis hypothesis. . . . Results have, in fact given a good deal of support to the opposite view . . . aggression stimulating effect has been most evident . . . when the witnessed aggression occurs in a justified context. This last point is particularly ironic in light of current media programming policies. In showing that "crime does not pay" by depicting the hero's successful and righteous use of violence against the "bad guys," the media may be creating those very conditions most conducive to the instigation of aggression.[35]

---

[32] Baker and Ball, *op. cit.,* p. 375.

[33] *Ibid.,* p. 152. The analogy is outdated, but it makes its point.

[34] *Ibid.,* p. 254.

[35] *Ibid.,* p. 456.

The Violence Commission itself concluded that the burden of proof must rest with the media rather than the researchers. Although research has still not conclusively defined the role of fictional violence in the media as the direct cause of real violence in society, the possibility that it *might* be responsible, even if only indirectly, for real-life violence seemed to the Commission too great a risk to ignore:

. . . we are deeply troubled by television's constant portrayal of violence not in any genuine attempt to focus artistic expression on the human condition, but rather in pandering to a public preoccupation with violence that television itself has helped to generate. . . .

We believe it is reasonable to conclude that a constant diet of violent behavior on television has an adverse effect on human behavior and attitudes. Violence on television encourages violent forms of behavior, and fosters moral and social values about violence in daily life which are unacceptable in a civilized society.[36]

24.7 / Perceptual Effects: Images, Realities, Values

Walter Lippmann introduced his pioneer study of public opinion with a chapter called "The World Outside and the Picture in Our Heads." Long before television, he was struck by the effect that still photos could have on how we perceive reality:

Photographs have the kind of authority over imagination today, which the printed word had yesterday, and the spoken word before that. They seem utterly real. They come, we imagine directly to us without human meddling, and they are the most effortless food of the mind conceivable.[37]

How much more an "effortless food of the mind" is television, of which Lippmann said nearly half a century later: "It makes everything simpler or more dramatic or more immediate than it is."[38]

Television provides a "window on the world," but a window whose flawed and wavy glass distorts the world that lies beyond. It mediates some small part of reality in the form of news and documentary material, but fictional material occupies by far the largest amount of time. It has always been assumed that the viewer's empathic identification with protagonists in popular dramatic fiction makes that form of entertainment especially influential in modelling values and even behavior, especially for children and others particularly susceptible to emotional involvement. For this reason production codes insist that good guys must always win—no matter what actually happens in real life.

Content analyses of popular fictional material (magazine stories, comic

---

[36] National Commission on the Causes and Prevention of Violence, *op. cit.,* pp. 160, 169–170.

[37] Walter Lippmann, *Public Opinion* (New York: Macmillan, 1922), p. 92.

[38] *New York Times Supplement,* September 14, 1969, p. 139.

books, radio dramas, television dramas, stage plays, motion pictures) invariably reveal gross differences between actuality and the mythical world of fiction. For example, if one analyzes the "population" represented by all the characters depicted in a body of fictional material and then compares its characteristics with those of the real population, little similarity between the two can be found. They differ markedly in all basic demographic features, such as age, social class, occupation, place of residence, and ethnic origin.[39]

Of course, such discrepancies are to be expected. To interest audiences, popular drama necessarily presents highly active characters involved in glamorous, exciting, and significant situations and events. Most people in the real world have unglamorous, dull, insignificant, repetitive jobs; therefore the proportion of people in fictional populations employed as policemen, criminals, lawyers, doctors, scientists, executives, and the like is unrealistically high. Most people in the real world solve their personal problems undramatically, even anticlimactically, by socially approved methods; fictional characters more often solve theirs by decisive, highly visible actions which entail some form of violence.

This is not to say that playwrights and novelists have any moral or artistic obligation to invent statistically representative models of the real world as the settings for their plays and stories.[40] Nevertheless, the unrealistic nature of dramatized life in television may have significant, if unintended, consequences.

The television world appears to serve quite literally as a model of reality for countless children and deprived adults (at home and abroad) who use no alternative information sources to correct or supplement the omissions and distortions in the world picture served up by television. Those too young to read, those who never learned to read, those who have no access to printed sources, and those who never acquired the habit of relying on print are the very ones who depend most heavily on television as a "real" picture of the world outside. A study made for the National Commission on Violence indicated that 15 per cent of a sample of middle-class white children perceived what they saw on television as "true to life." Thirty per cent of the poor white and 40 per cent of the poor black children believed they saw reality in television.[41]

On the other hand, perception of certain of the obvious disparities between the myth world of television entertainment and advertising and the real world surrounding much of the audience is presumed to have an effect on *expecta-*

---

[39] Baker and Ball, *op. cit.,* pp. 436–442, summarize some of this type of research. One recent study, for example, indicated (p. 440) that characters in a sample of television dramas used violence 58 per cent of the time to solve problems; "socially approved methods of achieving goals have the least likelihood of success."

[40] Some evidence can be found, however, to suggest that despite the surface discrepancies between the worlds of fiction and reality, underlying *values* of the two worlds may be rather consistent. See Sydney W. Head, "Content Analysis of Television Drama Programs," *The Quarterly of Film, Radio, and Television,* IX (Winter, 1954), 175–194.

[41] National Commission on the Causes and Prevention of Violence, *op. cit.,* p. 168.

tions. The sentimental stereotype of the hungry street urchin pressing his nose against the bakeshop window to get a glimpse of the forbidden goodies within has been replaced by a vision of the deprived and depressed multitudes of the world gazing through the window of television. They look not only hungrily, but angrily. They no longer regard the gap between their miserable surroundings and the affluence seen through the television window as either inevitable or tolerable. Thence the "revolution of rising expectations":

If, 400 years ago, the poorest Chinese had lived as well as the English duke, no one in England would have known about it. It would have been a traveller's tale on a par with stories about mermaids, unicorns, and other fables. Today, however, we see how other people live every day on the TV screen in our living room, as direct, personal, immediate experience. This is a gap within one and the same community, therefore.[42]

At another extreme, some observers believe that television has significantly altered our perception of some kinds of real-life events by throwing them into a unique new perspective. Before television, most Americans at home experienced war in terms of parades, statistics, patriotic drives, relatively painless but heart-warming self-denial. To the great majority who did not participate on the battlefield, the reality of battle came home vicariously, long after the event, in antiwar books and their film versions such as *All Quiet on the Western Front* and *The Naked and the Dead.*

Television brought the vicarious reality of Vietnam home even while the fighting went on. Vietnam became the "living-room war."[43] For the first time, people at home saw some of the pain, destruction, and ferocity of an overseas war *before* the boys came marching home. And for the first time, Americans found themselves deeply, even dangerously, divided about the wisdom of its pursuit. This division may have been due primarily to the intrinsic nature of the war, but many believed television was uniquely responsible for simultaneously revealing that nature. James Michener, for example, believes that similar coverage of previous wars would have altered the whole course of history:

Abraham Lincoln would not have been able to prosecute the Civil War to a successful conclusion had television been flooding the contemporary scene with daily pictures of the northern Copperheads who opposed the war, of the draft riots that rocketed through northern cities, and especially of the stark horror of Vicksburg. Sometime late in 1862 he would have been forced to capitulate, with the probability that slavery would have continued in the southern states till the early years of this century.[44]

---

[42] Peter Drucker, *The Age of Discontinuity* (New York: Harper & Row, 1969), p. 203.

[43] The title used by *New Yorker* critic Michael J. Arlen for a collection of his reviews (New York: Viking, 1969).

[44] James A. Michener, *The Quality of Life* (New York: J. B. Lippincott, 1970), p. 71.

24.8 / Shaping of Events

A miniscule fraction of the world's real events appear on the screen as the news of the day. All sorts of irrelevant and accidental circumstances help determine the selection and form of the final reporting of these events. One of these extraneous factors is television's demand for the *visual,* despite the fact that many significant news events have little or no intrinsic visual content.

Aside from this bias toward visually realizable news subjects, incessant demand for pictures also creates the temptation to enhance artificially the visual quality of events. The Kerner Commission, after studying the early ghetto riots, gave the press good marks on the whole, but nevertheless commented:

Most newsmen appear to be aware and concerned that their very physical presence can exacerbate a small disturbance, but some have conducted themselves with a startling lack of common sense. . . . Reports have come to the Commission's office of individual newsmen staging events, coaxing youths to throw rocks and interrupt traffic, and otherwise acting irresponsibly at the incipient stages of a disturbance.[45]

More subtle and pervasive, however, are the effects of ordinary editorial selection and shaping. Lang and Lang reported on a study of such effects in connection with remote television coverage of "MacArthur Day" in Chicago. General Douglas MacArthur, after his controversial dismissal by President Truman in 1951, made a triumphal tour, in the course of which he delivered the famous "old-soldiers-never-die" speech to Congress. Feelings ran high, and the media gave the impression that his subsequent Chicago appearance could precipitate violence.

The study compares the on-the-spot perception of the event by over a score of trained observers located at strategic points on the parade route with the perception of the event provided by television. By selective editing, television fulfilled expectations. It conveyed an impression of high tension and excitement. Observers on the scene perceived the event in quite different terms. For example, the crowds were both much smaller and less enthusiastic than made to appear on television. What does a television director do about empty bleachers? The fact of their emptiness is part of the story, yet dwelling on them could also seem like a form of editorializing.

Because of television's ability to move *with* the action, always selecting the high points, always able to zoom in to dramatic close shots, the home viewer experienced an artificially exciting, unified, continuous event. Each spectator at the scene, however, caught only one small and isolated fragment of the event as it passed him by. "The selectivity of the camera and the emphases of

---

[45] National Advisory Commission on Civil Disorders, *op. cit.,* p. 377. The networks and many stations later adopted guidelines to minimize the effect of their news-coverage activities on the course of events.

the commentary gave the televised event a *personal* dimension, nonexistent for the participant in the crowd."[46]

Thus a medium helps shape the nature of the events it reports in the very act of reporting them. The effects of this shaping tendency interact with the tendency of the sources of news to fabricate pseudo-events (Section 24.5.) This interaction affects in exceedingly complex ways the extent to which reportage can be taken as a picture of reality.

The tendency of the media to affect the events they report caused the denial of broadcast access to courtroom proceedings. All states except Texas and Colorado have adopted the American Bar Association's Canon 35. Originally passed in 1937 to keep news photographers out of the courtroom, Canon 35 was extended to television in 1963. It states, in part:

The taking of photographs in the courtroom during sessions of the court or recesses between sessions, and the broadcasting of court proceedings are calculated to detract from the essential dignity of the proceedings, degrade the court and create misconceptions with respect thereto in the mind of the public and should not be permitted.

In the *Estes* case, the Supreme Court voided a Texas court's conviction of Billie Sol Estes, charged with embezzlement and other crimes, on the grounds that the use of television in part of the trial had violated the defendant's rights of due process.[47]

24.9 / Gratification of Subjective Needs

The media form the core of our leisure time activities, and television is the heart of the core. For the average American, mass media usage occupies almost as much time as does work, and for some, appreciably *more* time is devoted to mass communications. For children, television alone occupies almost as much time as school in their first sixteen years of life.[48]

One cannot help feeling that any activity which takes up such a large part of a nation's time *must* have profound effects. At the very least, time spent watching television could be spent in some other way—perhaps more constructively or usefully. Some commentators beg this question by assuming that

---

[46] Lang and Lang, *op. cit.*, p. 60.

[47] *Estes* v. *State of Texas,* 381 U. S. 532 (1965). The Court divided five to four on the issue and wrote six different opinions. Although at first the television equipment had been distracting, later it was shown that coverage could—physically at least—be made completely inconspicuous.

[48] Baker and Ball, *op. cit.*, p. 239. The figure usually given for cumulative set use per home is six to seven hours per day. According to the Roper ten-year survey, the median hours of viewing *per adult person* increased between 1961 and 1968 by a half hour—from 2:17 to 2:47. Burns W. Roper, *A Ten-Year View of Public Attitudes Toward Television and Other Mass Media, 1959–1968* (New York: Television Information Office, 1969), p. 6.

any activity would be better than watching television. It has never been established that in fact television watching, for most people, actually displaces some more "useful" activity. Viewers have tended to do other things more efficiently and thus, in a sense, to create more available time.

Perhaps, too, time itself in this connection should be measured in psychological rather than physical terms. Subjective time is relative—sometimes it drags, sometimes it passes all too fast. Each hour of sidereal time has exactly the same value; not so each hour of human experience. Possibly the massive number of hours devoted to television has far less significance in psychological terms than its sheer numerical magnitude suggests.

Nor does it seem altogether justifiable to assume that time spent in watching television has value only if the programs watched uplift, educate, or inform. Possibly it has less conventional personal values for many viewers, for television seems to "succeed" everywhere, with everything. Program content seems almost of secondary importance as long as something fills the screen.

The entertainment that is television is not simply an accretion of entertainment programs; it is the television set and the watching experience that entertains. Viewers seem to be entertained by the glow and the flow. . . . Television succeeds "because it is there."[49]

According to this "glow-and-flow" concept, the act of watching television answers some kind of human need more general than the conscious desire to see particular programs. It has been suggested that, for media "addicts" at least, "watching and listening have become rewarding activities in their own right regardless of what is seen and heard."[50] Indeed, it seems unlikely that enough specific programs, deliberately selected for their own sake, could be found to fill all the time television viewing occupies.

Could this apparent transcendental need be for some people no more profound than a compelling need to kill time, to fill an unendurable void? Steiner, attempting to analyze the satisfactions people get from watching television, gathered such insights as this:

I'm an old man and all alone, and the TV brings people and music and talk into my life. Maybe without TV I would be ready to die; but this TV gives me life. It gives me what to look forward to—that tomorrow, if I live, I'll watch this and that program.[51]

More generally, Steiner's analysis elicited the suggestion that people may feel

---

[49] Rolf B. Meyersohn, "Social Research in Television," in Bernard Rosenberg and David M. White, eds., *Mass Culture: The Popular Arts in America* (Glencoe, Ill.: Free Press, 1957), p. 347.

[50] Philip Abrams, "The Nature of Radio and Television," in Alan Casty, ed., *Mass Media and Mass Man* (New York: Holt, Rinehart and Winston, 1968), p. 84.

[51] Viewer comment quoted in Gary A. Steiner, *The People Look at Television: A Study of Audience Attitudes* (New York: Alfred A. Knopf, 1963), p. 26.

more satisfied with *television* than with television *programs*. In answer to a question about what invention of the past twenty-five years has "done the most to make your life more enjoyable, pleasant, or interesting," over 60 per cent of the sample named television. But when asked which of five specified products or services they were "the most satisfied with," only 28 per cent of the men and 42 per cent of the women named television programs.[52] Respondents betrayed a somewhat similar ambivalence in responding to projective tests designed to probe their subjective feelings about the time they spent watching television: "a large number of respondents . . . were ready to say televison is both relaxing *and* a waste of time."[53]

The relaxing "glow-and-flow" function of television undoubtedly satisfies a therapeutic need for some people. We are told television is used "in every hospital and in every institution as an extremely effective nonchemical sedative."[54] In fact, as the psychiatrist views it, there is even a

. . . special set of needs television satisfies, needs centering around the wish for someone to care, to nurse, to give comfort and solace. . . . These infantile longings [in adults] can be satisfied only symbolically, and how readily the television set fills in. Warmth, sound, constancy, availability, a steady giving without ever a demand for return, the encouragement to complete passivity surrender and envelopment—all this and active fantasy besides. Watching adults, one is deeply impressed by their acting out with the television set of their unconscious longings to be infants in mother's lap.[55]

Barnouw extends the concept of therapeutic need gratification to the population as a whole, hypothesizing widespread feelings of repression and insecurity. He believes the act of participating in media consumption relieves these feelings. He sees the media functioning as "a vast extension of the adjustment mechanism within us. Wide success, far from being explainable in terms of superficiality, must be explained in opposite terms. Deep emotions are involved."[56]

The most detailed need-gratification analysis comes from Gerhart Wiebe, who feels that only by hypothesizing that the media have some "positive psychological utility" can one explain the immense popularity of low-quality materials.[57] Wiebe's theory rests on a fairly elaborate set of assumptions about the process of socialization (Section 24.3). In brief, the media help satisfy

---

[52] *Ibid.*, pp. 22–24, 28.

[53] *Ibid.*, p. 411.

[54] Eugene D. Glynn, "Television and the American Character—A Psychiatrist Looks at Television," in Casty, *op. cit.*, p. 79.

[55] *Ibid.*, pp. 77–78.

[56] Erik Barnouw, *Mass Communication: Television, Radio, Film, Press* (New York: Rinehart, 1956), p. 69.

[57] Gerhart D. Wiebe, "Two Psychological Factors in Media Audience Behavior," *Public Opinion Quarterly*, XXXIII (Winter 1969–1970), 523–536.

needs which arise because of the frustrations of socialization, which some psychologists think may require the individual ego to make a slower and more traumatic series of adjustments than was formerly supposed. The child starts life as a complete egocentric, with no concept of the "other." He is the sole occupant of his own world. Gradually he learns such behaviors as sharing, empathy, and service, which recognition of the "other's" existence demands. But adopting these behaviors requires repression of native egocentric impulses, which puts a strain on the individual. The media answer a need for relief from this tension. They "provide the sense of experience without the accommodation required in true participation." The media enable a special kind of inner relaxation, an "opportunity to enjoy the early pattern of taking without deference to the reciprocal needs of the giver."[58]

The second part of Wiebe's hypothesis concerns another aspect of resistance to socialization. In response to that "series of defeats and compromises," children "retreat and restore themselves somewhat through secret retaliation against authority figures." Now the media myth world, into which adults as well as children escape, provides just the kind of retaliative fantasies needed to offset the "strain of adapting, the weariness of conforming." These include: "crime, violence, disrespect for authority, sudden and unearned wealth, sexual indiscretion, freedom from social restraints."[59]

24.10 / Conclusion

The welter of speculations, theories, contentions, and contradictory conclusions about broadcasting effects indicates a need for some principle of delimitation. To fulfill all the roles ascribed to it, broadcasting would have to be all things to all men—father, mother, lover, big brother, baby-sitter, teacher, friend, salesman, philosopher, healer, critic, seer, entertainer, social worker, statesman, psychiatrist, nurse. What can be reasonably expected of broadcasting? What lies beyond its scope and responsibility?

Answering these questions seems to require first accepting that the medium works within boundaries implied by its own nature. Each method of communication has its characteristic limitations—"one cannot whistle an algebraic formula."[60] Some of the disillusionment about broadcasting comes from efforts at algebraic whistling.

The physical nature of the medium imposes a universal need to regulate such details as frequency, power, location, types of emission and equipment,

---

[58] *Ibid.,* p. 527.

[59] *Ibid.,* p. 532.

[60] Whitney J. Oates, "Classic Theories of Communication," in Lyman Bryson, ed., *The Communication of Ideas* (New York: Harper & Bros., 1948), p. 28. Of course you *can* whistle an algebraic formula and make yourself understood if you and at least one other person agree on a set of whistled symbols; the point is, however, that the medium of whistling is not well adapted to this purpose.

and times of operation. This need for regulation compels limitations not shared by other media. The American conception of the sociopolitical role of public communication, as implied by the First Amendment, in turn limits such regulation in characteristic ways. The fact that the frequency spectrum forms part of the country's natural resources governs the types of exploitation acceptable in each country. The fact that audience investment in receivers exceeds the broadcaster's investment in transmitters says something about relative economic rights in the medium. The fact that syndication provides the most workable solution to the economic problem of high production costs restricts programming essentially to types amenable to syndication. The fact of its being a home-consumption medium places inhibitions on permissible broadcasting content different from the inhibitions placed on other media.

These are only a few examples of the characteristic features of the medium the conscientious critic needs to consider. In tracing the events and describing the factors which have contributed to making broadcasting in America "the way it is," we have sought at each stage of the exposition to emphasize these unique characteristics of the medium—not only because they help explain its present condition, but also because they will help determine what broadcasting in America can become.

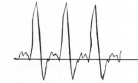

AFTERWORD

THE SECOND
FIFTY YEARS

Technology gives us television, and the imperatives of technology, unguided by other values, insist that we produce it and use it without attempting to consider what it should and should not be used for, what harm it might do, what controls are essential to its use. . . . It is the worst of all possible worlds: uncontrolled technology and uncontrolled profiteering combined into a force that is both immensely powerful and utterly irresponsible.[1]   CHARLES A. REICH

In the 1970's, American broadcasting is moving into its second half-century buffeted by the severest technological, legal, and doctrinal threats to its traditional form in its history. Broadcasting has always been at a storm center of controversy and technological innovation, but the winds of change in the 1970's are reaching velocities never before experienced.

On the physical side, knowledgeable observers freely predict that the convergence of sophisticated community-antenna cable systems, subscription programming, and video storage and access devices will soon make conventional open-circuit television, with its wasteful consumption of electromagnetic-spectrum space, obsolete.

On the legal side, the upsurge of "public-interest law" and concern for the environment, typified by Ralph Nader's Center for Study of Responsive Law, is investing the much-abused "public interest, convenience, and necessity" phrase with new meaning. Students and law professors are giving their time to investigating administrative agencies, corporations, and business practices. They are introducing innovative ways of applying existing laws to consumer-protection problems, as well as giving support to legal reforms.

Consumerism is affecting broadcasting on two fronts: as media consumers, members of the public are beginning to assert their right to participate actively in awarding and renewing broadcast licenses and in setting up programming policies and standards; as product and service consumers, members of the public are beginning more aggressively to assert their right to be protected from false, misleading, and injurious advertising. In 1970, a consumer group

---

[1] Charles A. Reich, *The Greening of America* (New York: Random House, 1970), p. 110.

sued a station on the ground that a violence-prone children's program infringed on Fifth Amendment rights by causing children mental harm. Another group petitioned the FCC to prohibit all advertising during two hours of children's programming each day. Only a few years before, such propositions would have been contemptuously dismissed by the broadcasting industry as the ravings of crackpot reformers. But the ban on broadcast cigarette advertising, effective in 1971, gave a measure of the realistic potentiality of such maneuvers in the 1970's.

After years of intransigent opposition to anything more than tokenism in educational broadcasting, the industry is suddenly finding itself not only cooperating with but even contributing to the emergence of a genuine second service in Public Television. Such noncommercial ventures as *Sesame Street* (children's programming), *The Forsyte Saga* (drama), *Civilisation* (art history), and *The Advocates* (public affairs) have proved the ability of the noncommercial service to reach audiences of significant size with programming significantly different from anything available commercially. Symbiotically, in 1970, *Sesame Street* characters and imitations thereof began to make appearances in commercial programs, while *Sesame Street* itself began to use stars from commercial programs as guests. Moreover, each of the networks responded to the challenge with innovative children's programming of its own, inspired by the *Sesame Street* example. There may even be an object lesson in the fact that one of the stars of the children's series was hounded out of commercial broadcasting during the blacklist era of the 1950's.

Less obvious and slower to take hold, perhaps, is the potential power of the noncommercial service to ameliorate the advertising excesses of commercial broadcasting. The relaxed example of noncommercial operations could hardly fail to make audiences increasingly impatient with commercial pile-ups and frequent arbitrary program interruptions for "messages."

All these changes, actual and potential, involve evolutionary adjustments "within the system." Even the predicted technological revolution would still take place within the existing basic legal, institutional, economic, and ethical framework. But in the 1960's, the system itself also came under increasingly sharp attack. When this happened, broadcasting stood out as one of the most vulnerable targets: not only is it the most conspicuous and advanced case of mass-produced technology; it is also the most influential merchandiser of materialistic culture. In 1970, Lewis Mumford wrote about the threat of the "megamachine" and Charles A. Reich about that of the "corporate state."[2] Different though each writer is, both blame runaway technology for the discontent of our age, and among technologies, both agree that television must bear a heavy load of responsibility. Basically, they carry forward Galbraith's thesis: that the media manufacture artificial consumer needs, enabling pro-

---

[2] Lewis Mumford, *The Myth of the Machine,* Vol. II: *The Pentagon of Power* (New York: Harcourt, Brace, Jovanovich, 1970); Reich, *op. cit.*

ducers to pour forth still more useless goods, creating ever-increasing environmental deterioration and maldistribution of resources.

They go on to some interesting further speculations. Mumford, for example, reminds us of the paradox that these very media that serve the megamachine also serve its enemies, the disaffected youth:

> . . . the electronic media, communication and record systems, even when operating mainly under centralized control, have given confidence and mutual support to otherwise isolated and seemingly lonely groups. Witness the way in which even the fundamentally dissolute Hippie movement has spread, through mimeographed "underground" papers, teletape records, and personal television appearances, throughout the world, even behind the Iron Curtain, without any extraneous organization.[3]

Reich makes a somewhat similar point in suggesting that, in their merchandising role, the media create desires which in fact *cannot* be satisfied—it turns out that the advertised mouthwash does not after all create instant popularity, the new-model automobile does not confer sexual potency, the prepackaged foods do not save marriages. Thus advertising's cumulative impact disillusions and dissatisfies. This is particularly true of young people, whom marketeers intensively cultivate as a special and highly profitable submarket:

> Here advertising is dealing with an unformed group in the society, and they are likely to be far more sensitive to the invitation to live *now* than their more settled elders. Thus, advertising is capable of creating a maximum of dissatisfaction and a minimum willingness to accept the drudgery of life, in the volatile "youth" market.[4]

The new social criticism attacks not only advertising and television; it questions *all* established institutions and habits of thought. The questioning is more fundamental and comes from a wider range of questioners than before. They ask what broadcasting contributes to the quality of life, and already changes have been wrought in American broadcasting which, even a decade previously, would have seemed wildly improbable. On the assumption that it is still not too late to curb "technocratic totalitarianism," as Theodore Roszak calls it,[5] without abandoning "the system" altogether, let us conclude by looking at some of the seminal changes which took place in American broadcasting during the 1960's and their probable significance for the future.

The predicted convergence of communications technologies could bring about a Big Brotherish, artificial extension of the human nervous system into which we could all become plugged—the ultimate horror for those who find life in the corporate state already drained of human meaning. A more optimis-

---

[3] Mumford, *op. cit.*, p. 376.

[4] Reich, *op. cit.*, p. 200.

[5] Theodore Roszak, *The Making of a Counter Culture: Reflections on the Technocratic Society and Its Youthful Opposition* (Garden City, N. Y.: Doubleday, 1969), p. xiii *et passim*.

tic view would stress the potentiality for improved communication to counteract the dehumanizing tendencies of technocracy. Certainly it would be a step in the right direction if, as outlined in Section 11.8, communication could be substituted for unnecessary physical travel, with its attendant environmental destruction.

As for the technology of broadcasting itself, the prospect seems to be less for outright obsolescence than for accommodation. Television needs to become less monolithic, more flexible and varied. Subscription programming, cable distribution, and storage-reproducing systems can help bring this about, without necessarily eliminating the essential broadcast elements of the service. Among these elements must be counted the fact, not often recognized, that stations and networks serve a useful purpose by imposing *organization* on programming. Complete freedom of program choice—the conversion of broadcasting into the equivalent of a book library, from which the reader can select at random any item desired at any time—might prove far less welcome than appears. Most listeners and viewers probably prefer *not* to have to make the affirmative decisions that completely random access to unlimited stores of program material would require. They may well prefer the more limited, negative decision making involved in the choice among a few *structured* program sequences selected and arranged by professionals.

Consumerism is here to stay, and many of the administrative-agency reforms mentioned in Section 21.7 can be expected to go into effect. This will mean increased public participation in licensing and other key FCC decisions. Similarly, more public participation in program decisions is likely to follow from the example of the kind of intervention represented by enforcement of the Fairness Doctrine and by program-policy covenants between licensees and citizens' groups, such as that pioneered in the KTAL-TV renewal case (Section 22.8). Some types of program content, notably violence in programs accessible during children's viewing hours, will probably be eliminated, either voluntarily or by legal restraints. Such restraints may be accompanied by a shift in the burden of responsibility from consumer to producer—it will be more up to the producer of questionable program material to prove it innocuous than up to audiences to prove it dangerous.

Advertising practices will need extensive overhauling before they can be considered a tolerable part of a healthful environment. Television has already gone a long way from the original radio-based concept of program sponsorship. This trend could well go all the way to complete disassociation of advertisers from program control or responsibility. Drastic reduction in the frequency of advertising interruption seems essential for the well-being of the medium. The FTC has already moved against rigged demonstrations in television advertising; it could conceivably also take steps to eliminate rigged psychological appeals. Banning all patent-medicine and proprietary-drug advertising is a possibility. Such products are among the most persistent, flagrant, and profitable violators of advertising laws. At the same time, their incessant promotion may encourage overdependence on chemicals as solutions

for real and imaginary ills. Again we have the example of the broadcast cig-
arette-advertising ban. For six years following the Surgeon General's report
on the link between lung cancer and smoking, the tobacco growers, the
cigarette makers, and the broadcasting industry lobbied to head off the ban.
They were opposed by a few consumer-oriented individuals without powerful
organizational backing (even the big health agencies like the American
Cancer Society hung back, apparently fearing failure and loss of standing with
broadcasters). Surprisingly, the big, heavily financed lobbies lost the contest.
Thomas Whiteside, after tracing the complex maneuvers that led up to the
ban, concluded:

> It may well be that the power inherent in these individual efforts on behalf of pub-
> lic health and against the merchandising of illusions bearing dangerous conse-
> quences is, collectively, a precursor of a far greater power now accumulating. To
> an increasing degree, citizens of the consumer state seem to be perceiving their
> ability to turn upon their manipulators, to place widespread abuses of commercial
> privilege under the prohibition of laws that genuinely do protect the public, and,
> in effect, to give back to the people a sense of controlling their own lives.[6]

Finally, the pluralism of which we spoke in Section P.6 will be needed to
ensure access to the media by most shades of opinion and most minority interests. Conventionally financed broadcasting stations remain highly vulnerable to local majoritarian pressures. Audience-supported radio stations, such
as the Pacifica group, seem able to survive in only a few very special environ-
ments. Pacifica's station in Houston, Texas, was bombed off the air twice in
1970. A few years earlier, a Ku Klux Klan boycott forced the owner of a commercial station in Bogalusa, Louisiana, out of business. This particular case
came to wide public notice only because the licensee refused to give in until reduced to only one local advertiser, and because his experience was spread on
the record in a House Un-American Activities Committee hearing. It takes
little imagination to surmise how many other owners must have quietly given
in to such pressures long before their advertisers deserted them.

Right-of-access guarantees, such as the Fairness Doctrine provides, will be
a partial answer to the problem of widening the spectrum of ideas and images
admitted to broadcasting. The noncommercial service promises, at the national
level, to be a significant leavening agent—though its eventual success depends
on the willingness of local affiliates to take on the responsibility of functioning as a genuine alternative service. Initially, at least, their record in this respect, as we pointed out in Section 16.7, was not perfect. Much depends on
how the noncommercial service progresses in terms of professionalization,
philosophical commitment, and—most important—financial independence.

Similarly challenging questions face American broadcasting in terms of its
overseas influence. Secton P.7 discussed the concern that American pro-

---

[6] Thomas Whiteside, "Annals of Advertising: Cutting Down," *The New Yorker,*
December 19, 1970, p. 95.

grams distributed abroad may do the country a disservice by projecting a misleading image of American culture and institutions. Perhaps we should be more concerned by foreign reaction to calculated exploitation of the media as instruments of policy. In the course of reviewing this trend, Herbert Schiller remarks, "Gunboat diplomacy is now an item in the antiquities showcase, but communications diplomacy is a very strong business of the moment."[7]

The drastic decline of American prestige abroad during the 1960's can be traced in part to exploitative uses of communications, such as those Schiller discusses. Many Americans at home find it incomprehensible that foreigners should ungratefully smash the windows in United States Information Service libraries. Sophisticated foreigners were not surprised, however, at the public disclosure in 1967 that the American Central Intelligence Agency was covertly supporting apparently voluntary, high-minded "people-to-people" programs, such as that of the National Student Association. These revelations lent color to a widespread suspicion that idealistic American undertakings such as aid to developing countries and the Peace Corps masked neoimperialistic designs.

Among the clandestine recipients of CIA support were Radio Free Europe and Radio Liberty, two broadcast services aimed at keeping alive resistance to communism behind the Iron Curtain and ostensibly supported entirely by voluntary public contributions. At the time of these disclosures, President L. B. Johnson directed that backdoor CIA funding of educational and voluntary projects should be stopped forthwith. Nevertheless, in 1971 a member of the Senate Appropriations and Foreign Relations Committee revealed that the two anticommunist broadcast services were still secretly receiving over $30 million a year from the intelligence agency, but very little indeed from much-publicized voluntary contributions.[8] But Radio Free Europe and Radio Liberty continued to be listed in international directories as being supported by "private persons and organizations."

In sum, broadcasting in America is facing its severest challenges as it enters its second half century in the 1970's. While the outlook seems not altogether grim, major adjustments seem needed for successful accommodation to the technological, social, and political innovations of the future.

---

[7] Herbert I. Schiller, *Mass Communications and American Empire* (New York: August M. Kellsey, 1969), p. 110.

[8] Benjamin Welles, "Case Would Bar C. I. A. Aid For Radio Free Europe," *New York Times,* January 24, 1971, pp. 1, 24.

BIBLIOGRAPHICAL NOTES

These incidental notes, arranged by section numbers of the text to which they apply, offer supplements (mostly recent) to the textual citations—without, however, trying to be a systematic bibliography.

Periodical abbreviations used: *EBR = Educational Broadcasting Review* (Washington: National Association of Educational Broadcasters); *JOB = Journal of Broadcasting* (Philadelphia: Temple University); *JQ = Journalism Quarterly* (Minneapolis: University of Minnesota); *POQ = Public Opinion Quarterly* (New York: Columbia University). All four carry reviews and booklists, but *JQ* is especially useful for annotated media bibliographies. See also Christopher H. Sterling, "Broadcast Bibliophiles' Booknotes" (Philadelphia: Temple University, monthly, mimeo.).

Prologue. Broadcasting in America—and the World

General

Lichty, Lawrence. *World and International Broadcasting: A Bibliography*. Washington: Association for Professional Broadcasting Education, 1971.

P.2 | National Systems

Emery, Walter B. *National and International Systems of Broadcasting: Their History, Operation, and Control*. East Lansing: Michigan State University Press, 1969.

Fischer, Heinz-Dietrich, and John C. Merrill, eds. *International Communications: Media, Channels, Functions*. New York: Hastings House, 1970.

Namurois, Albert. *Problems of Structure and Organization of Broadcasting in the Framework of Radiocommunications*. EBU Legal Monograph No. 2. Geneva: European Broadcasting Union, 1964.

Pons, Eugene. *General Considerations on License Fees for Radio and Television Sets*. EBU Legal Monograph No. 1. Geneva: European Broadcasting Union, 1964.

Siebert, Frederick S., Theodore Peterson, and Wilbur Schramm. *Four Theories of Communication*. Urbana: University of Illinois Press, 1956.

Periodicals: *EBU Review,* Part B, General and Legal (Geneva: European Broadcasting Union); *Radio and Television* (Prague: International Radio and Television Organization); *Telecommunication Journal* (Geneva: International Telecommunication Union).

P.4 | Paternalism

Mitchell, Jack. "BBC Goes Generic for the 70's." *EBR,* IV (June, 1970), 38–48.

Pryce-Jones, Alan. "Television in Great Britian." In Robert L. Shayon, *et al., The Eighth Art*. New York: Holt, Rinehart and Winston, 1962. Pp. 143–153.

P.7 | American Influences Abroad

Barnouw, Erik. *The Image Empire: A History of Broadcasting in the United States from 1953*. New York: Oxford University Press, 1970. Chapter 2, pp. 85–146, deals with U. S. overseas influence.

Dizard, Wilson P. *Television: A World View.* Syracuse, N. Y.: Syracuse University Press, 1966.

Henderson, John W. *The United States Information Agency.* New York: Praeger, 1969.

MacCann, Richard D. *Hollywood in Transition.* Boston: Houghton Mifflin, 1962. Chapter 5, "Hollywood Faces the World."

Schiller, Herbert I. *Mass Communications and American Empire.* New York: August M. Kellsey, 1969.

Steinberg, Charles S., ed. *Mass Media and Communication.* New York: Hastings House, 1966. Contains a section on international effects.

Chapter 3. The Television Service

General

Journal of the Society of Motion Picture and Television Engineers. Carries an annual survey of new equipment developments.

Spottiswoode, Raymond, ed. *The Focal Encyclopedia of Film and Television Techniques.* New York: Hastings House, 1969.

Chapter 8. Origins of Government Regulation of Broadcasting

8.4 / Origin of the Radio Act of 1927

Friedrich, Carl J., and Evelyn Sternberg. "Congress and the Control of Radio Broadcasting." *American Political Science Review,* XXXVII (October, 1943), 797–818; XXXVII (December, 1943), 1014–1026.

House Committee on Interstate and Foreign Commerce, Special Subcommittee on Legislative Oversight. *Regulation of Broadcasting: Half a Century of Government Regulation of Broadcasting and the Need for Further Legislation* ("McMahon Report"). Study on H. Res. 99. 85th Cong., 2d Sess. Washington: Government Printing Office, 1958.

Chapter 9. Radio's Golden Age

General

A revival of interest in radio programming of this period has increased availability of historically significant recorded material. See Lawrence W. Lichty, "A Brief Survey of Some Sources of Radio and Television Programs for Teaching and Research in Broadcasting History" (Madison: University of Wisconsin Press, n.d., mimeo.).

Buxton, Frank, and Bill Owen. *Radio's Golden Age.* New York: Easton Valley Press, 1966. Includes cast lists and other program data.

Mitchell, Curtis. *Cavalcade of Broadcasting.* New York: Benjamin, 1970. Industry Fiftieth-Anniversary volume.

Settel, Irving. *A Pictorial History of Radio.* New York: Grosset & Dunlap, 1967.

9.2 | Syndication

Austin, Henry R. "The Maddy-Petrillo Controversy." *JOB,* XIV (Summer, 1970), 287–296.

Lunde, Anders S. "The American Federation of Musicians and the Recording Ban." *POQ,* XII (1948), 45–56.

9.3 | Broadcast News

Lott, George E., Jr. "The Press-Radio War of the 1930's." *JOB,* XIV (Summer, 1970), 275–286.

Morris, Joe A. *Deadline Every Minute: The Story of the United Press.* New York: Doubleday, 1957.

White, Paul W. *News on the Air.* New York: Harcourt, Brace, 1947.

9.4 | Formats and Stars

Several volumes of radio plays are available, *e.g.:* Norman L. Corwin, *Thirteen by Corwin* (New York: Henry Holt, 1942); Douglas Coulter, ed., *Columbia Workshop Plays* (New York: McGraw-Hill, 1939); Arch Oboler, *Free World Theater: Nineteen New Radio Plays* (New York: Random House, 1944).

Harmon, Jim. *The Great Radio Heroes.* Garden City, N. Y.: Doubleday, 1967.
———. *The Great Radio Comedians.* Garden City, N. Y.: Doubleday, 1970.

Standard Rate and Data Service. *Spot Radio Rates and Data.* Skokie, Ill.: The Service, annually. Listings include brief descriptions of each station's program policy.

9.9 | Advent of FM

Siepmann, Charles. *Radio's Second Chance.* Boston: Little, Brown, 1946.

9.10 | The Noncommercial Service

Herman W. Land Associates. *The Hidden Medium: A Status Report on Educational Radio in the United States.* Washington: National Association of Educational Broadcasters, 1967.

Madden, Richard. "Educational Radio Bibliography, 1945–1967." *EBR,* II (October, 1968), 66–79.

Chapter 10. Television: The First Two Decades

10.7 | Programming Developments

Bailey, Robert L. "The Content of Network Television Prime-Time Special Programming: 1948–1968." *JOB,* XIV (Summer, 1970), 325–336.

Barnouw, Erik. *The Image Empire: A History of Broadcasting in the United States from 1953.* New York: Oxford University Press, 1970. The third and final volume of this history.

Blish, Edward, Jr. *In Search of Light: The Broadcasts of Edward R. Murrow, 1938–1961.* New York: Alfred A. Knopf, 1967.

Bluem, A. William. *Documentary in American Television: Form, Function, Method.* New York: Hastings House, 1965.

Chayefsky, Paddy. *Television Plays*. New York: Simon & Schuster, 1955.

Malone, Robert A. "Local TV: Public Service with a Capital P." *Broadcasting,* June 22, 1970, pp. 50–76.

Mayo, John B. *Bulletin from Dallas: The President is Dead*. New York: Exposition Press, 1967.

Michael, Paul, and Robert B. Parish. *The Emmy Awards: A Pictorial History*. New York: Crown, 1970.

Murrow, Edward R., and Fred Friendly. *See It Now*. New York: Simon & Schuster, 1955. Selections from the series with commentary and pictures.

10.8 | Noncommercial Stations

Koenig, Allen E., and Ruane B. Hill, eds. *The Farther Vision: Educational Television Today*. Madison: University of Wisconsin Press, 1967.

Schramm, Wilbur, Jack Lyle, and Ithiel de Sola Pool. *The People Look at Educational Television: A Report of Nine Representative ETV Stations*. Stanford, Cal.: Stanford University Press, 1963.

10.9 | The "Fourth Network"

Lippmann, Walter. "The Problem of Television." *New York Herald-Tribune,* October 27, 1959.

Chapter 11. Intermedia Relationships: Symbiosis and Convergence

11.1 | Media Symbiosis

Baumol, William J., and William G. Bowen. *Performing Arts: The Economic Dilemma*. New York: Twentieth Century Fund, 1966.

Levin, Harvey J. *Broadcast Regulation and Joint Ownership of Media*. New York: New York University Press, 1960.

11.2 | Whatever Happened to Radio?

Riggs, Frank L. "The Changing Role of Radio." *JOB*, VIII (Fall, 1964), 331–340.

11.4 | Print Media

Enoch, Kurt. "The Paper-Bound Book: Twentieth Century Publishing Phenomenon." *Library Quarterly*, XXIV (July, 1954), 211–255.

Ford, James L. C. *Magazines for Millions: The Story of Specialized Publications*. Carbondale: Southern Illinois University Press, 1969.

11.6 | Community Antenna Television

Seiden, Martin H. *An Economic Analysis of CATV Systems*. Report to the FCC. Washington: Government Printing Office, 1965.

11.8 | Convergence

Bagdikian, Ben H. *The Information Machines: Their Impact on Men and Media*. New York: Harper & Row, 1971.

Cordtz, Dan. "The Coming Shake-up in Telecommunications." *Fortune,* April, 1970, pp. 69–71, 158–164.

Herman W. Land Associates. *Television and the Wired City*. Washington: National Association of Broadcasters, 1968.

Chapter 12. The Economic Role of Advertising

General

Business Periodical Index. New York: H. W. Wilson.

Owen, Bruce M., David L. Grey, and James N. Rosse. "A Selected Bibiliography in the Economics of the Mass Media." Stanford, Cal.: Research Center in Economic Growth, August, 1970.

Topicator. Denver: Thompson Bureau. An index covering *JOB, EBR,* and *Broadcasting,* as well as advertising publications.

12.4 | The Case Against Advertising

de Grazia, Sebastian. *Of Time, Work, and Leisure.* New York: Twentieth Century Fund, 1962.

Turner, E. S. *The Shocking History of Advertising.* New York: Ballantine Books, 1953. Sound work with good bibliography, despite title.

12.5 | For the Defense

Bauer, Raymond A., and Stephen A. Greyser. *Advertising in America: The Consumer View.* Boston: Harvard Business School, 1968.

Chapter 13. Broadcast-Advertising Practice

13.4 | Bases of Advertising Rates

Kelley, William T. "How Television Stations Price Their Services." *JOB,* XI (Fall, 1967), 313–323.

Peterman, John L. "The Structure of National Time Rates in the Television Broadcasting Industry. *Journal of Law and Economics,* VIII (October, 1965), 77–131.

13.8 | Advertising Agencies

Agencies have been the subject or background of many novels, plays, and films, *e.g.,* Frederic Wakeman, *The Hucksters* (New York: Rinehart, 1946).

Several books by elder statesmen of the industry have been cited in the text. For an irreverent contrast, see Jerry Della Femina, *From Those Wonderful Folks Who Gave You Pearl Harbor: Front Line Dispatches from the Advertising War* (New York: Simon & Schuster, 1970).

Chapter 14. Tests and Measurements

General

Lichty, Lawrence, and Joseph Ripley II. *American Broadcasting: Introduction and Analysis, Readings.* Second Edition. Madison, Wis.: College, 1970. Facsimile reproduction of documents. Chapter V, pp. V202–V332, reproduces examples of the major rating services' reports.

Nafziger, Ralph O., and David M. White, eds. *Introduction to Mass Communications Research.* Revised Edition. Baton Rouge: Louisiana State University Press, 1963. Useful for introduction to statistical methods and overview of research techniques.

Chapter 15. Financial Organization of Broadcasting

15.3 | Economics of Networking
House Committee on Interstate and Foreign Commerce. *Televison Network Program Procurement.* House Report 281, prepared by FCC Office of Network Study. 88th Cong., 1st Sess. Washington: Government Printing Office, 1963.

15.4 | Network-Affiliation Contracts
FCC. "Option Time and the Station Right to Reject Network Programs." 28 *Fed. Reg.* 5501 (1963).

15.5 | Economics of Noncommercial Broadcasting
Bystrom, John W. "Public Broadcasting Systems: Plans and Realization." *EBR,* II (October, 1968), 23–34. Describes main proposed financing schemes.
Coase, R. H. "Who Should Pay." *Television Quarterly,* VII (Winter, 1968), 67–82. Opposes government financing of noncommercial broadcasting.
Louis Harris and Associates, Inc. "The Viewers of Public Television." Prepared for the Corporation of Public Broadcasting, November, 1969.
Siegle, Henry J. "A Look at the ETV Audience." *EBR,* III (October, 1969), 23–29. Based on an NAEB-sponsored study.

Chapter 16. Economic Constraints on Programming

16.2 | Service to Minorities
Garnett, Bernard E. "How Soulful is 'Soul' Radio?" Nashville Race Relations Center, March, 1970.

16.4 | Vulnerability to Pressure
Lamb, Edward. *Not for Slaughter: An Autobiography.* New York: Harcourt, Brace & World, 1963. Chapters 10–13 tell how the FCC attempted blacklist tactics to deprive an Ohio broadcaster of licenses.

16.5 | Affiliate Clearance of Network Programs
Barrett, Marvin, ed. *The Alfred I. Dupont-Columbia University Survey of Broadcast Journalism, 1968–1969.* New York: Grosset & Dunlap, 1969. Pp. 13–16.

16.6 | Economics of "Cultural Democracy"
Berelson, Bernard. "The Great Debate on Cultural Democracy." In Donald W. Barrett, ed. *Values in America.* South Bend, Ind.: University of Notre Dame Press, 1961.
Rothenberg, Jerome. "Consumer Sovereignty and the Economics of Television Programming." *Studies in Public Communication, No. 4.* Chicago: University of Chicago Press, 1962. Pp. 45–54.
Scitovsky, Tibor. "On the Principle of Consumers' Sovereignty." *American Economic Review: Papers and Proceedings,* LII (May, 1962), 262–268.
Steiner, Peter O. "Program Patterns and Preferences and the Workability of Competition in Radio Broadcasting." *Quarterly Journal of Economics,* LXVI (May, 1952), 194–223.

16.7 | Economic Constraints on Noncommercial Programming

Blanchard, Robert O. "Station Managers versus NET Producer: Conflict Over Subjectivity." *EBR,* IV (June, 1970), 3–6. See also "Letters to the Editor," *EBR,* IV (October, 1970), 15–16.

Waple, Ben F., and William R. Smith, Jr. "FCC Warns State Net About Decision Making." *EBR,* IV (October, 1970), 11–14. An exchange of letters between the FCC and the Mississippi ETV Authority re alleged discrimination against integrated cast of *Sesame Street.*

Chapter 17. The Law of Broadcasting

General

The conventions of legal bibliography provide a convenient short form for citing items in serial publications, consisting of (1) a number, representing the volume number in the series (sometimes calendar year); (2) abbreviated title of series; (3) page on which item begins; (4) calendar year. Example: "326 U. S. 1 at 20 (1945)" refers to page 20 of a Supreme Court decision which starts on page 1 of volume 326 of *United States Reports* (Washington: Government Printing Office).

The Communications Act is found in the *United States Code,* a Government Printing Office series which codifies all federal laws; the same laws, with explanatory notes and references, are published commercially as *United States Code Annotated* (St. Paul, Minn.: West). The background to legislation can be found in *United States Code Congressional and Administrative News* (West). Other background comes from reports of hearings and other transactions of Congressional committees, listed in the *Monthly Catalogue of United States Government Publications.*

Appeals against FCC decisions usually go to the District of Columbia District Court of Appeals, reported in the *Federal Reporter* (West), of which a second series was started in 1924 (cited "F. 2d"). Supreme Court reviews of District Court decisions are officially reported as noted above in *United States Reports;* commercial versions of these reports with annotations are also available.

FCC decisions, official notices, reports, and orders appear first in the *Federal Register,* a weekly compendium of such documents from all federal agencies, published by the National Archives since 1936. These are cumulated in *F.C.C. Reports,* of which a second series ("F.C.C. 2d") started in 1965. Commission Rules and Regulations appear in codified form in the official *Code of Federal Regulation (C.F.R.)*

The multiplicity of official sources and publication delays created a need for a single, composite, up-to-date source. This is supplied commercially by Pike and Fischer, of Washington, D.C. (sponsored by the F.C.C. Bar Association), in its *Radio Reports,* a compendium of all relevant materials with complete indexing and constant updating.

Articles in university law reviews provide valuable commentaries on broadcasting law. See Kenneth Gompertz, "A Bibliography of Articles About Broadcasting in Law Periodicals, 1956–1968," *JOB,* XIV, Part II (Winter, 1969–1970), 83–112; *Index to Legal Periodicals* (New York: H. W. Wilson).

Source Book

Kahn, Frank J., ed. *Documents of American Broadcasting.* New York: Appleton-Century-Crofts, 1968. Reprints basic primary materials on regulation, with helpful introductory notes.

17.3 | The "Public Interest, Convenience, and Necessity" Standard

Holt, Darrel. "The Origin of 'Public Interest' in Broadcasting." *EBR,* I (October, 1967), 15–19.

Schubert, Glendon A. *The Public Interest.* Glencoe: Free Press, 1960. Philosophical discussion.

17.9 | Comsat and Public Broadcasting

Schiller, Herbert I. *Mass Communications and American Empire.* New York: August M. Kellsey, 1969. See Chapter 9 for history and development.

17.11 | Other Laws Affecting Broadcasting

Ashley, Paul. *Say It Safely.* Seattle: University of Washington Press, 1966.

Codding, George A., Jr. *The International Telecommunication Union: An Experiment in International Cooperation.* Leyden: E. J. Bril, 1952.

Phelps, Robert H., and E. Douglas Hamilton. *Libel: Rights, Risks, Responsibilities.* New York: Macmillan, 1966.

Chapter 18. Administration of the Law: The FCC at Work

General

Sperry, Robert. "A Selected Bibliography of Works on the Federal Communications Commission, 1967–1969 Supplement." *JOB,* XIV (Summer, 1970), 377–389.

Chapter 19. Regulation: Enemy of Freedom

19.1 | The Dangerous Experiment

McCoy, Ralph E. *Freedom of the Press: An Annotated Bibliography.* Carbondale: Southern Illinois University Press, 1968.

Nelson, Harold L., and Dwight L. Teeter, Jr. *Law of Mass Communications: Freedom and Control of Print and Broadcast Media.* Mineola, N. Y.: Foundation Press, 1969.

19.2 | Censorable Matter: Obscenity in Print

De Grazia, Edward. *Censorship Landmarks.* New York: Bowker, 1970. Reprints full court reports dating back to 1663.

19.6 | The Inalienable Right to Speak

Brant, Irving. *The Bill of Rights: Its Origin and Meaning.* New York: Bobbs-Merrill, 1965. "Absolutist" position on speech freedom.

19.7 | New Media and "The Press"

Carmen, Ira H. *Movies, Censorship, and the Law*. Ann Arbor: University of Michigan Press, 1966. Includes unique materials based on interviews with censors themselves.

Hunnings, Neville M. *Film Censors and the Law*. London: George Allen & Unwin, 1967. International in scope.

Randall, R. S. *Censorship of the Movies: The Social and Political Control of a Mass Medium*. Madison: University of Wisconsin Press, 1967.

Rembar, Charles. *The End of Obscenity: The Trials of Lady Chatterly, Tropic of Cancer, and Fanny Hill*. New York: Random House, 1968. Rembar was the defense attorney in these cases.

Chapter 20. Regulation: Ally of Freedom

20.1 | The Marketplace of Ideas

Clark, David, and Earl R. Hutchinson. *Mass Media and the Law: Freedom and Restraint*. New York: Wiley-Interscience, 1970.

20.5 | Newspaper-Broadcasting Combinations

Lago, Armando M., and David P. Osborne. "A Quantitative Analysis of the Price Effects of Joint Mass Communication Media Ownership." Prepared for the National Association of Broadcasters. Bethseda, Md.: RMC Inc., March 1, 1971.

Owen, Bruce M. "Empirical Results on the Price Effects of Joint Ownership in the Mass Media." Stanford, Cal.: Research Center in Economic Growth, November, 1969.

20.9 | The Fairness Doctrine

Gillmor, Donald M., and Jerome A. Barron. *Cases and Comment on Mass Communication Law*. St. Paul, Minn.: West, 1969.

Kittross, John M., and Kenneth Harwood. *Free and Fair: Courtroom Access and the Fairness Doctrine*. Philadelphia: Temple University, 1970. Reprints articles from *JOB*.

Robinson, Glen O. "The FCC and the First Amendment: Observations on 40 Years of Radio and Television Regulation." *Minnesota Law Review*, LII (1967), 148–150. Opposes the *Red Lion* conclusion.

Chapter 21. Regulation and Public Interest: Facts and Fictions

21.1 | Defects of the Regulatory Agencies

Sperry, Robert. "A Selected Bibliography of Works on the Federal Communications Commission, 1967–1969 Supplement." *JOB*, XIV (Summer, 1970), 377–389.

21.6 | The Mythology of Regulation

Flynn, Patrick H. "Countervailing Power in Network Television." *JOB*, XIV (Summer, 1970), 297–305. Re inconsistency of regulatory concepts.

House Committee on Interstate and Foreign Commerce, Special Subcommittee on Investigations. *Analysis of FCC's 1970 Policy Statement on Comparative Hearings Involving Regular Renewal Applicants.* Staff Report. 91st Cong., 2d Sess. Washington: Government Printing Office, 1970. Attacks the FCC's tendency to favor incumbent licensees.

Lieban, Ruth. "Trouble in Paradise." In Marvin Barrett, ed. *The Alfred I. Dupont-Columbia University Survey of Broadcast Journalism, 1968–1969.* New York: Grosset & Dunlap, 1969. Pp. 112–121.

Stanley, Earl R. "Revocation, Renewal of License, and Fines and Forfeiture Cases Before the Federal Communications Commission." *JOB,* VIII (Fall, 1964), 371–382.

Stavins, Ralph L. "Television Today: The End of Communication and the Death of Community." Washington: Institute for Policy Studies, 1969. Report on methods used in assessing station performance to provide renewal-hearing evidence.

21.7 | Proposals for Reform

"Here, We Would Suggest, is a Program for the FCC." *Consumer Reports,* February, 1960, pp. 93–95.

Jones, William K. "Use and Regulation of the Radio Spectrum: Report on a Conference." *Washington University Law Quarterly,* Winter, 1968, pp. 71–115. Reviews concept of selling channels on open market.

Skornia, Harry J. *Television and Society: An Inquest and Agenda for Improvement.* New York: McGraw-Hill, 1965.

21.8 | The Federal Trade Commission

Alexander, George J. *Honesty and Competition: False-Advertising Law and Policy Under FTC Administration.* Syracuse, N. Y.: Syracuse University Press, 1967.

Gillmor, Donald M., and Jerome A. Barron. *Cases and Comment on Mass Communication Law.* St. Paul, Minn.: West, 1969. See "Advertising, the Media, and the Law," pp. 589–624.

Kintner, Earl W. "Federal Trade Commission Regulation of Advertising." *Michigan Law Review,* LXIV (1966), 1269–1284.

Millstein, Ira M. "The Federal Trade Commission and False Advertising." *Columbia Law Review,* LXIV (March, 1964), 439–499. In 1964, many law journals had special FTC fiftieth-anniversary issues.

Weston, Glen. "Deceptive Advertising and the F.T.C.: Decline of Caveat Emptor." *Federal Bar Journal,* XXIV (Fall, 1964), 548–578.

Chapter 22. Beyond the FCC: Nonregulatory Social Controls

22.2 | NAB Codes

Helffrich, Stockton. "The Radio and Television Codes and the Public Interest." *JOB,* XII (Summer, 1970), 267–274.

22.3 | Professionalism: Individualized Self-Regulation

Barrett, Marvin, ed. *The Alfred I. Dupont-Columbia University Survey of Broadcast Journalism, 1968–1969.* New York: Grosset & Dunlap, 1969. See "Broadcast Journalism and Advertising," pp. 50–58.

22.4 | *Education for Broadcasting*

Smith, Leslie. "Education for Broadcasting: 1929–1963." *JOB,* VIII (Fall, 1964), 383–398.

22.5 | *Professional Criticism of Broadcasting*

Most of the *JOB,* XI (Winter, 1966–1967) issue is devoted to criticism, *e.g.,* Maurice E. Shelby, Jr., "Patterns in Thirty Years of Broadcast Criticism," 27–39.

Ellison, Harlan. *The Glass Teat: Essays of Opinion on the Subject of Television.* New York: Ace, 1970.

Hada, Moses. "Climates of Criticism." In Robert L. Shayon, *et al. The Eighth Art.* New York: Holt, Rinehart and Winston, 1962. Pp. 15–21.

22.8 | *Broadcasting and Consumerism*

Baker, Robert K., and Sandra J. Ball. *Mass Media and Violence,* Vol. IX. A Report to National Commission on the Causes and Prevention of Violence. Washington: Government Printing Office, 1969. Pp. 386–393. Reviews previous proposals and makes its own.

Barber, Richard J. "Government and the Consumer." *Michigan Law Review,* LXIV (1966), 1203–1238.

Stavins, Ralph L. "Television Today: The End of Communication and the Death of Community." Washington: Institute for Policy Studies, 1969. Report on methods used to obtain evidence assessing station performance for use in renewal hearings.

Chapter 23. Mass-Media Effects: Research and Theory

General

Bauer, Raymond A., and Alice H. Bauer. "America, Mass Society and Mass Media." *Journal of Social Issues,* XVI (1960), 3–66.

Berelson, Bernard, and Gary A. Steiner. *Human Behavior: An Inventory of Scientific Findings.* New York: Harcourt, Brace & World, 1964. Chapter 13, pp. 527–555, deals with mass communication.

de Fleur, Melvin L. *Theories of Mass Communication.* New York: Donald McKay, 1966.

Gerbner, George. "Mass Media and Human Communication Theory." In F. E. X. Dance, ed. *Human Communications Theory.* New York: Holt, Rinehart and Winston, 1967. Pp. 40–60.

Hansen, D. A., and J. H. Parsons. *Mass Communication: A Research Bibliography.* Berkeley, Cal.: Glendessary Press, 1968.

23.2 | *Noncontent Influences on Effects*

Koch, Howard. *The Panic Broadcast.* Boston: Little, Brown, 1970. Story of the Orson Welles *War of the Worlds* broadcast by the script writer. (A recording of the program itself is available from Audio Rarities.)

23.5 | *Cultural-Effects Analysis*

Mendelsohn, Harold. *Mass Entertainment.* New Haven, Conn.: College and University Press, 1966. Distinguishes his subject from "culture."

Nye, Russell B. *The Unembarrassed Muse: The Popular Arts in America.* New York: Dial Press, 1970. Chapter 17, pp. 390–416, deals with broadcasting.

Phillips, Gifford. *The Arts in a Democratic Society.* Santa Barbara, Cal.: Center for the Study of Democratic Institutions, 1966. Pamphlet summarizing theories about cultural effects of the media.

Rosenberg, Bernard, and David M. White, eds. *Mass Culture: The Popular Arts in America.* Glencoe: Free Press, 1957.

Chapter 24. Effects of Broadcasting: Pragmatic Assessments

24.1 | Varieties of Broadcasting Effects

Catton, William R., Jr. "Mass Media as Producers of Effects: An Overview of Research Trends." In Robert K. Baker and Sandra J. Ball. *Mass Media and Violence,* Vol. IX. A Report to National Commission on the Causes and Prevention of Violence. Washington: Government Printing Office, 1969. Pp. 247–259. Counters some arguments in Joseph T. Klapper, *The Effects of Mass Communication* (New York: Free Press, 1960).

24.2 | Social Processes: Change and Conformity

Luter, John. "Investigative Reporting, 1968–1969." In Marvin Barrett, ed. *The Alfred I. Dupont-Columbia University Survey of Broadcast Journalism, 1968–1969.* New York: Grosset & Dunlap, 1969. Pp. 67–82.

Oshrin, Norm. "Broadcast News: Bending to the Times?" *Broadcasting,* October 12, 1970, pp. 56–59.

Trillin, Calvin. "U. S. Journal: Nampa, Idaho—Negative and Controversial." *The New Yorker,* October 31, 1970, pp. 104–109. Case history of how "hometownism" shapes a medium.

24.3 | Broadcasting's Socializing Role

Himmelweit, Hilde T., *et al. Television and the Child: An Empirical Study of the Effect of Television on the Young.* London: Oxford University Press, 1961. The British experience.

24.4 | Social Institutions: Political Campaigns

The *JOB,* XII (Summer, 1968) issue is devoted to political broadcasting.

Blumler, Jay G., and Denis McQuain. *Television and Politics: Its Uses and Influence.* Chicago: University of Chicago Press, 1969. About Britain.

Tull, Charles J. *Father Coughlin and the New Deal.* Syracuse, N. Y.: Syracuse University Press, 1965. Example of radio's demagogic potential.

24.6 | Behavioral Effects: Violence

Arnold, Arnold. *Violence and Your Child.* Chicago: Henry Regnery, 1969. Vigorous attack on the media researchers such as Schramm and Himmelweit.

Larsen, Otto N., ed. *Violence and the Mass Media.* New York: Harper & Row, 1968.

Schramm, Wilbur. *Motion Pictures and Real-Life Violence: What the Research Says.* Stanford, Cal.: Institute for Communication Research, 1968.

24.7 | *Perceptual Effects: Images, Realities, Values*

Greenberg, Bradley S., and Gerhard J. Hanneman. "Racial Attitudes and the Impact of TV Blacks." *EBR,* IV (April, 1970), 27–34.

Greenberg, Bradley S., and E. B. Parker. *The Kennedy Assassination and the American Public: Social Communication in a Crisis.* Stanford, Cal.: Stanford University Press, 1965.

24.8 | *Shaping of Events*

House Committee on Interstate and Foreign Commerce, Special Subcommittee on Investigations. *Deceptive Programming Practices: Staging of Marijuana Broadcast—"Pot Party at a University."* Hearings. 90th Cong., 2d Sess. Washington: Government Printing Office, 1968.

McGaffin, William, and Erwin Knoll. *Anything but the Truth: The Credibility Gap —How the News is Managed in Washington.* New York: G. P. Putnam's Sons, 1968.

Rovere, Richard H. "Television in Courts and Legislatures." In Robert L. Shayon, *et al. The Eighth Art.* New York: Holt, Rinehart and Winston, 1962. Pp. 135–142.

Small, William. *To Kill a Messenger: Television News and the Real World.* New York: Hastings House, 1970.

24.9 | *Gratification of Subjective Needs*

Burck, Gilbert. "There'll Be Less Leisure Than You Think." *Fortune,* March, 1970, pp. 87–89, 162–166.

de Grazia, Sebastian. *Of Time, Work, and Leisure.* New York: Twentieth Century Fund, 1962.

Emmett, B. P. "A New Role for Research in Broadcasting." *POQ,* XXXII (Winter, 1968–1969), 654–655.

Nordenstreng, Kaarle. "Comments on 'Gratification Research' in Broadcasting." *POQ,* XXXIV (Spring, 1969), 130–133.

AUTHORS CITED

FCC CITATIONS

LEGAL CITATIONS

INDEX

absorption, atmospheric, 35

access: to news, 170, 231–232; to use of media, 375, 444–446, 525; random, to media content, 101, 481, 524

Actors' Equity, 344

Administrative Procedures Act, 367, 447

advertisers, top ten, 288

advertising: advantages of, 13; amount of, in relation to other media content, 270; applied to social goals, 493–494; budgets, 285–286; on CATV, 236; in children's programs, 522; criticism of, 399; defense of, 256–260; economic value of, 493–495, 523; expenditure on, 247–249; FCC criteria for, 394; and First Amendment, 412–413; functions of, 250; impressions, 247; legal control of, 470; and mass consumption, 252–254; media of, 248–249; on noncommercial stations, 331–332; opposition to, 274; of patent medicines, 252, 254–255, 279; in program structure, 262–263; rates, 274–282, 329; reforms of, 260–261, 524–525; regulation of, 402–404; salience of, 261, 269–274; scientific, 249; self-regulation of, 260–261; social responsibility of, 256; as subsidy, 249–250; as synthesizer of wants, 253–254, 257–260, 522–523; unethical, 184, 255, 260, 383, 400, 401, 403–404, 465, 524–525. See also commercialism; demonstrations; FTC.

advertising agencies, 151, 202–203, 249, 285–290, 329, 341

Agnew, Vice-Pres. Spiro T., 434–435

Alexander bill, 139

Alexanderson, E. F. W., 189–190

Alexanderson alternator, 129, 130, 139–140

All-Radio Methodology Study (ARMS), 312–313

amateurs, 120, 133–136, 140

American Association of Advertising Agencies (AAAA), 289–290, 470

American Bar Association, 232, 463–464

American Broadcasting Company (ABC), 16, 175, 178, 184, 205, 218, 233; and blacklisting, 345; and ITT merger, 432; ratings of, 306, 310; and TV, 201, 203

American Council for Better Broadcasts, 484

American Federation of Musicians (AFM), 322

American Federation of Television and Radio Artists (AFTRA), 323, 344

American Forces Radio and Television Service (AFRTS), 3, 17

American Guild of Variety Artists, 323

American Marconi, 118, 128, 129, 130, 132, 139–142, 175

American Research Bureau (ARB), 293–294, 300, 303, 304, 311, 312, 313, 333

American Society of Composers, Authors, and Publishers (ASCAP), 168–169

American Telephone and Telegraph Company (AT&T), 85, 126, 130, 137, 138, 150, 159, 169, 170, 201, 215; cross-licensing, 143–150; development of, 112–114; and RCA, 141–143; and sound film, 224–225; theory of broadcasting, 144–146

amplitude, described, 26

amplitude-modulated link, 101

amplitude modulation (AM), 30–31, 32, 42. See also radio broadcasting, AM.

announcement program, 267–268

anomie, 495

antennas: directional, 35, 38, 47, 55, 85; AM, 44; FM, 49; shipboard, 121

appeal: law of, 363, 366–368; right of, 161

ARBitron, 303

areas of dominant influence (ADI), 293–294

Armstrong, Maj. Edwin, 48, 129, 179, 181

Armstrong Field Station for Electronic Research, 179

Army-McCarthy hearings, 206–207, 508

aspect ratio, 65, 226–227

Associated Press, 110, 170, 414

Association for Professional Broadcasting Education (APBE), 474–475

Atlantic cable, 109

attenuation of radio energy, 26, 35, 76–77, 85

audience: growth, 196; investment in broadcasting, 250–251. See also research.

audimeter, 293, 303

audion, 24–25, 122–123, 124–125

Audit Bureau of Circulation, 292–293

Austro-German Telegraphic Union, 154

authoritarian broadcasting philosophy, 7–8, 12

automation of stations, 322

auxiliary stations, 41

Avco rule, 402, 459